ECONOMICS of the PUBLIC SECTOR

THIRD EDITION

ECONOMICS of the PUBLIC SECTOR

THIRD EDITION

JOSEPH E. STIGLITZ

W.W. NORTON & COMPANY

NEW YORK / LONDON

The text of this book is composed in 10/12 New Baskerville with the display set in Frutiger.
Composition by UG/GGS Information Services, Inc.
Manufacturing by The Courier Companies
Book design by Martin Lubin Graphic Design
Editor: Ed Parsons
Associate Managing Editor: Jane Carter
Manufacturing Director: Roy Tedoff
Project Editor: Kate Barry
Editorial Assistant: Mark Henderson

Library of Congress Cataloging-in-Publication Data

Stiglitz, Joseph E.
    Economics of the public sector / Joseph E. Stiglitz.—3rd ed.
        p.   cm.
    Includes bibliographical references and index.
    ISBN 0-393-96651-8
    1. Finance, Public—United States.   2. Fiscal policy—United
States.   I. Title.
HJ257.2.S84   1999
336.73—dc21   98-34980

W. W. Norton & Company, Inc.
500 Fifth Avenue, New York, N.Y. 10110
www.wwnorton.com

W. W. Norton & Company Ltd.
Castle House, 75/76 Wells Street, London W1T 3QT

To My First Teachers,
Nat and Charlotte

CONTENTS

PART TWO
FUNDAMENTALS OF WELFARE ECONOMICS 53

3 MARKET EFFICIENCY 55

4 MARKET FAILURE 76

5 EFFICIENCY AND EQUITY 93

11 COST-BENEFIT ANALYSIS 271

12 HEALTH CARE 300

18 TAX INCIDENCE 482

APPENDIX: COMPARISON OF THE EFFECTS OF AN AD VALOREM AND SPECIFIC COMMODITY TAX ON A MONOPOLIST 515

19 TAXATION AND ECONOMIC EFFICIENCY 518

PREFACE

It has been a decade since the last revision of this textbook, and much has happened in the intervening ten years. I have been lucky enough to have been an active participant in many of these changes, as member and Chairman of the President's Council of Economic Advisers. This edition is written from the unique perspective of a public sector economist who had the chance to be involved in the decision-making process not only in the United States, but also in many other countries; following my stint at the White House, I moved to my current position as Chief Economist and senior vice president of the World Bank, which is involved in advising developing countries concerning their public sector policies. I have been able to participate in debates around the world on the central questions with which this book is concerned: What should be the role of the government? How should it design its programs in areas ranging from health and education, to social security and welfare? How should tax systems be designed to promote economic efficiency and to be consistent with basic views of fairness?

In one sense, my experiences confirmed many of the views and approaches that I had developed in the previous two editions. Indeed, it gave me great pleasure to see the extent to which the ideas and perspectives, many of which seemed so new when they were presented in the first edition of this book, were being so highly integrated into thinking about policy, not only in the United States, but throughout the world. I have increasingly become convinced that the kind of analysis presented in this book can—and has—significantly improved the formation of policies in the public sector.

The economics of the public sector is a subject that is always in flux. While there are some general principles that are as applicable today as they were two decades ago, new issues have arisen to the top of the policy agenda, and old issues have waned in importance. Debates today often hinge on different questions than they did even a decade ago. Even the language in which some of the debates are couched has changed. I have tried in this edition not only to incorporate the many changes in expenditure policies and tax laws, but also to reflect some of these changing approaches and themes. There is, for instance, an increased emphasis on understanding why government is often inefficient, and on improving the efficiency of government—to use the phrase popularized by the Clinton Administration, to "reinvent government."

My major aims in writing this edition remain the same as when I wrote the first: I wrote it in the belief that an understanding of the issues it addressed was central to any democratic society. Among the most important of these issues are the appropriate balance between the public and private sectors, the ways in which the public and private sector can complement each other, and how governments can more effectively meet their objectives, whatever those objectives are. Issues in public-sector economics often become highly charged politically, but I tried to present the analysis in an impartial manner, with a clear delineation between the analysis of the consequences of any policy and the value judgements associated with assessing the desirability of the policy. Inevitably, in the positions in which I have been placed in the last eight years, I have taken strong positions on a variety of public-sector issues. But I have always tried to be clear about what economic theory and empirical research has had to say *on all sides* of the debate, identifying where—and why—there is so frequently uncertainty about the outcomes of certain policies. In discussing with the President, for instance, the desirability of one course of action, part of my responsibility was to identify alternative policies, and to analyze the arguments that would be put forward for each. In this edition, I have continued with my commitment to present to the student a balanced account of these often heated debates. The favorable reception of the previous two editions by instructors of a wide variety of political persuasions suggests that they had succeeded in doing so. And the publication of so many foreign editions of the book, from large countries such as Russia, China, Japan, Germany, Italy, and Spain, to smaller ones such as Latvia, Turkey, and the Czech Republic, has shown that the approach has met with favor not just in the United States, but in countries facing quite different circumstances and problems.

My experiences, both at the White House and in the World Bank, have made me even more convinced of the importance of this endeavor. Democracies can only succeed if there is a meaningful public debate on the central public-policy issues of the day. Too often, in too many countries, good policies flounder because of a lack of widespread understanding of basic economic issues. Writing an undergraduate textbook such as this thus presents both a great challenge and a great opportunity; the challenge to present complex and complicated ideas in simple enough terms that they can be understood by someone with a relatively limited background in economics (at the most, a single year of a principles course); and opportunity, if one succeeds in doing so, of influencing the ways in which the public policy debates are approached.

Public-sector issues include some of the most exciting in all of economics. Health, defense, education, social security, welfare programs, and tax reform all receive steady attention in the news media. Economic analysis brings special insights to the debates. Should education be publicly provided? What is the long-term outlook for our social security program? How do current proposals for tax reform match our knowledge of who really bears the burden of the tax, of what determines the efficiency and equity consequences of various taxes? These kinds of questions breathe life into the course, which is why I give them careful attention.

Examining specific tax and expenditure programs offers an additional benefit: it underscores the importance of design features. One of the lessons we have learned in the past decade is that good intentions are not enough. Urban renewal programs, intended to revitalize our cities, had the unintended consequences of reducing the supply of housing to the poor. One of the major objectives of the tax reform of 1986 was to simplify the tax code, but it seems, instead, to have made it even more complex. There is little evidence that the tax provisions introduced in 1997 to encourage higher education will actually succeed in doing so. I use examples like these, of unintended consequences, not only to enliven the course, but also to instill in students the important habit of testing theory against the complex environment in which public-sector decisions are enacted and implemented.

The organization of this book is based on the principle of flexibility. The sequence I follow is, first, to introduce in Parts One and Two the fundamental questions, institutional details, and a review of the microeconomic theory underlying the role of the public sector. Part Three develops the theory of public expenditures, including public goods, public choice, and bureaucracy, while Part Four applies the theory of the five largest areas of public expenditure in the United States: health, defense, education, social security, and welfare programs. Parts Five and Six repeat this pattern, presenting the theory of taxation and its analysis, respectively. Part Seven takes up two further topics: issues concerning state and local taxation and expenditure and fiscal federalism; and issues concerning fiscal policy, with particular emphasis on the relation between microeconomic analysis and macroeconomic performance. One of the major changes since the last edition is that the deficits that were at the center of attention a decade ago have shifted—for the time being—to surpluses.

A perfectly workable alternative to this sequence would be to cover taxation before expenditures. Parts Five and Six have been carefully developed so that the teacher wishing to go straight to taxation after Part One can do so without loss of continuity. Further tips on how courses can be organized, as well as lecture notes, test questions, and coverage of advanced topics that some teachers may wish to include in their lectures, are contained in the *Instructor's Manual*.

The list of those to whom I am indebted is a long one. My teachers at Amherst College, James Nelson and Arnold Collery, not only stimulated my interest in economics, and in the particular subject of this course, but laid the foundations for my later studies. They also showed me, by example, what good teaching meant; I hope that some of what I learned from them is reflected in this book. At M.I.T. Dan Holland and E. Cary Brown introduced me to the formal study of public economics. Again, I hope some of the blend of policy, theory, and institutional detail that marked their work is reflected here. The insights of my colleagues and collaborators at the institutions at which I have worked (M.I.T., Yale University, Stanford University, Princeton University, Oxford University, Cambridge University, and the National Bureau of Economic Research) and the government agencies (Council of Economic Advisers, Treasury, Labor, Interior, Energy, Agency for International Development, State of Louisiana, State of Texas) and international organizations (World Bank, Interamerican Development Bank, Organization of Economic Cooperation and Development) for which I have worked and consulted have also proved invaluable. I should mention Henry Aaron (Brookings Institution), Alan J. Auerbach (Berkeley), Greg Ballantine (former Assistant Secretary of the Treasury for Tax Policy), William J. Baumol (Princeton University), Charles T. Clotfelter (Duke University), Partha Dasgupta (Cambridge University), Peter A. Diamond (M.I.T.), Avinash Dixit (Princeton University), Martin Feldstein (Harvard University), Harvey Galper (Brookings Institution), Robert E. Hall (Stanford University), John Hamilton (University of Florida), Arnold C. Harberger (University of Chicago and University of California, Los Angeles), Charles E. McClure (Hoover Institution; former Deputy Assistant Secretary of the Treasury), James A. Mirrlees (Cambridge University), Alvin Rabushka (Stanford University), Michael Rothschild (Princeton), Agnar Sandmo (Norges Handelshøgskole, Norway), Eytan Sheshinski (Hebrew University), Nick Stern (London School of Economics), Lawrence Summers (Harvard University), and in particular Anthony B. Atkinson (Oxford University), Peter Mieskowski (Rice University), Raj Kumar Sah (University of Chicago), and Steven L. Slutsky (University of Florida).

Comments and suggestions I have received from those who have taught from the book or read various stages of the manuscript have been enormously helpful in shaping this text. Here I particularly want to thank Donald N. Baum (University of Nebraska), Jim Bergin (Queens University, Canada), Michael Boskin (Stanford University), Lawrence Blume (Cornell University), David Bradford (Princeton University), Bradley Braun (University of Central Florida), Neil Bruce (University of Washington), John Burbidge (McMaster University), Paul M. Carrick (Naval Postgraduate School), Donald Cole (Drew University), Paul N. Courant (University of Michigan), Lieutenant Colonel Floyd Duncan (Virginia Military Institute), Stephen Erfle (Dickinson College), J. Eric Fredland (U.S. Naval Academy), Victor R. Fuchs (Stanford University), Don Fullerton (University of Texas–Austin), Roger Gordon (University of Michigan), William F. Hellmuth (Virginia Commonwealth University), Mervyn King (London School of Economics), Laurence J. Kotlikoff (Boston University), Robert J. Lampman (University of Wisconsin), Jerry Miner (Syracuse University), Joseph A. Pechman (Brookings Institution), Jim Poterba (M.I.T.), Anora Robbins (UNC Greensboro), Balbir S. Sahni (Concordia University, Montreal), Catherine Schneider (Boston College) Robert Sherry (Keene State College), John Shoven (Stanford University), Joel Slemrod (University of Michigan), Anne Winkler (University of Missouri at St. Louis), Sun-Tien Wu (Chung Hsing University, Taipei), and Qiang Zeng (Tsiing Hua University, Beijing).

In its Second Edition this book benefited tremendously from the insights of Karla Hoff, who served as both research assistant and critic. I hope this Third Edition lives up to the high standards of clarity, precision, and accessibility that Karla helped bring to its predecessor. In that effort I was aided by a group of outstanding graduate research assistants from University of Maryland: Amy Harris, Kosali Ilayperuma, Steven Karon, and Diana Stech. I also owe a special thanks to Janet McCubbin for her contributions on the first draft of the Third Edition. Janet read each word of the manuscript, and her invaluable feedback put the revision on a firm footing from the get go.

My indebtedness to Jane Hannaway is more than that customarily owed to a spouse, for her insights into the behavior of governments in general, and bureaucratic behavior in particular, have been instrumental in shaping my own views, although I am afraid I have had less influence on her than she has had on me.

Finally, I am deeply indebted to the fine people at W. W. Norton and Company, a truly outstanding publishing firm, who brought this project to fruition. Special thanks go to my editor, Ed Parsons, and his able assistants Mark Henderson and Claire Acher, manuscript editor Joan Benham, project editors Kate Barry and Margaret Farley, and proofreader Roseanne Fox. The book in your hands owes much to their excellent work and dedication.

Washington D.C.   J.E.S.
Fall, 1999

PART ONE INTRODUCTION

At the center of our country's political life are some basic economic questions: How does the government affect the economy? What should the government do? Why are some economic activities undertaken in the public sector and others in the private? Should government do more than it is currently doing, or less? Should it change what it is doing, and how it is doing it?

To answer these questions, we must begin by understanding what the government does today. How has the government grown over the past fifty years? How do the size and scope of government in the United States compare with government's size and scope in other countries?

Part One of this book provides this background. Chapter 1 gives an overall perspective on the economic role of government. It sets forth the basic questions that are addressed by public sector economists, and explains some of the reasons why there are disagreements among them about appropriate policies. Chapter 2 provides some of the basic data describing the public sector in the United States today.

1 The Public Sector in a Mixed Economy

FOCUS QUESTIONS

1 What are the central questions with which the economics of the public sector is concerned?

2 What are the differing views concerning the economic role of government? How have they changed over the years and what has given rise to those changes?

3 How do economists go about studying the economics of the public sector?

4 What are the principal sources of disagreement among economists about appropriate policies for government to pursue?

From birth to death, our lives are affected in countless ways by the activities of government.

• We are born in hospitals that are publicly subsidized, if not publicly owned. Our arrival is then publicly recorded (on our birth certificate), entitling us to a set of privileges and obligations as American citizens.

• Most of us (almost 90 percent) attend public schools.

• Virtually all of us, at some time in our lives, receive money from the government, through programs such as student loans, unemployment or disability payments, antipoverty programs, social security, and Medicare.

• All of us pay taxes to the government—sales taxes, taxes on such commodities as gasoline, liquor, telephones, air travel, perfumes, and tires, property taxes, income taxes, and social security (payroll) taxes.

• More than a sixth of the work force is employed by the government, and for the rest, the government has a significant impact on employment conditions.

• In many areas of production—be it cars, sneakers, or computers—profits and employment opportunities are greatly affected by whether the government allows foreign competitors to sell goods in America without a tariff or quota.

• What we eat and drink, where we can live and what kinds of houses we can live in are all regulated by government agencies.

• We travel on public roads and publicly subsidized railroads. In most communities our garbage is collected and our sewage is disposed of by a public agency; in some communities the water we drink is provided by public water companies.

• Our legal structure provides a framework within which individuals and firms can sign contracts with one another. When there is a dispute between two individuals, the two may turn to the courts to adjudicate the dispute.

• Without environmental regulations, many of our major cities would be choked with pollution, the water of our lakes and rivers would be undrinkable, and we could neither swim nor fish in them.

• Without safety regulations, such as those requiring seat belts, highway fatalities would be even higher than they are.

THE ECONOMIC ROLE OF GOVERNMENT

Why does government engage in some economic activities and not others? Why has the scope of its activities changed over the past hundred years, and why does it have different roles in different countries? Does the government do too much? Does it do well what it attempts to do? Could it perform its economic role more efficiently? These are the central questions with which the economics of the public sector is concerned. To address them, we will first consider the economic role of government in modern economies, how ideas about the role of government have emerged, and the changing role of government in the twentieth century.

**THE MIXED ECONOMY
OF THE UNITED STATES**

The United States has what is called a **mixed economy:** while many economic activities are undertaken by private firms, others are undertaken by the government. In addition, the government alters the behavior of the private sector through a variety of regulations, taxes, and subsidies.

By contrast, in the former Soviet Union, most economic activities were undertaken by the central government. Today, only North Korea and Cuba give the government such primacy. In many Western European economies, national governments have had a larger role in economic activity than in the United States. For instance, the government of France once participated in a range of economic activities, including the production of cars, electricity, and airplanes. Since the 1980s, however, **privatization**—converting government enterprises into private firms—has been the trend in Europe, although the economic role of government generally remains larger there than in the United States.[1]

The origins of the mixed economy of the United States lie in the origins of the country itself. In formulating the United States Constitution, the founders of the republic had to address explicitly key issues concerning the economic role of the new government. The Constitution assigned the federal government certain responsibilities, such as running the post office and printing money. It provided the foundations for what we now call "intellectual property rights" by giving the government the right to grant patents and issue copyrights to encourage innovation and creativity. It gave the federal government certain rights to levy taxes—though those did not include taxes on exports, income, or net wealth. Most importantly, for the future evolution of the country, under Article 1, Section 8, Clause 3, it gave the federal government the right to regulate interstate commerce. Since so much of economic activity involves goods produced in one state and sold in another, this clause, interpreted broadly, has been used to justify much of the federal government's regulatory activities.

Throughout the history of the United States, the economic role of the government has undergone important changes. For instance, one hundred years ago some highways and all railroads were private; today, there are no major private roads and most interstate railroad passenger travel is by Amtrak, a publicly established and subsidized enterprise. It is because mixed economies constantly face the problem of defining the appropriate boundaries between government and private activities that the study of the economics of the public sector in these countries is both so important and so interesting.

DIFFERENT PERSPECTIVES ON THE ROLE OF GOVERNMENT

To understand better contemporary perspectives on the economic role of government, it can be helpful to consider the different perspectives that have evolved in the past.[2] Some of the central ideas of the eighteenth and nineteenth centuries have been critical to economic history in the twentieth century, and continue to be important today.

One dominant view in the eighteenth century, which was particularly persuasive among French economists, was that the government should actively promote trade and industry. Advocates of this view were called **mercantilists.** It was partly in response to the mercantilists that Adam Smith (who is often viewed as the founder of modern economics) wrote *The Wealth of Nations* (1776), in which he argued for a limited role for govern-

---

[1] For more on the case of France, see H. Dumez and A. Jeunemaitre, "Privatization in France: 1983–1993," in *Industrial Privatization in Western Europe: Pressures, Problems, and Paradoxes,* ed. Vincent Wright (London and New York: Pinter Publishers, 1994), pp. 83–105, 194.

[2] See A. O. Hirschman, *Shifting Involvements: Private Interest and Public Action* (Princeton, N.J.: Princeton University Press, 1982). Hirschman has put forth an interesting theory attempting to explain the constant changes in views on the appropriate role of the government.

ment. Smith attempted to show how competition and the profit motive would lead individuals—in pursuing their own private interests—to serve the public interest. The profit motive would lead individuals, competing against one another, to supply the goods other individuals wanted. Only firms that produced what was wanted and at as low a price as possible would survive. Smith argued that the economy was led, as if by an invisible hand, to produce what was desired and in the best possible way.

Adam Smith's ideas had a powerful influence both on governments and on economists. Many of the most important nineteenth-century economists, such as the Englishmen John Stuart Mill and Nassau Senior, promulgated the doctrine known as **laissez faire.** In their view, the government should leave the private sector alone; it should not attempt to regulate or control private enterprise. Unfettered competition would serve the best interests of society.

Not all nineteenth-century social thinkers were persuaded by Smith's reasoning. The grave inequalities in income that they saw around them, the squalor in which much of the working classes lived, and the unemployment that workers frequently faced concerned them. While nineteenth-century writers like Charles Dickens attempted to portray the plight of the working classes in novels, social theorists, such as Karl Marx, Sismondi, and Robert Owen, developed theories that not only attempted to explain what they saw but also suggested ways in which society might be reorganized. Many attributed the evils in society to the private ownership of capital; what Adam Smith saw as a virtue they saw as a vice. Marx, if not the deepest of the social thinkers, was certainly the most influential among those who advocated a greater role for the state in controlling the means of production. Still others, such as Owen, saw the solution neither in the state nor in private enterprise, but in smaller groups of individuals getting together and acting cooperatively for their mutual interest.

On one hand, private ownership of capital and unfettered free enterprise, on the other, government control of the means of production—these contrary principles were to become a driving force for international politics and economics in the twentieth century, embodied in the Cold War. Today, the countries of the former Soviet Union and the Eastern bloc are in the midst of a monumental transition to market systems—a fundamental transformation of government's role in those economies. In the United States, the economic role of government has also changed, but the changes have arisen more gradually, in response to economic events throughout the century. There is now widespread agreement that markets and private enterprises are at the heart of a successful economy, but that government plays an important role as a complement to the market. The precise nature of that role remains, however, a source of contention.

AN IMPETUS FOR GOVERNMENT ACTION: MARKET FAILURES

The Great Depression, in which the unemployment rate reached 25 percent and national output fell by about a third from its peak in 1929, was the event that most fundamentally changed attitudes toward government. There was a (justified) widespread view that markets had failed in an important way, and there were enormous pressures for government to do something about this market failure. The great English economist John Maynard

Keynes, writing in the midst of the Great Depression, argued forcefully that the government not only should do something about economic slumps, but could. The belief that governments should and could stabilize the level of economic activity was eventually embedded in legislation in the United States, in the **Full Employment Act of 1946,** which at the same time established the Council of Economic Advisers, to advise the President on how best to accomplish these objectives.

The economy's seeming inability to provide jobs was not the only problem which drew attention. The depression brought to the fore problems that, in less severe form, had been there for a long time. Many individuals lost virtually all of their money when banks failed and the stock market crashed. Many elderly people were pushed into dire poverty. Many farmers found that the prices they received for their products were so low that they could not make their mortgage payments, and defaults became commonplace.

In response to the depression, the federal government not only took a more active role in attempting to stabilize the level of economic activity, but also passed legislation designed to alleviate many of the specific problems: unemployment insurance, social security, federal insurance for depositors, federal programs aimed at supporting agricultural prices, and a host of other programs aimed at a variety of social and economic objectives. Together, these programs are referred to as the New Deal.

After World War II, the country experienced an unprecedented level of prosperity. But it became clear that not everyone was enjoying the fruits of that prosperity. Many individuals, by the condition of their birth, seemed to be condemned to a life of squalor and poverty; they received inadequate education, and their prospects for obtaining good jobs were bleak.

These inequities provided the impetus for many of the government programs that were enacted in the 1960s, when President Lyndon B. Johnson declared his "War on Poverty." While some programs were aimed at providing a "safety net" for the needy—for instance, programs to provide food and medical care to the poor—others, such as job retraining programs and Head Start, which provides preschool education for underprivileged children, were directed at improving the economic opportunities of the disadvantaged.

Could government actions alleviate these problems? How was success to be gauged? The fact that a particular program did not live up to the hopes of its most enthusiastic supporters did not, of course, mean that it was a failure. Medicaid, which provides medical assistance to the indigent, was successful in narrowing the differences in access to medical care between the poor and the rich, but the gap in life expectancy between these two groups was not eliminated. Medicare, which provides medical care for the elderly, relieved the elderly and their families of much of the anxiety concerning the financing of their medical expenses, but it left in its wake a national problem of rapidly increasing medical expenditures. While the social security program provided the aged with an unprecedented level of economic security, it has run into financial problems that cast doubt on whether future generations will be able to enjoy the same benefits.

RENT CONTROL: A CASE STUDY IN GOVERNMENT FAILURE

In the aftermath of World War II and the Great Depression, a housing shortage developed in New York City. The failure to expand supply to keep pace with demand led to an increase in prices, as any economist would have predicted. The political response did not, however, take into account these underlying forces. When lawmakers passed rent control legislation, they failed to anticipate its full consequences, overlooking the fact that apartments were supplied by those who could turn elsewhere for better investment opportunities if the return to investments in housing fell. Advocates of rent control thus failed to anticipate that the supply of rental housing would decrease, and that

Thirty years after the War on Poverty began, poverty has not been eradicated from America. Both critics and supporters of the government's programs agree that good intentions are not enough: many programs designed to alleviate the perceived inadequacies of the market economy have had effects markedly different from those their proponents anticipated. Urban renewal programs designed to improve the quality of life in inner cities have in some instances resulted in the replacement of low-quality housing with high-quality housing that poor people cannot afford, thus forcing them to live in even worse conditions. Homelessness has become an increasing concern. Though many programs designed to promote integration of public schools have succeeded, because of residential segregation, public schools are no better integrated than private schools. A disproportionate share of the benefits of farm programs has accrued to large farms; government programs have not enabled many of the small farms to survive. Allegations that government welfare programs have contributed to the breakup of families and to the development of an attitude of dependency provided part of the rationale for the massive overhaul of the welfare system in 1996.

Supporters of continued government efforts claim that critics exaggerate the failures of government programs. They argue that the lesson to be learned is not that the government should abandon its efforts to solve the major social and economic problems facing the nation, but that greater care must be taken in the appropriate design of government programs.

GOVERNMENT FAILURES

While market failures led to the institution of major government programs in the 1930s and 1960s, in the 1970s and 1980s the shortcomings of many such programs led economists and political scientists to investigate government failure. Under what conditions would government programs not work well? Were the failures of government programs accidents, or did they follow predictably from the inherent nature of governmental activity? Are there lessons to be learned for the design of programs in the future?

There are four major reasons for the systematic failures of the government to achieve its stated objectives: the government's limited information,

the quality of services provided by landlords would deteriorate. Though the government attempted to control this deterioration by imposing standards on landlords, these attempts were only partially successful, and indeed exacerbated the decline in the supply of rental housing. There was little the city government could do to stop this, short of repealing the rent control statutes for new housing, which it eventually did, though numerous older buildings remain under rent control. Many more remain under "rent stabilization" legislation, which controls the rate of increase in rents.

its limited control over private responses to its actions, its limited control over the bureaucracy, and the limitations imposed by political processes.

1 *Limited information.* The consequences of many actions are complicated and difficult to foresee. The government did not anticipate the precipitous increase in expenditures on medical care by the aged that followed the adoption of the Medicare program. Often, government does not have the information required to do what it would like to do. For instance, there may be widespread agreement that the government should help the disabled, but that those who are capable of working should not get a free ride at public expense. However, limited information on the part of government may preclude it from distinguishing between those who are truly disabled and those who are pretending.

2 *Limited control over private market responses.* The government has only limited control over the consequences of its actions. For example, we noted earlier that the government failed to anticipate the rapid increase in health care expenditures after the adoption of the Medicare program. One reason for this is that government did not directly control the total level of expenditures. Even when it set prices—such as for hospital care and doctors' services—it did not control utilization rates. Under the fee-for-service system, doctors and patients determine how much and what kinds of services are provided.

3 *Limited control over bureaucracy.* Congress and state and local legislatures design legislation, but delegate implementation to government agencies. An agency may spend considerable time writing detailed regulations; how they are drafted is critical in determining the effects of the legislation. The agency may also be responsible for ensuring that the regulations are enforced. For instance, when Congress passed the Environmental Protection Act, its intent was clear—to ensure that industries did not pollute the environment. But the technical details—for instance, determining the admissible level of pollutants for different industries—were left to the Environmental Protection Agency (EPA). During the first two years of the Reagan administration, there were numerous controversies over whether the EPA

had been lax in promulgating and enforcing regulations, thus subverting the intentions of Congress.

In many cases, the failure to carry out the intent of Congress is not deliberate but rather a result of ambiguities in Congress's intentions. In other cases, problems arise because bureaucrats lack appropriate incentives to carry out the will of Congress. For instance, in terms of future job prospects, those in charge of regulating an industry may gain more from pleasing members of the industry than from pursuing consumer interests.[3]

4 *Limitations imposed by political processes.* Even if government were perfectly informed about the consequences of all possible actions, the political process through which decisions about actions are made would raise additional difficulties. For instance, representatives have incentives to act for the benefit of special interest groups, if only to raise funds to finance increasingly expensive campaigns. The electorate often has a penchant for looking for simple solutions to complex problems; their understanding of the complex determinants of poverty, for instance, may be limited.

Critics of government intervention in the economy, such as Milton Friedman, formerly of the University of Chicago, now at Stanford University, believe the four sources of government failure are sufficiently important that the government should be restrained from attempting to remedy alleged or demonstrable deficiencies in markets.

ACHIEVING BALANCE BETWEEN THE PUBLIC AND PRIVATE SECTORS

Markets often fail, but governments often do not succeed in correcting the failures of the market. Today economists, in ascertaining the appropriate role of government, attempt to incorporate an understanding of the limitations of both government and markets. There is agreement that there are many problems which the market does not adequately address; more generally, the market is fully efficient only under fairly restrictive assumptions (see Chapters 3 and 4).

But the recognition of the limitations of government implies that government should direct its energies only at those areas in which market failures are most significant *and* where there is evidence that government intervention can make a significant difference. Among American economists today, the dominant view is that *limited* government intervention could alleviate (but not solve) the worst problems: thus, the government should take an active role in maintaining full employment and alleviating the worst aspects of poverty, but private enterprise should play the central role in the economy. The prevalent view attempts to find ways for government and markets to work together, each strengthening the other. For instance, governments rely more heavily on markets and marketlike mechanisms.

But controversy remains over how limited or how active the government should be, with views differing according to how serious one considers the failures of the market to be and how effective one believes government is in remedying them. Economists such as Michael Boskin and John Taylor of Stanford University (who served on the Council of Economic Advisers dur-

---

[3] This view has been particularly argued by George Stigler. See, for instance, his "Theory of Regulation," *Bell Journal*, spring 1971, pp. 3–21.

THE MIXED ECONOMY

• The United States is a mixed economy, in which both the public and private sectors play an important role.

• The roles played by government—and views concerning what they should be—have changed markedly over time.

• An important motivation for government's undertaking certain activities is actual or perceived failures of the market.

• There has been increasing recognition of the limitations of government, of "government failures" as well as market failures, which arise from

Limited information

Limited control over private market responses

Limited control over the bureaucracy

Limitations imposed by the political process

ing the Bush administration) and Martin Feldstein of Harvard University (who served as chairman of President Reagan's Council of Economic Advisers) advocate a more limited role. On the other hand, economists who have served on the Council of Economic Advisers under Democratic administrations, such as Alan Blinder of Princeton, Laura D'Andrea Tyson of Berkeley, and Charles Schultz of the Brookings Institution, advocate a more active role.

**THE EMERGING
CONSENSUS**
As important as they are, the differences in views of government's economic role are far smaller than the differences a hundred years ago, when socialists advocated a dominant role for government and laissez-faire economists advocated no role for government at all. Contemporary rethinking of the role of government has been reflected in two initiatives, **deregulation** and privatization. The first, begun under President Carter, reduced the role of government in regulating the economy. For instance, the government stopped regulating prices for airlines and long-distance trucking. While Presidents Bush and Reagan criticized the regulatory burden imposed on business by government, regulations continue to grow, partly in response to the growing recognition of market failures, such as those associated with the environment and the near collapse of the banking system. The Democratic Congress, worried that a recalcitrant administration would refuse to implement the laws adequately, increasingly wrote legislation reducing the regulatory discretion of the executive branch. The Clinton administration sought a balance: while recognizing the need for regulation, it also recognized that many regulations were overly burdensome, their benefits less

than their costs, and that there might be more effective ways of obtaining the desired objectives. Major reforms were instituted in such areas as banking, telecommunications, and electricity. In some of these areas, such as telecommunications, it became clear that the scope for competition was far larger than had previously been thought. Parallel reforms occurred throughout the world. In some cases, the enthusiasm for deregulation seemed to be carried too far. The economic crisis in East Asia in 1997—as the savings and loan debacle in the United States, which cost taxpayers billions and billions of dollars, had done a decade earlier—brought home the importance of financial market regulation.

The second initiative, privatization, sought to turn over to the private sector activities previously undertaken by government. The privatization movement was much stronger in Europe, where telephones, railroads, airlines, and public utilities were all privatized. In the United States, since government ran few enterprises, there was much less scope for privatization. Perhaps the most important, and controversial, privatization was that of the United States Enrichment Corporation, the government agency responsible for enriching uranium. (Low-enriched uranium is used in nuclear power plants; highly enriched uranium is used to make atomic bombs. The same process and plants are used to make both.) The privatization, which was approved in 1997 and completed in 1998, raised profound implications for U.S. national security. For instance, it complicated subsequent nuclear disarmament discussions because of conflicts of interest between the privatized firm and national security. To many, this privatization appeared to be a case of the ideology of privatization gone amok—government had lost the sense of balance between the private and public sector required to make a mixed economy work.

WHAT OR WHO IS THE GOVERNMENT?

Throughout this chapter we have referred to "the government." But what precisely is the government? We all have some idea about what institutions are included: Congress and state and local legislatures, the President and state governors and mayors, the courts, and a host of the alphabet-soup agencies, such as the FTC (Federal Trade Commission) and the IRS (Internal Revenue Service). The United States has a *federal* governmental structure—that is, governmental activities take place at several levels: federal, state, and local. The federal government is responsible for national defense, the post office, the printing of money, and the regulation of interstate and international commerce. On the other hand, the states and localities have traditionally been responsible for education, police and fire protection, and the provision of other local services, such as libraries, sewage, and garbage collection. Though the Constitution asserts that all rights not explicitly delegated to the federal government reside with the states and the people, the Constitution has proven to be a sufficiently flexible document that the exact boundaries are ambiguous. While education is primarily a local responsibility, the federal government has become increasingly involved in its support.

The constitutional provision giving the federal government the right to control interstate business has provided the basis for federal regulation of almost all businesses, since almost all businesses are involved, in one way or another, in interstate commerce.

At the local level, there are frequently several separate governmental structures, each having the power to levy taxes and the responsibility for administering certain programs. In addition to townships and counties, there are school districts, sewage districts, and library districts. In 1992, there were 85,000 such governmental entities in the United States, down from 155,000 in 1942.[4]

The boundaries between what are public institutions and what are not are often unclear. When the government sets up a corporation, a public enterprise, is that enterprise part of the "government"? For instance, Amtrak, which was set up by the federal government to run the nation's interstate passenger railway services, receives subsidies from the federal government, but otherwise it is run like a private enterprise. Matters become even more complicated when the government is a major stockholder in a company, but not the only stockholder. For instance, prior to 1987 the British government owned up to 50 percent of the shares of British Petroleum.

What distinguishes those institutions that we have labeled as "government" from private institutions? There are two important differences. First, in a democracy the individuals who are responsible for running public institutions are elected, or are appointed by someone who is elected (or appointed by someone who is appointed by someone who is elected . . .). The "legitimacy" of the person holding the position is derived directly or indirectly from the electoral process. In contrast, those who are responsible for administering General Motors are chosen by the shareholders of General Motors, while those who are responsible for administering private foundations (such as the Rockefeller and Ford foundations) are chosen by a self-perpetuating board of trustees.

Secondly, the government is endowed with certain rights of compulsion that private institutions do not have. The government has the right to force you to pay taxes (and if you fail, it can confiscate your property and/or imprison you). The government has the right to seize your property for public use provided it pays you just compensation (this is called the right of eminent domain).

Not only do private institutions and individuals lack these rights, but the government actually restricts the rights of individuals to give to others similar powers of compulsion. For instance, the government does not allow you to sell yourself into slavery.

In contrast, all private exchanges are voluntary. I may need your property to construct an office building, but I cannot force you to sell it. I may think that some deal is advantageous to both of us, but I cannot force you to engage in the deal.

Government is thus fundamentally different from other institutions in our society. It has strengths—its ability to use compulsion means that it may

---

[4] *Statistical Abstract of the United States, 1997,* Table 474.

be able to do some things that private institutions cannot do. But it also has weaknesses, as we shall discuss in greater detail in later chapters. Understanding these strengths and weaknesses is an essential part of assessing what should be the role of the government in our mixed economy, and of determining how government can most effectively fulfill that role.

THINKING LIKE A PUBLIC SECTOR ECONOMIST

Economists study *scarcity*—how societies make choices concerning the use of limited resources—and they inquire into four central economic questions:

What is to be produced?

How is it to be produced?

For whom is it to be produced?

How are these decisions made?

Like all economists, public sector economists are concerned with these fundamental questions of choice. But their focus is the choices made within the public sector, the role of the government, and the ways government affects the decisions made in the private sector.

1 *What is to be produced?* How much of our resources should be devoted to the production of public goods, such as defense and highways, and how much of our resources should we devote to the production of private goods, such as cars, TV sets, and video games? We often depict this choice in terms of the **production possibilities schedule,** which traces the various amounts of two goods that can be produced efficiently with a given technology and resources. In our case, the two goods are public goods and private goods. Figure 1.1 gives the various possible combinations of public goods and private goods that society can produce.

Society can spend more on public goods, such as national defense, but only by reducing what is available for private consumption. Thus, in moving from G to E along the production possibilities schedule, public goods are increased, but private goods are decreased. A point such as I, which is below the production possibilities schedule, is said to be *inefficient:* society could get more public goods and more private goods. A point such as N, which is above the production possibilities schedule, is said to be *infeasible:* it is not possible, given current resources and technology, to have at the same time that quantity of public goods and that quantity of private goods.

2 *How should it be produced?* Under this question are subsumed such decisions as whether to produce privately or publicly, to use more capital and less labor or vice versa, or to employ energy-efficient technologies.

Other issues are also subsumed under this second question. Government policy affects how firms produce the goods they produce: environmental protection legislation restricts pollution by firms; payroll taxes that

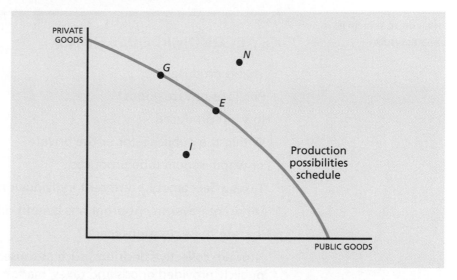

FIGURE 1.1 **Society's Production Possibilities Schedule** This depicts the maximum level of private goods that society can enjoy for each level of public goods. If society wishes to enjoy more public goods, it has to give up some private goods.

firms must pay on the workers they employ may make labor more expensive and thus discourage firms from using production techniques that require much labor.

3 *For whom is it to be produced: the question of distribution.* Government decisions about taxation or welfare programs affect how much income different individuals have to spend. Similarly, the government must decide what public goods to produce. Some groups will benefit from the production of one public good, others from another.

4 *How are choices made?* In the public sector, choices are made *collectively.* Collective choices are the choices that a society must make together—those, for instance, concerning its legal structure, the size of its military establishment, its expenditures on other public goods, etc. Texts in other fields of economics focus on how individuals make their decisions concerning consumption, how firms make their decisions concerning production, and how the price system works to ensure that the goods demanded by consumers are produced by firms. Collective decision-making is far more complicated, for individuals often disagree about what is desirable. After all, just as some individuals like chocolate ice cream and some like vanilla ice cream, some individuals get greater enjoyment out of public parks than do others. But while with private goods the individual who likes chocolate ice cream can simply buy chocolate ice cream and the individual who likes vanilla ice cream can buy vanilla ice cream, with public goods we must make a decision together. Anyone who has lived in a family knows something about the diffi-

KEY ECONOMIC QUESTIONS

- What is produced?

  Public or private goods?

- How is it produced?

  Within the public sector or the private?

- For whom should it be produced?

  Taxes affect amount different individuals have to spend.

  Different government programs benefit different groups.

- How are these decisions made?

  How are collective decisions, such as those concerning the supply of publicly provided goods and taxes, made?

culties of collective decision-making (should we go to the movies or go bowling?). Public decision-making is far more complex. One of the objectives of public sector economics is to study how collective choices (or, as they are sometimes called, social choices) are made in democratic societies.

The recognition of this divergence of views is important in itself. It should make us wary of expressions such as "It is in the public interest" or "We are concerned with the good of society." Different policies may be good for different individuals. One should carefully specify who will benefit from and who will be harmed by a given policy.

**ANALYZING THE
PUBLIC SECTOR**

In addressing each of the fundamental economic questions, there are four general stages of analysis: *describing* what the government does, *analyzing* the consequences of government action, *evaluating* alternative policies, and *interpreting* the political forces which underlie the decisions government makes.

1 *Knowing what activities the public sector engages in and how these are organized.* The complexity of the government's operations is so great that it is difficult to assess what its total expenditures are and what they go for. The budget of the federal government alone is a document that is more than 1000 pages, and within the budget, activities are not easily compartmentalized. Some activities are undertaken in several different departments or agencies. Research, for instance, is funded through the Department of Defense, the National Science Foundation, the National Institutes of Health, and the National Aeronautics and Space Administration, among others. Also, a department such as the Department of Health and Human Services undertakes a myriad of activities, some of which are only vaguely related to others.

Further, as was already noted, taxes and expenditures occur at several different levels: in some places, individuals pay not only federal and state taxes but separate taxes to their school district, their township, their county, the jurisdictions that provide their water and sewage, and their public library.

2 *Understanding and, insofar as possible, anticipating the full consequences of these governmental activities.* When a tax is imposed on a corporation, who bears the tax? At least part of the tax will be passed on to consumers through higher prices, or on to employees as wages fall. What are the consequences of the government's changing the age of retirement for social security? Of a tax credit or deduction for college tuition? Will universities respond by raising tuition so a college education will be hardly more affordable than before?

The consequences of government policies are often too complicated to predict accurately, and even after a policy has been introduced, there is often controversy about what its effects are. This book attempts not only to present all sides of some of the major controversies, but also to explain why such disagreements have persisted, and why they are difficult to resolve.

3 *Evaluating alternative policies.* To do this, we need not only to know the consequences of alternative policies, but to develop criteria for evaluation. First we must understand the objectives of government policy, and then we must ascertain the extent to which a particular proposal meets (or is likely to meet) those criteria.

Many government programs have multiple objectives. For example, the United States has a program to clean up hazardous waste sites, not only to protect health, but also because such sites may be an impediment to economic development. Some policies are better at achieving one objective, others may be better at achieving others. We need a framework for decision making in such situations: How do we think systematically about the trade-offs in evaluating alternative policies?

4 *Interpreting the political process.* Collective decisions, such as whether to subsidize farmers or to build a supercollider, or how much to spend on education, get made through political processes. How can we explain which alternatives are chosen? Economists identify the various groups that benefit

ANALYZING THE PUBLIC SECTOR

• Knowing what activities the public sector engages in and how they are organized

• Understanding and anticipating the full consequences of these government activities

• Evaluating alternative policies

• Interpreting the political process

or lose from a government program and analyze the incentives facing these groups to attempt to mobilize the political process to promote outcomes favorable to them. They also ask how the structure of government—the "rules of the game" (the rules by which Congress works, whether the President can veto specific items within a bill or only the bill as a whole, and so on)—affects the outcomes. Then they try to push the question further: What determines how the rules of the game are chosen? In addressing these questions, economics and political science merge. Economists, however, bring a distinct perspective to the analysis: they emphasize the importance of economic incentives in the behavior of participants in the political process, and therefore of economic self-interest in determining outcomes.

ECONOMIC MODELS

A central part of the analysis of the economics of the public sector is understanding the consequences of different policies. Economists, however, sometimes disagree over what those consequences will be. The standard way that science has found to test competing theories is to carry out an experiment. With luck, the results of the experiment will bear out the predictions of only one theory, while discrediting others. But economists ordinarily do not have the possibility of doing controlled experiments. Instead, what economists can observe are the uncontrolled experiments that are being done for us in different markets and in different time periods; the historical evidence, unfortunately, often does not permit us to resolve disagreements about how the economy behaves.

To analyze the consequences of various policies, economists make use of what are called **models**. Just as a model airplane attempts to replicate the basic features of an airplane, so too a model of the economy attempts to depict the basic features of the economy. The actual economy is obviously extremely complex; to see what is going on, and to make predictions about what the consequences of a particular change in policy will be, one needs to separate out the essential from the inessential features. The features one decides to focus on in constructing a model depend on the questions one wishes to address. The fact that models make simplifying assumptions, that they leave out many details, is a virtue, not a vice. An analogy may be useful. In going on a long road trip, you may use several maps. One map, depicting the interstate highway system, provides an overview, enabling you to see how to get from the general area where you are to the general area where you wish to go. You then use detailed maps to see how to get from your point of origin to the expressway, and from the expressway to your final destination. If the interstate highway map showed every street and road in the country, it would be so large that its usefulness would be limited; the extra detail, though important for some purposes, would simply get in the way.

All analysis involves the use of models, of simple hypotheses concerning how individuals and firms will respond to various changes in government policy, and how these responses will interact to determine the total impact on the economy. Everybody—politicians as well as economists—uses models in discussing the effects of alternative policies. The difference is that economists attempt to be *explicit* about their assumptions, and to be sure that their assumptions are consistent with each other and with the available evidence.

In their analysis, economists also try to identify carefully the points in their analysis where values enter in. When they describe the economy, and construct models that predict either how the economy will change or the effects of different policies, they are engaged in what is called **positive economics.** When they attempt to evaluate alternative policies, weighing up the various benefits and costs, they are engaged in what is called **normative economics.** Positive economics is concerned with what "is," with describing how the economy functions; normative economics deals with what "should be," with making judgments about the desirability of various courses of action. Normative economics makes use of positive economics. We cannot make judgments about whether a policy is desirable unless we have a clear picture of its consequences. Good normative economics also tries to be explicit about precisely what values or objectives it is incorporating. It tries to couch its statements in the form "If these are your objectives . . . , then this is the best possible policy."

Consider the positive and normative aspects of a proposal to levy a $1-per-case tax on beer. Positive economics would describe the effect the tax would have on the price of beer—would the price rise by the full $1, or would producers absorb some of the price rise? On the basis of that analysis, economists would go on to predict how much beer consumption would be reduced, and who would be affected by the tax. They might find, for instance, that since lower-income individuals spend a larger fraction of their income on beer, these people would be affected proportionately more. Studies may have indicated that there is a systematic relationship between the quantity of beer consumed and road accidents. Using this information, economists might attempt to estimate how the beer tax would affect the number of accidents. These steps are all part of describing the full consequences of the tax, without making judgments. In the end, however, the question is, *should* the tax be adopted? This is a normative question, and in responding to it economists will weigh the benefits of the tax revenue, the distortions it induces in consumption, the inequities caused by the fact that proportionately more of the tax is borne by lower-income individuals, and the lives saved in road accidents. Furthermore, in evaluating the tax, economists will also want to compare it with other ways of raising similar amounts of revenue.

This example is typical of many such situations that we face in economic policy analysis. Through positive economic analysis, we identify some gainers (the roads are safer) and some losers (consumers who pay higher prices, producers who have lower profits, workers who lose their jobs). Normative economics is concerned with developing systematic procedures by which we can compare the gains of those who are better off with the losses of those who are worse off, to arrive at some overall judgment concerning the desirability of the proposal.

The distinction between normative statements and positive statements arises not only in discussions of particular policy changes but also in discussions of political processes. For instance, economists are concerned with describing the consequences of the majority voting system in the United States, where the proposal that gets the majority of votes wins. A major

Richard Musgrave, one of the great public finance economists of the twentieth century, thought of the government as having three economic branches. The first was the *stabilization* branch; its responsibility was to ensure that the economy remained at full employment with stable prices. How this was to be done was the principal subject of courses in macroeconomics. The second branch was the *allocation* branch. Here, the government intervened in how the economy allocated its resources. It did this directly, by buying goods like defense and education, and indirectly, through taxes and subsidies, which encouraged some activities and discouraged others. The third branch, the *distribution* branch, was concerned with how the goods

group of economists, led by Nobel Prize winner James Buchanan of George Mason University, has focused on *describing* the impact of political processes on social choices (hence, these economists are often referred to as the *social choice school*).

What will be the consequences—in terms of patterns or levels of taxation or expenditure, or the speed with which these change in response to changed circumstances—of requiring a two-thirds majority for increments in public expenditures exceeding a certain amount? What will be the consequences of increasing politicians' pay? Of restricting private contributions to political campaigns? Of imposing campaign spending limits, or a variety of other proposals for reforming the financing and conduct of political campaigns? Of public support for political campaigns? But economists are also concerned with *evaluating* alternative political processes. Are some political processes better, in some senses, than others? Are they more likely to produce consistent choices? Are some political processes more likely than others to yield equitable or efficient outcomes?

DISAGREEMENTS AMONG ECONOMISTS

Unanimity is rare in the central questions of policy debate. Some individuals think affirmative action or bilingual education is desirable, some do not. Some think that the income tax should be more progressive (i.e., that wealthy individuals should pay a higher percentage of their income in taxes, while poor individuals should pay a lower percentage); some believe it should be less progressive. Some agree with the recent decision to provide a tax credit for college tuition; some believe the money could have been spent in better ways, including ways that are more effective in providing education for the poor. Some believe that capital gains should be taxed like any other form of income; others think capital gains should receive preferential treatment. One of the central concerns of policy analysis is to identify these sources of disagreement.

that were produced by society were distributed among its members. This branch was concerned with issues like equity, and the trade-offs between equity and efficiency. The economics of the public sector focuses on the latter two branches, though the issues arise in other economic courses as well, such as those that deal with regulation.

Today, we recognize that government activities in all three branches are intertwined, and cannot be neatly compartmentalized in the way that Musgrave envisaged. Still, his "three branches" provides a convenient way of looking at the myriad of activities in which the government is engaged.

Disagreements arise in two broad areas. Economists disagree about the consequences of policies (about the positive analysis) and about values (about the normative analysis).

DIFFERENCES IN VIEWS ON HOW THE ECONOMY BEHAVES

As we have seen, the first question economists ask in analyzing any policy is, what are its full consequences? In answering this question, they have to predict how households and firms will react. In 1696, England imposed a tax on windows, under the Act of Making Good the Deficiency of the Clipped Money. At the time windows were a luxury, and the houses of the wealthy had more windows than those of the poor. The window tax could be thought of as a rough substitute for an income tax, which the government did not have the authority to impose. The government should have asked, how much do people value light in their houses? One could imagine a policy debate among the king's advisers about what fraction of the population would value light so little that, rather than pay the tax, they simply would survive with windowless houses. At the time, there were no statistical studies upon which the king could rely. (In fact, many people did not value light highly, and so the government raised less revenue than anticipated, and more homes were darker than anticipated.)

Today, economists often disagree about the best model for describing the economy, and even after agreeing about the nature of the economy, they may disagree about quantitative magnitudes. For instance, they may agree that increased taxes discourage work, but disagree about the size of the effect.

A standard model that many economists employ assumes that there is perfect information and perfect competition—every firm and individual is so small that the prices it pays for what it buys and receives for what it sells do not depend at all on what it does. While most economists recognize that information and competition are both imperfect, some believe that the model of perfect information and perfect competition provides a close enough approximation to reality to be useful; others believe that—at least for some purposes, such as the health care market—the deviations are large, and that policy must be based on models which explicitly incorporate imperfect information and competition.

We cannot resolve these disagreements, but what we can do is to show how and when different views lead to different conclusions.

Even when economists agree about the kind of response a particular policy will elicit, they may disagree about the magnitude of the response. This was one of the sources of dispute about the consequences of President Clinton's 1993 health care proposals. Most economists believed that providing health insurance to more people would lead individuals who previously did not have insurance to consume more health care—one of the motivations of the program was that many of those without health insurance were getting inadequate care. But there was disagreement about how much more they would consume. The answer to this question affected what the cost of any program would be.

Although a central concern of modern economics is ascertaining the magnitude of the response of, say, investment, to an investment tax credit, of consumption to a change in the income tax rate, of savings to an increase in the interest rate, and so on, it is an unfortunate fact that various studies, using different bodies of data and different statistical techniques, come up with different conclusions. As economists obtain more data and develop better techniques for analyzing the limited available data, some of these disagreements may be resolved.

DISAGREEMENT
OVER VALUES

While the two previous sources of disagreement—concerning the best model for describing the economy and about quantitative magnitudes, such as the size of the response of savings to interest rates—arise within positive economics, the final source of disagreement lies within normative economics. Even if there is agreement about the full consequences of some policy, there may be disagreement about whether the policy is desirable. As has already been noted, there are frequently trade-offs: a policy may increase national output but also increase inequality; it may increase employment but also increase inflation; it may benefit one group but make another group worse off. Any policy, in other words, may have some desirable consequences and some undesirable consequences. Individuals may weigh these consequences in different ways, some attaching more importance to price stability than to unemployment, others attaching more importance to growth than to inequality.

On questions of values, there is no more unanimity among economists than there is among philosophers. This book will present the major views and assess some of the criticisms that have been leveled against each.

REVIEW AND PRACTICE

SUMMARY

1 In mixed economies, such as the United States, economic activity is carried on by both private enterprise and the government.

2 Since the time of Adam Smith, economic theory has emphasized the role of private markets in the efficient supply of goods. Yet economists and others have come to recognize important limitations in the ability of the

private sector to produce efficient outcomes and meet certain basic social needs. The attempt to correct these failures has led to the growth of government's role in the market economy.

3   The government, however, is not necessarily the solution to private sector failures. The failure of many public programs can be attributed to four factors: (a) The consequences of any action by the government are complicated and difficult to foresee. (b) The government has only limited control over these consequences. (c) Those who design legislation have only limited control over the implementation of the government programs. (d) Politicians may act to further special private interests; more generally, political processes are complicated and need not yield efficient outcomes.

4   The United States has a federal government structure, with certain activities primarily the responsibility of states and localities (such as education) and other activities primarily the responsibility of the federal government (such as defense).

5   Economics is the study of scarcity, how resources are allocated among competing uses. Public sector economics focuses on choices between the public and private sectors and choices within the public sector. It is concerned with four basic issues: what gets produced, how it gets produced, for whom it gets produced, and the processes by which these decisions are made.

6   In studying the public sector, positive economics looks at the scope of government activity and the consequences of various government policies. Normative economics attempts to evaluate alternative policies that might be pursued.

7   Disagreements about the desirability of policies are based on disagreements about the appropriate assumptions for describing the economy, such as how competitive the economy actually is, disagreements about how strongly the economy will respond to policy initiatives, and disagreements about values.

KEY CONCEPTS

Mixed economy	Deregulation
Privatization	Production possibilities schedule
Mercantilists	Economic models
Laissez faire	Positive economics
Full Employment Act of 1946	Normative economics

QUESTIONS AND PROBLEMS

1   Consider the following discussion of a program of price supports for farmers:

a The objective of our farm program is to ensure that all farmers have a reasonable standard of living. The way it does this is to ensure that farmers receive fair prices for their commodities. It is no more right that farmers should produce for substandard prices than that workers should work for substandard wages.

b Our farm program has been a failure. The benefits of the price subsidies accrue largely to large farmers (because they produce more). Many farmers still have incomes below the poverty line. The high prices have induced increased production, which has meant high costs for the government. Acreage restrictions have had only limited effect, since farmers have kept their best land in production. Direct grants to farmers would be preferable to our price support program.

Which of the statements in this discussion are normative, and which are positive? (The fact that you disagree with a normative statement or that you think a particular "positive" statement is inaccurate does not change the nature of the statement.)

Identify the sources of disagreement: Are they due to differences in values and objectives? To differences in perceptions about the nature of the economy? Or to a failure on one (or the other) side of the debate to take into account the full consequences of the government's action?

2 For each of the following programs, identify one or more "unintended" consequences:

    a Rent control

    b Minimum wages

    c Medicare (free hospital care to the aged)

    d Improved highways making suburbs more accessible to the city

    e Forced integration of central-city schools

    f Agricultural price supports

    g Lowering the speed limit to 55 miles an hour to save on gasoline

    h Providing health insurance to children who currently are underinsured

    i Banning advertising of cigarettes (Hint: Consider the consequences of increased life spans for the social security system.)

    j National testing standards for schools

3 There has been considerable concern that our social security (old-age and survivors insurance) program is not adequately financed: with expected birth rates, death rates, and increases in payroll tax collections, the current level of benefits can only be sustained with increases in tax rates. Some believe that the appropriate response is to reduce the current level of bene-

fits, others that the appropriate response is to increase taxes in the future. Still others, worried about the effects of even higher tax rates but believing that lowering the benefits of those presently receiving social security would be unfair, argue that benefits in the future should be cut.

In this discussion, separate out the positive statements from the normative statements. To what extent are the disagreements attributable to differences in views of the economy?

2 The Public Sector in the United States

FOCUS QUESTIONS

1 What are the principal activities of government?

2 What does government spend its money on? How have these expenditure patterns changed over time, and how do they compare across countries? Which expenditures occur at the federal level, which at the state and local level?

3 How does the government finance its expenditures? How do the sources of tax revenues differ between the federal government and the state and local governments? How have they changed over time?

A central topic of debate in the United States, and in other mixed economies, is the appropriate size of the public sector. Some believe that the public sector is too large. They are skeptical of government's ability to solve social and economic problems because of the kinds of government failures we discussed in Chapter 1—for example, government's limited control over private market responses. Or they may believe in limited government on philosophical grounds, because of a fear that big government undermines economic and political freedom.[1] Others believe that the public

---

[1] A leading proponent of this view, a form of libertarianism, is Robert Nozick. His ideas are summarized in the preface of his *Anarchy, State, and Utopia* (Oxford: Basil Blackwell, 1974). See also Milton Friedman, *Capitalism and Freedom* (Chicago: University of Chicago Press, 1962).

sector is too small. In their view, greater government spending could solve the problems of blighted inner cities and inadequate schools.

Whatever view you take, there is no doubt that the government today is far larger than it was before World War I. In 1997, tax revenues (and other nontax receipts)[2] collected at all levels of government were $2.6 trillion, or 32 percent of total U.S. production, and government expenditures were about the same.[3] By contrast, in 1913, prior to World War I, taxes and government expenditures were less than 10 percent of total production. How do we account for this dramatic change in the size of government? What does the government spend all this money on?

This chapter gives an overview of the scope of the U.S. public sector and how it has broadened over time. It also shows the ways in which government actions affect private markets. Chapter 4 will take up the economic rationale for government intervention in markets. These chapters will not resolve the debate over whether the U.S. public sector is too big or too small, but they provide a basis for formulating a reasonable position on this issue.

TYPES OF GOVERNMENT ACTIVITY

A primary role of government is to provide the legal framework within which all economic transactions occur. Beyond that, the activities of government fall into four categories: (a) the production of goods and services; (b) the regulation and subsidization of private production; (c) the purchase of goods and services, from missiles to the services of street cleaners; and (d) the redistribution of income, that is, payments, such as unemployment benefits, to particular groups of individuals that enable them to spend more than they could otherwise. Payments that transfer money from one individual to another—but not in return for the provision of goods or services—are called **transfer payments.**

These four categories—production, regulation, purchase, and redistribution—are simply a convenient way of grouping the vast array of government activities. But they do not correspond to the way the federal government organizes its budget or divides responsibilities between its various departments—Commerce, Health and Human Services, Interior, and so on. Moreover, government activities are undertaken at the state and local levels as well as at the federal level, with the relative importance of state, local, and federal expenditures of various types having changed over time.

A final complication is that the nature of some government expenditures is ambiguous. For example, government subsidies to small farmers could be considered a production subsidy or a redistributive (transfer) payment. Pension payments to military retirees are often counted as transfer payments, but they are more appropriately treated as part of the cost of national defense, just as the pension costs of a private firm are counted among its labor costs.

---

[2] Nontax receipts include, for instance, fees the government receives for various services.

[3] *Survey of Current Business,* May 1998, Table 3.1.

Thus, the task of constructing a quantitative description of the government's activities is a formidable one.

PROVIDING A LEGAL SYSTEM

An important activity of the government, but one that accounts for very little expenditure, is the establishment of the legal framework within which firms and individuals can engage in economic interactions. Economists and philosophers often try to imagine what life would be like in the complete absence of government. Without laws defining property rights, only the exercise of force would stop one individual from stealing from another. Without the ability to protect property, individuals would have little incentive to accumulate assets. Needless to say, economic activities would be severely restricted.

The U.S. legal system does much more than just protect property rights. It enforces contracts between individuals. It also imposes restrictions on the kinds of contracts that are legally enforceable. Our bankruptcy laws limit the liability of investors. Product liability laws have an important effect on the quality of goods produced. Antitrust laws attempt to encourage competition among firms: they restrict mergers, acquisitions, and unfair business practices.

The effects of our criminal justice system are pervasive, but expenditures for running it are relatively small: less than 5 percent of total government expenditures.[4]

GOVERNMENT PRODUCTION

The United States government directly undertakes certain types of production. Much of this is similar to corresponding activities carried out by private firms. For instance, both private and government enterprises produce and sell electricity (the most famous of the latter is perhaps the Tennessee Valley Authority). Also, under the Constitution, the federal government takes responsibility for running the postal service and for printing money.[5]

At the local level, many communities provide water and collect garbage, services which in other communities are provided by private firms. Most elementary and secondary school students go to public schools—schools run by the government—though others go to private schools, some of which are run by nonprofit organizations like churches, and a few of which are even run on a for-profit basis.

Comparing the public and private sectors in various countries, we see that some industries frequently fall within the public sector, while other industries seldom do. Agriculture and retail trade are seldom in the public sector. On the other hand, in most countries, at least part of the radio and

---

[4] Based on 1992 data, the most recent available. See *Economic Report of the President, 1998*, Table B-84, and Bureau of Justice Statistics, *Justice Expenditure and Employment Extracts, 1992*, Table A, p. 1.

[5] Though the U.S. Postal Service has a monopoly on the delivery of first-class mail, private carriers, such as United Parcel Service, Federal Express, and others, play a major role in the delivery of parcels and express mail.

TV broadcasting industry lies in the public sector. In many countries, the banking system is at least partially owned and operated by the government; in the United States it is closely regulated but privately owned.[6]

The line between public and private production shifts over time. During the past fifteen years in Europe, many countries have converted public enterprises into private enterprises, a process called privatization. (The process of converting private enterprises to government enterprises is called **nationalization**.) For instance, the British government has privatized enterprises in industries ranging from telecommunications to energy, automobiles, aerospace, and steel. In France, a wave of privatization began in 1986, which included the privatization of enterprises that had been nationalized earlier in that decade when the socialist party was in power.[7]

For technical reasons, the best way to measure the size of government production is to look at employment, as in Figure 2.1 shown on page 30. In 1997 public employees (including public education and the armed forces) represented 15.9 percent of total employment. This was almost double the percentage in 1929 (when it was 9 percent of the labor force). The figure shows a marked increase in the ratio of public employment from 1929 through 1936 (both in the Hoover and Roosevelt administrations), a burst of public employment during World War II, and a return to pre-War levels by 1952. Though there was a slight decrease in the pace of growth during the Eisenhower years, employment in the public sector did not begin to decline until the Nixon and Ford administrations. This decline has continued. In fact, as a percentage of civilian employment, by 1997 federal government employment was comparable to that of the early 1930s, before the New Deal.

It is also important to note the variations in the relative roles played by the federal, state, and local governments, as suggested by the bottom line in Figure 2.1. Comparing it to the top line, we see that total government employment and federal government employment do not always move together. While federal employment as a percentage of total employment declined in the early 1970s, this decline was offset by the rise in employment at the state and local level. It is important to bear this in mind: reductions in federal expenditures or employment do not of themselves necessarily imply a reduction in government expenditures or employment. More of a burden may simply be placed on states and localities.

[6] The Federal Reserve Banks, which are responsible for the management of the banking system, are publicly owned. Their profits are turned over to the U.S. Treasury. In 1997 these amounted to $21.5 billion. (*Survey of Current Business*, May 1998, Table 3.2, p. D-8.)

[7] For more on privatization, see William L. Megginson et al., "The Financial and Operating Performance of Newly Privatized Firms: An International Empirical Analysis," *Journal of Finance* 49, no. 2 (1994), and Pierre Guislain, *The Privatization Challenge: A Strategic, Legal, and Institutional Analysis of International Experience* (Washington, D.C.: World Bank, 1997).

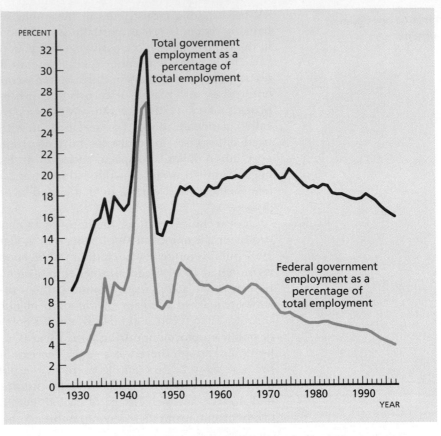

PERCENT

YEAR

FIGURE 2.1   **Government Employment as a Percentage of Total Employment, 1929–1997**
Government employment as a percentage of all employment provides a view
of the government's role as producer. Employment is defined here as the
number of full-time equivalent employees.

SOURCES: U.S. Department of Commerce, *National Income and Product Accounts, 1929–1958*,
Tables 1.7, 6.5A; *National Income and Product Accounts, 1959–1988*, Tables 1.7, 6.5B, 6.5C;
Survey of Current Business, July 1992, Tables 1.7, 6.5C; *Survey of Current Business*, January
1999, Table B.9.

**GOVERNMENT'S
INFLUENCE ON
PRIVATE PRODUCTION**

In industries in which the government is neither a producer nor a consumer, it may nevertheless have a pervasive effect on the decisions of private
producers. This influence is exercised through subsidies and taxes—both
direct and indirect—and through regulations. There are many motives for
such government influence. There may be dissatisfaction with particular actions of firms, such as pollution. There may be concern about the monopoly
power of some firms. Special interest groups may convince Congress that
they are particularly deserving of help. Private markets may fail to provide
certain goods and services that are felt to be important.

SUBSIDIES AND TAXES Government subsidizes private production in three
broad ways: direct payments to producers, indirect payments through the tax

system, and other hidden expenditures. The most extensive of the U.S. government's subsidy programs is that for agriculture. Direct payments to farmers rose precipitously during the 1980s, from $1.3 billion in 1980 to a peak of $16.7 billion in 1987. In 1987, direct payments amounted to 37 percent of income from wheat, 40 percent of income from rice, and 20 percent of income from all crops. At least one of every five dollars in farm income was a gift from the government. The size of agricultural subsidies has fallen since 1987, and fluctuates markedly from year to year. Under the new farm bill passed in 1996, these subsidies are scheduled to decline over the coming years.[8]

The tax system also sometimes serves to subsidize production. If the government gives a grant to a producer to assist her in buying a machine, it appears as an expenditure. But suppose the government allows her to take a tax credit on her expenditures on machines—that is, if she buys a $100 machine with a 7 percent tax credit, she will get a $7 tax credit, which reduces the taxes she otherwise would have paid by $7. Though it is not accounted as such, for all intents and purposes the tax credit is equivalent to a government expenditure, and is thus referred to as a *tax expenditure*. The value of federal tax expenditures has become very large in recent years: amounting to in excess of 34 percent of direct expenditures for fiscal year 1998.[9]

Finally, many government subsidies show up neither in the statistics on government expenditures nor in those on tax expenditures. For instance, when the government restricts the importation of some foreign good or imposes a tariff on its importation, this raises the prices of that good in the United States. American producers of competing goods are helped. In effect, there is a subsidy to American producers, paid not by the government but directly by consumers.

GOVERNMENT CREDIT A special type of subsidy is government provision of credit below market interest rates, in the form of low-interest loans and loan guarantees. Government subsidies tend to lead to the expansion of the subsidized industry, by lowering its cost of doing business. This is as true for subsidies to credit as it is for other forms of subsidies. Though such subsidies were once hidden, the Credit Reform Act of 1990 required the government to treat as expenditures any difference between the interest rates it paid and the interest rates it charged (taking into account the probability that the borrower might not repay).

In addition to loan subsidies, other government programs affect the allocation of credit, and thus of productive resources. In the United States, the subsidies are often to buy particular goods and services. For instance, government-sponsored enterprises (called GSEs) encourage lending to enable people to buy homes and go to school. In 1993, the Clinton administration began directly lending funds to college students.

[8] United States Department of Agriculture, Economic Research Service, *Economic Indicators of the Farm Sector: National Financial Summary, 1992,* January 1994, Tables 14 and 22, and *Survey of Current Business,* June 1997, Table B-10, p. D-24.

[9] *Budget of the United States Government, Fiscal Year 1999,* Table 5-1, Analytical Perspectives; Historical Tables, Table 3.1.

REGULATING BUSINESS Government regulates business activity in an attempt to protect workers, consumers, and the environment, to prevent anticompetitive practices, and to prevent discrimination.

The Occupational Safety and Health Administration attempts to ensure that workers' places of employment meet certain minimal standards. The National Labor Relations Board attempts to ensure that management and unions deal fairly with each other. The Federal Trade Commission attempts, among other things, to protect consumers from misleading advertising. The Environmental Protection Agency attempts to protect certain vital parts of our environment by regulating, for instance, emissions from automobiles and toxic waste disposal.

In addition to these broad categories, there are regulations that apply to specific industries. The banking industry is regulated both by the Federal Reserve Board and the Comptroller of the Currency. Trucking is regulated by the Federal Highway Administration. The airlines are regulated by the Federal Aviation Administration. The telecommunications industry is regulated by the Federal Communications Commission. The securities industry is regulated by the Securities and Exchange Commission.

Beginning in the late 1970s, there was a concerted effort to reduce the extent of federal regulation. As noted earlier, the process of reducing or eliminating regulations is referred to as deregulation. There has been deregulation in the airline industry (with the elimination of the Civil Aeronautics Board in 1984), in natural gas (gas prices have been allowed to rise gradually to market levels), in trucking, and in banking (the range of services that banks are now allowed to provide has been greatly increased).

In 1993, the Clinton administration initiated a systematic effort to reexamine all government regulations, to ascertain whether they were still required and whether they achieved their objectives in the most cost-effective way. The initiative was called "re-inventing government" or "National Performance Review," and focused on making government agencies more client oriented and employing more marketlike regulatory mechanisms. Legislation in 1996 provided for major changes in the regulation of telecommunications; it recognized the increased scope for competition, but that nevertheless competition in certain segments of the industry remained limited. New regulations in electricity in the mid-1990s expanded the scope for competition in that sector.

While the overall trend entailed reduced regulation, there were some instances of tightened regulation: the massive failure of the savings and loan associations in the 1980s was attributed in part to lax banking regulation, and legislation enacted in 1989 provided for heightened scrutiny. In other cases, the focus was on changing regulation to reflect changing circumstances. For example, while several cases of deaths from food poisoning reinforced the importance of food safety regulations, there was increasing recognition that the visual inspection system (did the meat smell and look rotten?) that had been employed since the beginning of the twentieth century needed to be replaced with a more scientific process.

Federal outlays for the regulatory agencies are minuscule relative to the rest of the budget. But these expenditures do not give an accurate view of the impact of the federal regulatory agencies. The extent to which these agencies influence virtually every aspect of business practices goes well beyond the simple measure of government expenditures. Many regulations have effects that are similar to those of taxes and subsidies. For example, regulations on utility prices may reduce prices for certain users below the free-market level, while raising the price to other users.

GOVERNMENT PURCHASES OF GOODS AND SERVICES

Every year the government buys billions of dollars' worth of goods and services. It does this to provide for our national defense, to maintain a network of highways, to provide education, police protection, fire protection, and parks. These purchases of goods and services amount to nearly one-fifth of the total production in the United States. In 1997, total government purchases were $1.2 trillion. Of these purchases, 15.3 percent was for investments, for expenditures, for instance, on roads and bridges and buildings that increase the economy's future productivity.[10]

What we characterize as government purchases are amounts spent for goods and services made available to the public, such as national defense, public schools, and highways. Government payments to the aged through the Medicare program to finance their hospital expenses or to the poor through the food stamp program are categorized as transfer payments, not as direct government purchases. They are discussed in the next section, on government redistribution of income.

GOVERNMENT REDISTRIBUTION OF INCOME

The government takes an active role in redistributing income, that is, in taking money away from some individuals and giving it to others. There are two major categories of explicit redistribution programs: public assistance programs, which provide benefits to those poor enough to qualify; and social insurance, which provides benefits to the retired, disabled, unemployed, and sick.

As we saw above, outlays for explicit redistribution programs are called *transfer payments*. These expenditures are qualitatively different from government spending on, say, roads or bombers. Transfer payments are simply changes in who has the right to consume goods. In contrast, a government outlay for a road or a bomber reduces the amount of other goods (e.g., private consumption goods) that society can enjoy. Transfer payments affect the way in which society's total income is divided among its members, but (neglecting here losses of output due to distorted incentives associated with transfers) transfers do not affect the total amount of private goods that can be enjoyed.

PUBLIC ASSISTANCE PROGRAMS Public assistance programs take two forms. Some provide cash, while others provide payment only for specific services or commodities. The latter are referred to as **in-kind benefits.** Of the cash

---

[10] The investment numbers do not include investments in people—human capital, for either education or health—but they do include investments in military aircraft and other hardware that enhance the country's future defense capabilities; in transportation infrastructure, such as highways and airports; and in natural resource investments, such as pollution control facilities.

PROGRAM	DATE ENACTED	1990 OUTLAY	1996 OUTLAY
CASH BENEFITS			
AFDC	1935	26,034	24,220
SSI	1972	21,162	31,064
General assistance		3,591	2,946
Earned income tax credit*	1975	6,512	22,061
Other assistance		8,221	9,010
IN-KIND BENEFITS			
Medicaid	1965	89,020	163,013
Food stamps	1964	21,718	27,971
Low-income housing assistance	1937	12,989	15,360
National School Lunch Program	1946	3,873	4,894
TOTAL		193,120	300,539

*Includes only the refunded portion.
SOURCE: *Statistical Abstract of the United States,* 1998, Table 605.

programs, the largest are Temporary Assistance to Needy Families (TANF), the program that in 1997 replaced the long-standing Aid to Families with Dependent Children (AFDC), and Supplemental Security Income (SSI), which provides cash to the poor who are aged, blind, or disabled. The largest in-kind public assistance program is Medicaid, which covers the medical costs of the poor, and accounts for about one half of total public assistance.

Table 2.1 lists the main public assistance programs with their date of enactment and their benefits. (In-kind benefits are valued at government cost in the table; we will see later that this may be different from their value to the recipients.) The table shows that most benefits (roughly two thirds) were in-kind, not cash.

SOCIAL INSURANCE PROGRAMS **Social insurance** differs from public assistance in that an individual's entitlements are partly dependent on his or her contributions, which can be viewed as insurance premiums. To the extent that what individuals receive is commensurate with their contributions, social insurance can be viewed as a government "production activity" not a redistribution activity. But since what some receive is far in excess of what they contribute (on an actuarial basis), there is a large element of redistribution involved in government social insurance programs.

The largest of these programs is the Old-Age, Survivors, and Disability Insurance Program (OASDI, the proper name for social security). It provides income not only for the retired, but also to their survivors (in particular, widows and widowers) and to the disabled. The other major social insurance programs are workers' compensation, which provides compensation for workers injured at work; unemployment insurance, which provides temporary benefits after an individual loses a job; and Medicare. The Medicare program, providing medical services to the aged, has (like Medicaid) grown rapidly since it was first introduced in 1965, and now is the second largest program. Figure 2.2 gives the relative size of the various social insurance and public assistance programs.

The social security and Medicare programs are sometimes referred to as **middle-class entitlement programs,** because the main beneficiaries are the middle class, and benefits are provided not on the basis of need but because

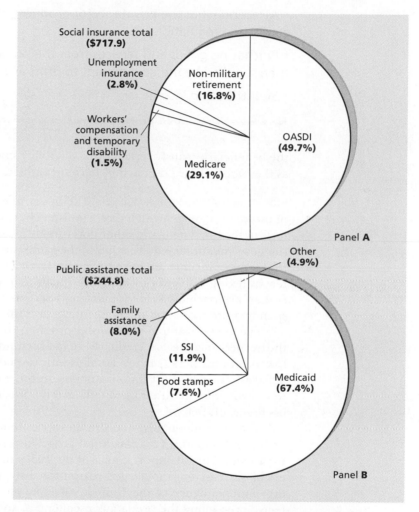

FIGURE 2.2   **Relative Importance of Social Insurance and Public Assistance Programs, 1996** Social Security (OASDI) is by far the largest social insurance expenditure, and the largest overall transfer program. Medicaid is the largest public assistance expenditure. (Workers' compensation includes Workers' Compensation, Temporary Disability, and Black Lung benefits. Other retirement includes Railroad Retirement and Pension Benefit Guaranty.)

SOURCE: *Survey of Current Business*, August 1998, Table 3.1, 65.

GOVERNMENT ACTIVITIES

- Providing a legal system—required if a market economy is to function
- Producing goods—defense, education, mail
- Affecting what the private sector produces, through subsidies, taxes, credit, and regulation
- Purchasing goods and services from the private sector, which are then supplied by the government to firms and households
- Redistributing income

the beneficiaries satisfy certain other eligibility standards (e.g., age). As soon as they satisfy these criteria, they become entitled to receive the benefits.

HIDDEN REDISTRIBUTION PROGRAMS The government affects the distribution of income not only through direct transfers but also through the indirect effects of the tax system and other government programs. One could imagine the government taxing everyone at the same rate but then giving grants to those whose income fell below a certain level. This would have the same effect as taxing the lower-income individuals at a lower rate. Thus, there is a certain arbitrariness in distinguishing between transfer payments through spending programs and the implicit transfers through the tax system.[11]

The major example of a transfer program run through the tax system is the earned income tax credit (EITC), which actually provides income to low-income earners (such as families with two children with income under $28,000). Under the Clinton administration, expenditures for the EITC were expanded in an effort to enhance the incentives for low-skilled workers to stay off welfare.

The government also redistributes income in the guise of subsidy programs and quotas. Our agricultural programs in effect redistribute income to farmers. The oil import quotas of the 1950s redistributed income to owners of oil reserves. The alleged reason for the quotas was to ensure the energy independence of the United States; nonetheless the redistributive effects were among the primary consequences, and they may indeed provide the true motivation for the legislation.

Spending for goods and services also has its redistributive consequences: subsidies to urban bus transport may help the poor, while subsidies to suburban rail lines may help the middle class.

[11] Some of the tax expenditures can be viewed explicitly as forms of social insurance. The fact that unemployment insurance and social security are only partially taxed, and disability benefits not taxed at all, means that a dollar of direct expenditures for those purposes goes further than it would if subjected to taxation.

We can now put together the discussion of purchases and transfers to get an overview of government expenditures. Figure 2.3 shows the distribution of government expenditures in 1997. In panel A, which combines outlays at all levels of government, we can see that purchases of goods and services, pri-

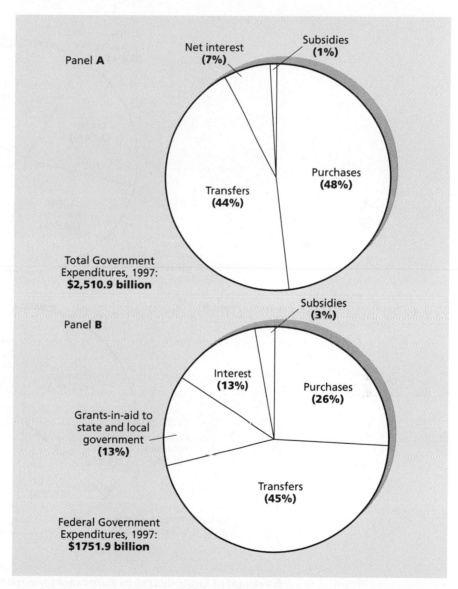

Panel **A**

Net interest (7%)

Subsidies (1%)

Purchases (48%)

Transfers (44%)

Total Government Expenditures, 1997: **$2,510.9 billion**

Panel **B**

Subsidies (3%)

Interest (13%)

Purchases (26%)

Grants-in-aid to state and local government (13%)

Transfers (45%)

Federal Government Expenditures, 1997: **$1751.9 billion**

FIGURE 2.3   **Government Expenditures by Type** Today, almost half of all government expenditures at the federal, state, and local levels are transfers. As a result of the huge deficits accumulated since 1981, almost one out of every seven dollars goes to pay interest on the government debt.

SOURCE: *Economic Report of the President,* 1998, Tables B-82, B-84.

marily for defense and education, constitute almost half of expenditures, and transfer payments comprise the bulk of the rest.

Figure 2.4 shows the purpose of the expenditures by broad categories, both for the federal government's expenditures and for all government expenditures. Note that at the federal level, social security (OASDI) and de-

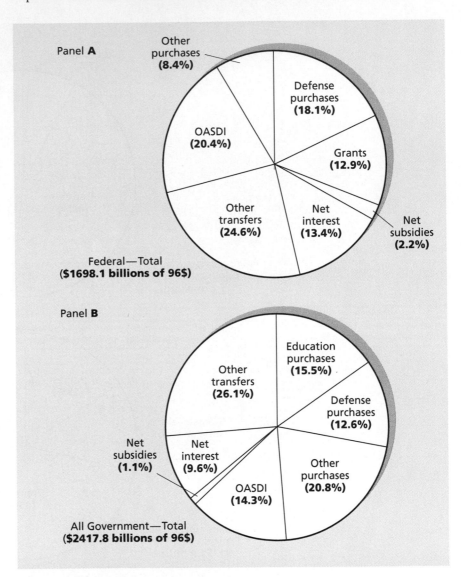

Panel **A**

Other purchases (8.4%)

Defense purchases (18.1%)

OASDI (20.4%)

Grants (12.9%)

Other transfers (24.6%)

Net interest (13.4%)

Net subsidies (2.2%)

Federal—Total ($1698.1 billions of 96$)

Panel **B**

Education purchases (15.5%)

Other transfers (26.1%)

Defense purchases (12.6%)

Net subsidies (1.1%)

Net interest (9.6%)

Other purchases (20.8%)

OASDI (14.3%)

All Government—Total ($2417.8 billions of 96$)

FIGURE 2.4 **Government Expenditures by Purpose** At the federal level, the most important expenditures, other than transfers, are for defense; at the state and local level, the most important expenditures are for education.

Source: *Survey of Current Business*, October 1997, Tables 3.1, 3.15, 3.16, 3.17.

fense purchases play major roles. For total government expenditures, education appears as a major category because it is the largest type of expenditure at the state and local level.[12]

There have been marked changes in the relative importance of expenditures at different levels of government over the past century. For instance, the federal share of all non-defense government spending grew from slightly less than a fifth in 1902 to more than 60 percent in 1997.

GAUGING THE SIZE OF THE PUBLIC SECTOR

Since the government's impact on the private economy depends on its regulatory and tax policies as well as on its outlays, no single number can provide an accurate indicator of the government's effect on the economy. Nonetheless, one indicator that economists have found particularly convenient to use is the size of public expenditures relative to the size of the total economy. A standard measure of the size of the total economy is gross domestic product (GDP), which is a measure of the value of all the goods and services produced in the economy during a given year.

GROWTH IN EXPENDITURES AND THEIR CHANGING COMPOSITION During the past fifty years, public expenditures as a share of GDP have grown rapidly. In 1940 they were 10 percent of GDP. In 1997, they represented 31 percent of GDP, as we see in Figure 2.5.[13]

DEFENSE EXPENDITURES Figure 2.5 also shows that between 1967 and 1979 defense expenditures as a percentage of GDP declined from 9 percent to 4.9 percent. They then increased during the Reagan years until 1986, peaking at 6.2 percent, but after the end of the Cold War they once again declined to a projected 3 percent of GDP in 2000.

In order to avoid the misleading impressions that can be caused by failing to take account of inflation, economists like to express expenditures in dollars of constant value. Thus, if last year the government spent $1 billion on some program, and this year it spends $1.1 billion, but prices have increased by 10 percent, we say that the current expenditures (measured in last year's prices) are $1 billion—in constant dollars expenditures have not increased at all. Thus, in constant 1997 dollars, defense expenditures shrank from an average of $353 billion in 1967–1969 to $263 billion in

[12] Note that there is some inherent imprecision in any classification. For instance, veterans' benefits, which are typically not included in defense expenditures, can be thought of as expenditures for previously delivered defense services. Some of the expenditures on space are motivated by defense concerns.

[13] Recall from the earlier discussion the arbitrariness of this measure. For instance, if the government switches from providing aid to education through direct grants to providing it through tax expenditures, these statistics would show a fall in the share of public expenditures.

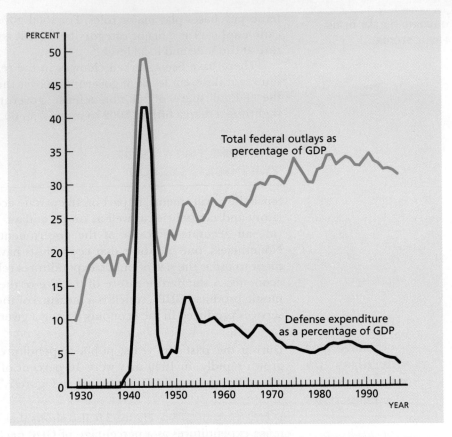

FIGURE 2.5 **Federal Defense Outlays and Total Federal Outlays as a Percentage of Gross Domestic Product (GDP), 1929–1999** Total government expenditures as a percentage of GDP have increased markedly since 1929.

SOURCES: *National Income and Product Accounts, 1929–1958*, Tables 1.7, 3.1, 3.2, 3.15; *National Income and Product Accounts, 1959–1988*, Tables 1.7, 3.15; *Survey of Current Business*, July 1992, Tables 1.7, 3.15; *Survey of Current Business*, August 1997, Tables 1.7, 3.15; *Survey of Current Business*, May 1998, Table 3.10.

1976, but they increased to a post–Korean War high of $412 billion in 1987. Subsequently, they declined to a projected level of $269 billion by 2000.

TRANSFER PAYMENTS AND INTEREST Growth in expenditures for social security, Medicare, and interest account for much of the increase in public expenditures since 1950. (See Figure 2.6.) The increase in interest payments is a consequence of the huge deficits that began under President Reagan, as the government spent more than it received. It was not until Clinton succeeded in passing a deficit reduction act in 1993 that the deficit was brought under control; interest payments actually came down, as interest rates fell by more than the deficit increased. Though public assistance is often blamed for the growth

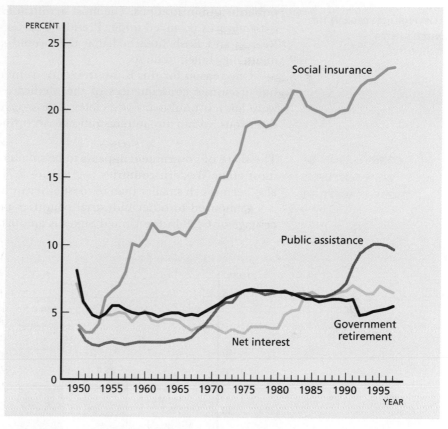

FIGURE 2.6 **Government Transfer and Interest Payments as a Percentage of Total Expenditures, 1950–1997** Social insurance payments (largely OASDI) have grown from less than 5 percent of expenditures in 1950 to over 23 percent of expenditures in 1997. Interest payments grew from a low of 3.5 percent of expenditures in 1975 to a high of 7.1 percent in 1991. Government retirement in this graph includes retirement benefits for civilian and military personnel and veterans' benefits.

SOURCES: *National Income and Product Accounts, 1929–1958*, Tables 3.1, 3.12; *National Income and Product Accounts, 1958–1988*, Tables 3.1, 3.12; *Survey of Current Business*, July 1992, Tables 3.1, 3.12; *Survey of Current Business*, August 1997, Tables 3.1, 3.12; *Survey of Current Business*, May 1998, Table 3.1; *Survey of Current Business*, August 1998, Table 3.12.

in public expenditures, its share of total government expenditures only increased from 4 percent of expenditures in 1950 to about 10 percent in 1996.

A major source of increased expenditure during the past two decades has been health care—Medicaid and Medicare—and there is real concern that these expenditures will continue to soar in coming decades as well.

Figures 2.5 and 2.6 tell one other interesting story. Total non-defense expenditures as well as social insurance expenditures increased rapidly from the mid-1960s through the mid-1970s, under both Democratic and Republican administrations. The most significant break in the *rate of increase* of expenditures occurred under President Carter (1976–1980). And although Reagan and Bush preached that they would cut back the size of government, they failed to do so.

One reason for this is the tremendous inertia in the fiscal system. The full economic consequences of the Medicare program, enacted in 1965, were not felt until many years later. The scope for discretion, for changing directions, within any administration is accordingly limited.

COMPARISON OF EXPENDITURES ACROSS COUNTRIES

The share of government appears to be smaller in the United States than in most other Western countries (see Figure 2.7), and its relative growth has also been much smaller than in most other industrialized countries.

Compared to other industrial countries public expenditures as a percentage of GDP in the United States is among the lowest. Because defense

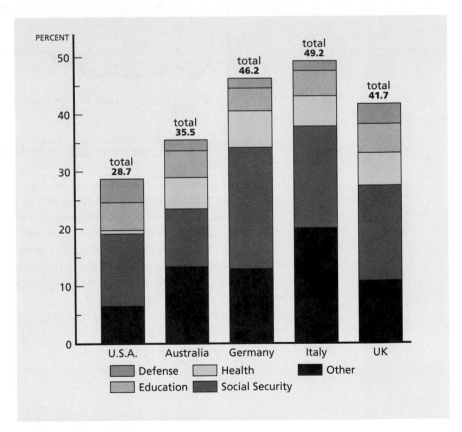

FIGURE 2.7   **Government Programs as a Percentage of GDP in Five Countries** Despite the growth of government in the United States, it has the smallest public sector of the five countries shown here.

SOURCES: Organization for Economic Cooperation and Development, *National Accounts, Detailed Tables*, vol. 2, 1983–1995, Tables for Specific Countries; *Survey of Current Business*, October 1997, Table 3.15.

GAUGING THE SIZE OF GOVERNMENT

• The size of the U.S. government today is much larger than it was a hundred years ago.

  • During the past fifty years, public expenditures as a share of GDP have grown rapidly. In 1940, they were 10 percent of GDP. In 1997, they represented 31 percent of GDP.

  • Growth in expenditures for social security, Medicare, and interest account for much of the increase in public expenditures since 1950.

• The size of government relative to the economy is much smaller in the United States than in most European countries.

expenditures play a larger role in the United States, the relative size of non-defense expenditures is particularly low, viewed from this international perspective.[14]

GOVERNMENT REVENUES

Now that we have examined what the government spends its money on, we will briefly survey the methods by which government raises revenue to pay for these expenditures. The government levies a variety of taxes. When the revenues that it receives from taxes are less than its planned expenditures, it must either cut back expenditures or borrow the difference.[15]

TAXES AND THE CONSTITUTION

The issue of taxation was very much in the thoughts of the founders of the republic. Indeed, the American Revolution began as a tax revolt with the Boston Tea Party, which was a protest against the tax on tea, and with the slogan "Taxation without representation is tyranny." The first article of the Constitution provides that "The Congress shall have power to levy and collect Taxes, Duties, Imposts, and Excises, to pay the Debts and provide for the Common Defense and General Welfare of the United States."

[14] Comparisons across countries always need to be treated with caution. Particular problems are raised by the treatment of public enterprises. The fact that tax expenditures are relatively more important here than abroad may result in an understatement of the "effective" relative size of the public sector in the United States. On the other hand, regulations are perhaps less important in the United States than in most other developed countries.

[15] In many countries, when there is a gap between expenditures and revenues, the difference is financed by printing money. This is how the Continental Congress financed the Revolutionary War. (The expression "not worth a continental" arose from the fact that the currency was not highly valued.)

Three restrictions were imposed: The government could not levy taxes on exports; "all Duties, Imposts, and Excises" had to be "uniform throughout the United States" (referred to as the uniformity clause); and "no capitation or other direct tax shall be laid, unless in proportion to the Census or Enumeration herein before directed to be taken" (referred to as the apportionment clause). (A capitation tax is a tax levied on each person. These taxes are also called head taxes or poll taxes. They are no longer levied by any state.)

The constitutional provision restricting direct taxes proved to be a problem. Congress levied an income tax during the Civil War, and reenacted it in 1894 as a tax on very high incomes. But it was declared unconstitutional by the Supreme Court in 1895. The Court held that the individual income tax was, in part, a direct tax, which the Constitution stipulates must be apportioned among the states according to their population. Widespread criticism of this rule led to a constitutional amendment. The Sixteenth Amendment, ratified in 1913, declares that "Congress shall have the power to levy and collect taxes on incomes, from whatever sources derived, without apportionment among the several states, and without regard to census or enumeration."

The apportionment provision, however, still may restrict Congress's ability to impose some taxes. Several countries impose national property taxes or wealth taxes. But these are likely to be considered direct taxes, and thus precluded in the United States by the apportionment provision.

FEDERAL TAXATION TODAY

The federal government currently relies on five major forms of taxation: (1) the individual **income tax,** (2) **payroll taxes** (to finance social security and Medicare benefits), (3) **corporate income taxes,** (4) **excise taxes** (taxes on specific commodities, such as gasoline, cigarettes, airline tickets, and alcohol), and (5) **customs taxes** (taxes levied on selected imported goods). The individual income tax is the single largest source of tax revenue for the federal government, accounting for almost half of government revenues in recent years. In 1997, social security taxes accounted for another 37.5 percent, the corporation income tax 12.3 percent, and customs and excise taxes 4.5 percent of federal government revenue.[16]

Just as there has been a marked shift in the composition of expenditures over the past fifty years, so too there has been a marked change in the source of government revenues. With the two exceptions mentioned above, the federal government did not impose any income tax on individuals before 1913. The individual income tax accounted for 30 percent or less of government tax revenues before the 1940s, when rates were quadrupled to pay for World War II.[17] Since that war, the individual income tax has been the largest single source of federal revenues, as shown in Figure 2.8. The

[16] *Survey of Current Business,* May 1998, Table 3.2, p. D-8.
[17] For a historical summary of the major federal taxes, see Joseph Pechman, *Federal Tax Policy,* 5th ed. (Washington D.C.: Brookings Institution, 1987), Appendix A.

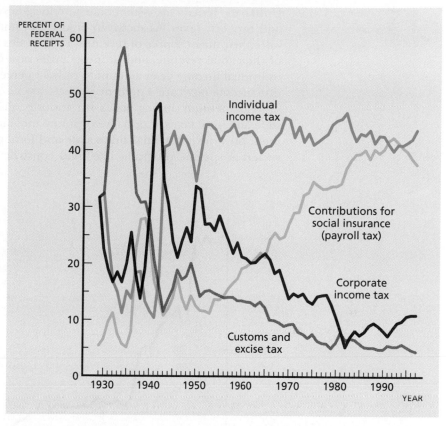

PERCENT OF FEDERAL RECEIPTS

Individual income tax

Contributions for social insurance (payroll tax)

Corporate income tax

Customs and excise tax

YEAR

FIGURE 2.8 **Distribution of Federal Receipts by Source, as Percentages of Total Federal Receipts** The individual income tax and contributions to social insurance (primarily social security payroll taxes) are now by far the most important source of federal revenue. The shares of revenue provided by the corporate income tax and by customs and excise taxes have fallen sharply over the past forty years.

SOURCES: *National Income and Product Accounts, 1929–1982*, Table 3.2; *Survey of Current Business*, July 1986, Table 3.2; *Survey of Current Business*, July 1989, Table 3.2; *Survey of Current Business*, July 1992, Table 3.2; *Survey of Current Business*, August 1997, Table 3.2; *Survey of Current Business*, May 1998, Table 3.2.

corporation income tax has played a decreasing role, falling from 36 percent of federal revenues in 1927 to 23 percent in 1960 and 12.3 percent in 1997.

Between 1789 and 1909, the federal government received almost all of its revenues from excise taxes and customs. Today, those taxes are relatively unimportant. On the other hand, the payroll tax, which was introduced by the Social Security Act of 1935, increased from 18 percent of federal revenues in 1960 to 37.5 percent in 1997.

Unlike the federal tax system, state and local tax systems rely heavily on sales and property taxes. As shown in Figure 2.9, until the 1970s property taxes were their major source of revenue. Today, sales taxes amount to 24 percent of their total revenue, and property taxes raise 22 percent. State and local individual income taxes amount to only 14 percent of the total, while corporate income taxes are 4 percent.

Competition among states for industry discourages the use of some state and local taxes, especially corporate income taxes. The federal government provides substantial aid to state and local governments, much of it directed at specific programs like road construction, mass transit, bilingual

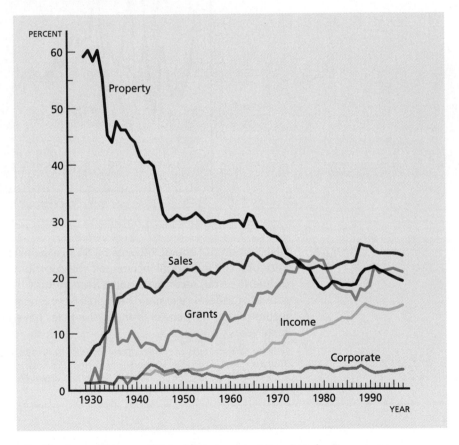

FIGURE 2.9   **Distribution of State and Local Government Receipts by Source, as Percentages of Total** Federal grants and individual income taxes have increased in importance while property taxes have decreased in importance as a source of state and local revenues.

SOURCES: *National Income and Product Accounts, 1929–1982*, Table 3.3; *Survey of Current Business*, July 1986, Table 3.3; *Survey of Current Business*, July 1989, Table 3.3; *Survey of Current Business*, July 1992, Table 3.3; *Survey of Current Business*, August 1997, Table 3.3; *Survey of Current Business*, May 1998, Table 3.3.

education, vocational education, and libraries. In 1996, federal grants to state and local governments provided one-fifth of their revenue.

Patterns of taxation differ from country to country. While in most European countries the individual income tax is less important than in the United States—it averages only 27 percent of government revenues throughout the European Union—taxes on goods and services are more important. Outside the United States, the **value-added tax** (a tax imposed on the value of the output of a firm less the value of goods and services purchased from other firms) is a major source of revenue. Social security taxes comprise about the same share of government revenues in Japan, Europe, and the United States.[18]

DEFICIT FINANCING

The major source of financing of government expenditures is taxes. But many governments, especially in recent years, have found tax revenues insufficient to pay for their expenditures. A **deficit** in any period is the excess of spending over revenues. A deficit is financed by borrowing. The cumulative value of borrowing by a firm, household, or government is its debt.

A firm or household that runs a deficit cannot continue to borrow indefinitely, but will be forced into bankruptcy once its debt gets too large. Because of the federal government's ability to tax, and the huge potential revenue sources it can tap, its deficits do not cause the same kinds of problems that large debts incurred by private firms or individuals would. Lenders will continue to willingly finance the federal government's debt, provided the interest rate is high enough.

In the early 1980s, the size of the federal deficit, both in dollar terms and, more importantly, as a fraction of GDP and of the budget, reached all-time highs (for peacetime); see Figure 2.10. The size of the deficits in the 1980s caused great consternation both in and outside of Washington. In order to finance the deficit, the role of the federal government as a *borrower* in U.S. credit markets soared.

The dollar value of the debt goes up each year by the amount of that year's federal deficit (a federal surplus reduces the federal debt). But the *real* value of the debt also depends very much on inflation. To see what this means, assume you promise to pay someone $100 next year. If the prices of all goods and services rise by 10 percent, next year that person will be able to purchase with $100 the same goods that he could have purchased with $91 this year. The "real value" of what you have to pay him has declined by $9.

---

[18] *OECD in Figures*, pp. 45–46, accessed at *Statistics at the OECD* (http://www.oecd.org/std/), April 7, 1998. Percentages reflect tax revenues in 1994.

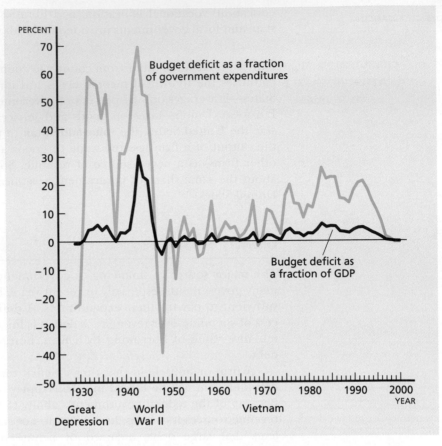

PERCENT

Budget deficit as a fraction of government expenditures

Budget deficit as a fraction of GDP

Great Depression

World War II

Vietnam

YEAR

FIGURE 2.10   **The Federal Budget Deficit as a Percentage of Expenditures and of GDP, 1929–2000** The deficit increased markedly during the early 1980s, fell, and then increased again during the early 1990s. A federal budget surplus is projected after 1998. Note that figures for 1998–2000 are estimates.

SOURCE: *Budget of the United States Government, Fiscal Year 1999*, Historical Tables, Tables 1.1, 1.2.

Figure 2.11 traces the changes since 1940 in the real value of the federal debt owed to U.S. citizens and foreigners—known as the publicly held federal debt. In real terms, the increase in the debt after 1980 is dramatic. As a result of the high deficits and the fall in the inflation rate, the period 1980–1986 saw a near doubling of the publicly held real debt, from $1,147 billion in 1980 to $2,264 billion in 1997 (both amounts measured in 1997 prices). To put it another way, in the first six years of the Reagan administration, the total increase in *real* debt of the federal government was nearly equal to the total real debt accumulated over the first two hundred years of this country, including the entire debt required to finance U.S. participation in World War II.

In 1998, the expanding economy (which had grown strongly since 1993), the tax increases enacted in 1993, and the limitations on expendi-

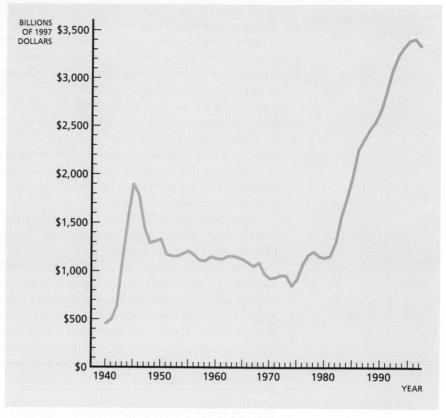

FIGURE 2.11   **Gross Federal Debt Held by the Public (1997 prices)** Government debt has grown enormously since 1974.

Source: *Budget of the United States Government, Fiscal Year 1999*, Historical Tables.

tures that had been imposed for almost a decade, beginning in 1990, finally achieved their long sought goal: there was a $70 billion surplus. Further surpluses were projected for the following years, though the President and Congress quickly began a heated discussion of what should be done with those surpluses, in particular, whether they should be primarily used for tax cuts or for ensuring the viability of social security.

PLAYING TRICKS WITH THE DATA
ON GOVERNMENT ACTIVITIES

The budgets of the federal, state, and local governments set out their expenditures and receipts. As we have seen, however, budgets provide only a partial view of the size of government and the effect of government on economic activity. As a result, one must treat with caution any comparisons of the size of the public sector either over time or across countries.

Earlier in this chapter the sections on government subsidies and credits discussed how tax expenditures may result in misleading conclusions concerning not only the size of the public sector but also the composition of its expenditures. If the federal government wishes to hide the size of its subsidies to business, it provides tax credits to businesses. It hides the extent of its subsidies to states and localities by providing "tax expenditures" in the form of tax deductions on the federal individual income tax for most state and local taxes and tax exemption for interest on state and local bonds.

There is a second method by which the budget may be manipulated: by recording the revenues obtained when assets are sold, but not the cost—the reduction in the assets of the government. Such tricks were important in Reagan's attempt to reduce the deficit. For instance, he accelerated the sale of offshore oil and gas leases.

Speeding tax collections by increasing withholding or by increasing penalties for failing to pay taxes in a timely fashion is another one-time way of reducing a current deficit.

The overall size of the public sector (but not the deficit) can be decreased by the setting up of independent agencies and enterprises. It makes no real difference whether the post office is a department of the U.S. government or, as is the case today, a separate "corporation" receiving a subsidy from the federal treasury. But if it is a department, all of its income and all of its expenditures will be included in the government budget; if it is a separate enterprise, only the deficit (the difference between its expenditures and income) is recorded.

Though these problems provide considerable room for politicians to select statistics to support their views, the pattern of changes in the level and structure of expenditures and taxation in the United States over the past twenty-five to fifty years has been significant enough that there can be little question about three major observations that have been made in this chapter:

1 The public sector exerts a major influence on the production of goods and the distribution of income in the United States.
2 Social insurance has been the fastest-growing category of government expenditures in the past thirty years. Since 1960, the rapid growth in non-defense expenditure by government was largely accounted for by social security, government retirement programs, Medicare, and interest.
3 The individual income tax has become the principal source of federal revenue, and the role of the corporation income tax as a revenue source has dwindled.

REVIEW AND PRACTICE

SUMMARY

1 The government performs many roles:
    a It provides the basic legal framework within which we live.
    b It regulates economic activities. It encourages some activities by subsidizing them and discourages others by taxing them.

c It produces goods and provides credit, loan guarantees, and insurance.

d It purchases goods and services, including many that are produced by private firms (such as weapons manufacturers).

e It redistributes income, transferring income from some individuals to others.

f It provides social insurance, for retirement, unemployment, disability, and medical care for the aged.

2 The size of the government relative to GDP is much larger now than it was forty years ago. Much of this increase is accounted for by increased payments for social insurance.

3 The relative size of the public sector in the United States is smaller than in most Western European countries.

4 The three major areas of government expenditures are defense, social insurance, and education. Together, these accounted for 65 percent of governmental expenditures in 1996.

5 The major source of revenue for the federal government is the individual income tax, followed by the payroll tax, corporation tax, and customs and excise taxes.

6 The major sources of revenue for state and local government are the sales tax, the property tax, and the income tax.

7 The Constitution provides the basic framework for the government of the United States. It provides some restrictions on the taxes that can be imposed, but no effective restrictions on what the government can spend its money on.

8 The deficit—the difference between the government's expenditures and revenues—grew enormously, beginning in 1981, with the total real debt accumulated between 1981 and 1987 alone equaling the total real debt accumulated over the first two hundred years of the country. Deficit reduction measures, begun in 1990 and extended in 1993, combined with a growing economy, enabled a surplus to be achieved in 1998.

KEY CONCEPTS

Transfer payments	Social security (payroll) tax
Nationalization	Corporate income tax
In-kind benefit	Excise tax
Social insurance	Customs tax
Middle-class entitlement programs	Value-added tax
Income tax	Deficit

1   To see what is going on, economists often "adjust" the data to reflect changes in the economy. For instance, in the text, we discussed the adjustments in dollar amounts made to correct for inflation. Another adjustment that is frequently made is to take into account the increase in population. What adjustments might you make in looking at education expenditures? At social security expenditures?

2   In each of the following areas, give one or more examples (where possible) in which the government is involved as a producer; a regulator; a purchaser of final goods and services distributed directly to individuals or used within government:

   a Education

   b Utilities

   c Transportation

   d Credit markets

   e Insurance markets

   f Food

   g Housing

3   In each of the following areas, give an example of a tax expenditure and a conventional expenditure. Explain how the same results could be obtained by converting the tax expenditure into a conventional expenditure.

   a Medicine

   b Housing

   c Education

4   Assume you were President and your planned expenditures exceeded your receipts. Describe some of the tricks you might use to reduce the apparent budget deficit while maintaining current levels of services and transfers (subsidies).

   Assume, on the other hand, that you had run on a platform of keeping the growth in total governmental expenditures down to 3 percent. Once in office, you see, however, that you would like expenditures to rise by 5 percent. How might you do this while appearing to keep your election promises?

PART TWO FUNDAMENTALS OF WELFARE ECONOMICS

Most economies today are mixed economies, in which
there is both a private and a public sector. At the core of
the economy are profit-maximizing firms interacting with
households in competitive markets. Under certain
idealized conditions, a competitive economy is efficient. If
those conditions were satisfied, there would be a very
limited role for government. To understand the role of the
public sector, then, we have to understand when markets
work well, and when, and in what ways, they do not. That
is the objective of this part of the book.

Chapter 3 explains what is entailed by efficiency, and why,
under idealized conditions, competitive economies are
efficient. Chapter 4 then explains the variety of reasons
why and circumstances in which markets may fail to
produce efficient outcomes, and why, even if the economy
were efficient, there might be a role for government in
redistributing income.

The hardest choices facing the public sector involve trade-
offs—in particular, trade-offs between increased efficiency

and a more equitable distribution of income. Chapter 5 provides a conceptual framework for thinking about these trade-offs, as well as some tools that are used by governments in attempting to quantify them.

3 Market Efficiency

FOCUS QUESTIONS

1 What do economists mean when they say the economy is efficient?

2 What conditions have to be satisfied if markets are to be efficient?

3 Why is there a general presumption that competitive markets result in efficiency?

In most modern industrial economies, primary reliance for the production and distribution of goods lies in the private rather than the public sector. One of the most enduring tenets of economics holds that this form of economic organization leads to an efficient allocation of resources. But if private markets are efficient, why should there be an economic role for government? To answer this question a precise understanding of the meaning of economic efficiency is needed. That is the aim of this chapter. The next chapter will consider why private markets may fail to achieve efficient outcomes and how government may respond to these market failures.

THE INVISIBLE HAND OF COMPETITIVE MARKETS

In 1776 Adam Smith, in the first major work of modern economics, *The Wealth of Nations*, argued that competition would lead the individual in the pursuit of his private interests (profits) to pursue the public interest, as if by an invisible hand:

> ... he intends only his own gain, and he is in this, as in many other cases, led by an invisible hand to promote an end which was no part of his intention. Nor is it always the worse for the society that it was no part of it. By pursuing his own interest he frequently promotes that of the society more effectually than when he really intends to promote it.[1]

The significance of Smith's insight is clarified by a look at the views about the role of government commonly held prior to Smith. There was widespread belief that achieving the best interests of the public (however that might be defined) required an active government. This view was particularly associated with the mercantilist school of the seventeenth and eighteenth centuries, which argued that government should promote industry and trade. Indeed, many European governments had actively promoted the establishment of colonies, and the mercantilists provided a rationale for this.

Some countries (or some citizens within them) had benefited greatly from the active role taken by their government, but other countries, whose governments had been much more passive, had also prospered. And some countries with strong, active governments had not prospered, as their resources were squandered on wars or on a variety of unsuccessful public ventures.

In the face of these seemingly contradictory experiences, Smith addressed himself to the question: Can society ensure that those entrusted with governing actually pursue the public interest? Experience had shown that while at times the policies governments pursued seemed consistent with the public good, at other times the policies pursued could not by any reasonable stretch of the imagination be reconciled with the public good. Rather, those in the position of governing often seemed to pursue their private interests at the expense of the public interest. Moreover, even well-intentioned leaders often led their countries astray. Smith argued that it was not necessary to rely on government or on any moral sentiments to do good. The public interest, he maintained, is served when each individual simply does what is in his own self-interest. Self-interest is a much more persistent characteristic of human nature than a concern to do good, and therefore provides a more reliable basis for the organization of society. Moreover, individuals are more likely to ascertain with some accuracy what is in their own self-interest than they are to determine what is in the public interest.

The intuition behind Smith's insight is simple: If there is some commodity or service that individuals value but that is not currently being produced, then they will be willing to pay something for it. Entrepreneurs, in their search for profits, are always looking for such opportunities. If the value of a certain commodity to a consumer exceeds the cost of production,

[1] Adam Smith, *The Wealth of Nations* (New York: Modern Library, 1937). Originally published in 1776.

there is a potential for profit, and an entrepreneur will produce the commodity. Similarly, if there is a cheaper way of producing a commodity than that which is presently employed, an entrepreneur who discovers this cheaper method will be able to undercut competing firms and make a profit. The search for profits on the part of enterprises is thus a search for more efficient ways of production and for new commodities that better serve the needs of consumers.

Notice that in this view, no government committee needs to decide whether a commodity should or should not be produced. It will be produced if it meets the market test—that is, if what individuals are willing to pay exceeds the costs of production. Nor does any government oversight committee need to check whether a particular firm is producing efficiently: competition will drive out inefficient producers.

There is widespread consensus among economists that competitive forces do lead to a high degree of efficiency, and that competition does provide an important spur to innovation. However, over the past two hundred years economists have come to recognize that in some important instances the market does not work as perfectly as the more ardent supporters of the free market suggest. Economies have gone through periods of massive unemployment and idle resources; the Great Depression of the 1930s left many who wanted work unemployed; pollution has choked many of our larger cities; and urban decay has set in on others.

WELFARE ECONOMICS AND
PARETO EFFICIENCY

Welfare economics is the branch of economics that focuses on what were termed normative issues in Chapter 1. The most fundamental normative issue for welfare economics is the economy's organization—what should be produced, how it should be produced, for whom, and who should make these decisions. In Chapter 1, we noted that the United States and most other economies today are *mixed*, with some decisions made by the government but most left up to the myriad of firms and households. But there are many "mixes." How are we to evaluate the alternatives? Most economists embrace a criterion called **Pareto efficiency,** named after the great Italian economist and sociologist Vilfredo Pareto (1848–1923). Resource allocations that have the property that no one can be made better off without someone being made worse off are said to be **Pareto efficient,** or **Pareto optimal.** Pareto efficiency is what economists normally mean when they talk about efficiency.

Assume, for instance, that the government is contemplating building a bridge. Those who wish to use the bridge are willing to pay more than enough in tolls to cover the costs of construction and maintenance. The construction of this bridge is likely to be a **Pareto improvement,** that is, a change which makes some individuals better off without making anyone worse off. We use the term "likely" because there are always others who might be adversely affected by the construction of the bridge. For example,

While finding Pareto improvements is difficult, economists are constantly on the lookout for such opportunities. Two recent proposals illustrate some of the problems that may be encountered.

One proposal concerned offshore oil wells. The federal government leases the land to oil companies in return for a royalty, usually around 16 percent. The oil companies compete for these leases in competitive auctions; the lease goes to the firm offering the highest bid. As oil wells get old, the cost of extraction increases, often to the point where, with the royalty taken into account, it pays to shut down the well. If the price of oil is $20 a barrel, and there is a 16 percent royalty, it pays to shut down the well when the cost of extraction exceeds $16.80. ($16.80 plus the $3.20 royalty equals the $20 received.) This seems inefficient, since the value of the oil ($20) exceeds the cost of production. Hence, there have been proposals to eliminate royalties on old wells and to allow the oil companies to pay a fixed up-front fee. The government is no worse off (since if the well is shut down it receives no revenue), and, provided the fee is set low enough, the oil company is better off (since if the well is shut down it receives nothing). The oil companies have resisted the proposal: they prefer that the government simply eliminate royalties. Although the proposal is a Pareto improvement over the status quo, they would

if the bridge changes the traffic flow, some stores might find that their business is decreased, and they are worse off. Or an entire neighborhood may be affected by the noise of bridge traffic and the shadows cast by the bridge superstructure.

Frequently on summer days, or at rush hour, large backups develop at toll booths on toll roads and bridges. If tolls were raised at those times and the proceeds used to finance additional toll booths or more peak-time toll collectors, everyone might be better off. People would prefer to pay a slightly higher price in return for less waiting. But even this change might not be a Pareto improvement: among those waiting in line may be some unemployed individuals who are relatively little concerned about the waste of time but who are concerned about spending more money on tolls.

Economists are always on the lookout for Pareto improvements. The belief that any such improvements should be instituted is referred to as the **Pareto principle.**

"Packages" of changes together may constitute a Pareto improvement, when each change alone might not. Thus, while reducing the tariff on steel would not be a Pareto improvement (since steel producers would be worse off), it might be possible to reduce the tariff on steel, increase income taxes slightly, and use the proceeds to finance a subsidy to the steel industry; such

prefer to garner for themselves more of the potential gains from the increased economic efficiency.

A second proposal involved allowing private companies to construct improved turbines at hydroelectric sites, increasing the energy output. They would be allowed to sell the electricity at market prices. Hydroelectric energy is particularly attractive, since it generates no pollution. There would be no adverse environmental impacts, since the developments would occur only at sites already being used. This too appeared to be a Pareto improvement: economic efficiency would be increased as cheaper hydroelectric power replaced power relying on fossil fuels; the benefits of the improved efficiency would be shared between consumers, investors, and the government; future generations would be better off as a result of the more favorable environmental impacts. This proposal was opposed by utility companies who currently get electricity from these dams at below-market prices. Though the proposal did not alter the current level of preferential treatment, they were worried that once the principle that electricity from hydroelectric sites could be sold at market prices was established, their preferential treatment would be threatened. Though the proposal as framed was a Pareto improvement, they saw the long-run consequences of the proposal as a gain in efficiency at the expense of their future welfare.

a combination of changes might make everyone in the country better off (and make those abroad, the foreign exporters of steel, also better off).

PARETO EFFICIENCY AND INDIVIDUALISM

The criterion of Pareto efficiency has an important property which needs comment. It is *individualistic,* in two senses. First, it is concerned only with each individual's welfare, not with the relative well-being of different individuals. It is not concerned explicitly with inequality. Thus, a change that made the rich much better off but left the poor unaffected would still be a Pareto improvement. Some people, however, think that increasing the gap between the rich and the poor is undesirable. They believe that it gives rise, for instance, to undesirable social tensions. Less developed countries often go through periods of rapid growth during which all major segments of society become better off but the income of the rich grows more rapidly than that of the poor. To assess these changes, is it enough simply to say that everyone is better off? There is no agreement on the answer to this question.

Second, it is each individual's perception of his or her own welfare that counts. This is consistent with the general principle of **consumer sovereignty,** which holds that individuals are the best judge of their own needs and wants, of what is in their own best interests.

Two of the most important results of welfare economics describe the relationship between competitive markets and Pareto efficiency. These results are called the **fundamental theorems of welfare economics.** The first theorem tells us that if the economy is competitive (and satisfies certain other conditions), it is Pareto efficient.

The second theorem asks the reverse question. There are many Pareto efficient distributions. By transferring wealth from one individual to another, we make the second individual better off, the first worse off. After we make the redistribution of wealth, if we let the forces of competition freely play themselves out, we will obtain a Pareto efficient allocation of resources. This new allocation will be different in many ways from the old. If we take wealth away from those who like chocolate ice cream and give it to those who like vanilla, in the new equilibrium, more vanilla ice cream will be produced and less chocolate. But no one can be made better off in the new equilibrium without making someone else worse off.

Let's say there is a *particular* distribution which we would like to obtain. Assume, for instance, that we care particularly about the aged. The second fundamental theorem of welfare economics says that the *only* thing the government needs to do is redistribute initial wealth. *Every Pareto efficient resource allocation can be obtained through a competitive market process with an initial redistribution of wealth.* Thus, if we don't like the income distribution generated by the competitive market, we need not abandon the use of the competitive market mechanism. All we need do is redistribute the initial wealth, and then leave the rest to the competitive market.

The second fundamental theorem of welfare economics has the remarkable implication that every Pareto efficient allocation can be attained by means of a **decentralized market mechanism.** In a decentralized system, decisions about production and consumption (what goods get produced, how they get produced, and who gets what goods) are carried out by the myriad firms and individuals that make up the economy. In contrast, in a **centralized allocation mechanism,** all such decisions are concentrated in the hands of a single agency, the central planning agency, or a single individual, who is referred to as the central planner. Of course, no economy has even come close to being fully centralized, though under communism in the former Soviet Union and some of the other Eastern bloc countries, economic decision making was much more concentrated than in the United States

FUNDAMENTAL THEOREMS OF WELFARE ECONOMICS

• Every competitive economy is Pareto efficient.

• Every Pareto efficient resource allocation can be attained through a competitive market mechanism, with the appropriate initial redistributions.

and other Western economies. Today, only Cuba and North Korea place heavy reliance on central planning.

The second fundamental theorem of welfare economics says that to attain an efficient allocation of resources, with the desired distribution of income, it is not necessary to have a central planner, with all the wisdom an economic theorist or a utopian socialist might attribute to him: competitive enterprises, attempting to maximize their profits, can do as well as the best of all possible central planners. This theorem thus provides a major justification for reliance on the market mechanism. Put another way, if the conditions assumed in the second welfare theorem were valid, the study of public finance could be limited to an analysis of the appropriate governmental redistributions of resources.

Why the competitive market, under ideal conditions, leads to a Pareto optimal allocation of resources is one of the primary subjects of study in standard courses in microeconomics. Since we will be concerned with understanding why under some circumstances competitive markets do not lead to efficiency, we first need to understand why competition under ideal conditions leads to efficiency. But before turning to this, it is important to emphasize that these results are *theorems;* that is, logical propositions in which the conclusion (the Pareto efficiency of the economy) follows from the assumptions. The assumptions reflect an ideal competitive model, in which, for instance, there are many small firms and millions of households, each so small that it has no effect on prices; in which all firms and households have perfect information, say, concerning the goods that are available in the market and the prices which are being charged; and in which there is no air or water pollution.[2] The accuracy of these assumptions in portrayal of our economy and the robustness of the results—the extent to which the conclusions change when the assumptions change—are two of the main subjects of debate among economists. In the next chapter we will look at some of the important ways in which markets fail to deliver efficient outcomes; that is, we will identify important circumstances in which the ideal conditions underlying the fundamental theorems of welfare economics are not satisfied.

We can see why competition results in economic efficiency using traditional demand and supply curves. The demand curve of an individual gives the amount of the good the individual is willing to demand at each price. The market demand curve simply adds up the demand curves of all individuals: it gives the total quantity of the good that individuals in the economy are willing to purchase, at each price. As Figure 3.1 illustrates, the demand curve is normally downward-sloping: as prices increase, individuals demand less of the good. In deciding how much to demand, individuals equate the

---

[2] There are also a number of technical assumptions.

[3] This is often called the partial equilibrium approach, in contrast to the general equilibrium approach, which looks at all markets simultaneously. We take the latter approach in the next section.

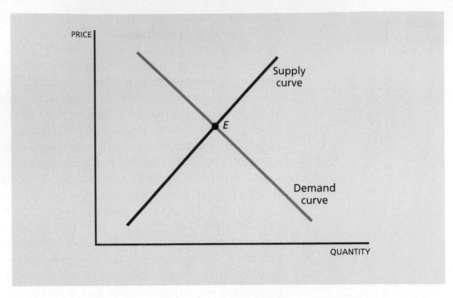

PRICE

Supply
curve

E

Demand
curve

QUANTITY

FIGURE 3.1 **Efficiency from the Perspective of a Single Market** In deciding how much to demand, individuals equate the marginal benefit they receive from consuming an extra unit with the marginal cost, the price they have to pay. In deciding how much to supply, firms equate the marginal benefit they receive, which is just the price, with the marginal cost. At the market equilibrium, where supply equals demand, the marginal benefit (to consumers) is equal to the marginal cost to firms—and each equals the price.

marginal (additional) benefit they receive from consuming an extra unit with the **marginal (additional) cost** of purchasing an extra unit. The marginal cost is just the price they have to pay.

The supply curve of a firm gives the amount of the good the firm is willing to supply at each price. The market supply curve simply adds up the supply curves of all firms: it gives the total quantity of the good that firms in the economy are willing to supply, at each price. As Figure 3.1 illustrates, the supply curve is normally upward-sloping: as prices increase, firms are willing to supply more of the good. In deciding how much of a good to produce, competitive firms equate the marginal (additional) benefit they receive from producing an extra unit—which is just the price they receive—with the marginal (additional) cost of producing an extra unit.

Efficiency requires that the marginal benefit associated with producing one more unit of any good equal its marginal cost. For if the marginal benefit exceeds the marginal cost, society would gain from producing more of the good; and if the marginal benefit was less than the marginal cost, society would gain from reducing production of the good.

Market equilibrium occurs at the point where market demand equals supply, point E in Figure 3.1. At this point, the marginal benefit and the marginal cost each equal the price; thus the marginal benefit equals the marginal cost, which is precisely the condition required for economic efficiency.

ANALYZING ECONOMIC EFFICIENCY

To develop a deeper analysis that goes beyond the basic supply and demand framework just presented, economists consider three aspects of efficiency, all of which are required for Pareto efficiency. First, the economy must achieve **exchange efficiency,** that is, whatever goods are produced have to go to the individuals who value them most. If I like chocolate ice cream and you like vanilla ice cream, I should get the chocolate cone and you the vanilla. Second, there must be **production efficiency.** Given the society's resources, the production of one good cannot be increased without decreasing the production of another. Third, the economy must achieve **product mix efficiency** so that the goods produced correspond to those desired by individuals. If individuals value ice cream a lot relative to apples, and if the cost of producing ice cream is low relative to apples, then more ice cream should be produced. The following sections examine each of these types of efficiency in turn.

THE UTILITY
POSSIBILITIES CURVE

In preparation for learning what is entailed by each of the three aspects of Pareto efficiency, the concept of the **utility possibilities curve** is useful. Economists sometimes refer to the benefits that an individual gets from consumption as the *utility* that she gets from the combination of goods she consumes.[4] If she gets more goods, her utility has increased. The utility possibilities curve traces out the maximum level of utility that may be achieved by two consumers. Figure 3.2 shows a utility possibilities frontier for Robinson Crusoe and Friday, showing Friday's maximum level of utility, given Crusoe's level of utility (and vice versa). Recall the definition of Pareto efficiency: An economy is Pareto efficient if no one can be made better off without making someone else worse off. That is, we cannot increase the utility of Friday without decreasing the utility of Crusoe. Thus, if an economy is Pareto efficient, it must be operating along the utility possibilities frontier. If the economy were operating at a point below the utility possibilities frontier, such as at point *A* in Figure 3.2, it would be possible to increase the utility of Friday or Crusoe without decreasing the utility of the other, or to increase the utility of both.

The first fundamental theorem of welfare economics says that a competitive economy operates along the utility possibilities frontier; the second

---

[4] Note that the concept of utility is only a useful way of thinking about the benefits that an individual gets from consumption. There is no way of measuring utility (other than indirectly, by looking at what individuals are willing to pay), no machine which can ascertain the number of "utiles" (or whatever the unit of measurement of utility might be called) derived from eating a pizza or listening to a CD.

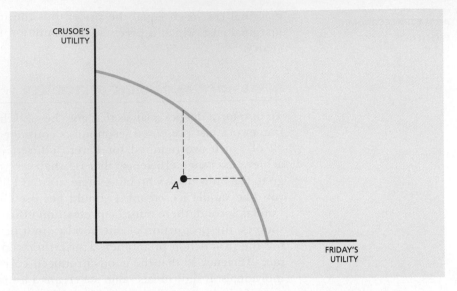

CRUSOE'S
UTILITY

A

FRIDAY'S
UTILITY

FIGURE 3.2   **The Utility Possibilities Curve** The utility possibilities curve gives the maximum level of utility that one individual (Friday) can achieve, given the level of utility of the other individual (Crusoe). Along the frontier, it is not possible for Crusoe to consume more unless Friday consumes less. Therefore, the utility possibilities curve is downward-sloping: the higher Crusoe's utility, the lower the maximum level of Friday's utility.

fundamental theorem of welfare economics says that we can attain any point along the utility possibilities frontier using competitive markets, provided we redistribute initial endowments appropriately.

EXCHANGE EFFICIENCY   Exchange efficiency concerns the distribution of goods. Given a particular set of available goods, exchange efficiency provides that those goods are distributed so no one can be made better off without someone else being made worse off. Exchange efficiency thus requires that there is no scope for **trades,** or exchanges that would make both parties better off.

Assume that Robinson is willing to give up one apple in exchange for one orange, or to get one apple in exchange for giving up one orange. Assume that Friday, on the other hand, is willing to give up three apples if he can get one more orange. At the margin, Friday values oranges more highly than does Robinson. Clearly, there is room for a deal: if Robinson gives Friday one of his oranges, and Friday gives Robinson two of his apples, both are better off. Robinson would have required only one apple to make him just as well off, but he gets two in exchange for his orange. Friday would have been willing to give up three apples; he only gave up two, so he is clearly better off.

The amount of one commodity which an individual is willing to give up in exchange for a unit of another commodity is called the **marginal rate of**

substitution. So long as Robinson and Friday's marginal rates of substitution differ, there will be room for a deal. Thus, exchange efficiency requires that all individuals have the same marginal rate of substitution.

We now will see why competitive economies satisfy this condition for exchange efficiency. To do so, we need to review how consumers make their decisions. We begin with the budget constraint—the amount of income a consumer can spend on various goods. Robinson has $100, which he can divide between apples and oranges. If an apple costs $1 and an orange $2, Robinson can buy 100 apples or 50 oranges, or combinations in between, as illustrated in Figure 3.3. If Robinson buys one more orange, he has to give up two apples. Thus, the slope of the budget constraint is equal to the ratio of the prices.

Robinson chooses the point along the budget constraint that he most prefers. To see what this entails, we introduce a new concept: **Indifference curves** give the combinations of goods among which an individual is indifferent or which yield the same level of utility. Figure 3.4 shows indifference curves for apples and oranges. For example, the indifference curve I_0 gives all those combinations of apples and oranges that the consumer finds just as attractive as 80 apples and 18 oranges (point A on the indifference curve). If points A and B are on the same indifference curve, the consumer is indifferent between the two combinations of apples and oranges represented by the two points. The indifference curve also shows how much of

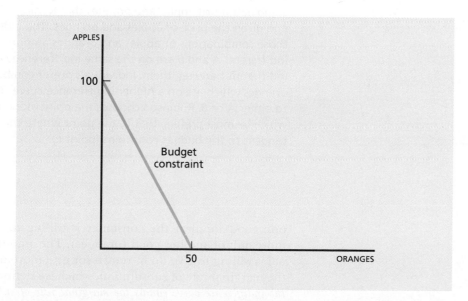

FIGURE 3.3   **Robinson's Budget Constraint** Given income of $100, the price of oranges of $2, and the price of apples of $1, an individual can purchase any combination of apples and oranges along or to the left of the budget constraint. Any combination to the right of the budget constraint is unaffordable. The slope of the budget constraint is based on the relative price of oranges and apples.

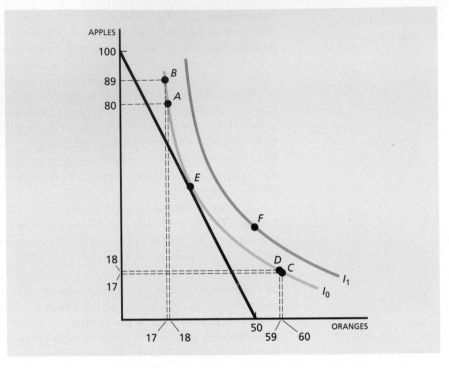

FIGURE 3.4   **The Consumer's Choice Problem** The budget constraint gives the combinations of apples and oranges that Robinson can buy, given his income and given the price of apples and oranges. The indifference curve gives those combinations of apples and oranges among which Robinson is indifferent. *A* and *B* are on the same indifference curve; Robinson is indifferent between them. Individuals prefer combinations of apples and oranges which are on a higher indifference curve. Thus, point *F* is preferred to either *A* or *B*. Robinson chooses the point along the budget constraint which he most prefers, that is, the point where the indifference curve I_0 is tangent to the budget constraint (point *E*).

one good (apples) the consumer is willing to give up in return for one more unit of another good (oranges). The amount of one good the individual is willing to give up in return for one more unit of another good is just the marginal rate of substitution, which we defined earlier. Thus, *the slope of the indifference curve equals the marginal rate of substitution*. In Figure 3.4, in moving from point *A* to point *B*, Robinson gives up one orange, but he is just as well off if he is compensated with nine extra apples. Note that the number of apples that he needs to compensate him for having one less orange is much higher when he moves from *A* to *B* than when he moves from *C* to *D*. When he has 60 oranges, he is much more willing to give up one of his oranges: he only needs one more apple to compensate him. Thus the marginal rate of substitution diminishes as the number of oranges which Robinson consumes increases. This explains why the indifference curves have the shape depicted.

Clearly, individuals are better off if they have more apples and oranges; that is why combinations of goods along a higher indifference curve give a higher level of utility. Thus, any of the points on I_1 are more attractive than the points on I_0. By definition, a consumer does not care which point along an indifference curve he is at; but he wants to be along the highest indifference curve possible. Robinson would like to get to any point along the indifference curve I_1, but he cannot: all of these points lie above the budget constraint, and so are not feasible. The best that Robinson can do is to choose point E, where the indifference curve is tangent to the budget constraint.

At the point of tangency, the slope of the indifference curve is identical to the slope of the budget constraint. But the slope of the indifference curve is the marginal rate of substitution, and the slope of the budget constraint is the price ratio. Thus, individuals choose a combination of apples and oranges where the marginal rate of substitution is equal to the price ratio.

Because all consumers face the same prices in a competitive economy, and each sets his or her marginal rate of substitution equal to the price ratio, they all have the same marginal rate of substitution. Earlier, we showed that the condition for exchange efficiency was that all individuals have the same marginal rate of substitution. Thus **competitive markets have exchange efficiency.**

Another way to represent exchange efficiency is illustrated in Figure 3.5. For simplicity, we continue the example of Robinson Crusoe and Friday. Whatever Crusoe does not get, Friday gets. Thus we can represent all possible allocations in a box (called an Edgeworth-Bowley Box, after two early-twentieth-century English mathematical economists), where the horizontal axis represents the total supply of oranges and the vertical axis represents the total supply of apples. In Figure 3.5, what Crusoe gets to consume is measured from the bottom left corner (O), and what Friday gets is measured from the top right corner (O'). At the allocation denoted by the point E, Crusoe gets OA oranges and OB apples, while Friday gets the remainder ($O'A'$ oranges and $O'B'$ apples). We then draw Crusoe's indifference curves, such as U^c. We have also drawn Friday's indifference curves. His indifference curves look perfectly normal if you turn the book upside down.

Let us now fix Crusoe's utility. Pareto efficiency requires us to maximize Friday's utility, given the level of utility attained by Crusoe. Thus we ask, given that Crusoe is on the indifference curve U^c, what is the highest indifference curve that Friday can get to? Remember that Friday's utility increases as we move down and to the left (Friday is getting more goods, Crusoe fewer goods). Friday attains his highest utility where his indifference curve is *tangent* to Crusoe's, at E. At this point, the slopes of the indifference curves are the same, that is, their marginal rates of substitution of apples for oranges are the same.

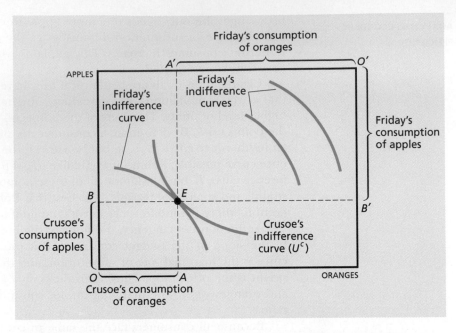

FIGURE 3.5 **Exchange Efficiency** The sides of this Edgeworth-Bowley Box give the available supplies of apples and oranges. *OA* and *OB* give Crusoe's consumption of the two commodities. Friday gets what Crusoe does not consume, that is, *O′A′* and *O′B′*. Pareto efficiency requires the tangency of the two indifference curves (one such point is at *E*), where the marginal rates of substitution of apples for oranges are equal.

PRODUCTION EFFICIENCY

If an economy is not productively efficient, it can produce more of one good without reducing production of other goods. Along the production possibilities frontier in Figure 3.6, the economy cannot produce more of one good without giving up some of another good, given a fixed set of resources.[5]

The analysis used to determine whether an economy is productively efficient is similar to the one we used above for exchange efficiency. Consider Figure 3.7. In place of the budget constraint we have an **isocost line,** giving the different combinations of inputs that cost the firm the same amount. The slope of the isocost line is the relative price of the two factors. The fig-

---

[5] The production possibilities schedule has the shape it does because of the law of diminishing returns. As we try to produce more and more oranges, it becomes harder and harder to produce an additional orange. Thus, as we give up apples, we get more oranges, but for each additional apple we give up, we get fewer and fewer extra oranges.

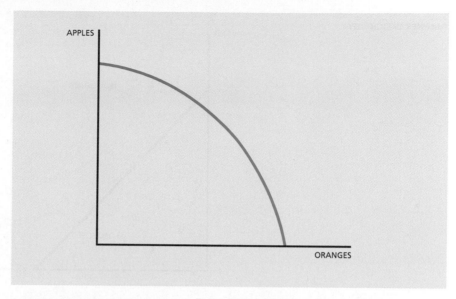

FIGURE 3.6 **Production Efficiency and the Production Possibilities Frontier** Points inside
the frontier are attainable but inefficient. Points along the frontier are
feasible and efficient. Points outside the frontier are unattainable, given the
resources of the economy.

ure also shows two **isoquants**. These trace out the different combinations of
inputs—in this case, land and labor—that produce the same quantities of
outputs. Thus, isoquants are to the analysis of production what indifference
curves are to the analysis of consumption. Economists call the slope of an
isoquant the **marginal rate of technical substitution.** In Figure 3.7, the marginal rate of technical substitution is the amount of land required to compensate for a decrease in the input of labor by one unit. When relatively little labor is being used, it is hard to economize further in its use, so if one
less worker is used, there must be a large increase in land if output is to remain unchanged. That is why the isoquants have the shape they do. There is
a diminishing marginal rate of technical substitution.

Just as exchange efficiency required that the marginal rate of substitution between any pair of commodities be the same for all individuals, production efficiency requires that the marginal rate of technical substitution
be the same for all firms. Assume the marginal rate of substitution between
land and labor is 2 in producing apples and 1 in producing oranges. That
means if we reduce labor by one in oranges, we need one more unit of land.
If we reduce labor by one in apples, we need two more units of land. Conversely, if we increase labor by one in apples, we need two fewer units of
land. Thus, if we take one worker from producing oranges and put him to

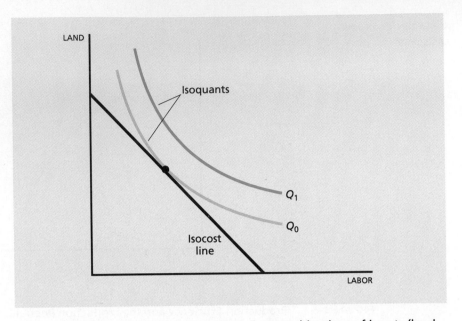

FIGURE 3.7 **Isoquants and Isocost Lines** An isoquant gives combinations of inputs (land and labor) which yield the same output. The isoquant labeled Q_1 represents a higher level of output than the isoquant labeled Q_0. The slope of the isoquant is the marginal rate of technical substitution. The isocost line gives those combinations of inputs which cost the same amount. The slope of the isocost line is given by the relative prices of the two inputs. The firm maximizes its output, given a particular level of expenditures on inputs, at the point where the isoquant is tangent to the isocost line. At that point, the marginal rate of technical substitution equals the relative price.

work in apples, and we take one unit of land, and switch it from producing apples to producing oranges, production of oranges is unchanged but production of apples is increased. Whenever the marginal rates of substitution differ, we can switch resources around in a similar way, to increase production.

A firm maximizes the amount of output that it produces, at a given level of expenditures on inputs, by finding the point where the isoquant is tangent to the isocost line. At the point of tangency, the slopes of the two curves are the same—the marginal rate of technical substitution is equal to the ratio of the prices of the two inputs. In a competitive economy all firms face the same prices, so all firms using labor and land will set their marginal rate of technical substitution equal to the *same* price ratio. Hence all will have the same marginal rate of technical substitution—the condition that is required for production efficiency.

In Figure 3.8 we see the same principle diagrammatically using another Edgeworth-Bowley Box. We wish to know how to allocate a fixed supply of inputs to ensure productive efficiency. We represent the fixed supply of the

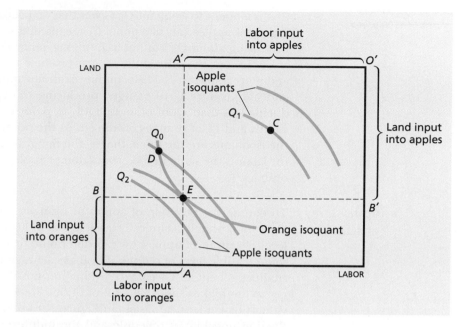

Production Efficiency The sides of this Edgeworth-Bowley Box give the available supply of resources—land and labor. Resources used in the production of oranges are given by *OA* and *OB*; resources not used in the production of oranges are used in the production of apples, *O'A'* and *O'B'*. Production efficiency requires the tangency of the isoquants. At tangency points, such as *E*, the marginal rate of substitution of land for labor is the same in the production of apples and oranges.

two inputs by a box, with the total available supply of land measured along the vertical axis and the total supply of labor along the horizontal axis. We measure inputs into orange production from the bottom left-hand corner. Thus, point *E* means that the amount *OB* of land is used in orange production, and *OA* of labor. That in turn means that the *remaining* inputs are used in the production of apples. Thus, we measure inputs into apples from the upper right-hand corner. At *E*, the amounts *O'B'* of land and *O'A'* of labor go into apple production.

The isoquants also appear in the figure. Q_0 gives a typical orange isoquant. Remember that the quantities of inputs going into apple production are measured from *O'*. That is why the isoquants for apples have the shape they do; they look perfectly normal if you turn the book upside down. Clearly, production efficiency requires that for any level of production of oranges the output of apples is maximized. As we move down and to the left in the box, more resources are being allocated to apple production; hence, isoquants through those points represent higher levels of apple output. If we fix the output of oranges at the level corresponding to isoquant Q_0, it is clear that the output of apples is maximized by finding the apple isoquant that is tangent to isoquant Q_0. Given that we produce Q_0 of oranges, producing Q_1 of apples (at, say, point C) means that some resources are unused. Producing along Q_0, but not at E (at, say, point D), means that all resources are used, but not efficiently; we can produce the same number of oranges and more apples at E. The economy cannot produce more than Q_1 of apples and still produce Q_0 of oranges; producing Q_2 of apples would require producing less than Q_0 of oranges. Only at point E are all resources used efficiently and Q_0 of oranges produced. At the point of tangency, the slopes of the isoquants are the same, that is, the marginal rate of substitution of land for labor is the same in the production of apples as it is in the production of oranges.

PRODUCT MIX EFFICIENCY

To choose the best mix of apples or oranges to produce, we need to consider both what is technically feasible *and* individuals' preferences. For each level of output of apples, we can determine from the technology the maximum feasible level of output of oranges. This generates the production possibilities schedule. Given the production possibilities schedule, we wish to get to the highest possible level of utility. For simplicity, we assume all individuals have identical tastes. In Figure 3.9 we have depicted both the production possibilities schedule and the indifference curves between apples and oranges. Utility is maximized at the point of tangency of the indifference curve to the production possibilities schedule. The slope of the production possibilities schedule is called the **marginal rate of transformation;** this tells us how many extra apples we can have if we reduce production of

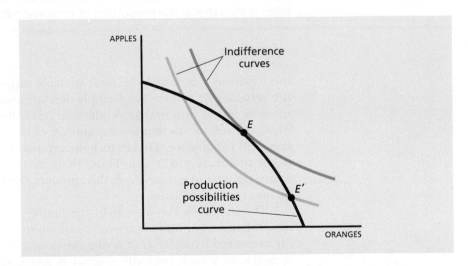

FIGURE 3.9　**Product Mix Efficiency Requires that the Marginal Rate of Transformation Equal Consumers' Marginal Rate of Substitution** In order to reach the highest level of consumers' utility, the indifference curve and the production possibilities schedule must be tangent (point *E*). At any other point, such as *E'*, consumer utility is lower than at *E*.

BASIC CONDITIONS FOR PARETO EFFICIENCY

1 Exchange efficiency: Marginal rate of substitution between any two goods must be the same for all individuals.

2 Production efficiency: Marginal rate of technical substitution between any two inputs must be the same for all firms.

3 Product mix efficiency: Marginal rate of transformation must equal marginal rate of substitution.

Competitive economies satisfy all three conditions.

oranges by one. At the point of tangency, E, the slopes of the indifference curve and the production possibilities schedule are the same, that is, the marginal rate of substitution of apples for oranges is equal to the marginal rate of transformation.

Under competition, the marginal rate of transformation will be equal to the relative price of apples to oranges. If, by reducing production of apples by one, firms can increase the production of oranges by, say, one, and sell the oranges for more than the price of apples, profit-maximizing firms will clearly expand production of oranges. We have shown why under competition consumers' marginal rates of substitution will equal the price ratio. Since both the marginal rates of substitution and the marginal rate of transformation will equal the price ratio, the marginal rate of transformation must equal consumers' marginal rates of substitution. Hence, under ideal competitive markets, all three conditions required for Pareto efficiency are satisfied.

REVIEW AND PRACTICE

SUMMARY

1 Resource allocations that have the property that no one can be made better off without someone else being made worse off are called Pareto efficient allocations.

2 The Pareto principle is based on individualistic values. Whenever a change can make some individuals better off without making others worse off, it should be adopted. Most public policy choices, however, involve trade-offs, where some individuals are better off and others are worse off.

3 The principle of consumer sovereignty holds that individuals are the best judges of their own needs and pleasures.

4 Pareto efficiency requires exchange efficiency, production efficiency, and product mix efficiency.

5 The fundamental theorems of welfare economics provide conditions under which a competitive economy is Pareto efficient, and under which every Pareto efficient allocation can be obtained through markets, provided that there is the appropriate redistribution of initial endowments (incomes).

6 Exchange efficiency means that, given the set of goods available in the economy, no one can be made better off without someone else being made worse off; it requires that all individuals have the same marginal rate of substitution between any pair of commodities. Competitive markets in which individuals face the same prices always have exchange efficiency.

7 Production efficiency requires that, given the set of resources, the economy not be able to produce more of one commodity without reducing the output of some other commodity; the economy must be operating along its production possibilities curve. Production efficiency requires that all firms have the same marginal rate of technical substitution between any pair of inputs; competitive markets in which firms face the same prices always have production efficiency.

8 Product mix efficiency requires that the marginal rate of transformation—the slope of the production possibilities curve—equal individuals' marginal rate of substitution. Competitive markets have product mix efficiency.

KEY CONCEPTS

Invisible hand	Marginal cost
Pareto efficiency	Exchange efficiency
Pareto principle	Production efficiency
Consumer sovereignty	Product mix efficiency
Fundamental theorems of welfare economics	Utility possibilities curve
	Marginal rate of substitution
Centralized allocation mechanism	Marginal rate of technical substitution
Marginal benefit	Marginal rate of transformation

QUESTIONS AND PROBLEMS

1 Explain why an economy in which airlines charge different passengers different prices for the same flight will not have exchange efficiency.

2 Doctors often charge patients different amounts depending on their judgment concerning their ability to pay. What implications does this have for exchange efficiency?

3 Can you think of other common practices and policies that might interfere with exchange efficiency?

4 Explain why a tax which is only levied on the use of capital by corporations will interfere with the production efficiency of the economy. (Compare the marginal rates of technical substitution between corporations and unincorporated enterprises.)

5 Advocates of small businesses often argue that they should receive special tax treatment. Assume that small businesses had to pay only half the social security tax that is imposed on large corporations. What effect would that have on production efficiency?

6 Consider an economy which produces two goods, cars and shirts. Explain why if a tax is imposed on the consumption of cars but not on shirts, the economy will not exhibit product mix efficiency.

7 An individual is indifferent among the combinations of public and private goods shown in the following table.

COMBINATION	PUBLIC GOODS	PRIVATE GOODS
A	1	16
B	2	11
C	3	7
D	4	4
E	5	3
F	6	2

Draw the individual's indifference curve. Assuming that the economy can produce one unit of public goods and ten units of private goods, but that it can produce one more unit of public goods by reducing its production of private goods by two units, draw the production possibilities schedule. What is the maximum production of private goods? The maximum production of public goods? Can it produce five units of public goods and one unit of private goods? Which of the feasible combinations maximizes utility?

4 Market Failure

FOCUS QUESTIONS

1 What are the principal reasons why markets fail to produce efficient outcomes?

2 What role does government play in making it possible for markets to work at all?

3 Why might the government intervene in the market's allocation of resources, even when it is Pareto efficient? What are merit goods? What is government's role in redistribution?

4 What is the "market failures" approach to the role of government? What are alternative perspectives in thinking about the role of government?

The last chapter explained why markets play such a central role in our economy: under ideal conditions, they ensure that the economy is Pareto efficient. But there is often dissatisfaction with markets. Some of the dissatisfaction is of the "grass is always greener on the other side" variety: people like to think that an alternative way of organizing the economy might make them better off. But some of the dissatisfaction is real: markets often seem to produce too much of some things, like air and water pollution, and too little of others, such as support for the arts or research into the nature of matter or the causes of cancer. And markets can lead to situations where some people have too little income to live on. Over the past fifty years, economists have devoted enormous efforts to understanding the circumstances under which markets yield efficient outcomes, and the circumstances in which they fail to do so.

This chapter will look both at these market failures and at the reasons why governments intervene in markets *even when they are efficient.*

PROPERTY RIGHTS AND CONTRACT ENFORCEMENT

Chapter 3 explained why markets result in Pareto efficient outcomes. But even for markets to work, there needs to be a government to define property rights and enforce contracts. In some societies, land is held in common; anyone can graze their cattle and sheep on it. Since no one has the property right to the land, no one has an incentive to ensure that there is not overgrazing. In the former communist countries, property rights were not well defined, so people had insufficient incentive to maintain or improve their apartments. In market economies, the benefits of such improvements are reflected in the market price of the property.

Similarly, if individuals are to engage in transactions with each other, the contracts they sign must be enforced. Consider a typical loan, where one person borrows money from another, and signs a contract to repay it. Unless such contracts are enforced, no one would be willing to make a loan.

At an even more primitive level, unless there is protection of private property, people will have insufficient incentive to save and invest, since their savings might be taken away.

Government activities aimed at protecting citizens and property, enforcing contracts, and defining property rights can be thought of as providing the foundations on which all market economies rest.

MARKET FAILURES AND THE ROLE OF GOVERNMENT

The first fundamental theorem of welfare economics asserts that the economy is Pareto efficient only under certain circumstances or conditions. There are six important conditions under which markets are not Pareto efficient. These are referred to as **market failures,** and they provide a rationale for government activity.

1 FAILURE OF COMPETITION

For markets to result in Pareto efficiency, there must be **perfect competition**—that is, there must be a sufficiently large number of firms that each believes it has no effect on prices. But in some industries—supercomputers, aluminum, cigarettes, greeting cards—there are relatively few firms, or one or two firms have a large share of the market. When a single firm supplies the market, economists refer to it as a **monopoly;** when a few firms supply the market, economists refer to them as an **oligopoly.** And even when there are many firms, each may produce a slightly different good and may thus

77

perceive itself facing a downward-sloping demand curve. Economists refer to such situations as **monopolistic competition.** In all of these situations, competition deviates from the ideal of perfect competition, where each firm is so small that it believes there is nothing it can do to affect prices.

It is important to recognize that under these circumstances, firms may still seem to be competing actively against each other, and that the market economy may seem to "work" in the sense that goods are being produced which consumers seem to like. The first fundamental theorem of welfare economics—the result that market economies are Pareto efficient—requires more than just that there be *some* competition. As we saw in the last chapter, Pareto efficiency entails stringent conditions, like exchange, production, and product mix efficiency, and these conditions typically are satisfied only if each firm and household believes that it has *no* effect on prices.

There are a variety of reasons why competition may be limited. When average costs of production decline as a firm produces more,[1] a larger firm will have a competitive advantage over a smaller firm. There may even be a **natural monopoly,** a situation where it is cheaper for a single firm to produce the entire output than for each of several firms to produce part of it. Even when there is not a natural monopoly, it may be efficient for there to be only a few firms operating. High transportation costs mean that goods sold by a firm at one location are not perfect substitutes for goods sold at another location. Imperfect information may also mean that if a firm raises its price it will not lose all of its customers; it only faces a downward-sloping demand curve.

Firms may also engage in strategic behavior to discourage competition. They may threaten to cut prices if potential rivals enter, and such threats may both be credible and serve to discourage entry.

Finally, some imperfections of competition arise out of government actions. Governments grant patents—exclusive rights to an invention—to innovators. While patents are important in providing incentives to innovate, they make competition in the product market less than perfect. The market dominance of such firms as Xerox, Alcoa, Polaroid, and Kodak was based on patents. Of course, even without patents, the fact that an innovator has some information (knowledge) that is not freely available to others may enable it to establish a dominant market position.

It is easy to see why imperfect competition leads to economic inefficiency. We saw earlier that under competition, firms set output at the Pareto efficient level. They set price equal to the marginal cost of production. Price can be thought of as measuring the marginal benefit of consuming an extra unit of the good. Thus, with competition, marginal benefits equal marginal costs. Under imperfect competition, firms set the extra revenue they obtain from selling one unit more—the **marginal revenue**—equal to the marginal cost. With a downward-sloping demand curve, the marginal revenue has two components. When a firm sells an extra unit, it receives the

---

[1] Declining average costs correspond to increasing returns: doubling inputs more than doubles output.

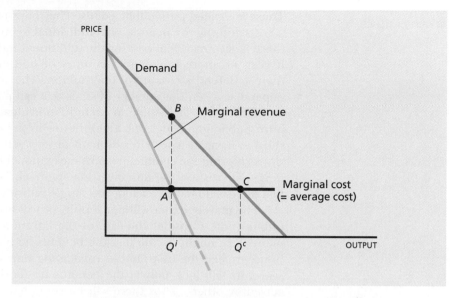

PRICE

Demand

B Marginal revenue

C
A   Marginal cost
(= average cost)

Q^i Q^c OUTPUT

FIGURE 4.1   **Monopoly Pricing** Monopoly output is lower than competitive output, or the output at which profits are zero. There is a resulting welfare loss.

price of the unit; but to sell the extra unit, it must lower the price it charges on that and all previous units—the demand curve is downward-sloping. The revenue gained from selling the extra unit is its price minus the revenue foregone because the expansion in sales lowers the price on all units. Thus, marginal revenue is less than price. Figure 4.1 shows the demand curve facing a firm and the marginal revenue, which lies below the demand curve. Competitive equilibrium occurs at Q^c, while the imperfect competition equilibrium occurs at Q^i, a much lower level of output. This reduction in output is the inefficiency associated with imperfect competition.

Of course, if there is a natural monopoly, with declining average costs, and with marginal costs below average costs,[2] competition is not viable; if a firm charged price equal to marginal cost (as would be the case under competition), it would operate at a loss, since the marginal cost is lower than the average costs. Even then, however, a private monopoly would typically charge more than a government-run monopoly; the private monopoly would seek to maximize profits, while the government-run monopoly which did not receive any subsidy would only seek to break even.

2 PUBLIC GOODS   There are some goods that either will not be supplied by the market or, if supplied, will be supplied in insufficient quantity. An example on a large scale is national defense; on a small scale, navigational aids (such as a buoy).

[2] When average costs are declining, marginal costs always lie below average costs; it is the low value of the marginal cost—the cost of producing the last unit—which brings down the average costs.

These are called **pure public goods.** They have two critical properties. First, it costs nothing for an additional individual to enjoy their benefits: formally, there is zero marginal cost for the additional individual enjoying the good. It costs no more to defend a country of one million and one individuals than to defend a country of one million. The costs of a lighthouse do not depend at all on the number of ships that sail past it. Secondly, it is in general difficult or impossible to exclude individuals from the enjoyment of a pure public good. If I put a lighthouse in a rocky channel to enable my ships to navigate safely, it is difficult or impossible for me to exclude other ships entering the channel from its navigational benefits. If our national defense policy is successful in diverting an attack from abroad, everyone benefits; there is no way to exclude any single individual from these benefits.

The market either will not supply, or will not supply enough of, a pure public good. Consider the case of the lighthouse. A large shipowner with many ships might decide that the benefits he himself receives from a lighthouse exceed the costs; but in calculating how many lighthouses to put in place, he will look only at the benefits he receives, not at the benefits received by others. Thus there will be some lighthouses for which the total benefits (taking into account *all* of the ships that make use of the lighthouse) exceed the costs but for which the benefits of any single shipowner are less than the costs. Such lighthouses will not be put into place, and that is inefficient. The fact that private markets will not supply, or will supply too little of, public goods provides a rationale for many government activities. Public goods are discussed in detail in Chapter 6.

3 EXTERNALITIES

There are many cases where the actions of one individual or one firm affect other individuals or firms; where one firm imposes a cost on other firms but does not compensate them, or alternatively, where one firm confers a benefit on other firms but does not reap a reward for providing it. Air and water pollution are examples. When I drive a car that is not equipped with a pollution control device, I lower the quality of the air, and thus impose a cost on others. Similarly, a chemical plant that discharges its chemicals into a nearby stream imposes costs on downstream users of the water, who may have to spend a considerable amount of money to clean up the water to make it usable.

Instances where one individual's actions impose a cost on others are referred to as **negative externalities.** But not all externalities are negative. There are some important instances of **positive externalities,** where one individual's actions confer a benefit upon others. If I plant a beautiful flower garden in front of my house, my neighbors may benefit from being able to look at it. An apple orchard may confer a positive externality on a neighboring beekeeper. An individual who rehabilitates his house in a neighborhood that is in decline may confer a positive externality on his neighbors.

There are a large number of other examples of externalities. An additional car on a crowded highway will add to road congestion, both reducing the speed at which other drivers can travel safely and increasing the probability of an accident. An additional fisherman fishing in a given pond may reduce the amount of fish that others will be able to catch. If there are several oil wells drilled in the same oil pool, taking more oil from one of the wells may reduce the amount of oil extracted by the other wells.

Whenever there are such externalities, the resource allocation provided by the market will not be efficient. Since individuals do not bear the full cost of the negative externalities they generate, they will engage in an excessive amount of such activities; conversely, since individuals do not enjoy the full benefits of activities generating positive externalities, they will engage in too little of these. Thus, for example, without government intervention of some kind, the level of pollution would be too high.

Externalities and environmental policy are discussed in detail in Chapter 9.

4 INCOMPLETE MARKETS

Pure public goods and services are not the only goods and services that private markets fail to provide adequately. Whenever private markets fail to provide a good or service even though the cost of providing it is less than what individuals are willing to pay, there is a market failure that we refer to as **incomplete markets** (because a complete market would provide all goods and services for which the cost of provision is less than what individuals are willing to pay). Some economists believe that private markets have done a particularly poor job of providing insurance and loans, and that this provides a rationale for government activities in these areas.

INSURANCE AND CAPITAL MARKETS The private market does not provide insurance for many important risks that individuals face, though insurance markets are much better today than they were seventy-five years ago. The government has undertaken a number of insurance programs, motivated at least in part by this market failure. In 1933, following the bank failures of the Great Depression, the government set up the Federal Deposit Insurance Corporation. Banks pay the corporation annual premiums, which provide insurance for depositors against a loss of savings arising from the insolvency of banks. The government has also been active in providing flood insurance. Following urban riots in the summer of 1967, most private insurance companies refused to write fire insurance in certain inner-city areas, and again the government stepped in.

Similarly, government has provided farmers with crop insurance, partly because of the failure of markets to do so; it provides unemployment insurance; and until Medicare, the government health insurance program for the aged, was introduced in the 1960s, many of the elderly found it difficult to procure health insurance in the market. Most recently, beginning in January 1997, the government began offering inflation-protected bonds—bonds on which the returns are guaranteed against the effects of inflation.

In recent decades, the government has taken an active role not only in remedying deficiencies in risk markets but in ameliorating the effects of imperfect capital markets. In 1965 the government passed legislation providing for government guarantees on student loans, making it less difficult for individuals to obtain loans to finance their college education. But this is only one of several government loan programs. The government, through the Federal National Mortgage Association (referred to as Fanny Mae), provides funds for home mortgages; it provides loans to businesses engaged in international trade through the Export-Import Bank; it provides loans for small business through the Small Business Administration; and so forth. In each of these credit markets, there were allegations that access to credit was restricted prior to the introduction of the government program.

The question of why capital and insurance markets are imperfect has been the subject of extensive research during the past two decades. At least three different answers have been put forward; each may have some validity. One focuses on *innovation:* we are used to new products, such as VCRs and laser discs, constantly coming onto the market; but there are also innovations in how the economy functions—innovations in creating new markets, including inventing new securities and new insurance policies. Indeed, those working in the insurance and securities industries refer to these advances as new products.

The introduction of many of these new products is related to the second explanation: *transactions costs.* It is costly to run markets, to enforce contracts, and to introduce new insurance policies. An insurance firm may be reluctant to go to the trouble of designing a new insurance policy if it is unsure whether anyone will buy the policy. There is no effective "patent protection," and as a result, there will be underinvestment in innovation.

The third set of explanations centers around *asymmetries of information* and *enforcement costs.* The insurance company is often less informed about the nature of some risks than the person purchasing insurance. When the two parties to a transaction have different information of this kind, we say that there is an information asymmetry. Thus, a firm might well wish to buy insurance against the risk that the demand for its product will decline. But the insurance firm may well reason: I want to estimate the risk, and charge a premium based on that estimate. But if I overestimate the risk, the premium will be too high, and the firm will refuse to buy my policy; while if I underestimate the risk, the premium will be too low; the firm will buy my policy, but on average, I will lose money. I am in a heads-you-win, tails-I-lose situation. When information asymmetries like this are large, markets will not exist.

Similarly, in capital markets, lenders worry about getting repaid. They may not be able to tell which borrowers are likely to repay. This is particularly a problem with loans, such as student loans, where there is no collateral. (In the case of a loan on a house, if the borrower defaults, at least the lender can sell the house and recoup most or all of what it has put out.) The bank finds itself in a dilemma: If it increases the interest rate to reflect the fact that many loans are not repaid, it may find that the default rate actually increases; those who know that they are going to repay refuse to borrow, while those who are not planning to repay care very little about the amount the lender is nominally charging, since in all likelihood they will not pay that amount anyway. The phenomenon is called **adverse selection;** as we shall see in Chapter 12, it plays an important role in health insurance markets. It may turn out that there is no interest rate which the bank can charge for, say, student loans (without a government subsidy) at which it can reap an *expected return* commensurate with what it can obtain on other investments.

This basic principle—that when there are asymmetries of information and enforcement problems markets may not exist—has been shown to provide part of the explanation of many missing markets.[3] We shall examine these problems in greater depth in the context of health insurance, in Chapter 12.

The reasons why markets do not exist may have implications for how governments might go about remedying the market failure. Government too faces transactions costs, enforcement problems, and asymmetries of information, though in many instances they are different from those faced by the private sector. Thus, in designing loan programs or interventions in capital markets, governments need to bear in mind that they too are often less informed than the borrower.

COMPLEMENTARY MARKETS Finally, we turn to the problems associated with the absence of certain complementary markets. Suppose that all individuals only enjoy coffee with sugar. Assume, moreover, that without coffee there is no market for sugar. Given that sugar was not produced, an entrepreneur considering whether to produce coffee would not do so, because he would realize that he would have no sales. Likewise, given that coffee was not produced, an entrepreneur considering whether to produce sugar also would not do so, since he too would realize that he would have no sales. If, however, the two entrepreneurs could get together, there would be a good market for coffee and sugar. Each *acting alone* would not be able to pursue the public interest, but acting together they could.

This particular example is deliberately quite simple, and in this case coordination (between the potential sugar producer and the potential coffee producer) might easily be provided by the individuals themselves without government intervention. But there are many cases where large-scale coordination is required, particularly in less developed countries, and this may require government planning. Similar arguments have been put forward as justification for public urban renewal programs. To redevelop a large section of a city requires extensive coordination among factories, retailers, landlords, and other businesses. One of the objectives of government development agencies is to provide that coordination (if markets were complete, the prices provided by the market would perform this "coordination" function).

5 INFORMATION FAILURES

A number of government activities are motivated by imperfect information on the part of consumers, and by the belief that the market, by itself, will supply too little information. For instance, the Truth-in-Lending bill requires lenders to inform borrowers of the true rate of interest on their loans. The Federal Trade Commission and the Food and Drug Administration have both adopted a number of regulations concerning labeling, dis-

---

[3] The literature in this area is extensive. The basic articles are George Akerlof, "The Market for Lemons: Qualitative Uncertainty and the Market Mechanism," *Quarterly Journal of Economics* 84 (1970): 488–500; and Michael Rothschild and Joseph Stiglitz, "Equilibrium in Competitive Insurance Markets: An Essay on the Economics of Imsperfect Information," *Quarterly Journal of Economics* 90 (1976): 629–50.

closure of contents, etc. At one time, the Federal Trade Commission proposed that used-car dealers be required to disclose whether they had tested various parts of the car, and if so, what the outcome of the test was. These regulations generated a considerable amount of controversy, and under pressure from Congress, the FTC was forced to back down.

Opponents of regulations on information disclosure contend that they are unnecessary (the competitive market provides incentives for firms to disclose relevant information), irrelevant (consumers pay little attention to the information the law requires firms to disclose), and costly, both to government, which must administer them, and to the firms which must comply with the regulations. Proponents of these regulations claim that, though difficult to administer effectively, they are still critical to the affected markets.

The government's role in remedying information failures goes beyond these simple consumer and investor protections, however. Information is, in many respects, a public good. Giving information to one more individual does not reduce the amount others have. Efficiency requires that information be freely disseminated or, more accurately, that the only charge be for the actual cost of transmitting the information. The private market will often provide an inadequate supply of information, just as it supplies an inadequate amount of other public goods. The most notable example of government activity in this area is the U.S. Weather Bureau. Another example is the information provided to ships by the U.S. Coast Guard.

There are various other market failures associated with imperfect information. One of the assumptions that went into the proof of the fundamental theorems of welfare economics was that there was perfect information, or more precisely, that nothing firms or households did had any effect on beliefs or information. In fact, much economic activity is directed at obtaining information—from employers trying to find out who are good employees, to lenders trying to find out who are good borrowers, investors trying to find out what are good investments, and insurers trying to find out who are good risks. Later, we shall see that information problems lie behind several government programs. For instance, many of the problems in the health sector in general and health insurance markets in particular can be traced to problems of information.

Resources devoted to producing new knowledge—**research and development (R&D)** expenditures—can be thought of as a particularly important category of expenditures on information. Again, the fundamental theorems of welfare economics, which form the basis of our belief in the efficiency of market economies, simply assume that there is a given state of information about technology, begging the question of how the economy allocates resources to research and development. Chapter 13 will explain why the market, on its own, may engage in an insufficient amount of at least certain types of R&D.[4]

[4] For an extended discussion of the market failures associated with incomplete markets and imperfect information, see B. Greenwald and J. E. Stiglitz, "Externalities in Economies with Imperfect Information and Incomplete Markets," *Quarterly Journal of Economics* (May 1986): 229–264.

Perhaps the most widely recognized symptoms of market failure are the periodic episodes of high unemployment, both of workers and machines, that have plagued capitalist economies during the past two centuries. Though these recessions and depressions have been greatly moderated in the period since World War II, perhaps partly because of government policies, the unemployment rate still climbed over 10 percent in 1982; that is low, however, compared to the Great Depression, when unemployment reached 24 percent in the United States. While by these standards the recession of 1991–1992, in which the country's average unemployment rate peaked at over 7 percent, was relatively mild, in some states, such as California, more than one out of ten workers was out of work. And unemployment rates in Europe have remained persistently high—in some cases in excess of 15 percent or even 20 percent—for the past two decades.

Most economists take the high levels of unemployment as prima facie evidence that *something* is not working well in the market. To some economists, high unemployment is the most dramatic and most convincing evidence of market failure.

The issues raised by unemployment and inflation are sufficiently important, and sufficiently complicated, that they warrant a separate course in macroeconomics. But some aspects of these issues are touched on in Chapter 28, which is concerned with the consequences of government deficits and attempts to survey some of the important ways that these macroeconomic considerations affect the design of tax policy.

**INTERRELATIONSHIPS
OF MARKET FAILURES**

The market failures we have discussed are not mutually exclusive. Information problems often provide part of the explanation of missing markets. In turn, externalities are often thought to arise from missing markets: if fishermen could be charged for using fishing grounds—if there were a market for fishing rights—there would not be overfishing. Public goods are sometimes viewed as an extreme case of externalities, where others benefit from my production of the good as much as I do. Much of the recent research on unemployment has attempted to relate it to one of the other market failures.

SIX BASIC MARKET FAILURES

1 Imperfect competition

2 Public goods

3 Externalities

4 Incomplete markets

5 Imperfect information

6 Unemployment and other macroeconomic disturbances

MARKET FAILURES: EXPLANATIONS OR EXCUSES?

The agricultural price support program provides an illustration of an instance where the appeal to market failures is more of an excuse for a program than a rationale. There are important market failures in agriculture. Prices and output are highly variable. Farmers typically cannot buy insurance to protect them against either price or output fluctuations. Though they could reduce their exposure to price risk somewhat by trading in futures and forward markets, these markets are highly speculative, and farmers worry that they are at a marked disadvantage in trading in them. For example, there are five very large traders in wheat who have access to more information; as a result farmers view trading on futures markets with these informed traders as playing on an unlevel playing field.

What farmers really care about, of course, is not price variability, but income variability. Programs to stabilize prices do not fully stabilize income, since income depends both on the price received and the quantity produced. Indeed, in some cases, stabilizing prices may actually increase the variability of income. Normally, prices rise when, on average, quantities fall. If prices rise proportionately, then income may vary very little, with price increases just offsetting quantity

REDISTRIBUTION AND MERIT GOODS

The sources of market failure discussed thus far result in economic inefficiency in the absence of government intervention. But even if the economy were Pareto efficient, there are two further arguments for government intervention. The first is income distribution. The fact that the economy is Pareto efficient says nothing about the distribution of income; competitive markets may give rise to a very unequal distribution, which may leave some individuals with insufficient resources on which to live. One of the most important activities of the government is to redistribute income. This is the express purpose of welfare activities, such as food stamps and Medicaid. How we think systematically about issues of distribution is the subject of the next chapter.

The second argument for government intervention in a Pareto efficient economy arises from concern that individuals may not act in their own best interests. It is often argued that an individual's perception of his own welfare may be an unreliable criterion for making welfare judgments. Even fully informed consumers may make "bad" decisions. Individuals continue to smoke even though it is bad for them, and even though they know it is bad for them. Individuals fail to wear seat belts, even though wearing seat belts increases the chances of survival from an accident, and even though individuals know the benefits of seat belts. There are those who believe that

decreases. In such a situation, stabilizing prices will increase income variability.

Price support programs are also justified as helping poor farmers—reflecting the failure of markets to provide an appropriate distribution of income. But, critics ask, why are poor farmers particularly deserving of aid, rather than poor people in general? Moreover, the price support programs give aid on the basis of how much a farmer produces. Thus, large farmers gain far more than small farmers.

If the objective of the farm programs were to address these market failures, then the farm program would be designed in a markedly different manner. In fact, a major objective of the farm program is to transfer resources—to subsidize farmers (and not just poor farmers)—not to correct a market failure. The program is designed to keep a large part of its cost hidden: only a part of the cost is reflected in the federal budget; the rest is paid for by consumers in the form of higher prices. The market failure approach has provided some of the rhetoric for the program, but not the rationale. For that, we have to look into politics and the role of special interest groups.

the government should intervene in such cases, where individuals seemingly do not do what is in their own best interest; the kind of intervention that is required must be stronger than simply providing information. Goods that the government compels individuals to consume, like seat belts and elementary education, are called **merit goods.**

The view that the government should intervene because it knows what is in the best interest of individuals better than they do themselves is referred to as **paternalism.** The paternalistic argument for government activities is quite distinct from the externalities argument discussed above. One might argue that smoking causes cancer, and that since individuals who get cancer may be treated in public hospitals or financed by public funds, smokers impose a cost on nonsmokers. This, however, can be dealt with by making smokers pay their full costs—for instance, by imposing a tax on cigarettes. Alternatively, smoking in a crowded room does indeed impose a cost on nonsmokers in that room. But this, too, can be dealt with directly. Those who take a paternalistic view might argue that individuals should not be allowed to smoke, even in the privacy of their own homes, and even if a tax which makes the smokers take account of the external costs imposed on others is levied. Though few have taken such an extreme paternalistic position with respect to smoking, this paternalistic role undoubtedly has been important in a number of areas, such as government policies toward drugs (illegalization of marijuana) and liquor (prohibition in the 1930s).

In contrast to the paternalistic view, many economists and social philosophers believe that the government should respect consumers' preferences. Though there may occasionally be cases that merit a paternalistic role for the government, these economists argue that it is virtually impossible to distinguish such cases from those that do not. And they worry that once the government assumes a paternalistic role, special interest groups will attempt to use government to further their own views about how individuals should act or what they should consume. The view that government should not interfere with the choices of individuals is sometimes referred to as **libertarianism.**

There are two important caveats to economists' general presumption against government paternalism. The first concerns children. Someone must make paternalistic decisions on behalf of children, either the parents or the state, and there is an ongoing debate concerning the proper division of responsibility between the two. Some treat children as if they were the property of their parents, arguing that parents alone should have responsibility for taking care of their children. But most argue that the state has certain basic responsibilities, such as, for instance, ensuring that every child gets an education and that parents do not deprive their children of needed medical care or endanger them physically or emotionally.

The second caveat concerns situations where the government cannot, at least without difficulty, commit itself to refrain from helping individuals who make poor decisions. For instance, individuals who do not save for their retirement become a burden on the government, and this provides part of the rationale for social security. There are other instances in which individuals who fail to take appropriate precautions become a burden to society—and a sense of compassion makes it difficult in the face of a crisis to simply say, "you should have taken appropriate precautions." Government accordingly responds by *forcing* or at least *encouraging* precautionary behavior. Individuals who neither buy earthquake insurance nor build homes that can withstand the effects of an earthquake become a burden on the government when an earthquake strikes. The government finds itself compelled to act compassionately, even if the victims' dire situation is partly of their own making. Recognizing this, the government may compel individuals to take adequate precautions against the event of an earthquake by, for instance, enforcing high standards for earthquake-resistant construction and making mandatory the purchase of earthquake insurance.

TWO PERSPECTIVES ON
THE ROLE OF GOVERNMENT

We saw in Chapter 1 that there are two aspects of the analysis of public sector activities: the normative approach, which focuses on what the government should do, and the positive approach, which focuses on describing and explaining both what the government actually does and what its consequences are. We can now relate our discussion of market failures, redistribution, and merit goods to these two alternative approaches.

NORMATIVE ANALYSIS

The fundamental theorems of welfare economics are useful because they clearly delineate a role for the government. In the absence of market failures and merit goods all the government needs to do is worry about the distribution of income (resources). The private enterprise system ensures that resources will be used efficiently.

If there are important market failures—imperfect competition, imperfect information, incomplete markets, externalities, public goods, and unemployment—there is a presumption that the market will not be Pareto efficient. This suggests a role for the government. But there are two important qualifications.

First, it has to be shown that there is, at least in principle, some way of intervening in the market to make someone better off without making anyone worse off, that is, of making a *Pareto improvement*. Secondly, it has to be shown that the actual political processes and bureaucratic structures of a democratic society are capable of correcting the market failure and achieving a Pareto improvement.

When information is imperfect and costly, the analysis of whether the market is Pareto efficient must take into account these information costs; information is costly to the government, just as it is to private firms. Markets may be incomplete because of transactions costs; the government too would face costs in establishing and running a public insurance program. These costs must be considered in the decision to set up such a program.

Recent research has established a variety of circumstances under which, although the government has no advantage in information or transactions costs over the private market, the government could, in principle, bring about a Pareto improvement. The fact that there may exist government policies that would be Pareto improvements does not, however, necessarily create a presumption that government intervention is desirable. We also have to consider the consequences of government intervention, in the form it is likely to take, given the nature of our political process. We have to understand how real governments function if we are to assess whether government action is likely to remedy market failures.

In the 1960s, it was common to take a market failure, show that a government program could lead to a Pareto improvement (someone could be made better off without making anyone worse off), and conclude that government intervention was called for. When programs were enacted and failed to achieve what they were supposed to, the blame was placed on petty bureaucrats or political tampering. But, as we shall see in Chapters 7 and 8, even if bureaucrats and politicians behave honorably, the nature of government itself still may help explain government's failures.

Public programs—even those allegedly directed at alleviating some market failure—are instituted in democracies not by ideal governments or benevolent despots but by complicated political processes.

The market failure approach to understanding the role of the government is largely a normative approach. The market failure approach provides a basis for identifying situations where the government *ought* to do something, tempered by considerations of government failure.

The popularity of the market failure approach has caused many programs to be justified in terms of market failures. But this may simply be rhetoric. There is often a significant difference between a program's stated objective (to remedy some market failure) and its design. Political rhetoric may focus on the failure of markets to provide insurance against volatile prices and the consequences that this has for small farmers, but government agricultural programs may in practice transfer income to large farmers. Insight into the political forces at work and the true objectives of the programs may be gained more easily by looking at how the programs are designed and implemented than by looking at the stated objectives of the legislation.

Some economists believe that economists should focus their attention on positive analysis, on describing the consequences of government programs and the nature of the political processes, rather than on normative analysis, what the government should do. However, discussions by economists (and others) of the role that government *should* play constitute an important part of the political process in modern democracies. Beyond that, an analysis of institutional arrangements by which public decisions get made may lead to designs which enhance the likelihood that the public decisions will reflect a broader set of public interests, and not just special interests. These matters will be taken up in further detail in later chapters.

REVIEW AND PRACTICE

SUMMARY

1 Under certain conditions, the competitive market results in a Pareto efficient resource allocation. When the conditions required for this are not satisfied, a rationale for government intervention in the market is provided.

2 Government is required to establish and enforce property rights and enforce contracts. Without this, markets by themselves cannot function.

3 There are six reasons why the market mechanism may not result in a Pareto efficient resource allocation: failure of competition, public goods, externalities, incomplete markets, information failures, and unemployment. These are known as market failures.

4 Even if the market is Pareto efficient, there may be two further grounds for government action. First, the competitive market may give rise to a socially undesirable distribution of income. And second, some believe that individuals, even when well informed, do not make good judgments concerning the goods they consume, thus providing a rationale for regulations restricting the consumption of some goods, and for the public provision of other goods, called merit goods.

5 Though the presence of market failures implies that there may be scope for government activity, it does not imply that a particular government program aimed at correcting the market failure is necessarily desirable. To evaluate government programs, one must take into account not only their objectives but also how they are implemented.

6 The normative approach to the role of government asks, how can government address market failures and other perceived inadequacies in the market's resource allocation? The positive approach asks, what is it that the government does, what are its effects, and how does the nature of the political process (including the incentives it provides bureaucrats and politicians) help explain what the government does and how it does it?

KEY CONCEPTS

Natural monopoly	Incomplete markets
Marginal revenue	Merit goods
Pure public goods	Paternalism
Externalities	Libertarianism

QUESTIONS AND PROBLEMS

1 For each program listed below, discuss what market failures might be (or are) used as a partial rationale:

    a Automobile safety belt requirements

    b Regulations on automobile pollution

    c National defense

    d Unemployment compensation

    e Medicare (medical care for the aged)

    f Medicaid (medical care for the indigent)

    g Federal Deposit Insurance Corporation

    h Federally insured mortgages

    i Law requiring lenders to disclose the true rate of interest they are charging on loans (truth-in-lending laws)

    j National Weather Service

    k Urban renewal

    l Post office

    m Government prohibition of the use of narcotics

    n Rent control

2 If the primary objective of government programs in each of these areas is the alleviation of some market failure, how might they be better designed?

    a Farm price supports

    b Oil import quotas (in the 1950s)

    c Special tax provisions for energy industries

3 Many government programs both redistribute income and correct a market failure. What are the market failures associated with each of these programs, and how else might they be addressed if there were no distributional objectives?

    a Student loan programs

    b Public elementary education

    c Public support for universities

    d Social security

4 Draw the average and marginal cost curves for a natural monopoly. Draw the demand and marginal revenue curves.

    a Show the efficient level of output, at which price equals marginal cost. Explain why if the firm charged a price equal to marginal cost, it would operate at a loss. Show diagrammatically the necessary subsidy.

    b Show the monopoly level of output, at which marginal revenue equals marginal cost. Explain why the monopoly level of output is smaller than the efficient level of output.

    c Show the level of output of a government monopoly which was instructed to just break even. How does this level of output compare with the efficient level of output and the private monopoly level of output? (Show diagrammatically.)

5 Efficiency and Equity

FOCUS QUESTIONS

1 How do economists think systematically about how to make social choices when there are trade-offs, that is, when after finding all possible Pareto improvements, gains to the welfare of one individual must come at the expense of the welfare of others? What is the social welfare function, and why do economists find this concept useful?

2 How do economists think systematically about the trade-offs between efficiency and inequality? How do they measure poverty or inequality? How do they measure efficiency?

3 As a practical matter, how do governments translate these general principles into a form which can actually be used in decision making?

Chapter 3 took up Pareto efficiency, the condition in which no one can be made better off without making someone else worse off. It showed that in the absence of market failures, a free market would be Pareto efficient. But even if the competitive economy is efficient, the distribution of income to which it gives rise may be viewed as undesirable. One of the main consequences, and main objectives, of government activity is to alter the distribution of income.

The evaluation of a public program often entails balancing its consequences for economic efficiency and for the distribution of income. A central objective of welfare economics is to provide a framework within which these evaluations can be performed systematically. This chapter shows how economists conceptualize the trade-offs between efficiency and equity.

EFFICIENCY AND DISTRIBUTION TRADE-OFFS

Consider again a simple economy with two individuals, Robinson Crusoe and Friday. Assume initially that Robinson Crusoe has ten oranges, while Friday has only two. This seems inequitable. Assume, therefore, that we play the role of government and attempt to transfer four oranges from Robinson Crusoe to Friday, but in the process one orange gets lost. Hence Robinson Crusoe ends up with six oranges, and Friday with five. We have eliminated most of the inequity, but in the process the total number of oranges available has been diminished. There is a **trade-off** between efficiency—the total number of oranges available—and equity.

The trade-off between equity and efficiency is at the heart of many discussions of public policy. Two questions are debated. First, there is disagreement about the nature of the trade-off. To reduce inequality, how much efficiency do we have to give up? Will one orange or two be lost in the process of transferring oranges from Crusoe to Friday?

Second, there is disagreement on the relative value to be assigned to a decrease in inequality compared to a decrease in efficiency. Some people claim that inequality is the central problem of society, and society should simply minimize the extent of inequality, regardless of the consequences to efficiency. Others claim that efficiency is the central issue. They argue that even if one wishes to help the poor, in the long run, the best way to do that is not to worry about how the pie is to be divided but to increase the size of the pie, to make it grow as rapidly as possible, so that there are more goods for everyone.

These disagreements relate to social choices between equity and efficiency. We now take a closer look at these choices.

ANALYZING SOCIAL CHOICES

When economists analyze consumer choice, the opportunity set is defined by the consumer's budget constraint, and the consumer's preferences are described by indifference curves (see Chapter 3, pp. 94–96). The individual chooses the point on the budget constraint which is tangent to an indifference curve—this puts him on the highest indifference curve feasible, given the budget constraint.

Economists have tried to use the same framework for analyzing social choices. The utility possibilities curve, introduced in Chapter 3, describes the opportunity set. It gives the highest level of utility (or welfare) attainable by one individual, given the levels of utility attained by others. An economy is Pareto efficient if and only if it is operating along the utility possibilities schedule. The first fundamental theorem of welfare economics says that competitive economies are always on the utility possibilities schedule. The second fundamental theorem of welfare economics says that every point on the utility possibilities schedule can be attained through a competitive market process if the government redistributes initial endowments accordingly. How does society select a point along the utility possibilities curve? Just as indifference curves for individuals describe how they make trade-offs between different goods, **social indifference curves** describe how society might make trade-offs between utility levels of different individuals. A social indifference curve gives those combinations of utility of, say, Crusoe and Friday, between which society is indifferent.

The two central questions of welfare economics can now be restated in terms of this social choice framework. Assume the current competitive market equilibrium is represented by the point A on the utility possibilities schedule depicted in Figure 5.1. Suppose society decides to move, say, from point A to point B along the utility possibilities schedule, representing an increase in Friday's utility and a reduction in Crusoe's utility. The first question is: What is the trade-off? The utility possibilities curve gives the answer by showing the increase in Friday's utility from U^F_0 to U^F_1 and the decrease

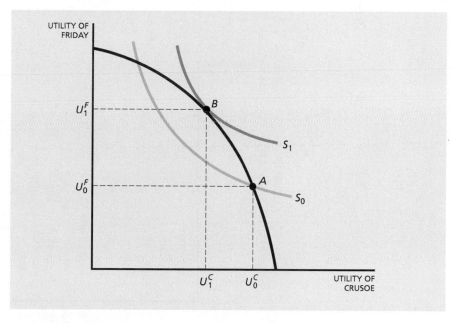

FIGURE 5.1   **Social Indifference Curves** The social indifference curves describe how society evaluates trade-offs between Friday and Crusoe; it gives the combinations of utilities between which society is indifferent. Society is better off on a higher social indifference curve, just as an individual is better off on a higher individual indifference curve. And just as the individual chooses the point on the budget constraint at which the indifference curve is tangent to the budget constraint, society's preferred point on the utility possibilities curve is the point at which the social indifference curve is tangent to the utility possibilities curve.

in Crusoe's utility from U^C_0 to U^C_1. The second question concerns social preferences: How does society evaluate the trade-off? The slope of the social indifference curves gives the trade-offs for which society is indifferent. Point B is on the social indifference curve S_1, which is tangent to the utility possibilities curve, and lies on a higher indifference curve than S_0. Point B is therefore preferred by society.

The next two sections take a closer look at each of these questions regarding trade-offs and the economist's framework for analyzing social choice.

DETERMINING THE TRADE-OFFS

As we saw in Figure 5.1, the utility possibilities schedule shows us the trade-offs of transferring utility from Crusoe to Friday. The shape of the utility possibilities schedule tells us something more about those trade-offs. Consider the utility possibilities schedule shown in Figure 5.2. Assume that the economy lies at point A, where Crusoe enjoys much more utility than Friday. Moving up and to the left along the schedule increases Friday's utility and decreases Crusoe's. Suppose we transfer oranges from Crusoe to Friday by moving in two steps, from point A to B to C. Clearly, this makes Crusoe

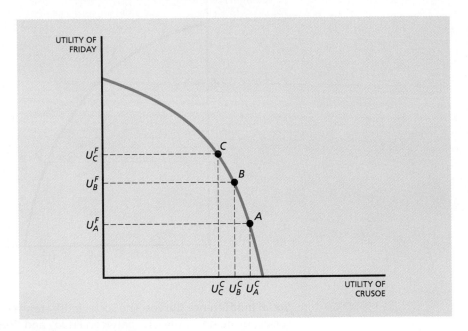

FIGURE 5.2 **Crusoe's and Friday's Utility Possibilities Curve** As oranges are transferred from Crusoe to Friday, Crusoe's utility is decreased and Friday's increased. In moving from point A to B the gain in Friday's utility appears much greater than the loss in Crusoe's utility. That is because Friday is so much worse off than Crusoe. In moving from B to C, the gain in Friday's utility is still larger than the loss in Crusoe's utility, but the trade-off has changed so that Friday's gain is smaller than the gain from A to B.

worse off. As depicted in the figure, the decreases in Crusoe's utility are small in comparison to the increases in Friday's utility.

Utility theory helps explain this outcome. Economists use the term **utility function** to describe the relationship between the number of oranges and Friday's level of utility; the extra utility Friday gets from an extra orange is called his **marginal utility**. These are shown in panels A and B of Figure 5.3. At each point, marginal utility is the slope of the utility function—the

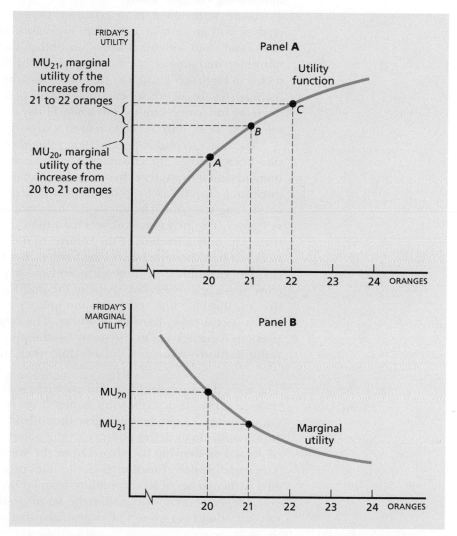

FIGURE 5.3   **The Utility Function and Marginal Utility** Panel A shows the utility function. As we give Friday more oranges, his utility increases, but each additional orange leaves him less extra utility. Panel B shows marginal utility: the extra utility Friday gets from an extra orange decreases as the number of oranges increases, corresponding to the decreasing slope of the utility function.

change in utility from a unit change in orange consumption. Notice that as more oranges are consumed, utility rises more slowly, and marginal utility falls. (Thus, the slope of the utility function at point C is less than the slope at A or B.) This is because Friday enjoys the first orange very much, the next one a little less, and additional oranges still less. Finally, he becomes satiated and derives very little additional enjoyment from an additional orange. As an individual consumes more of any good, the extra gain from having one extra unit of that good becomes smaller. This phenomenon is referred to as **diminishing marginal utility.**[1]

By the same token, as we take away oranges from Crusoe, his utility decreases; and as we take away more and more oranges, the extra utility he loses from each additional loss of an orange increases. That is why with diminishing marginal utility, the utility possibilities schedule has the shape depicted in Figures 5.1 and 5.2. This shape says that when Friday has very little income (few oranges), we can increase his utility a great deal with a small decrease in Crusoe's utility, but when Friday is much better off, we can increase his utility only a little with even a large decrease in Crusoe's utility.

There is a second important determinant of the shape of the utility possibilities schedule—the efficiency with which we can transfer resources from one individual to another. In our society, the way we transfer resources from one group (say, the rich) to another (say, the poor) is by taxing the rich and subsidizing the poor. The way we do that normally interferes with economic efficiency. The rich may work less hard than they would otherwise, because they reap only a fraction of the returns to their effort; while the poor may work less hard because by working harder, they may lose eligibility for benefits. The magnitude of these disincentives—a subject of considerable controversy—affects the entire shape of the utility possibilities schedule. In Figure 5.4, the blue line represents the utility possibilities schedule assuming that it is costless to transfer resources. The black line, lying far below the previous locus, except at the point C—the point which occurs without any redistribution—represents the schedule when transfers are very costly.

EVALUATING THE TRADE-OFFS

The second basic concept used in analyzing social choices is the social indifference curve. As described in Chapter 3, an indifference curve gives those combinations of goods which give the individual the same level of utility. Just as individuals derive utility from the goods they consume, we can think of society as deriving its welfare from the utility received by its members. The **social welfare function** gives the level of social welfare corresponding to a particular set of levels of utility attained by members of society. The *social indifference curve* is defined as the set of combinations of utility of different individuals (or groups of individuals) that yields equal levels of welfare

---

[1] We write the utility function as $U = U(C_1, C_2, \ldots, C_n)$, where $C_1, C_2, \ldots, C_n$ represent the quantities of consumption of the various goods. Marginal utility of, say, C_1, is then simply the increase in U (utility) from an increase in consumption of C_1. Diminishing marginal utility implies that successive increments in C_1 yield successively smaller increments to U.

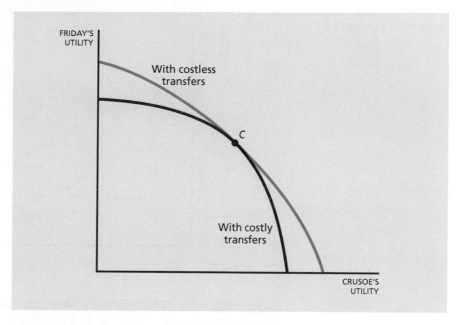

FRIDAY'S UTILITY

With costless transfers

C

With costly transfers

CRUSOE'S UTILITY

FIGURE 5.4 **Utility Possibilities Schedule with Costly Transfers** The set of points we can achieve through redistribution, when transfers are costly, lies within the utility possibilities curve, given costless transfers.

to society—for which, in other words, the social welfare function has the same value.

The social welfare function provides a basis for ranking any allocation of resources: we choose those allocations which yield higher levels of social welfare. The **Pareto principle** says that we should prefer those allocations in which at least some individuals are better off and no one is worse off. It says that if some individuals' utility is increased and no one else's utility is decreased, social welfare increases. Thus, in Figure 5.5 those combinations to the northeast of A make everyone better off, and hence satisfy the Pareto principle.

Unfortunately, most choices involve trade-offs, with some individuals being made better off and others worse off. At point B the second group is better off than at A, but the first group is worse off. We thus need a stronger criterion, and this is what the social welfare function provides. The social indifference curves provide a convenient diagrammatic way of thinking about the kinds of trade-offs society faces in these situations. Thus, in Figure 5.5 all combinations of the utilities of Groups 1 and 2 that are on the social indifference curve labeled W_2 yield a higher level of social welfare than those combinations on the curve labeled W_1. This shows that B is preferred to A.

Social welfare functions can be thought of as a tool economists use to summarize assumptions about society's attitudes toward different distributions of income and welfare. If society is very concerned about inequality, it might not care that Crusoe has to give up seventy oranges for Friday to get

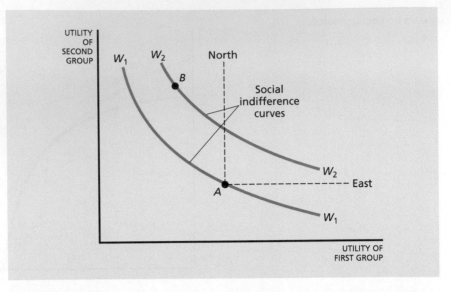

FIGURE 5.5 **Social Indifference Curves** Society is willing to trade off some decrease in one group's utility for an increase in another's. A social indifference curve gives those combinations of utilities of Group 1 and Group 2 between which society is indifferent. Points on the social indifference curve labeled W_2 yield a higher level of social welfare than do points on the social indifference curve labeled W_1.

one orange, "since Crusoe has so many to begin with." So long as Friday is poorer than Crusoe, any sacrifice on Crusoe's part that makes Friday better off would be justified. On the other hand, society might not care at all about inequality; it could value an orange in the hands of Friday exactly the same as an orange in the hands of Crusoe, even though Friday is much poorer. In that case it would focus only on efficiency, on the number of oranges available. No redistribution of oranges from Crusoe to Friday would be justified if, in the process, a single orange was lost.

UTILITARIANISM Social welfare functions—and the associated social indifference curves—can take a variety of shapes, as illustrated in Figure 5.6. Panels A and B illustrate two different cases. In panel A the social indifference curve is a straight line, implying that no matter what the level of utility of Friday and Crusoe, society is willing to trade off one "unit" of Friday's utility against one unit of Crusoe's. The view represented by this social indifference curve has a long historical tradition. Jeremy Bentham was the leader of a group, called **utilitarians,** which argued that society should maximize the sum of the utilities of its members; in our simple example with two individuals, the social welfare function is

$$W = U_1 + U_2.$$

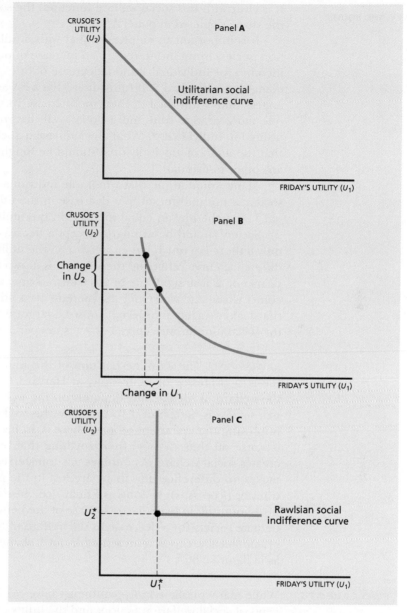

FIGURE 5.6 **Alternative Shapes of Social Indifference Curves** (A) A utilitarian is willing to give up some utility for Crusoe so long as Friday gains at least an equal amount of utility. The social indifference curves are straight lines. (B) Some argue that society requires more than an equal increase in the utility (U_2) of a rich individual to compensate for a decrease in the utility (U_1) of a poor individual. (C) Rawls maintains that no amount of increase in the welfare of the rich can compensate for a decrease in the welfare of the poor. This implies that the social indifference curves are L-shaped.

It is clear with this social welfare function, the social indifference curve has the shape depicted in panel A.

It is important to emphasize that with a utilitarian social welfare function, society is not indifferent to an increase of one orange (or one dollar of income) for Individual 1 and a decrease of one orange (or one dollar of income) for Individual 2. If Individual 1 has a lower level of income (fewer oranges) than Individual 2, then the increase in utility of Individual 1 from one more orange (one more dollar) will be greater than the decrease in utility for Individual 2. What the utilitarian social welfare function says is that the *utility* of any individual should be weighted equally to the utility of any other individual.

Many would argue that when one individual is worse off than another, society is not indifferent to a decrease in the utility of the poorer (Individual 1) matched by an equal increase in the utility of the richer (Individual 2). Society should be willing to accept a decrease in the utility of the poor only if there is a much larger increase in the utility of the rich. The social indifference curve reflecting these values is drawn in Figure 5.6B, where it appears not as a straight line but as a curved one; as the poorer individual becomes worse and worse off, the increment in utility of the richer individual that makes society indifferent must be larger and larger (i.e., the slope of the social indifference curve becomes steeper and steeper).

RAWLSIANISM The extreme position of this debate has been taken by John Rawls, a professor of philosophy at Harvard University. Rawls argues that the welfare of society only depends on the welfare of the worst-off individual; society is better off if you improve his welfare but gains nothing from improving the welfare of others. There is, in his view, no trade-off. If Friday is worse off than Crusoe, then anything that increases Friday's welfare increases social welfare. As oranges are transferred from Crusoe to Friday, it makes no difference how many are lost in the process (how inefficient the transfer process is), so long as Friday gets *something*. To put it another way, no amount of increase in the welfare of the better-off individual could compensate society for a decrease in the welfare of the worst-off individual. Diagrammatically, this is represented by an L-shaped social indifference curve, as in Figure 5.6C[2].

TWO CAVEATS While many public sector economists have made extensive use of the concepts of social welfare functions and the utility possibilities curve, these concepts have also been extensively criticized, on several grounds.

INTERPERSONAL COMPARISONS We assume that when an individual consumes more, her utility rises. But we cannot measure the level of utility or the

---

[2] The social welfare function is written:

$$W = \min \{U_1, \ldots U_n\}.$$

Social welfare reflects only the utility of the worst-off member of society.

SOCIAL CHOICE IN THEORY

1 *Construct the opportunity set.* The utility possibilities schedule describes how much one person's utility has to be decreased when another's is increased.

2 *Define preferences.* Social indifference curves describe how much society is willing to decrease one person's utility to increase another's by a given amount.

3 *Adopt programs that increase social welfare.* Find the programs that put society on the highest social indifference curve.

change in utility. Social welfare functions seem to assume not only that there is a meaningful way of measuring an individual's utility,[3] but that there is a meaningful way of comparing the utility of different individuals. For example, with the utilitarian social welfare function we add up the utility of the different members of society. Because we add Crusoe's and Friday's utility together, we are, in effect, assuming that somehow we can compare *in a meaningful numerical way* their level of utility. But when we transfer an orange from Robinson to Friday, how can we compare in an objective way the value of Friday's gain and Robinson's loss?

The same problem arises with a Rawlsian social welfare function, where we are told to maximize the welfare of the worst-off member of society. To judge who is worst off, we must somehow compare utilities.

Many economists believe these **interpersonal comparisons** cannot be made in any meaningful way. I may claim that although I have a much higher income than my brother, I am unhappier; not only that, I may claim that I know how to spend income so much better that the extra increment in my utility from a dollar given to me is much greater than the extra increment in utility that he would get from receiving an extra dollar. How could anyone prove that I was wrong (or right)? Because there is no way of answering this question, economists argue that there can be no scientific basis for making welfare comparisons.

Since there is no "scientific" basis for making such welfare comparisons, many economists believe economists should limit themselves to describing the consequences of different policies, pointing out who are the gainers and who are the losers, and that should be the end of their analysis. They believe the only circumstances in which economists should make welfare

---

[3] In some situations, it may be possible to use the amount of money an individual would be willing to pay for an object as a *measure* of the utility of that object. But this does not resolve the problem of comparing utilities across individuals.

COMPARING INDIVIDUAL AND SOCIAL CHOICES

INDIVIDUAL CHOICES	SOCIAL CHOICES
STEP ONE: DEFINE OPPORTUNITY SET	
Budget constraint	Utility possibilities curve
STEP TWO: DEFINE PREFERENCES	
Individual indifference curve	Social indifference curve
STEP THREE: CHOOSE PREFERRED POINT	
Tangency between individual indifference curve and budget constraint	Tangency between social indifference curve and utility possibilities curve

judgments is when the policy change is a Pareto improvement. Unfortunately, as we have said, few policy changes are Pareto improvements, and hence without making interpersonal comparisons of welfare, economists have little to say regarding policy.

WHENCE SOCIAL WELFARE FUNCTIONS? The second set of objections concerns the very nature of social welfare functions. Individuals have preferences; they can decide whether they prefer some combination of apples and oranges to another combination. Society consists of many individuals; but society itself does not have preferences. We can describe the preferences of each individual, but whose preferences does the social welfare function represent? If there were a dictator, the answer to that question would be easy: the social welfare function would reflect the preferences of the dictator. But in a democratic society, there is no easy answer to the question. Some individuals—particularly the rich—may care little for redistribution, while others—particularly the poor—may argue that greater weight should be placed on redistribution.

As a descriptive matter—as part of a positive analysis—societies seldom exhibit consistency. One of the results to be described in Chapter 7 explains why this is not unexpected. Most economists think of the concepts we have described—as part of a normative analysis—as tools that help us think systematically about the trade-offs society constantly must face. And, as we noted earlier, the systematic analysis of these trade-offs actually constitutes an important part of the process by which decisions get made.

SOCIAL CHOICES IN PRACTICE

In practice, government officials do not derive utility possibilities schedules, nor do they write down social welfare functions. But their approach to deciding whether, say, to undertake any particular project does reflect the concepts we have introduced.

First, they attempt to identify and measure the net benefits (benefits minus costs) received by different groups. Second, they ascertain whether the project is a Pareto improvement, that is, whether everyone is better off. If so, clearly the project should be undertaken (this is the Pareto principle).

If the project is not a Pareto improvement, matters are more difficult. Some gain, some lose. The government needs to make an overall judgment. One commonly used approach looks at two summary statistics, describing "efficiency" and "equity" effects. *Efficiency* is measured by simply summing the gains or losses for each individual (which are calculated in a manner to be described shortly). *Equity* is measured by looking at some overall measure of inequality in society. If a project has net positive gains (positive efficiency effects) and reduces measured inequality, it should be undertaken. If a project has net positive losses and increases measured inequality, it should not be undertaken. If the efficiency measure shows gains but the equality measure shows losses (or vice versa), there is a trade-off, which is evaluated using a social welfare function: how much extra inequality is society willing to accept for an increase in efficiency?

There are numerous examples where choices between equality and efficiency have to made. For instance, in general, the more a tax system redistributes income, the greater the inefficiencies it introduces. There is a trade-off between equality and efficiency. There are, of course, important instances of poorly designed tax systems; such tax systems put the economy below its utility possibilities schedule. In such cases, it may be possible to increase both equality and efficiency.

We now take a closer look at how economists measure efficiency and inequality.

MEASURING BENEFITS

The first problem is how to measure the benefits of some program or project to particular individuals. In the discussion of utility theory above, we described how giving Friday more oranges increased his utility. But how do we measure this?

The standard way this is done is in terms of *willingness to pay*. We ask how much an individual would be willing to pay to be in one situation rather than another. For example, if Joe likes chocolate ice cream more than vanilla, it stands to reason that he would be willing to pay more for a scoop of chocolate ice cream than for a scoop of vanilla. Or if Diane would rather live in California than in New Jersey, it stands to reason that she would be willing to pay more for the West Coast location.

Notice that how much a person is willing to pay is different from how much he *has* to pay. Just because Joe is willing to pay more for chocolate ice cream than for vanilla does not mean he will have to pay more. What he has to pay depends on market prices; what he is willing to pay reflects his preferences.

Using willingness to pay as our measure of utility, we can construct a diagram like panel A of Figure 5.7, which shows the level of utility Mary receives from sweatshirts as the number of sweatshirts she buys increases. This

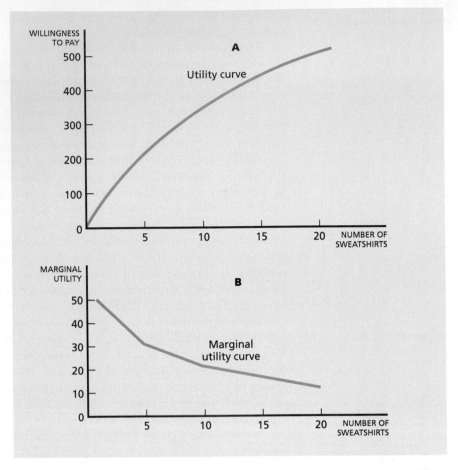

WILLINGNESS
TO PAY

A

Utility curve

NUMBER OF
SWEATSHIRTS

MARGINAL
UTILITY

B

Marginal
utility curve

NUMBER OF
SWEATSHIRTS

FIGURE 5.7 **Utility and Marginal Utility** Panel A shows that utility increases continually with consumption but tends to level off as consumption climbs higher. Panel B explicitly shows marginal utility; notice that it declines as consumption increases.

information is also given in Table 5.1. Here we assume that Mary is willing to pay $200 for five sweatshirts, $228 for six sweatshirts, $254 for seven sweatshirts, and so on. Thus, five sweatshirts give her a utility of 200, six a utility of 228, and seven sweatshirts a utility of 254. Mary's willingness to pay increases with the number of sweatshirts, reflecting the fact that additional sweatshirts give her additional utility. The extra utility of an additional sweatshirt measured here by the additional amount she is willing to pay, is the marginal utility. The numbers in the third column of Table 5.1 give the marginal (or extra) utility she received from her last sweatshirt. When Mary owns five sweatshirts, an additional sweatshirt yields her an additional or marginal utility of 28 (228 − 200); when she owns six sweatshirts, an additional one

TABLE 5.1	NUMBER OF SWEATSHIRTS	MARY'S WILLINGNESS TO PAY (UTILITY)	MARGINAL UTILITY
Utility and	0	0	
Marginal Utility	1	50	50
	2	95	45
	3	135	40
	4	170	35
	5	200	30
	6	228	28
	7	254	26
	8	278	24
	9	301	23
	10	323	22
	11	344	21
	12	364	20
	13	383	19
	14	401	18
	15	418	17
	16	434	16
	17	449	15
	18	463	14
	19	476	13
	20	488	12

gives her a marginal utility of only 26 (254 − 228). Panel B traces the marginal utilities of each of these increments.[4]

ORDINARY AND COMPENSATED DEMAND CURVES

We can use the concept of willingness to pay to construct a demand curve. We have already asked how much Mary is willing to pay for each additional sweatshirt. If the price of sweatshirts is $29, then she will buy five sweatshirts. She would have been willing to pay $30 for the fifth sweatshirt, so clearly, the marginal benefit of the fifth sweatshirt exceeds its cost; but she is only willing to pay $28 for the sixth sweatshirt, so the marginal benefit is less than the cost. Thus, the marginal utility curve drawn in panel B in Figure 5.7 can also be thought of as the demand curve.

But it is a special demand curve, called the **compensated demand curve,** which differs slightly from the **ordinary demand curve.** Recall that we constructed the compensated demand curve by asking how much Mary would

[4] Since marginal utility is the extra utility from an extra unit of consumption, it is measured by the slope of the utility curve in panel A.

be willing to pay for each additional sweatshirt; thus, as we give her more sweatshirts, we are always keeping her at exactly the same level of utility.

To construct the ordinary demand curve we need to know how many units of the commodity Mary would buy at each price. As the price is lowered, Mary not only demands more, but is made better off. As prices are lowered, individuals substitute the cheaper good for others goods. If the price of sweatshirts is lowered, Mary will substitute sweatshirts for sweaters. This is called the **substitution effect.** Because of the lower price, Mary is better off; if she bought exactly the same amount of goods that she did before, she would have money left over. She spreads this money around. Some of it is spent on buying sweatshirts. The increase in demand for sweatshirts as a result of the fact that Mary is better off—it is *as if* she had more income—is called the **income effect.** If we take away this extra money, we have the compensated demand curve; we eliminate the income effect. Thus, the compensated demand curve reflects only the substitution effect. In most cases, the differences between the two are negligible. If Mary spends one-tenth of 1 percent of her income on sweatshirts, taking away the extra income has almost no effect on her demand for sweatshirts, or any other commodity. Thus, Figure 5.8 shows the ordinary and compen-

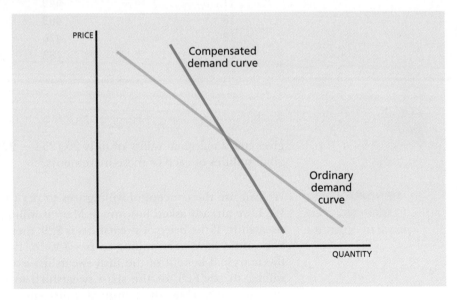

FIGURE 5.8   **Compensated versus Uncompensated Demand Curves** The compensated demand curve gives the demand for a good assuming, as price is changed, that money is taken away or given to the individual to leave him just as well off as he was before the price change. It thus measures only the substitution effect associated with the price changes. Because as price is lowered individuals are better off, and as a result buy slightly more of (normal) commodities, the ordinary demand curve is slightly flatter than the compensated demand curve.

sated demand curves as being almost the same, with the ordinary demand curve being slightly flatter (lowering the price from its current level, P_0, results in a slightly greater increase in the quantity demanded, and raising the price from its current level results in a slightly greater decrease in quantity demanded).

CONSUMER SURPLUS

The difference between what an individual is willing to pay and what he has to pay is called his **consumer surplus.** Mary would have been willing to pay $50 for the first sweatshirt, $45 for the second, $40 for the third, and so on. But if the market price is $29, that is all she has to pay for each sweatshirt. Thus, on the first sweatshirt she gets a surplus of $21 ($50, what she was willing to pay, minus $29, what she actually pays); on the second sweatshirt she gets a surplus of $16; on the third sweatshirt she gets a surplus of $11, and so on. The total consumer surplus is thus the sum: $21 + $16 + $11 + $6 + $1 = $55.

Diagrammatically, the consumer surplus is depicted in Figure 5.9 as the shaded area under the compensated demand curve and above the price line. Of course, since the compensated and uncompensated demand curves are almost the same, typically, we calculate the consumer surplus simply by looking at the area under the ordinary demand curve above the price line.

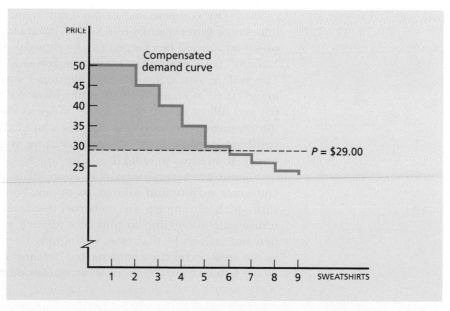

FIGURE 5.9   **Graphical Representation of Consumer Surplus** An individual's surplus is the difference between what he is willing to pay (represented by the area beneath the demand curve) and what he actually pays (the area under the price line). The consumer surplus here is indicated by the shaded region.

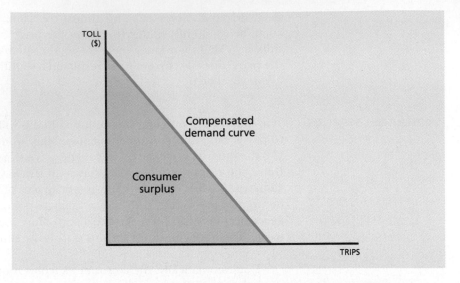

FIGURE 5.10   **Measuring the Benefits of a Government Project: Building a Bridge** The benefits of a bridge for which no tolls will be charged can be measured by the total area under the demand curve—the total consumer surplus.

USING CONSUMER SURPLUS TO CALCULATE THE BENEFITS OF A GOVERNMENT PROJECT The compensated demand curve can be useful for measuring the benefits of government projects. For instance, constructing a bridge upon which no toll will be charged can be thought of as lowering the price from "infinity" (one simply can't buy trips across a nonexistent bridge) to zero. The welfare gain is just the total consumer surplus, the area under the demand curve in Figure 5.10. This measures the maximum individuals could pay and still be as well off with the bridge as they were without it. Clearly, if the consumer surplus is less than the cost of the bridge, it does not pay to construct it, while if the consumer surplus is greater than the cost of the bridge, it does pay to build it.

There are several ways that economists go about trying to measure consumer surplus and willingness to pay. For many goods, there are data with which economists can construct the demand curve (the quantity that individuals are willing to purchase at each price) and the compensated demand curve.[5] In that case, willingness to pay can be calculated simply as the area under the compensated demand curve. For some goods, such as the Grand Canyon, there is no market demand curve. Yet the govern-

---

[5] As was noted previously, for most goods the compensated and uncompensated demand curves are very similar. If the *income elasticity* (the percentage increase in the demand for the good when income increases by 1 percent) is known, one can calculate the compensated demand curve from the uncompensated demand curve.

ment still might want to know how much citizens are willing to pay to preserve it in its pristine condition. Economists have designed elaborate survey techniques to elicit meaningful answers from individuals concerning their willingness to pay. These methods are discussed at greater length in Chapter 11.

MEASURING AGGREGATE SOCIAL BENEFITS

We have now described how we can measure the benefits that an individual receives. Social benefits are typically measured by adding up the benefits received by all individuals. The numbers obtained represent the total willingness to pay of all individuals in society. The difference between the total willingness to pay and the total costs of a project can be thought of as the net "efficiency" effect of the project. It is a dollar value of the net benefits.

MEASURING INEFFICIENCY

In assessing alternative policies, economists have put particular emphasis on economic efficiency. Taxes are criticized for discouraging work effort, monopolies for restricting production and driving up prices. To measure the dollar value of an inefficiency, economists use exactly the same methodology they use to measure the dollar value of a new project. There, we calculated the consumer surplus associated with the project. Here, we calculate the consumer surplus associated with the elimination of the inefficiency. That is, economists ask: "How much would an individual be willing to give up to have the inefficiency eliminated?" Consider the inefficiency caused by a tax on cigarettes. We ask each individual how much he would be willing to pay to have the tax on cigarettes eliminated. Say his answer is $100. Thus eliminating the cigarette tax and imposing in its place a $100 **lump-sum tax** (that is, a tax that the individual would have to pay regardless of what he did) leaves his welfare unchanged. The difference between the revenue raised by the cigarette tax (say, $80) and the lump-sum tax that the individual would be willing to pay is called the **deadweight loss** or **excess burden** of the tax. It is the measure of the inefficiency of the tax. Taxes, other than lump-sum taxes, give rise to a deadweight loss because they cause individuals to forgo more-preferred consumption in favor of less-preferred consumption in order to avoid payments of the tax. Thus, even a tax that raises no government revenue—because individuals completely avoid purchasing the taxed commodity—can have a substantial excess burden.

We can calculate the deadweight loss using compensated demand curves. Assume the cost of producing a cigarette is c_0, and the tax raises the price from c_0 to $c_0 + t$, where t is the tax per pack. We assume the individual consumes q_0 packs of cigarettes with the tax, and q_1 after the tax has been removed (but replaced by a lump-sum tax that leaves him no better or no worse off than when there was a cigarette tax). We have drawn the resulting compensated demand curve in Figure 5.11. The deadweight loss is measured by the shaded area *ABC*, the area under the compensated de-

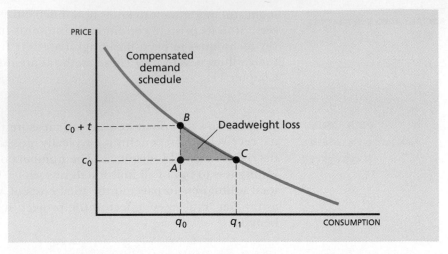

PRICE

Compensated
demand
schedule

B

Deadweight loss

$c_0 + t$

C

c_0

A

q_0 q_1 CONSUMPTION

FIGURE 5.11   **Measuring Inefficiencies** The area ABC measures the deadweight loss, the efficiency loss as a result of a cigarette tax. A lump-sum tax that would have the same effect on the individual's welfare as the cigarette tax would raise an additional revenue of ABC.

mand schedule and above c_0, between the output with and without the tax.

The triangle ABC is sometimes called a **Harberger triangle,**[6] in honor of Chicago economist Arnold Harberger, who used such triangles not only to measure the inefficiencies associated with distortionary taxation but also to measure other inefficiencies, such as those associated with monopoly. Why does the Harberger triangle provide a measure of deadweight loss? The price tells us the value of the last unit consumed; that is, at q_0, the individual is willing to trade off $p_0 = c_0 + t$ units of "income" (with which he could have purchased other goods) for one more pack of cigarettes. Of course, when the individual has $q_0 + 1$ packs of cigarettes, he will value an additional pack of cigarettes less than when he has q_0 packs, and so the price he is willing to pay will fall.

Assume that initially consumption is 100 packs, and consumption increases by 10 packs when the tax is removed; the tax is 10 cents, and the cost of production is $1.00 per pack. (Tax revenue is 100 packs times 10 cents per pack, or $10.) The individual is willing to pay $1.10 for the first additional pack, $1.09 for the second, $1.08 for the third, and so on. If the tax

[6] See for instance, A. Harberger, "Taxation, Resource Allocation and Welfare," in *The Role of Direct and Indirect Taxes in the Federal Revenue System,* ed. J. Due (Princeton, N.J.: Princeton University Press, 1964), reprinted in A. Harberger, *Taxation and Welfare* (Chicago: University of Chicago Press, 1974).

CONSUMER SURPLUS

• Measured by the area under the (compensated) demand curve

• Used to measure the value of a government project or assess the magnitude of an inefficiency

were eliminated, and the price fell to c_0, the cost of production ($1.00 a pack), the total amount that the individual would be willing to pay would be 10 cents times 100 packs = $10 (the amount he saves on the first 100 packs he has purchased, which is equal to the tax revenue); plus 10 cents for the 101st pack (the difference between how much he values the 101st pack and what he must pay), 9 cents for the 102nd pack, etc. Remember, we are calculating how much *more* he would be willing to pay beyond the $1.00 that he will have to pay for each pack. The total he would be willing to pay is thus $10.50. Since the tax raised a revenue of $10, the deadweight loss is 50 cents. This is, of course, just the area under the compensated demand curve and above c_0, between q_0 and q_1.

QUANTIFYING DISTRIBUTIONAL EFFECTS

Assessing the distributional effects of a project or a tax is often far more complex than assessing the efficiency effects. There are many groups in a society, and each may be affected differently. Some poor individuals may be hurt, some helped; some middle-income individuals may be helped, others hurt. In some cases the rich may be helped the most, the poor helped moderately, and the middle class made only slightly worse off.

In practice, governments focus on a few summary measures of inequality. Since the poor are of particular concern, they receive special attention. The **poverty index** measures the fraction of the population whose income lies below a critical threshold; below that threshold, individuals are considered to be in poverty. In 1997, the poverty threshold for a family of four was $16,404.[7]

Another measure is the **poverty gap.** The poverty index only counts the number of individuals who are below the poverty threshold; it does not look at how far below that threshold they are. The poverty gap asks, how much income would we have to give to the poor to bring them all up to the poverty threshold?

Two other measures are briefly discussed in the appendix to this chapter.

---

[7] This is an estimate for 1997. U.S. Bureau of the Census, Current Population Survey, accessed at the U.S. Census Bureau web site (http://www.census.gov) on 9/4/98.

DRAWING A POVERTY LINE

The official poverty line determines how many people the government counts as poor. But what determines the poverty line itself?

In the late 1960s, an official at the Social Security Administration, Molly Orshansky, developed a method of measuring poverty from a survey of household expenditures. She found that a typical family spent one-third of its income on food. She then gathered information on minimum food budgets for families of various sizes, and multiplied that number by 3 to get an estimate of the poverty line for the different family sizes. With minor changes, Orshansky's poverty line was officially adopted in 1969 and it has been increased by the overall rate of inflation since then.

There are a number of questions one can ask about how poverty is measured: here are three.

First, the survey Orshansky relied on to find that households spent one-third of their income on food was taken in 1955. Since then, household expenditures have shifted. Households now spend a much lower percentage of income on food, perhaps one-fourth or one-fifth. If the minimum food budget were accordingly multiplied by 4 or 5, the poverty line would be much higher.

Second, the poverty line does not take in-kind benefits into account. In-kind benefits include any benefits that are not received in cash form, like Medicaid, food stamps, and subsidized school lunches. If those benefits are measured as additional income, the number of people below the poverty line falls by about 20 percent.

THREE APPROACHES TO SOCIAL CHOICES

We now have the basic tools for describing social choices in those difficult cases where the project does not constitute a Pareto improvement. There are three approaches, which we shall refer to as the *compensation principle*, *trading-off measures*, and the *weighted benefits approach*.

THE COMPENSATION PRINCIPLE

What happens if the total willingness to pay exceeds the total costs, but the costs borne by some individuals exceed their willingness to pay? Should the project be undertaken? The **compensation principle** says that if the aggregate willingness to pay exceeds the cost, the project should be undertaken. Most economists criticize this principle, for it ignores distributional concerns. Only if the compensation is actually paid to those adversely affected can we be sure that the project is desirable, for then it is a Pareto improvement.

Finally, some critics have proposed that poverty should be thought of as a relative rather than an absolute concept. They argue that those at the bottom of society, say, the bottom 5 or 10 or 20 percent, are poor relative to everyone else. Poverty is more appropriately viewed as an extreme case of inequality.

For many, this last criticism goes too far. They fear that a relative concept of poverty could reduce the moral urgency of fighting poverty. There is broad social support for efforts to assure that people have basic levels of food, housing, clothing, and medical care, even if defining those amounts is controversial.

In 1995, a National Academy of Sciences study proposed major revisions in how we measure poverty. While there was agreement about including noncash income, the difficult problems of how best to include health care expenditures were not fully resolved. Should a sick, poor person who receives $150,000 for a kidney transplant have that added to his income, in which case he now appears to be in an upper income bracket? The study proposed an adjustment in the poverty level that went beyond just taking into account inflation, but it did not propose increasing the poverty level in proportion to increases in average income, which would have made poverty a purely relative phenomenon. But even this compromise generated a strong dissent from one of the members of the Academy's panel.

SOURCES: Joyce E. Allen and Margaret C. Simms, "Is a New Yardstick Needed to Measure Poverty?" *Focus*, February 1990, pp. 6–8; *Measuring Poverty: A New Approach* (Washington, D.C.: National Academy of Sciences, 1996).

Because the compensation principle does not pay adequate attention to distributional concerns, economists have turned to two other approaches.

TRADE-OFFS ACROSS MEASURES
With a measure of efficiency (net benefits) and a measure of inequality, public decision-making, conceptually at least, should be easy: one simply evaluates whether the increase in efficiency is worth the increase in inequality, or vice versa.

The previous two sections have described how we measure total efficiency and inequality. These are just statistics, numbers that help to summarize the impacts of a project or program. Such summary statistics, while useful, often submerge some of the detailed information which is important in public decision-making. Ideally, we would look at the impacts on each individual, and then use the social welfare function to add up the effects. In practice, the government doesn't attempt to identify impacts on every individual, but it does at-

SOCIAL CHOICE IN PRACTICE

• Identify Pareto improvements.

• If some individuals are better off while others are worse off, identify groups of individuals who are better off and groups that are worse off (by income, region, age), and gains and losses of each major group.

> • Ascertain whether aggregate net benefits are positive (compensation principle).

> • Look at change in measure of efficiency and measure of inequality, and evaluate trade-offs.

> • Calculate weighted net benefits, weighting gains and losses to poor more heavily than those to rich, according to the social welfare function.

tempt to ascertain the effects on each major group. For instance, it may look at the impact on individuals in different income categories—say, families with incomes below $10,000, between $10,000 and $20,000, and so forth.

WEIGHTED NET BENEFITS This may be all the information required for policy makers to make a decision. If the aggregate net benefits (the sum of the willingnesses to pay minus costs) is positive, and if the poor are net beneficiaries and the rich are net losers, then the project increases both efficiency and equity and should be adopted. But often, matters are more complicated. For instance, the poor and the rich may be worse off, but middle-income individuals better off. How do we assess such a change? Again, we turn to our social welfare function to add up the effects. We assign weights to the net gains of different groups to summarize the impacts in a single number. The social welfare function tells us how to do that. Because of the concern for equity, effects on higher-income groups are weighted less heavily. How much less heavily may determine whether it is desirable to undertake a project. For instance, a project that helps the middle class but hurts the poor and the rich might not be undertaken if we weight the losses of the poor much more heavily than the gains to the middle class.[8]

[8] Given the importance of these weights in social decision-making, economists have looked for a rational basis for assigning weights. One way is to think about how rapidly marginal utility diminishes with increased income. Inferences about this can be made from observing individual behavior in risky situations: if marginal utility diminishes very rapidly, individuals will be very averse to undertaking large risks, and will be willing to pay large premiums to divest themselves of risk. On the basis of this evidence, most economists argue that a doubling of income will lower the marginal utility of income by a factor of between 2 and 4, so that a change in the income of a middle-class individual with an income of $30,000 should be weighted half to a quarter of the same change in income of a poor individual with an income of $15,000.

The use of weights can be thought of as based on three assumptions: first, that there is diminishing marginal utility; second, that different individuals have the same relation between utility and income; and third, that society is concerned with total utility—the sum of the utilities of all individuals (the utilitarian social welfare function). While each of these assumptions may be questioned, we can also think of these procedures as simply a convenient way to summarize data that decision makers often find helpful.

REVIEW AND PRACTICE

SUMMARY

1 Welfare economics—or normative economics—is concerned with criteria for evaluating alternative economic policies. In general, it takes into account both efficiency *and* equity.

2 The social welfare function provides a framework within which the distributional consequences of a policy may be analyzed. It specifies the increase in utility of one individual that is required to compensate for a decrease in utility of another.

3 In the utilitarian social welfare function, social welfare is equal to the sum of the utilities of the individuals in society. In the Rawlsian social welfare function, social welfare is equal to the utility of the worst-off individual in society.

4 The concept of consumer surplus—how much individuals are willing to pay for a project or program in addition to what they have to pay—is used to measure the aggregate benefits of a project or program. The concept of deadweight loss is used to measure the inefficiency of a tax; it asks how much extra revenue could have been generated by a lump-sum tax that would have left individuals just as well off as the tax that was imposed.

5 As a practical matter, in evaluating alternative proposals we do not detail the impact each proposal has on each individual in society, but rather we summarize its effects by describing its impact on some measure of inequality (or on some well-identified groups) and describing the efficiency gains or losses. Alternative proposals often present trade-offs between efficiency and distribution; to get more equality one has to give up some efficiency. Differences in views arise concerning the nature of the trade-offs (how much efficiency one needs to give up to get some increase in equality), and values (how much efficiency one should be willing to give up, at the margin, to get some increase in equality).

6 Three approaches for making social choices when there is not a Pareto improvement are:

   a the compensation principle

   b trade-offs across measures of efficiency and equality

   c the weighted benefits approach

7 The poverty index measures the fraction of the population whose income lies below some threshold.

Social indifference curves	Deadweight loss
Diminishing marginal utility	Excess burden
Social welfare function	Poverty index
Utilitarianism	Poverty gap
Rawlsianism	Compensation principle
Interpersonal utility comparisons	Weighted benefits approach
Rawlsian social welfare function	

1 Assume that Friday and Crusoe have identical utility functions described by the following table.

Utility Functions for Friday and Crusoe

NUMBER OF ORANGES	UTILITY	MARGINAL UTILITY
1	11	
2	21	
3	30	
4	38	
5	45	
6	48	
7	50	
8	51	

Draw the utility function. Fill in the marginal utility data in the table above, and draw the marginal utility function.

2 Assume that there are eight oranges to be divided between Friday and Crusoe. Take a utilitarian view—assume that social welfare is the sum of the utilities of the two individuals. Using the data from Problem 1, what is the social welfare corresponding to each possible allocation of oranges? What allocation maximizes social welfare? Show that it has the property that the marginal utility of an extra orange given to each individual is the same.

3 Now take a Rawlsian view and assume that the social welfare function is the level of utility of the individual with the lowest utility level. Using the data from Problem 1, and again assuming there are eight oranges, what is the social welfare associated with each allocation of oranges? What allocation maximizes social welfare?

4   Draw the utility possibilities schedule based on the data from Problem 1. Mark the points that maximize social welfare under the two alternative criteria from Problems 2 and 3.

5   Assume that Crusoe's and Friday's utility functions are described in Problem 1. But assume now that initially Crusoe has six oranges and Friday two. Assume that for every two oranges taken away from Crusoe, Friday gets only one, an orange being lost in the process. What does the utility possibilities schedule look like now? Which of the feasible allocations maximizes social welfare with a utilitarian social welfare function? With a Rawlsian social welfare function?

6   If marginal utility did not decrease at all for both Friday and Crusoe, what would the utility possibilities schedule look like?

7   Consider an accident where an individual loses his leg. Assume that it lowers his utility at each level of income but increases his marginal utility (at each level of income), though only slightly. Show diagrammatically the utility functions before and after the accident. Show that if you were a utilitarian, you would give more income to the individual after the accident, but that even after the transfer, the individual with the accident is worse off than before. Show the compensation that a Rawlsian would provide.

Is it possible for a utilitarian to give more to the individual who had experienced the accident than a Rawlsian?

Under what circumstances would a utilitarian give nothing to an individual who had experienced an accident?

8   For each of the following policy changes, explain why the change is or is not likely to be a Pareto improvement:

   a Building a park, financed by an increase in the local property tax rate.

   b Building a park, financed by the donation of a rich philanthropist; the city acquires the land by exercising the right of eminent domain.[9]

   c Increasing medical facilities for lung cancer, financed out of general revenues.

   d Increasing medical care facilities for lung cancer, financed out of an increase in the cigarette tax.

   e Replacing the system of agricultural price supports with a system of income supplements for poor farmers.

   f Protecting the automobile industry from cheap foreign imports by imposing quotas on the importation of foreign cars.

_____

[9] The right of eminent domain gives public authorities the right to take property, with compensation, for public uses.

g Increasing social security benefits, financed by an increase in the payroll tax.

h Replacing the primary reliance at the local level on the property tax with state revenues obtained from an income tax.

i Eliminating rent control laws.

In each case, state who the losers (if any) are likely to be. Which of these changes might be approved under the compensation principle? Which might be approved under a Rawlsian social welfare function?

9 Assume you are shipwrecked. There are ten of you in a lifeboat; you know that it will take ten days to reach shore and that there are only rations for ten man-days. (The ration is the minimum amount needed for survival.) How would a utilitarian allocate the rations? How would a Rawlsian? Some people think that even Rawlsian criteria are not sufficiently egalitarian. What might an extreme egalitarian individual advocate? What does Pareto efficiency require? In each case, state what assumptions you need to make to make the decision.

ALTERNATIVE MEASURES OF INEQUALITY

In the text, we introduced the two most commonly used measures of inequality. These measures are criticized, however, for focusing exclusively on the impact on the very poor. In this appendix, we discuss two more-inclusive measures.

THE LORENZ CURVE

Economists often represent the degree of inequality in an economy by a diagram called the **Lorenz curve,** shown in Figure 5.12. The Lorenz curve shows the cumulative fraction of the country's total income earned by the poorest 5 percent, the poorest 10 percent, the poorest 15 percent, and so on. If there were complete equality, then 20 percent of the income would accrue to the lowest 20 percent of the population, 40 percent to the lowest 40 percent. The Lorenz curve would be a straight line, as depicted in panel A. On the other hand, if incomes were very concentrated, then the lowest 80 percent might receive almost nothing, and the top 5 percent might receive 80 percent of total income; in this case, the Lorenz curve would be bowed, as illustrated in panel B. When there is a great deal of inequality, the shaded area between the 45-degree line in panel B and the Lorenz curve is large. When there is complete equality, as in panel A, this area is zero. Twice the area between the 45-degree line and

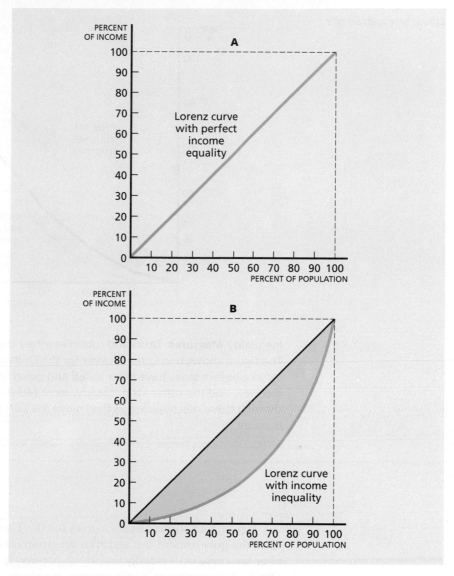

FIGURE 5.12 **The Lorenz Curve** Panel A shows a Lorenz curve for an economy in which income is evenly distributed. The bottom 20 percent of the economy has 20 percent of income, the bottom 40 percent has 40 percent of income, and so on. Panel B depicts a Lorenz curve for an economy where income is unequally distributed. The curvature of the line indicates that now the bottom 20 percent has less than 20 percent of income, the bottom 40 percent has less than 40 percent of income, and so on.

the Lorenz curve is a commonly employed measure of inequality, called the **Gini coefficient.**

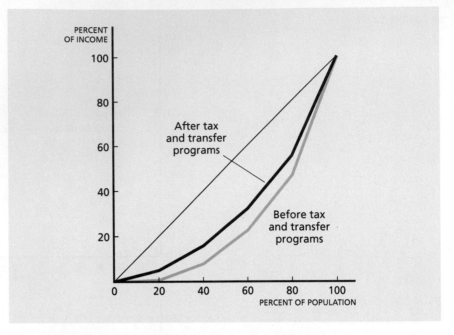

FIGURE 5.13 **Inequality Measures** Taxes and subsidies affect the distribution of income. The figure shows two Lorenz curves for the United States in 1995, one for income before taxes have been levied and government transfers have been received, and the other after. Clearly, some redistribution does take place through these mechanisms, as they move the Lorenz curve toward greater equality.

SOURCE: U.S. Census Bureau, *Current Population Survey*, March 1996, Table E.

Figure 5.13 shows Lorenz curves for the United States, both before and after the government tax and transfer programs have had their effect. The after-tax curve is decidedly inside the pre-tax, indicating that the combined effect of government redistribution programs is to make incomes more equal than the market would have made them. Thus, while the efficiency costs are less clear-cut, the redistributive gains are undeniable.

THE DALTON-ATKINSON MEASURE

There is another measure, first introduced by Sir Hugh Dalton, a professor of public finance at the London School of Economics who went on to become the Chancellor of the Exchequer for the United Kingdom. This measure was based on the premise that societies prefer more egalitarian distributions. Figure 5.14 shows two distributions of income. In distribution *B*, more of the income is concentrated at the center, and for societies that value equality, this is the preferred distribution. We can ask, if society could move from its current distribution to a situation where income was completely equally distributed, what fraction of its total income would it be willing to give up? This fraction is called the Dalton-Atkinson measure of inequality. Of course, different individuals might have different views on the amounts that society should be *willing* to give up (this says nothing about how much they would *have* to give up to accomplish the redistribution). The amount society would be willing to give up depends on its social welfare function. With a Rawlsian social welfare function, the amount would be much larger than with a utilitarian social welfare function. An-

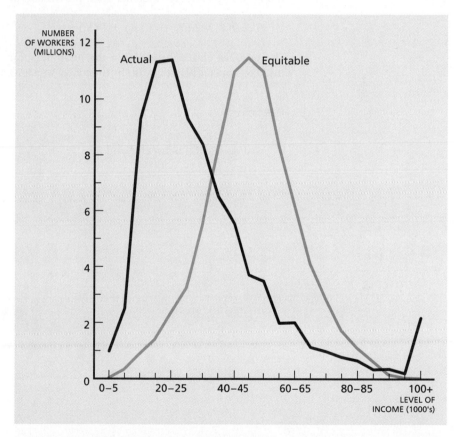

FIGURE 5.14   **Toward a More Egalitarian Income Distribution** The dark line *A* represents the actual income distribution of full-time, permanent U.S. workers in 1995. The shaded line *B* represents what the income distribution might look like under a more egalitarian setting.

SOURCE: U.S. Bureau of Labor Statistics and Bureau of the Census, *Annual Demographic Survey, March 1997 Supplement.*

123

thony Atkinson, of Nuffield College, Oxford, argued that the amount was significant, often between a quarter and a third of total income in more developed economies. Changes in the Dalton-Atkinson measure can be used to assess the impact on inequality of any proposed government program.[10]

[10] Formally, the Dalton-Atkinson measure can be defined as follows. Assume a utilitarian social welfare function

$$W = U(Y_1) + U(Y_2) + U(Y_3) + \ldots$$

and let Y be the average income. Then the Dalton-Atkinson measure D is given by

$$U((1 - D)Y) = U(Y_1) + U(Y_2) + U(Y_3) + \ldots$$

The measure clearly depends on the utility function. Atkinson, in his analysis, focused on constant-elasticity utility functions, which have the form

$$U = \frac{Y^{1-\alpha}}{1 - \alpha}$$

He used values of α between 1 and 2.

PART THREE

PUBLIC EXPENDITURE THEORY

This part is concerned with the basic theory of public expenditures. Chapter 6 explains what public goods are and describes what it means to have an under- or oversupply of public goods. How the level of expenditures on public goods is determined, is the subject of Chapter 7, with particular focus on the consequences of majority voting.

Governments both provide goods and produce them. Some of the goods they provide are privately produced; some of the goods they produce are sold, just like private goods. Chapter 8 is concerned with the government as a producer. It asks, for instance, whether there are reasons one might expect the government to be less efficient than private firms.

In recent years, governments have taken an increasingly active role in attempting to control the adverse effects of a number of important externalities, including air and water pollution. Chapter 9 discusses the merits of alternative public remedies to the problems posed by externalities.

6 Public Goods and Publicly Provided Private Goods

FOCUS QUESTIONS

1 What distinguishes public goods, those goods which are typically provided by governments, from privately provided goods? What do economists mean by *pure public goods*?

2 Why will private markets undersupply pure public goods? What is the free rider problem?

3 Why do governments provide goods which are not pure public goods?

4 What determines an efficient supply of pure public goods? How is the efficient supply affected by concerns about income distribution? How is it affected by the fact that taxes required to pay for the public good typically introduce distortions in the economy?

5 In what sense is efficient government a public good?

The government supplies a wide variety of goods, from national defense to education to police and fire protection. Some of these goods, like education, are also provided privately; others, like national defense, are the exclusive province of government. What are the economic properties of such goods? How do they differ from goods such as ice cream, automobiles, and the myriad of other goods that are provided principally through private markets?

Earlier chapters noted the central role played by prices in market economies. Because of the price system, markets result in an efficient allocation of resources. Prices ration private goods. Those consumers who are willing and able to pay the requisite price obtain the good. This chapter asks: What is distinctive about the goods typically provided by government? What prevents them in many cases from being provided privately? And if they are provided privately, why is the private supply likely to be inadequate?

PUBLIC GOODS

To distinguish between private and public goods, economists ask two basic questions. First, does the good have the property of rival consumption? **Rival consumption** means that if a good is used by one person, it cannot be used by another. For instance, if Lynn drinks a bottle of apple juice, Fran cannot drink that same bottle of apple juice. By contrast, **non-rival consumption** refers to cases for which one person's consumption does not detract from or prevent another person's consumption.

The classic example of non-rival consumption is national defense. If the government creates a military establishment that protects the country from attack, all citizens are protected. National defense costs are essentially unaffected when an additional baby is born or an additional individual immigrates to the United States. This stands in sharp contrast to private goods. It costs additional resources to provide another bottle of apple juice so that both Lynn and Fran can have one. This is the only way for Lynn and Fran each to enjoy a bottle of apple juice. For a non-rival good, such as a lighthouse, though it would indeed cost more to build more lighthouses, there is essentially no additional cost for an additional ship to make use of an existing lighthouse.

The second question we ask to distinguish between private and public goods relates to the property of **exclusion**. Is it possible to exclude any individual from the benefits of the public good (without incurring great costs)? A ship going past a lighthouse, for instance, cannot be excluded from the benefits the lighthouse provides. Likewise, if the country is defended against attack by foreigners, then all citizens are protected; it is difficult to exclude anyone from the benefits. Clearly, if exclusion is impossible, then use of the price system is impossible, because consumers have no incentive to pay. By contrast, private goods always have the property of excludability: individuals can be excluded from enjoying the good unless they pay for it.

Generally speaking, private goods have the properties of rival consumption and excludability; public goods are characterized by non-rival consumption and non-excludability. Goods for which there is *no* rivalry in consumption and for which exclusion is *impossible* are **pure public goods.** To develop a more complete picture of public goods (and pure public goods), we now examine the properties of non-rivalry and non-exclusion in greater detail. We will see how these properties may lead to market failures, creating a rationale for the public provision of public goods.

In order to isolate the role of excludability and rivalrousness in consumption, we consider instances in which a good has one property but not the other. For some goods, consumption is non-rival but exclusion is possible. For instance, the marginal cost of an additional individual turning on his television and watching a show is zero; the number of times I watch *Seinfeld* does not detract from the number of times you can watch it. But exclusion is possible (though costly), through signal scramblers, as illustrated by pay-TV.

Even if exclusion were possible, when a good is non-rival, there is no impetus for exclusion from the standpoint of economic efficiency. Charging a price for a non-rival good prevents some people from enjoying the good, even though their consumption of the good would have no marginal cost. Thus, charging for a non-rival good is inefficient because it results in underconsumption. The marginal benefit is positive; the marginal cost (of the extra person watching the show) is zero. The underconsumption is a form of inefficiency.

But if there is no charge for a non-rival good, there will be no incentive for supplying the good. In this case, inefficiency takes the form of undersupply.

Thus, there are two basic forms of market failure associated with public goods: **underconsumption** and **undersupply.** In the case of non-rival goods, exclusion is undesirable because it results in underconsumption. But without exclusion, there is the problem of undersupply.

If exclusion is possible, even if consumption is non-rival, governments often charge fees, called **user fees,** to those who benefit from a publicly provided good or service. Toll roads are financed by user fees. The airline ticket tax can be thought of as a user fee; revenues from the ticket tax (currently 10 percent of the price of the ticket) go to finance airports and the air traffic control system. User fees are often thought of as an equitable way of raising revenues, since those who use the public facility the most (and therefore presumably benefit from it the most) pay the most. However, when consumption is non-rival, user fees introduce an inefficiency. We can use the sort of analysis introduced in Chapter 5 to measure the inefficiency.

This is illustrated in Figure 6.1 for the case of a bridge. We have drawn the demand curve for the bridge, describing the number of trips taken as a function of the toll charged. Lowering the toll results in increased demand for the bridge. The capacity of the bridge is Q_c; for any demand below Q_c, there is no congestion and no marginal cost associated with use of the bridge. So long as the bridge is operating below capacity, consumption is non-rival; additional consumption by one individual does not detract from what others can enjoy. Since the marginal cost of usage is zero, efficiency requires that the price for usage be zero. But clearly, the revenue raised by the bridge will then be zero.

This is where the difference between *public provision* and private is clearest: with a single bridge, the monopoly owner would choose a toll to maximize his revenue, and would build the bridge only if those revenues equaled or exceeded the cost of the bridge. The government would face a more

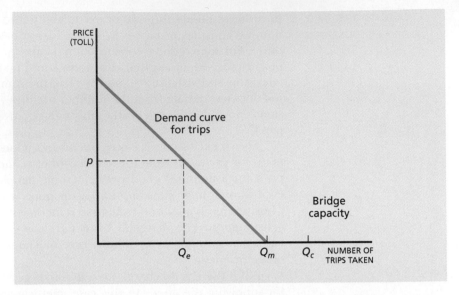

FIGURE 6.1 **Bridges: How a User Fee Can Result in Underconsumption** If the capacity is large enough, the bridge is a non-rival good. While it is possible to exclude people from using the bridge by charging a toll, p, this results in an underconsumption of the good, Q_e, below the non-toll level of consumption, Q_m.

complicated set of calculations. It might charge the toll required to just cover the costs of construction, to break even. In doing so, it would recognize that with any toll, the usage of the bridge would be reduced, and some trips whose benefits exceed the social cost (here zero) would not be undertaken. Thus, it might charge a toll less than required to break even, raising the revenue required to finance the bridge in some other way. It might not even charge any toll. In making these decisions, it would weigh equity considerations—the principle that those who benefit from the bridge should bear its costs—with efficiency considerations. The distortions arising from the underutilization of the bridge would need to be compared with the distortions associated with alternative ways of raising revenues (for example, taxes) to finance the bridge. Finally, the government might build the bridge even if the maximum revenue it could obtain from the tolls was less than the cost of the bridge, since it recognizes that there is some consumer surplus from the bridge: the amount that at least some individuals might be willing to pay for the bridge may be considerably greater than even the amount raised by the revenue-maximizing toll.

THE FREE RIDER PROBLEM

Many of the most important publicly provided goods—such as public health programs and national defense—have the property of non-excludability, making rationing by the price system unfeasible. For instance, the international vaccine program against smallpox virtually wiped out the disease, to the benefit of all, whether they contributed to supporting the program or not. While national defense has the property of non-excludability and zero marginal cost, there are a few goods which have the property of at least high costs of exclusion, even though the marginal cost of using the good is positive. Congested urban streets are an example: under current technology, it is expensive to charge for the use of the street (someone could collect tolls at each corner, but the cost would be extremely high); but the throughput of the street may be limited, so if one more person uses it, another is displaced—indeed, in some cases, as more people attempt to use the street, the total throughput of the street may even be decreased, as gridlock sets in.

The infeasibility of rationing by the price system implies that the competitive market will not generate a Pareto efficient amount of the public good. Assume that everyone valued national defense, but the government did not provide for it. Could a private firm enter to fill this gap? To do so, it would have to charge for the services it provided. But since every individual would believe that he would benefit from the services provided regardless of whether he contributed to the service, he would have no incentive to pay for the services *voluntarily*. That is why individuals must be forced to support these goods through taxation. The reluctance of individuals to contribute voluntarily to the support of public goods is referred to as the **free rider problem.**

An example will help to illustrate the nature of this problem. In many communities, fire departments are supported voluntarily. Some individuals refuse to contribute to the fire department, yet, in an area where buildings are close together, the fire department will usually put out a fire in a non-contributor's building because of the threat it poses to adjacent contributors' structures. Knowing that they will be protected even if they do not pay induces some people to be free riders.

Clearly, if it is not possible to use price to ration a particular good, the good is not likely to be provided privately. If it is to be provided at all, government will have to take responsibility.

There are a few cases where non-excludable public goods are provided privately. Usually this is because there is a single, large consumer whose direct benefits are so large that it pays him to provide it for himself. He knows that there are free riders benefiting from his actions, but in deciding how much to supply, he looks only at his own direct benefit, not at the benefits that accrue to others. For instance, a large shipowner might find it worthwhile to install a lighthouse and light buoys, even if others cannot be excluded from enjoying the benefits. But in deciding how many lighthouses and buoys to construct, he looks only at the benefits which accrue to his own ships. The total benefit of an additional buoy—including the benefits both to his own ships and to others, for instance—might be considerable, even though the direct benefit to his own ships might not warrant the additional cost. In that case he would not put the additional buoy into place. Thus, even if there is *some* private provision of public goods, there will be an undersupply.

ECONOMISTS AND THE FREE RIDER PROBLEM

The free rider problem is just a reflection of an important incentive problem that arises in the case of public goods: If the good is going to be provided anyway, why should I pay? What I would contribute would be negligible, and hardly alter the aggregate supply. To be sure, if everyone reasoned the same way, the good would not be supplied. That is one of the arguments for government's providing these goods, because government has the power to compel people to contribute (through taxes).

But there are many instances of public goods being supported voluntarily: volunteer fire departments, local charities, hospitals, public TV, and many others. How do we explain these? Perhaps

PURE AND IMPURE PUBLIC GOODS

A pure public good is a public good where the marginal costs of providing it to an additional person are strictly zero and where it is impossible to exclude people from receiving the good. National defense is one of the few examples of a pure public good. Many public goods that government provides are not *pure* public goods in this sense. The cost of an additional person using an uncrowded interstate highway is very, very small, but not zero, and it is possible, though relatively expensive, to exclude people from (or charge people for) using the highway.

Figure 6.2 compares examples of goods that are often publicly provided with the strict definition of a *pure* public good. It shows the ease of exclusion along the horizontal axis and the (marginal) cost of an additional individual's using the good along the vertical axis. The lower left-hand corner represents a pure public good. Of the major public expenditures, only national defense comes close to being a pure public good. The upper right-hand cor-

PUBLIC GOODS

Pure public goods have the properties of perfectly non-rival consumption and non-excludability.

With non-rival consumption, it is not desirable to exclude anyone from the benefits. With private provision, there will be underconsumption and/or undersupply.

With non-excludability, it is not feasible to exclude anyone from the benefits of the good. There will be a free rider problem. Such goods typically cannot be provided by the market, and when they are privately provided, they will be undersupplied.

economists have overemphasized the "selfish" nature of man? Several recent studies in experimental economics have suggested that this might be the case. These experimental situations are designed to make individuals face situations where they could free ride if they wanted to; alternatively, they could cooperate in providing for a public good. Systematically, more cooperative behavior and less free riding is observed than economists' analysis of selfish incentives would suggest. Interestingly, when economists participate in these experiments, their behavior systematically comes much closer in accord with the predictions of their theory.

ner represents a good (ordinary health services) where the cost of exclusion is low and the marginal cost of an additional individual using the good is high. It is easy to charge each patient for health services, and it costs a doctor twice as much to see two patients as to see one—there are significant marginal costs of providing health services to additional individuals.

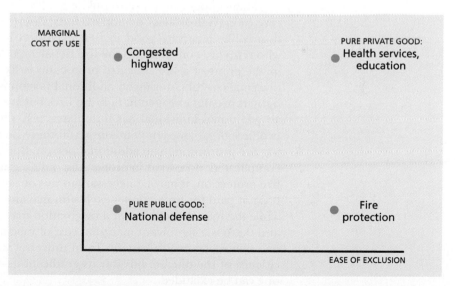

FIGURE 6.2 **Publicly Provided Goods** Pure public goods are characterized by non-rival consumption (the marginal cost of an additional individual's enjoying the good is zero) and non-excludability (the cost of excluding an individual from enjoying the good is prohibitively high). Goods provided by the public sector differ in the extent to which they have these two properties.

PROPERTY RIGHTS, EXCLUDABILITY, AND EXTERNALITIES

Some problems of excludability arise not from the *feasibility* of exclusion, but from imperfections in the legal structure which make exclusion difficult. Some economists, such as Nobel Prize–winning economist Ronald Coase, have argued that many public-good and externality problems would be resolved if property rights, which allow exclusion, were established.

Consider a crowded room. The air in the room is a public good: all persons in the room breathe essentially the same air. When any individual smokes, he creates an externality on others. In the absence of property rights, he would fail to take that into account in his decision to smoke. But if property rights were assigned, the problem would (so the argument goes) be resolved. Assume the "rights" to the air were given to a particular individual. (Coase argues that, apart from distribution, to whom it is given makes no difference.) He would then conduct an auction: he would ask the smokers how much they would be willing to pay to allow smoking, and he would ask the nonsmokers how much they would be willing to pay to prohibit

Many goods are not pure public goods but have one or the other property (non-rivalrousness or non-excludability) to some degree. Fire protection is like a private good in that exclusion is relatively easy—individuals who refuse to contribute to the fire department could simply not be helped in the event of a fire. But fire protection is like a public good in that the marginal cost of covering an additional person is low. Most of the time, firefighters are not engaged in fighting fires but are waiting for calls. Protecting an additional individual has little extra cost. Only in that rare event when two fires break out simultaneously will there be a significant cost to extending fire protection to an additional person. But even here, matters are more complicated: if we want to protect the building next door which has paid for fire protection, it may be necessary to put out the fire in the building which has not paid for protection—exclusion may not really be feasible. Similarly, while the main beneficiary of a vaccination may be the individual protected, and there is a significant marginal cost of vaccinating an additional individual, the public health benefits from universal vaccination—the reduced incidence of the disease, possibly its eradication—are benefits from which no one can be excluded.

Sometimes the marginal cost of using a good to which access is easy (a good that possesses the property of non-excludability) will be high. When an uncongested highway turns congested, the costs of using it rise dramatically, not only in terms of wear and tear on the road but in terms of the time lost by drivers using the road. It is costly to exclude by charging for road use—as a practical matter, this can only be done on toll roads, and, ironi-

smoking. He would then offer the air for sale to those for whom the value was highest. This would be efficient.*

But this "solution" ignores the free rider problem: individual smokers have an incentive not to reveal the full value of the right to smoke (if they might actually have to pay that amount); and similarly individual nonsmokers have an incentive not to reveal the full value of clean air.

While there are some important cases where assigning property rights would reduce or eliminate externalities or public good problems, in some of the most important cases, assigning property rights is either impracticable or would not resolve the underlying problems.

*The resource allocation would be Pareto efficient, *given the assignment of the property right of the air to a single individual.* But, of course, if the smokers bid more than the nonsmokers, the smoker who winds up having to pay for the right to smoke is worse off relative to the initial situation where he could smoke without paying anything. Though in this example, the smokers could have compensated the nonsmokers, such compensation may well not be made.

cally, the tollbooths often contribute to the congestion. New technologies, which automatically bill regular users of the road, have radically reduced these costs.

COSTS OF EXCLUSION For many goods, the issue is not so much the feasibility of rationing, but the cost. Thus, TV and radio provided over the airwaves has one of the two properties of a public good: consumption is non-rival. But it may be feasible to exclude some consumers, as in the use of TV scramblers for pay-TV, even though it is costly to do so. In the case of pay-TV, though there is a cost to exclusion, there is no benefit to society from doing so. In other cases, such as a slightly crowded highway, there is a cost to exclusion (the cost of collecting tolls), and some benefit (less congestion).

There are, of course, costs associated with exclusion for private goods as well as for public goods. Economists call these **transactions costs.** For example, the salaries of checkout clerks at grocery stores and collectors of tolls along toll highways and at toll bridges are transactions costs, part of the administrative costs associated with operating a price mechanism. But while the costs of exclusion are relatively small for most private goods, they may be large (prohibitive) for some publicly provided goods.

EXTERNALITIES AS IMPURE PUBLIC GOODS Pure public goods have the property that if one individual purchases more of it, all individuals' consumption of that good increases by the same amount. (Individuals may, of course, differ

135

in how they value the increased consumption.) Pure private goods have the property that if one individual purchases more of it, others are (at least directly) unaffected. Goods for which there are externalities in consumption have the property that others are affected, but not necessarily in the same amount. Externalities can thus be viewed as a form of impure public goods (or perhaps better stated, public goods can be viewed as an extreme form of externalities).[1]

PUBLICLY PROVIDED PRIVATE GOODS

Publicly provided goods for which there is a large marginal cost associated with supplying additional individuals are referred to as **publicly provided private goods.** Though the costs of running a market provide one of the rationales for the public supply of some of these goods, it is not the only or even the most important rationale. Education is a publicly provided private good in the sense defined above—if the number of students enrolled doubles, costs will roughly double (assuming that quality, as reflected in class size, expenditures on teachers and textbooks, and so on, are kept roughly the same). One of the usual explanations given for public provision of education is concerned with distributive considerations; many feel that the opportunities of the young should not depend on the wealth of their parents.

Sometimes when the government provides a private good publicly (like water), it simply allows individuals to consume as much as they want without charge. Remember, for these goods, there is a marginal cost associated with each unit consumed. It costs money to purify water and to deliver it from the source to the individual's home. If a private good is freely provided, there is likely to be overconsumption of the good. Since the individual does not have to pay for the good, he will demand it until the point where the marginal benefit he receives from the good is zero, in spite of the fact that there is a positive marginal cost associated with providing it. In some cases, such as water, satiation may be quickly reached, so that the distortion from overconsumption may not be too large (Figure 6.3A). In other cases, such as the demand for certain types of medical services, the distortion may be very large (Figure 6.3B). The welfare loss can be measured by the difference between what the individual is willing to pay for the increase in output from Q_e (where price equals marginal cost) to Q_m (where price equals zero) and the costs of increasing production from Q_e to Q_m. This is the area of the shaded triangles in Figure 6.3.

---

[1] This is sometimes expressed by saying that for private goods, J's individual utility depends only on his own purchases, X^J. For a pure public good, J's utility depends on the *sum* of the purchases of all individuals: $X^1 + X^2 + \ldots + X^J + \ldots \ldots$ When there is an externality, J's utility may depend more heavily on his own purchases, but it may also depend on others' more weakly; for instance, it might depend on $aX^1 + aX^2 + \ldots + X^J + \ldots \ldots aX^n$, where a is a small number.

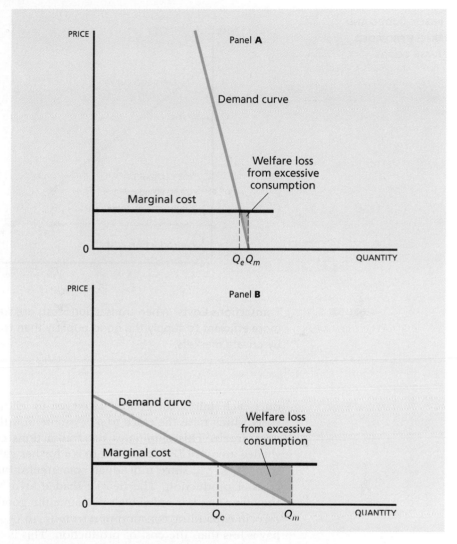

FIGURE 6.3 **Distortions Associated with Supplying Goods Freely** (A) For some goods, such as water, supplying the good freely rather than at marginal costs results in relatively little additional consumption. (B) For other goods, such as certain medical services, supplying the good freely rather than at marginal costs results in extensive overconsumption.

RATIONING DEVICES FOR PUBLICLY PROVIDED PRIVATE GOODS

When there is a marginal cost associated with each individual using a good, if the costs of running the price system are very high, it may be more efficient simply to provide the good publicly and to finance the good through general taxation, even though providing the good publicly causes a distortion. We illustrate this in Figure 6.4, where we have depicted a good with constant marginal costs of production, c. (It costs the firm c dollars to pro-

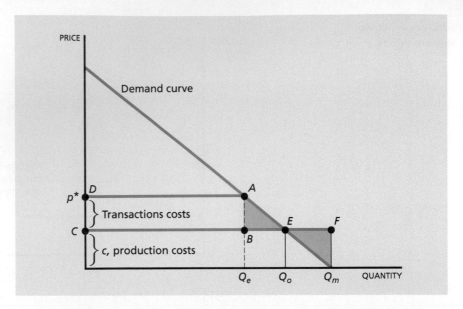

FIGURE 6.4 **Transactions Costs** When transactions costs are sufficiently high, it may be more efficient to supply the good publicly than to have the good supplied by private markets.

duce each unit of the good.)[2] However, to sell the good entails transactions costs, which raise the price to p^*. Assume now the government supplies the good freely. This eliminates the transactions costs, and the entire lightly shaded area $ABCD$ is saved. There is a further gain as consumption increases from Q_e to Q_o, since individuals' marginal valuations exceed the marginal costs of production. The heavily shaded area ABE measures the gain. On the other hand, if individuals consume the good until the marginal value is zero, in expanding consumption from Q_o to Q_m, the marginal willingness to pay is less than the cost of production. This is obviously inefficient. To decide whether the good should be provided publicly, we must compare the savings in transactions costs plus the gain from increasing consumption from Q_e to Q_o with (1) the loss from the excessive consumption of the good (the shaded area EFQ_m in Figure 6.4), plus (2) the loss from the distortions created by any taxes required to finance the provision of the good publicly.

The high costs of private markets' providing insurance has been used as one of the arguments for the public provision of insurance. For many kinds of insurance, the administrative costs (including the selling costs) associated with providing the insurance privately are more than 20 percent of the benefits paid out, in contrast with the administrative costs associated with public insurance, which (ignoring the distortions associated with the taxes re-

[2] We assume, moreover, that the demand curve does not shift significantly as we raise taxes.

quired to finance the administrative costs of the social insurance programs) are usually less than 10 percent of the value of the benefits.

Given the inefficiencies arising from overconsumption when no charges are imposed for publicly provided private goods, governments often try to find some way of limiting consumption. Any method restricting consumption of a good is called a **rationing system.** Prices provide one rationing system. We have already discussed how user fees may be employed to limit demand. A second commonly employed way of rationing publicly provided goods is **uniform provision:** supplying the same quantity of the good to everyone. Thus, we typically provide a uniform level of free education to all individuals, even though some individuals would like to have more and some less. (Those who would like to purchase more may be able to purchase supplemental educational services on the private market, such as tutoring.) This, then, is the major disadvantage of the public provision of goods; it does not allow for adaptation to differences in individuals' needs and desires as does the private market.

This is illustrated in Figure 6.5, where the demand curves for two different individuals are drawn. If the good was privately provided, Individual 1, the high demander, would consume Q_1, while Individual 2, the low demander, would consume the much smaller quantity Q_2. The government chooses to supply each individual with a quantity that is somewhere in between, Q^*. At this level of consumption, the high demander is consuming less than he would like; his marginal willingness to pay exceeds the marginal cost of production. On the other hand, the low demander is consuming more than the efficient level; his marginal willingness to pay is less than the marginal cost. (But since he does not have to pay anything for it, and still values the good positively, he, of course, consumes up to Q^*.)

For certain types of insurance (say, social security for retirement), the government provides a basic, uniform level. Again, those who wish to purchase more can do so, but those who wish to purchase less cannot. The dis-

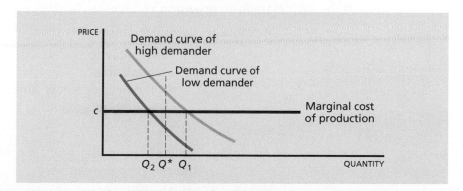

FIGURE 6.5 **Distortions Associated with Uniform Provision** When the publicly provided private good is supplied in equal amounts to all individuals, some get more than the efficient level and some get less.

tortion here may not, however, be very great; if the uniform level provided is sufficiently low, then relatively few individuals will be induced to consume more than they would otherwise, and the savings in administrative costs that we referred to earlier may more than offset the slight distortion associated with the uniform provision of the basic level of insurance. On the other hand, the system of combining public and private provision may increase total transactions (administrative) costs over what they would be if only the public sector or private sector took responsibility.

A third method of rationing that is commonly employed by the government is **queuing:** rather than charging individuals money for access to the publicly provided goods or services, the government requires that they pay a cost in waiting time. This allows some adaptability of the level of supply to the needs of the individual. Those whose demand for medical services is stronger are more willing to wait in the doctor's office. It is claimed that money is an undesirable basis upon which to ration medical services: Why should the wealthy have a greater right to good health than the poor? Queues, it is argued, may be an effective device for discriminating between the truly needy (who are willing to wait in line) and those who are less needy of medical care. But queues are a far from perfect way of determining who is deserving of medical care, since those who are unemployed or re-

---

THREE METHODS OF RATIONING PUBLICLY PROVIDED GOODS

1 User charges

Advantage: Those who benefit bear the costs.

Disadvantages: Results in underconsumption.
   Administering pricing system adds transactions costs.

2 Uniform provision

Advantage: Saves on transactions costs.

Disadvantages: Leads some to underconsume, others to overconsume.
   High demanders may supplement public consumption, increasing total transactions costs.

3 Queuing

Advantage: Goods (like health care) allocated not necessarily on basis of who is wealthiest.

Disadvantages: Alternative basis of allocation (who has time to spare) may be undesirable.
   Time is wasted.

---

tired, but are not so needy of medical care, may be more willing to wait than either the busy corporate executive or the low-paid worker holding down two jobs. In effect, willingness to pay has been replaced as a criterion for allocating medical services by willingness to wait in the doctor's office. There is, in addition, a real social cost to using queuing as a rationing device—the waste of time spent queuing; this is a cost that could be avoided if prices were used as a rationing device.

EFFICIENCY CONDITIONS FOR PUBLIC GOODS

A central concern is how large the supply of public goods should be. What does it mean to say that the government is supplying too little or too much of a public good? Chapter 3 provided a criterion that enables us to answer this question: a resource allocation is Pareto efficient if no one can be made better off without someone else's becoming worse off. There we established that Pareto efficiency in private markets requires, among other criteria, that the individual's marginal rate of substitution is equal to the marginal rate of transformation.

In this section of the chapter, we characterize what is required for Pareto efficiency in the supply of pure public goods, and in particular, goods for which the marginal cost of an additional individual enjoying them is zero. *Pure public goods are efficiently supplied when the sum of the marginal rates of substitution (over all individuals) is equal to the marginal rate of transformation.* The *marginal rate of substitution* of private goods for public goods tells how much of the private good each individual is willing to give up to get one more unit of the public good. The sum of the marginal rates of substitution thus tells us how much of the private good all the members of society, together, are willing to give up to get one more unit of the public good (which will be jointly consumed by all). The *marginal rate of transformation* tells us how much of the private good must be given up to get one more unit of the public good. Efficiency requires, then, that the total amount individuals are willing to give up—the sum of the marginal rates of substitution—must equal the amount that they have to give up—the marginal rate of transformation.

Let's apply this efficiency condition to national defense. Assume that when we increase production of guns (national defense) by one, we must reduce production of butter (basic consumer products) by one pound (the marginal rate of transformation is unity). Guns used for national defense are a public good. We consider a simple economy with two individuals: Crusoe and Friday. Crusoe is willing to give up one-third of a pound of butter for an extra gun. But his one-third pound alone does not buy the gun. Friday is willing to give up two-thirds of a pound of butter for an extra gun. The total amount of butter that this small society would be willing to give up, were the government to buy one more gun, is $1/3 + 2/3 = 1$.

The total amount they would *have to* give up to get one more gun is also one. Thus, the sum of the marginal rates of substitution equals the marginal rate of transformation; their government has provided an efficient level of national defense. If the sum of the marginal rates of substitution exceeded unity, then, collectively, individuals would be willing to give up more than they had to; we could ask each of them to give up an amount slightly less than the amount that would make them indifferent, and it would still be possible to increase the production of guns by one unit. Thus they could all be made better off by increasing the production of the public good (guns) by one.

**DEMAND CURVES FOR
PUBLIC GOODS**

Individuals do not buy public goods. We can, however, ask how much they would demand if they had to pay a given amount for each extra unit of the public good. This is not a completely hypothetical question, for as expenditures on public goods increase, so do individuals' taxes. We call the extra payment that an individual has to make for each extra unit of the public good his **tax price.** In the following discussion, we shall assume the government has the discretion to charge different individuals different tax prices.

Assume that the individual's tax price is p, that is, for each unit of the public good, he must pay p. Then, the total amount the individual can spend, his *budget constraint*, is:

$$C + pG = Y,$$

where C is his consumption of private goods, G is the total amount of public goods provided, and Y is his income. The budget constraint shows the combinations of goods (here, public and private goods) that the individual can purchase, given his income and his tax price. The budget constraint is represented in Figure 6.6A by the line BB. Along the budget constraint, if government expenditures are lower, consumption of private goods is obviously higher. The individual wishes to obtain the highest level of utility he can, consistent with his budget constraint. Figure 6.6A also shows the individual's indifference curves between public and private goods. The individual is willing to give up some private goods if he gets more public goods. The quantity of private goods he is willing to give up to get one more unit of public goods is his marginal rate of substitution. As he gets more public goods (and has fewer private goods), the amount of private goods he is willing to give up to get an extra unit of public goods becomes smaller—that is, he has a diminishing marginal rate of substitution. Graphically, the marginal rate of substitution is the slope of the indifference curve. Thus as the individual consumes more public goods and fewer private goods, the indifference curve becomes flatter.

The individual's highest level of utility is attained at the point of tangency between the indifference curve and the budget constraint, point E in panel A. At this point, the slope of the budget constraint and the slope of the indifference curve are identical. The slope of the budget constraint tells us how much in private goods the individual must give up to get one more unit of public goods; it is equal to the individual's tax price. The slope of

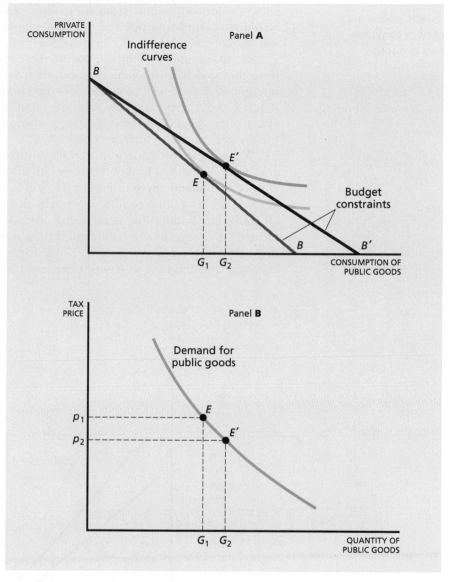

FIGURE 6.6
Individual Demand Curve for Public Goods The individual's most preferred level of expenditure is the point of tangency between the indifference curve and the budget constraint. As the tax price decreases (the budget constraint shifts from *BB* to *BB'*), the individual's most preferred level of public expenditure increases, generating the demand curve of panel B.

the indifference curve tells us how much in private goods the individual is willing to give up to get one more unit of public goods. Thus at the individual's most preferred point, the amount that he is *willing* to give up to get an additional unit of public goods is just equal to the amount he *must* give up to get one more unit of the public good. As we lower the tax price, the bud-

143

get constraint shifts out (from *BB* to *BB'*), and the individual's most pre-ferred point moves to point *E'*. The individual's demand for public goods will normally increase.

By raising and lowering the tax price, we can trace out a demand curve for public goods, in the same way that we trace out demand curves for pri-vate goods. Figure 6.6B plots the demand curve corresponding to panel A. Points *E* and *E'*, from panel A, show the quantity of public goods demanded at tax prices p_1 and p_2. We could trace more points for panel B by shifting the budget constraint further in panel A.

We can use this approach to trace out the demand curves for public goods of Crusoe and Friday. Then we can add them *vertically* to derive the **collective demand curve** in Figure 6.7. Vertical summation is appropriate because a pure public good is necessarily provided in the same amount to all individuals. Rationing is infeasible and is also undesirable, since one individual's usage of the public good does not detract from any other in-dividual's enjoyment of it. Therefore, for a given quantity we add up everyone's willingness to pay to calculate the total willingness to pay; by

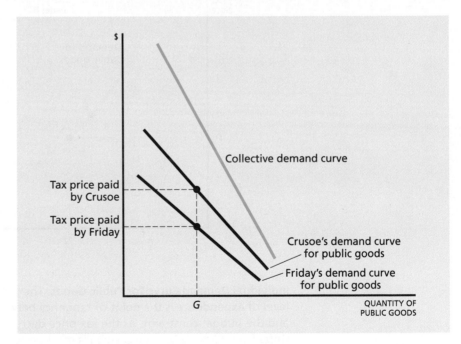

FIGURE 6.7   **Collective Demand for Public Goods** Since at each point on the demand curve the price is equal to the marginal rate of substitution, by adding the demand curves vertically we obtain the sum of the marginal rates of substitution, the total amount of private goods that the individuals in society are willing to give up to get one more unit of the public good. The vertical sum thus can be thought of as generating the collective demand curve for the public good.

calculating this amount at every quantity, we trace out the collective de-mand curve.[3]

The demand curve can be thought of as a "marginal willingness to pay" curve. That is, at each level of output of the public good, it says how much the individual would be willing to pay for an extra unit of the public good. (Remember, the tax price for the public good faced by the individual is set equal to his marginal rate of substitution, which simply gives how much of the private good he is willing to give up for one more unit of the public good.) Thus, the vertical sum of the demand curves is just the sum of their marginal willingnesses to pay, that is, it is the total amount that all individuals together are willing to pay for an extra unit of the public good. Equivalently, since each point on the demand curve of an individual represents his marginal rate of substitution at that level of government expenditure, by adding the demand curves vertically we simply obtain the sum of the marginal rates of substitution (the total marginal benefit from producing an extra unit). The result is the collective demand curve shown in Figure 6.7.

We can draw a supply curve just as we did for private goods; for each level of output, the price represents how much of the other goods have to be forgone to produce one more unit of public goods; this is the marginal cost, or the marginal rate of transformation. At the output level where the collective demand is equal to the supply (Figure 6.8), the sum of the marginal willingnesses to pay (the sum of the marginal rates of substitution) is just equal to the marginal cost of production or the marginal rate of transformation. Since at this point, the marginal benefit from producing an extra unit of the public good equals the marginal cost, or the sum of the marginal rates of substitution equals the marginal rate of transformation, the output level described by the intersection of the collective demand curve and the supply curve for public goods is Pareto efficient.

Though we constructed each individual's demand curve for public goods in a manner analogous to the manner in which we could construct his demand curve for private goods, there are some important distinctions between the two. In particular, while market *equilibrium* occurs at the intersection of the demand and supply curves, we have not provided any explanation for why the equilibrium supply of public goods should occur at the intersection of the demand curve we have constructed and the supply curve. We have only established that if it did, the level of production of the public good would be Pareto efficient. Decisions about the level of public goods are made publicly, by governments, and not by individuals; hence, whether

---

[3] The collective demand curve is also sometimes referred to as the *aggregate demand curve* (not to be confused with the same term used in macroeconomics), and is the analog to the market demand curve for private goods. When constructing the market demand curve for private goods, we add up the quantities demanded for a given price, because all individuals face the same price but may consume different amounts. The *market demand curve* is thus derived by adding up the individual demand curves horizontally.

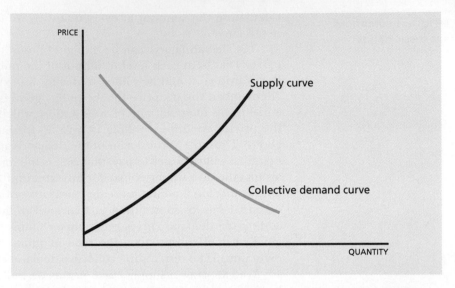

FIGURE 6.8 **Efficient Production of Public Goods** An efficient supply of public goods occurs at the point of intersection of the demand curve and the supply curve. The collective demand curve gives the sum of what all individuals are willing to give up, at the margin, to have one more unit of public goods (one more gun), while the supply curve gives the amount of other goods that have to be given up to obtain one more unit of the public good.

production occurs at this point depends on the nature of the political process, a subject discussed at length in the next chapter.

Moreover, while in a competitive market for private goods all individuals face the same prices but consume different quantities (reflecting differences in tastes), a pure public good must be provided in the same amount to all affected individuals, and we have hypothesized that the government could charge different tax prices for the public good. One way of thinking about these prices is to suppose that each individual is told beforehand the

EFFICIENCY CONDITION FOR PURE PUBLIC GOODS

Efficient production requires that the sum of the marginal rates of substitution equal the marginal rate of transformation.

Efficient production occurs at the intersection of the collective demand curve, formed by vertically adding the demand curves for each individual, with the supply curve.

share of public expenditures that he will have to bear. If some individual has to bear 1 percent of the cost of public expenditures, then an item that costs the government $1.00 costs him 1 cent, while if an individual has to bear 3 percent of the cost of public expenditures, then an increase in public expenditures by $1.00 costs that individual 3 cents.

Finally, we should emphasize that we have characterized the Pareto efficient level of expenditure on public goods corresponding to a particular distribution of income. As we shall see in the next section, the efficient level of expenditure on public goods generally depends on the distribution of income.

PARETO EFFICIENCY AND INCOME DISTRIBUTION

Recall from our discussion of Chapters 3 and 5 that there are many Pareto efficient resource allocations; any point on the utility possibilities schedule is Pareto efficient. The market equilibrium in the absence of market failures corresponds to just one of those points. By the same token, there is not a unique Pareto optimal supply of public goods. The intersection of the demand and supply curves in Figure 6.8 is one of these Pareto efficient levels of supply, but there are others as well, with different distributional implications.

To see how the efficient level of public goods depends on the distribution of income, assume the government transferred a dollar of income from Crusoe to Friday. This would normally shift Crusoe's demand for public goods (at any price) down and Friday's up. In general, there is no reason why these changes should exactly offset each other, so that the aggregate level of demand will normally change. With this new distribution of income, there is a new efficient level of public goods. But efficiency is still characterized by the sum of the marginal rates of substitution equaling the marginal rate of transformation. To put it another way, each point on the utility possibilities schedule may be characterized by a different level of public goods, but at each point the sum of the marginal rates of substitution equals the marginal rate of transformation.

The fact that the efficient level of public goods depends, in general, on the distribution of income has one important implication: one cannot separate out efficiency considerations in the supply of public goods from distributional considerations. Any change in the distribution of income, say, brought about by a change in the income tax structure, will thus be accompanied by corresponding changes in the efficient levels of public-goods production.[4]

---

[4] Some economists have suggested that decisions concerning the efficient level of public-goods production and distribution of income can be separated; for instance, there is a view that concerns about the distribution of income should be reflected in tax schedules and welfare programs, but that decisions concerning the supply of public goods can and should be made quite independently of such considerations. There are some cases where the decisions can be separated (see Atkinson and Stiglitz, *Lectures in Public Economics* [New York: McGraw-Hill, 1980] or L. J. Lau, E. Sheshinski, and J. E. Stiglitz, "Efficiency in the Optimum Supply of Public Goods," *Econometrica* 46 [1978]: 269–84), but these are indeed special.

Governments, in evaluating the benefits of a public program, often seem to be particularly concerned with the question of *who* benefits from the program. They seem to weight benefits that accrue to the poor more heavily than benefits that accrue to the rich. Yet the previous analysis suggested that one should simply add up the marginal rates of substitution, the amounts that each individual is willing to pay at the margin for an increase in the public good, treating the rich and the poor equally. How can these approaches be reconciled?

In Chapter 5, we saw how we could trace out the utility possibilities schedule simply by taking away resources from one individual and giving them to another. Recall our parable of the Robinson Crusoe economy, where in the process of transferring oranges from Crusoe to Friday some of the oranges are lost. In the U.S. economy, we use primarily the tax system and welfare system to redistribute resources. Not only are the administrative costs of running these systems large, but they have important incentive effects—for instance, on individuals' savings and work decisions. The fact that redistributing resources through the tax and welfare systems is costly implies that the government may look for alternative ways to achieve its redistributive goals; one way is to incorporate redistributive considerations into its evaluation of public projects.

The fact that the revenue raised to finance public goods is raised through distortionary taxes, such as the income tax, has some important implications for the efficient supply of public goods. The amount of private goods that individuals must give up to get one more unit of public goods is greater than it would be if the government could raise revenue in a way that did not entail distortionary incentive effects and that was not costly to administer.

We can define a **feasibility curve,** giving the maximum level of private-goods consumption consistent with each level of public goods, for our given tax system. The tax system introduces inefficiencies, so this feasibility curve lies inside the production possibilities schedule, as in Figure 6.9.

The amount of private goods we have to give up to obtain one more unit of public goods, taking into account these extra costs, is called the **marginal economic rate of transformation,** as opposed to the **marginal physical rate of transformation** we employed in our earlier analysis. The latter is completely determined by *technology*, while the marginal economic rate of transformation takes into account the costs associated with the taxes required to finance increased public expenditure. Thus we replace the earlier condition that the marginal physical rate of transformation must equal the sum of the marginal rates of substitution with a new condition, that the marginal economic rate of transformation must equal the sum of the marginal rates of substitution.

Since it becomes more costly to obtain public goods when taxation imposes distortions, normally this will imply that the efficient level of public goods is smaller than it would have been with nondistortionary taxation.

Indeed, it appears that much of the debate about the desirable level of public goods provision centers around this issue. Some believe that the dis-

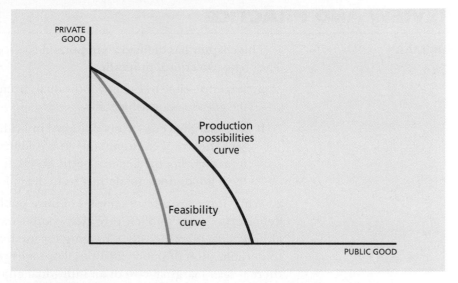

FIGURE 6.9 **The Feasibility Curve** The feasibility curve gives the maximum output (consumption) of private goods for any level of public goods, taking into account the inefficiencies that arise from the taxes that must be imposed to raise the requisite revenue. The feasibility curve lies below the production possibilities schedule.

tortions associated with the tax system are not very great, while others contend that the cost of attempting to raise additional revenues for public goods is great. They *may* agree on the magnitude of the social benefits that may accrue from additional government expenditures, but disagree on the costs.

EFFICIENT GOVERNMENT AS A PUBLIC GOOD

One of the most important public goods is the management of the government: we all benefit from a better, more efficient, more responsive government. Indeed, "good government" possesses both of the properties of public goods we noted earlier: it is difficult and undesirable to exclude any individual from the benefits of a better government.

If the government is able to become more efficient and reduce taxes without reducing the level of government services, everyone benefits. The politician who succeeds in doing this may get some return, but this return is only a fraction of the benefits that accrue to others. In particular, those who voted against the politician who succeeds in doing this gain as much as those who worked for his election, and the individual who did not vote, who attempted to free ride on the political activities of others, benefits as much as either.

149

REVIEW AND PRACTICE

SUMMARY

1 This chapter has defined an important class of goods, pure public goods. They have two critical properties:

   a It is impossible to exclude individuals from enjoying the benefits of the goods (non-excludability).

   b The marginal cost of an additional individual enjoying the good is zero (non-rival consumption). It is undesirable to exclude individuals from enjoying the benefits of the goods, since their enjoyment of these goods does not detract from the enjoyment of others.

2 While there are a few examples of pure public goods, such as national defense, for many publicly provided goods exclusion is possible, although frequently costly. Charging for use may result in the underutilization of public facilities. For many publicly provided goods, there is *some* marginal cost of an individual enjoying the good. While the marginal cost of an individual using a completely uncongested road may be negligible, if there is some congestion, the marginal cost may be more significant.

3 Private markets either will not supply or will provide an inadequate supply of pure public goods.

4 The problem with voluntary arrangements for providing public goods arises from individuals trying to be *free riders* and enjoying the benefits of the public goods paid for by others.

5 For many publicly provided goods, consumption is rivalrous; consumption by one individual reduces that of another; or the marginal cost of supplying an extra individual may be significant, equal to, or even greater than, the average cost. These are called publicly provided private goods. If they are supplied freely, there will be overconsumption.

6 For publicly provided private goods, some method of rationing other than the price system may be used; sometimes queuing is used, while at other times the good is simply provided in fixed quantities to all individuals. Both of these entail inefficiencies.

7 Pareto efficiency requires that a public good be supplied up to the point where the sum of the marginal rates of substitution equals the marginal rate of transformation. Different Pareto efficient levels of consumption of the public good will be associated with different distributions of income.

8 The basic rule for the efficient level of supply of public goods must be modified when there are costs (distortions) associated with raising revenue and redistributing income.

9 Efficient management of the government is a public good in itself.

KEY CONCEPTS

Exclusion

Pure public goods

User fees

Free rider problem

Transactions costs

Publicly provided private goods

Rationing system

Tax price

Collective demand curve

Feasibility curve

Marginal economic rate of transformation

Marginal physical rate of transformation

QUESTIONS AND PROBLEMS

1 Where should each of the following goods lie in Figure 6.2? Explain why each is or is not a pure public good. Where applicable, note instances where the good is both publicly and privately provided:

a College education

b A local park

c Yosemite National Park

d Sewage collection

e Water

f Electricity

g Telephone service

h Retirement insurance

i Medicine

j Police protection

k TV

l Basic research

m Applied research

2 What happens to the efficient allocation between public and private goods as an economy becomes wealthier? Can you think of examples of public goods, the consumption of which would increase more than proportionately to the increase in income? Less than proportionately to the increase in income?

3 The government rations a variety of publicly provided private goods and impure public goods (in which there is congestion) in a variety of ways. Discuss how each of these is rationed, and consider the effect of alternative rationing systems:

a Public higher education

b Health services in the United Kingdom

c Yellowstone National Park

What happens to a publicly provided good in which congestion can occur (such as a highway or swimming pool on a hot, sunny day), but in which no direct rationing system is employed?

4 To what extent do you think differences in views between advocates of less spending on public goods and advocates of more spending can be attributed to different assessments of the marginal cost of public goods,

including the increased distortions associated with the additional taxes required to finance public goods? What are other sources of disagreement?

5 What implications might the fact that efficient government is a public good have for the efficiency with which governments function?

6 Discuss the issue of vaccination from the perspective of public goods/externalities. Why might individuals not voluntarily consent to be vaccinated?

7 There has been increasing concern about increased atmospheric concentrations of greenhouse gases, such as carbon dioxide, which are likely to lead to global warming. Discuss the world's atmosphere as an "international" public good. What are some of the problems of ensuring that individuals and countries take actions to reduce emissions of greenhouse gases?

8 Discuss how changes in income, technology, or other changes in the economic environment may lead to changes in the balance between public and private provision. Illustrate, for instance, by a discussion of the role of public parks.

APPENDIX A   THE LEFTOVER CURVE

In this appendix we provide an alternative, diagrammatic exposition for the basic efficiency condition for public goods:

Sum of marginal rates of substitution = Marginal rate of transformation.

In Figure 6.10A we have superimposed Crusoe's indifference curve on the production possibilities schedule. If the government provides a level of public goods G, and wishes, at the same time, to ensure that Crusoe attains the level of utility associated with the indifference curve U_1 drawn in the figure, then the amount of private good that is "left over" for Friday is the vertical distance between the production possibilities schedule and the indifference curve. Accordingly, we call the (vertical) difference between the two the **leftover curve.** This curve is plotted in Figure 6.10B. We now superimpose on Figure 6.10B Friday's indifference curves. The highest level of utility he can attain, consistent with the production possibilities schedule, and consistent with the prespecified level of utility of Crusoe, is at the point of tangency between his indifference curve and the leftover curve.

There is a simple way to express this tangency condition. Since the leftover curve represents the difference between the production possibilities schedule for the economy and the first individual's indifference curve, the

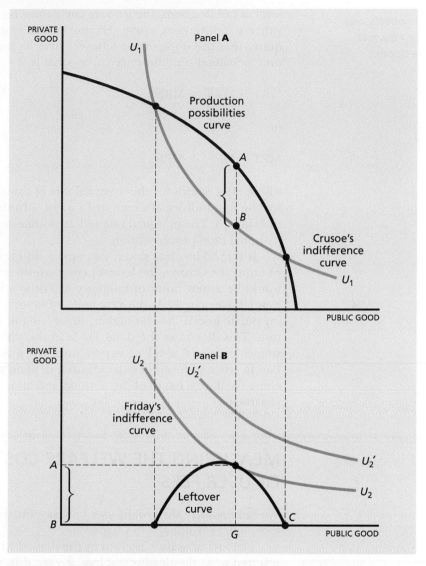

FIGURE 6.10 **Determination of the Efficient Level of Production of Public Goods**
(A) If the level of public goods is G, and the first individual is to get level
of utility U_1, then the distance AB represents the amount of private
goods left over for the second individual. (B) The second individual's
welfare is maximized at the point of tangency of his indifference curve
and the "leftover" curve.

slope of the leftover curve is the difference between the slope of the production possibilities schedule and the slope of the first individual's indifference
curve. The slope of the production possibilities schedule is, as we just saw,
the marginal rate of transformation, while the slope of the first individual's
indifference curve is his marginal rate of substitution. If G is the optimal

level of public goods, the leftover curve must be tangent to the second individual's indifference curve. Hence Pareto efficiency of the economy requires that the slope of the leftover curve be equal to the slope of the second individual's indifference curve—that is,

$$MRT - MRS^1 = MRS^2$$

or

$$MRT = MRS^1 + MRS^2,$$

where MRT stands for the marginal rate of transformation and MRS^1 stands for the first individual's marginal rate of substitution, MRS^2 for the second individual's. The marginal rate of transformation must equal the sum of the marginal rates of substitution.

It should be clear that if we chose a different (say, higher) initial level of utility for Crusoe, the leftover curve would be shifted (down), and there would be a new point of tangency of Friday's indifference curve with the new leftover curve. At the new point of tangency, the level of expenditure on public goods may be higher, lower, or the same as in the initial situation. This illustrates the point made in the text: There is not necessarily a single "efficient" level of expenditure on public goods; there are many Pareto efficient levels of expenditures, depending on the distribution of income (welfare). Issues of distribution and allocation cannot, in general, be separated.

APPENDIX B

MEASURING THE WELFARE COST OF USER FEES

We can measure the cost of user fees, say, for the use of a bridge, using the techniques introduced in Chapter 5.

The loss in welfare is given by the shaded triangle in Figure 6.11. This is referred to as the **deadweight loss.** To see this, we recall that the points on the demand curve measure the individual's marginal willingness to pay for an extra trip at different quantities. Assume a price, p, was charged for the use of the bridge. The number of trips taken would then be Q_e. The welfare loss from not taking the trip is the difference between what he is willing to pay (his marginal benefit) and the marginal cost. The willingness to pay at Q_e is p, and the cost of providing an extra trip is zero; thus the welfare loss is just p. At slightly higher levels of usage, the loss is still the marginal willingness to pay, but this is now smaller. To find the total welfare loss, we simply add up the welfare loss associated with each of the trips *not* taken as a result of charging the toll. At a zero price, Q_m trips are taken. At a price of p, Q_e trips are taken. Hence, the toll results in $(Q_m - Q_e)$ trips not being taken. The loss in welfare from the first trip not taken is p; the loss in welfare from

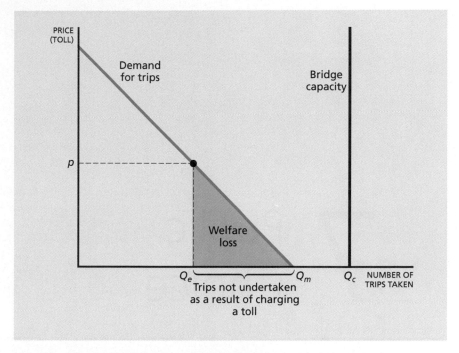

FIGURE 6.11 **Bridges: How a User Fee Can Result in Welfare Loss** As a result of a toll, *p*, some trips across the bridge are not taken even though they would be beneficial to society as a whole. The total welfare loss created by the toll is represented by the shaded region.

the last trip not taken is zero (his willingness to pay for one additional trip at Q_m is zero). The *average* welfare loss from each trip not taken is thus $p/2$; and the total welfare loss is $p(Q_m - Q_e)/2$, the area of the shaded triangle in Figure 6.11.[5]

[5] Recall from Chapter 5 that this is only an approximation for the deadweight loss. The correct calculation entails using the *compensated* demand schedule, not the ordinary demand schedule. However, if the fraction of income spent on traveling across the bridge is small, the two demand curves differ by very little.

7 Public Choice

FOCUS QUESTIONS

1 In what ways does *collective* decision-making—such as determining the level of public goods—differ from standard decision-making within a household? What is the problem of eliciting preferences? When individuals differ in what they want—say, about the level of expenditures on a public good—how are those differences resolved? What is meant by the problem of "aggregating preferences"?

2 Why may there not be a well-defined outcome when majority voting is used to resolve differences in views? Is there any voting procedure that yields a well-defined outcome in all situations? When there is a well-defined outcome, is it necessarily efficient?

3 What are alternative ways for determining the level of public goods expenditures? Are there ways which ensure an efficient level of expenditures on public goods?

4 What are some of the ways in which politics affects the outcomes of public decision-making about resource allocation?

Unlike expenditures on conventional private goods, which are determined through the price system, expenditures on public goods are determined through a political process. This chapter examines some models of that political process, bringing us to the border between political science and economics.

PUBLIC MECHANISMS FOR ALLOCATING RESOURCES

Chapter 3 explained how the market economy depends on the price system to arrive at efficient resource allocations in the production of private goods. The price system provides incentives for firms to produce goods that are valued and a basis for allocating the goods that are produced among consumers. We often speak of the important role prices play in conveying information: from consumers to producers concerning the value they attach to different commodities; between producers and from producers to consumers concerning the costs of production and the scarcity of these commodities.

Equilibrium in private markets is determined at the intersection of the demand curve and the supply curve. When, for one reason or another, the demand for a commodity increases, its demand curve shifts up, the price rises, and this induces firms to produce more. Thus, the price system conveys information about a change in individuals' tastes to firms. Similarly, when, for one reason or another, a commodity becomes less costly to produce, its supply curve will shift down, the price will fall, and individuals will be induced to shift their consumption toward the now-cheaper commodity. Again, the price system has conveyed information about the change in technology from firms to consumers. Indeed, one of the central results of modern welfare economics, as was pointed out in Chapter 3, is that in a competitive economy, the resulting resource allocations are efficient.

Decisions about resource allocations in the public sector are made in quite a different manner. Individuals vote for elected representatives, these elected representatives in turn vote for a public budget, and the money itself is spent by a variety of administrative agencies. Thus there is a major difference between how an individual decides to spend his own money and how, say, Congress decides to spend the public's money. A member of Congress, when she votes, is supposed to reflect the views of constituents, not just her own views. In deciding how to vote, she faces two problems: first she must ascertain what the views of her constituents are; second, since these views are likely to differ, she must decide how much weight to assign to various positions.

THE PROBLEM OF PREFERENCE REVELATION

While individuals may express their views about the desirability of one private good versus another by a simple action—by buying the good or not—there is no comparably effective way that individuals can express their views about the desirability of one public good versus another. Elections of public officials convey only limited information about voters' attitudes toward specific public goods; at best, they convey a general notion that voters prefer more or less government spending.

Even if individuals were asked directly what their preferences are, would they truthfully and meaningfully reveal them? In recent years, politicians have increasingly turned to polls to ascertain voters' preferences, and while they have found the polls to be useful, they have come to treat the results with extreme caution. For instance, in the early 1990s, in the period of exploding government deficits, polls consistently showed strong sentiment toward reducing the deficit. But no consistent picture emerged concerning the trade-offs: some polls suggested that voters would be willing to pay higher taxes or accept expenditure cuts to reduce the deficit, but other polls (confirmed to some extent by voting patterns) suggested otherwise. While in polls voters consistently say they believe the government should spend less on assistance to foreign countries, when asked how much should be spent, they give a number considerably in excess of what the United States is currently spending.

Unless individuals are faced with concrete trade-offs, where they actually have to give up something to get more, say, of another good, it is difficult to get them to think hard about their choices. And there are special problems in inducing individuals to reveal truthfully their preferences concerning public goods. If what they have to pay does not depend on their answer, then there is a tendency to ask for more of the good: one would normally like more public goods so long as one doesn't have to pay for them. But if what an individual says affects how much he has to pay, there is an incentive to pretend that he enjoys the good much less than he really does—he knows that his answer will have a negligible effect on the total amount supplied, and he would like to be a free rider.[1]

In private decisions the decision maker knows his own preferences. In public decisions the decision maker has to ascertain the preferences of those on whose behalf he is making the decision. This is the first important difference between public and private resource allocations.

INDIVIDUAL PREFERENCES FOR PUBLIC GOODS

Collective decision-making is difficult because different individuals have different views, for instance, about how much should be spent on public goods. They differ for three reasons. Sometimes there are simply differences in tastes. Just as some individuals prefer chocolate ice cream and others vanilla, some people prefer public parks and education, while others prefer private goods, like video games and cars. This book will not have much to say about these matters of tastes.

The other two sources of differences are incomes and taxes. Richer individuals have higher incomes, so normally they prefer to spend more on all goods, both public and private. But when the government spends more on public goods, richer individuals often have to pay a relatively large share of the additional cost. In the case of private goods, rich and poor individuals typically pay the same price; with public goods, in effect, richer individuals typically have to pay a higher price. The **tax price** is the additional amount an individual must pay when government expenditures increase by one dollar. The tax price times total government expenditures equals the individual's tax payment. A higher tax price by itself means that richer individuals

---

[1] Economists have devised some clever ways of getting around these problems *in principle*, but in practice, no government has actually implemented them. See the appendix to this chapter.

would want a lower level of expenditures on public goods. With an income effect leading to a higher desired demand, however, and a price effect leading to a lower desired demand, the net effect is ambiguous.

To see these effects, consider first a situation where there are N people and each must pay the same amount, regardless of income. Under this system of **uniform taxation** the tax price is just $1/N$ and the tax payment is G/N.[2] With **proportional taxation,** everyone pays the same percentage of income. The tax price can be easily calculated. If $\bar{Y}$ is *average* income, $N\bar{Y}$ is total income; if t is the tax rate, then $tN\bar{Y}$ is total government revenue. This must equal government expenditures:

$$G = tN\bar{Y}.$$

Thus, the tax rate is

$$t = G/N\bar{Y}.$$

The tax *payment* of an individual with income Y_i is

$$tY_i = \frac{GY_i}{N\bar{Y}}.$$

If government expenditures increase by a dollar, the individual's incremental tax—his tax price—is just $Y_i/N\bar{Y}$. Thus, an individual with average income $(Y_i - \bar{Y})$ faces a tax price of $1/N$, an individual with above-average income (where $Y_i > Y$) faces a higher tax price, and an individual with below-average income faces a lower tax price.

A **progressive** tax system is one in which tax payments increase more than proportionately with income, a **regressive** tax system one in which they increase less than proportionately. Accordingly, the tax price for a high-income individual under a progressive tax system is typically greater than $Y_i/N\bar{Y}$.

Given the individual's tax price, we can derive his preferred level of public goods expenditure, as illustrated in Figure 7.1. Individuals with different incomes face different budget constraints; the preferred levels of public goods expenditure are at the tangencies of the indifference curves with the budget constraints.

Different individuals will differ with respect to their preferred level of expenditures. With proportional taxation, poorer individuals face lower tax prices, and on that account, their preferred level of expenditures, G_P, is higher. But poorer individuals have lower incomes, and with lower incomes

---

[2] No government today imposes uniform taxation (that is, taxes which do not depend on income). However, many "clubs," which can be thought of as voluntary collective organizations, do charge uniform fees; and there are some dedicated taxes—gasoline taxes which are used for road construction, for example—which do not depend directly on income.

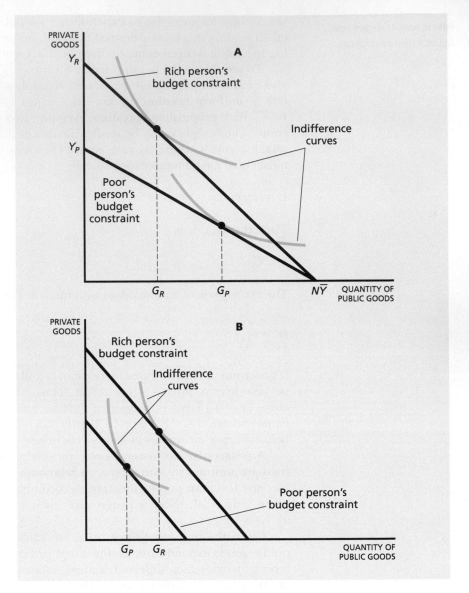

FIGURE 7.1 **Individual's Choice of "Most Preferred" Level of Government Expenditures**
The individual's most preferred level of government expenditures occurs at
the tangency between the budget constraint and the indifference curve. With
proportional taxation, individuals with lower incomes face a lower tax price
(flatter budget constraint), as shown in panel A. The income and substitution
effects work in opposite directions, so that it is ambiguous whether the most
preferred level of government expenditure is higher or lower. With uniform
taxation, as shown in panel B, all individuals face the same tax price, so there
is only an income effect. Rich individuals prefer higher levels of expenditure.
(In this example, the rich and poor are assumed to have the same indifference
curves (preferences); they differ only with respect to the budget constraints.)

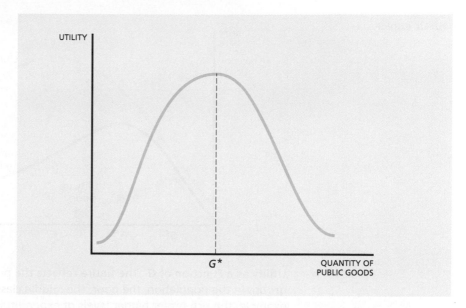

UTILITY

G^*

QUANTITY OF
PUBLIC GOODS

FIGURE 7.2   **Utility Depends on Level of Government Expenditure** Utility is maximized at
the point of tangency between the indifference curve and the budget
constraint. The further away the actual level of expenditures from the
preferred level of expenditures, G^*, the lower the level of utility.

they demand less public as well as private goods. The net effect is ambiguous. Figure 7.1A illustrates the case where the substitution effect (lower tax price) dominates the income effect, and so the poorer individual does prefer a higher level of public goods than the richer person.

With uniform taxation, there is only an income effect, so high-income individuals will prefer higher levels of public expenditure (Figure 7.1B); with progressive income taxation, lower-income individuals will face a lower tax price than with proportional taxation, so their preferred level of expenditures will be even higher than with proportional taxation.

Figure 7.2 shows how utility depends on the level of government expenditures. The individual's most preferred level of expenditures occurs at G^*, but utility is maximized under a budget constraint, at the point of tangency with the indifference curve. The further away the actual level of expenditures is from the preferred level of expenditures, G^*, the lower the level of utility.

Figure 7.3 shows the relationship between the level of utility and the level of public goods expenditure for three different groups—the rich, the poor, and the "middle," assuming a particular tax system. Each has its own preferred outcome, and utility decreases both as expenditures deviate above or below that level. For expenditures above, the marginal benefits of increased public expenditure are less than the marginal costs the individual bears in additional tax payments, while the converse holds for expenditures below the preferred level.

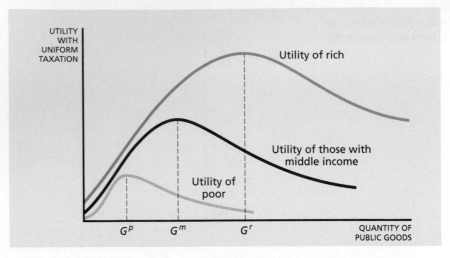

FIGURE 7.3   **Utility as a Function of G.** The figure reflects the preferences of three groups in the population, the poor, the middle class, and the rich. In this example, the rich prefer higher levels of expenditure to the middle class, who prefer higher levels than the poor.

THE PROBLEM OF AGGREGATING PREFERENCES   In the private market, the firm does not have to balance the claims and interests of one group against those of another. If an individual is willing to pay a price for the commodity that exceeds the marginal cost of production, it pays for the firm to sell the commodity to the individual. Decisions are made on an individual basis. In the public sector, on the other hand, decisions are made collectively—when a politician votes to increase expenditure on some public good, it is not as if he has to pay for the good himself. His vote is intended to represent the interests of his constituents, but their opinions are not likely to

CENTRAL PROBLEMS OF PUBLIC CHOICE

Preference Revelation:

- Ascertaining the desired level of public goods of each individual

Aggregating Preferences:

- Different individuals have different preferred levels of public expenditure.
- Preferred level depends both on individual's income and tax system.
- Other things being equal, rich typically prefer higher levels.
- But cost of increased public expenditure may be higher for rich.

be unanimous. Some individuals would like more military spending, others less. Some individuals would like more expenditures on welfare, others less.

The problem of reconciling differences arises whenever there must be a collective decision. Popular political discussions often refer to what "the people" want. But since different people want different things, how, out of these divergent views, can a social decision be made? In a dictatorship, the answer is easy: the dictator's preferences dominate. But there is no such easy resolution in a democracy. A number of different voting rules have been suggested, among them unanimity voting, simple majority voting, and two-thirds majority voting. Of these, perhaps the most widely employed rule for decision making in a democracy is simple majority voting.

MAJORITY VOTING AND THE VOTING PARADOX

We all know how majority voting works. Suppose you and two friends are trying to decide whether to go to a movie or a basketball game. You take a vote: if the movie gets two votes, you go to the movie; if the basketball game gets two votes, you go to the game. But sometimes majority voting does not lead to such a clear outcome when there are more than two alternatives. A majority voting equilibrium requires that there is one alternative which can win a majority in a contest against *any* alternative. As early as the eighteenth century, the famous French philosopher Condorcet noted that *there may not exist any majority voting equilibrium.* The problem may be seen in the following simple example, where there are three voters and three alternatives, denoted A, B, and C. A could be going to a movie, B to a basketball game, C renting a video; or A could be spending more money on health care for children, B reducing the deficit, C cutting taxes.

Voter 1 prefers A to B to C.
Voter 2 prefers C to A to B.
Voter 3 prefers B to C to A.

Assume we vote on A versus B. Voters 1 and 2 vote for A, so A wins. Now we vote on A versus C. Voters 2 and 3 prefer C to A, so C wins. It appears that C should be the social choice. C wins against A, which wins against B. But let us now have a direct confrontation between C and B. Both Voter 1 and Voter 3 prefer B to C. This is referred to as the **voting paradox,** or the paradox of cyclical voting. There is no clear winner. B beats C and C beats A but A beats B. Assume we began by saying we were going to first vote on B versus C, and put the winner against A. B beats C, and then A beats B. But just to check that we had made the right decision (A), we decide to put A against C. C beats A. So we think C is the winner. But then we check that by challenging C with B. B beats C—which was our original vote. B again appears to be the winner. But just to check, we again challenge it with A. A again beats B, as we knew from our earlier vote. The voting process goes on and on.

Often, to avoid these voting cycles, democracies organize their decision making as a sequence of votes, for instance, A against B, and the winner of that vote will be put against C, with the final determination depending on the outcome of that vote, with no further contests. In that case, it may be very important to control the agenda, the order in which the votes occur.

RANK-ORDER VOTING FAILS "INDEPENDENCE OF IRRELEVANT ALTERNATIVES"

John and Jim prefer a swimming pool to a library to a tennis court.

Tom prefers a tennis court to a swimming pool to a library.

Lucy and Jill prefer a tennis court to a swimming pool to a library.

Majority voting: Three prefer a tennis court to a swimming pool.

Three prefer a tennis court to a library.

Five prefer a swimming pool to a library.

TENNIS COURT WINS.

Rank order (lowest sum of ranks wins): Tennis nine; swimming pool eight; library thirteen.

SWIMMING POOL WINS.

Rank order in choice between tennis court and swimming pool (library not an option): Tennis seven; swimming pool eight.

TENNIS COURT WINS.

Adding "irrelevant choice"—library—alters outcome.

For instance, as just depicted, we know that A would defeat B, and C would defeat A, so C would be the decision. But suppose instead we structured the election as first a contest between B and C, and then the winner of that contest against A. A would win that election. Finally, suppose we structured the election as first a contest between A and C, and the winner of that election against B. Then clearly B would win. Thus the winner of each of these elections is determined solely by the order in which the pair-wise comparisons were made.

Note, too, that if individuals realize there is going to be a particular sequence of votes, they may wish to vote strategically. That is, in the first round of the vote, Voter 1 may not vote her true preferences on, say, A versus B, but think through the *consequences* of that for the eventual equilibrium. She may vote for B, even though she would prefer A, knowing that in a contest between C and B, B will win, while in a contest between A and C, C might win. Since she prefers B to C, she votes initially for B.

This analysis leads to two questions. First, are there voting rules that will ensure a determinate outcome for any vote? Second, are there any circumstances under which simple majority voting will yield a determinate outcome? We take up these two questions in the next two sections. It turns out that the voting paradox cannot be resolved through voting rules, but there are indeed circumstances in which majority voting yields clear decisions.

ARROW'S IMPOSSIBILITY THEOREM

An endless cycle of voting is clearly an unsatisfactory state of affairs. It is natural to ask, then, whether there is any other political mechanism, any other set of rules for making social decisions, that eliminates this problem. An ideal political mechanism should have four characteristics:

1 *Transitivity.* If the rule shows that A is preferred to B, and B is preferred to C, then A should be preferred to C. As we have seen, simple majority voting lacks this essential property. Without this property, we can get into cyclical voting.

2 *Nondictatorial choice.* There is a simple way of avoiding voting cycles: give all decision-making powers to a dictator. As long as the dictator has consistent preferences, then there will never be a voting cycle. But in a democratic society, a meaningful political mechanism must ensure that the outcomes do not simply reflect the preferences of a single individual.

3 *Independence of irrelevant alternatives.* The outcome should be independent of irrelevant alternatives; that is, if we have to make a choice between, say, a swimming pool and a tennis court, the outcome should not depend on whether there is a third alternative (such as a new library).

4 *Unrestricted domain.* The mechanism must work no matter what the set of preferences and no matter what the range of alternatives over which choices are to be made.

In looking for a system that would satisfy all four of these properties, a number of alternative rules were examined, but each fails one or more of the requirements. For instance, *rank-order voting* (in which individuals rank the alternatives, the ranks assigned by all individuals are added together, and the alternative with the lowest score wins) does not satisfy the "independence of irrelevant alternatives" criterion.

The quest for an ideal system came to an end with the findings of Nobel laureate Kenneth Arrow of Stanford. He showed that there was no rule that would satisfy all of the desired characteristics. This theorem is referred to as **Arrow's impossibility theorem.**[3]

Arrow's impossibility theorem has one further interesting and important implication. We often hear expressions such as: "The government seems to be acting in an inconsistent manner . . . ," or "Why doesn't the gov-

---

[3] Kenneth Arrow, *Social Choice and Individual Values,* 2nd ed. (New York: Wiley, 1963).

ernment determine its priorities and then act upon them?" This language personifies the government, treats the government as if it were an individual. Language is important: although we all know that the government is not a single individual, speaking of it as if it were frequently leads us to think of it in such facile terms. We come to expect that government should act consistently like a rational individual. But Arrow's impossibility theorem suggests that, unless some individual is granted dictatorial powers, the government should not be expected to act with the same degree of consistency and rationality as an individual.

In the earlier example in which there was no majority voting equilibrium, we saw the importance of control of the agenda. We also saw that it can be beneficial for individuals to vote strategically, that is, to vote not according to their true preferences, but to take into account how the outcome of the current vote will affect the final outcome. Just as Arrow established that there does not exist any way of adding together the preferences of different individuals to satisfy all of the desired characteristics of a choice mechanism, it has been shown that there does not, in general, exist any voting system[4] in which individuals will always vote their true preferences.

SINGLE-PEAKED PREFERENCES AND THE EXISTENCE OF A MAJORITY VOTING EQUILIBRIUM

Though Arrow's impossibility theorem shows that there is no voting rule which *always* satisfies the desirable properties of a social choice mechanism described earlier, there are some conditions under which the simple system of majority voting yields a determinate outcome.

Figure 7.3 showed the level of utility as a function of the level of expenditure on public goods. There, each individual has a single peak to his preference profile. This property of **single-peakedness** is enough to guarantee the existence of a majority voting equilibrium. Note that the peak need not be "interior" but may lie on the "end," so that preferences such as those in Figure 7.4A are also consistent with single-peakedness.

On the other hand, preferences such as those illustrated in Figure 7.4C are not consistent with single-peakedness. Both 0 and G_1 are (local) peaks. Unfortunately, such examples arise naturally in considering many public choice problems.

For instance, consider the problem of an individual's attitudes toward expenditures on public education. If the level of expenditure on public education is below a certain minimum level, a rich individual may prefer sending his children to private schools. If he does this, any increase in expenditure on public schools simply increases his taxes; he gets no direct benefits. Thus his utility decreases with government expenditures up to a critical level at which he decides to send his children to public school. For increases beyond that level, he derives some benefit. Of course, beyond some point,

---

[4] A voting system is any set of voting rules by which a group of individuals tries to reach a decision—for instance, by dropping from consideration the alternative with the lowest number of votes or by giving individuals several votes and allowing them to assign as many as they like to each alternative.

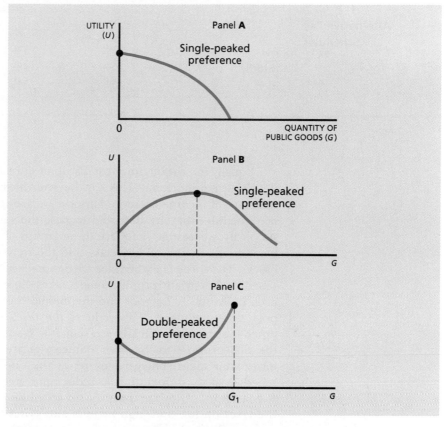

FIGURE 7.4   **Single-Peaked and Double-Peaked Preferences** With single-peaked preferences (panels A and B), there always exists a majority voting equilibrium. Without single-peakedness (panel C), there may not exist a majority voting equilibrium.

the increases in taxes more than offset the benefits. For this individual, a high level of expenditure is preferred to no expenditure, but no expenditure is preferred to an intermediate level of expenditure. There may be no majority voting equilibrium in this case.

Although preferences for a *single* public good (with no private good option, unlike education) are usually single-peaked, when we have to rank choices involving more than one public good, those rankings are seldom single-peaked.[5] To obtain single-peakedness, we have to restrict ourselves to voting on one issue at a time.[6]

[5] See G. Kramer, "On a Class of Equilibrium Conditions for Majority Rule," *Econometrica* 41 (1973): 285–97.

[6] See S. Slutsky, "A Voting Model for the Allocation of Public Goods: Existence of an Equilibrium," *Journal of Economic Theory* 11 (1975): 292–304.

TABLE 7.1	PAID IN TAXES		FRACTION OF INCOME	
Alternative Tax Schedules		A	B	C
	Poor	20%	18%	17%
	Middle	20%	18%	21%
	Rich	20%	23%	22%

Equally important, for most distribution issues there will not be a majority voting equilibrium.[7] This can be seen most clearly in considering the structure of income taxation. Suppose we are voting between three income tax schedules that are designed to raise the same amount of revenue. For simplicity, we assume there are three groups of individuals with equal numbers: the poor, the middle class, and the rich—and that they vote in solid blocks. The three tax schedules are denoted as A, B, and C in Table 7.1. Tax schedule A is strictly proportional; it takes the same fraction of income from each individual. The poor and the middle class then get together and propose tax schedule B. This reduces the taxes they pay but taxes the rich much more heavily. Clearly, tax schedule B will win a majority over A. Now the rich propose to the poor: "Since you are more needy, why don't we lower your taxes somewhat more; at the same time, we'll adjust the tax schedule at the upper end, to reduce the inequities associated with excessive taxation." Thus they propose tax schedule C, which, relative to B, lowers the taxes on low and high income and raises them on middle income, so that now both the middle- and upper-income individuals pay a larger proportion of their income in taxes than do the poor. Clearly, tax schedule C wins a majority over B. Now, however, the middle class proposes going back to straight proportional taxation. Since both the upper- and middle-income individuals prefer schedule A, A defeats C. We again get a cyclical pattern of voting.[8]

THE MEDIAN VOTER

When preferences are single-peaked, we asserted that there is a well-defined majority voting equilibrium. What does it look like? And how does it correspond to the *Pareto efficient* equilibrium that we described in the previous chapter?

[7] See D. K. Foley, "Resource Allocation and the Public Sector," *Yale Economic Essays* 7 (1967): 45–98.

[8] If we restrict the set of tax schedules over which voting occurs to, for instance, tax schedules with an exemption level and a fixed marginal tax rate (these are called flat-rate tax schedules), there may be a majority voting equilibrium. See T. Romer, "Individual Welfare, Majority Voting, and the Properties of a Linear Income Tax," *Journal of Public Economics* 4 (1975): 163–85.

TABLE 7.2	Lucy	Tom	Jim	John	Jill
Preferred Levels of Expenditure on Public Goods	$600	$800	$1000	$1200	$1400
	Jim is median voter				

When preferences are single-peaked, we can rank individuals by their preferred levels of, say, expenditure on the public good, from the individual who prefers the least to the individual who prefers the most. The *median* individual is the individual such that half prefer less and half prefer more than he does. In Table 7.2 Jim is the median voter. *The outcome of majority voting corresponds to the preferences of the median voter.* In this case, it is Jim's preferred level, $1000, that wins. The reason is simple: if any level of expenditure below $1000 is voted on against $1000, Jim plus all of those who want more than $1000 vote for $1000; since Jim is the median voter, a majority cast their vote for $1000. If any level of expenditure above $1000 is voted on against $1000, Jim and all of those who want less than $1000 vote for $1000. Again, $1000 wins.

THE INEFFICIENCY OF THE MAJORITY VOTING EQUILIBRIUM

Since the median voter determines the level of expenditure on public goods, to ascertain whether there is too much or too little expenditure we need only examine how he votes, and contrast that with the conditions for efficiency discussed in Chapter 6. The median individual is assumed to compare only the benefits he receives with the costs that he bears. His benefits are lower than total social benefits (which includes all the benefits that accrue to others), but so are his costs. Whether there is too much or too little expenditure on public goods thus depends on whether his share of total (marginal) costs is less than or greater than his share of total (marginal) benefits.

For a wide variety of public goods, with proportional or progressive taxation majority voting will result in an oversupply of public goods. To see this, assume there are N individuals. With uniform taxation, the tax price for each individual would be $1/N$; with proportional taxation, it would be $Y_m/\overline{Y}N$, where Y_m is the income of the median voter and $\overline{Y}$ is average income; and with progressive taxation, the tax price would be still lower. With a symmetric distribution of income, as illustrated in panel A of Figure 7.5, the income of the median individual equals the average income, that is, $Y_m = \overline{Y}$; but in fact, most income distributions are skewed, as in panel B. There are a few very rich individuals which increase the average income. As a result, average income exceeds the income of the median individual, $Y_m < \overline{Y}$, so that with proportional taxation the tax price is even less than $1/N$.

The question, then, is what fraction of the total marginal benefits accrues to the median voter. If the marginal benefits are uniform, then the median voter gets $1/N$ of the total marginal benefits, so that with uniform

169

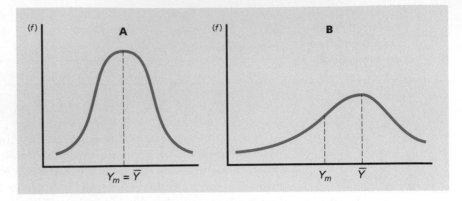

FIGURE 7.5   **Income Distributions** Panel A shows a symmetric income distribution; the median income, Y_m, equals the average income, $\overline{Y}$. Panel B shows a skewed income distribution more typical of the United States. Because there are a few very rich individuals, the average income exceeds the median income.

taxation the median voter would get $1/N$th of the total social benefits and bear $1/N$th of the total costs. Therefore he would vote for an efficient level of expenditure. But with proportional or progressive taxation, his share of the cost would be smaller than his share of the benefits, and he would vote for excessive expenditures—that is, for a level of expenditure where the sum of the marginal benefits is less than the total marginal cost to society.

Some forms of public expenditures are actually enjoyed disproportionately by the poor: in many cities the rich may make less use of public parks, for instance, because they have large yards of their own. According to the median voter theory, there is an especially large tendency for an oversupply of such goods. In many cases, it is difficult to ascertain the balance: the median voter gets a smaller share of the benefits and bears a smaller share of the costs.

In the examples discussed so far, the median voter corresponds to the voter with the median income. This is often, but not necessarily, the case. Higher-income individuals normally demand more of all goods, including public goods, *if they face the same prices*; but the tax price faced by higher-income individuals is typically higher, so that in some cases, very high income individuals may actually prefer lower levels of public expenditures on certain goods than do middle-income individuals.

Median voter theory says that to understand collective choices, we should focus our attention on the median voter and how a particular policy affects him. Consider what the median voter theory says about support for, and consequences of, abolishing the deductibility of state and local income and property taxes for purposes of the federal income tax, a proposal which is frequently raised in the context of tax reform. Most individuals do not itemize; that is, in calculating their taxable income, they subtract a "standard deduction" rather than listing all the allowable deductions, including local and state taxes. Accordingly, they would be unaffected directly, though the increased federal revenue, which could be used to reduce the deficit or taxes, would be a benefit. Thus, the median voter should support this reform. Yet it has been repeatedly defeated—suggesting that there are other considerations that go into determining outcomes in political processes, as we note later in this chapter.

One of the worries of state governors has been that if state taxes are made non-deductible, the "tax price" for state expenditures will go up. Now, in effect, the federal government subsidizes the state. If a New York voter who pays 28 percent of his income to the federal government in income taxes pays $1000 more in state taxes, and he can deduct that expenditure from his income, his federal tax liability goes down by $280, and the *net cost* to him is only $720. With a higher tax price, demand for state-provided goods and services would normally be expected to decrease. The median voter theory says "not to worry": since the median voter in the state does not itemize, tax deductibility has no effect on the level of state-provided goods and services.

THE TWO-PARTY SYSTEM AND THE MEDIAN VOTER

We noted earlier that an elected representative bears a negligible fraction of the costs of, and receives a negligible fraction of the benefits from, an increase in government expenditure. What can economic theory say about how he should vote? A natural supposition is that the politician wishes to stay in office and that, accordingly, he wishes to maximize his votes, given the position taken by his rival. A vote-maximizing voting strategy can easily be defined as follows: Assume there are two parties, "R" and "D." Party R takes the position of Party D as given. Focusing on a single issue, the level of expenditure, denote by G_R the position of Party R (that is, the level of public expenditure advocated by the party) and by G_D the position of Party D. For each value of G_D there is an optimal (i.e., vote-maximizing) position for G_R.

Under the hypothesis that each party seeks to maximize its vote given the position of its rival, what will each party do? Let G_m be the preferred level of expenditure of the median voter. Suppose Party D chooses $G_D > G_m$. Then if Party R takes a position between G_m and G_D, it will get all the voters who prefer an expenditure level less than or equal to G_m, and some who prefer slightly more. Thus Party R gets over 50 percent of the votes and wins. In response, Party D will choose a position, G_D', between G_m and G_R, which wins against G_R. But then Party R chooses a position, G_R', between G_D' and G_m. The process continues until both parties stand for the same position: that of the median voter (G_m). (See Figure 7.6.)

This result is consistent with the widely observed allegation that with our two-party system voters get no choice: both parties take a "middle-of-the-road" position. This is precisely what the theory predicts.[9]

[9] This general theory is due to Harold Hotelling, a pioneer in mathematical economics who taught at Columbia and North Carolina State Universities. See H. Hotelling, "Stability in Competition," *Economic Journal* 39 (March 1929): 41–57.

SOCIAL CHOICE THEORY

The hypothesis that government actions can be explained as the outcome of individuals' acting rationally in their own self-interest, in response to the political "rules of the game," is a central tenet of social choice theory. James Buchanan, currently at George Mason University, received a Nobel Prize in 1986 for his pioneering work in this area. In this view, designing the rules of the game—the constitution—is critical. An important part of the rules of the game is the imposition of constraints on government (such as limits on deficit financing). Without some form of constraints, the incentive of the majority to redistribute income in their favor, away from the minority, or of special interest groups to try to induce elected representatives to act in *their* interests, rather than in the general interest, is too great to be resisted.

Even acts of Congress which seem to go against the special interest groups appear in a different light when viewed from this perspective. Consider the 1986 tax reform, which attempted to strip out of the tax law many of the favorable provisions which special interest groups had succeeded in putting in. Professor Buchanan argues that this action should be viewed from the self-interest of Congress: the tax system had become so overladen with special provisions that the cost of granting further special benefits was rising sharply. The tax reform enabled Congress to start with a clean slate: there was now greater opportunity for introducing *new* special benefits. The greater

There are, however, some important limitations of the theory that need to be borne in mind. First, we noted earlier that in general, there may not exist a majority voting equilibrium. There does if individuals have single-peaked preferences. In the present context, this requires that we should be

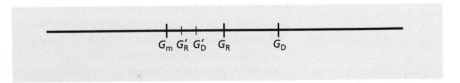

| FIGURE 7.6 | **Two-Party System** If both parties in a two-party system try to maximize their votes, taking the position of the rival as fixed, in equilibrium both parties will adopt the position of the median voter. |

opportunity for Congress to dispense special favors was of immense benefit to Congressmen.*

One issue addressed by Nobel laureate Gary Becker, of Chicago and Stanford Universities, is how to explain the seemingly disproportionate influence of certain small interest groups. Farmers, though they constitute less than 2 percent of Americans, have succeeded in getting huge subsidies from the federal government. The answer Becker suggests is that with small groups, the free rider problem that we encountered in Chapter 6 is smaller. "Bribing" representatives to support one's special interest is a public good: all wheat farmers benefit from a wheat subsidy; all steel or car producers benefit from trade barriers that keep out less expensive foreign steel or cars. The smaller the group, the easier it is to persuade all members to contribute to the cost of lobbying. Each of these programs has losers—and not only are the losers far more numerous, but their aggregate losses exceed the benefits of the special interest groups. But each of the losers loses a little. Opposing the special interest groups is also a public good, and each opponent has an incentive to be a free rider.

*James M. Buchanan, "Tax Reform as Political Choice," *Journal of Economic Perspectives* 1 (summer 1987), pp. 29–35.

able to arrange issues along a single dimension—for example, conservative–liberal. If, however, there are a variety of dimensions—some individuals are liberal on some issues and conservative on others—then the median voter is not well defined, and there may be no equilibrium to the political process.

Secondly, we have ignored questions of participation in the political process. There are, for instance, costs associated with becoming informed and voting. These costs are sufficiently great relative to the perceived benefits that slight changes in the weather, making it slightly less pleasant to go outside to vote, have significant effects on voter participation. In particular, voters whose preferences are near the median have little incentive to be active politically, particularly if they believe that the political process will reflect their preferences anyway. Thus, it may be in the interests of those who are more extreme to attempt to pull their party away from the center. This tendency for greater political activism at the extremes may partially offset the median-directed tendencies noted earlier.

MAJORITY VOTING

Proposal which gets a majority against all other wins

WHEN MAJORITY VOTING EQUILIBRIUM EXISTS, REFLECTS PREFERENCES OF MEDIAN VOTER

- In two-party system, both parties will converge to position of median voter.
- Majority voting equilibrium is not in general Pareto efficient.

MAJORITY VOTING EQUILIBRIUM MAY NOT EXIST

- Proposal A defeats B, C defeats A, but B defeats C.
- Majority voting equilibrium exists if preferences are single peaked.

ARROWS IMPOSSIBILITY THEOREM: THERE DOES NOT EXIST AN ALTERNATIVE VOTING MECHANISM THAT AVOIDS PROBLEMS OF MAJORITY VOTING (AND SATISFIES CERTAIN OTHER DESIRED PROPERTIES).

ALTERNATIVES FOR DETERMINING PUBLIC GOODS EXPENDITURES

We have identified several major problems with the most commonly employed way of making collective decisions, majority voting: there may not be a determinate outcome; even when there is, it may not be efficient; and voters may vote strategically, not revealing their true preferences. Even if there is no ideal system, are there perhaps systems that resolve one or the other of these problems? Economists have looked for such alternative systems.

LINDAHL EQUILIBRIUM   The most famous is called the Lindahl solution, after the great Swedish economist Erik Lindahl, who first proposed it in 1919.[10] He was looking for a system that would yield efficiency; he paid little attention to the other problems listed earlier. Lindahl's system attempts to mimic, as far as possible, the way that the market works in providing private goods. Remember, market equilibrium for private goods is described by the intersection of the demand and supply curves. All individuals face the same price. The sum of the quantities they demand is equal to the sum of the quantities supplied by firms.

[10] E. Lindahl, "*Positive Lösung, Die Gerechtigkeit der Besteuerung,*" translated as "Just Taxation—A Positive Solution" in *Classics in the Theory of Public Finance,* ed. R. A. Musgrave and A. T. Peacock (New York: St. Martin's Press, 1958).

One of the ways we can characterize the efficient level of public goods is as the intersection of the "collective" demand curve (formed by adding vertically each individual's demand curve) with the supply curve. The demand curves are generated by asking the individual how much of the public good he would demand if he were to pay so much for each unit produced; that is, in Figure 7.7A if the first individual faced a tax price of, say, p_1, he would demand G^*.

The Lindahl equilibrium is illustrated in Figure 7.7C. We add vertically the demand curves for Individuals 1 and 2 illustrated in Figure 7.7A and 7.7B, obtaining the collective demand. The Lindahl equilibrium occurs at the intersection of this curve with the supply curve. Price, along the supply curve, measures the marginal cost of production. p_1 measures the first individual's marginal benefit (marginal willingness to pay for an additional unit of government expenditure) at G^*, and what he has to pay, and p_2 measures the same thing for the second individual. At G^*, the sum of the marginal benefits (the total marginal willingness to pay) just equals the marginal cost. The Lindahl equilibrium is thus a set of tax prices (the amount each individual has to pay if one more unit of the public good is produced) adding up to the marginal cost of production, such that, given those tax prices, every individual prefers the same level of expenditures, G^*. Since at the Lindahl equilibrium the sum of the marginal benefits equals the marginal cost, the Lindahl equilibrium is Pareto efficient.

We noted earlier, however, that there were in fact a whole range of Pareto efficient resource allocations, with one individual better off in some, another better off in others. Almost by definition, there cannot be unanimity about which, among these points, is preferred. The Lindahl equilibrium picks one of the Pareto efficient points; but individuals who are disadvantaged by this particular Pareto efficient point will not agree to the use of this mechanism for determining the allocation of public goods; indeed, they would prefer Pareto inefficient allocations so long as the level of utility they obtain is higher.

The most telling criticism of the Lindahl solution is that *individuals do not have an incentive to tell the truth because their tax price increases as their stated demand does.* That is, the higher their stated demand (given the demand statements of others), the higher the equilibrium expenditures on public goods will be. Higher expenditures on public goods necessitate, of course, higher equilibrium tax prices. The demand curves that are used in the Lindahl analysis were drawn under the hypothesis that individuals face a given tax price; they believe that nothing they say will alter what they have to pay per unit of public expenditure. But if they understand the Lindahl mechanism, they will realize that what they say does alter what they have to pay per unit of public expenditure, and thus they will not truthfully reveal their demands.

Let us briefly review the two sets of processes by which collective decisions concerning public goods could be determined, majority voting and the Lindahl equilibrium. Voting, as we have seen, may not yield an equilibrium, and when it does, it is in general not Pareto efficient. We saw earlier that there existed no democratic mechanism which fully resolved the problem of

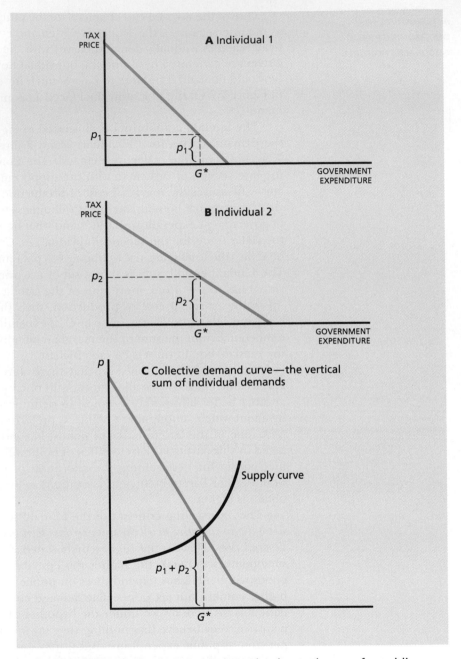

FIGURE 7.7   **Lindahl Equilibrium** Panels A and B show the demand curves for public
goods; demand depends on the tax price faced by the individual. In panel C
the two demand curves are added *vertically*, that is, at each level of
government expenditures, the tax prices of Individuals 1 and 2 are added
together. The Lindahl equilibrium is the level of expenditures G^* at which
the collective demand curve thus constructed intersects the supply curve. At
the intersection, the sum of the tax prices equals the supply price.

COMPARISON OF PUBLIC CHOICE MECHANISMS

Majority voting

- Equilibrium may not exist
- When equilibrium exists, not in general Pareto efficient

Lindahl equilibrium

- Equilibrium always exists
- Equilibrium always Pareto efficient
- Individuals do not have incentive for truthful revelation of preferences

the nonexistence of a voting equilibrium. The Lindahl equilibrium will be efficient, but individuals do not have an incentive to be honest in providing the information required to implement it. The next natural question is, are there more general plausible ways of organizing collective decision-making which yield efficient outcomes, which do not have the problems we have encountered in the case of majority voting and the Lindahl equilibrium? Though economists have devised complicated schemes that have *some* desirable properties, or that may work in *some* circumstances, it appears that there is no *perfect solution to* the problem of collective decision-making in democratic societies. The appendix to this chapter describes one scheme which, while it induces individuals to reveal honestly their preferences, has other problems which perhaps explain why it is not commonly used.

POLITICS AND ECONOMICS

The preceding discussion of the political process differs markedly from the kind of analysis one might typically find in a political science course. There, one might discuss the roles of special interest groups and political institutions. A full discussion of the relationship between economic theories of the political process and other theories of the political process would take us beyond the scope of this book. In the following pages, we touch on some economic interpretations of certain political phenomena.

WHY DO INDIVIDUALS VOTE? In many elections voter participation rates are low, and are sensitive to such chance occurrences as changes in the weather. The reason for this, as we have noted, is that the benefits of voting for the individual are low—there is little chance of one person affecting the outcome. The alternatives may differ so little that the outcome is inconsequential, and, though the costs of voting are relatively low, they are not low in relation to the benefits. Indeed, in a fully rational calculation, no one would vote: the probability that an individual's vote would make a difference to the outcome (since in most cases the individual cares only about whether her candidate wins or loses, not the magnitude of the win or loss) is essentially zero. Yet individuals do vote.[11]

This paradox is resolved, in a somewhat tautological manner, simply by assuming that individuals get utility out of voting, or more generally, out of participation in the political process. More to the point, considerable time and energy are devoted to inculcating into our children notions of civic responsibility, and among these civic responsibilities is the responsibility to be an informed voter.

The same considerations imply that when the individual votes, she may not act in the narrowly self-interested manner that we have assumed in our discussion so far. Individuals may support representatives who vote for closing some loophole in the income tax system because it would result in a more equitable distribution of the tax burden, even though their personal tax liability might thereby be increased.

ELECTIONS AND SPECIAL INTEREST GROUPS

The political models we have discussed thus far have assumed that all individuals are well informed about the consequences of all alternatives under consideration, that all individuals vote, and that they cast their votes on the basis of the implications that each alternative has for their own (private) welfare.

There are many who believe that this does not provide an adequate description of the political process. Although constitutionally each person has one vote, some votes seem more effective than others. The outcome of the political process, in this view, reflects the political power of special interest groups.

Assessing the validity of these views is beyond the scope of this chapter. Instead we will focus on a more narrow set of questions: What can economic theory say about the kinds of interest groups that are likely to be effective? And how can we reconcile the effectiveness of special interest groups with the fact that each individual does, in the United States, have only one vote?

The answer to these questions is related to our discussion in the previous chapter of the public interest as a public good. We saw there that the efficient management of the public sector was a public good. Similarly, when others choose elected officials who are competent and who reflect values similar to our own, we benefit as well. This may reduce our incentive to become informed voters, and encourage us instead to "free ride."

At the same time, we should note that the free rider problem may not be as serious in small groups as it is in large. It is easier to form an interest group of a small number of steel producers to attempt to persuade Congress to restrict steel imports than it is to form an interest group of the large number of steel users who would be adversely affected by such restrictions. Each of the producers has more to gain than each of the consumers has to

---

[11] In U.S. presidential elections since 1932, between 49 percent and 63 percent of the voting age population has voted. In elections of U.S. representatives to Congress, participation has been somewhat lower (33 percent to 59 percent) (*Statistical Abstract of the United States, 1997,* p. 289). In local school board elections, often less than 10 percent of the eligible voters vote.

lose, though the aggregate gains of producers may, in fact, be less than the aggregate losses to consumers.

Trade unions, recognizing the nature of the free rider problem, have long sought closed shops, in which all workers must support the activities the union believes to be in their collective interests. Once they have this power, they can attempt to use it not only at the bargaining table but also in the political arena, where they act as a special interest group.

THE POWER OF SPECIAL INTEREST GROUPS

How are interest groups able to exercise power? There appear to be at least three mechanisms. First, as we noted before, individuals have little incentive to vote or to become informed concerning the issues. Interest groups can attempt to lower the costs of voting and information, particularly for those voters who are likely to support them. They do so by making information (obviously, that supporting their own views) readily available; and they often assist directly by providing transportation, child care, and so on, on polling day.

Secondly, we noted the difficulty that politicians have in obtaining information about the preferences of their constituents. There is no simple demand-revealing mechanism for public goods, as there is for private goods. Interest groups attempt to provide such information. Politicians may lack the technical information required to make informed political decisions—for example, they may not know the consequences of continued imports of cheap foreign cars or clothing. Interest groups are a primary source of information, and it is through providing information that they often exercise influence.

The third mechanism is through direct and indirect bribery of the politician. Direct bribery does not occur often, at least in most jurisdictions in the United States. (Presumably, this may not be due to the purity of our politicians so much as to the costs associated with being caught.) But indirect bribery is important: special interest groups provide financial and other forms of support for politicians who support their interests; this support is viewed to be essential in running a successful political campaign.

There has been increasing recognition of the power of contributions, reaching a crescendo after the 1996 elections, in which the President was accused of "selling" nights in the Lincoln bedroom and seats on Air Force One in return for large contributions. But in spite of rhetorical support for campaign finance reform from both parties, Congress has failed to pass legislation.

THE ALTRUISTIC POLITICIAN?

An alternative view holds that many politicians do not behave in as self-interested a way as we have assumed throughout this chapter. Just as individuals behave altruistically as private citizens, and give to charity, so too do they behave as public citizens, in their capacity as elected officials. In our society considerable status and respect are accorded to public officials and public service. Effective government depends on the quality of these public servants.

However, being disinterested does not suffice to ensure that politicians will make a wise decision: as has been noted, even a well-intentioned public official may have a difficult time ascertaining the preferences of his constituents. Further, even if the electorate would like to chose altruistic repre-

CAMPAIGN REFORM

Behind the power of many special interest groups is the power of money—especially money to support candidates whom they favor. Traditionally, the Democratic Party has had less access to money; and its members have been particularly concerned that the power of money has created an unlevel playing field, where the voices of rich individuals and corporations are heard more clearly than the voices of the poor and middle class. But incumbents of any party, who typically have better access to financial support, are usually less enthusiastic about reform than those trying to get elected. This helps explain in part why Congress has, at least in the past, had only limited enthusiasm for strong reforms.

Some reforms have focused on limiting the amount of money that any organization can give to any candidate. Such reforms typically have been subverted: if a corporation cannot give money directly, it may still encourage its employees to contribute. If they cannot give money to a candidate, they give money to the candidate's party. Even were they restricted in their contributions to his party, they could give

---

sentatives who vote exclusively on principle, attempting to ensure that there is an "efficient" supply of public goods, they face a difficult problem: So long as not all individuals running for office are disinterested, the voters must select between those who are and those who are not. If voters believe that it is better to be a "disinterested" public servant than a selfish politician, then self-interested politicians will all attempt to resemble a disinterested public servant. How are voters to choose among them on the basis of the limited information they normally have available?

There are numerous instances where politicians seem to act "on principle," voting in a way that is inconsistent not only with their own narrowly defined self-interest, but also with the wishes of their voters. They thus risk not getting elected (though often the electorate respects such shows of "independence" and "principle").

While altruistic behavior on the part of politicians is to be preferred to corruption, or even to lesser forms of self-aggrandizement, economists have long worried about the reliability of seemingly altruistic behavior in the pursuit of the common interest. Indeed, it was the seeming capriciousness of the actions taken by political leaders (often allegedly in the public interest) that led Adam Smith to suggest that there was a better way that the public interest might be served: by each individual's pursuing his private interest. Unfortunately, though Adam Smith's invisible hand may work well for most goods, it does not work well for public goods. Still, at least to a limited degree, self-interest on the part of politicians—their desire to get re-elected—serves an important function: it induces them to try to elicit accurately the

money to some group identified with a position of the candidate. If the National Rifle Association were limited in the amount it gave to pro-gun representatives, it could still mount a campaign against their opponents who advocate gun control.

Some critics of campaign reform worry that it will create an unlevel playing field of a different sort. Groups that can mobilize thousands of volunteers and huge letter-writing campaigns, such as senior citizen advocates or labor unions, will still be able to exercise political influence.

There is also a worry that any restrictions on contributions to parties or causes would be in effect a restriction on First Amendment (free speech) rights: in a democracy, individuals should not be restricted in what they say, how they say it, or to whom they say it. Campaign finance mainly goes to support the dissemination of views—though to be sure, questions may be raised at the extent to which a thirty-second spot ad on TV promotes intelligent decision-making.

---

preferences of their (voting) constituents and to vote for measures that reflect those preferences. It is this form of self-interest that lies behind the analysis of the two-party model presented earlier.

THE PERSISTENCE OF INEFFICIENT EQUILIBRIUM

In recent years, the prices of commodities—from cars to corn to aluminum to uranium to tomatoes—have been higher as a result of trade restrictions, or the threat of imposition of trade restrictions. When special interest groups manage to impose trade restrictions or to obtain subsidies for themselves, the resulting resource allocations not only violate generally accepted standards of equity and fairness but also are frequently inefficient. There are alternative allocations that could make everyone better off. Why, in the face of this, don't individuals get together and propose one of these Pareto-dominating alternatives, to which, presumably, all would agree? There is no universally agreed-upon answer to this puzzle. Several "partial" answers may be suggestive.

First, as we have already seen, the public interest is a public good. Since the efforts to maintain a good government must come from private individuals, there will be an undersupply of this (as any other) privately provided public good.

Secondly, many of the distributive implications of public programs undertaken at the behest of special interest groups are far from obvious—and this is deliberately so. It is unlikely, for instance, that the American voters would deliberately vote to transfer resources (give a public gift) to *rich* rice farmers. For these individuals to receive a transfer at the public expense, they must be included in a broader-scale program, of which they appear to be almost accidental beneficiaries. Thus, rich rice farmers become advocates of federal aid to rice farmers, singling out, in their public rhetoric, the benefits that would accrue to poor rice farmers from such a program. A Pareto improvement might, for instance, entail giving each rice farmer a fixed sum, which would leave him free to move into some other occupation where his productivity might be higher. Although such direct grants could be structured to make everyone better off, they would expose the true distributive implications of the program—that is, that most of the benefits accrue not to poor rice farmers, but to rich ones. Since the likely result would be weakened political support for subsidies to rice farmers, this Pareto improvement would not receive the backing of rich rice farmers.

REVIEW AND PRACTICE

SUMMARY

1 Collective decision-making, such as determining the level of public goods, differs from standard decision-making within a household in two important ways: First, there is a problem of eliciting preferences. If the amount that individuals have to pay depends on their statements, they may tend to understate their true preferences. If the amount that individuals have to pay does not depend at all on their statements, they may tend to overstate their true preferences.

Second, there is a problem of resolving differences in preferences: how much should be provided, if different individuals desire that the government should, for instance, spend different levels on providing public goods?

2 Majority voting is the simplest way by which such differences are resolved. Unfortunately, there may not exist a majority voting equilibrium.

3 Arrow's impossibility theorem demonstrates the impossibility of finding an alternative, nondictatorial political mechanism that resolves this problem of majority voting and that satisfies certain other properties that one would desire of any political mechanism (such as independence of irrelevant alternatives).

4 The majority voting equilibrium exists if preferences are single-peaked.

5 Preferences for a single public good will usually be single-peaked. Preferences will not be single-peaked if:

    a there is more than one public good, and the vote is taken over packages, rather than over a single good at a time;

    b voting is over a publicly provided private good, for which there exists a private alternative, such as education;

    c voting is over distributional questions, such as the structure of the income tax schedule.

6 The majority voting equilibrium, when it exists, reflects the preferences of the median voter.

7 In a two-party system, there will be a convergence of positions of the two parties toward that of the median voter.

8 The majority voting equilibrium does not, in general, result in an efficient supply of public goods; there may be either an undersupply or an oversupply.

9 The Lindahl equilibrium is the level of public goods provision in which the sum of the tax prices equals the marginal cost of production. While the Lindahl equilibrium is Pareto efficient, there is no incentive for individuals to tell the truth concerning their preferences.

10 In many elections, voter participation is low. In fact, economists are puzzled why individuals bother to vote at all, since the expected private benefit—given the low probability that they affect the outcome—is typically less than the private cost.

11 Special interest groups often exercise strong influences over the outcome of political processes.

KEY CONCEPTS

Preference revelation

Aggregating preferences

Voting paradox

Arrow's impossibility theorem

Single-peaked preferences

Median voter

Lindahl equilibrium

QUESTIONS AND PROBLEMS

1 Assume that some individual's marginal valuation of public goods increases. What does this do to the Pareto efficient level of public expenditures? If this individual is not the median individual, what will happen in a two-party system to the equilibrium level of expenditure on public goods? If the equilibrium was originally Pareto efficient, will it still be?

2 Assume that all individuals have identical preferences but some individuals are wealthier than others. Assume there is a single public good and a single private good.

   a Show diagrammatically how you derive the demand curve for the public good, as a function of the tax price charged the individual.

   b Assume that the demand function is of the form

   $G = kY/p,$

   where k is a constant (less than 1), Y is income, and p is the tax price. This says that when income doubles the demand for public goods doubles, but when the tax price doubles the demand is cut in half. If the tax price is proportional to the individual's income (as with proportional taxation), how will demand for public goods differ among those with different incomes?

3 Assume instead there is uniform taxation, so that all individuals face the same tax price. Recall that along each individual's demand curve, the price equals the marginal rate of substitution. Thus,

$$MRS = p = kY/G,$$

the marginal rate of substitution is proportional to income. Assume that income is symmetrically distributed, so that mean income equals the median. Explain why the majority voting equilibrium will be Pareto efficient. Now assume that income is not symmetrically distributed, but rather is skewed toward higher incomes, as in Figure 7.5B. Will the majority voting equilibrium still be efficient? Will there be an under- or oversupply of public goods?

4 Demand curves are said to be *income elastic* if the demand for the good increases more than proportionately with income. For instance, with the demand curve

$$G = kY^2/p$$

the demand for public goods increases with the *square* of income. Draw the marginal rate of substitution as a function of income (for a fixed level of expenditure on public goods). Assume income is symmetrically distributed. What is the relationship between the average value of the marginal rate of substitution and the marginal rate of substitution of the median individual? What does this imply about the equilibrium supply of public goods under majority voting with uniform taxation?

5 In the text, we suggested that for well-off individuals, with uniform taxation, preferences for education were not single-peaked. Why might preferences for local parks and for urban public transportation systems (buses and subways) also not be single-peaked?

6 Is the median voter always the voter with the median income? Give examples.

7 How might the majority voting model be used to explain the growth of government expenditures?

a Should changes in median or average income better explain increases in the demand for government services?

b What should be the effect of an increase in the costs of producing public good caused by government inefficiency? Would it make a difference if the increase in cost is a result of government paying above-market wages (wages higher than those paid comparable workers in the private sector)? (Does your answer to the last question depend on whether the median voter is a government employee?)

c Why might you expect that if income per capita remains the same but the number of individuals in the economy increases, the demand for public goods would increase?

8 One popular voting scheme is rank-order voting, where individuals assign a rank (1, 2, 3) to the possible alternatives; the assigned ranks are then added up, and the alternative with the lowest sum wins. Consider a choice among four alternative ways of spending public funds (a library, a ski slope, a swimming pool, a garbage dump). Can you construct an example in which the outcome (the most preferred alternative) is, say, a library, if the vote is among the first three alternatives, while the outcome is a ski slope if the vote is among all four alternatives? This voting scheme thus violates the principle that the chosen outcome should be independent of irrelevant outcomes (the garbage dump was not chosen in either situation).

9 Median voter theory says that to predict changes in collective decision-making, one should focus on the median voter. Between 1973 and 1993, average incomes in the United States increased, while the income of the median family remained roughly stagnant. (Since then, the median income has increased slightly, but not enough to erase the increased gap of the previous two decades.) How might an economist focusing on median voter behavior and an economist focusing on average incomes differ in their predictions concerning changes in the level and composition of public expenditures?

APPENDIX   NEW PREFERENCE-REVELATION MECHANISMS

This appendix describes a simple procedure which induces individuals to reveal truthfully their demands, provided there is no collusion among individuals. Everyone is asked to give his demand curve for public goods, just as in the Lindahl equilibrium. As before, the equilibrium will be at the intersection of the collective demand (formed by adding vertically the demand curves of each individual) and the supply curve. For simplicity, we assume that the marginal cost of production of the public good is constant, so the supply curve is horizontal. But now, there is a different rule for determining the individual's tax liability.

We first add up the demand curves for *all other* individuals (vertically). The collective demand curve of all *others* intersects the supply curve at G_0 in Figure 7.8. This is what the level of public goods would be if the individual said that he got no value out of the public good. He is told that for each unit beyond G_0 that the government produces, he will have to pay the difference between the marginal costs of production and the collective valuation (demand) of all others. If the equilibrium entailed an output of $G_0 + 1$, the

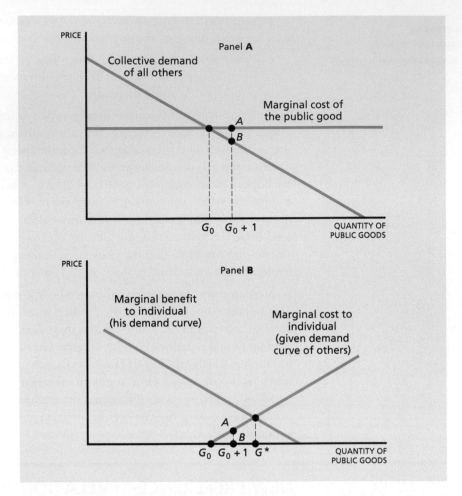

FIGURE 7.8 **New Preference-Revelation Mechanism** Panel A shows the collective demand of all but one individual for the public good (the sum of their marginal valuations) and the marginal cost of production. If the last individual placed no value on the public good, the level of production of the public good would be G_0, where the sum of the marginal valuations equals the marginal cost. As the level of expenditure increases beyond G_0, the last individual is required to pay, for each additional unit, the difference between the collective (marginal) valuation of all others and the marginal cost. Thus, if $G_0 + 1$ is produced, he must pay the amount denoted by AB. Panel B shows, at each level of output, the *marginal* cost that the (last) individual must pay for each extra unit of output. Thus, to have the economy go from producing G_0 to producing $G_0 + 1$ requires that he pay AB. Panel B also shows the last individual's marginal valuation of the public good (his demand curve). The individual's most preferred level of expenditure is where his marginal benefit from increased expenditures (given by his demand curve) exactly equals his marginal cost, that is G^*. If the government sets public expenditures at G^*, the individual will be induced to reveal truthfully his demand.

individual would have to pay *AB*, the distance between the marginal cost curve and the others' collective demand curve.

The individual is in a position to determine the level of public goods simply by his announcement of how much they are valued to him. Clearly, he will try to increase *G* to the point where the marginal cost to him of increasing *G* is equal to his marginal benefit. This can be seen in two alternative ways. First, in Figure 7.8B, we have plotted the marginal cost to the individual from each additional unit of production beyond G_0, given others' demands. Since his marginal cost is the difference between the cost of production and others' demand, the marginal cost of the *G* + 1st unit is equal to *AB*. In panel B we have also drawn the individual's demand curve; the individual will wish point *G** to be chosen, where *his* demand curve intersects *his* marginal cost curve.

We now show that each individual has an incentive to reveal honestly his demand for public goods, and that the equilibrium is Pareto efficient. To see this, we look at the individual's budget constraint. The individual faces a budget constraint as depicted in Figure 7.9. The extra amount that the individual has to give up for each extra unit of public goods beyond G_0 is the marginal cost minus the others' collective demand (marginal valuation). Thus he sets his marginal rate of substitution equal to the marginal cost minus the others' collective demand, point *E* in Figure 7.9. It is clear

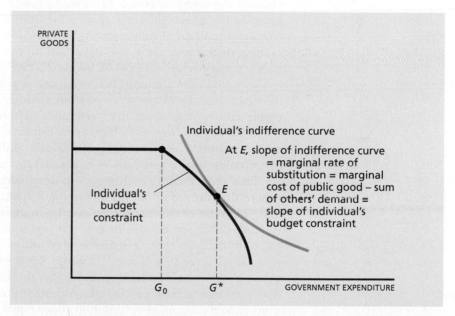

FIGURE 7.9   **Choice of Optimal *G* by Individual** If the individual must pay the difference between marginal cost and others' demands, and others have honestly revealed their demands, the level of public goods will be Pareto efficient. From Figure 7.8, the price the individual has to pay for each increment in public goods expenditure increases. That is why the individual's budget constraint has the shape depicted.

that the individual has no incentive to misrepresent his preferences. If he asked for any level of public goods other than G^* he would be worse off.

Assume now that each individual honestly announces his demand curve. Recall that in constructing the demand curve, the tax price for each individual (the slope of his budget constraint) was set equal to the individual's marginal rate of substitution. Hence, when the demand curves are added vertically, the sum of the marginal rates of substitution are just the sum of the tax prices, and at the Pareto efficient allocation that equals the marginal cost (the marginal rate of transformation):

$$MRS_1 + MRS_2 + \ldots = MC.$$

In other words, each individual's marginal rate of substitution is equal to the marginal cost of the public good minus the sum of the marginal rates of substitution of others (the sum of their tax prices). For instance, for the first individual,

$$MRS_1 = MC - (MRS_2 + MRS_3 + \ldots).$$

But this is exactly the point we described earlier, where the marginal cost to the individual of further increases in government expenditure (which equaled the marginal cost of production minus the sum of others' demand prices at the given quantity) equaled the marginal benefit to the individual (his marginal rate of substitution). We have just shown that by honestly revealing his demand curve, the individual maximizes his own utility, and the allocation of resources to public goods will be Pareto efficient.

In spite of the attention that revelation mechanisms such as the one we have just described have received from economic theorists, there is considerable controversy about their relevance. There are several objections to them, besides their possibly high administrative costs and the fact that they are susceptible to collusion (two individuals could get together, agree to distort what each said, and each be better off).

Like the Lindahl equilibrium we described earlier, these mechanisms ensure that the condition for a Pareto efficient allocation—that the sum of marginal rates of substitution equals the marginal rate of transformation—is satisfied. But some individuals might prefer another, Pareto inefficient allocation that gives them a higher level of utility. Hence, it is not obvious that they would agree to a decision to adopt this mechanism, knowing that they would thereby be disadvantaged. Finally, the mechanisms do not, in general, guarantee a balanced budget. Although the sum of the marginal valuations (marginal rates of substitution) does equal the marginal cost, the total amount paid may well differ from the total costs of the public good.

8 Public Production and Bureaucracy

FOCUS QUESTIONS

1 What is the role of government in production? What is the rationale behind government production of goods and services such as electric utilities and water? Why are these called natural monopolies, and what are alternative ways by which abuses of monopoly power might be prevented?

2 Why is production in the public sector often less efficient than production in the private sector? What are the dangers and limits of privatization?

This chapter is concerned with the role of government in production. Chapter 4 identified several market failures. When there is a market failure, some form of government intervention is required. For instance, Chapter 6 explained why there will be an undersupply of public goods, and described the efficient level of provision of public goods. But government does not have to produce these goods; all it has to do is pay for them. There are many public goods which are privately produced. There are also many private goods which are publicly produced, such as postal services and utilities.

Even though market failures provide a rationale for some form of government intervention, they do not, by themselves, provide a rationale for government production. Yet there are certain areas in which government production dominates, and others in which it is very commonly used. For instance, with few exceptions, governments have not relied on mercenary armies. In most countries governments run the school systems, and in almost all countries, the postal system. And, until a few years ago, in most countries governments ran public utilities such as telecommunications.

Two common threads run through these examples. First, in many of these cases, competition is not viable. Remember, markets result in efficiency *when they are competitive.* Historically, only one firm has provided postal services and one company has provided telephone services. Without government intervention one firm, or a few firms, would be able to exercise market power and exploit consumers. Governments have intervened in two ways. In the past, most governments have chosen to take charge of the industry directly, providing telephone services or electricity. As an alternative to producing the goods itself, however, government can regulate private firms—for example, by controlling their prices—to ensure that they do not exercise their monopoly power. In the last several years, there has been a shift away from public production toward private production with regulation. This process of **privatization** has been particularly marked in Europe and Japan, and in utilities (like gas, electricity, and telecommunications) and transportation (railroads and airlines).

The other common thread in many of the examples of government production is that the public interest has many dimensions. Will the actions of profit-maximizing firms reflect these broader public interests? There is often no simple way government can intervene to ensure that they do. This is why the government does not contract out to private firms to run the national defense system. It does contract out specific activities, such as building ships or airplanes. But it does not say to a private firm, "Run our defense establishment in Europe." Similarly, some believe that schools serve a variety of social functions, which go beyond conveying skills and knowledge. They transmit national values and help form a sense of nationhood. There is concern that a private school system, as effective as it might be in imparting skills, might not work as effectively in advancing this broader set of public objectives.

While limitations of markets (such as limited competition) and concerns about broader objectives provide motivations for public production, there is one compelling argument against public production: Often, governments seem to be inefficient producers. Thus, identifying when government should engage in production and when it should use private firms involves a balancing. To understand better the nature of the balance, we begin by taking a look at government production of private goods, where issues of "social values" enter in a much more limited way. The primary concern is that the private good—electricity, mail service, or telephone service—be provided in the most efficient way at the lowest possible cost to consumers.

NATURAL MONOPOLY: PUBLIC PRODUCTION OF PRIVATE GOODS

The most important market failure that has led to public production of private goods arises when markets are not competitive. This provides at least part of the explanation for government production in postal services, telecommunications, water, harbors, electricity. As we saw in Chapter 4, a common reason why markets may not be competitive is the existence of increasing returns to scale; that is, the average costs of production decline as the level of production increases. In that case, economic efficiency requires that there be a limited number of firms. Industries where increasing returns are so significant that only one firm should operate in any region are referred to as **natural monopolies.**

Water is a good example. The major cost associated with delivering water is the network of pipes. Once pipes have been installed, the additional costs of supplying water to one extra user are relatively insignificant. It would clearly be inefficient to have two networks of pipes, side by side, one delivering to one home, the next to a neighbor's. The same is true of electricity, cable TV, and natural gas.

THE BASIC ECONOMICS OF NATURAL MONOPOLY

The average cost curve and the demand curve for a natural monopoly are represented in Figure 8.1. Since the average costs of production decline as the level of production increases, it is efficient to have only one firm. In the case depicted, there is a whole range of viable outputs (where the firm makes a profit). The maximum viable output (without subsidies) is Q_1, where the demand curve intersects the average cost curve.

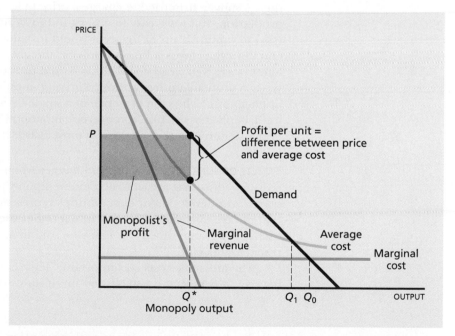

FIGURE 8.1   **Natural Monopoly** With no sunk costs and potential entry, a natural monopolist would operate at Q_1, the lowest price consistent with at least breaking even. With sunk costs, the price will be higher. The monopolist unconcerned with the threat of entry operates at Q^*, where marginal revenue equals marginal cost.

In these situations, we cannot rely on the kinds of competitive forces that we discussed earlier to ensure that the industry operates at the efficient level. Efficiency requires that price equal marginal cost (at quantity Q_0). But if the firm charges a price equal to marginal cost, it will suffer a loss, since marginal cost is lower than average cost for industries with declining average cost.

One common recommendation in this situation is for the government to provide a subsidy to the industry and insist that the firm charge a price equal to the marginal cost. This policy ignores, however, the question of how the revenues required to pay the subsidy are to be raised; in particular, it assumes that there are no costs associated with raising this revenue. Moreover, it assumes that the government knows the magnitude of the subsidy that will enable the firm to be viable.

In practice, most governments have attempted to make such industries pay for themselves. (They may also be concerned with the equity of making general taxpayers pay to subsidize a private good that is enjoyed by only a portion of the population, or enjoyed by different individuals to different extents.) Thus they have insisted on government-managed natural monopolies operating at the intersection of their demand curves and their average cost curves (Q_1 in the figure). This is called the **zero profit point.**

The zero profit point is precisely the point where natural monopolies may operate, under the assumption that there is effective potential competition. Assume a firm tried to charge a price that exceeded the average cost of production. If it were easy to enter (and exit) from an industry, a firm that tried to capture a profit for itself would instantaneously be threatened with entry by other firms willing to provide the given service or commodity at a lower price. New firms could come in and provide the services or commodities at a profitable price, without worrying unduly about the reactions of the original firm.[1] Thus the presence of a single firm in an industry does not, in itself, imply that the firm can exercise monopoly power. So long as there are potential entrants, that single firm must charge a price equal to average cost.

EFFECTS OF SUNK COSTS All of this changes when there are **sunk costs.** Sunk costs are costs that are not recoverable upon the exit of the firm. Most research and development expenditures represent sunk costs. But a building that can be converted costlessly into another use does not represent a sunk cost. An airplane, which can easily be sold to another airline, does not represent a sunk cost.

Why are sunk costs so important? They create an essential asymmetry between a firm that is established in an industry, and one that is not. The

---

[1] In the recent literature on industrial organization, markets with decreasing average costs but no sunk costs, in which price is maintained at a level equal to average costs, are referred to as *contestable.* See W. J. Baumol, J. Panzar, and R. Willig, *Contestable Markets and the Theory of Industrial Organization* (New York: Harcourt Brace Jovanovich, 1982). For a simple exposition of the theory of contestable markets, see W. J. Baumol, "Contestable Markets: An Uprising in the Theory of Industry Structure," *American Economic Review* 72 (1982): 1–15.

potential entrant is not in the same position as the firm already in the industry, for the firm already in the industry has expended funds that it cannot recover. In deciding whether to enter, a firm does not look at the level of current profits and prices, but at what prices and profits will be *after* entry. Even if prices currently are considerably above average costs (so profits are large), a potential entrant may well believe that the firm already in the industry will respond to entry not by exiting the industry but by lowering its price; at the lower price, entry no longer is profitable. Moreover, when sunk costs are significant, an entrant worries that it will not be able to recover all the expenditures it makes upon entry. Thus, it will be reluctant to gamble that the current firm will either exit or leave its prices at their currently high levels. Accordingly, sunk costs act as a barrier to entry and allow the established firm a degree of monopoly power that it could not exercise otherwise.

Since virtually all natural monopolies entail important sunk costs, the government cannot simply rely on the threat of potential competition. The fact that a single firm controls consumers' water or electricity gives rise to concern: the monopolist is in a position to exploit its consumers. The monopolist who is unconcerned about entry by other firms charges a price that maximizes its profits, the price where the marginal revenue it gets from selling an additional unit is equal to the marginal costs (output Q^* in Figure 8.1). Its profit per unit of output is the difference between the price it charges and the average costs.

MULTIPRODUCT NATURAL MONOPOLIES So far, we have focused on a natural monopoly producing a single commodity. If the industry is not to be subsidized, it must charge a price in excess of marginal cost.

On what principle should prices be set when a natural monopoly produces several commodities? Prices, on average, will still need to exceed marginal cost, if the firm is to break even. Should, for instance, the ratio of the price to marginal cost be the same for all the firm's products? Should higher charges on some services be used to subsidize other services?

For example, the U.S. Postal Service imposes uniform charges for delivering mail, even though the marginal cost of delivering mail to a rural household in North Dakota may be much higher than the cost of delivering a letter in Chicago. If the post office is to break even, there must be a **cross-subsidy,** a subsidy from one user (product) to another user (product).

The issue is obviously very political; the elimination of cross-subsidies will affect some groups adversely. When pricing decisions are made politically, these groups will attempt to persuade those in charge to lower the prices to them, implicitly raising prices to others.

The analysis of pricing decisions involves both efficiency and distributional considerations. Economists have been particularly concerned with the efficiency costs of politically determined pricing policies. When prices are raised on some service, the consumption of that service declines, but a 1 percent price increase reduces demand more for some goods than for other goods. Goods for which demand is more sensitive to price increases are said to be **price elastic.** Figure 8.2A shows an inelastic demand curve, for which a change in price does not result in a very large change in consumption,

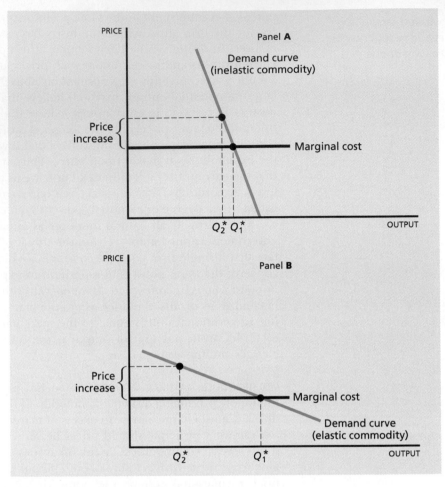

FIGURE 8.2   **Pricing in a Multi-Commodity Natural Monopoly** (A) With an inelastic demand, an increase in the price above marginal cost results in a relatively small decline in output. (B) With an elastic demand, an increase in price above marginal cost results in a large decline in output.

while in Figure 8.2B the demand is very elastic; a change in price results in a large change in consumption.

If a natural monopoly is to break even (without government subsidies), it obviously must charge a price in excess of marginal cost. If the government increased price above marginal cost by the same percentage for all commodities, clearly consumption of goods with elastic demand would be reduced by more than consumption of goods with inelastic demand. Under some circumstances it can be shown to be desirable to charge prices such that consumption of every good is reduced by the same percentage (from what it would be if price equaled marginal cost). If the government wishes to do this, it should increase the price (above marginal cost) more for commodities whose demand is inelastic than for commodities whose demand is elastic.[2]

REGULATION AND
TAXATION (SUBSIDIES)
When there is a natural monopoly with sunk costs, there is a danger that the monopolist will take advantage of its position and charge a high price. One way of addressing this concern, as we have seen, is for government to take over production. But there has been increasing concern that governments do not do a good job at managing production. Rather than attempting to produce the good itself, the government may leave production to the private sector, but regulate prices to ensure that the firm does not take advantage of its monopoly position. Moreover, it can use subsidies to encourage the firm to provide services that might not be profitable privately but are viewed as socially desirable, such as providing postal service to rural areas.

Those who advocate **regulation** and subsidies (or taxes) as remedies for market failures believe that they have three major advantages over public ownership. First, they allow for a more consistent and efficient national policy. Assume that it is desirable to locate firms in some area with high unemployment. Because of this, government-run firms are often told to locate in such areas. It is, however, better to provide a general subsidy, with those firms for whom the move has the least cost taking advantage of the subsidy, than to simply impose the burden on those firms that happen to be government run.

Second, the utilization of tax and subsidy schemes allows a clearer estimate of the costs associated with pursuing a given objective. It may be desirable to reduce the level of pollution, but how much is it worth? It may be desirable to locate a firm in an area where there is high unemployment, but

---

[2] This policy will minimize the deadweight loss resulting from price exceeding marginal cost. The problem of how to set prices for a multi-commodity public monopoly was first solved in 1956 by Marcel Boiteux, who served as the director of Electricité de France, the government agency in France responsible for producing electricity. For an English translation, see "On the Management of Public Monopolies Subject to Budgetary Constraints," *Journal of Economic Theory* 3 (1971): 219–40. This question of the determination of prices for different commodities turns out to be equivalent to a similar question posed some twenty-five years earlier by the great British economist Frank Ramsey: If the government must raise a given amount of revenue by distortionary taxation, how should it raise the revenue? Should it, for instance, charge a uniform tax on all commodities, so that the ratio of the price to marginal cost would be the same for all commodities? Would there then be no relative distortions? Ramsey showed that, as plausible as that might seem, a uniform tax was not the correct answer; it was preferable to charge a higher tax on a commodity whose demand was inelastic. Both Ramsey and Boiteux ignored the distributional issues that are central to most of the political debate. These were introduced into the analysis by M. Feldstein, "Distributional Equity and the Optimal Structure of Public Prices," *American Economic Review* 62 (1973): 32–36; and (in the context of taxation) by P. Diamond and J. Mirrlees, "Optimal Taxation and Public Production," *American Economic Review* 61 (1971): 261–78, and A. B. Atkinson and J. E. Stiglitz, "The Structure of Indirect Taxation and Economic Efficiency," *Journal of Public Economics* (1972): 97–119 and "The Design of Tax Structure: Direct versus Indirect Taxation," *Journal of Public Economics* 6 (1976): 55–75. See also below, Chapter 20.

how much is it worth? It is often difficult to ascertain the additional costs of government enterprises' pursuing alternative objectives; providing direct government subsidies brings the costs more into the open and thus allows a more rational decision concerning whether the costs are worth the benefits.

Third, there is a widespread belief that incentives for efficiency are greater with private firms, even with regulation.

In the case of natural monopolies, the United States has long relied on regulation (though there is some government production, particularly of hydroelectric power and water), in contrast to Europe, which until recently relied on government ownership. Regulation is not without its problems: there are significant costs to administering the regulations, and almost any regulatory scheme gives rise to distortions (that is, deviations in their behavior from what efficient, competitive firms would do), as private firms try to maximize their profits, given the regulatory rules. Thus, if regulations allow a particular return on capital, there may be an incentive to invest too heavily in capital; if they allow more generous depreciation allowances for one type of capital than another, this too may distort the investment decisions. In spite of these problems, beginning in the 1970s and 1980s there was a major movement throughout the world toward privatization, that is, the selling off of government-owned enterprises, and subjecting them to regulation. The advantages of gains in efficiency overwhelmed any disadvantages associated with regulation.

NO GOVERNMENT INTERVENTION

Some economists, including Harold Demsetz of the University of California at Los Angeles and the late George Stigler of the University of Chicago, question whether it might be better in most cases to just let the private sector alone, even with natural monopoly. Monopolists are efficient; the only problem with them is that they charge too high a price, and accordingly produce too little. But Arnold Harberger, in a famous calculation, estimated that the loss from monopoly pricing is relatively small (less than 3 percent of the value of output). Monopolies reduce production relative to the efficient level; but the resources not used by the monopolist go elsewhere in the economy. The loss is the difference in the marginal values of the two uses. The cumulative loss in efficiency from either regulation[3] or government production, these economists believe, may be much greater.

---

[3] Stigler has argued, further, that regulation may be ineffective, as the regulated group "captures" the regulators, partly because the only people who are well informed on the highly technical matters of regulation are the regulated parties; and partly because the regulators often get lucrative jobs in the regulated industry after they leave their regulatory positions.

Though the regulations may be ineffective in limiting the regulated entity's profit, the regulations may still be highly distortionary. In recent years, there have been problems on the other side: elected regulators may follow populist policies, driving down prices to the point that the utility has little incentive to invest further.

George J. Stigler, "Free Riders and Collective Action: An Appendix to Theories of Economic Regulation," *Bell Journal of Economics and Management Science* 5, autumn 1974, pp. 359–65; and "The Theory of Economic Regulation," *Bell Journal of Economics and Management Science* 2, spring 1971, pp. 3–21.

GOVERNMENT PRODUCTION OF PRIVATE GOODS

Examples:	Postal Service, utilities
Rationale:	Market failure—lack of competition associated with natural monopoly
Problems:	Inefficiencies associated with government production
	Cross-subsidization issues
	Intervention of political concerns
Alternatives:	Regulation
	Ignoring problem (all known cures worse than disease)
Current trends:	Privatization
	Focusing government involvement on natural-monopoly core, encouraging competition where feasible

Most economists remain skeptical. They see larger losses from natural monopolies, partly because managers in industries not subject to competition (and not subject to the scrutiny of regulators) have a tendency to become lax, and partly because, in the absence of competition, incentives to innovate may be limited.

Whether for these or for other reasons, popular support for *eliminating* regulations of natural monopolies remains limited. But there remains considerable interest in *narrowing* the scope of regulation. It is now recognized that there is more scope for competition than had been previously realized—for instance, several firms now provide long-distance telephone service, and there is a multitude of generators of electricity. There is still some natural monopoly—only a single firm provides local telephone service or electricity to most homes. Today, regulation is focused on ensuring that there is competition where competition is viable, and that those parts of the system where

NATURAL MONOPOLY

- Efficient production entails only a single firm.
- Market equilibrium will be characterized by a lack of competition.
- Provides rationale for government production or regulation.

NATIONAL PERFORMANCE REVIEW

The problems of government inefficiency, particularly arising out of procurement and personnel policies, were the subject of a major review under the direction of Vice President Albert Gore. A report was issued in September 1993. The basic theme was that procurement and personnel policies had to be revised substantially in the process of *reinventing government.* The report emphasized greater reliance on performance measures, greater use of market incentives, and greater use of commercial procurement practices:

> Our government, built around a complex cluster of monopolies, insulates both managers and workers from the power of incentives. We must force our government to put the customer first by injecting the dynamics of the marketplace. The best way to deal with monopoly is to expose it to competition.

Elsewhere, the report argued that "competition is the one force that gives public agencies no choice but to improve."

Competition is enough to force the private sector constantly to "reinvent" itself, to look for better and more efficient ways of doing what it does. But it is political pressures—including the pressure of a

there is a natural monopoly do not abuse their monopoly power, either by leveraging their monopoly power to gain further control or by raising prices to make high rates of return. Major reforms in telecommunications and in electricity regulation in 1996 reflected these changed perspectives.

COMPARISON OF EFFICIENCY IN THE PUBLIC AND PRIVATE SECTORS

Anyone who follows the news media has encountered shocking stories of government inefficiency, often citing misguided procurement policies featuring $1000 toilet seats, $400 hammers, and the like. Similar accounts have been issued from the private sector, such as the quest of cigarette companies to create a smokeless, safe cigarette. While stories of government inefficiency draw enormous attention, and have helped create an image of inefficient government, there is some systematic evidence that reinforces the anecdotal evidence. Comparisons of costs of government and private firms engaged in similar activities tend to show substantially lower costs for private firms, whether in housing, garbage collection, bus transportation, payroll processing, or environmental cleanups.

Even so, hard evidence on government inefficiency is difficult to come by. For the most part, the government and the private sector do not pro-

huge government deficit—that provide the incentive to reinvent government. And it is often political pressure from special interest groups that prevents the process of reinvention from succeeding. There are many examples of this. For over a hundred years, government has been responsible for meat inspection. Americans want to know that the meat that they are eating is safe. But when the system of government inspectors was established after Upton Sinclair's graphic description of Chicago's stockyards,* all that was available was a system of visual inspection: did the meat look rotten? Today, we know that most problems arise from microbes that are invisible to the eye, and there are advanced ways of both detecting and dealing with these microbes. Yet, despite the existence of systems which could do a better job at lower costs—and of private firms ready and able to perform these tasks—the meat inspectors' union worries that its workers will lose their jobs, and politicians worry that the union will mount a scare campaign—so the inefficient system of visual inspection survives.

*Upton Sinclair, *The Jungle* (New York: Doubleday, Page & Company, 1906).

duce the same commodities, so direct comparisons are hard to make. When they do produce similar commodities—such as education—it is hard to measure both the inputs (with education, the quality of students) and the outputs (tests adequately capture only some dimensions of student achievement; creativity and citizenship values, both of which schools strive to promote, are typically left out).

Although the weight of the available evidence, both in the United States and abroad, suggests that government enterprises are less efficient than their private counterparts, some evidence shows that this need not be the case. The French-run public enterprises have long been held up as models of efficiency. For instance, the French electricity company developed a single design of a nuclear power plant, which they replicated throughout the country, pushing costs significantly below those associated with American nuclear power plants, where there used to be many different designs. Within the United States, state-run liquor stores charge prices that are 4 to 11 percent lower than those charged by private retailers.[4] While administrative costs of the Social Security Administration are less than 1 percent of the ben-

[4] Sam Peltzman, "Pricing in Public and Private Enterprises: Electric Utilities in the United States," *Journal of Law and Economics* 14, no. 1 (April 1971): 109–47. This article discusses both electric utilities and liquor stores.

efits paid, private insurance companies frequently spend as much as 30 to 40 percent of the amount provided in benefits in administrative and sales costs.

Admittedly, it is difficult to measure the productivity of many government workers, those who are engaged in administrative activity; there is no good measure of their output. But there are some indirect indicators. Since 1992, the number of government public employees in the United States has been brought down dramatically, to the level of the early 1960s, and as a percentage of the civilian labor force, to a level comparable to the early 1930s; in the same period, there has been a huge increase in government service and an increase in the populations served—suggesting an increase in productivity.[5]

The Postal Service provides an example in the United States of how difficult it is to draw general conclusions. In areas of direct competition, such as overnight mail and parcel post, the post office has not fared well in recent decades. On the other hand, in its main line of business, the post office has shown remarkable increases in productivity in the last twenty years—three times the pace of business sector productivity.

Of all the comparative productivity studies, one of the most telling was that between private and public railroads in Canada. One of the two major rail systems is private, the other public. The study concluded that there was no significant difference in the efficiency of the two systems. Evidently, competition between the two provides strong incentives for efficiency in both.[6]

SOURCES OF INEFFICIENCY IN THE PUBLIC SECTOR

There are several reasons why we might expect public enterprises to be systematically less efficient than private enterprises. These have to do with incentives and restrictions at both the individual and organizational levels.

ORGANIZATIONAL
DIFFERENCES

ORGANIZATIONAL INCENTIVES Because public enterprises are not driven by the profit motive, they have little incentive to maximize productivity. Indeed, they are often driven by political concerns—such as providing jobs, especially in regions where there is an unemployment problem—which work against productivity. In some countries, public enterprises may not even worry about making a loss, since they cannot go bankrupt, and any losses are made up out of government revenues. They face, in other words, a **soft**

---

[5] Prior to the 1990s, productivity growth in the government may also have been greater than in the private sector. See Nancy Hayward and George Kuper's detailed study over the period of 1967 to 1978, "The National Economy and Productivity in Government," *Public Administration Review* 38 (1978); and U.S. Office of Personnel Management, *Measuring Federal Productivity*, February 1980.

[6] D. W. Daves and L. R. Christensen, "The Relative Efficiency of Public and Private Firms in a Competitive Environment: The Case of Canadian Railroads," *Journal of Political Economy* 88 (1980): 958–76.

budget constraint. And they often operate in an environment with limited competition.

PERSONNEL RESTRICTIONS Worry that public employees might abuse their position and power—to the detriment of taxpayers who might have to pay more for the services than they should—has resulted in the imposition of numerous constraints. Private firms can hire whomever they like and pay whatever salaries they like; the owners suffer if a firm pays someone more than their worth. But the taxpayer suffers if a government agency pays someone more than their worth. We find it particularly objectionable when a public official does not act fairly; equity is an essential part of public trust. Thus, we have imposed strong *civil service* rules, which are designed to ensure that the government hires and promotes the most qualified individuals and that their pay is appropriate. But while such rules serve an important function, they introduce rigidities: it is difficult for a government agency to fire an incompetent worker, and this attenuates incentives. It is difficult for the government to compete with private companies for the best brains; these often command a high wage premium, well beyond the civil service scales for someone with the same qualifications.

PROCUREMENT RESTRICTIONS Similarly, to avoid abuses in the government's purchase of billions of dollars of goods and services every year, procedures have been designed to ensure that the government is not taken for a ride, but their effect is often to raise costs. In buying a jet engine, these procedures reportedly result in cost increases of as much as one-third. In many areas, the government insists on competitive bidding. But to do this, the government must specify in minute detail what it is purchasing. A T-shirt may take thirty pages of fine print, detailing the quality of thread, the shape, and so on. But since the specifications required by the government typically differ in several ways from those the T-shirt company makes for the private market, firms will have to have separate production runs to meet the government specifications. Relatively few companies will find complying with all the government regulations worthwhile; competition will thus be restricted, and the prices bid will reflect these high costs of complying with the government specifications and regulations. As a result, the government may end up paying substantially more than it would have to pay for comparable products off-the-shelf. Off-the-shelf purchasing—a well-informed consumer using the discipline of the market combined with product testing—may save considerable money. Procurement reform enacted in 1994 along these lines has saved billions of dollars.[7]

---

[7] For instance, within two years of the reform's passage, the Defense Department reported saving $4.7 billion from the new procurement programs. (U.S. Department of Defense, "Defense Acquisition Pilot Programs Forecast Cost/Schedule Savings of Up to 50 Percent from Acquisition Reform," News Release No. 138–96, March 14, 1996.)

BUDGETING RESTRICTIONS Another way government agencies differ from private firms is in budgeting, particularly in making long-term investments. It took the airlines many years and hundreds of millions of dollars to develop their airline reservation systems; but they could easily budget for what they knew was an important capital expenditure. The air traffic control system—which makes sure that airplanes do not crash into each other—is run by the Federal Aviation Administration. To keep up with the immense increase in air traffic, and to update the controllers' obsolete computers, will require investments in the billions of dollars. But Congress only makes appropriations on an annual basis, and given the tight budgetary situation, it never appropriates enough to fund fully the rapid modernization. It does not look at the matter as a business would, assessing the return on the investment. The result has been a near disaster: computers that still use vacuum tubes, which have to be purchased in Poland since they are no longer made in the United States, and a system stretched to its limits.

**INDIVIDUAL
DIFFERENCES**

Many of these organizational differences have immediate impacts on individuals. Because individuals cannot be fired, and cannot be rewarded for good performance with the kinds of bonuses that private firms pay, there are neither the carrots nor the sticks to provide as strong individual incentives. Because public agencies have less incentive for efficiency or for ensuring that they are attentive to their "customers," what powers to provide incentives they do have often are not directed at those objectives, but rather at more political goals.

There is a whole set of traits that are normally associated with **bureaucratic behavior.** Bureaucrats may not receive larger paychecks or bigger dividends from increased efficiency, but they often seem to act as if they enjoy the power and prestige associated with being in charge of a larger organization. They thus may try to maximize the size of their bureaucracy; if the demand curve for their services has less than unitary elasticity, by reducing efficiency—increasing the price per unit service provided—they actually can increase total expenditures on their agency, and its size. (See Figure 8.3.) What stops bureaucrats from doing this is competition—competition between bureaucracies. W. A. Niskanen, a member of the Council of Economic Advisers in the Reagan administration and currently president of the Cato Institute, a conservative think tank, has argued that the increasing centralization of government bureaucracies—in the attempt to ensure that two government agencies do not perform duplicative functions—while intended to enhance efficiency, has reduced competition, thereby giving bureaucrats more scope to pursue their interests at the expense of efficiency and the public interest.

The problem to which Niskanen called attention—that government bureaucrats may act in their own interests, and not necessarily in the interests of the citizens whom they are supposed to serve—is an example of a general class of problems called **principal-agent problems.** The principal-agent problem is simply the familiar problem of how one person gets another to do what he wants. Here, the problem is, how do citizens (the "principals") get their employees, public servants (the agents), to act in their interests?

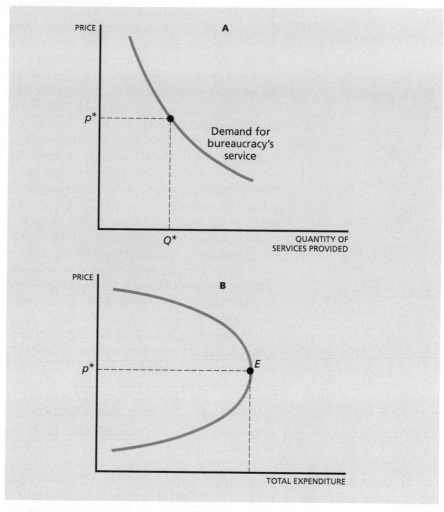

FIGURE 8.3 **Maximizing a Bureaucracy's Size** Panel A shows a demand curve for a bureaucracy's service. As the price of the service (cost per unit) declines, the quantity of services demanded increases. The bureaucrat can calculate the total expenditures—price times quantity—at each level of price (panel B). In the absence of competition, the bureaucrat can choose the price—and he will choose the price which maximizes total expenditures (the size of his bureaucracy). At p^*, expenditures are maximized.

(The analogous problem in the private sector is, how do shareholders (the principals) get their employees, the managers and workers in the firms they own (the agents), to act in the shareholders' interests?)

Principal-agent problems arise in all organizations, whether public or private. Managers always face the problem of ensuring that their employees' behavior conforms with their wishes; and unless the firm is owned by managers, the owners always have a problem in ensuring that managers act in their interests. The problems of controlling employees are particularly acute in large organizations, and the problem of controlling managers is perhaps as serious in a large corporation where there is no large shareholder as it is in a government enterprise. British Petroleum, when it was government owned, acted little differently from any other large oil company, with diffuse ownership, such as Texaco (though in some ways, both may have acted differently from a large oil company controlled by a single family, such as Getty). What difference does it make if there are private shareholders or if there is a single shareholder, the government? Some contend that managers of public enterprises may behave in much the same way that managers of large private enterprises do. In both cases, managers have a large amount of discretion, allowing them to pursue their own interests, often at the expense of the public interest (in the case of public enterprises) or shareholder interests (in the case of private enterprises). Recent payoffs, called "green-mail," out of the corporate purse to those attempting to take over a firm have confirmed these views; such payments, as well as the provisions that management has attempted to put into their corporate charters making takeovers more difficult, have preserved management's prerogatives, but at the shareholders' expense.

In large organizations, principal-agent problems are never fully resolved. Incentive structures—rewards for "good" performance (often financial rewards) and punishments for "bad" performance (being fired)—represent the most effective ways of aligning incentives. Though both public and private sectors face problems in designing incentives that fully resolve agency problems, these problems seem more formidable within the public sector, partly because of restrictions on how public agencies can compensate their employees.

BUREAUCRATIC PROCEDURES AND RISK AVERSION

Bureaucrats' desire to increase the size of their budget seems to provide an explanation of many aspects of bureaucratic behavior. Other aspects of bureaucratic behavior can best be explained by another important aspect of the incentives bureaucrats are given. Though bureaucrats' pay may not be closely and directly related to their performance, in the long run their promotion is at least partially dependent on observed performance.

A bureaucrat can absolve herself of responsibility for mistakes by following certain bureaucratic procedures that ensure that all of her actions are reviewed by others. Although this process of group decision-making also reduces the claims the individual can make for any success, bureaucrats seem willing to make this trade-off. We say they are **risk averse.** This is what gives rise, in part, to the nature of bureaucracies: everything must pass through the appropriate channels (red tape).

Two other factors contribute to the prevalence of bureaucratic procedures. First, many of the costs associated with engaging in risk-averse activities are not borne by bureaucrats themselves. Rather, they are borne by society as a whole, through the taxes required to pay the extra personnel. Further costs are imposed on those dealing with the bureaucracy in the

EXPLANATIONS OF INEFFICIENCY IN THE PUBLIC SECTOR

Organizational differences

• Soft budget constraint (government subsidies, no bankruptcy)

• Role of political concerns

• Absence of competition

• Additional restrictions

On personnel (civil service—hard to fire, pay competitive wages)

On procurement

On budgeting (hard to do long-term budgeting required for large capital investments)

Individual differences

• Absence of incentive pay, difficulty of firing reduces incentives (removes carrots and sticks)

• Principal-agent problems

Pursuit of bureaucratic objectives—maximizing size of organization

Excessively high levels of risk aversion—leading to a focus on following procedures (red tape)

form of delays, paperwork, and so on. (Indeed, there are those who claim that bureaucrats may actually enjoy the bureaucratic process.)[8]

Second, the prevalence of set routines that must be followed entailing the approval of any proposal by several different individuals has a positive aspect as well; it is not just a consequence of bureaucrats' pursuing their own self-interest. It follows naturally from the fiduciary relationship between government bureaucrats and the funds they allocate. That is, government bureaucrats are not spending their own money; they are spending public resources. It is generally accepted that an individual should have more discretion—should take greater care—in spending the money of others than in spending his own money. Again, what is implied by taking greater care is that certain routines are followed; these ensure that the funds are spent not according to the whim of any single individual. They also reduce the possibility of corruption. Since many individuals must give approval, it is usually

---

[8] There are alternative, more psychologically or sociologically based theories of why bureaucrats behave bureaucratically.

not within the power of any individual to give a contract at an above-market price and thus receive a kickback.

Two examples of bureaucratic routines are the use of cost-benefit analyses and environmental impact statements. The intent behind such procedures is clear. On the other hand, because the data on which an assessment can be firmly established are rarely available, the studies often become pro forma exercises with predictable outcomes. Occasionally they serve as the basis for attempts by opponents of a project to delay the project and thereby to increase the costs to the point where the project is no longer economically feasible. There is a social loss in these delaying practices.

CORPORATIZATION

The last section explored a number of the reasons why government enterprises are often less efficient than their public counterparts. We have seen that a host of regulations and restrictions, on hiring and promotion, on procurement, and on budgeting for long-term investment—for all of which there may be good reasons—inhibit efficiency. But enterprises do not have to be turned over to the private sector—privatized—to address these concerns. The United States and other countries have experimented with forms of organization that lie between conventional public agencies and private companies, including **government corporations** and **performance-based organizations.**

There are many examples of government corporations: the Postal Service, the Tennessee Valley Authority (the nation's largest producer of electricity), the Saint Lawrence Seaway, and until 1998, the U.S. Enrichment Corporation (USEC), which converts natural uranium into enriched uranium used in nuclear reactors and atomic bombs, are among the most widely known. These corporations are owned by the U.S. government, so typically their boards of directors and president are appointed by the President; but they are intended to be nonpolitical, with a term of office that does not necessarily coincide with that of the President. Like ordinary firms, they raise their revenues by selling their products or services. Most importantly, they are freed from most of the restrictions imposed on government agencies—they can borrow and lend, and they have considerable discretion in pay (the president of USEC receives a higher salary than the President of the United States) and procurement. By and large, they act much like private corporations.

Typically, before a government enterprise is privatized, it goes through the intermediate stage of **corporatization.** Most of the efficiency gains seem to occur in this stage, though there is controversy about why. Some argue that the freedom from government personnel, procurement, and budget restrictions is all that is required; under corporatization, effective incentive schemes can be put into place. Others argue that without the profit motive—derived from private ownership—these gains could not be sustained; often the managers of government enterprises do well after privatization, becoming highly paid executives in the new private company and/or receiving hefty shares or options in the newly privatized company—and it is these economic returns which drive them to improve efficiency during the corporatization stage.

Performance-based organizations (PBOs) are government agencies that remain more firmly within the public sector, but in which agency officials are rewarded on the basis of performance. In the United Kingdom the Patent Office became a PBO, and a similar proposal has been made in the United States.

Many countries are involved in a lively debate: When should a government agency be privatized, corporatized, or converted into a PBO? In all three cases, the agency's output has to be measurable. In the case of privatization or corporatization, the agency has to produce a product which can be sold, or there at least has to be a source of revenue related to its activities. The TVA sells electricity; the Postal Service, stamps. Many countries have privatized their air traffic control systems, and the Clinton administration proposed corporatizing it; it could easily be financed either through a ticket tax or through landing or takeoff fees.

Why not privatize everything, or at least everything for which a charge could be imposed? The answer is that there are public objectives that may not be well addressed by a private firm, and that cannot be well addressed through regulation. One might not want a profit-maximizing firm in the business of producing enriched uranium which could be used to make atomic bombs—though curiously, the Bush administration proposed doing precisely that, and the Clinton administration actually did it in 1998. If the Postal Service were privatized, concern would arise that it might raise prices in an attempt to exercise its monopoly power and that it might not serve rural areas as well. (While the government might require that it serve those areas, stipulating how it should do so, and then monitoring the quality of the service, might be difficult.)

Issues of public interest are often complex, hard to measure, and difficult to reflect adequately in the design of performance-based organizations. One wants the Patent Office to be not only fast, but accurate; that is, one does not want it to deny patents that should be granted, or to grant patents that will be overturned by the courts. Unfortunately, the appeal process often takes years, and accordingly, it may take years to know how good a job the Patent Office has done. Moreover, there are fundamental *public* issues associated with, for instance, the scope of a patent: Should a patent for a new genetically altered tomato be limited to that tomato breed, or to all genetically altered tomatoes, or to all genetically altered plants? Typically, such decisions are made now on a case-by-case basis. There is concern that if the Patent Office became a performance-based organization, it might not make these decisions in a way which best reflected the national interest.

More recently, privatization has been pushed even further. Some states already have privatized prisons (see box), and Texas has proposed privatizing the administration of welfare programs. The federal government said that Texas could not do so, on the grounds that the private welfare agency might have an incentive to deny benefits to those who were really eligible for benefits. Critics of the federal government's decision argue that an in-

PRIVATIZING PRISONS

Prisons may seem among the least likely candidates for privatization. After all, a for-profit company would have every incentive to reduce services, such as the quality of food, to the bare minimum; the "customers" might complain, but they really have nowhere else to go. And indeed, though private prisons are not new—dating back to colonial times—they have had a somewhat spotty history. But recently, they have been gaining favor, so that by 1996 almost 48,500 prisoners were in prisons owned or managed by private companies.

Remarkably, many of the prisons have earned high marks both from prisoners and from those responsible for overseeing their function: not only are costs down, but services, such as educational training and drug treatment programs, are improved. The leading corporation,

centive scheme could be found which would address these concerns—for instance, by imposing a sufficiently large fine on the private welfare agency in those instances where its denial of benefits was overturned upon appeal.

A GROWING CONSENSUS ON GOVERNMENT'S ROLE IN PRODUCTION

The role of the government in production will remain an area of active debate. Today, there is growing consensus that government should not be involved in the production of ordinary private goods. And there is a consensus that government should not privatize national defense (though the United States did hire mercenaries during the Revolutionary War). Even in these areas, however, government can purchase many goods and services from private contractors. While it has long purchased airplanes and tanks, it is turning increasingly to private firms for housing and other services.

Some of the arguments against further privatization are political: opponents of privatizing the TVA and the other government hydroelectric projects fear that prices would rise to market level; a hidden subsidy would be eliminated. Opposition to privatizing—or even corporatizing—the air traffic control system arises from owners of corporate jets and from general aviation, which currently receive these services without paying their fair share of the costs—they receive a subsidy estimated at as much as $2 billion a year.

But in other cases, there is real concern that with privatization, the broader range of public objectives would not be pursued. And it is in this arena that the debate is likely to be most lively: Should prisons, welfare agencies, schools, or the production of the material to make nuclear bombs be privatized? Or can most of the gains in efficiency be achieved simply by corporatizing, rewarding performance, and encouraging public agencies to think about those they serve as customers and clients?

Corrections Corporation of America, has done this partly by "reinventing" prisons—for instance, redesigning them so that fewer guards can supervise more people. They have also recognized that with less tension in the prison, not only are prisoners better off, but fewer guards are required, and absenteeism rates are far lower than in conventional prisons. The 1994 Crime Bill provides billions of dollars for additional prison construction, and it is anticipated that many of these prisons will be either privately owned or managed.

SOURCE: Charles Thomas, Dianne Bolinger, and John Badalamenti, "Private Adult Correctional Facility Census," Private Corrections Project, Center for Studies in Criminology and Law, University of Florida, March 1997, p. iv.

To what extent can government, by imitating the private sector—for instance, by making more extensive use of incentive pay—achieve comparable efficiencies? And to what extent are observed inefficiencies in the public sector an inherent consequence of the nature of what the public sector does? It is, for instance, difficult to measure performance in many areas of administrative work; certainly, one does not want to measure performance

ALTERNATIVE ORGANIZATIONAL FORMS

Private firms

Government corporations

Performance-based organizations

Conventional government agencies

Criteria for privatization:

    Source of revenue (related to its functions)

    Possible to deal with "externalities" and other public interest issues (such as safety, abuse of monopoly power) in satisfactory manner, such as through regulation

Criteria for performance-based organization:

    Possible to measure performance

    Possible to deal with public interest issues in satisfactory manner

by the number of pages of paper produced or processed! In many areas, there cannot be competition, or competition might be feasible but undesirable. Do we want two competing armed forces? Two competing judicial systems? To be sure, there are instances where competition can be introduced, especially where the government has maintained a state monopoly—the examples in broadcasting, in telephone service, in health, and in education have been promising. But even after competition is introduced, there remain vexing questions: How do we ensure that the public and private firms are on a level playing field, that there are not hidden subsidies in the government's operation?

While a consensus has emerged that private firms should have an expanded role in production—and that the government's role should be contracted—in the future the locus of controversy is likely to be in those areas, such as prisons, schools, and welfare services, once thought to be part of the central provenance of government.

REVIEW AND PRACTICE

SUMMARY

1   In the United States, the government has played an important role in production in several sectors, though its role is far more limited than in most other countries. Market failures provide an explanation for government intervention, but not an explanation for government production.

2   Natural monopolies are industries in which it is efficient to have only one producer; in such situations, there is unlikely to be effective competition in the market equilibrium. This lack of competition provides a major reason for government production of private goods. An alternative to public production is government regulation. While the United States has, for the most part, addressed the problem of natural monopolies through regulation, until recently, in Europe, telephone and other natural monopolies were government controlled. More recently, many have been privatized.

3   There is some limited evidence that governments on average are less efficient than private enterprises in providing comparable services. But there are important exceptions, suggesting that government enterprises are not necessarily less efficient than their private counterparts.

4   Government enterprises differ from private enterprises in several respects: While private enterprises maximize profits, government enterprises may pursue other objectives; government enterprises often face soft budget constraints and limited competition; and they face additional constraints, in personnel policy (pay and firing), procurement, and budgeting. While there may be good reasons for these restrictions, they nonetheless interfere with economic efficiency.

5   These differences lead to differences in individual incentives. Bureaucrats often try to maximize the size of their organization and to avoid risk.

At the same time, public organizations share with private firms the principal-agent problem, the problem of ensuring that their employees act in the interests of the organization, or more broadly, that managers and workers in firms act in ways which are congruent with the interests of shareholders, and that public servants act in ways which are congruent with the interests of citizens.

6   There are a number of organizational forms that lie between conventional public agencies and private corporations, including government corporations and performance-based organizations. They may be able to achieve many of the efficiency benefits of private organizations, and at the same time pursue public interests more effectively than purely private firms subject to regulations. Much of the debate in the future will be about the extent of utilization of these organizational forms and whether private firms should enter into areas, such as prisons and social services, previously thought of as core government functions.

KEY CONCEPTS

Privatization

Natural monopoly

Zero profit point

Sunk costs

Cross-subsidy

Regulation

Soft budget constraint

Bureaucracy

Principal-agent problem

Risk aversion

Corporatization

QUESTIONS AND PROBLEMS

1   In the past two decades there has been extensive privatization of public enterprises. The U.S. government sold Conrail, the French government sold off many of its banks, and the British government partly sold off its telephone services. In each of these cases, outline the major arguments in favor of and against privatization. Do you feel differently about the three cases? Why?

2   Under the Reagan administration, the Interior Department greatly increased the rate at which it leased offshore oil and gas. This had the effect of significantly reducing the prices that the government received for these leases. (Though the leases are sold by auction, on more than two-thirds of the tracts there was only a single bidder.) Discuss the distributional and efficiency consequences of this policy.

3   The Postal Service claims that one reason why it cannot provide services as cheaply as private firms is that it is required to provide services to rural areas but cannot charge them more than the urban areas. The private companies "skim" the low-cost markets. (Effectively, urban areas are subsidizing rural areas.) Discuss the efficiency and equity consequences of this kind of cross-subsidization.

Some have argued that if it is desirable as a matter of national policy to subsidize rural post offices, the subsidies should be paid out of general tax revenue, not by the other users of the postal system. Discuss the advantages and problems of such an alternative subsidy scheme.

4   There are many private security firms, and many large housing developments have police protection provided by such private firms. Yet few towns contract out their police department. Why do you think this is so? What would be the advantages and disadvantages of doing so? Recently, however, many communities have contracted to have their prisons run by private firms. What advantages or problems might you anticipate from this?

5   The military buys most of its equipment from private contractors but does not use private contractors to man its ships or fly its airplanes. What differences in the nature of the services provided might account for these differences?

6   There have been recurrent proposals for education voucher schemes, in which the government provides a voucher that can be used to purchase education from either a public provider (the local town) or a private provider. The GI Bill effectively provided such vouchers for veterans of the Korean War and World War II. In the 1996 presidential campaign, Senator Dole proposed that the federal government finance a limited number of such vouchers. What do you see as the advantages and disadvantages of these voucher schemes? Are there some circumstances (some kinds of educational services) for which vouchers seem more attractive?

7   Discuss what organizational form (private firm, government corporation, or normal government production) you think might be appropriate for each of the following. In each case, discuss problems of designing appropriate incentives and effective regulatory systems.

  a   Public housing
  b   Production of enriched uranium to be used in atomic bombs or nuclear power plants
  c   Production of helium, sometimes used by the government for military purposes
  d   Air traffic control system
  e   The Patent and Copyright Office
  f   Prisons

g Job placement services

h Administering the welfare program

i Administering the food stamp program

8 Recently, there have been several proposals to privatize the social security system, and some countries have actually privatized part or all of their social security system. What arguments might be put in favor or against doing this?

9 Externalities and the Environment

FOCUS QUESTIONS

1 What are externalities?

2 How do private markets respond to externalities? What are the limitations of these private remedies?

3 What are the principal ways by which the public sector attempts to deal with externalities? What are the advantages and disadvantages of these alternative approaches?

4 What currently are the major environmental public policy issues? What policies regarding these issues have succeeded and what policies have failed? What are some of the current controversies in environmental public policy, and what insights does economic analysis provide into these controversies?

While the federal government has long had an interest in environmental policy—the earliest federal action appears to have been the Refuse Act of 1899, designed to rid navigable waters of debris—the modern era of federal environmental regulation began with the Water Pollution Control Act of 1948, the first of a series of acts to protect the water we drink and the lakes and rivers in which we swim and fish.

Government activity on behalf of the environment has clearly had some beneficial effect. The quality of air in major industrial cities such as Pittsburgh and Gary has improved noticeably since passage of the Clean Air Act of 1963. Lakes such as Lake Erie, which once faced the prospect of becoming so polluted that much marine life would be extinguished, have been saved.

Still, problems remain. On some days Los Angeles is blanketed by smog despite stringent California regulations on air pollution. Dangerous poisons from chemical dumps have threatened many communities. In 1985, scientists discovered that chlorofluorocarbons (used in such products as spray cans) had caused a hole in the ozone layer, a part of the atmosphere that shields the Earth's surface from harmful radiation. An international convention (treaty) signed in 1990 in Montreal, Canada, bans the use of ozone-depleting chemicals. By 1992 an international consensus concerning the threat of global warming caused by carbon dioxide and other chemicals had developed, and another international agreement was signed in Rio de Janeiro, Brazil.

While it is increasingly agreed that government actions are required to preserve our environment, the extent and form of those actions remain a subject of debate. This chapter will describe the economic rationale for government intervention in the environment, and review the major government programs and policy issues related to environmental intervention.

THE PROBLEM OF EXTERNALITIES

Air and water pollution are two examples of a much broader range of phenomena that economists refer to as **externalities,** one of the market failures discussed in Chapter 4. Whenever an individual or firm undertakes an action that has an effect on another individual or firm, for which the latter does not pay or is not paid, we say there is an externality. Markets affected by externalities result in inefficient resource allocations. Levels of production as well as expenditures directed at controlling the externality will be incorrect. For instance, consider a firm that could, by expending resources, reduce its level of pollution. Although there would be a large social benefit, there is no private incentive driving the firm to spend the money.

In some cases, the actions of an individual or firm confer (uncompensated) benefits on others; these are called *positive* externalities. A homeowner who maintains his property, including planting attractive flowers in front, provides a positive externality. Actions that adversely affect others are called *negative* externalities.

The level of production of negative externality–generating commodities will be excessive. Figure 9.1 shows conventional demand and supply curves. We argued earlier that, in the absence of externalities, the resulting market equilibrium, Q_m, was efficient. The demand curve reflected the individual's marginal benefits from the production of an extra unit of the commodity, and the supply curve reflected the marginal costs of producing an extra unit of the commodity. At the intersection of the two curves, the marginal benefits just equal the marginal costs. Now, with externalities, the industry's supply curve will not reflect marginal *social* costs, only marginal private

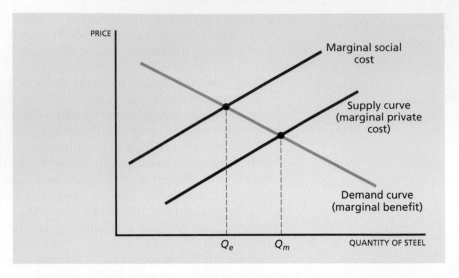

FIGURE 9.1   **Excessive Production of Goods Yielding Negative Externalities** The presence of a negative externality means that marginal social costs exceed marginal private costs, and the market equilibrium will entail an excessive production of the commodity. Q_m is market equilibrium, Q_e is the efficient level of output.

costs—those borne directly by the producers. If the expansion of steel production increases the level of pollution, there is a real cost to that expansion in addition to the costs of the iron ore, labor, coke, and limestone that go into the production of steel. But the steel industry fails to take the cost of pollution into account. Thus Figure 9.1 also shows the **marginal social cost curve,** giving the total extra costs (private and social) of producing an extra unit of steel. This cost curve lies above the industry supply curve. Efficiency requires that marginal social cost equal the marginal benefit of increasing output: production should occur at Q_e, the intersection of the marginal so-

EXTERNALITIES

Externalities arise whenever an individual or firm undertakes an action that has an effect on another individual or firm, for which the latter does not pay or is not paid.

Consequences:

1 Overproduction of goods generating negative externalities

2 Undersupply of goods generating positive externalities

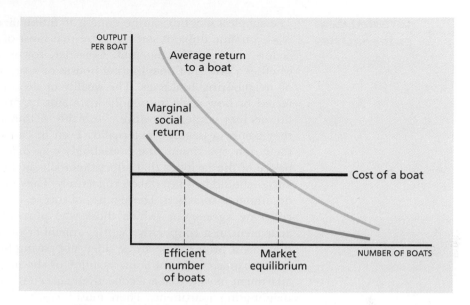

OUTPUT PER BOAT

Average return to a boat

Marginal social return

Cost of a boat

Efficient number of boats

Market equilibrium

NUMBER OF BOATS

FIGURE 9.2   **Common Resource Problem Leads to Excessive Fishing** The extra output of an additional boat is less than the average output. There will be an excessive number of boats.

cial cost curve and the demand curve. The efficient level of production is lower than the market equilibrium level.

An important class of externalities arises from what is referred to as **common resource problems.** Their central characteristic is that they pertain to a pool of scarce resources to which access is not restricted. Consider a lake in which the total number of fish caught increases with the number of fishing boats, but less than proportionately, so that the number of fish caught per boat decreases as the number of boats increases. Each additional boat reduces the catch of other boats. This is the externality. The marginal social benefit of an additional boat is thus less than the average catch of each boat, as shown in Figure 9.2; some of the fish that the additional boat catches would have been caught by some other boat. The private return to an additional individual deciding whether to purchase a boat is simply the average return (once they are on the lake, all boats catch the same number of fish), which is much more than the marginal social return. Thus, while the private market equilibrium entails average returns equal to the cost of a boat (assumed to be constant), social efficiency requires that the marginal social return be equal to the cost of a boat.

In general, when there are externalities, the market equilibrium will not be efficient.

PRIVATE SOLUTIONS TO EXTERNALITIES

Under some circumstances, private markets can deal with externalities without government assistance.

The simplest way this can be done is to **internalize** the externality by forming economic units of sufficient size that most of the consequences of any action occur within the unit. Consider, for instance, any community—whether a group of neighboring houses or a set of apartments in the same or neighboring buildings. The quality of life in the neighborhood is affected by how each household maintains its property. If someone plants flowers they confer a positive externality; if they let their house run down, they confer a negative externality. Even in cases where each family owns their own apartment, the households may *collectively* decide that maintenance of the facilities that affect them all—including the external appearance—should be undertaken collectively. They form a cooperative or a condominium association. There must, of course, be some way of enforcing the collective agreement (which those who purchase a condominium or an apartment in a cooperative sign). A member of the condominium association might prefer to be a free rider, not paying her share of the cost of the maintenance of the common facilities; or she might refuse to maintain her apartment in ways that are collectively agreed upon and that adversely affect neighboring apartments. There must be recourse to the legal system, which ensures that the terms of the agreement—by which those living near each other attempt to deal with some of the externalities they impose upon each other and to provide what are "public goods" to the group—are adhered to.

THE COASE THEOREM

As we have noted, externalities arise when individuals do not have to pay for the full consequences of their actions. There is excessive fishing in a common pool because individuals do not have to pay for the right to fish. Frequently, externalities can be dealt with by the appropriate assignment of **property rights.** Property rights assign to a particular individual the right to control some assets and to receive fees for the property's use.

Consider the problem of oil pools. Oil is usually found in large pools beneath the ground. To obtain access to a pool, all one needs to do is to buy enough land to drill a well and equipment for the drilling. The more oil that one well takes out of the pool, the less there is for others to take.[1] The total extra oil obtained as a result of drilling an extra well—the marginal social benefit—is thus less than the amount obtained by the additional well. Too many wells will be drilled.

The reason for this is that no one has the property right to the entire pool of oil. When the oil pool is controlled by a single individual, he has an incentive to make sure that the correct number of wells is drilled. Since economic efficiency is enhanced by having a single firm control the entire pool, any firm could buy the land over the pool from its present owners (at what they would have received from selling the oil) and wind up with a profit. In this view, no outside intervention would be required to ensure that an efficient pattern of property rights emerged.

---

[1] There is another externality: as oil is removed, the costs of pumping out additional oil rise, because underground pressure is reduced. Additional wells may actually reduce the total amount that will be extracted.

Even when property rights for a common resource are not assigned to a single individual, the market may find an efficient way of dealing with the externality. Owners of oil wells frequently get together to **unitize** their production, thus making it less likely that too many wells will be drilled.[2] And fishermen using the same grounds may get together to devise mutually agreed-upon restrictions to prevent excess fishing.

The assertion that whenever there are externalities, the parties involved can get together and make some set of arrangements by which the externality is internalized and efficiency is ensured, is referred to as the **Coase theorem.**[3]

For instance, when there are smokers and nonsmokers in the same room, if the loss to the nonsmokers exceeds the gains to the smokers, the nonsmokers might get together and "bribe" (or, as economists like to say, "compensate") the smokers not to smoke. Or say the smokers are in a nonsmoking compartment of a train, and the restriction on smoking (which can be viewed as an externality imposed on the smokers by the nonsmokers) takes away more from their welfare than the nonsmokers gain. Then the smokers might get together and "compensate" the nonsmokers in order to allow themselves to smoke.

Of course, the determination of who compensates whom makes a great deal of difference to the distributive implications of the externality. Smokers are clearly better off in the regime in which smoking is allowed unless they are paid not to smoke, compared to the regime in which smoking is banned unless they compensate nonsmokers.

USING THE LEGAL SYSTEM

Even when property rights are not perfectly defined, the legal system can provide protections against externalities. Our system of common law does not allow one party to injure another, and "injury" has been interpreted to include a variety of economic costs imposed on others. Implicitly, courts have given individuals some property rights—say, in the waters which they rely upon for fishing. And those injured have increasingly turned to courts to enforce those property rights.

When the Exxon tanker *Valdez* spilled oil into Alaska's Prince William Sound in 1989, those damaged by the spill—the fishermen whose catch was diminished, as well as those in the tourist industry who depend on sports fishermen—successfully sued Exxon. Many Americans believed that by spoiling one of the relatively pristine environments in the country, the spill hurt them too. They valued the *existence* of these natural resources, even if they did not immediately enjoy the benefits by visiting Alaska; to that extent

---

[2] Under unitization, the development of an oil or gas reservoir is put under a single management, with proceeds distributed according to a formula specified in the unitization agreement. This unitization is not done to reduce competition (it occurs even among small oil companies who take the price of oil as given, unaffected by their actions) but to increase efficiency.

[3] R. H. Coase, "The Problem of Social Cost," *Journal of Law and Economics* 3 (1960): 1–44.

THE EXXON *VALDEZ* OIL SPILL

Oil tankers have long been a major source of ocean pollution. The potential for damage was forcefully brought home with the grounding of the Exxon *Valdez* in Alaska's Prince William Sound in March 1989. Nightly pictures on TV depicted graphically the massive death of wildlife, including sea otters, salmon, birds, and seals. How long the devastation would last—or whether nature would ever fully recover—was not clear.

Exxon was made to pay more than $1 billion, most of which was to be spent on correcting the environmental damage; and the company claimed to have spent more than $2 billion beyond that in the months immediately after the spill, trying to limit the extent of damage. Even so, there was debate over whether the amount paid by Exxon was adequate: how much should Americans be compensated for the damage of the spill?

To answer this question, a study was done in which individuals were asked questions about how much they would be willing to pay to preserve a natural habitat, such as that which was harmed by the *Valdez* spill. Just as opinion polls, by sampling a thousand individuals, can provide an accurate forecast about how the entire population will vote, so too a sample of individuals can provide an accurate estimate for the value that would be assigned by the entire population. Some individuals will assign a high value, others a relatively low value, but these differences will be reflected in the sample. By projecting the distribution of values in the sample to the entire population, one can calculate the total value for the nation. In the case of the *Valdez* oil spill, the value estimated in this way was about $3 billion. This methodology for assessing existence values is called contingent valuation.

the *Valdez* oil spill had an externality effect upon them too. Courts have recognized these **existence values**—in the *Valdez* case, the State of Alaska, acting as trustee, collected over a billion dollars in compensation.

To reduce the uncertainty about these often imperfectly defined property rights, government has tried to clarify them and to specify more precisely the nature and amount of damages that can be collected. Thus, more recent legislation and regulation has recognized the importance of existence values; the government, as "trustee" for the country's natural resources, has the right to sue for damages, though under current legislation the amount recovered has to be used for restoration.

The more fundamental question was how to prevent such disasters, or more accurately, how to make their occurrence less likely and the consequences less severe. As long as oil is transported, there is some risk of a spill, and no one has contemplated a complete ban on shipping oil. But shippers may not have the appropriate incentives to avoid a spill, because they do not bear the full consequences. This is a particularly severe problem, since many shipping companies are poorly capitalized, and in the event of an accident they would simply go bankrupt. Only a company as large and strong as Exxon could pay out $3 billion; yet almost any large oil tanker could do comparable damage.

To rectify this problem, Congress passed the Oil Pollution Act of 1990. This combined a system of incentives with regulations. Vessels had to be double-hulled, thus reducing the likelihood of spillage.

One criticism that economists have raised is that the funds paid in compensation for damage, in general, have to be used for cleanups. This constraint induces an inefficiency. The amount that vessels that have spills are required to pay should be designed to provide the corrective incentive to avoid spills. This may be more than the amount that is appropriately spent on cleanup. For instance, suppose that the consequences of a spill would be rectified by nature on its own in a year, and that it would cost an enormous amount to speed up the restoration process. We still would want to penalize firms that spill, but we might not want to spend the money to speed the restoration, since there would be little benefit.

FAILURES OF PRIVATE SOLUTIONS

If the arguments asserting that private markets can internalize externalities are correct, is there any need for government intervention, other than to establish clear property rights? And if these arguments are correct, why is it that cooperative agreements have failed to take care of so many externalities?

There are several reasons why government intervention is required. The first has to do with the public goods problem discussed in Chapter 6. Many (but far from all) externalities involve the provision of a public good, such as clean air or clean water: in particular, it may be very costly to exclude anyone from enjoying the benefits of these goods. If nonsmokers get

PRIVATE SOLUTIONS TO EXTERNALITIES

1 Internalize externality.

2 Assign property rights (Coase theorem).

3 Use the legal system.

together to compensate smokers for not smoking, it pays any individual nonsmoker to claim that he is almost indifferent to letting others smoke. He will attempt to be a free rider on the efforts of other nonsmokers to induce the smokers not to smoke.

The problems of arriving voluntarily at an efficient solution are exacerbated by the presence of imperfect information. Smokers will try to persuade nonsmokers that they require a lot of compensation to induce them not to smoke. In any such bargaining situation, one party may risk the possibility of not arriving at a mutually advantageous agreement in order to get more out of any bargain that might be made.

Problems may arise even in cases where markets are well established. Consider the problem of an oil pool, the land above which is owned by several individuals. Efficiency can be obtained by bringing all the land covering an oil pool under a single unitized management and control—called unitization. However, if all but one of the landowners unitize, it may not pay the last owner to join. He knows that production on the unitized portion will be reduced, thus enabling him to increase his production. He will join only if he receives more than a proportionate share of the revenues. But each

FAILURES OF PRIVATE REMEDIES FOR EXTERNALITIES

- Public good (free rider) problems
- Compounded by imperfect information problems

  How much does the individual need to be compensated for externality?

  Incentive not to reveal truth
- Transactions costs
- Additional problems with litigation

  Uncertainty about outcomes

  Differential access

small owner may believe he can gain by holding out to be the last to join the unitization agreement (or to sell to a large firm attempting to purchase all the small owners). States have therefore found it necessary to pass legislation requiring unitization.

Another reason for government intervention concerns transactions costs. The costs of getting individuals together to internalize externalities voluntarily is significant. The provision of those organizational services itself is a public good. Indeed, the government may be looked upon as precisely the mechanism that individuals have set up to reduce the welfare losses from externalities.

Transactions costs are a major disadvantage of dealing with externalities through judicial processes. For many externalities, the losses involved may simply be too small to justify undertaking litigation. Since those generating externalities know that litigation is expensive, they may be inclined to generate their externality just up to the point where it pays the injured party to sue—giving rise to considerable inefficiencies. One way of partially dealing with this is to charge anyone shown to have imposed an externality on another a multiple of the estimated value of the damages. But this gives rise to a countervailing danger of unwarranted lawsuits, with defendants settling claims simply to avoid the enormous litigation costs.

Uncertainty about the extent of the injury frequently compounds the problem of transactions costs, and there is also some ambiguity about the outcome of most suits. If litigation costs are large, the uncertainty acts as a further deterrent to individuals contemplating using the court system to deal with externalities.

The high litigation costs and uncertain outcome of the litigation process imply that there is, in effect, differential access to legal remedies—poor people may not be able or willing to bear the risks of litigation—a situation which conflicts with our usual notion of justice in a democracy. Because the legal system and the other private methods of addressing externalities so often work so poorly and so inequitably, there has been increasing reliance on public remedies.

PUBLIC SECTOR SOLUTIONS TO EXTERNALITIES

Public sector solutions to environmental externalities fall into two broad categories: market-based solutions and direct regulation. Market-based solutions attempt to influence incentives to ensure economically efficient outcomes. For instance, fines for polluting can be used to present firms with the true social costs of their actions, thereby diminishing their incentive to pollute. By contrast, government has used direct regulations to limit externalities, as in the case of mandatory emissions standards for automobiles.

Before comparing the merits of these different approaches, we should first dispel the common fallacy which asserts that an individual or firm should never be allowed to impose a negative externality on others. For example, it is sometimes asserted that a firm should never be allowed to pollute the air and water. In the view of most economists, such absolutist positions make no sense. There is indeed a social cost associated with pollution (or any other negative externality), but the cost is not infinite; it is finite. There is some amount of money that people would be willing to receive in compensation for having to live in a community with dirtier air or dirtier water. Thus we need to weigh the costs and benefits associated with pollution control, just as we need to weigh the costs and benefits associated with any other economic activity. The problem with the market is *not* that it results in pollution; there is, indeed, a socially efficient level of pollution. The problem rather is that firms fail to take into account the social costs associated with the externalities they impose—in this case, pollution—and as a result, the level of pollution is likely to be excessively high. The task of the government is to help the private sector achieve the socially efficient level of pollution, to make individuals and firms act in such a way that they are induced to take into account the effects of their actions on others.

In the ensuing discussion the focus will be on pollution externalities. The arguments, however, extend in a straightforward way to other categories of externalities.

MARKET-BASED SOLUTIONS

Even when markets themselves do not lead to efficient resource allocations—as when there are externalities—economists tend to believe that marketlike mechanisms can be used to ensure efficient behavior. Market-based solutions to environmental externalities take three forms: fines and taxes, subsidies for pollution abatement, and marketable permits. We now consider each of these solutions in turn.

FINES AND TAXES The simplest form of market-based solution involves levying fees or taxes in proportion to the amount of pollution emitted. In general, whenever there is an externality, there is a difference between the social cost and the private cost, and between the social benefit and private benefit. A properly calculated fine or tax presents the individual or firm with the true social costs and benefits of its actions. Fines of this sort—designed to make marginal private costs equal marginal social costs, and marginal private benefits equal to marginal social benefits—are called **corrective taxes,** or sometimes **Pigouvian taxes,** after A. C. Pigou, a great English economist of the first half of the twentieth century.[4]

Consider the example, discussed earlier, of steel producers polluting the air. We showed that because firms were concerned only with private marginal costs, not the social marginal costs (the two differing by the marginal costs of pollution), output of steel would be excessive. By charging each firm an amount equal to the marginal cost of pollution, the marginal private costs and marginal social costs are equated. In Figure 9.3 we have assumed that the amount of pollution is proportional to the level of output, and the marginal cost of each unit of pollution is fixed; hence by imposing

[4] Pigou argued persuasively for the use of corrective taxes in his book, *The Economics of Welfare* (London: Macmillan, 1918).

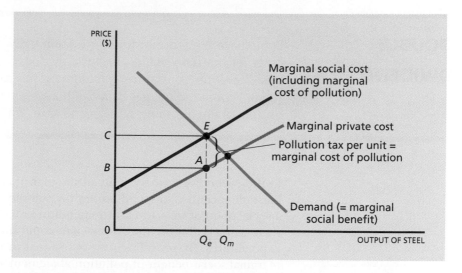

PRICE ($)

Marginal social cost (including marginal cost of pollution)

Marginal private cost

Pollution tax per unit = marginal cost of pollution

Demand (= marginal social benefit)

OUTPUT OF STEEL

FIGURE 9.3 **Market Equilibrium With and Without Fines** In the absence of a tax on pollution, firms will set price equal to marginal private cost. There will be excessive production (Q_m). By setting a tax equal to the marginal pollution cost, efficiency is obtained.

a fixed charge per unit of output, equal to the marginal social cost of pollution, each firm will be induced to produce the socially efficient level of output. In the figure, the distance *EA* represents the pollution tax per unit output, and the area *EABC* represents the total pollution taxes paid.

Firms can reduce pollution by producing less, or by changing production methods. Changes in production methods may entail direct expenditures for pollution control devices, or changes in the input mixes and other alterations in the production process. Fines related directly to the amount of pollution ensure that firms will undertake the pollution abatement in the least costly—most efficient—manner possible. Assume that there is a given, known marginal social cost imposed on others by each unit of pollution (measured, say, by the number of particles added to the air per unit of time). It is costly to reduce pollution; and we assume that at any given level of production, it costs more to reduce pollution more. In other words, the *marginal* cost of pollution control is rising. This is depicted in Figure 9.4, where we measure along the horizontal axis the *reduction* in pollution (from what it would be if the firm spent nothing on pollution abatement). Efficiency requires that the marginal social benefits associated with further pollution abatement expenditures just equal the marginal social costs, point P^* in the diagram. If the firm is charged a fine, f^*, equal to the marginal social cost of pollution, the firm will undertake the efficient level of expenditure on pollution abatement.

SUBSIDIZING POLLUTION ABATEMENT Since a firm is likely to receive a negligible direct benefit from pollution abatement (most of the benefits accruing

225

Some have argued that there is a double dividend from imposing taxes (or fines) on pollution. Not only does it discourage pollution, it raises revenue, so that the government has to rely less on distorting taxes. Those who believe that the tax system is distorting—with taxes on capital discouraging savings and taxes on labor discouraging

to those who live in the vicinity of the plant), absent a fine on pollution, it has little incentive to spend money on pollution abatement. There is, from a social point of view, too little expenditure on pollution abatement. Rather than taxing pollution, the government could subsidize pollution abatement expenditures. By providing a subsidy equal to the difference between the marginal social benefit of pollution abatement and the firm's marginal private benefit, the efficient level of pollution abatement expenditures can be attained. This is illustrated in Figure 9.5. (Note that the marginal cost of pollution depicted in Figure 9.4 is directly related to the marginal benefit of pollution abatement depicted in Figure 9.5. While in Figure 9.4 we assumed a fixed marginal social cost of pollution, and hence a fixed marginal social

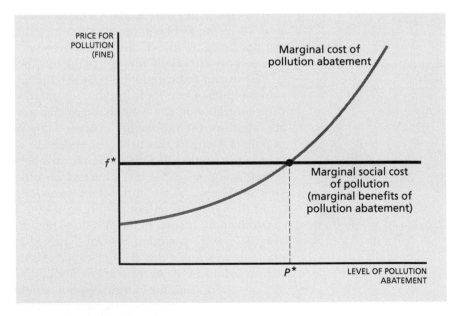

FIGURE 9.4   **Efficient Control of Pollution** The efficient level of pollution can be attained either by charging firms a fine of *f** per unit of pollution (say, measured by the number of particles added to the air) or by imposing a regulation that firms have a pollution abatement level *P**.

work—emphasize this double dividend. Not only will national output *as conventionally measured* go up, but *true* output—which takes account of the pollution and degradation of the environment—goes up even more than conventionally measured output, as the tax or fine discourages pollution.

benefit from pollution abatement, in Figure 9.5, as pollution decreases, the marginal social benefit from further pollution abatement decreases. Similarly, in Figure 9.4 we have assumed rising costs of pollution abatement, while in Figure 9.5 marginal costs are constant. Either case may hold in a real situation.)

This remedy does not, however, attain a socially efficient resource allocation. The reason is simple: the total marginal social costs of producing steel include the costs of the government subsidies for pollution abatement. Firms fail to take this into account in deciding on the level of production. Thus, as before, the marginal social cost of steel production exceeds the marginal private cost. The pollution abatement subsidy reduces the marginal social cost of output (from the dashed line to the solid black line in

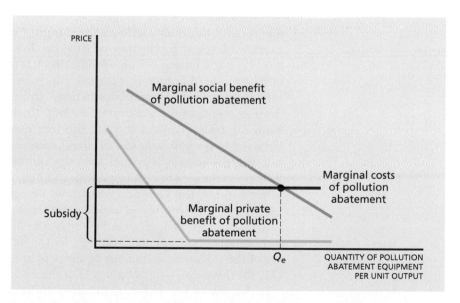

FIGURE 9.5 **Pollution Abatement Subsidies** By subsidizing the purchase of pollution abatement equipment (by the difference between marginal social benefit of pollution abatement and marginal private benefit), an efficient level of expenditure on pollution abatement can be attained.

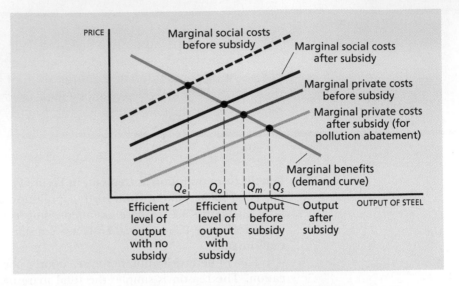

PRICE

Marginal social costs
before subsidy

Marginal social costs
after subsidy

Marginal private costs
before subsidy

Marginal private costs
after subsidy (for
pollution abatement)

Marginal benefits
(demand curve)

Q_e Q_o Q_m Q_s

Efficient
level of
output
with no
subsidy

Efficient
level of
output
with
subsidy

Output
before
subsidy

Output
after
subsidy

OUTPUT OF STEEL

FIGURE 9.6   **Market Equilibrium with Pollution Abatement Subsidies** Even after the pollution abatement subsidy, the equilibrium level of output of steel is still inefficient; the firm fails to take into account the extra costs of public subsidies for pollution abatement associated with increased output of steel as well as the marginal social cost of any remaining pollution.

Figure 9.6). But it also reduces the marginal private costs. There is still an excessive level of production of steel, as illustrated by point Q_s in Figure 9.6.[5] Q_m is the output before subsidy, which is markedly greater than Q_e, the efficient level of output with the subsidy. A well-designed subsidy lowers the total marginal social cost of production—there is less pollution, and though there is a cost of the abatement subsidy (including the distortions arising from the taxes required to raise the revenues to finance it), the benefits from the lower pollution exceed these costs; hence the optimal level of output with the subsidy is greater than the optimal level of output when firms have no incentives to reduce pollution. Thus, Q_o is greater than Q_e. On the other hand, if the pollution abatement equipment confers some ancillary benefits to the firm, it may simultaneously reduce the firm's marginal private costs of production, as indicated by the light gray line. Thus, the firm's output level also increases, from Q_m to Q_s. Since, however, the main benefits of the pollution abatement equipment are to reduce pollution, presumably the distortion—the magnitude of the excess production—is reduced.

The reason why polluters prefer subsidies for pollution abatement over fines is clear: profits are higher under the former system than under the lat-

[5] If the level of pollution of a firm cannot be directly monitored, a desirable policy would entail a subsidy for expenditures on pollution abatement combined with a tax on output. The tax on output (if set at the appropriate rate) reduces the level of output to the socially efficient level.

ter. The distributional consequences are not limited to the polluting firms and their shareholders. Because output will be smaller under the system of fines, prices will be higher, and consumers of the polluting firm's products will be worse off. On the other hand, those who have to pay the taxes to finance the subsidies for pollution abatement are clearly better off under the system of fines. It should be emphasized, however, that the choice between subsidies and fines is not just a distribution issue. As we have seen, under the pollution abatement subsidy scheme, producers do not face the true social cost of their production; there is an inefficiency. By contrast, with an appropriately designed system of fines, producers do face the true social costs.

MARKETABLE PERMITS An increasingly popular market-based solution involves **marketable permits.** These limit the amount of pollution that any firm can emit. For instance, each firm may be allowed to emit 90 percent of the amount it emitted last year. Thus, a firm is granted a permit to emit so many units of pollutants. Since what the government cares about is the total amount of emission reduction, it allows firms to trade permits. A company that cuts its emissions in half could sell some of its permits to another company that wants to expand production (and hence increase its emission of pollutants).

Under this system, firms will be willing to sell permits so long as the market price of the permit is greater than the marginal cost of reducing pollution, and firms will be willing to buy permits so long as the marginal cost of reducing pollution is greater than the market price of the permit. Thus, in equilibrium, each firm will reduce pollution to a level such that the marginal cost of pollution reduction is equal to the market price of the permit. Like fines, marketable permits use the market mechanism to ensure economic efficiency in the reduction of pollution: the marginal cost of reducing pollution is the same for every firm.

However, marketable permits have one advantage over fines. With fines, the government may not be sure about the level of emissions that firms will choose to produce. If the pollution level is too high, it will have to increase the fines. Finding the right "price" may take a long time.

If the government believes it knows the right *quantity*, the amount to which pollution should be restricted,[6] then tradable permits are a way of using the market mechanism without bearing the risk of excessive pollution.

There are two problems with tradable permits. The first is making the initial assignments. While the system of assigning firms a fraction of their current levels of pollution might at first glance seem reasonable, it causes a major equity problem: "good" firms which have spent large amounts on pollution control are given fewer permits, and, if they have already installed state-of-the-art technology, will have a harder time reducing pollution. An alternative system bases permits simply on the level of production. This system is basically the one used when tradable permits were introduced to control acid rain. When Los Angeles introduced tradable permits in 1994, its

---

[6] That is, if it knows, for instance, the amount of pollution which the system can absorb without posing a serious threat to health.

assignments took into account both the levels of output and pollution and the state of the firm's current technology.

The second problem is more subtle. Tradable permits work well only where the location of the pollutant makes no difference. In many situations, this is not the case. Thus, air pollution is much more serious near large cities. Moreover, with prevailing winds blowing from west to east, pollution along the East Coast may be little problem, since most of it gets blown immediately out to sea; but pollution in the Midwest may have adverse effects on all the eastern states. The marketable permits that were introduced to control acid rain did not fully take this problem into account.

REGULATION

Most economists believe that market-based solutions provide the most promise for curbing environmental externalities, but government traditionally has relied upon direct regulation. It has set emission standards for automobiles; put forth detailed regulations relating to the disposal of toxic chemicals; outlawed smoking on domestic airline flights; imposed laws requiring oil companies with wells in the same oil pool to unitize their production; imposed restrictions on fishing and hunting to reduce the inefficiencies associated with excessive utilization of these common resources. These examples illustrate the myriad forms that regulation may take.

Advocates of regulations argue that they provide greater certainty: if firms are prohibited from emitting more than a given level of pollution into the water, then one knows the maximum level of pollution; with fines, the level of pollution depends on the costs of reducing the pollution level. But advocates of fines argue that one can easily adjust fines to induce firms to lower pollution to the desired level. And marketable permits provide a market-based way to attain efficient pollution reduction *and* certainty of outcome. Indeed, a major criticism of regulations is that they do not reduce pollution in the most efficient way: different firms may face different marginal costs of further pollution abatement. And regulations typically provide little or no incentive for firms to reduce pollution below the standard that has been set, regardless of how low the cost of doing so.

In the case of pollution, we should distinguish between two important classes of regulations. Recall that the market-based mechanisms discussed earlier focus on the *amount* of pollution; to pollute more, a firm must pay more in fines or buy more permits. This is a performance-based system, since the government only cares about the final outcome—how much pollution is produced. There are many **performance-based regulations,** such as regulations on automobile emissions, that also focus on the final outcome. However, much of pollution regulation has focused on standards, practices, and inputs, rather than performance. For instance, the government may prohibit the use of certain grades of coal, or it may require firms to employ scrubbers and other pollution abatement devices, or to construct smokestacks to specific heights. These are called **input regulations.** Market-based mechanisms may also focus on inputs and practices in this way; for example, a tax may be levied on high-sulfur coal, rather than on the pollution emitted.

Where feasible, it is preferable to focus on performance, either for regulations or for market-based mechanisms. The one argument for focusing on inputs and practices is that they may be more easily monitored. Thus, it may be difficult to measure the amount of pollution coming out of a smokestack, but it is certain that if scrubbers (devices that reduce the amount of sulfur being emitted by a coal-burning electric power plant) are used, the amount being emitted will be less than if scrubbers are not used.

While there may be good reasons for these policies, in some cases politics rather than policy has dominated the decision. In the case of coal, had a performance-based standard been used, eastern coal producers would have been disadvantaged relative to western coal producers, because eastern coal contains more sulfur. To attain the same level of sulfur, firms using eastern coal would have had to use scrubbers, while those using western coal would not. Eastern coal producers successfully lobbied for the universal imposition of the requirement to use scrubbers.

INNOVATION

One of the reasons for performance-based regulation (as opposed to input standards) and pollution-based taxes (as opposed, say, to subsidies for particular forms of abatement equipment) is that they directly address what is of concern—the level of pollution—and they may induce innovations, such as new ways of producing that generate less pollution or new techniques for abating pollution at lower costs. Although today, the level of pollution cannot be directly measured, a well-designed regulatory framework, focusing on performance, may be able to provide incentives for innovations enhancing the ability to monitor.

There has been considerable controversy over the best way to stimulate innovation and about the scope for innovation. Some environmentalists are less convinced than economists of the power of normal economic forces. Many believe that industry needs to be *forced* to innovate. Thus, by imposing extremely stringent standards—for instance, that cars get at least 40 miles per gallon—they will force industry to develop a product meeting these standards. Implicitly, they believe that the benefits of the innovation would outweigh the costs, but that the incentives that could be provided by the price system—charging car companies taxes in proportion to the amount of pollution—simply do not suffice to warrant their attention on this area.

In practice, the success of this strategy has been mixed. In some cases, rather than inducing innovation, stringent regulations have induced litigation: it may appear cheaper to a firm to try to persuade a court that the regulation is unreasonable than to spend the money to meet the standards imposed by the regulation. In some cases, firms have played a game of chicken, gambling that if they fail to meet the standards, the government will not shut them down, for fear of a political backlash from workers who are put out of a job. But in some cases, industry unity has been broken by an innovative firm that showed that the standards are indeed attainable. For instance, Honda developed an automobile engine in the 1970s (introduced with the 1976 Honda Accord) that readily met the efficiency standards—miles per gallon—imposed by the U.S. government. This put the government in an awkward position, for if it strictly enforced the regulations, U.S. firms would be put at a disadvantage relative to the foreign competitor.

Environmentalists who doubt the effectiveness of market incentives by themselves in inducing innovation often point to the large gap between best practices—which often seem to be the most cost-effective practices—and what actually occurs. They point out, for instance, that there are energy-efficient lightbulbs which more than pay for their higher costs in terms of reduced usage costs. They argue that there are win-win regulations, where efficiency is enhanced at the same time that environmental costs, especially those associated with the use of energy, are reduced. Most economists have been skeptical. They argue, for instance, that the reason why energy-efficient lightbulbs are more prevalent in Japan than in the United States is simply that the price of electricity is higher there. In between these two camps are those who argue that there are information barriers and other types of barriers to the adoption of these cost-efficient energy-saving technologies, and that the government can help promote the diffusion of these technologies by disseminating information; typically, however, they believe that the gains to be had are likely to be modest and slow. Today, labels on many electric products identify energy usage and costs, helping buyers make more intelligent decisions about lifetime costs of different products. Slight modifications in construction practices—the color of roof shingles or the planting of trees—can have a noticeable effect on energy consumption.

Critics of approaches focusing on inputs rather than performance argue that such approaches not only are not efficient, but stifle innovation and push it in the wrong direction. Rather than seeking the most effective way of reducing emissions from coal-burning power plants, research is focused on making a cheaper scrubber. Moreover, research directed at improving the ability to monitor outputs accurately—thus reducing the necessity of relying on input regulations—is not encouraged.

INFORMATION DISCLOSURE

In some areas, governments have been experimenting with another approach, focusing on public pressure rather than the heavy hand of government. Government's role would be limited to requiring firms to disclose, for instance, the potentially cancer-inducing chemicals that they discharge into the water or emit into the air. Government would not even comment on the extent of scientific evidence concerning the impact of the chemicals on humans. Critics of this approach often argue that the costs of such information disclosures can be high; but their real concern is that government would be encouraging a scare campaign. Most people would simply assume that if a chemical is listed as dangerous, it must be dangerous—or in any case, why risk it? People in the neighborhood would put enormous pressure on the firm to eliminate the chemical, without any assessment of the costs or benefits of doing so. There could be enormous adverse economic effects. Particularly troubling is the evidence of one study by the Environmental Protection Agency which showed the magnitude of popular misconceptions about environmental risks. Scientists and nonscientists were asked to rank a number of different potential environmental health hazards, and there was little correlation between the two. Among the risks rated most highly by the nonscientists were several that were ranked at the bottom by the scientists, and vice versa.

So far most of our discussion has focused on the *efficiency* of alternative ways of controlling pollution (externalities). But much of the debate is about *distribution*—who bears the costs. Different systems of controlling pollution may have markedly different distributive consequences. Subsidies for pollution abatement equipment may result in a less efficient resource allocation

ASSESSING ALTERNATIVE APPROACHES TO CONTROLLING EXTERNALITIES

Performance-based versus input-based

- Performance-based is more efficient when performance can be measured.
- Costs of monitoring inputs may be lower.

Regulation versus fines

- Fines related to costs of pollution provide appropriate incentives.
- But there may be greater uncertainty about the actual level of pollution.
- Regulations provide greater certainty, strong incentives to meet the regulatory standards, but no incentive to reduce pollution below the standard, regardless of how low the cost is to do so.

Marketable permits versus fines

- Both can result in efficient reductions in pollution levels.
- Marketable permits provide greater certainty about the level of pollution.
- Marketable permit systems face difficult problems in allocating initial permit rights.
- There are further problems if the costs of pollution depend on *where* it occurs.

Subsidies for pollution reductions versus fines for pollution

- Both can induce reductions in pollution levels and even achieve efficient levels of pollution abatement. But the level of production of the pollution-inducing industry will be too high, since the firm will not take into account full costs—including costs of pollution abatement. Firms prefer pollution abatement subsidies.

than a system of fines for polluting; but firms will clearly prefer subsidies. Greater efficiency means that in principle, the overall gains to society from using the more efficient system are such that the gainers could compensate the losers. Why then do governments so often resort to inefficient systems, like abatement subsidies? The reason is that the compensation is typically not paid. Partly this is because it is often difficult to measure the gains and losses to each individual—the information required to implement the desired compensations is simply not available. And partly it is because those who benefit from the inefficient system are more politically organized. The losers from a system of fines are clear—both the owners of the polluting firms, who see their profits decreased, and the consumers of their products, who see their prices increased. The gainers are more dispersed—all the taxpayers who bear the burden of the taxes used to pay the subsidies, and all the consumers of all the other products who might see their prices rise slightly as production shifts slightly toward the subsidized industry. As is so often the case, the losers are much easier to identify than the gainers; thus, it is much easier for the losers to get together and use the political process to argue for a system which, while inefficient, makes them bear less of the cost of reducing pollution.

PROTECTING THE ENVIRONMENT: THE ROLE OF GOVERNMENT IN PRACTICE

We now look more closely at the actual policies that the government undertakes to protect the environment. For convenience, we divide them into three categories: those directed primarily at air, at water, and at land. There are, of course, important interactions between these pieces of our environment, so that several of the policies affect two or more of these categories.

AIR　The air we breathe has been taken for granted since the beginning of time, but by the middle of the twentieth century this was no longer possible in many major cities. London became famous for its pea-soup fog generated by pollution; Los Angeles for its life-threatening smog; Gary and Pittsburgh for their brilliant red overcast skies, a product of the steel mills upon which those cities' economy depended. People with weak respiratory systems knew the dangers of living in these cities, but the fact that *all* individuals faced greater health risks was recognized only slowly.

There are several aspects of the nation's attempt to control air pollution. Two have been marked by considerable success; over a third one, there is heated controversy; and in the fourth, progress remains slight.

The most marked success is associated with ozone depletion and chlorofluorocarbons.

OZONE DEPLETION　The Earth's atmosphere has a thin layer of ozone, which shields us from harmful solar radiation. In the late 1980s it became clear that a hole was appearing in the ozone layer over Antarctica, and that the cause of the hole was chlorofluorocarbons (CFCs). The nations of the world responded in 1990 with a treaty signed in Montreal, Canada. This treaty, the Montreal Protocol, required the production and consumption levels of CFCs to be cut in half by 1999. Signatories to the agreement have consistently met targets, although illicit trade in CFCs—called CFC smuggling—has become a growing concern.

ACID RAIN The control of sulfur dioxide, which gives rise to acid rain, and which is emitted especially by coal-burning power plants, is another success story. In the 1970s, we became aware that the leaves on the trees in many of our forests were turning yellow and many of our lakes seemed to be devoid of fish. The Acid Precipitation Act of 1980 and the Clean Air Act Amendments of 1990 began a program to control these emissions. A program of tradable permits was introduced, and these are estimated to have significantly reduced the overall cost of bringing down the level of pollution. A system of tradable permits for nitrogen oxide—another pollutant—is now on the drawing board.

CLEAN AIR ACT The Clean Air Act, including its 1990 amendments, while having brought great benefits in terms of reduced pollution, has become the subject of considerable controversy. In 1997, Carol Browner, administrator of the Environmental Protection Agency, proposed tightening significantly the standards for particulates in the air. These particulates do have adverse health consequences—both to asthmatic children (a number of whom are forced to have brief periods of hospitalization as a result) and to the very elderly, some of whom may actually die. The large increase in the rate of incidence of asthma, and the especially high rates in poor neighborhoods, have reinforced concerns about these particulates. The controversy concerns the cold calculations of costs and benefits, the costs of reducing the level of particulates versus the health benefits. As hard as it is to quantify these benefits, there are standard procedures by which this is done; such calculations are made routinely in evaluating how much to spend to make a safer highway, a safer car, or a safer airplane. These changes can result in a slightly smaller probability of an accident—from which one can calculate, *on average*, how many lives will be saved. The government has to have a systematic way of deciding whether the benefits exceed the costs, and to do so, it places a value on life—in the range of two to eight million dollars. By most accounts, the costs of the proposed particulate standards far exceed the benefits—though the law itself did not allow such a cost-benefit calculation to be made (a major criticism of the law from the perspective of most economists). Caught between pressure from the business community and the environmentalists, the Clinton administration at first vacillated, but finally came down in support of the stronger regulations. It will take years to see whether the dire economic consequences forecast by businesses will be realized.

GLOBAL WARMING The one area in which little progress has been made is global warming and greenhouse gases. The burning of carbon—coal, gas,

235

and oil—adds carbon dioxide to the atmosphere. The current level of concentration of carbon dioxide is substantially greater than it was at the beginning of the industrial revolution, and it continues to grow. To many, this is a risky experiment with our planet Earth. Moreover, climate scientists believe that this increased carbon dioxide is leading to a warming of the planet (the carbon dioxide leads to what is called a "greenhouse" effect, with energy from the sun being trapped inside the Earth's atmosphere) and to a rise in the sea level. There will be some severe adverse effects from this warming, especially on the tropics, and the increase in sea level will obviously have adverse effects on low-lying islands and countries, such as Bangladesh and the Netherlands. Other predicted effects include an increase in the variability of weather. While there is clear evidence for the increase in greenhouse gases, and there is a general (but not universal) consensus on the long-run effects, there is more controversy over whether the effects are already being felt. There is evidence, for instance, of a marked increase in losses from weather—far greater than the increased losses from nonweather events such as earthquakes. And there is some disagreement among economists about the magnitude of the overall costs—with some countries in cold climates actually benefiting.

Faced by the mounting scientific evidence concerning the long-run effects, in a convention (treaty) signed in Rio de Janeiro in 1992 the developed countries committed themselves to reducing their level of emissions to 1990 levels by the year 2000. The developing countries argued that the whole problem had been caused by the profligacy of the advanced countries, that their own contributions to the greenhouse gases were relatively small, and that they were too poor to devote much of their resources to reducing their emissions below the level which economics dictated.

In 1997, the countries of the world met again, in Kyoto, Japan, to assess their progress and to make plans for the future. The progress had been limited. Few countries were on track to meeting their targets. The less developed countries were no more willing to make commitments than before, but now it had become increasingly clear that within a short period of time, the greenhouse gas contributions of these countries, especially China and India, would in total exceed those of the advanced countries—though not on a per capita basis. The developed countries made binding commitments for the future; but the less developed countries saw no reason to accept commitments that allowed the United States a far higher level of per capita emissions. While the developed countries nontheless accepted binding commitments upon themselves, the treaty provided no enforcement mechanism. To reduce the overall costs, the countries agreed at Kyoto to explore more market-based mechanisms—tradable permits and a variant called "the clean development mechanism" or **joint implementation.** (Since one country would "buy" the greenhouse gas reduction from another, in effect paying for it, they could be thought of as "jointly" implementing the greenhouse gas reduction.) Some critics suggested that the United States was advocating joint implementation not out of a commitment to economic efficiency, but because it could not or would not take measures that would reduce greenhouse gases within its own borders.

TABLE 9.1		TAX PER LITRE IN U.S. DOLLARS
Gasoline Taxes across the World	France	.87
	Germany	.67
	Italy	.81
	Spain	.54
	United Kingdom	.99
	Japan	.42
	Canada	.19
	United States	.10

SOURCE: *International Energy Agency Monthly Oil Report*, June 1998, Table 9, accessed at http://www.iea.org/oil.htm on August 10, 1998.

The United States was caught in a bind. Though the Clinton administration was committed to reducing greenhouse gases, the easiest and most cost-effective way of reducing emissions would be a carbon or energy tax. The administration had proposed such a tax in 1993, only to have it adamantly opposed by the powerful gas, coal, and oil interests, and soundly defeated. As it is, gasoline taxes in the United States are markedly lower than in Europe and most other industrialized countries, as shown in Table 9.1.[7]

WATER   The debate over clean air today centers not around whether pollution should be controlled, but rather how and at what levels. Likewise, in the case of water there is consensus that the controls that have been put in place for drinking water make sense, but controversy remains over the benefits relative to costs of stringent regulations attempting to reduce pollution in streams and rivers. Much of today's water pollution comes not from factories, which can be more easily controlled, but from difficult-to-control sources such as runoff from farms. Controlling such pollution would require controlling the use of fertilizers and pesticides. And while price mechanisms (taxes) might discourage the use of fertilizers and pesticides, it would be virtually impossible to differentiate between usages which contribute to pollution and usages which do not. Moreover, there is controversy over some of the benefits. How worried should we be about the pollution of groundwater that will almost surely never be used for drinking and that is unlikely to seep into wells or springs? Some environmentalists believe that we should never spoil a part of our natural heritage; keeping groundwater clean has nothing to do with the use to which groundwater might be put. Others take a very risk-averse stance: how can we be sure that the groundwater

[7] As this book goes to press, the Kyoto convention has not been ratified by the United States, and Congress remains firmly opposed so long as the developing countries do not make commitments that go well beyond what they currently are willing to make.

237

will never be used for drinking? Controversy over these issues has prevented the reauthorization of the Clean Water Act in recent years.

TOXIC WASTES

Newspapers have presented graphic stories of rivers, canals, and land that chemical companies have turned into toxic waste sites, subjecting those who come into contact with them on a regular basis to increased risk of cancer. Americans had nightmares about discovering that their homes had been built over toxic waste sites. In response, in 1980 Congress passed a law, called **Superfund** after the fund it established (based partially on a tax on chemical companies), to help clean up these sites. But the law was badly designed. It was based on the principle that those who contributed to the pollution should pay for its cleanup; but it provided that anyone who had contributed at all to the particular site was liable for the entire cleanup costs. This enabled the government to go after large corporations—those with "deep pockets"—forcing them to pay for the cleanup and letting them sue the other polluters to recover their shares. (This is called the **system of joint and several liability.**) And it provided for perpetual liability: even after the site was cleaned up, it was always possible that on the site another chemical with adverse effects would be discovered—the guilty party never got complete freedom. To make matters worse, the polluters' insurance companies argued that their general liability policies did not cover pollution other than that which originated as a result of an accident. In several states the courts supported the insurance companies, while in other states, the courts said that the insurance companies were liable. The upshot was litigation: between the government and the polluters, between the different polluters, and between the polluters and their insurance companies. The lawyers made out like bandits, but the toxic wastes did not get cleaned up. Over 70 percent of insurance company expenditures went to legal fees, and more than a quarter of what the polluters spent went to lawyers. Worse still, property owners had a new nightmare to worry about: that toxic waste would be discovered on their property that might not hurt their health but would definitely hurt their pocketbook. They would be responsible for cleaning it up, and the EPA often set standards where the costs simply could not be justified by the benefits. In some places, the result was "gridlock" in the land market: no one would buy potentially polluted sites, which hampered efforts to redevelop inner-city areas. Banks would not make loans, lest they wind up holding the property (and being responsible for the cleanup) in case of a default. America's landscape was scarred with such "brownfields" (as they came to be called), and America's firms had to get out to find green fields to build their new factories. A law intended to preserve and protect the land had led to opposite results.

Thirteen years after the bill had passed, only one out of seven major sites that had been identified had been cleaned up. Four years later, the administration was claiming that two-thirds of the sites had been, or were on the way to being, cleaned up. But even if these statistics prove accurate, the other problems—such as the brownfields and the inequities associated with joint and several liability—persisted. While there was universal agreement that reforms were needed, the differing perspectives of environmentalists, insurance companies, and polluters made resolution of these problems difficult. There were conflicts about both the standards of cleanup and about who should pay. While forcing those who pollute to pay provides strong incentives not to pollute, there was controversy over whether it was right to force people to pay for actions that were not illegal at the time they occurred, and whose consequences might not even have been apparent. Indeed, the worst effects of the powerful chemicals that dry cleaners had used was probably not on the land onto which some of these chemicals spilled, but on the owners and workers who spent their lives working in these cleaning plants, unaware of the health effects. They had already paid a high price—and given the competitive nature of the industry, the benefits of their using the chemicals were received by their customers: had they been required to dispose of the chemicals in another way, they would have done so and passed the costs on to their customers. And in any event, in many cases it was not the polluter who would actually pay, but their insurance companies—thus undermining the moral argument that polluters should pay.

By the spring of 1994, the Clinton administration had managed to get the various parties together on a compromise bill; but while the bill received bipartisan support in the House committee which had to approve it, as the November 1994 election approached, politics took over. And after the election, the business groups hoped for a better deal and abandoned support for the compromise. The stalemate persisted, and as this book goes to press, no reform bill has been passed.

ENDANGERED SPECIES

There has been concern not only to protect the environment from pollution, but also to preserve it. As populations expand, they crowd out nature. Throughout the world, a multitude of species are threatened with extinction. At the global level, international treaties have been signed to combat these threats; 1992 was marked not only by a treaty on global warming, but also by a treaty intended to preserve the world's biodiversity—plants as well as animals. Particularly powerful in this debate was the recognition that within this diverse biological heritage might lie cures for a myriad of diseases. Other international treaties are directed at preventing the extinction of whales, trade in ivory (which might encourage the extinction of elephants) and in rhinoceros horn (highly valued in certain parts of the world for its alleged powers in enhancing sexual potency).

The United States in 1973 passed the Endangered Species Act. The legislation has been highly controversial because of its potentially strong economic impact. For instance, logging in large parts of Washington and Oregon was halted because of a concern over the destruction of the habitat of the spotted owl, an endangered species; and in Texas, development of areas near Austin was halted over fear of destroying the habitat of some endangered species of spiders.

Critics argue that the preservation of these species is a public good, but a public good which owners of these particular parcels of land are made to pay for. If the public wants these species to be preserved, it should buy the land. Prohibiting owners from developing the land is almost tantamount to seizing it. Indeed, many argue that any restrictions on usage represent a

239

"taking" of property; and just as the government cannot simply take away your property without compensation, it should not be allowed to take away the uses to which you can put your property without compensation. There is a fundamental difference between laws which stop a person from imposing an externality on others, and laws which require a person to provide a public good (the protection of an endangered species) to others.

Supporters of the endangered species legislation, even when they recognize these arguments, say that there simply isn't enough money available to provide owners compensation; the choice is a pragmatic one—allow the species to become extinct, or impose these mandates on property owners. Besides, the longer the law is on the books, the less these arguments on "takings" become relevant; those who buy property know that their use may be encumbered by the Endangered Species Act, and this is reflected in the price which they pay upon purchase. The cost was effectively borne by the owners of the land at the time the law was enacted; if anyone should be compensated, it is the former owners, not the current ones.

While the specifics of environmental legislation—how best to improve the environment and how high to set the standards—are likely to remain contentious, there is a growing consensus on a set of general principles: The environment is of critical importance; markets alone will not provide efficient outcomes because of important externalities; some form of government action is required; and when possible, interventions should be performance based and market oriented.

REVIEW AND PRACTICE

SUMMARY

1 Externalities are actions of an individual or firm that have an effect on another individual or firm for which the latter does not pay or is not paid.

2 Sometimes economic efficiency can be attained without resort to government intervention: a) By establishing sufficiently large economic organizations, the externalities can be internalized. b) By establishing clear property rights, private parties can bargain toward an efficient solution, as suggested by Coase. c) By using the legal system, imposers of externalities can be forced to compensate victims.

3 There are important limitations to each of these private remedies. For instance, public goods problems and transactions costs impede efficient bargaining solutions in the manner suggested by Coase. These failures necessitate a greater role for government in remedying the problems of externalities.

4 There are four methods by which the government has attempted to induce individuals and firms to act in a socially efficient manner: fines and taxes, subsidies, tradable permits, and regulation.

5 When there is good information about the marginal social cost of the externality (as with pollution), and the fines can be adjusted to reflect

those costs, then a fine system can attain a Pareto efficient outcome. Subsidies to pollution abatement, while enabling the efficient level of pollution abatement to be attained, will result in excessive production of the pollution-generating commodity. In principle, the gainers under the fine system could more than compensate the losers, but in practice these compensations are seldom made. Thus, the choice of the system for controlling externalities has important distributional consequences.

6 Tradable permits can also result in efficient pollution abatement.

7 Regulations focusing on inputs or standards are likely to result in inefficiency.

8 The Clean Air Act has greatly reduced the level of pollution in the air. There is increasing concern about greenhouse gas emissions, which may lead to global warming.

9 The Clean Water Act has greatly reduced water pollution. Controversy remains over whether standards are excessively stringent, so that at the margin, costs exceed benefits.

10 The Superfund program, which is intended to clean up toxic waste sites, faces several problems, including excessive litigation costs and slow cleanups. Remedies include reforms in the legal system and the cleanup standards, and must address the problem of who should bear the costs of cleanup.

11 There has been increasing interest in preserving biodiversity, protecting endangered species. There is concern, however, that restrictions on land usage required to protect endangered species constitute an unfair "taking" of property.

KEY CONCEPTS

Externalities	Coase theorem
Common resource problems	Corrective taxes
Internalizing externalities	Superfund
Property rights	

QUESTIONS AND PROBLEMS

1 Make a list of the positive and negative externalities that you generate or that affect you. For each, discuss the advantages and disadvantages of each of the remedies discussed in the text.

2 An important class of externalities to which attention has recently been directed is called *information externalities*. The information produced by one individual or firm generates benefits for others. The success of an oil well on one tract of land increases the likelihood of oil's being found on an

adjacent tract, and hence increases the value of that tract. Can you think of other examples of information externalities? What are the likely consequences of information externalities for the efficiency of resource allocations? Discuss the possibilities of private market solutions to these problems.

3 Explain why subsidies for pollution abatement equipment, even if they result in an efficient level of pollution abatement, will not result in an efficient resource allocation.

4 Assume that there is uncertainty about the value of pollution control (as a result, for instance, of uncertainty about the costs of pollution). Draw two different "demand curves" (or benefit curves) for pollution, showing the marginal benefit of reducing pollution by one unit more decreasing as the level of pollution reduction increases. Assume that the marginal cost of pollution abatement increases as the level of pollution abatement increases.

    a Assume the government can regulate the amount of pollution control *after* it knows what the benefits are. Show what the level of pollution control will be in each situation.

    b Assume the government can impose a tax on pollution *after* it knows what the benefits are. Show what the level of tax (or fine) will be in each situation. Is there any difference between regulations and fines in these circumstances?

    c Now assume that the government must set the level of allowable pollution before it knows what the benefits are. How will it set the level of allowable pollution? (Hint: there is a deadweight loss from allowing too much pollution if it turns out the benefits of pollution reduction are high, and from being too restrictive if it turns out the benefits are low. How do you minimize the sum of these two deadweight losses?

    d Now assume the government must set the level of fine before it knows what the benefits are. How will it set the fine? Is there a difference between fines and regulations here?

    e Now assume that marginal benefits of pollution abatement are unknown. Assume also that when marginal benefits are high, the marginal costs are also high, and similarly, costs are low when benefits are low. Contrast a system of fines and regulations under these circumstances, where the level of fine or regulation must be set before costs are known.

5 Assume there are two types of communities in the United States, those in which there is a high benefit of pollution control and a high cost of pollution control, and those in which there is a low benefit of pollution control and a low cost of pollution control. Assume that the government must set either uniform regulations (a uniform level of pollution control)

or a uniform fine for pollution. Show diagrammatically that a regulatory scheme may be preferable to a system of fines. How does your answer change if communities in which there is a high marginal cost of pollution control happen to be communities in which there is a low marginal benefit; and communities with a low marginal cost of pollution control happen to be communities in which there is a high marginal benefit?

6 The impact of some externalities is very local, such as noise from airplanes landing and taking off at an airport. Such externalities depress the value of the immediately surrounding real estate. We say that the cost of the externality is *capitalized* in the value of the property. Assume that poor individuals are more willing to accept the high level of noise pollution, in return for the much lower rents they have to pay for housing. Describe the *incidence* of a regulation lowering the noise level surrounding the airport, that is, who benefits. (Hint: What will happen to land values? To rents?)

7 Zoning laws, which restrict how individuals can use their land, are sometimes justified as a means of controlling externalities. Explain. Discuss alternative solutions to these externalities.

8 What is the externality associated with an additional individual's driving on a congested road? How do tolls help alleviate this externality? How should the toll be set?

9 Explain why a system of joint implementation for reducing greenhouse gases is more efficient than if each country must reduce its pollution by a fixed amount.

10 Many economists are worried that unless all countries are required to reduce their levels of greenhouse gas emissions, reductions in emissions in one country may be partially offset by increases in another. Explain how this might occur.

11 Global warming is related to the concentration of greenhouse gases in the atmosphere. Once in the atmosphere, gases remain there for long periods of time (centuries). Greenhouse gases include carbon dioxide and methane.

    a Assume the effect on global warming of a given amount of carbon dioxide is four times that of methane. What should be the relative fine (tax) on emissions of the two gases?

    b How should the tax vary over time?

    c A carbon tax is a tax related to the amount of carbon dioxide that burning gas, oil, or coal adds to the atmosphere. With a carbon tax, coal is taxed very heavily (relative to the amount of energy put out) and natural gas relatively lightly. A BTU (British thermal unit) tax is a tax related to the amount of energy produced, for instance, by burning gas, oil, or coal. If one is concerned about greenhouse gas warming, why is a carbon tax preferable to a BTU tax?

12 Two different strategies are debated for reducing greenhouse gas emissions. One is that all the countries in the world should adopt common measures, such as a carbon tax. The other is that all countries in the world should adopt common goals, such as reducing the level of emissions to the levels of 1990. Explain the distribution and efficiency aspects of these two strategies.

13 CAFE (company average fuel economies) standards stipulate the average fuel efficiency (miles per gallon) of cars produced by each manufacturer. That is, the average fuel efficiency of cars sold by GM, Ford, Chrysler, Toyota, and so forth must be at least equal to the standard set by the government. Explain why such a system introduces both inefficiencies and inequities among different automobile manufacturers. (Hint: Consider a company that specializes in small cars versus one that specializes in large cars.)

14 Discuss some of the problems with CAFE standards. How might a system of "tradable CAFE standards" be designed, and why might such a system improve efficiency?

15 To resolve the controversy over insurance coverage of Superfund sites, it has been proposed that the insurance industry be taxed to create a fund out of which claims would be paid. What difference does it make if the tax is levied on the basis of:

    a Insurance premiums as of 1980?

    b Current insurance premiums?

Which insurance companies might be expected to prefer each way of levying the tax? (You can use a supply and demand diagram to illustrate the answers. How does each form of tax affect the supply curve of insurance?)

16 One proposal to reduce automobile emissions involves "pay at the pump insurance," under which individuals would pay, say, 25 cents per gallon of gasoline, with the proceeds going toward an insurance fund. What might be the environmental effects of such a proposal? Can you think of other grounds on which such a proposal might be attractive?

PART FOUR EXPENDITURE PROGRAMS

In this part, we show how the theoretical models we developed in previous chapters can be used to analyze a variety of public expenditure programs: national defense, health care, education, welfare, and social insurance. These particular programs were chosen for two reasons. They are among the most important programs: in terms of dollars spent they account for more than two-thirds of federal expenditures as well as of total public expenditures in the United States. And the examination of these particular programs brings out most of the critical issues in expenditure analysis; other programs can be analyzed using the basic framework and tools of analysis that we develop here. The first two chapters are devoted to explaining our basic approach to the analysis of public expenditures: Chapter 10 develops a general framework, while Chapter 11 shows how the benefits and costs of different government programs may be quantified. Chapters 12–16 then apply this framework.

10 The Analysis of Expenditure Policy

FOCUS QUESTIONS

1 What are the major steps in the analysis of a public expenditure program?

2 What are some of the reasons why the actual effects of a government program are different from those that are intended, or those that are apparent at first sight? What is meant by the incidence of a program?

3 Why are some programs said to be inefficient?

4 How in practice are the distributional impacts of a program assessed?

5 What is meant by the trade-off between equity and efficiency? Is there always such a trade-off?

6 Why might an understanding of the political process be relevant for an understanding of the design of government programs?

At least since the beginning of the 1990s, there have been calls for change in major segments of the American economy—its health care and education systems; for major reforms in welfare and social security; for cutbacks in some programs, such as defense, and expansions in others, such as those aimed at developing new technologies. This chapter provides a framework for thinking systematically about such policies: questions that need to be asked, and methods that can be employed to help answer them.

Policy makers need such a framework in order to address increasingly complex issues. Indeed, the complexity of most government programs is so great that Congress delegates responsibility for working out most of the details (within guidelines Congress has set up) to the executive branch. In a process called rule making, agencies of the executive branch (like the Environmental Protection Agency or the Department of Transportation) spell out these details, and the public is given time to comment. The Office of Management and Budget (OMB) within the Office of the President provides guidance to the agencies in how to go about this process. Currently, OMB guidance closely reflects the framework discussed in this chapter.

This framework for analyzing public expenditures provides guidelines for applying the efficiency and equity criteria presented in Chapters 3 and 5. It is not a simple formula that can be applied blindly to all problems, but rather a list of considerations that should be raised. Some may be more relevant to certain government programs than to others. The kinds of questions we are ultimately interested in addressing are:

• Why is there a government program in the first place?

• Why does the government program take on the particular form that it takes?

• How does the government program affect the private sector?

• Who gains and who loses as a result of the government program? Are the gains greater than the losses?

• Are there alternative programs that are (Pareto) superior to current government programs (that is, in which some individuals can be made better off without adversely affecting anyone else)? Are there alternative programs that have different distributional consequences but that at the same time achieve the program's primary objectives? What are the impediments to the introduction of these alternative programs?

We begin by breaking down the analysis of public expenditures into ten steps: (1) the need for a program; (2) market failures addressed by the program; (3) alternatives to the program; (4) particular design features of the program; (5) private sector responses; (6) efficiency consequences; (7) distributional consequences; (8) equity-efficiency trade-offs; (9) public policy objectives; and (10) the political process.

NEED FOR PROGRAM

It is often useful to begin the analysis of a public program by investigating the program's history and the circumstances under which it arose. Who were the individuals or groups who pressed for its passage, and what were the perceived needs that it supposedly addressed?

For instance, when the bill establishing the social security program was passed in 1935, the United States was in the midst of the Great Depression. Up to that time, few employers provided adequate pensions for their employees, and the private market for annuities (insurance policies that provide individuals with a given annual income from retirement until death, regardless of how long they live) was undeveloped; many individuals had failed to save adequately for their retirement, and many who had saved had found their savings wiped out by the stock market crash in 1929. The failure to have adequate savings was not as irrational and improvident as it appears to us today; in those days, many individuals continued to work until they died. They needed life insurance to look after their family after their demise, but not pensions for themselves. But in the Great Depression, many of these individuals lost their jobs and had no unemployment insurance. It was widely felt that society had to make some provision for them and that it was preferable to do so on a systematic basis rather than just to solve the immediate problems of the time.

MARKET FAILURES

The second step in the analysis of public programs is to attempt to relate the need, the source of demand, to one or more of the market failures discussed in Chapter 4: imperfect competition, public goods, externalities, incomplete markets, and imperfect information. In addition, we saw in Chapter 4 that even if the economy is Pareto efficient, there are two further arguments for government intervention: first, that the distribution of income emerging from the market economy may not be socially equitable; and second, that an individual's own perceptions of her welfare may be an inappropriate or inadequate criterion for making welfare judgments. There are merit goods, which the government should encourage, and merit bads, which the government should discourage or prohibit.

In some cases, the nature of the market failure is obvious: national defense is a pure public good, and as we argued earlier, in the absence of public provision, such goods will always be in undersupply. In other cases the answers are not so obvious, and economists may not agree about the nature of the market failure. Some economists believe that education is a public good, for example. But most economists argue that it is essentially a private good (in the technical sense defined in Chapter 6) and that to find an explanation for its public provision one must look elsewhere: for instance, at capital market imperfections; at the distributive consequences of public provision; or at education as a merit good, essential for the functioning of a democratic society.

The fact that there is a demand for the public provision of some good or service does not in itself imply that there has been a market failure. Some demands for public provision arise from an inadequate understanding of the market and of the government's capabilities for making things better. Identifying whether there is or is not a market failure is an essential step in identifying the appropriate scope for government action.

HIGHER EDUCATION IN THE UNITED STATES

In the United States, higher education illustrates several of the alternative forms of government involvement. It is publicly produced: every state has its own system of universities, colleges, and junior colleges. Though direct aid to private universities is limited in the United States, in other countries (such as Canada) it is common, and is granted on the basis of the number of students enrolled. In the United States the federal government provides considerable aid to research universities through a variety of programs of support for basic and applied research. Most federal support to higher education, however, takes the form of support to the consumers, the students. Though there have been no general programs of support, there have been three major selective programs. First, since World War II a large number of veterans have

ALTERNATIVE FORMS OF GOVERNMENT INTERVENTION

Once a market failure has been identified, a variety of government actions might address the problem. The three major categories of government action are public production; private production with taxes and subsidies aimed at encouraging or discouraging certain activities; and private production with government regulation aimed at ensuring that firms act in the desired way.

If the government decides to bear responsibility for production, it must decide on how the output is to be allocated. It can charge for the good at market prices; it can charge for the good at something approximating the cost of production, as it typically does for electricity; it can charge for the good, but the charges can be much less than the cost of production, as it typically does for higher education; it can provide the good free of charge and uniformly, as it does for elementary school and secondary school education; or it can allocate the good or service in some way corresponding to a perceived need or benefit. In countries like Britain, where medicine is provided for free, it is obviously not provided equally to all individuals. Needs differ. The decision as to who gets how much of the available supply of medical services is left to doctors (operating within guidelines set up by the government, in consultation with them).

Similarly, if the good is to be privately produced, the government must decide whether to: (a) contract directly for the commodity but retain responsibility for distributing it; (b) provide a subsidy to producers, with the hope that some of the benefits will be passed on to consumers through lower prices; or (c) provide a subsidy to consumers. And if some form of subsidy is desired, government must decide whether it should be provided through the tax system or through a direct grant. If a subsidy is granted, the

attended colleges and universities at government expense. Second, federally guaranteed loans to lower- and middle-income individuals, often at subsidized rates, have made higher education more financially accessible. In 1993, these loan programs were greatly expanded; the government now directly provides loans, and it has introduced new, more flexible, loan programs (where repayment rates depend on income). Third, the government provides grants to low-income individuals (called Pell Grants) to enable them to go to college.

In 1997 a new form of federal support was introduced, a tuition tax credit for the first two years of college for lower- and middle-income families.

terms have to be decided upon—for example, how restrictive eligibility standards should be. All of these possible forms of government action are observed.

The importance of identifying alternative programs is increasingly recognized. Frequently new programs can be devised that attain the objectives of older programs at less cost and more effectively. "Social innovation" is no less important than technological innovation. Today, there is increasing emphasis on the use of markets and marketlike mechanisms.

ALTERNATIVE FORMS OF GOVERNMENT INTERVENTION

1 Public Production

    Free distribution

    Distribution at below cost of production

    Distribution at cost

2 Private Production

    Government subsidies to (taxes on) producers

    Government subsidies to (taxes on) consumers

    Direct government distribution

    Government regulation

THE IMPORTANCE OF PARTICULAR
DESIGN FEATURES

The detailed provisions of a program, for instance the precise statements concerning the eligibility standards, are often crucial in determining the efficiency and equity consequences of the program. Fairness and efficiency require making a number of distinctions that, though clear in principle, are difficult to apply in practice. The distinction between those who are hungry and those who are not is an important one, but devising a program to provide food for the hungry requires some easy way of identifying who the hungry are. Too narrow a definition will result in many of those who are needy not receiving aid. Too broad a set of eligibility standards will result in many individuals who are not needy receiving aid, much to the objections of other taxpayers who are having to contribute to these individuals' support. Thus, because of the impossibility of identifying perfectly those who are truly deserving of aid, there is a trade-off, when designing regulations, between two types of errors: denying aid to those who are deserving and granting aid to those who are not deserving (see Figure 10.1). Different individuals may judge the importance of these two kinds of errors differently.

The design of eligibility standards has further effects, as individuals may alter their behavior to gain eligibility or to receive larger benefits. There has been concern, for instance, that welfare programs that provide funds only to single mothers discourage marriage. Food stamps, which provide assistance to people with low available income, offer another example of altered

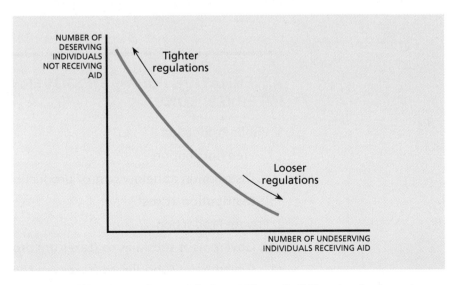

FIGURE 10.1   **The Trade-off in Designing Regulations** When eligibility standards are loose, many individuals who are undeserving will qualify for aid. When standards are tight, many deserving individuals will not qualify for aid.

incentives. To calculate the amount of income available for spending on food, expenditures on housing are subtracted from the individual's take-home pay. But this may alter behavior: the individual who spends more on housing receives more in food stamps. Food stamps, a program intended to encourage better nutrition among the poor, may—because of the particular way it has been designed—encourage more expenditure on housing.

PRIVATE SECTOR RESPONSES
TO GOVERNMENT PROGRAMS

One of the central features of a mixed market economy like that of the United States is that the government has only a limited degree of control over it. The private sector may, for instance, react to any government program in such a way as to undo many of its alleged benefits. For example, when the government increases social security benefits, the welfare of the aged may not increase in the long run by the full corresponding amount; individuals may be induced to reduce their own savings for retirement, and children may be induced to provide less support for their aging parents. Public support may thus **"crowd out"** private support, eroding the impact of the program.

In considering the consequences of a government program, one needs to look at the long-run consequences, after all producers and consumers have adjusted their behavior, as well as the immediate impact. One of the major impacts of rent control, for instance, is that the supply of new housing dries up, the effects of which are felt only gradually.

Calculating the full private-sector responses is often one of the most difficult and contentious aspects of analyzing a government program. To what extent, for instance, will a government subsidy to builders of lower-income housing result in higher profits, thus benefiting the building industry? To what extent will competition in the industry bid these profits away, lowering the price and increasing the supply, thus benefiting the intended beneficiaries? The answers depend on views concerning the housing and construction markets. How competitive is the building industry? If it is competitive, what is the elasticity of supply? What is the elasticity of demand?[1]

As we have already noted, the effects of a government program may hinge critically on seemingly innocuous design features. Economists look for *marginal incentive* effects. Two programs giving the same average subsidy can have quite different marginal incentive effects. A food stamp program with a $200 cap on benefits may have no *marginal* effect for those individuals who spend more than $200 on food. An analysis of the magnitude of the demand and supply responses from the private sector—and thus of the effects on price and quantities—must pay careful attention to these marginal incentives.

---

[1] Elasticity of supply is defined as the percentage change in quantity supplied as a result of a 1 percent change in price; elasticity of demand is defined as the percentage change in quantity demanded as a result of a 1 percent change in price.

EFFICIENCY CONSEQUENCES

The next steps in expenditure policy analysis entail identifying the efficiency and distributional consequences of each alternative program and assessing the extent to which alternative programs can meet the objectives of public policy.

Government programs may result in inefficiencies both in the production of a good or service and in levels of consumption. In Chapter 8 we suggested that the government's decision to produce a good or service itself, to purchase the good or service from private firms but distribute it itself, or to have private firms produce it and market it subject to government regulation may significantly affect the costs associated with producing and delivering the given good or service.

We also suggested that when consumers had an element of choice, the competition among providers would likely increase the efficiency with which the goods or services were provided as well as make what was produced more responsive to the needs and desires of consumers. These arguments are less persuasive if consumers have limited information concerning the product they are purchasing (such as medical care), or if consumer concern about costs is reduced because the government pays all, or a substantial part of the costs (again, as in the case of medical care).

For many programs, it is useful to distinguish between **substitution effects** and **income effects.** Whenever a government program lowers the price of some commodity, there is a substitution effect: the individual substitutes the cheaper good for other goods. For example, with tuition subsidies for higher education individuals substitute education for other goods they might have spent their money on. On the other hand, grants to individuals that make them better off but do not alter the relative prices of different commodities result in an income effect: an individual changes his expenditure pattern because he is better off. In many cases, there is both an income effect and a substitution effect, and both alter the individual's behavior. Normally, however, it is only the substitution effect that we associate with *inefficiency*.

To see this, assume that the government gives an individual food stamps to buy $10 worth of groceries every week. Prior to this, the individual's budget constraint was the lower one in Figure 10.2. By giving up $1 of groceries the individual could acquire $1 more of other goods. The food stamp program shifts his budget constraint to the right. If the individual now wants to consume more than $10 worth of groceries, he still must give up $1 of other goods for each extra dollar of groceries consumed; there is no substitution effect. There is, however, an income effect—the individual now has $10 extra to spend. The effect on food consumption is the same as giving the individual an equivalent amount of income (except in the case where the individual would prefer to consume less than $10 worth of food each week). The food stamp program has altered his behavior; he consumes more food (*B*) than he previously did (*A*). But notice that he does not increase his food consumption by the full $10; he spreads this extra income between food and all other goods, just as he would have with $10 more of income. Because there is no substitution effect, there is no inefficiency associated with this food stamp program.

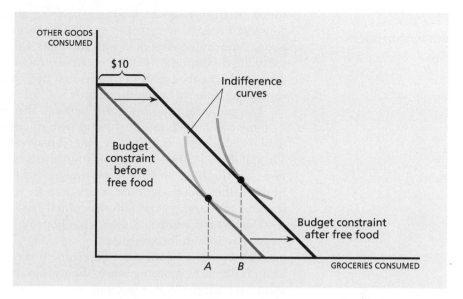

FIGURE 10.2   **Income Effect** Giving free food has an income effect but no substitution effect: its effects are identical to giving an individual extra income.

To see the substitution effect, assume, in contrast, that the government has agreed to pay for 30 percent of food purchases. This lowers the cost of food. The new budget constraint is shown in Figure 10.3. Now there is a sub-

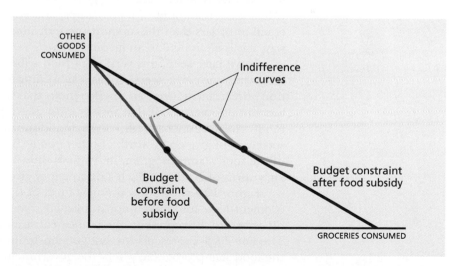

FIGURE 10.3   **Substitution Effect** When government pays a part of the costs of food, there is a substitution effect. The slope of the budget constraint changes. In this figure, the government pays a fixed fraction of the cost of food, regardless of the amount the individual consumes.

stitution effect. Food is cheaper relative to all other goods, so the budget constraint rotates as shown. Note that in Figure 10.2, by contrast, the new budget constraint associated with the food stamps is parallel with the original budget constraint. (There is also an income effect in Figure 10.3, because with cheaper food the individual not only consumes more food, he can consume more of all other goods.)

It is important to distinguish between income and substitution effects. In some cases, the government may wish to encourage or discourage a particular economic activity; in that case, it may want a large substitution effect. Thus, if there is a belief that poor individuals do not attach sufficient importance to housing, and the government wishes to improve the quality of housing they purchase, then a program in which the government pays a fraction of housing expenditures (which has, as a result, a substitution effect) will be more effective than a flat housing grant, which (unless it is very large) has only an income effect.

On the other hand, if the government is primarily concerned with how well off different individuals are, then programs that do not alter marginal incentives are preferable; such programs do not cause the inefficiencies associated with the substitution effect.

Returning to the case of food stamps, we can see how a change in the design of the program avoids the inefficiency generated by the substitution effect. When the program was established in 1964, participants purchased food stamps at a discount from their face value, so the government paid a fraction of the costs of stamps. Thus, food stamps worth $100 might cost a poor person $70; she might be allowed to buy, say, up to $2000 of food stamps. She might, in fact, purchase only $1000 worth of food stamps—for a total subsidy of $300. Today, the government simply gives a low-income individual a fixed amount of food stamps, and so long as the amount given is equal to or less than the amount the individual would spend on food anyway, this is equivalent to an income grant.

As we have seen, this version of food subsidies has only an income effect, while the earlier version has a substitution effect as well. The substitution effect introduces an inefficiency: the true cost of groceries—the amount of other goods that society must give up to obtain an extra unit of food—remains unchanged. For each additional dollar of food consumed, society must give up $1 worth of other goods. But under the original version of the food stamp program, individuals only had to pay 30 cents for a dollar's worth of groceries. Such a discrepancy gives rise to inefficiency.

Figure 10.4 shows how the new form of the program can cost the government less—and leave poor individuals receiving the subsidy just as well off as before. *BB* represents the budget constraint before any food subsidies. The line *BKB′* represents the budget constraint under the original form of the food stamp program, where the government pays for a fixed fraction of the costs of groceries, up to some limit. After that limit is reached (represented by the point *K*) individuals have to pay the full price of groceries. The individual chooses the point *E*, where her indifference curve is tangent to the budget constraint. The magnitude of the subsidy is the difference between what the individual has to pay and what society has to forgo; it corre-

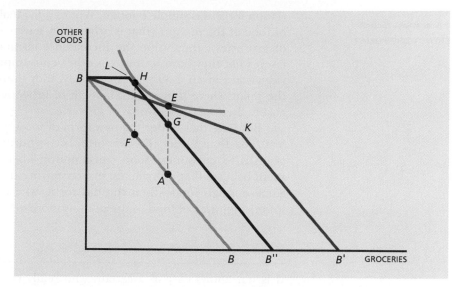

FIGURE 10.4 **Inefficiency Associated with Old-Style Food Stamp Program** Under the original form of food stamps, the government paid a fixed fraction of the costs of groceries, up to some limit, generating the budget constraint *BKB'*. The new form (*BLB''*), where the government pays for a fixed amount of food, can make individuals just as well off, but cost less. The "savings" is represented by the distance *EG*.

sponds to the vertical distance between the before-subsidy budget constraint and the after-subsidy budget constraint at the equilibrium level of consumption of groceries, the distance *AE*.

Figure 10.4 also includes a budget constraint for the food stamps given in the form of a fixed amount to be spent on food. How do we know that the individual is just as well off? Because the income grant was set so that the budget constraint it produced would be tangent to the indifference curve through *E*. By definition of indifference curves, then, the individual is just as satisfied at *H* as at *E*. But the income grant costs the government less. Again, the cost of the program is represented by the vertical distance between the before-subsidy and after-subsidy budget constraints. The size of the grant, *HF*, is smaller than the size of the 30 percent subsidy, *AE*.[2] The

---

[2] To see this, note that the budget constraint segment *LB''* is parallel to the budget constraint *BB*—the individual has to pay the full marginal cost of food, and so the trade-off between food and other goods is unchanged. Thus, *AG* = *FH* (the vertical distance between two parallel lines is everywhere the same). The inefficiency associated with the 30 percent subsidy is thus measured by *EG*; the government must spend that amount extra to leave the individual just as well off as he would have been with an income grant. *EG* is the deadweight loss associated with the inefficient subsidy.

reason for this is simple enough: When individuals have to pay the full price of food at the margin (that is, when they have to pay $1 for $1 more worth of groceries), they value the increased consumption of groceries by precisely what they have to forgo in other consumption goods. But when individuals are given a 30 percent subsidy, they then purchase groceries up to the point where they value $1 worth of groceries at 70 cents, which is the cost to them of the $1 worth of groceries.

But note that under the new form of food stamps, individuals consume less food than under the old form. If the purpose of the food stamp program is to encourage food consumption—because, for instance, government believes that individuals, in maximizing their own utility, will not consume enough food—then the old form, where the government in effect lowers the price of food to the poor, is more effective.

DISTRIBUTIONAL CONSEQUENCES

It is not always easy to ascertain who really benefits from a given government program. Consider, for instance, the Medicare program, under which government finances most medical care for the aged. The aged clearly benefit greatly from the program; but to some extent, the federal aid substitutes for money that families of the elderly would have contributed (public expenditures thus crowd out private expenditures), and to that extent, the true beneficiaries of the program are not the elderly but their children. With this sort of analysis, economists seek to identify a property they call the **incidence** of a government expenditure program or tax, that is, they seek to answer the question of who really benefits from, is hurt by, or bears the burden of the program or tax.

Government programs often induce a variety of responses from the private sector which result in changes in prices. Thus, a program's effects can extend well beyond the people directly affected, and often the beneficiaries are different from those that were intended. There has been considerable concern that, at least in the short run, federal subsidies for private housing for the poor simply increase the price of housing, making the true beneficiaries the slum landlords, not the poor.

The effect of a government subsidy is illustrated in Figure 10.5, which shows the demand and supply curves for housing. In the short run (panel A), the supply of housing is assumed to be very inelastic because it takes some time for new housing to be constructed. Assume the government has passed a general subsidy for housing, the effect of which is to increase the demand for housing (the demand curve shifts up). Note that in the figure, almost the entire subsidy is reflected in the increased price of housing; the actual level of housing services provided increases very little. In the long run, of course, the supply response is likely to be larger; hence in Figure 10.5B the long-run supply curve is fairly flat, showing that a small percentage increase in the price, given enough time, elicits a fairly large increase in the supply of housing. In the short run, the beneficiaries of housing subsidies are the current owners of houses; renters find that virtually their entire

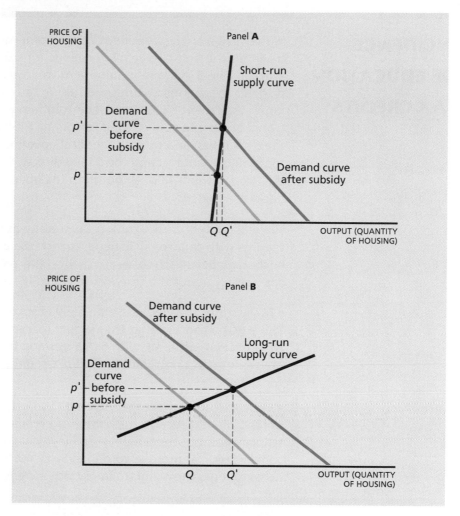

FIGURE 10.5 **Short-Run and Long-Run Incidence of Expenditure Program** (A) In the short run, a subsidy may increase price more than quantity. Thus landlords may benefit from a housing subsidy given to help the poor acquire better housing. (B) In the long run, the output response will be larger and the price response smaller.

subsidy is reflected in higher rents (the shift from p to p'). In the long run, however, renters are better off, as the increase in the quantity of housing supplied (from Q to Q') serves to limit the price increase.

Mass transit subsidies provide another example: Who benefits from a new subway system? At first glance, the answer seems obvious: subway riders. But this may be incorrect. Those who own houses or apartments near the subway will find that their houses and apartments are more sought after; the increased demand for these residences will be reflected in the rents that the

INCIDENCE OF EDUCATION TAX CREDITS

In the 1996 election, President Clinton proposed a $1500 tuition tax credit for the first two years of college for students who obtained a B average. The B average requirement was intended to encourage students to work hard. With the tuition tax credit, a middle-income family that spent $2000 in college tuition on their freshman daughter would be able to reduce their tax bill by $1500. It was as if they paid their full taxes, and then the federal government sent them a check for $1500. By subtracting the $1500 directly from the tax payment, this "round trip"—money going to the government and then coming back—is avoided.

While the intent of the tuition tax credit was to help middle-class families with children in college, to increase enrollment, and to encourage better school performance, there was considerable controversy about the true incidence.

• Many states charged less than $1500 for community colleges. There was a concern that they would (perhaps gradually) raise their tuition—after all, with $1500 coming from the federal government in tax credits, individuals could afford to pay more for tuition.

• Colleges could offset the increased tuition costs for those whose parents did not receive the tuition tax credit by giving them scholarships; but they might not, in which case some kids would find college less, not more, affordable. Since most A and B students already go to college, the program might not increase enrollment much

owners can charge (and in the market value of the houses and apartments). The commuter who owns no real estate finds that he is better off because of the better subway service, but worse off because of the higher rents, and the two effects are likely to cancel out. The true beneficiaries are the property owners near the subway lines.

The subway example illustrates a general principle: The benefits of government programs are often **capitalized** in the value of scarce assets associated with obtaining those benefits (land near the subway stops). In that case, the true beneficiaries are those who own the asset at the time the program was announced (or passed, or when it came to be believed that the program would pass). By the same token, the costs of a program are often capitalized, so that a tax on land is reflected in the value of the land; the true costs are borne by those who own the asset at the time the tax was announced (or passed, or when it came to be believed that the tax would be passed). When those who benefit from a government program are different

among them, but it might reduce enrollment among C students. Alternatively, teachers might worry that by giving a low grade—even a C—they might shut off a kid's chance of staying in college, by cutting off the tuition tax credit. There may be grade inflation. But with grade inflation, better students may have less incentive to work hard.

• If states did raise their tuition, then at least some of the benefits would accrue to state governments, rather than to the taxpayers. This is the "true" incidence. Education still might be helped, if the state spent most of the increased tuition revenue on education; on the other hand, the state might reduce its educational expenditures, and give a tax cut to its taxpayers. Then the true incidence would be on the states' taxpayers in general, not just those who had children in college. If the state reduced taxes at the top, then what had appeared to be a middle-class tax break would become a tax break for upper-income individuals, as a result of shifting.

• Similarly, private schools might be induced to raise their tuitions, enabling them to pay higher faculty salaries or support more research. Again, the incidence is markedly different from that intended.

As a result of concern about some of these perverse incentive effects—as well as complications in implementation—when the tuition tax credit was enacted in 1997, the B requirement was dropped. It is too soon to tell to what extent the tuition tax credit will lead to higher tuitions.

from those that the program was intended to help, we say that the benefits have been **shifted,** or that the *actual incidence* (those on whom the benefits actually fall) is different from the intended one. Considerable research in recent years has been devoted to determining the actual incidence of government programs.

EVALUATING THE DISTRIBUTIONAL CONSEQUENCES

As we have noted, different individuals receive different benefits from a given government program. Although it is obviously not possible to identify how much *each* individual benefits, it may be important to know how different groups in society are differentially affected. Which groups we focus on may vary from program to program, and benefits may vary within a particular income group. Thus, a program of rebates for heating-oil expenditures for people whose income falls below a particular level obviously benefits the poor more than the rich, but it benefits some poor (those who consume a lot of heating oil, those who live in the Northeast) more than others (those who live in the Sun Belt). If the variability of consumption of heating oil among the poor is very large, this rebate program may be viewed as an unfair way of helping the poor, unless those who consume a lot of heating oil are viewed as particularly deserving of assistance.

In other cases, we may attempt to identify how producers are affected differentially. This typically is the focus of analysis in the evaluation of programs aimed at aiding particular industries, such as agricultural price supports. In still other cases, such as the social security program, we may be concerned with the differential impact on the present elderly versus the impact on the young—the elderly of the future. We refer to these impacts as the program's **intertemporal distribution effects**—distribution effects over time. In still other cases, we may wish to identify the regional impact or the impact on cities versus suburbs, or urban versus rural areas.

When a program's benefits accrue disproportionately to the poor (they receive more than their contribution to the costs of the program through the tax system), we say that its distribution effect is **progressive.** If the benefits accrue disproportionately to the rich, we say that the program's distribution effect is **regressive.**

There are often controversies about who are the real beneficiaries of a program, and one's perspective on its distributive impact is determined in large part by the group one is focusing on. For instance, government support for higher education is often viewed as enabling the children of the poor to go to college, and thus is viewed to have a positive redistributive impact. But children of the middle and upper-middle classes are more likely to avail themselves of a higher education. Thus, *general* subsidies—such as reduced tuition for all students—disproportionately benefit children of middle- and upper-income families. Indeed, by some calculations they benefit more than their share of taxes—educational subsidies to higher education are thus regressive. This is in contrast to *targeted* subsidies—such as scholarships for children from low-income families. Even then, it is not clear that parents' income provides the appropriate focus of attention; the beneficiaries of education are not the parents but the children; it is they who will receive higher wages as a result of their increased level of education.[3] Those who hold to this view often favor student loan programs. Let us contrast the distributional consequences of direct state support for universities (allowing them to charge a low tuition) with the distributional consequences of a student loan program. Those who avail themselves of higher education will, on average, have a much higher income than those who do not. A loan program may thus be more progressive than the current system, where even low-wage high school dropouts are called upon to provide some support for higher education. Loan programs introduced in 1993, which allowed repayments to be related to students' incomes, increased progressivity still fur-

---

[3] With middle- and upper-income parents who would have sent their children to college anyway, the true beneficiaries may be the parents, who save on the money they otherwise would have spent; but to the extent that parents use this money to increase the bequest they leave to their children, it is the children who really benefit.

ther, since students who wind up making higher incomes in effect pay more than those who receive low incomes. As this example makes clear, one's view of the distributional impact of a government program depends not only on what groups one focuses upon but also on the available alternatives to a given program. The relevant choice is seldom one program versus no program, but one *type* of program versus another. Thus, the present state system of aid to higher education*may* be more progressive than a totally private education system; but its distributional impact may look less favorable when contrasted with a system of loans for higher education.

**FAIRNESS AND
DISTRIBUTION**

Political discussions commonly focus on the equity of various proposals, with each side claiming that its proposals are more fair. Notions of fairness, unfortunately, are not well defined; different individuals may have conflicting views of what is fair. A middle-class couple who love children but have decided for financial reasons to limit the number of children they have to two may feel that it is unfair for them to have to support a child from a family of ten children whose parents don't want to use modern birth control methods and cannot afford to send their kids to college without government assistance. A couple who have saved $40,000 to put a child through college may feel that it is unfair that they are not entitled to receive a government grant or loan, when their next-door neighbors, with the same income (who have put nothing aside for their children's education), enjoy expensive vacations every winter and are entitled to a government grant (which depends not only on family income, but on assets).

CONSEQUENCES OF PUBLIC PROGRAMS

1 Government programs may crowd out private actions; equivalently, private actions may largely offset public actions, resulting in a small net effect.

2 Government programs give rise to income and substitution effects. The substitution effect is related to the magnitude of the marginal incentives.

3 Inefficiencies in public programs are related to the magnitude of the substitution effect.

4 The incidence of a program describes who actually benefits from, or is hurt by, the program. The actual incidence is often markedly different from the intended or apparent incidence.

5 The benefits of a program may be capitalized, in which case the true beneficiaries are those who own the asset in which they are capitalized at the time the program was started (or announced).

An unmarried person and a family with both spouses working may both think it unfair that their expected returns from social security are so much lower than those of an individual whose spouse does not have a job outside the home. But an individual whose spouse does not work outside the home may feel that it is fair that he receive more, since his family has not had the benefit of a second income.

EQUITY-EFFICIENCY TRADE-OFFS

Because of the ambiguities associated with using the term "fair," economists try to avoid it in their analysis; rather, they focus on identifying the impact of programs. Economists begin their analysis of any program by looking for Pareto or near-Pareto improvements, changes in the program which make someone, or some groups, better off, without making anyone, or almost anyone, worse off. Rent control, it is argued, in the long run fails to benefit renters, as the supply of housing dries up. There are better ways of helping low-income individuals obtain housing. Welfare programs that create a sense of dependency among welfare recipients do not serve the beneficiaries well. If taxpayers invested a little more money in training and education, in the long run, beneficiaries would be better off, and the tax burden resulting from support of the welfare population might actually be reduced. There are alternative market-based ways of dealing with pollution, such as fines and tradable permits (see Chapter 9) which can achieve higher levels of pollution reduction than a system of strict regulation, at lower costs—benefiting both the environment and the economy.

Unfortunately, while there is considerable scope for such Pareto or near-Pareto improvements, in many expenditure programs trade-offs exist between the objectives of efficiency and equity (redistribution of income or benefits to the needy). It may be possible to design a more progressive expenditure program, but only at some cost. An increase in social security benefits may be desirable from the perspective of certain distributional goals, but the increased benefits may lead to earlier retirement, and the higher taxes required to finance them may decrease work incentives. Higher unemployment compensation may provide increased income to some who are among the most needy, but unemployment insurance may make some individuals feel disinclined to find another job.

Disagreements about the desirability of different programs often arise from disagreements not only about values, the relative importance of equity versus efficiency considerations, but also about the nature of the trade-offs, how much loss of efficiency would result from an attempt to change a program's structure of benefits to make its distributional impact more progressive.

Figure 10.6 shows the equity-efficiency frontier for a hypothetical program and the indifference curves for two individuals. In panel A, Scrooge is much less willing to give up efficiency for a gain in equity than is his brother, Spendthrift. E_1 represents the point on the trade-off curve that is optimal as Spendthrift sees it, while E_2 is optimal from the point of view of Scrooge. Not surprisingly, Scrooge chooses a point with higher efficiency but lower equity

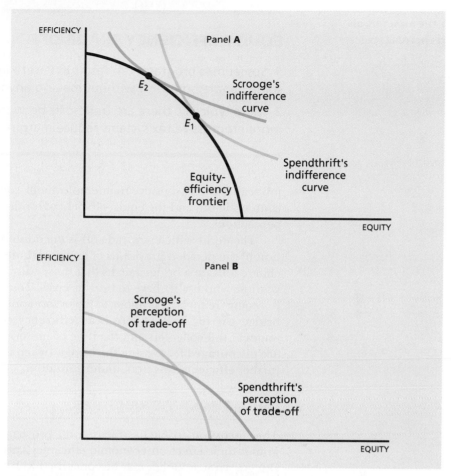

FIGURE 10.6 **Sources of Differences in Views Concerning Public Programs** (A) Scrooge and Spendthrift have the same perceptions concerning trade-offs but differ in values (indifference curves). (B) Scrooge and Spendthrift differ in their perception of the nature of the efficiency-equity trade-off.

than does Spendthrift. Thus in panel A, the source of the disagreement about policy is a difference in the values held by the two individuals.

On the other hand, panel B depicts a situation where the differences about policy arise from differences in judgments concerning the nature of the trade-off. Scrooge thinks that to get a slight increase in equity one must give up a lot of efficiency. On the other hand, Spendthrift thinks that one can get a large increase in equity with just a slight loss in efficiency.

For instance, if the main reason that unemployed individuals do not obtain jobs is that there are no jobs available, then the size of unemployment insurance may have little effect on search. But if unemployment insurance has little effect on job search, there is not much trade-off between efficiency and equity, and the frontier is consistent with Spendthrift's perceptions; if

265

EQUITY-EFFICIENCY TRADE-OFF

1 Sometimes programs can result in Pareto improvements, making some people better off without making anyone worse off.

2 More typically, there are trade-offs between equity and efficiency; more progressive tax systems reduce marginal incentives to work.

job search is very sensitive to unemployment compensation, there is a significant trade-off, and the equity-efficiency frontier is consistent with Scrooge's perceptions.

The equity-efficiency trade-off is encountered repeatedly in the evaluation of the detailed provisions of any government program. The decision to charge tolls on a bridge means that those who benefit from the bridge (that is, those who use it) have to bear its costs. To many people, this is desirable for equity reasons; it is unfair to make someone who does not drive over the bridge pay for it. But there is an efficiency cost in money and time: the wages of toll collectors and the time of motorists. Moreover, if some drivers are discouraged from using the bridge (when it is below capacity), there is a further efficiency loss from underutilization.

PUBLIC POLICY OBJECTIVES

The discussion so far has focused on two bases for evaluating public programs: their effect on economic efficiency and their effect on distribution. But government policy may be concerned with a broader range of objectives. For instance, government may be concerned with the extent to which individuals of different racial, ethnic, and class backgrounds are mixed together in schools. It may be concerned not just with the income of the poor but with the physical appearance of the housing in which they live. When these alternative objectives are fairly well defined, the government can still make use of a variety of instruments for attaining them; it can, for instance, still make use of private producers, by imposing regulations on them, or by setting standards that have to be met for individuals or firms to be eligible to receive subsidies. Thus the government has specified that institutions receiving federal grants must comply with certain affirmative action regulations.

In some cases, however, it may be difficult for the government to specify clearly (and in advance) all of its objectives, or to articulate them in the form of a set of regulations or standards. There is widespread belief that private producers, in the absence of well-articulated and enforced regulations, will simply pursue profit-maximizing behavior, regardless of alternative objectives that they may affirm. In such circumstances, there is an argument for the government to assume direct responsibility for the activity. But to the extent that this is true, it may be difficult for Congress or the executive branch to clearly specify the objectives it wishes the bureaucrats responsible for implementing its programs to pursue. In that case, the bureaucrats will be left with considerable discretion, and the discrepancies between how they exercise that discretion and the intent of, say, Congress may be significant.

Similarly, there is concern that whenever the government finances an activity, it will almost inevitably impose a set of regulations, some of which may have adverse effects, particularly on economic efficiency; thus many of the alleged efficiency advantages of private production may be lost. These concerns have been raised, for instance, in discussions of school voucher programs, which would provide students with funds that could be used at any school, private or public.

POLITICAL PROCESS

In a democracy, the design and adoption of any public expenditure program involves many individuals and groups, with various objectives and various beliefs about how the economy works. The program that eventually is adopted represents a compromise among their views; it probably will not conform to the views of any one individual and may seem to be inconsistent with any single set of objectives. If two chefs disagree about the appropriate liquid to add to a sauce, one arguing for lemon juice and the other for cream, the compromise solution of adding a little of both may be disastrous, with results inconsistent with any culinary objective.

The study of the political process by which a particular expenditure program was adopted may be insightful for several reasons. First, we may be able to understand why the program looks the way it does. Consider the government program to stabilize farmers' prices. There is a market failure that this program addresses: the inability of individuals to obtain insurance for many of the important risks they face, including the risks associated with the variability of prices.[4] But a closer examination of the price stabilization program suggests that if that were the only objective, it would be designed in a quite different way. What farmers care about is *income* risk—not just the variability of price, but the variability of all the factors that go into determining net income (including output and costs). In some cases, the price stabilization program may actually increase income variability. In fact, reducing risk is probably not the true objective: the real objective is to transfer resources (income) to farmers from the rest of the population. Yet if that is the objective, there are more efficient ways of transferring resources to the farmers; outright grants would be preferable to the present program. But if that objective were made explicit—if the transfers were made conspicuous—they might not get approved. Voters in urban districts might strongly oppose them, while they do not oppose the present form of inefficient subsidies, simply because they are not fully aware of the nature of the transfers.

Particular provisions of public programs are likely to have strong distributional consequences for particular groups in the population. If one group

---

[4] Futures markets now enable farmers to divest themselves of some of the risks associated with price variability.

can be suitably organized, it will attempt to induce the political process to adopt provisions that are to its benefit. In Chapter 9 we discussed the regulations providing for scrubbing the smoke emitted from burning coal. These regulations may have an enormous effect on the relative demand for hard (or western) coal and bituminous coal, and hence on the incomes of both miners and coal producers in different parts of the country. The shape of environmental legislation and regulation may be affected as much by these particular distributional consequences as by overall efficiency considerations.

A second reason why it may be helpful to study an expenditure program's adoption process is that in democracies, programs respond at least in part to the desires and perceptions of voters. Because programs have to be explained and "sold" to voters, there is a premium on simplicity. Also, programs often look different from the way that economists think they should be designed because voters often do not understand the true incidence of a program. For instance, most voters think that half of the cost of social security is paid for by contributions from the employer; most economists believe that the true incidence is the same as it would be if social security contributions were paid entirely by workers. In this case, the confusion over incidence has few consequences, but in many other programs, this confusion can have significant impacts, as we shall see in later chapters.

Finally, the design of programs may affect the extent to which they are subjected to political pressures or corruption. Corruption is an increasing concern in many countries. It can take a variety of forms. In modern democracies, special interests contribute to campaigns, often in an attempt to "buy" legislation that favors them; in many countries, bureaucrats use their discretionary powers to extend favors in return for bribes. In New York City, there have been extensive reports of bribes to building inspectors, more to ensure that they inspect the building in a timely way (so that there will not be costly interruptions to construction) than to give approval to a substandard building. The more discretion that is left to bureaucrats, the more potential there is for the exercise of political influence and corruption.

Accordingly, in evaluating alternative policies, one needs to take into account the political process, what the legislation might look like after it has been subjected to the political process, and what the consequences of the program will be, knowing that it will be administered by bureaucrats, probably not unlike those administering other government programs, and subject to the same kinds of incentives.

REVIEW AND PRACTICE

SUMMARY

There are ten major elements in the analysis of public expenditure programs:

1 Identifying a need, the source of demand for the government program;

2 Identifying a market failure (if it exists) and ascertaining whether what is at issue is a concern for (the consequences of) the distribution of income or the provision of a merit good;

3 Identifying alternative programs that might address the perceived problems;

4 In ascertaining and evaluating the impacts of alternative programs, paying attention to the importance of particular design features;

5 Identifying private sector responses;

6 Identifying the efficiency consequences of alternative programs;

7 Identifying the distributional consequences of alternative programs;

8 Identifying the trade-offs between equity and efficiency considerations;

9 Identifying the extent to which alternative programs achieve public policy objectives; and

10 Identifying how the political process affects the design and implementation of public programs.

KEY CONCEPTS

Crowding out	Shifting
Substitution effect	Intertemporal distribution effects
Income effect	Progressive
Incidence	Regressive
Capitalization	

QUESTIONS AND PROBLEMS

1 Explain how the following actual design features have an important effect on the consequences of government programs:

   a The income ceiling for eligibility for food stamps is reduced by expenditures on housing.

   b Until recently, whether an individual between sixty-five and seventy was eligible for social security benefits depended on her income calculated on a month-by-month basis.

   c An ex-spouse becomes eligible for social security benefits only if the marriage lasted at least ten years.

Can you think of other instances where particular design features have seemingly unintended consequences?

2 Who may be the actual beneficiaries of the following government program or proposed programs; that is, taking into account how individuals respond to the government program, who is actually better off as a result of the program?

   a Medicare

   b Housing subsidies for the poor

   c Education loans

269

Can you think of other programs whose actual beneficiaries may differ from those the program seemingly intended?

3   In Chapters 12 to 16, we will use the framework we have discussed in this chapter to analyze several different government programs. Before reading those analyses, see if you can answer the following questions for each program:

  a   What were the original sources of demand for the program? What perceived need was it intended to address?

  b   What are the market failures that gave rise to the program?

  c   What are the possible forms of government intervention? Are there particular design features that have had, or currently have, an important impact on the program's effectiveness? How do private sector responses weaken, or reinforce, the intended effects of the program? What is the true incidence of the program?

  d   What are the major efficiency consequences of the program?

  e   Does the program entail any effective redistribution of income?

  f   Are there important instances of trade-offs between equity and efficiency in the program's design?

  g   What are some alternatives for meeting the program's objectives? To what extent might they do a better job—for example, by reducing distortions and increasing the equity of the programs?

  h   How has the political process affected the nature of the present program?

4   Draw the budget constraint between housing and "other consumption" for an individual on food stamps, where the amount of food stamps the individual receives depends on his income net of housing costs. Does it make a difference whether the individual is consuming an amount of food equal to, less than, or greater than his food stamp allotment?

5   State governments effectively subsidize tuition in state universities and colleges. How might this affect the amount of education that individuals get? Is there a substitution effect? Is there a market failure that this program might be addressing? Are there alternative ways of addressing it?

11 Cost-Benefit Analysis

FOCUS QUESTIONS

1 What is cost-benefit analysis and why is it useful? What are the basic steps in cost-benefit analysis?

2 How does private cost-benefit analysis differ from social cost-benefit analysis?

3 What is consumer surplus and what role does it play in cost-benefit analysis?

4 How does the government value nonmarketed benefits of a project (such as time or lives saved)?

5 What discount rates should be used for valuing future benefits and costs in social cost-benefit analysis?

6 How should risks be treated in cost-benefit analysis? How should distributional concerns be brought into the analysis?

The preceding chapter set out the basic framework for the analysis of government expenditure policies. In many cases, government wants more than a qualitative analysis; it needs a quantitative analysis. It needs to know not only that there is a rationale for government action; it needs to know whether the benefits of the particular government action (project, regulation) exceed the costs. For example, should the government:

- Build a bridge and, if so, of what size?

- Construct a dam and, if so, of what size?

- Institute more stringent regulations for flammability of mattresses?

- Institute more stringent regulations for licensing drugs?

- Extend the Washington, D.C., subway system?

- Declare certain portions of the Cape Cod seashore a national park?

This chapter describes how the government goes about making these evaluations. First, however, it is instructive to consider how a private firm makes decisions concerning which projects to undertake.

PRIVATE COST-BENEFIT ANALYSIS

Private firms continually have to decide whether to undertake investments. The procedures they follow can be characterized in four steps:

1   Identify the set of possible projects to be considered. If a steel firm wishes to expand its production capacity, there may be a number of ways it can do this. There may be alternative technologies available for smelting iron ore, and there may be a number of alternative specialized forms of steel that can be produced. The first stage, then, is to list the various major alternatives.

2   Identify the full consequences of each alternative. The firm is primarily concerned with its inputs and outputs. Thus, it will determine the labor, iron ore, coal, and other materials required for each production alternative; it will assess the quality of steel that will be produced under each alternative; it will determine the quantity of various wastes that will be produced.

3   Assign a value to each input and output. The firm will estimate the costs of various kinds of labor (with various skills) over the lifetime of the plant; the costs of other inputs, such as coal and iron ore; the prices at which it can sell the steel (which will depend on the quality of the steel produced, which may in turn vary from project to project); and the costs of disposing of wastes.

4   Add up the costs and benefits to estimate the total profitability of the project. The firm will undertake the project with the highest profit (the maximum difference between benefits and costs)—provided, of course, that profits are positive (taking appropriate account of the **opportunity costs,** the return the firm's resources could obtain elsewhere). If profits for all contemplated projects are negative, the firm will undertake no project; it will invest its funds elsewhere.

The procedures described above seem simple and straightforward. Only one part requires some elaboration. The benefits and costs of the steel mill occur over an extended period of time. Surely the firm is not indifferent when it comes to choosing between receiving a dollar today and receiving one in twenty-five years. How are the benefits and costs that accrue at different dates to be valued and compared?

The method used is based on the premise that *a dollar today is worth more than a dollar tomorrow.* Suppose the interest rate is 10 percent. If the firm receives $1 today, it can take it down to the bank, deposit it, and have $1.10 at the end of the year. Thus $1 today is worth $1.10 next year. The firm is just as well off receiving $1 today as $1.10 next year. If the firm invests the $1.10, it will have at the end of the following year $1.21. Accordingly, the firm is indifferent between receiving $1 today and $1.21 in two years' time.

To evaluate projects with receipts and expenditures in future years, the firm multiplies those receipts and payments by a **discount factor,** a number (less than 1) that makes those future receipts and payments equivalent to current receipts and payments. The discount factor is smaller the further into the future the benefit is received. The discount factor for payments in one year is just $1/1 + r$, where r is the rate of interest[1] (in our example $r = .10$, so the discount factor is $1/1.1 = .9$); for payments in two years' time it is just $1/(1 + r)^2$ (in our example it is $1/1.21$). The value *today* of $100 to be received two years in the future is thus $100/1.21 = $82.64. We then add up the value of what is to be received (or paid out) in each year of the project. The sum is called the **present discounted value** of the project, often abbreviated as PDV. If R_t is the *net* receipts from the project in period t, and r the rate of interest, then if the project lasts for N years, its PDV is given by

$$\text{PDV} = R_0 + \frac{R_1}{1 + r} + \frac{R_2}{(1 + r)^2} + \cdots \frac{R_t}{(1 + r)^t} \cdots \frac{R_N}{(1 + r)^N}$$

Table 11.1 provides an illustration of how this might be done for a hypothetical steel mill lasting five years. (Most steel mills last much longer than that; this makes the calculations more complicated, but the principle is the same.) For each year, we multiply the net receipts of that year by the discount factor for that year. Notice the large difference between undiscounted profits ($1000) and discounted profits ($169). This difference is

---

[1] To see this, compare what the firm has at the end of the year if it receives $100 × $1/(1+ r)$ today. It takes the $100 × $1/(1 + r)$ and invests it, receiving a return of r. Thus, at the end of the year, it has

$100 × 1/(1+r)$ the original amount
$+$ $r × $100 × 1/(1+r)$ the interest
     $(1 + r) × ($100 × 1/(1 + r)) = $100.$

Therefore, the firm is indifferent between receiving $100 × $\frac{1}{1 + r}$ today, and $100 next year.

YEAR	BENEFITS (RECEIPTS)	COSTS	NET PROFITS	DISCOUNT FACTOR	NET DISCOUNTED PROFITS
1		3000	−3000	1	−3000
2	1200	200	1000	$1/1.1 = .909$	909
3	1200	200	1000	$(1/1.1)^2 = .826$	826
4	1200	200	1000	$(1/1.1)^3 = .751$	751
5	1200	200	1000	$(1/1.1)^4 = .683$	683
Total	4800	3800	1000		169

likely to be particularly large for long-lived projects entailing large initial investments; the benefits for such projects occur later in time (and are therefore worth less) than the costs, which occur earlier in time.

SOCIAL COST-BENEFIT ANALYSIS

The government goes through basically the same procedures in evaluating a project. There are, however, two critical differences between social and private cost-benefit analyses.

First, while the only consequences of a project that are of concern to the firm are those that affect its profitability, the government may be concerned with a much broader range of consequences. For example, it may be concerned with the ecological effects of a dam, and with the impact of the dam on the river's recreational uses.

Second, whereas the firm uses market prices to evaluate what it has to pay for its inputs and what it receives for its outputs, there are two instances in which the government might not use market prices in evaluating projects: (a) When the outputs and inputs are not sold on the market, market prices do not exist. Market prices do not exist for clean air, for lives saved, or for the preservation of wilderness in its natural state. (b) When there is a market failure, market prices do not represent a project's true marginal social costs or benefits. The prices the government uses to evaluate its projects must reflect the market failure. (Recall from Chapter 3 that in the absence of market failures, market prices do reflect marginal social costs and benefits; accordingly, in the absence of market failure, the government should use market prices in evaluating its projects.)

Social cost-benefit analysis is concerned with developing systematic ways of analyzing costs and benefits when market prices do not reflect social costs and benefits. In the following sections, we will look at how the government values benefits that are typically not monetized—like the value of the environment, or of lives—and how the government values marketed goods and services when there are reasons to believe that important market failures exist, such as massive unemployment, which result in market prices that do not reflect social benefits and costs.

MAJOR DIFFERENCES BETWEEN SOCIAL AND PRIVATE COST-BENEFIT ANALYSIS

1 Social cost-benefit analysis takes into account a wider range of impacts, not just profits.

2 In social cost-benefit analysis, market prices may not exist for many benefits and costs, and market prices may not be used because of market failures (so, market prices do not reflect marginal social benefits and costs).

CONSUMER SURPLUS AND THE DECISION TO UNDERTAKE A PROJECT

Before turning to these issues, there is, however, one other set of situations where cost-benefit analysis plays an important role. Even when the price system is working well, so that prices reflect marginal benefits and costs, a project may not break even—and thus would not be provided by the market—and yet total benefits exceed costs, so the project *should* be undertaken. Typically, these are projects that have large fixed costs, such as a bridge, or more generally, projects that are large enough to have an effect on prices. Thus market prices can be used for valuing projects only when projects are sufficiently small that they have a negligible effect on prices. In the case of a bridge, while it may leave prices in general unchanged, the "price" of crossing the river at that particular place can be thought of as being reduced from infinite (the good simply is not available) to zero.

Figure 11.1 shows the demand curve for a bridge. Even at a price of zero, only a certain number of trips across the bridge will be taken—denoted by point E. Assume the capacity of a minimal-size bridge is C, which exceeds E, and that the marginal cost of using the bridge is zero. Then efficient utilization of the bridge requires a zero toll (price); any higher price will restrict usage, when the marginal cost of usage is zero. But clearly, at a zero price, no private firm would undertake the bridge.

But while the marginal value of a trip is zero, the total value of the bridge is clearly positive. The question is, is the total value large enough to offset the costs of the bridge? To find the total value of the bridge, we ask a simple question: How much, in total, would individuals be willing to pay to have the bridge (with a toll of, say, zero)? As we saw in Chapter 5, the total amount that individuals *would be willing to pay* in excess of *what they have to pay* is called the **consumer surplus.** There, we showed that consumer surplus is measured as the difference between the area under the compensated demand curve and what they actually have to pay for the

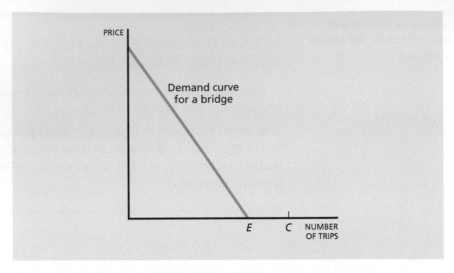

FIGURE 11.1 **Efficient Utilization of a Bridge** If the minimum scale capacity for a bridge, *C*, exceeds the demand at a zero price, *E*, then efficiency requires that no toll be charged, but it still may be worth constructing the bridge.

good.[2] Figure 11.2 shows the compensated demand curve—everywhere along it each individual's welfare is the same as it would have been if no bridge had been constructed. If no tolls were charged, the consumer surplus would be the entire area under the demand curve, the area of the triangle *AFE*. This would measure the entire amount that all individuals would be willing to pay to have the bridge—say, the value of the savings in time and driving costs of using that bridge rather than using the

[2] Recall that along the compensated demand curve, the individual's welfare (utility) is constant. The compensated demand curve tells us the quantity of the good which the individual demands at each price if, as the price is lowered, we take away just enough income to leave him no better off as a result of the price decrease. If the individual consumes relatively little of the good, then the amount we have to take away is relatively small. The difference between the compensated and uncompensated demand is the result of the "income effect"—the change in demand (here, for trips) from taking away this small amount of income. Accordingly, the difference between the compensated and uncompensated demand curves for an item like a bridge is typically small. See R. Willig, "Consumer's Surplus without Apology," *American Economic Review* 66 (1976): 589–97. Obviously, in other cases—such as the supply of labor (demand for leisure)—the difference could be large. See J. Hausman, "Exact Consumer's Surplus and Deadweight Loss," *American Economic Review* 71 (1981): 662–76. Whether economists *should* ignore the income effect or not, in practice they frequently do, because of difficulties in quantifying its magnitude. (As a matter of terminology, the area under the ordinary demand curve is often called the consumer surplus, as opposed to the *exact* consumer's surplus, the area under the compensated demand curve. The exact consumer's surplus is what is relevant for project evaluation.)

CONSUMER SURPLUS AND
THE DECISION TO UNDERTAKE
A PROJECT

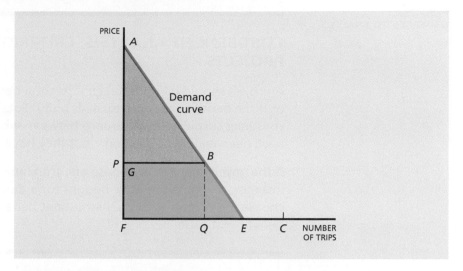

FIGURE 11.2   **Calculation of Consumer Surplus** The consumer surplus is the area under the (compensated) demand curve. If a zero toll is charged, the bridge should still be constructed if the consumer surplus exceeds the cost of the bridge. (If a toll of *P* is charged, then the consumer surplus is the area *AGB*, and the bridge should be constructed if the consumer surplus, which is now only *AGB*, plus the revenues raised, *FGBQ*, exceed the cost of the bridge.)

bridge one mile downstream. If a toll *P* is charged, then the total people are willing to pay still exceeds the amount actually paid by the amount of the triangle *AGB*.

The decision to build the bridge is then a simple one: Do the total benefits (revenues *plus* consumer surplus) exceed the total costs (including any costs incurred in raising the revenue to finance the bridge)?[3]

Sometimes economists look at the ratio of benefits to costs. The criterion for undertaking any project for which benefits, *B*, exceed costs, *C*,

Undertake a project if $B > C$

can be rewritten: Undertake any project for which the ratio of benefits to costs exceeds unity:

Undertake a project if $B/C > 1$.

Often, governments must choose *which* project among several to undertake. There may be a dam site on which only one dam can be constructed.

[3] There is one subtlety: The total costs should include not only the expenditures on the bridge, but the *additional* costs associated with raising the required tax revenues to finance it.

277

COST-BENEFIT ANALYSIS: CRITERION FOR ACCEPTING PROJECTS

A project should be undertaken if its total benefits exceed total costs, or if the benefit-cost ratio exceeds unity. Total benefits include the consumer surplus, the difference between what individuals would have been willing to pay and what they have to pay.

If the government must choose one from among a set of projects (for instance, several alternative designs for a dam to construct), it should choose the project with the highest net benefits, not the highest benefit-cost ratio.

Different dams may have different benefits and costs. In this particular case, the government should undertake the project in which the total *net benefit* from the project, the difference between the benefits and costs, is largest.

Note that choosing the project that maximizes the difference between benefits and costs is *not* the same as choosing the project that maximizes the benefit-cost ratio. A very small project with a small benefit and an even smaller cost could have a very high benefit-cost ratio, and yet yield relatively small net benefits.[4]

MEASURING NON-MONETIZED COSTS AND BENEFITS

For many of the costs and benefits associated with government projects and regulations—such as lives saved, or environments protected—there are not market prices. Economists have developed systematic procedures for estimating these values. In some cases, such as the value of time, we can make inferences about individuals' evaluations from market data and from their observed behavior in other contexts. In other cases, such as the value of the Grand Canyon, survey techniques have been employed. Many of these valuation techniques remain controversial.[5]

---

[4] The problem is that we have not included in our cost measure the opportunity cost of the dam site. If we correctly calculate the opportunity cost of the dam site, then there will be only one project for which the benefits exceed the total costs; this is, of course, the same project that we identified before as maximizing the net benefits from the dam site.

[5] For more on determining the benefits of environmental goods, see Maureen L. Cropper and Wallace E. Oates, "Environmental Economics: A Survey," *Journal of Economic Literature* 30 (June 1992): 675–740. Also see the Symposium on Contingent Valuation in the *Journal of Economic Perspectives* 8, no. 4 (fall 1994).

VALUING TIME   The old adage "time is money" describes how most economists evaluate the savings in time resulting from an improved transportation system, such as a better subway system or road network. The typical approach is to attempt to ascertain the wage rate of those who use the transportation system; under certain ideal conditions, the wage provides a measure of an individual's evaluation of her own time. In simple economic models, an individual is pictured as making a choice between the amount of leisure and the amount of work that she undertakes. As a result of giving up one more hour of leisure, she gets an increase in consumption goods equal to her hourly wage. In equilibrium, she is indifferent when choosing whether to give up one more hour of leisure and increase her consumption by an amount equal to her hourly wage, or to reduce her work (increase her leisure) by an hour and decrease her consumption by an amount equal to her hourly wage. Thus her wage provides a monetary valuation of her time. If a faster subway reduces commuting time by twenty minutes, and the wage is $9 an hour, the value of the time saved is $3. We calculate the value of time saved by each individual and add the values together to obtain the total value of time saved.

Some claim that this overestimates the value of time: many individuals would like to work more at their wage rate but are unable to find additional employment at that wage; the job restricts the number of hours that they can work. The individual's valuation of his leisure is thus fairly low; the compensation that would be required for reducing an individual's leisure by one hour is, in this view, much less than the wage that the individual receives for the work that he is able to obtain.

Others claim that the wage may underestimate the value of leisure for some individuals and overestimate the value of leisure for other individuals. They point out that professors, for instance, have chosen a comparatively low-wage job relative to other options available to them because of the great nonmonetary benefits associated with the job. The value of their leisure exceeds the wage they receive. On the other hand, the wage of the coal miner or the garbage collector includes some compensation for the unattractive features of those jobs and hence represents an overestimate of the value of leisure.

VALUING LIFE   Probably no subject in public cost-benefit analysis has engendered so much emotional discussion as economists' attempts to place a monetary value on life. As distasteful as such a calculation may seem, it is necessary, in a variety of circumstances, for governments to face up to this problem. There is virtually no limit to the amount that could be spent to reduce the likelihood of an accident on a road, or of death from some disease. Yet at some point a judgment must be made that the gain from further expenditures is sufficiently small that additional expenditures are not warranted. An individual who otherwise would not have may die as a result of this decision. Yet we cannot spend 50 percent of our national income on transportation safety, or 50 percent of our national income on health.

CHILDREN, CAR SAFETY, AND THE VALUE OF LIFE

Even though life is priceless, economists have used the methodologies described in the text (and others) to put a dollar number on it. Different studies produce different results, with a range of between $1 million to $20 million, but most studies show numbers at the lower end of that range, between $2 million and $8 million (in 1997 dollars).*

The U.S. government has debated whether to use a single number for cost-benefit analyses in all agencies. So far, different agencies use different numbers—with the Environmental Protection Agency typically using numbers considerably larger than those employed by the Department of Transportation—and larger than those substantiated by most outside studies.

Those who argue against using a single number suggest that there are a number of other factors that should go into the analysis, such as whether the death resulted from an action voluntarily engaged in (such as driving).

One of the most difficult questions in valuing lives is whether the life of a child should be valued differently than the life of an adult, or of an 80-year-old. The issue comes up repeatedly: How should we allocate money between two cancer research programs, one targeting

Two methods have been used for estimating the value of life. The first is the *constructive method*—that is, we estimate what the individual would have earned had he remained alive (until his "normal" age of death). To do this, we extrapolate his employment history, comparing it to that of individuals in similar positions.

This method fails to distinguish between the value of life and the livelihood that goes with it. It thus suggests that after retirement, an individual's life has zero value, since there is no loss of earnings. This seems clearly wrong. (It confuses means and ends: Income is earned in order to provide

ALTERNATIVE METHODS OF VALUING LIFE

1 Constructive method: What would the individual have earned had she remained alive?

2 Revealed preference method: How much extra income do individuals need to compensate them for an increase in the chance of death, as reflected in market wages for riskier jobs?

a cancer typically found in children, the other a form of cancer that typically only shows up among the elderly?

The Department of Transportation (DOT) is responsible for imposing regulations to ensure the safety of cars. In imposing regulations, it looks at the costs and benefits. In the mid-1990s, DOT addressed whether to strengthen the standard for car frames that would largely affect deaths in the rear seat in side collisions. A disproportionate fraction of those saved would be children (since they more often ride in the rear seat). This raised the issue of whether to employ a different value of life instead of the one used elsewhere, when those saved were more typically adults. When a child's life is saved, more "life-years" are saved than when the life of an 80-year-old is saved. DOT has continued to use the traditional method for valuing life, which treats all lives the same. Even so, an alternative methodology, which focused on life-years saved rather than lives, was sanctioned in new federal guidelines established in 1995.

*For surveys of the value of life, see pages 713–15 in M. Cropper and W. Oates, "Environmental Economics: A Survey," Journal of Economic Literature 30, no. 2 (June 1992): 675–740; and Peter Dorman, Markets and Mortality: Economics, Dangerous Work, and the Value of Human Life (Cambridge, England; New York; and Melbourne: Cambridge University Press, 1996).

consumption; producing income is not presumably the *object* of life, and therefore not the basis of valuing it.)[6]

There is an alternative, indirect method that does recognize the natural desire to live longer. In some occupations, there is a much higher chance of death than in others. For instance, the accident rates for coal miners are higher than for college professors, and the death rates for workers in asbestos factories and jackhammer operators are much higher than for clerical workers. Individuals who undertake riskier occupations normally require compensation for assuming these additional risks. By choosing the riskier occupation, they are saying that they are willing to face a higher chance of death for a higher income while they are alive. The second method calculates the value of life by looking at how much extra income individuals need to compensate them for an increase in the chance of death. There is considerable controversy about this second method, however, just as there is about the first. Some believe that it grossly underestimates the value of life; they argue that individuals are not well informed concerning the risks they

[6] For an early critique of this method and one of the first developments of the second, indirect method, see T. Schelling, "The Life You Save May Be Your Own," reprinted in T. Schelling, *Choices and Consequences* (Cambridge, Mass.: Harvard University Press, 1984).

face.[7] Also, for well-known psychological reasons, individuals attempt to ignore what information they do have concerning the riskiness of their jobs.

As controversial as the estimates of the value of life may be, there appears to be no alternative to using them in the evaluation of projects that affect the likelihood of death.

VALUING NATURAL RESOURCES

A question of increasing concern is how to value impacts on the environment. That issue was raised forcefully by the 1989 Exxon *Valdez* oil spill. Network news reports on the millions of dying otters, salmon, and birds brought into every American home the impact of the spill in a relatively remote area. If people had died, it is clear that Exxon would have owed the families huge amounts of money in compensation. Obviously, the relatives of the animals that had been killed had no standing in court to demand compensation. But many Americans felt that Exxon should pay something, both to deter others from taking actions which might damage the environment, and to compensate them for their perceived loss from the environmental injury. Using a relatively new technique called **contingent valuation,** courts valued the compensation that Exxon would have to pay at approximately $1 billion. This was compensation that went beyond the direct economic injury, for instance, to fishermen who lost their livelihood.

In contingent valuation, individuals are asked a series of questions intended to elicit how much they value the environmental damage or the preservation of some species. Many (but not all) individuals seem willing to pay something, for instance, to preserve whales or the spotted owl or other endangered species, or the Arctic National Wildlife area, even if they themselves do not directly come into contact with the species or do not visit the preservation area. These values are referred to as **existence values.** Even if each individual is willing to pay only a little, say, $5 or $10, when added up over all Americans, the values may be significant—in excess of $1 billion. This is what the court found in the *Valdez* case.

Though there is considerable controversy over the accuracy of these methods, a special panel set up by the National Oceanic and Atmospheric Administration, which included distinguished Nobel Prize winners Kenneth Arrow of Stanford and Robert Solow of MIT, recommended cautious use of the methodology by the government. In 1994, the government proposed new regulations implementing the new methodology.[8]

---

[7] Several studies have attempted to estimate the magnitude of workers' misperceptions and suggest that they may not be too large. See, for instance, W. K. Viscusi, *Risk by Choice: Regulating Health and Safety in the Workplace* (Cambridge, Mass.: Harvard University Press, 1983).

[8] See M. Common, I. Reid, and R. Blaney, "Do Existence Values for Cost-Benefit Analysis Exist?" *Journal of Environmental and Resource Economics* 9, no. 2 (1997): 225–38; John Duffield, "Nonmarket Valuation and the Courts: The Case of Exxon *Valdez,*" *Contemporary Economic Policy* 15, no. 4 (October 1997): 98–110; Kenneth J. Arrow et al., "Is There a Role for Benefit-Cost Analysis in Environmental, Health, and Safety Regulation," *Environment and Development Economics* 2, no. 2 (May 1997): 196–201; and Paul R. Portney, "The Contingent Valuation Debate: Why Economists Should Care," *Journal of Economic Perspectives* 8, no. 4 (fall 1994): 3–17.

SHADOW PRICES AND MARKET PRICES

Whenever there is a market failure, market prices may not reflect true marginal social costs or benefits. In such circumstances, economists attempt to calculate the true marginal social costs or benefits—for instance, of hiring an additional worker, or of importing or exporting additional goods. They call these "social prices" or "shadow prices." The term **shadow price** reminds us that while these prices do not really exist in the market, they are the true social costs and benefits, reflected imperfectly in the market price.

In the absence of a market failure, the price of something equals its opportunity cost, what is forgone in alternative uses. In an economy in which there is massive unemployment, the market wage exceeds the opportunity cost—indeed, what is forgone is the individual's leisure—but when workers are unemployed involuntarily, the market wage exceeds the value of this forgone leisure often by a considerable amount. The shadow price of labor when there is massive unemployment is the low value of the forgone leisure, not the market wage.

Similarly, in an economy in which capital markets work very imperfectly, and firms cannot raise additional capital at the "market rate of interest," the shadow cost of capital—what is forgone by using capital in one use rather than another—may exceed the market rate of interest by a considerable amount.

DIFFERENCES BETWEEN MARKET PRICES AND SHADOW PRICES

Shadow prices reflect true marginal social costs. When there are market failures, market prices may not fully reflect social costs.

Examples are shown below.

MARKET	DIFFERENCE BETWEEN MARKET AND SHADOW PRICES	EXPLANATION
Labor	Shadow wage is less than market wage when there is unemployment.	No loss in output elsewhere when individual is hired; hence marginal social cost of hiring worker is less than wage.
Capital	Shadow interest rate exceeds market interest when there is rationing in capital markets.	Firm's expected return exceeds interest rate (firm would like to borrow more at given interest rate, but can't). Thus opportunity cost of funds is greater than the interest rate.
Steel	Shadow price exceeds market price.	Steel producer fails to value marginal social cost of pollution resulting from increased production.

DISCOUNT RATE FOR SOCIAL COST-BENEFIT ANALYSIS

Our discussion of private cost-benefit analysis noted that a dollar next year or the year after is not worth as much as a dollar today. Hence, income to be received in the future or expenses to be incurred in the future have to be discounted. In deciding whether to undertake a project, we look at its present discounted value. The discount rate private firms use is r, the rate of interest the firm has to pay. What discount rate should the government use? The discount rate used by the government is sometimes called the **social discount rate.** The central question of concern is the relationship between this rate and the interest rate faced by consumers, on the one hand, and the rate faced by producers, on the other.

For evaluating long-lived projects, such as dams, the choice of the discount rate is crucial: a project that looks very favorable using a 3 percent interest rate may look very unattractive at a 10 percent rate. If markets worked perfectly, the market interest rate would reflect the opportunity cost of the resources used and the relative evaluation of income at different dates. But there is a widespread belief that capital markets do not work well. Moreover, taxes may introduce large distortions, with large differences between before- and after-tax returns. Thus it is not clear which of the various market rates of interest, if any, should be used: for instance, should it be the rate at which the government can borrow, or the rate at which the typical taxpayer can borrow?

If the individuals who benefit from the project are the same as those who pay the costs, we can simply use their *marginal rate of substitution,* how they are willing to trade off the reduction in current consumption for gains in future consumption. Since their marginal rate of substitution will be directly related to the rate of interest at which they can borrow and lend, in this case we can use that market rate of interest for evaluating costs and benefits in different periods. But often, the project has further ramifications—a public project may, for instance, displace a private project—and we then have to look at *all* of the consequences, the *net* change in consumption.

If a public project displaces a private project of the same size, then the net reduction in consumption today from the project is zero. If both the public and private projects yield all of their returns in the same period, then we can easily decide whether to undertake the project: we should undertake it if its output exceeds that of the private project; or equivalently, if its rate of return exceeds that of the private project. In this view, which, not surprisingly, is called the **opportunity cost view**—because the private project is the opportunity cost of the public project—it is the producer's rate of return that should be used in project evaluation.

Focusing on opportunity costs and focusing on consumers' marginal rates of substitution yield exactly the same result in economies in which there are no market failures, for then the marginal rate of substitution (which equals the rate of interest facing consumers) equals the rate of return on capital, or the producers' rate of interest (the opportunity cost). Problems arise when there are market failures or taxes; and/or when those who benefit from a project are different from those who pay for them.[9] Today many economists argue that the appropriate rate of interest for government discounting may be *none* of the observed market rates of interest. More generally, it is recognized that choosing the appropriate interest rate is an exceedingly complex matter.[10]

In the more general case, there is no presumption that the ratio of the marginal valuation of an increase in consumption by one generation to that of another is related to *any* interest rate. One approach, in that case, is to use *social welfare functions.* We first introduced the concept of a social welfare function in Chapter 5 as a way of formalizing how consumption or income of different individuals could be compared. Exactly the same principles apply in comparing individuals over time as in comparing individuals at the same point of time, with one difference. In both cases, there is *diminishing marginal utility,* so that if future generations have higher incomes than the current generation, the marginal valuation of a dollar of consumption to them is lower. But some economists believe that the welfare of individuals of future generations *at the same level of income* should be weighted less than the welfare of the current generation, simply because it exists in the future. The rate at which future generations' welfare should be discounted is referred to as the **pure discount rate.** Other economists, such as the distinguished Cambridge economist Frank Ramsey, argued that all generations should be given equal weight.

[9] There are a few special cases where the fact that the benefits may accrue to different generations poses no problem. If the government has engaged in optimal **intergenerational redistribution of income,** then the marginal value of a dollar to every generation will be equal to the market rate of interest, and so long as the project is relatively small, we can evaluate the marginal benefits received by different generations using market rates of interest, just as we can when the impacts are felt by a single individual. Similarly, if society consists of a set of family dynasties, in which each family optimally redistributes income from the current generation to succeeding generations, then the marginal value of a dollar to every generation should equal the consumer rate of interest. (See R. Barro, "Are Government Bonds Net Wealth," *Journal of Political Economy* 82, 1974: 1095–1117.) The validity of this model has been strongly questioned. It implies, for instance, that when the government ran huge deficits in the 1980s, individuals increased their savings in a fully offsetting way. Thus, it implies that in the absence of these deficits, personal savings would have been negative. For an extensive discussion of these issues, see the symposium in the *Journal of Economic Perspectives* 3, no. 2 (spring 1989).

[10] There are a few special cases where there is a simple and clear solution—for instance, if the *only* imperfection in the market is *optimally chosen taxes* (in later chapters, we shall describe in detail what is entailed by optimal taxes; for now, we simply note that actual tax systems seldom comport even closely with optimal tax structures) then the producer's rate of return should be used in project evaluation. (See P. Diamond and J. Mirrlees, "Optimal Taxation and Public Production," *American Economic Review* 61 (1971): 261–78.) For a discussion showing how even slight changes in assumptions can lead to markedly different conclusions, see J. E. Stiglitz and P. Dasgupta, "Differential Taxation, Public Goods, and Economic Efficiency," *Review of Economic Studies* 39 (1971): 151–74.

CLIMATE CHANGE AND DISCOUNT RATES

One important policy issue facing the world over coming decades will be how to respond to the threat of global warming as a result of the increased concentrations of greenhouse gases (such as carbon dioxide) in the atmosphere. The effects go beyond just an increase in temperature: there are concerns about the rise in the level of seawater and increased weather variability.

A series of scientific panels (the International Panel on Climate Change—the IPCC) was convened to assess the scientific evidence concerning global warming. Atmospheric concentrations of greenhouse gases had increased substantially since the beginning of the industrial revolution (mainly as a result of the burning of fossil fuels for energy)—and if unabated would within 150 years exceed two to three times the level at that time. Though no one could be sure about the magnitude of the effects on the climate, there was a consensus that it could be significant. While some cold-climate countries might gain, on average there would be losses, and for some countries—low-lying countries such as Bangladesh and the Pacific Islands—the impact could be disastrous. The reports of the IPCC led to increasing consensus that concerted international action was required, and in 1992 the nations of the world signed an agreement at Rio de Janeiro (called the Rio Convention) intended to reduce the emissions of carbon dioxide and other greenhouse gases. The U.S. Senate ratified the Rio Convention in 1992. In 1997 in Kyoto a further agreement was signed, calling for binding commitments of the industrialized countries to reduce their emissions of greenhouse gases below their 1990 levels. As this book goes to press, prospects for ratification of the Kyoto Convention by the U.S. Senate remain bleak.

In spite of these agreements, within the United States there has been controversy about what should be done about greenhouse gases—how much should be spent to reduce emissions. The controversy arises

To see what is implied by this approach, assume that per capita income is increasing at the rate of 1.5 percent, and the *elasticity of marginal utility* is 1. (The elasticity of marginal utility is the percentage decrease in marginal utility from a 1 percent increase in consumption. As we saw in Chapter 5, economists usually assume the elasticity of marginal utility is between 1 and 2.) Then if the pure discount rate is zero, the social rate of discount is 1.5 percent, roughly equal to the real interest rate on safe (government) securities, but considerably below the opportunity cost of capital.

in part because of discounting: most of the effects of global climate change will not be felt for 100 years—and at a 7 percent discount rate, the value of $100 a hundred years from now is less than 10 cents. It clearly won't be worth spending much today to avert even large costs in the future. On the other hand, at a 1 percent discount rate, $100 a hundred years from now is worth more than $30.

A special working group of economists of the IPCC, including Nobel Prize winner Kenneth Arrow and the chairman of the Council of Economic Advisers of the United States, Joseph Stiglitz, argued that the appropriate methodology implied using a low interest rate for purposes of discounting for costs and benefits associated with climate change.* Future generations would be adversely affected if actions mitigating the pace of emissions of greenhouse gases were not undertaken, and there were no ethical grounds for valuing their welfare substantially less than the welfare of the current generation. Critics of this view argued that future generations could be made whole, "simply" by setting aside money today, investing it at the market rate of interest, and letting the amount accumulate to be used to address the costs of climate change. The worry, however, was that not only might estimates of future damage repair costs be too low, and more fundamentally, that there might be some damage that was irreparable at any cost, but also that countries would not set aside the funds. If they did not, then the appropriate trade-off was that analyzed by the IPCC committee, between consumption of the current generation and the welfare of future generations which would be adversely affected by climate change.

*Climate Change 1995: Economic and Social Dimensions of Climate Change. Contribution of Working Group III to the Second Assessment Report of the Intergovernmental Panel on Climate Change. Edited by J. Bruce, Hoesung Lee, and E. Haites. (Cambridge, England, and New York: (Cambridge University Press, 1996.) More information on the IPCC can be found on the Internet at: http://www.usgcrp.gov/ipcc/

The question of the appropriate social rate of discount has become a hotly contested political issue. Those who are concerned about the environment and who see environmental impacts stretching out over decades, for example, believe strongly in low discount rates. For instance, in their view, simply because the effects of nuclear waste can be postponed for fifty or a hundred years is no reason to essentially ignore them—which a 10 percent discount rate effectively tells us to do.

Today, the federal government uses a 7 percent discount rate as its basic "guideline." This partially reflects the opportunity cost view—the *aver-*

age rate of return across all sectors of the economy is estimated to be around 7 percent. But for long-lived projects, particularly where there are long-lived environmental impacts, it is likely that lower interest rates will be used in the future.[11]

TABLE 11.2 Sources of Disagreement in Discount Rates	**HIGH DISCOUNT RATE** (OPPORTUNITY COST OF CAPITAL)	**LOW DISCOUNT RATE** (SOCIAL RATE OF DISCOUNT)
	1 Government investment tends to displace private investment.	1 Assessing *net* impacts is typically far more complicated than just assuming a dollar of public investment displaces a dollar of private investment.
	2 Even in a world with distortions, everyone could be made better off if efficiency is maintained—this entails the rate of return on public projects' equaling that on private projects.	2 Assessing the desirability of a project must take into account *intergenerational distributional* effects as well as *efficiency* effects. a) Programs' beneficiaries are often different from those who bear the costs. b) Even if the government *could* in principle make everyone better off, the required compensations (for instance, to those who are adversely affected) are seldom made.
	3 Even in the absence of government intergenerational redistributions, if parents leave bequests to their children, marginal valuations of consumption of different generations will be equalized (the dynastic model).	3 In the absence of optimal intergenerational redistribution, market rates of interest do not reflect marginal social valuations of dollars to different generations. Further, the dynastic model is implausible.
	4 When market distortions are caused by optimal taxes, then efficiency is still desirable, so the government should use the opportunity cost of capital.	4 With market distortions, marginal rates of substitution (how individuals value a marginal dollar in different years) and marginal rates of transformation (the trade-offs facing firms) may differ markedly. With distortionary taxes, efficiency—as exemplified by using the private sector's opportunity cost of capital in the public sector—is desirable only under highly restrictive conditions.

[11] The guidelines for cost-benefit analysis issued by the federal government in 1995 allowed for the use of lower discount rates for long-lived projects with impacts over many generations.

THREE VIEWS ON THE SOCIAL DISCOUNT RATE

1 Reflects consumers' rate of time preference (the consumers' borrowing rate).

2 Reflects opportunity cost of capital (the producers' borrowing rate).

3 May reflect neither: for example, in long-lived projects affecting different generations, where social marginal valuation of consumption of different generations may have nothing to do with observed interest rates, in the absence of optimal intergenerational redistribution of income.

It is not surprising that the discount rate should be a subject of such *political* controversy. But why can't economists agree among themselves? Our discussion has highlighted several sources of disagreement about the economy and about the government, summarized in Table 11.2.

THE EVALUATION OF RISK

The most common mistake in trying to cope with the uncertainties of the benefits and costs of a project is to argue that in the face of risk, the government should use a higher discount rate. Recall that the discount rate relates the value of a dollar at one date to its value at a later date. To see how increasing the discount rate may lead to absurd results, consider a project that, at termination, requires an expenditure (say, an automobile has to be towed to the junkyard). Assume that there is some uncertainty about the magnitude of that cost. We would normally think that this uncertainty would make the project less attractive than if we knew for sure what the termination costs were. But consider what happens if we use a higher discount rate to offset the risk: the discount factor is lower, the present value of those costs is reduced, and the project looks more, not less, attractive. To use a higher discount rate confuses the evaluation of income at different dates with the evaluation of risk; these are two separate issues.

To evaluate risks, economists introduce the concept of **certainty equivalents.** Assume there is some risky project. Next year the output of the project may be worth $0 or $100; there is a fifty-fifty chance of each outcome. The *average* value is just $50 ($\frac{1}{2} \times \$100 + \frac{1}{2} \times \$0 = \$50$). If we dislike risk, however, we would clearly prefer a project whose return was a certain $50. In fact, we would prefer a project with a smaller average value, so long as the risk was smaller. If we would be indifferent in choosing between the risky project with an average value of $50 and a perfectly safe project with a value of $45, we would say that $45 is the certainty equivalent of the risky project with an average value of $50. To evaluate risky projects, then, we simply take the present discounted value of the certainty equivalents.[12]

Thus risky projects have to earn a higher return than safe projects with the same certainty equivalent to be acceptable. The extra amount a risky project must earn to compensate is its **risk premium.**

We illustrate the procedure in Table 11.3, for a five-year project. We have assumed that the initial investment in the first period is certain. The benefits that accrue in years 2, 3, and 4 are increasingly uncertain, reflected in the certainty equivalents. The final year, the project is scrapped; there are large costs associated with the termination of the project. (Consider the problem of what to do with a nuclear power plant when its useful life has come to an end.) But these costs are uncertain. Hence its certainty equivalent exceeds the $50 expected cost. (In contrast, had we employed a higher time discount rate to take account of risk, these uncertain scrapping costs would not have weighed very heavily in our cost-benefit calculation.)

To obtain the present discounted value of the certainty equivalent net benefit at any date, we multiply it by the time discount factor. To obtain the present discounted value, we add up the discounted certainty equivalent net benefits for the life of the project.

How should the government evaluate the risks associated with various projects? In some cases, such as the risks associated with the generation of electricity, it can look to how private markets value risks. But for risks for which there is no comparable private project, matters are more difficult. Some, such as a flood control project, serve to *reduce* the risks individuals face, and for these projects, the risk premium is negative. Individuals are willing to pay something to reduce the risk of flood. Since the government can spread risks over the entire population, when the project neither serves an insurance function (reducing the risks individuals would other-

			TIME DISCOUNT	DISCOUNTED VALUE
		CERTAINTY	FACTOR (10 PERCENT	OF CERTAINTY
	EXPECTED NET	EQUIVALENT	INTEREST RATE)	EQUIVALENT NET BENEFIT
YEAR	BENEFIT	NET BENEFIT		
1	$-100	$-100	1	$-100
2	100	90	.91	81.90
3	100	80	.83	66.40
4	100	75	.75	56.25
5	-50	-75	.68	-51
Total	150	70		53.55

TABLE 11.3
Example of Cost-Benefit Analysis for Risky Investment

[12] This methodology is not perfectly general. It requires that we be able to separate the analysis of risk at one date from that at other dates. For most practical purposes, however, it is sufficiently general.

wise face) nor provides a return that is correlated with income from other sources (that is, the return to the project is neither particularly high nor particularly low when the economy is, say, healthy), the government should employ no risk premium.

RISK ASSESSMENT

An area of increasing scrutiny—and controversy—in risk analysis is the risks to health, safety, and indeed life, that are posed, for instance, by hazardous wastes, pesticides, and fungicides. Chemicals in the water and air increase the likelihood of cancer and a variety of other ailments, often life-threatening. About this there is little doubt. The debate has focused on **risk assessment,** on how the magnitude of these risks is assessed and how priorities for reducing these risks should be established.

For instance, many risks are related to exposure. A chemical in dirt that is sealed under a thick layer of concrete is unlikely to impose significant risks; there would be a much higher risk if that same dirt were directly ingested by a child. In assessing the overall risk, one must take into account the probability of different levels of exposure, as well as the risks associated with each level of exposure.

The Environmental Protection Agency, in setting its priorities and its standards—for instance, for cleaning up hazardous wastes—has been criticized on several grounds. Rather than analyzing the effects of compounding of probabilities in the way that students are typically taught in modern statistics courses, the EPA uses a "worst case scenario analysis," which looks at the risks associated with the worst case. For example, what would be the risk assuming that the concrete seal around the dirt cracked, and a child wandered into the site? There have been some famous stories of the EPA insisting on cleanups to the standard that a child could eat the dirt for a six-week period without having any significant increase in health risk.[13] In setting priorities, there has been concern that the government has not gone after the highest risks, but rather the risks which have the most "popular appeal." The risks that are addressed by the EPA are often far lower than the risks which individuals take in their day-to-day lives, for instance, from drinking alcohol moderately, let alone from smoking. There is, however, one critical distinction: The risks upon which the EPA focuses are those (like air and water pollution) over which individuals have no choice; they are incurred involuntarily, as opposed to the risks associated with smoking and drinking. Still, the fact that individuals seem willing to incur certain risks reveals information about their *valuation* of the risks, a fact which government should presumably take into account when adopting environmental risk standards. Recent government regulations have put greater emphasis on assessments of comparative risks; there is a reluctance to impose costly regulations to reduce risks which are of the size that individuals seem willing to accept in ordinary circumstances.

---

[13] See Stephen G. Breyer, *Breaking the Vicious Circle: Toward Effective Risk Regulation* (Cambridge, Mass.: Harvard University Press, 1993), p. 12.

There has been increasing concern that environmental risks are borne disproportionately by the poor, who often live in industrial areas with heavier pollution. This is not surprising, since land in such areas typically is less valuable, so that they can obtain housing at lower costs. Early in 1994, President Clinton signed an executive order on **environmental justice,** instructing agencies to ascertain the distributional impact of various environmental measures that they might undertake.

DISTRIBUTIONAL CONSIDERATIONS

The benefits of any given public project are not uniformly distributed across the population. Some projects, such as a dam, have benefits that are limited geographically. Other projects, such as the bilingual education program and jobs retraining program, are directed mainly at the poor. The government is clearly concerned about the impact of its programs on the distribution of income.

Should these distributional effects be taken into account in cost-benefit analysis? If so, how can they be quantified?

The issue of whether government should take distributional effects into account is analogous to the issue of whether, in choosing a social discount rate, the government needs to be concerned with the impact on different

KEY ISSUES IN MEASURING A PROJECT'S BENEFITS

1 Measuring consumer surplus

2 Measuring non-pecuniary benefits:

Valuing time

Valuing life

Valuing the environment

3 Valuing marketed goods in the presence of market failure:

Using shadow prices to measure marginal social costs when market prices do not accurately measure it

4 Valuing consumption (output) at different dates:

Choosing the right discount rate

5 Valuing risk

6 Valuing distributional considerations:

How are impacts on different groups to be compared?

generations. *If* the government has already "optimally" redistributed income, then the "social" marginal value of a dollar to all individuals is the same, and we can simply add up the dollar value of the impacts on consumption of different individuals. But there is a widespread presumption that the social marginal value of a dollar to a poor individual is greater than it is to a rich individual.

The first step in any distributional analysis is to ascertain as precisely as possible how the program affects individuals in different circumstances. Typically, the focus is placed on individuals of different incomes, though frequently regional impacts are also taken into account. Of two programs with similar overall impact, the one in which more of the benefits and fewer of the costs accrue to poor individuals would presumably be preferred, if society cares about distribution.

Often, however, there is a desire to go beyond simply enumerating the impacts on different groups, to obtain a broader picture. This is done in two different ways. The first uses the social welfare function approach referred to earlier. It recognizes that the marginal valuation of a dollar is greater to a poor person than to a rich person, and uses the concept of the elasticity of marginal utility to quantify the extent to which this is so. For example, using an elasticity of unity (1), and giving a weight of unity to those at median income, impacts on those with half median income receive a weight of 2, while impacts on those with twice median income receive a weight of ½. Using these weights, the total "weighted benefit" is calculated, and of two programs with the same costs, the one with the highest weighted benefit is undertaken.

The second approach looks at the impact on the overall distribution of income or wealth.[14] But this approach lends itself only to major programs with the capacity for substantial distributional effects, such as changing the welfare system or the tax system. Most projects undertaken by the government are smaller in scale.

COST EFFECTIVENESS

In some cases, there are difficulties in comparing costs and benefits. The benefits may be improved health, the costs are dollars expended. Though we have emphasized the necessity of making hard—monetary—judgments concerning life and health, the political process often tries to avoid making such judgments, where possible. **Cost effectiveness** analysis provides a way of doing this by looking at programs with the same (or similar) benefits, and asking which produces those benefits at the least cost.

---

[14] This approach relies on measures like the Gini coefficient, discussed in the appendix to Chapter 5.

Assume that we wish to avoid the problems associated with valuing lives while helping the government assess a variety of ways of reducing highway deaths. We could calculate the costs associated with each of several methods of accomplishing the same goal. Or we might simply show the marginal costs associated with incremental reductions in the death rate under each method, and leave it to the legislators to determine which point along the curve should be chosen (and therefore what method of improving traffic safety should be chosen).

When the Occupational Safety and Health Administration considered standards for noise pollution, it did a cost effectiveness study, calculating how many extra workers would be protected from hearing loss as a result of alternative standards. It then calculated the cost associated with each standard. From this information, it calculated the marginal gross and net costs (taking into account the fact that hearing losses reduce productivity) associated with different levels of protection, as depicted in Figure 11.3. The curve shows that there are significant extra costs of trying to protect additional individuals from hearing loss. On the basis of this, one study concluded, "an effectively administered hearing-protector program could provide most of the benefits at much lower cost in comparison with an industrywide engineering-only noise standard. . . . an 85-decibel hearing-protector standard [has] the relatively reasonable marginal cost of about $23,000 per hearing impairment avoided. . . ." In ordinary English, the study recommended the use of ear plugs rather than the drastic changes in plants and equipment that would be required to implement the same level of hearing protection. Table 11.4 shows another example of cost effectiveness studies, this time comparing the effectiveness of alternative medical interventions (see page 296). There is an enormous range of cost effectiveness ratios, from $2158 per life-year saved for administering a low dose of the drug lovastatin to reduce cholesterol for heart attack survivors between 55 and 64 who had a high cholesterol level, to $41,000 for annual breast examination and mammography for females, age 55–65, to $88,000 for a coronary artery bypass graft for someone with a single-vessel disease with moderate heart weakness, to $335,000 for the use of an exercise cardiogram as a screening test for heart disease for 40-year-old females.

Though cost effectiveness analysis is simpler than cost-benefit analysis, because it avoids all the problems of measuring and valuing benefits, most of the issues discussed in measuring and valuing benefits remain, scaled down, for measuring and valuing costs. For instance, shadow prices for inputs may differ from market prices; a social discount rate must be used to value costs incurred at different dates; and there is considerable uncertainty—for example, we might be unsure of the exact degree to which hearing loss hurts productivity, or how much it will cost to bring a new weapon to completion, or how much it will cost firms to comply with stricter environmental standards.

Cost-benefit and cost effectiveness analysis are important tools used by policy makers throughout the world. They provide discipline to the decision-making process. While critics complain that they reduce everything to cold calculations, they can be used to bring systematically into the analysis

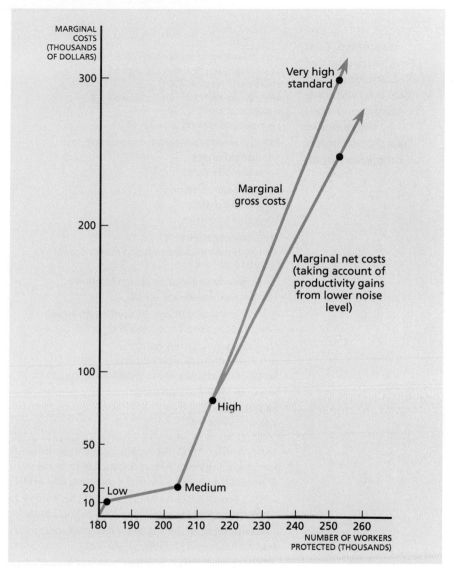

FIGURE 11.3 **Comparison of Alternative Standards for Occupational Noise Exposure**
Higher standards cost more and protect more workers from hearing loss.

SOURCE: J. R. Morrall III, "Exposure to Occupational Noise," in *Benefit-Cost Analyses of Social Regulation*, ed. James C. Miller III and Bruce Yandle (Washington, D.C.: American Enterprise Institute for Public Policy Research, 1979).

not only economic costs and benefits, but also concerns about the environment, health, and distribution. While there never will be complete precision, especially in these hard-to-quantify areas, judgments will be made weighing these various considerations, and quantification can be a helpful step in resolving the complicated trade-offs that have to be faced.

TABLE 11.4	INTERVENTION	COST/LIFE-YEAR ($1993)
Estimated Cost Effectiveness of Commonly Used Medical Interventions. (all interventions compared to "usual care" unless otherwise noted)	*Low-dose lovastatin for high cholesterol[a]*	
	Male heart attack survivors, age 55–64, cholesterol level ≥ 250	2,158
	Male heart attack survivors, age 55–64, cholesterol level < 250	2,293
	Female nonsmokers, age 35–44	2,023,440
	Exercise electrocardiogram as screening test[b]	
	40-year-old males	124,374
	40-year-old females	335,217
	Hypertension screening[c]	
	40-year-old males	27,519
	40-year-old females	42,222
	Breast cancer screening[d]	
	Annual breast examination and mammography, females age 55–65	41,008
	Physician advice about smoking cessation[e]	
	1% quit rate, males age 45–50	3,777
	Pap smear starting at age 20, continuing to 74[f]	
	Every 3 years, versus not screening	24,011
	Coronary artery bypass graft[g]	
	Left main coronary artery disease	8,768
	Single-vessel disease with moderate angina	88,087
	Neonatal intensive care units[h]	
	Infants 1000–1500 g	10,927
	Infants 500–999 g	77,161

[a] L. Goldman, M. C. Weinstein, et al., "Cost-Effectiveness of HMG-CoA Reductase Inhibition for Primary and Secondary Prevention of Coronary Heart Disease," *Journal of the American Medical Association*, 265 (1991): 1145–51.

[b] H. C. Sox, Jr., B. Littenberg, et al., "The Role of Exercise Testing in Screening for Coronary Artery Disease," *Annals of Internal Medicine*, 110 (1989): 456–69.

[c] B. Littenberg, A. M. Garber, et al., "Screening for Hypertension," *Annals of Internal Medicine* 112 (1990): 192–202.

[d] D. M. Eddy, "Screening for Cervical Cancer," *Annals of Internal Medicine* 113 (1990): 214–26.

[e] S. R. Cummings, S. M. Rubin, et al., "The Cost-Effectiveness of Counseling Smokers to Quit," *Journal of the American Medical Association* (1989) 261: 75–79.

[f] D. M. Eddy, "Screening for Breast Cancer," *Annals of Internal Medicine* 111 (1989): 389–99.

[g] M. C. Weinstein, "Economic Assessment of Medical Practices and Technologies," *Medical Decision Making* 1 (1981): 309–30.

[h] M. H. Boyle, G. W. Torrance, J. C. Sinclair, and S. P. Horwood, "Economic Evaluation of Neonatal Intensive Care of Very-Low-Birth-Weight Infants," *New England Journal of Medicine* 308 (1983): 1330–37.

SOURCE: Alan M. Garber and Charles Phelps, "Economic Foundations of Cost-Effectiveness Analysis," *Journal of Health Economics* 16, no. 1 (1997): 1–31.

REVIEW AND PRACTICE

SUMMARY

1   Cost-benefit analysis provides a systematic set of procedures by which a firm or government can assess whether to undertake a project or program and, when there is a choice among mutually exclusive projects or programs, which one to undertake.

2   Private cost-benefit analysis entails determining the consequences (inputs and outputs) associated with a project, evaluating these using market prices to calculate the net profit in each year, and, finally, discounting profits in future years to calculate the present discounted value of profits.

3   Social cost-benefit analysis involves the same procedures as private cost-benefit analysis, except that a broader range of consequences is taken into account, and the prices at which inputs and outputs are evaluated may not be market prices, either because the inputs and outputs are not marketed (so market prices do not exist) or because market prices do not accurately reflect marginal social costs and benefits, due to a market failure.

4   When the government makes available a good or service that was not previously available (e.g., constructs a bridge across a river), the value of the project to an individual is measured by the consumer surplus it generates; this is the area under the (compensated) demand curve.

5   The government has to make inferences (based on market data or observed behavior) concerning the valuation of nonmarketed consequences—e.g., lives and time saved, or impacts on the environment.

6   The rate of discount used by the government to evaluate projects may differ from that used by private firms.

7   To evaluate risky projects, the certainty equivalent of the benefits and costs needs to be calculated.

8   Distributional considerations may be introduced into evaluations, either by weighting the benefits accruing to different groups differently or by assessing the impact of the project on some measure of inequality.

KEY CONCEPTS

Opportunity costs	Opportunity cost view
Discounting, discount factor	Intergenerational distribution
Present discounted value	Pure discount rate
Consumer surplus	Certainty equivalent
Contingent valuation	Risk premium
Existence values	Risk assessment
Shadow prices	Cost effectiveness
Social discount rate	

1 Consider a project that costs $100,000 and yields a return of $30,000 for five years. At the end of the fifth year, there is a cost of $20,000 to dispose of the waste from the project. Should the project be undertaken if the discount rate is 0? 10 percent? 15 percent? The interest rate at which the net present discounted value of the project is zero is referred to as the *internal rate of return* of the project.

2 Assume there is uncertainty about the costs of disposing of the waste: there is a fifty-fifty chance that they will be $10,000 or $30,000. Discuss how this uncertainty affects the cost-benefit calculation, if the government is risk neutral, that is, it requires no risk premium to compensate it for bearing risk; if it is very risk averse, that is, if it requires a large risk premium to compensate it for bearing risk.

3 Assume now that there are two groups in the population. Each contributes equally to the cost of the project, but two-thirds of the benefits accrue to the richer group. Discuss how this alters the cost-benefit calculation. Under what circumstances will the decision to undertake the project be altered?

4 Assume that the government now has a choice between undertaking the project described in problem 1 and undertaking a larger project. If it spends an additional $100,000, returns will be increased by $25,000 per year and disposal costs in the final year will increase by $20,000. Which project should be undertaken if the discount rate is 0? 10 percent? 15 percent? In the case where there are two groups in the population, how are your answers affected if two-thirds of the incremental benefits go to the poor (with the incremental costs being shared equally, as before)?

5 Discuss why, under each of these circumstances, a social cost-benefit analysis might differ from a private cost-benefit analysis:

   a The unemployment rate is 10 percent.

   b The government has imposed a tariff on the importation of textiles.

   c The government has imposed a quota on the importation of oil.

   d The government has imposed a tax on interest income.

   e The government has imposed price controls on natural gas.

   f The government has regulated airlines, so that prices exceed the competitive levels.

6 For each of the following projects, what benefits or costs might be included in a social cost-benefit analysis that might be excluded from a private cost-benefit analysis:

   a A hydroelectric project

   b A steel mill

   c A chemical plant

d A project to improve car safety

e A training program to improve the skills of minority workers in a firm

How might your answers be affected by changes in legislation (e.g., concerning manufacturers' liabilities for automobile accidents, legislation imposing fines on polluters)?

7 How might the techniques used to analyze the distributional consequences in cost-benefit analysis be employed to ensure that concerns about environmental justice are incorporated into the analysis?

8 How are issues of incidence analysis and capitalization (discussed in the previous chapter) incorporated into cost-benefit analysis? For each case below, does it make a difference to your answer whether poor individuals own or rent their houses? In particular, if you wished to incorporate the distributional consequences of the following policies and programs, how might you do so?

a A government regulation which reduces the allowable level of noise for aircraft. (Assume that those who live in the neighborhood of the airport are relatively poor.)

b A subway line intended to make it less expensive for those in low-income neighborhoods to get to jobs in the center city.

c The Superfund program is intended to clean up toxic waste sites. Currently, a disproportionate number of poor people live near toxic waste sites.

9 The government is debating whether to spend $100 billion to reduce global warming damage 100 years from now. It is estimated that $800 billion of damage will be averted. A critic of the expenditure says that it would be far better to take the $100 billion, invest it in the stock market, earning an average return of 6 percent per year, and use the proceeds of the investment in 100 years to repair the damage. Should the project be undertaken?

12 Health Care

FOCUS QUESTIONS

1 What are the fundamental problems facing the health care system today?

2 What role does the government play in the health care sector today?

3 What are the reasons for government action? What are the market failures? What are the ways in which the market for health care differs from markets for other commodities? Why do concerns about distribution play a particularly large role in health care?

4 What are some of the problems that arise from the fact that a large fraction of health care costs are covered by insurance? What problems confront insurance providers?

5 What are the key public policy issues today? What are some ways in which costs can be contained or insurance coverage extended? What are some of the major proposed reforms to Medicare and Medicaid?

Reform of the health care sector was one of the key issues in Bill Clinton's presidential campaign of 1992. The subsequent failure of President Clinton's health care reform in 1994 is generally thought to have fueled the gains of the Republican Party in the congressional elections of that year. Ensuing years did see important changes in the private health care sector, though large-scale reform of the entire health care system moved off the political agenda. Today there is broad agreement that the public health care programs—**Medicare,** providing health care to the aged, and **Medicaid,** providing health care to the poor—will face substantial reform in the years ahead.

Three separate, and somewhat conflicting, concerns about the U.S. health care system continue to inform the debate over health care: excessive costs, limited insurance coverage, and the fiscal strains providing health care imposes on government.

Health expenditures as a percentage of GDP are higher in the United States than in any other country, amounting to more than $1 trillion in 1997—about 14 percent of GDP, or close to $4000 per capita. Even so, health status, as recorded by such measures as life expectancy and infant mortality, is actually lower here than in many countries that spend considerably less. Furthermore, expenditures are rising rapidly, partly due to increased quantity of services, and partly due to prices increasing faster than the price level in general, as indicated in Figure 12.1.[1]

A second problem is that many individuals lack health insurance. Health insurance coverage has declined in the United States in recent years. Slightly more than one out of eight people were uninsured in 1987, but today nearly one in six are uninsured. Lack of coverage has become a major political issue because of the anxiety that it imposes, especially on middle-class workers. Since most health care insurance is provided by employers, if a worker loses his job, he loses his insurance. The poor typically are covered by public programs, such as Medicaid. It is typically workers in low-paying jobs, workers without regular employment, and the self-employed who are left uncovered. While those without coverage can get access to health care services—hospitals do not normally turn away those who need care, regardless of whether they have insurance or can pay themselves—they often delay getting adequate treatment, raising the total costs of the treatment. Since those without coverage do eventually get treatment, for which they may not pay, lack of coverage also results in **cost shifting,** a shift of the costs of unpaid bills to others.

Soaring health costs put a strain on government budgets, pushing up government expenditures on Medicare and Medicaid. As the federal budget deficit soared in the 1980s and early 1990s, these rising government expenditures for health care, illustrated in panel A of Figure 12.1 and, for the two principal government programs, Medicare and Medicaid, in Figure 12.2, became an increasing source of concern. But even as the deficit has turned into a surplus in the late 1990s, projected future increases in costs remain a concern. Government expenditures on Medicare and Medicaid, which in 1996 accounted for 3.9 percent of GDP, are projected to grow to 14 percent

---

[1] Changes in the quality of health care services pose serious measurement problems. Most economists agree that conventional price measures overstate the rate of inflation in health care costs, though there is little consensus over the magnitude of the measurement errors.

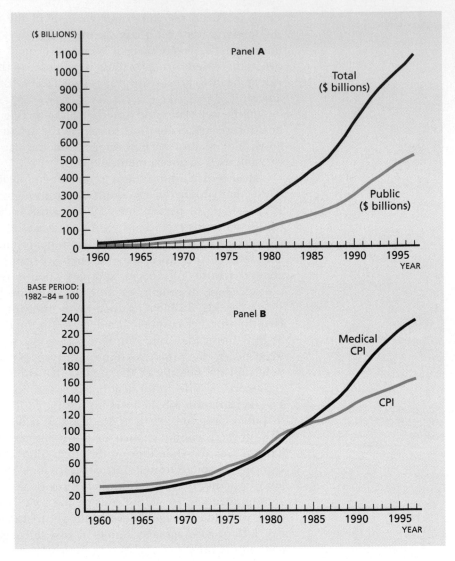

FIGURE 12.1   **Soaring Health Care Costs and Expenditures, 1960–1997**   Panel A: Health care expenditures have been rising rapidly, faster than GDP, so the percentage of GDP devoted to health care has been rising at least until the mid-1990s. Panel B: This is partly because volume of services has increased, and partly because health care prices (measured by the medical consumer price index or the medical CPI) have been rising faster than prices in general (measured by the CPI).

SOURCES: *Economic Report of the President, February 1998*, Table B-60; Health Care Financing Administration, Office of the Actuary, Office of National Health Statistics.

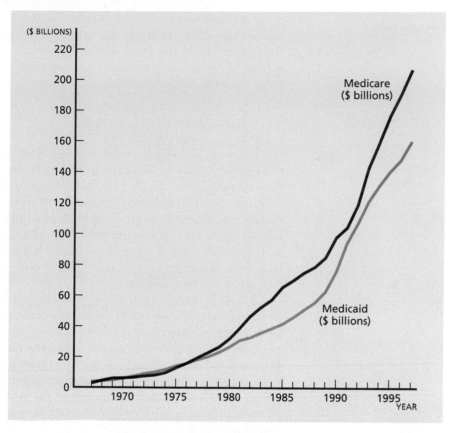

FIGURE 12.2 **Medicare and Medicaid Expenditures, 1966–1997** Expenditures on Medicare and Medicaid, the two major government health programs, have been rising rapidly and are imposing large fiscal strains, which will continue to grow in coming decades.

SOURCES: Executive Office of the President, Office of Management and Budget, *Budget of the United States Government, Fiscal Year 1999*, Historical Tables; Health Care Financing Administration, Office of the Actuary, Office of National Health Statistics.

of GDP by 2050. This growth is due to an increasing number of aged, increasing quantities of services being used by the aged, and health care prices that are anticipated to rise faster than the rate of inflation. Combined with social security, total expenditures on these programs will grow to 20.3 percent of GDP.[2] (To put this into perspective, *total* federal expenditures have historically amounted to about 20 percent of GDP.) If such expenditures do grow unchecked, then either taxes will have to be raised, the deficit will soar, or other government programs will have to be cut back.

[2] See *Economic Report of the President, 1997*, Chart 3-4, p. 97. The percentage is projected to increase still further, to 28 percent of GDP, by 2070.

This chapter provides an overview of the U.S. health care system. It examines how different market failures have shaped the role of government in the system; tracks the sources of the problems of excessive costs, limited insurance coverage, and fiscal strains; and takes up the different efforts to reform the system in recent years.

THE HEALTH CARE SYSTEM IN THE UNITED STATES

Governments may be involved in the health care system in a variety of ways: directly paying for health care, subsidizing individual purchases of health care and health insurance, providing health care services, financing and conducting research, preventing the spread of communicable diseases, and regulating drugs and medical devices. In the United States, the government is involved in each of these areas, but to a lesser extent than in many other countries. For instance, in Great Britain, the major health care delivery system is run by the government.

The U.S. health care system, with its mix of public, private, and non-profit providers, is also one of the most complex systems in the world. Most health care consumers in the United States fall into one of four groups: the poor, who receive medical care through the federal government's Medicaid program; the aged, whose basic medical costs are paid by Medicare, another program of the federal government; employed individuals covered by employer-provided health insurance; and the uninsured, who sometimes purchase health care services directly, but who often receive **uncompensated care,** the cost of which is passed on to others. In addition, a small number of those who do not enjoy employer-provided insurance purchase their own insurance.

For virtually everyone, a substantial part of health care is paid not by the individual receiving the treatment, but by a third party—the government or a health insurance provider. As Figure 12.3 shows, consumers prepay (directly or through their employers) 32 percent of the cost of health care in the form of private insurance premiums. Another 45 percent of health care costs are paid by the government. Only 19 percent of the money spent on medical care comes from direct payments by consumers.[3] The percentage of total expenditures which individuals bear themselves has declined steadily over the past quarter century. Total **third-party payments** (govern-

---

[3] These figures on the overall sources of funds disguise the fact that the share of out-of-pocket costs varies a great deal among consumers (depending on their insurance plan) and among kinds of health expenditures. For example, in 1995 only 3 percent of national hospital costs were paid directly by consumers, compared to 18 percent of doctors' fees and 37 percent of nursing home costs.

What matters, of course, is not just the average amounts paid by consumers but their marginal costs. At the margin, what fraction of incremental costs do consumers bear? On average, the share of *marginal* costs borne by individuals is likely to be less than these numbers indicate.

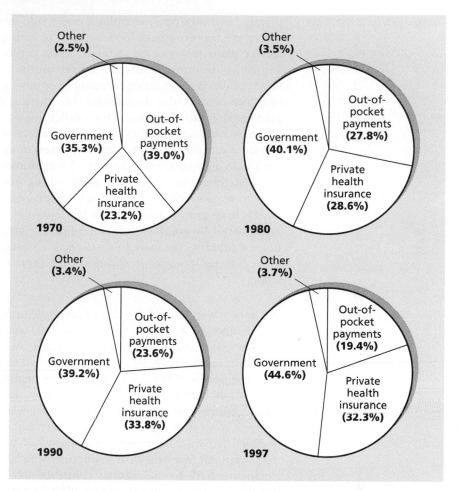

FIGURE 12.3   **Sources of Funds for Personal Health Care Expenditures, Selected Years**
Americans pay a relatively small percentage of health care costs out-of-pocket, and the share of such payments has been falling in recent decades. "Other" includes spending by charitable organizations and industrial on-site health services.

SOURCE: Health Care Financing Administration web site, Table 4, accessed at http://www.hcfa.gov/stats/nhe-oact/tables/t12.htm.

ment and health insurance) in 1980 amounted to 69 percent of total personal health care expenditures; by 1997, they were close to 80 percent. And while 50 percent of total *private* health care expenditures were met by private insurance in 1980, by 1997 that number had increased to more than 60 percent.[4]

[4] U.S. Health Care Financing Administration, *Health Care Financing Review*, fall 1996 (cited in *Statistical Abstract of the United States, 1997*, p. 114).

305

Private insurance providers play a major role in the U.S. health care system. There are two dominant forms of private insurance. In one, called **fee-for-service plans,** doctors are reimbursed on the basis of the service provided. Typically, insurance reimburses a fixed amount of the total bill, up to some limit. Often, the insurance company only pays an amount in excess of a certain level, called the **deductible;** the fraction of the excess over this deductible that the individual pays is called his **co-payment.** Insurance policies also have caps on what they will pay for certain services. In the other form of private insurance, called **health maintenance organizations (HMOs),** the patient pays a fixed annual fee, called a **capitation fee,** to cover the medical costs. Members of an HMO must go to the doctors of that HMO. In addition, to see a specialist, they must be referred by their HMO family doctor.[5] HMOs have grown rapidly in the last few years, especially among those who are covered by employer-provided health plans, mainly because they have helped contain cost increases. (Indeed, employer health care costs in 1996 were essentially stagnant, though since then they have begun to increase again.)

THE ROLE OF GOVERNMENT

We have already noted the large role of government in the U.S. health care system, and the huge growth over the last two decades of the two most important government programs, Medicare and Medicaid. Both programs were motivated largely by a concern that two major segments of the population, the poor and the aged, did not have health insurance coverage (and in many cases could not have obtained it, or at least not at premiums that could generally be regarded as affordable). The larger of the two programs is Medicare, which provides medical care for everyone over 65 and certain disabled persons. Medicare is composed of two parts—hospital insurance and supplementary medical insurance, which pays for physicians' services. Recipients have to make some contributions to supplementary insurance, but their contribution covers only about a quarter of the costs of even this part of Medicare. The rest comes from general tax revenues. Hospital costs are covered by a 2.9 percent payroll tax (paid by working people as part of the social security tax, though half is nominally paid by employers). The money from the 2.9 percent payroll tax goes into a trust fund, which has been near exhaustion a number of times. Each time quick fixes have enabled the fund's life to be extended.

Medicaid provides medical care for certain low-income families with dependent children, and for most poor aged, blind, and disabled persons. Unlike Medicare, Medicaid is administered by the states. The eligibility standards are set by each state within federal guidelines, and the states and local communities are required to pay for between 20 and 50 percent of the ben-

---

[5] There are also hybrids of the two systems. An example is **preferred provider plans.** Such plans pay for all the costs of visits to its preferred providers. If the member goes to another provider, the plan pays for only a fraction of the costs. Similarly, many HMOs allow patients to go to other doctors, but reimburse only a fraction of the costs.

efits, depending on the per capita income of the state. The federal portion is paid out of general tax revenues. States also pay 50 percent of administrative costs. The rapid growth in these costs has imposed serious problems for states and localities.

OTHER EXPENDITURE PROGRAMS

Three other categories of direct expenditures should be mentioned: the Public Health Service, VA hospitals, and expenditures on medical research and teaching. The Public Health Service, which traces its roots to 1798 with the establishment of the Marine Health Service, was created in part to address important externalities associated with communicable diseases. (If individuals have a contagious disease, they impose an externality on others by increasing the likelihood that the disease will spread.) The Public Health Service played a pivotal role in reducing or eliminating contagious diseases such as smallpox and measles.

Another major government medical program is the VA hospitals run by the Veterans Administration. Dating back to the establishment of the Veterans Administration in 1930, the VA hospitals provide medical care for those injured while serving in the armed forces and for other veterans. As those who fought in World War II have grown older, requiring more medical care, increasing demands have been imposed on the system. VA expenditures reached $16.6 billion in 1997.[6]

Expenditures for medical research and teaching are another important category of expenditures. The government runs some very successful research laboratories (the National Institutes of Health) and in addition supports extensive research in universities and medical schools. Medical research expenditures amounted to $18 billion in 1997.

TAX EXPENDITURES

For more than three decades, there has been concern about the uninsured. Without insurance, a serious illness or accident can cause a huge financial burden. Accordingly, the government has encouraged employers to provide insurance by giving their employees a significant tax advantage: employees do not have to pay taxes on the value of their employer-provided health benefits. In 1997, the value of this tax break was estimated to be $70 billion.

Government provides a second tax break for health expenditures: Medical expenses in excess of 7.5 percent of income are deductible from income. The estimated value of this tax break in 1997 was $4 billion. The rationale for this provision is that taxes should be based on some measure of ability to pay, and that large medical expenses—to the extent that they are not voluntary—reduce an individual's ability to pay.

These **tax expenditures** encourage both health insurance purchases and medical expenditures. They effectively lower the price an individual must pay for insurance, and health insurance lowers the price individuals have to pay for medical care.

[6] Health Care Financing Administration web site, www.hcfa.gov/stats/nhe-oact/tables/t18.htm, accessed January 1997.

There is concern not only about the efficiency consequences of our tax expenditures—that is, the excessive consumption of medical services that is induced—but also about their equity. Tax benefits are clearly larger for those at higher marginal tax rates—that is, for wealthier individuals. The unemployed and those at low-paying jobs with few or no benefits obviously do not enjoy the tax expenditures associated with employer-provided medical insurance.

Prior to 1981 the tax expenditures were so regressive that total federal expenditures (including tax expenditures) per capita on high-income individuals actually exceeded those on middle-income individuals, even though direct expenditures (i.e., through Medicare and Medicaid) were considerably lower on a per capita basis for upper-income groups. In fact, expenditures per capita on the middle-income group were lower than those on any other group. Changes to the tax code in the 1980s reduced marginal tax rates and increased the minimum expenditure required for tax deductibility of medical expenses. These changes made health expenditures less regressive.[7]

RATIONALE FOR A ROLE OF GOVERNMENT IN THE HEALTH CARE SECTOR

At the beginning of this chapter we noted that rising costs are a major concern about the U.S. health care system. Typically, an increase in the price of some commodity is not by itself taken as grounds for government intervention. Market prices change in response to demand and supply, resulting in changes in scarcity.[8] Similarly, the fact that Americans spend more on health care (as a percent of GDP) than other countries may simply be a reflection of preferences. (We would not infer from the fact that Americans prefer larger cars that there is something wrong with the U.S. automobile market requiring government intervention.) But in fact, the health care market is rife with imperfections, and some of these do indeed lead to excessive expenditures. In this section we begin with general theory, and then focus on two special aspects of the U.S. health care market.

We will first discuss four market failures. The first two, imperfect information and limited competition, were discussed in general terms in Chap-

[7] See Gail R. Wilensky, "Government and the Financing of Health Care," *American Economic Review* 72, no. 2 (May 1982): 205; Jonathan Gruber and James Poterba, "Tax Incentives and the Decision to Purchase Health Insurance: Evidence from the Self-Employed," *Quarterly Journal of Economics* 109, no. 3 (August 1994): 701–33; Charles E. Phelps, *Health Economics* (New York: Harper Collins, 1992).

[8] In competitive markets, increases in expenditures can result either from a shift in the demand curve along a given supply curve, and/or from an upward shift in the supply curve along an inelastic demand curve. Both of these may well have occurred, with demand shifting as Americans have become more health conscious, and the supply curve shifting as health care costs have been rising faster than the costs of goods and services in general. As we comment below, however, the concern is that the increases in health care expenditures do not reflect the normal workings of competitive markets.

ter 4. The two others relate to the large roles of nonprofit institutions and of the insurance industry in the health care sector.

But even if there were no market failures, there might be a role for government: some people might have such a low income that they could not afford or chose not to get adequate health care. The final section addresses these concerns about the provision of health care to the poor.

IMPERFECT INFORMATION

When consumers go to a doctor, in large measure they are buying the doctor's knowledge and/or information. As a patient, the consumer must rely on the doctor's judgment as to what medicine is required or whether an operation or other procedure is advisable. Because they lack medical expertise, patients cannot effectively assess and evaluate their doctors' advice. They may not even be able to tell whether a doctor is qualified. This explains why government has long taken a role in licensing doctors and regulating the drugs they can administer to their patients.[9]

These information problems are far more severe than those faced by consumers in other areas. In the case of repeat purchases, like groceries, consumers either are able to judge the quality of the products themselves or come to rely on a grocery store (say, for the freshness of its vegetables). But typically, individuals do not have repeat purchases of medical procedures such as kidney replacements, heart bypass surgery, or even ulcer treatments. In the case of products like cars, there are independent rating agencies, such as Consumers Union (which publishes *Consumer Reports*), that test the product and describe its strengths and weaknesses. But there are simply too many doctors and hospitals and too many procedures for that to be feasible in the health care sector: a hospital may be good at one procedure and weak at another. Success may depend on subjective factors, like a doctor's personal manner, which may work well with some individuals and not with others. Even "report cards"—say, the fraction of heart bypass patients that survived one year—may not be fully informative, because hospitals in one region may have an intake of sicker patients than hospitals in another.

Insurance companies also encounter information problems relating to doctors and patients. Like patients, they must rely largely on doctors to determine what procedures are necessary and useful. Imperfect information about patients creates problems in the market for insurance, as discussed below (see the section on adverse selection).

LIMITED COMPETITION

Imperfect information decreases the effective degree of competition.[10] A firm selling a standard commodity, like a Sony television, knows that it can attract customers away from other stores by lowering its price. Customers can easily ascertain where they are getting the best value for their money.

---

[9] Kenneth Arrow has emphasized the importance of imperfect information in medical markets. See K. J. Arrow, "Uncertainty and Welfare Economics of Medical Care," *American Economic Review* 53 (1963): 941–73.

[10] See, for instance, S. Salop, "Information and Monopolistic Competition," *American Economic Review*, May 1976, pp. 240–45.

By contrast, potential patients who see a doctor with lower prices than her competitors may infer that she is not in great demand and is therefore trying to attract more customers; but the apparent lack of demand for her services may suggest to them that she is not a good doctor.

By the same token, the heterogeneity of medical services makes price and quality comparisons difficult and thus inhibits the effective dissemination of information. My neighbor may be pleased with the medical treatment that he obtained from his doctor, but if his medical problems are different from mine, his satisfaction is no assurance that I will be pleased if I go to the same doctor. And if I hear that one doctor charges more than another doctor, to evaluate whether one is a better buy I have to know precisely what services were performed.

The practices of the medical profession may compound the inevitable limitations of competition resulting from imperfect information. Doctors used not to be allowed to advertise. In other contexts, restrictions on advertising have been shown to raise prices (because they inhibit competition). Thus, several states now allow advertising for eyeglasses, and in those states, there has been a dramatic decrease in the price of eyeglasses. In many states, doctors and hospitals have been allowed to advertise. But it has not become a common practice, and the effects on competition are not yet clear.

There are other measures by which doctors can attempt to restrict price competition. It has been suggested, for instance, that "lowering fees might provoke one's colleagues to deny a surgeon hospital privileges or seek to damage his reputation."[11]

Finally, in many small communities there are few doctors from which to choose. The grouping together of doctors in HMOs and preferred provider plans may actually be significantly lessening competition in these areas.

Moreover, there is also limited competition among hospitals. Most smaller communities have at most only a few hospitals. In the event of an emergency, an individual seldom is in a position to choose from among many. And even when there is time to make a choice, the choice is made not by the individual but by his doctor.

ABSENCE OF PROFIT MOTIVE

Another important difference between medical markets and standard competitive markets is the large role of not-for-profit organizations in the provision of health care. Until recently, not-for-profit hospitals vastly outnumbered their for-profit counterparts, and even today, the majority of hospitals in the United States are not-for-profit institutions. Such institutions do not view their objective as simply minimizing the cost of delivering medical care, or maximizing profits. The consequences of this absence of profit incentives have been exacerbated by the manner in which hospitals have been reimbursed for their expenses by government and by private insurance companies: in most cases, hospitals were paid whatever they charged.

[11] V. Fuchs, *Who Shall Live? Health Economics and Social Choice* (New York: Basic Books, 1975).

In contrast, for-profit hospital chains respond more clearly to incentives for efficiency, and several large for-profit hospital chains, such as Humana, have achieved a reputation not only for efficiency but for innovativeness as well.[12] Even so, there remain concerns about perverse incentives for lowering quality, especially in circumstances where quality is hard to judge. For instance, for-profit blood providers earned a reputation for gathering blood from drug addicts and others whose blood was more likely to carry disease. As a result, that market has been dominated by not-for-profit firms.

Incentive problems encountered with both for-profit and not-for-profit providers arise in large measure from imperfect information. If consumers could easily ascertain the quality of what they purchased, both types of providers would have stronger incentives to achieve efficiency and high quality. A key part of Clinton's proposed health care reforms was improved information, with more extensive attempts at gathering data and more public disclosure of hospital performance and consumer satisfaction.

SPECIAL CHARACTERISTICS OF THE U.S. MARKET

Two characteristics of the U.S. health sector exacerbate the problems identified thus far: the prevalence of third-party payments and the fee-for-service system.

THIRD-PARTY PAYMENT For an ordinary commodity, for which the consumer directly pays the full price, it can be taken for granted that the consumer believes that the benefits of the commodity are at least as great as its cost. Health care differs from an ordinary commodity in that consumers are insulated from cost considerations at the point of consumption, partly through private insurance, and partly through government programs. As we have noted, individuals pay for less than a quarter of all health care costs, an even smaller fraction of doctor costs, and a negligible fraction of hospital costs (around 3 percent). Because so much of medical expenditures are paid for by third parties, consumers have little incentive to be cost conscious. The force of the price system is greatly diminished.

FEE FOR SERVICE The fee-for-service system which is prevalent in the United States may also exacerbate the problems arising from imperfectly informed consumers. The patient goes to the doctor for advice about what medical services are necessary and appropriate. But the doctor, like any purveyor of services, has a vested interest in selling more of his services. The more services the doctor provides, the higher his income. The threat of **malpractice suits** (see box) also encourages doctors to be very cautious. In addition, patients tend to be risk averse, and to demand any test or treatment which might protect their health. As a result, there is a tendency for doctors to recommend and patients to accept high levels of service. These problems are exacerbated by the fact that a third party (the insurance company or the government) pays the costs.

---

[12] Most notably, in the implanting of an artificial heart in 1986 in their Louisville, Kentucky, hospital.

MALPRACTICE SUITS

Uninformed consumers are frequently disappointed with what they purchase. In the context of health care, people who believe they have received poor medical treatment often file malpractice suits against physicians and health care providers. The number of such suits filed doubled during a five-year span in the early 1980s, and the size of settlements also increased. Since then, their rate of growth has moderated.

Though it is difficult to get data on the total value of malpractice suits, since out-of-court settlements typically are not recorded or are kept confidential, one indicator is provided by a recent Government Accounting Office report showing that during a short period from fiscal 1990 to 1994, malpractice claims at VA medical centers went from $678 million to $978 million. During that period, claimants received over $200 million in payments.

In some medical specialties, such as obstetrics, the cost of the malpractice insurance that covers doctors against the risk of suits has reached such high levels that many doctors have closed their practices and younger physicians are reluctant to enter those specialties.

A doctor can be sued if she fails to prescribe some drug, even if the probability of its having a beneficial effect is low, or if she fails to administer some test, even if the costs relative to the information it yields are high. Since third parties bear most of the costs of such drugs and tests, doctors and their patients have every incentive to make use of them. This is called "defensive medicine." The problem is further exacerbated as the defensive practices become widely used, and thus become the standard of practice against which malpractice is judged.

HMOs may resolve some of these problems by altering the incentives faced by doctors and patients. Evidence shows that there are important differences in the care provided and utilized under the fee-for-service and HMO systems. Generally, utilization of health care services is reduced when doctors are compensated with salaries or capitation systems, as is common in HMOs.[13]

[13] L. DeBrock and R. J. Arnould, "Utilization Control in HMOs," *Quarterly Review of Economics and Finance* 32, no. 3 (autumn 1992). See also Laurence Baker, "HMO's and Fee-For-Service Health Care Expenditures: Evidence from Medicare," NBER Working Paper 5360, November 1995, p. 27; and David M. Cutler, "A Guide to Health Care Reform," *Journal of Economic Perspectives* 8, no. 3 (summer 1994): 13–29.

It is difficult to estimate the total cost of defensive medicine, but with medical malpractice insurance now running $5 billion a year, the costs of defensive medicine are probably quite high. One study of defensive medicine suggested that the nation could save $41 billion over five years if aggressive malpractice reforms were instituted.

Many economists believe that malpractice suits play a major role in the high cost of U.S. health care, and that they should be curtailed. But what trade-offs would arise from limiting malpractice suits? On the one hand, a system that limits malpractice suits (or the magnitude of rewards) might result in some individuals' not being adequately compensated for their injuries. On the other hand, economic efficiency would probably be increased through a reduction in needless expenditures. Excessive legal expenditures, which now amount to about one dollar for every dollar (net of legal fees) received by plaintiffs in such cases, would be reduced, as would excessive expenditures designed to forestall malpractice suits.

Many states have amended their laws to discourage liability suits. However, these reforms seem to have had the most pronounced effect on general liability cases and less effect on medical malpractice cases.

SOURCES: U.S. Department of Justice, Tort Policy Working Group, *An Update on the Liability Crisis* (Washington, D.C.: U.S. Government Printing Office, 1987), p. 52; K. Viscusi et al., "The Effects of 1980s Tort Reform Legislation on General Liability and Medical Malpractice," *Journal of Risk and Uncertainty,* April 1993, pp. 165–86; HEHS 96-24, VA Health Care: Trends in Malpractice Claims, GAO; Robert J. Rubin and Daniel N. Mendelson, "Defensive Medicine: At What Cost?" *Journal of American Health Policy* 4, no. 4 (July 1994); Daniel Kessler and Mark McClellan, "Do Doctors Practice Defensive Medicine?" *Quarterly Journal of Economics* 111, no. 2 (1996).

One of the concerns with HMOs is that their incentives may lead to underprovision of services. This concern has grown recently as competition among HMOs has intensified, and profit margins have been cut.

THE ROLE OF THE HEALTH INSURANCE INDUSTRY

Individuals are risk averse; that is why they buy insurance. They would rather pay a certain amount every year to the health insurance company than go one year with few expenditures because they are lucky and have no illness or accident, and another year with high expenditures when they are less lucky. This is all the more so because when expenditures are very high income may be particularly low, since they may not be able to work. Indeed, if on average individuals expect to pay $4000 in medical bills, most individuals are even willing to pay an insurance company more, "a risk premium," to avoid the risk. Thus, even if there are substantial transactions costs (the costs of filing and processing insurance claims), insurance may be desirable.

There has been considerable dissatisfaction with the insurance provided by the market. The complaints are that (a) some people buy too much insurance, and insurance induces excessive expenditure on health care; (b) many people cannot obtain insurance (there is too little coverage) or can obtain it only at an excessive cost; and (c) transactions costs are excessive.

INSURANCE AND EXCESSIVE EXPENDITURES ON HEALTH CARE When individuals buy insurance, they no longer pay the full costs of health care. If illnesses simply happened, unaffected by the actions of the individual, and if doctors faced no choices in how much to spend to deal with the illness, then there would be no problem. But individuals can affect their likelihood of needing health care, by taking preventive actions. (As a result of insurance their incentives to do so are reduced, though this effect may not be too significant, since most of the "costs" of an illness are probably the discomfort costs and risks borne by the individual, not the doctors' and hospitals' medical bills.)

More important, however, is the fact that there is considerable discretion in treatment. There may be some benefit from staying in a hospital an extra day, but the benefit may be far less than the cost. A very expensive drug may represent a very, very slight improvement over a very cheap drug. A patient might not be willing to pay the cost himself, but would not turn it down if offered the more expensive drug for nothing, or for pennies.

The demand curve for health services, like the demand curve for any other commodity, is downward-sloping; and because it is downward-sloping, lowering the *marginal* cost paid by the patient increases the utilization. With many medical plans, patients pay only 20 percent of the true marginal costs; with some, they pay essentially none of the costs. (Demand is still limited, because there is a time and discomfort cost to spending time in the hospital or going to the doctor.) Figure 12.4 shows a downward-sloping demand curve, and how consumption is increased from what it would be if individuals paid the full marginal cost. The magnitude of the increase depends on the elasticity of demand. A recent estimate puts the demand elasticity for medical care at .14, so that with a 20 percent co-payment (where the individual pays 20 percent of the marginal cost) demand is increased by 11.2 percent (price is lowered by 80 percent, so demand is increased by .14 × .80).[14]

The problem is not so much the increase in the health care expenditures, but the fact that *at the margin* the social benefits of the extra expenditures are less than the costs. Indeed, at the margin, the marginal benefit (with a 20 percent co-payment) is only equal to 20 percent of the marginal cost.

The problem that with insurance, individuals spend too much on health care is called the **moral hazard** problem. The insurance industry has

[14] Joseph P. Newhouse, *Free for All? Lessons from the RAND Health Insurance Experiment,* a RAND study (Cambridge and London: Harvard University Press, 1993), p. 120.

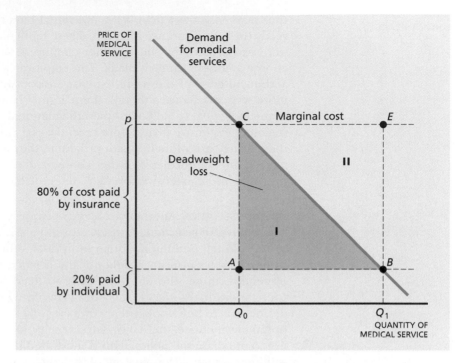

FIGURE 12.4 **Insurance and the Utilization of Health Care Services** Insurance lowers the price paid by the individual and thus increases the quantity of health care services consumed, from Q_0 to Q_1. For these additional expenditures, marginal costs (reflected in the market price p) exceed the marginal benefit to the individual (reflected in his willingness to pay, as evidenced by his demand curve). The area ABC measures the deadweight loss from excessive consumption.

long worried that insurance would increase the likelihood of whatever was insured against; it thought of this as a *moral* problem—with excessive fire insurance, an owner of a property might even be induced to burn down his building. But economists view the issue simply as one of *incentives*. With insurance, incentives to maintain health and control health expenditures are attenuated. There is a trade-off. The more insurance, the less risk the individual buys, but the weaker are incentives, and thus the greater the overall costs. Optimal insurance balances off these trade-offs.[15]

There is a concern that government policies have led to excessive insurance, and because insurance is excessive, expenditures on health care are excessive. The tax system subsidizes insurance. Employer-provided insurance premiums are essentially a tax-free form of compensation. The marginal cost of providing health care through employer-provided insurance is

[15] That is, with optimal insurance, individuals will spend more on health care than they would with no insurance, but this is the "price" that must be borne in order to reduce the risks they face.

315

thus markedly lower than if the individual buys the health care services directly (or buys insurance directly). These tendencies for excessive insurance were exacerbated by the way that employers used to allow employees to choose among insurance plans. The employer would pay a fraction of the additional costs of the more expensive plan (which traditionally provided more services). Thus, although the marginal benefit of the extra insurance to the individual could be less than the marginal cost, she would still choose the more expensive plans. More recently, as many firms have worried about the soaring costs of their health programs, they have required individuals to pay the full marginal costs if they choose a plan costing more (and typically providing more extensive coverage) than the basic plan offered by the firm.

ADVERSE SELECTION Another problem which arises in many insurance markets is **adverse selection.** Consider a simple situation where the insurance firm could tell nothing about an individual, other than that he was willing to purchase an insurance policy at the premium being offered. At higher premiums, those who are least likely to need medical care—say, healthy young individuals—decide it is not worth paying the premium. Or they may decide only to buy a policy that covers very large medical expenses. Thus, as premiums increase, there is an adverse selection effect: the best risks decide not to purchase the policy. This is illustrated in panel A of Figure 12.5. But with the best risks dropping out of the market, the average cost per policy issued increases. Panel B of the figure illustrates the competitive market equilibrium, which occurs when the premium equals the expected payout per policy. Because there are few highly risk-averse individuals who are willing to pay a large amount in excess of their expected costs, a small fraction of the population obtains insurance.

Insurance firms do not, of course, sit idly by, accepting anyone who applies. They actively attempt to increase the "quality" of those they insure. They do this in several ways, each of which has adverse effects on the effectiveness of insurance. First, they often will not provide insurance for "pre-existing conditions"—for instance, illnesses whose onset occurred before the purchase of insurance. In some cases, insurance firms simply refuse to insure those with a bad health history. These provisions have a particularly adverse effect on the ability of individuals to switch jobs; if anyone in the worker's family has an illness, the worker can become locked into his current job, for if he moves, the insurance at his new company often will not cover the medical costs of that illness. Secondly, they impose limits on the extent of coverage. Thus, while insurance is supposed to cover big losses—those losses which individuals are least able to bear—in fact insurance markets simply fail to cover these losses. Even insurance designed to cover major medical losses typically have caps on claims, for instance at $1 million. Thirdly, they may concentrate their selling efforts in low-risk communities. Health status varies greatly across different communities; the incidence of malnutrition, violence, drugs, and alcoholism—all of which can lead to high medical costs—is much higher among some socioeconomic groups than others.

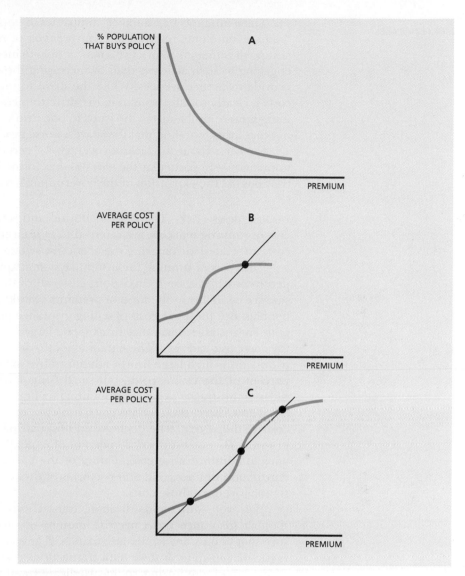

FIGURE 12.5   **Adverse Selection** As the premium rises, the percentage of the population
purchasing insurance decreases, with the best risks—those with the least
chance of needing insurance—dropping out of the market first. As a result,
the average payout increases as the premium increases. Panel B shows the
market equilibrium, where the premium equals the average payout. In
equilibrium, either relatively few or relatively many individuals may remain
uncovered. Panel C shows that indeed there may be multiple equilibria; in the
high-price equilibrium, relatively few people are covered, in the low price,
most people are covered.

These attempts by insurance companies to improve the mix of those covered are sometimes referred to as *cherry picking* or *cream skimming*. The important point is that insurance firms may be able to increase their profits more by engaging in such activities than by increasing the efficiency with which they provide insurance services. While the drive to increase profits by reducing costs is clearly socially beneficial, the drive to increase profits by cream skimming is more problematic: the gains to one firm occur largely at the expense of other firms, who find that they have a worse mix of insured individuals.[16]

Concern about the lack of coverage for certain high-risk groups in the population—in particular the elderly—has formed one of the strongest motivations for the expansion of the government's role in health care.

TRANSACTIONS COSTS The costs of buying and selling goods, including the cost of running markets, are referred to as **transactions costs.** These are the costs associated with making the economic system work.

The costs of running the insurance system appear to be high. In a competitive world without transactions costs, all of the money going into an insurance company in the form of premiums would be paid out in the form of benefits. But there are costs of selling insurance policies and paying the benefits. For instance, insurance firms spend large amounts in the effort to identify good and bad risks. These transactions costs are relatively low for policies provided through large firms—administrative expenses amount to about 5.5 percent of the claims paid—but small firms face a much heavier burden, with administrative expenses amounting to 40 percent of the claims paid.[17]

These direct transactions costs, however, are not the entire transactions costs of the system. The doctors and hospitals have to fill out vast numbers of forms. By one estimate, 20 percent of expenditures on hospitals actually goes to administrative costs. Critics of the current system argue that standardization of forms and other reforms of the health care system could substantially reduce those costs.

But even with standardization, transactions costs would likely be substantial. Insurance firms need to monitor doctors and hospitals to make sure that claims are legitimate. Critics of government insurance programs argue that in spite of their high transactions costs, they have done an ineffective job of monitoring, so that Medicare fraud and abuse has mounted to billions of dollars annually.[18]

[16] The issue is somewhat more complicated, because there can be efficiency gains from sorting individuals according to their risks. For instance, it may be useful to ascertain that some individuals are bad drivers, in order to discourage them from driving. Charging higher premiums for health insurance to those who smoke or drink may similarly have beneficial incentive effects. However, this is not the case for most of the sorting that occurs in health insurance markets.

[17] *Economic Report of the President, 1994,* p. 140 (Washington, D.C.: U.S. Government Printing Office).

[18] For a discussion of these estimates, see U.S. Congress, House Committee on Commerce, Subcommittee on Oversight and Investigation, *Medicare Waste, Fraud, and Abuse,* Hearings, September 27, 1998.

PROBLEMS WITH MARKET-PROVIDED HEALTH INSURANCE

Moral hazard—Reduced incentive to avoid insured-against event.

Trade-off between risk and incentives.

Insurance firms try to limit through use of co-payments and deductibles.

Adverse selection—Those who choose a particular policy may have risk characteristics that differ from the population as a whole.

As price of insurance increases, best risks may decide not to apply.

Insurance firms have incentive to try to insure only low-risk individuals—"cherry picking" or "cream skimming."

Transactions costs.

Because of the incentive effects and large transactions costs typically associated with insurance, most economists believe that insurance markets should focus on large losses, those which the individual would find difficult bearing himself. Unfortunately, many individuals feel that they are not getting their "money's worth" from insurance unless they regularly get at least something back; insurance companies have thus found customers attracted to covering small losses (such as, in automobile insurance, towing).

CONSEQUENCES OF INEFFICIENCIES IN HEALTH CARE MARKETS

Failures in health care markets lead to inefficiencies and may contribute to the rising costs which have fueled recent public policy debates. Two important examples of such inefficiencies are the excessive provision of health care services and the provision of inappropriate care.

SUPPLY CREATES ITS OWN DEMAND Conventional competition theory predicts that an increase in the supply of doctors will lower the price of medical services. But during the 1970s, the number of doctors almost doubled. Even though this expansion was far greater than the increase in population or income, prices for medical services did not fall. One explanation for this was discussed earlier: Because of their limited information, patients judge quality partly on the basis of price, and so doctors are reluctant to cut prices, lest they get a reputation as second-rate.

For a conventional commodity, if supply increases and price does not fall, there will be *excess supply*. There is some evidence of this occurring in medical practice; one detailed study in a suburban New York community showed surgeons having a workload only one-third of what experts viewed as a full schedule. These results were consistent with similar findings based on aggregate statistics of the number of surgeons and operations.

But in health care, there is another possible response: Since patients do not know what care is necessary and appropriate, and since they pay little of the cost of their care, doctors may increase the demand for their services. *Supply creates its own demand.* There is some evidence, in fact, that increasing the number of surgeons leads to an increase in the number of operations even when prices do not change at all.[19]

Indeed, there is even evidence of what might be viewed as a backward-bending supply curve. In Canada, as the government has attempted to ratchet health care costs down, it has reduced the fees paid doctors for each service performed. Doctors have responded by performing more services. (To some extent, the doctor may not actually be performing more services, but rather billing more of the services actually performed. Thus, a doctor who might have treated a patient for two maladies at the same time, and billed her for one office visit, might ask the patient to come back to take a more careful look at the second malady.)

Questions of whether an operation is advisable or necessary are, of course, debatable. Most doctors do not recommend operations simply to increase their own income. But in making a professional judgment about whether an operation is desirable, time constraints and the demands of other patients facing a doctor have important effects. And patients with limited information are likely to have surgery if their surgeon recommends it.[20]

INAPPROPRIATE CARE There is considerable evidence that much of medical care expenditures may in fact be inappropriate. Perhaps the most telling are the data comparing practices in different locations. For instance, the average length of a hospital stay in New York is almost twice that in Utah.[21] This large difference cannot be accounted for by differences in the populations. One classic study showed that the chances of a child's having his tonsils removed varied in towns across Vermont from 7 percent to 70 percent.[22] Huge practice differences occur across states as well as countries. Appendectomies occur twice as frequently in the United States as in Norway, and

[19] See V. Fuchs, *Who Shall Live?*; W. McClure, "Buying Right: The Consequences of Glut," *Business and Health*, September 1985, pp. 43–46; and Victor R. Fuchs, "The Supply of Surgeons and the Demand for Operations," in V. Fuchs, *The Health Economy*, (London and Cambridge: Harvard University Press, 1986), pp. 126–47.

[20] Although seeking second opinions before undergoing surgery may improve matters, it is far from a solution. In a community in which there is an increased supply of physicians, diagnostic criteria may change, so that a second opinion would merely reflect the same general inclination to recommend surgery more frequently.

[21] Milliman and Robertson, *Hospital Length of Stay Efficiency Indices*, web site accessed at http://www.op.net/~jcookson/home.html.

[22] John Wennberg and Alan Gittelsohn, "Small Are Variations in Health Care Delivery," *Science* 182 (1973): 1102–08, cited in C. E. Phelps, "Diffusion of Information in Medical Care," *Journal of Economic Perspectives* 6, no. 3 (summer 1992): 25.

hysterectomies occur more than six times as frequently in the United States as in Japan.[23]

These variations lead to huge cost differences. Boston residents spend 87 percent more per person per year on hospital care than do those in New Haven, with most of the variation occurring in minor surgery and medical (nonsurgery) cases. It is generally agreed that differences in age and other demographic characteristics of the population fail to explain most of the variation in practices. The aggregate annual loss from practice variations across regions just in hospital care has been estimated to exceed $7 billion.[24]

POVERTY, INCOMPLETE COVERAGE, AND THE ROLE OF GOVERNMENT

Most of our discussion so far has focused on market failures, such as inefficiencies in the market arising from imperfections of information and competition. But one of the principal reasons for government action in health care has nothing to do with efficiency; even if markets were perfectly efficient, there would be a concern that those who are very poor do not receive adequate health care.

Many believe that no individual, regardless of his income, should be denied access to adequate medical care. If choices have to be made, they should be made on the basis not of wealth but of other attributes, such as age, or the likelihood of success of the operation, or perhaps random selection. This view holds that medical services are different from clothes, movies, automobiles, and most other commodities. Just as the right to vote should not be subject to the marketplace (individuals are not allowed to buy and sell their votes), and just as when there was a draft, individuals were not allowed to buy their way out of their military obligations (though during the Civil War they were), the right to live—access to medical services—should not be controlled by the market. The view that there are goods and services, such as health care, whose availability to different individuals should not just depend on their income, is known as **specific egalitarianism.**[25]

Not all economists agree about whether medical services should be treated differently than other commodities. Many hold that they should not: those who have more money and want to spend it on getting health care should be allowed to do so. Those who hold this view often point out that the relationship between medical care and life (death) is very weak: other factors, such as smoking, drinking, and eating patterns (consumption of vegetables and fruits) have greater effects on longevity. If one wanted to

[23] Klim McPherson, "International Differences in Medical Care Practices," *Health Care Financing Review*, 1989 Annual Supplement, p. 14; H. J. Aaron, *Serious and Unstable Condition*, (Washington, D.C.: Brookings Institution, 1991).

[24] C. E. Phelps and S. T. Parente, "Priority Setting for Medical Technology and Medical Practice Assessment," *Medical Care* 28, no. 8 (August 1990): 702–23.

[25] J. Tobin, "On Limiting the Domain of Inequality," *Journal of Law and Economics* 13 (1970): 263–77.

improve the health status of the poor, one could do so in a more cost-effective way by waging campaigns against smoking and drinking, raising taxes on tobacco and alcohol, and encouraging the consumption of fruits and vegetables.

Still a third view—toward which many Western democracies seem to be gravitating—is that everyone should have the right to a certain minimal level of care. The provision of Medicaid can be thought of as reflecting that view.

REFORMING HEALTH CARE

Recent efforts in health care reform have targeted the big issues identified at this chapter's outset: high costs, limited health insurance coverage, and growing fiscal strains. This section describes some of the most important attempts to counter these problems.

COST CONTAINMENT

Economists look to improved incentives as the primary way in which costs can be contained.

ELIMINATING TAX DISTORTIONS Eliminating the tax incentives associated with employer-provided insurance has met with strong resistance from labor unions, largely because they have made more extensive health care a major thrust of labor negotiations over the last two decades, accepting better health benefits in lieu of higher wages. (While total compensation—including health benefits—has increased roughly in line with productivity, real wages have increased more slowly, in some cases, especially for unskilled workers, actually falling.) There is also worry that without such tax incentives, the number of uninsured would increase, exacerbating other problems in the health care system. A compromise proposal is to cap the tax deductibility, so that at the margin, individuals and firms face the correct incentives, and to make it a condition for eligibility for tax deduction that if employees are given a choice of plans, they must face the full marginal costs of the more expensive plans.

MORE EXTENSIVE USE OF MANAGED CARE As we noted, **managed care** has grown extensively, to the point where the vast majority of those with employer-provided coverage are in HMOs. Ironically, the debate about managed care has shifted. Originally, there was concern about whether it would simply reduce costs by, say, 15 percent, leaving the rate of increase unchanged, or whether it could reduce the rate of increase. The experience in the nineties, while it left this longer-range question unsettled, demonstrated clearly that HMOs could reduce costs markedly.[26] But as they reduced costs,

---

[26] Critics noted that some of the cost savings came from the fact that HMOs that owned their own hospitals managed to reduce the amount of uncompensated care which they provided.

concerns were expressed about whether they had too strong incentives for cost containment, unbalanced by commitment to the quality of care. The issue became cystallized in a debate over "drive-by deliveries" in which HMOs allowed new mothers only a twenty-four-hour hospital stay after the delivery of a baby. Other practices, such as a reluctance to pay for expensive new experimental procedures, also drew widespread media attention. Drive-by deliveries were banned, and many states proposed a stronger role of government in regulating HMOs.

MEDICAL SAVINGS ACCOUNTS Legislation passed in 1996 established **medical savings accounts (MSAs).** These were intended to encourage individuals to buy insurance policies with larger deductibles and co-payments, and thus fewer incentives for moral hazard. Funds allocated to these accounts are tax deductible. Annual contributions to MSAs are limited, but if the amount in the account reaches beyond a certain level, funds may be withdrawn and used for other purposes. Thus, the accounts link the desire to increase savings with the goal of creating a more efficient health care system. They also eliminate one of the distortions of the existing system, under which health care paid for through insurance companies is, in effect, tax deductible, but direct payments are not.

One criticism of MSAs relates to the relative strength of the incentive effects for reducing moral hazard, compared to the adverse selection effects. Clearly, those who thought it unlikely that they would need much medical care, and rich individuals better able to bear the risk of paying a large deductible or co-payment and for whom the tax break was particularly significant, would be much more attracted to the MSAs. If healthier individuals were attracted to the MSAs, then those not having MSAs would face higher insurance premiums.

Thus, for some individuals, MSAs might prove very attractive; their overall medical costs—insurance plus out-of-pocket expenses—might well go down. The unanswered question was, to what extent were those lower costs a reflection of greater efficiency (a reduction in the distortions arising from moral hazard) and to what extent were they a reflection of cream skimming? The 1996 legislation provided a limited experiment. Unfortunately, the experiment was not designed in ways which would necessarily shed light on this critical question. Advocates of the experiment—including the insurance firms that planned to cash in on these new accounts—hoped that it would prove so popular that the accounts would be made permanent.

EXTENDING INSURANCE COVERAGE

As we noted at the beginning of this chapter, many people in the United States have no health insurance. A number of reform efforts have attempted to address the problem of the uninsured.

MANDATED HEALTH INSURANCE Extending health insurance was central to the ill-fated Clinton health care reform of 1993–1994. Today, most employers provide health insurance to their employees; the Clinton administration proposed that every employer would have to provide health insurance.

Many advocates of universal health insurance favored a **single payer system** such as Canada's, which works much like Medicare, with the government paying medical bills. But financing such a system would have required new taxes, a political impossibility at the time. Instead, the mandated system would have constituted a hidden tax, since ultimately the mandate would have imposed insurance costs on firms and consumers.

A host of regulatory and finance issues undermined the Clinton reform bill and its proposed insurance mandate. Even as the legislation grew to 1300 pages, the Department of Health and Human Services was assigned enormous responsibilities for writing further regulations. Many saw in the proposal the heavy hand of government, and these fears led to the bill's defeat.

PRE-EXISTING CONDITIONS As noted earlier, many insurance firms have refused to cover health conditions existing prior to the beginning of the insurance coverage. Thus, a worker with a kidney problem would find it impossible to change jobs because the new insurance policy would not cover the costs of continued treatment. Legislation passed in August of 1996—called the Kennedy-Kassebaum bill after the senators who wrote it—was devised to prevent insurers from excluding pre-existing conditions from coverage. A number of questions were raised with the passage of the legislation: How much would insurance firms have to raise premiums to extend this coverage? Would employers, concerned that hiring a worker with a pre-existing condition would lead to soaring premiums, discriminate against job candidates they suspected of having such conditions? So far, it appears that the bill's impact on either the insurance or labor market has been limited.

FILLING IN THE GAPS Another set of reforms was designed to extend coverage to particular groups of the uninsured. In his 1996 budget, President Clinton proposed extending coverage to those temporarily unemployed. Since most individuals receive health care through their employers, when they lose their job they also lose their health care benefits—at precisely the time they are least able to pay for such insurance themselves.

A more ambitious proposal focuses on extending health care coverage to all uninsured children. Already, most poor children are covered by Medicaid. While there is general support for the overall objective, there is real concern about the costs in relation to the benefits. The problem is that those who are not covered are very much like those who are; there is no way of effectively targeting them. Providing health insurance to all uninsured children would result in a large incentive for firms that currently provide such insurance to drop their coverage of children. If they did that, then the government would end up paying the cost of almost all children, and the cost per additional child covered would be very high.

Because it is so difficult to extend coverage in this way, some have proposed more extensive use of publicly financed free clinics in poor neighborhoods, or more extensive provision of health services through the schools.

Still another proposal, presented in Clinton's 1998 State of the Union Address, focuses on retired individuals. Today, many individuals retire before they are eligible for Medicare. Under Clinton's proposal, they would be able to buy Medicare coverage. Critics worry that even if initially they would be required to pay the full costs of Medicare, over time subsidies would be introduced, further undermining the financial viability of the program.

MEDICARE REFORM: EASING LONG-TERM FISCAL STRAINS

The long-run fiscal strains arising from the health care system are largely the result of growing Medicare expenditures. Efforts to reform Medicare focus on three issues: improved incentives, better management of health care provision, and more competition.

IMPROVED INCENTIVES The Medicare program itself has large co-payments and deductibles; but most elderly buy, at quite moderate costs, **medigap** insurance, that is, insurance which covers most of these out-of-pocket costs. For individuals with medigap insurance, there are few incentives to economize on the use of medical care. Those who buy medigap insurance do not pay the full incremental cost associated with the policy; because of reduced incentives to economize on health care, those with medigap insurance make more demands on the Medicare system itself. Medigap premiums cover the direct costs incurred by the insurance companies, but not the additional costs imposed on the government because of increased utilization. One set of reform proposals thus would either restrict the coverage which can be provided by such policies or force them to pay the full incremental costs.

One of the fastest-growing parts of the Medicare system is home health care. There are many individuals who do not need to stay in hospitals or long-term-care facilities, so long as they have some limited assistance at home. Home health care provides that assistance. But home health care has been subject to extensive abuse. Unlike doctors, nurses, and other traditional health care providers, who must pass stringent standards, relatively few skills are required of home health care providers, and entry into the business appears easy. And while the demand for heart surgery may be relatively insensitive to price (and in any case would be limited even at a zero price), almost anyone offered free assistance would find it useful. Ironically, however, while the Medicare system has deductibles and co-payments associated with most medical treatments, it has not imposed any co-payments on home health services.

IMPROVED MANAGEMENT As costs soared soon after the Medicare program was begun, attention focused on providing better incentives to the providers. Initially, Medicare had simply reimbursed hospitals for whatever costs they incurred. Such a system clearly provides perverse incentives. In 1983 Medicare switched to a system in which hospitals were reimbursed a fixed amount for the treatment of a particular illness. Overall, the system, called **DRGs** (for **diagnostically related groups**), has worked well. Initially, there was concern that hospitals might refuse to provide treatment in areas

325

where the reimbursement rate was too low, or that they would be tempted to cheat on the diagnoses or to cut corners on the services provided, adversely affecting the quality of the care. (Of course, the intent of the system was to cut *unnecessary* costs, such as hospital stays that were longer than needed. The problem is that it is often difficult to distinguish between cutting corners and cutting unnecessary expenditures.) Neither of these fears has come true.

One ongoing concern, however, is the ballooning of out-of-hospital costs. Hospitals have tried to push patients out of the hospital as quickly as possible. Thus, while hospital costs have been contained, overall health costs have not performed as well. This has prompted some to suggest an extension of the system, called **bundling,** to include all of the treatment associated with an illness, both in hospital and out of hospital.

STRENGTHENED COMPETITION While there are many doctors and hospitals in the country as a whole, competition within a given locale may be very limited. Providers have sought immunity from (or at least a loosening of) antitrust provisions, which would reduce competition even further. So far, these pressures have been resisted. Such immunity might, for instance, allow all the X-ray labs in an area to get together to set prices, or a single health provider (HMO or preferred provider organization) to sign up all the bone specialists in a community.

Some have argued that the government should strengthen competitive forces by having competitive bidding for the supply of Medicare services. The winning bidder would, in effect, become a **preferred provider,** with the government paying 100 percent of its bid. Other providers might be reimbursed a fixed amount up to a fixed percentage of the winning bid. Critics of such plans worry about ensuring quality and about the development of a two-tier system, in which poor individuals would go to the preferred provider, while wealthier individuals would go to higher-priced providers.

FINANCIAL REFORMS The reforms just described are directed at improving the efficiency with which Medicare services are provided. There is another set of reforms focused more narrowly on lowering the financial drain on the government, either by reducing benefits—such as by increasing the age of eligibility from 65 to, say, 67, just as the normal age of retirement has been increasing under social security—or by imposing more of the costs on recipients. Particularly troublesome is the fact that the Medicare subsidies are extended to all participants, regardless of their income, which means that a millionaire retiree is being subsidized by a $20,000-a-year worker. Pressure to increase payments at least for higher-income beneficiaries has been mounting in recent years, particularly as some recent studies suggest that the Medicare program overall is regressive. With taxes proportional to income, and all individuals having the same entitlement, it had been thought that Medicare was highly progressive. But when account is taken of the fact that richer individuals tend to live longer and are better capable of extracting services out of the Medicare system, it turns out that the rich get more, so much more that it more than offsets their higher Medicare tax contributions.

Medicaid provides medical assistance to the poor and to the disabled, and long-term nursing care to the aged. Each of these comprises about a third of the program. The long-term nursing program has been a particular source of concern. While Medicaid began as a program for the destitute, today about half of all nursing home expenditures are paid by Medicaid. Many elderly individuals transfer wealth to their children in order to qualify to receive these benefits. While the government has attempted to limit these transfers (typically, funds transferred within three years of entering a nursing home are treated as if they were available to pay for nursing home care), it has had only limited success. These expenditures are expected to soar as the number of very old Americans—those over 85—increases. And while just 5 percent of the general population over 65 are in nursing homes, a quarter of those over 85 are. The average cost of a skilled nursing home in 1996 was over $35,000 per year.

The private insurance market for long-term nursing care was slow to develop. In 1994, only 3 percent of nursing home expenditures were paid for by private insurance. Part of the reason is that the public provision—through Medicaid—reduces the incentive to purchase this insurance. In 1994, the government reduced incentives further: Some states had provided "asset protection"—individuals who purchased a minimal amount of nursing home insurance could keep a certain amount of assets to pass on to their heirs or for other expenses without losing eligibility for Medicaid when their insurance ran out. Some members of Congress viewed this as a benefit to the rich, rather than as an incentive that might actually save the government money, and Congress banned any additional states from providing this asset protection.

There have been three major groups of proposals to reduce government costs, all based on the premise that most individuals should make provision for themselves, but if they do not, it is difficult for the government not to provide assistance. One proposal is to mandate insurance: every individual would have to purchase, either privately or through the government, long-term nursing care insurance. Providing it through the government would entail effectively expanding the social security program. To finance long-term nursing care would require an increase in the social security tax of around 1 to 1.5 percentage points. The second proposal is to increase incentives—both carrots and sticks—to purchase insurance, by providing tax preferences and asset protection, and by reducing the magnitude of public support for nursing care. The third proposal is to assist the private sector in providing meaningful long-term nursing care insurance, by providing reinsurance against large losses (associated with long stays) or against hard-to-anticipate long-term trends, either in longevity or overall nursing home care expenses.

REVIEW AND PRACTICE

SUMMARY

1   Though decisions about health are difficult, resource allocations—choices among alternative uses of funds—must be made. Economic analysis may be useful in making those decisions in a systematic and consistent way.

2   Medical expenditures represent the third largest category of public expenditures, after defense and education. The government now pays more than two-fifths of all health expenditures. The four major public programs are Medicare, Medicaid, health care for veterans, and public support for research and development. In addition, there are two major categories of tax expenditures: employer-financed health insurance and tax deductibility of medical expenses exceeding a certain level.

3   Three fundamental problems facing the health care system in the early 1990s were:

   a   A large and growing population of uninsured

   b   High and rising health care costs

   c   Growing federal health care expenditures.

4   Among the reasons why markets may not provide an efficient allocation of resources in the health care sector are:

   a   Consumers and insurers have limited information.

   b   Competition is limited.

   c   Many of the key providers operate on a nonprofit basis.

   d   Only a small fraction of health care costs are paid directly by the consumer.

5   Health insurance is associated with the problems of adverse selection and moral hazard. Insurance reduces individuals' incentives to take care of themselves and to economize on health care services, and insurance firms may increase their profits more by ensuring that they cover only the most healthy, than by increasing their efficiency.

6   The tax system encourages excessive purchase of insurance and excessive consumption of health care services. Tax expenditures for health amount to billions of dollars. Most economists believe that these tax benefits should be capped, so that individuals will more nearly pay the full marginal costs of services.

7   Concern that the fee-for-service system leads to excessive consumption of health care has led to rapid growth of health maintenance organizations. More recently, there has been a concern that HMOs have been too zealous in controlling costs, sacrificing quality and service.

8   Since the failure of comprehensive health care reform in 1994, which would have mandated that all employers provide medical insurance to their employees, attention has focused on incremental reforms, such as

extending insurance coverage to the unemployed and to children, eliminating restricted coverage of pre-existing conditions, and providing medical savings accounts to encourage individuals to purchase policies with larger deductibles and co-payments.

9 Proposals to reform Medicare focus on improving incentives, introducing better management of health care providers, ensuring more effective competition, and placing more of the financial burden on beneficiaries.

10 The major concern today about Medicaid is the growing burden of nursing home care.

KEY CONCEPTS

Medicare	Moral hazard
Medicaid	Adverse selection
Cost shifting	Transactions costs
Uncompensated care	Specific egalitarianism
Third-party payment	Managed care
Fee-for-service plan	Medical savings accounts (MSAs)
Deductible	Single payer system
Co-payments	Medigap
Health maintenance organizations (HMO)	Diagnostically related groups (DRGs)
Capitation fees	Bundling
Tax expenditures	Preferred provider plans
Malpractice suits	

QUESTIONS AND PROBLEMS

1 List the various distortions in incentives that arise in the health care sector. (Be sure to include those that affect the purchase of insurance as well as the purchase of health care services directly.)

2 In what ways is the purchase of medical services similar to the purchase of a car? In what ways is it different?

3 We have noted that there is extensive disagreement on what should be done about the way medical care is provided in the United States. To what extent is this disagreement due to differences in judgments concerning how the market for medical services functions? Be specific. To what extent is the disagreement due to differences in values?

4 Consider the "market failures" that arise in medical markets and current proposals for altering how medical care is provided in the United States.

Discuss the extent to which each of the proposals is aimed at remedying particular market failures.

5   During the past thirty-five years there has been a decline in community-run hospitals and an increase in private (for-profit) hospitals. Are there reasons why hospitals should be particularly suited or unsuited to being run publicly? What do you think accounts for these trends?

6   Critics of malpractice suits claim that they have contributed significantly to the rise of medical costs and want legislation that would limit the size of awards and lawyers' fees, or otherwise discourage such suits. Many lawyers are concerned that any such legislation would impair the rights of victims of malpractice to be justly compensated for the damages they have suffered. Discuss the equity-efficiency trade-offs. What do you think should be done?

7   Assume that medical expenditures are fully deductible from taxes. Show diagrammatically the effect on the demand for medical services. If the elasticity of demand with respect to price is .7, what is the effect of deductibility on an individual in the 15 percent marginal tax bracket; in the 28 percent marginal tax bracket; in the 40 percent marginal tax bracket?

8   Some states have proposed requiring community rating, that is, insurance companies would not be allowed to charge individuals different premiums, regardless of their health, age, or sex; everyone in the community would pay the same premium. Discuss the possible consequences of community rating. Evaluate such proposals from the perspective of equity and efficiency.

9   Many employers offer their employees a choice of plans, paying a fixed share of the cost of each. What inefficiencies does this introduce? Some employers, such as Stanford University, have instead offered a fixed payment, regardless of the plan chosen, and have insisted that all programs offer identical coverage. Within three years, the cost of providing this standard coverage fell by 20 percent in real terms. Explain why this may have happened.

10 Economists have criticized the tax treatment of health insurance. Why have unions resisted changing this tax treatment? What are the equity and efficiency consequences of capping the tax deductibility at some number, say, $5000, representing the average costs of health benefit plans in unionized firms?

13 Defense and Technology

FOCUS QUESTIONS

1 How do we go about deciding how much to spend on national defense? What is the role of marginal analysis?

2 What are the current key issues concerning defense strategy and their implications for the level and allocation of defense expenditures?

3 What are some of the key ways by which the Defense Department is currently attempting to increase its efficiency?

4 What is the rationale for government actions to promote research and new technologies?

5 What are intellectual property rights? How well do they address the problem of underinvestment in research?

6 What are the other ways by which government encourages the private production of knowledge? Why does government provide direct support to research?

The end of the Cold War, marked by the demise of the Gorbachev regime in the Soviet Union in 1991, had profound consequences for the U.S. economy. At the time, defense had long been the largest single item of public expenditures in the United States. In the late 1950s, defense spending reached 10 percent of GDP. In the aftermath of the Vietnam War, defense

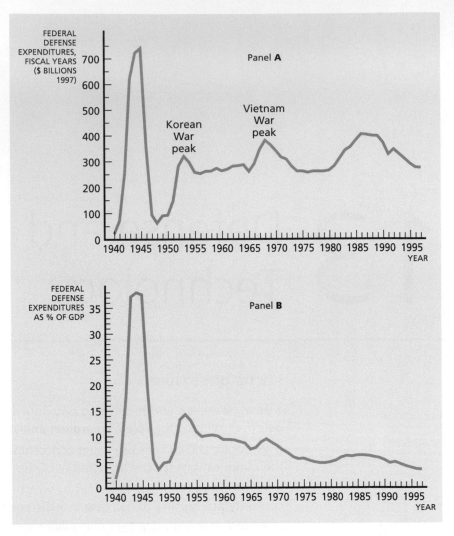

FIGURE 13.1   **U.S. Defense Expenditures** Panel A shows federal defense expenditures in 1997 dollars. Panel B shows federal defense expenditures as a percentage of GDP.

SOURCES: *Economic Report of the President, 1998*, Tables B-79, B-80; Bureau of Labor Statistics.

expenditures had been reduced to under 5 percent of GDP, but during the 1980s, they increased to 6.2 percent of GDP in 1986 and 1987.

After the collapse of the Soviet empire, there was excitement in the United States about a "peace dividend." Defense expenditures dropped so that by 1998 they were projected to be just over 3 percent of GDP (see Figure 13.1). These spending reductions were critical to the successful effort to reduce the federal budget deficit during the Clinton administration. Even so, in the years following the end of the Cold War, excitement about the **peace dividend** was rapidly subdued. Conflicts in Bosnia, the Persian Gulf War, problems in Somalia, Haiti, and Zaire, along with the threat of nuclear proliferation, made it clear that the United States would need a substantial peacetime army. In some quarters, there was concern that defense had been reduced excessively.

Another consequence of the end of the Cold War related to the federal government's expenditures on research and development (R&D). For decades, defense spending and R&D spending had been closely intertwined. Indeed, in 1997, 57 percent of the federal government's expenditures on R&D were defense related. There had been great spin-offs to the commercial sector—from advances in computer technology to advances in ceramics—but U.S. commercial interests almost surely did not benefit from these expenditures to the same extent that they would have if more of government R&D expenditures had been directed at commercial uses. Nondefense R&D expenditures lagged behind those of the country's competitors, and in the long run this could have significant adverse effects on U.S. competitiveness. There was thus a need for a new U.S. technology policy.

This chapter discusses these two important areas of government expenditure.

DEFENSE EXPENDITURES

Even though defense has long been the major item of expenditure at the federal level, it has traditionally received little attention from economists. Instead, military experts have led the way in determining how to achieve the country's defense objectives. But defense spending is fundamentally a question of resource allocation—the country wishes to receive the best defense for the money spent—and therefore hinges on economic reasoning.

As the defense budget was being cut in the 1990s, the fundamental question was: How much? Conventional economic analysis—focusing on marginal benefits and costs—is essential to answering this question. Yet the most difficult questions go beyond simple economics. How do we assess the magnitude of the benefits from defense expenditures, and how should an appropriate military strategy be selected? The next two sections take up these questions. Later sections consider how to increase the efficiency of our defense expenditures and how to address the problems associated with downsizing the military.

THE VALUE OF MARGINAL ANALYSIS

In allocating a given defense budget, one needs to consider the effect of the expenditures on various defense objectives. In evaluating whether we should spend more on defense, we similarly need to know how much extra "protection" we get from an extra expenditure of $1 billion.

The following example, provided by Charles Hitch, who was assistant secretary of defense in the Kennedy-Johnson administration, illustrates the role of marginal analysis.[1] Assume each missile has a 50 percent probability of success in killing its target. We have 100 targets that we would like to de-

---

[1] From C. J. Hitch, *Decision Making for Defense* (Berkeley: University of California Press, 1966), pp. 50–51.

GAME
THEORY, THE
ARMS RACE,
AND THE
THEORY OF
DETERRENCE

The 1994 Nobel Prize in economics was awarded to three economist/mathematicians who pioneered in the development of game theory: John Nash of Princeton, John Harsanyi of the University of California at Berkeley, and Reinhold Selten of Rheinische Friedrich-Wilhelms-Universität in Bonn, Germany.

Most of game theory is based on the postulate of rationality. Each individual not only plays to win, but believes his opponent plays to win, and believes his opponent believes that he is playing to win, and

stroy. One hundred missiles sent at the targets would "achieve an expectancy of 50 kills, 200 missiles—75 kills, 300 missiles—87 kills," as depicted in Figure 13.2. Clearly, there are very strong diminishing returns. Each target can be destroyed only once, and some of the additional missiles will land on a target already destroyed. While the first 100 missiles give us 50

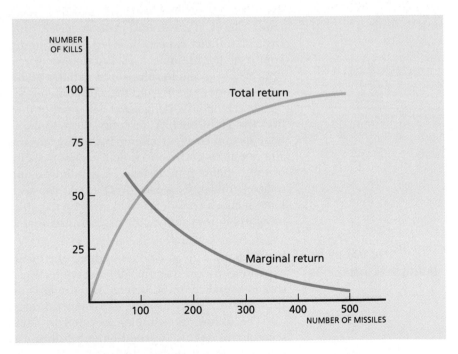

FIGURE 13.2 **The Role of Marginal Analysis in Defense** The relevant question is not whether we should have 500 missiles or no missiles, but how many extra kills we get from each additional missile. There may be sharply diminishing returns.

so forth. Thus, each player in deciding what to do puts himself in his rival's shoes: if I do X, what will my rival do? But in putting himself in his rival's shoes, he reasons that his rival will be thinking about what he would do, assuming he is rational.

Much of the development of game theory was supported by the Department of Defense, in an attempt to understand better how the Soviet Union would respond to what the United States did. Game theory was used both as the basis of the theory of deterrence, which underlay American defense strategy, and to explain the arms race.

kills, increasing the number of missiles from 400 to 500 increases the number of kills by only 3. We need to ask ourselves not whether it is worth the cost of 500 missiles to get 97 kills but whether it is worth the cost of 100 additional missiles to get 3 extra kills.

This kind of analysis is not easy. But by relating expenditures to objectives, and by showing what one gets from additional expenditures, one can hope to make more rational decisions concerning how much is enough.

In making these assessments, however, one set of considerations is particularly hard to evaluate: deterrence.

DEFENSE STRATEGY   In the 1960s and 1970s, defense focused on **deterrence**—establishing a strong enough force that no one would contemplate attacking. Under President Ronald Reagan, another approach was advocated, called the **Strategic Defense Initiative** (**SDI**), which attempted to provide a fail-safe defense capability. Today, the focus of debate is on two other issues: the capability of fighting two wars simultaneously; and nuclear proliferation, terrorism, and chemical and germ warfare.

DETERRENCE The existence of strong capacities for retaliating serves to deter others from "misbehaving." This thinking was central to the defense strategy of the United States and the Soviet Union after World War II. It was believed that with a large enough capacity to destroy the opponent, there would be little incentive for it to attack. The capability of retaliating depended on the number of missiles that survived the first strike, known as the **second strike capability.** Since the number that survived depended on the size of the first strike, each side had a strong incentive to create a larger arsenal. Thus was the arms race born.

STRATEGIC DEFENSE INITIATIVE President Reagan, in his famous "Star Wars" speech in March 1983, proposed a basic change in U.S. strategy, from a policy of deterrence to strategic defense (hence the new program's official title, Strategic Defense Initiative). The objective of this program was to develop weapons systems that would protect against a nuclear attack, thus rendering nuclear weapons "impotent and obsolete." As one commentator put it, "the promise of 'assured survival' would displace the threat of 'assured destruction.'"

The program was strongly criticized, because of doubts about its technical feasibility and about its costs, and because it raised the specter of increased, not reduced, vulnerability. The worry was that if the Soviet Union believed that we would become invulnerable in, say, fifteen years, while it would take them some time longer to achieve the same defense capability, they would have every incentive to attack us *before that time.* Even if they had no offensive interest in the United States, if they believed that the United States had offensive interests against them, they would recognize that their best strategy would be to launch a preemptive strike.

There was, however, another rationale for SDI: It was viewed as a bargaining ploy. Because of the fundamentally weaker economy of the Soviet Union, it was recognized that they would have a hard time keeping pace with the United States. By increasing our defense expenditures, we would force them to the bargaining table. This argument had considerable validity. Indeed, a major step was taken in 1987 when the United States and the Soviet Union agreed to withdraw all short- and medium-range missiles from Europe. More fundamentally, there is some evidence that the arms race greatly weakened the Soviet Union, contributing to its eventual collapse.

TWO-THEATRE CAPABILITY With the threat of massive nuclear war subsiding, attention has focused on regional wars—a conflict in the Persian Gulf or on the Korean peninsula. There is a widespread view among military experts that we should have the capability of fighting at least two such localized wars simultaneously.

The problem is analogous to that facing larger communities in how large a fire department to have. Assume it takes twenty men to fight a moderate-size fire. Most of the time, there will be no fires. Occasionally, there will be a fire, and it is surely worthwhile to have a fire department ready for that emergency. For simplicity, we assume it takes two hours to contain a fire. Assume that the community has ten thousand buildings, and that the chance of any building's catching fire in any two-hour span is one in a thousand. There is a small probability that in any two-hour span more than one fire will occur. The question is, is it worth having a second fire department, an additional twenty men, on reserve for this small-probability event? It may or may not be. If it is, we then need to ask, is it worth having a third fire department on reserve for the very slight chance that there will be three or more fires? The probability of using each additional fire department—and thus the expected benefit—diminishes markedly.

In one respect, the fire analogy is inappropriate. Typically, we do not worry about an arsonist waiting to light a fire until the fire department is busy putting out a fire elsewhere. But in the area of defense, this is a real concern: potential enemies or troublemakers may wait until the United States is occupied with fighting in one theatre to start trouble in another. Many worry that without a two-theatre capacity, the United States would be inviting trouble. From this perspective, the major role of the **two-theatre capability** is its role as a deterrent.

Currently, the dominant view is that the United States should have the capacity to fight two localized wars of moderate scale simultaneously. It is the ability to fight the second war which is compromised when the defense budget is cut.

Of course, matters are seldom clear-cut. One of the main bottlenecks in fighting a war is logistics, in particular, getting troops and equipment to the scene of battle. These bottlenecks are likely to be particularly binding in the early stages of a war, and at times when troops and equipment must be deployed rapidly. Given a span of a few months, ships being used for other purposes can be converted into transports for military equipment and personnel. This can be done even when troops need to be deployed quickly, provided there is willingness to force the domestic economy to undertake greater short-run costs: the military could, for instance, order civilian aircraft to transport troops. Thus, greater expenditures for defense readiness reduce the costs should a crisis occur; the question is, how much of an "insurance premium" are we willing to pay?

The issue, then, is not (as it is sometimes put) simply whether the United States could fight on two fronts simultaneously, but rather, what would be the additional costs and risks on the second front? Almost all of the serious conflagrations that the United States has faced in the past fifty years have lasted months, if not years. If this is the likely pattern in the future, then the need for a full capacity for rapid deployment on a second front may not be a high imperative.

ARMS PROLIFERATION Since the fall of the Soviet empire, attention has focused on denuclearizing Ukraine and Kazakhstan (the two former Soviet republics, besides Russia, that inherited nuclear weapons), reducing the number of nuclear warheads in Russia, and arms proliferation. The arms industry is a profitable one, and one of the few in which Russia has real strength. With many small countries interested in buying weapons, there is real danger that the arms will feed the ethnic and political struggles that seem to be proliferating around the world. Since the United States has itself been a major arms supplier to the rest of the world, it is difficult for this country to criticize others for doing as it does, though it claims to be more responsible in its arms sales.[2]

The United States and seventy-nine other countries signed a nonproliferation treaty in 1968, attempting to restrict access to nuclear weapons and the methods of delivering them.[3] The United States has used the threat of

---

[2] In 1995, the United States exported $15.6 billion worth of weapons. U.S. arms exports were higher than those of any other country, and accounted for 49 percent of the world total. (*Source:* U.S. Arms Control and Disarmament Agency, *World Military Expenditures and Arms Transfers,* 1996, Table 2.)

[3] By 1997, 186 countries were members of the nonproliferation treaty. See Stockholm International Peace Research Institute, *World Armaments and Disarmaments: SIPRI Yearbook* (New York: Oxford University Press, 1968/69 issue, pp. 320–31, and 1997 issue, pp. 533–45).

economic sanctions to enforce the agreement. Thus, in 1993 and again in 1996, in retaliation for exporting missiles to Pakistan, China was threatened with losing its most favored nation status—under which its exports to the United States faced the lowest tariffs that the United States imposes on any country (other than Canada and Mexico). A military confrontation between North Korea and the United States was avoided when, in October 1994, North Korea and the United States signed an agreement providing for substantial aid by the United States in return for a substantial dismantling by North Korea of its nuclear potential. In May 1998, India and Pakistan both successfully tested nuclear bombs, joining the exclusive nuclear club. In response, the United States and other countries imposed sanctions on both countries, cutting off non-humanitarian assistance and restricting loans to the Indian and Pakistani governments. Critics of the sanctions worried that they might further destabilize the region, a particularly disturbing prospect now that the countries had nuclear weapons; advocates hoped that the sanctions would force the parties to come to agreements restricting further testing and deployment.

CHEMICAL AND BIOLOGICAL WEAPONS AND TERRORISM The 1991 Gulf War focused attention more broadly on the threat of rogue states, and their use of terrorism and chemical and biological weapons. That a small vial containing a deadly virus could cause massive death is a frightening prospect. And even if Iraq had not engaged in biological warfare, the numerous maladies plaguing those returning from the Gulf War were a constant reminder of the threat of chemical weapons. A bipartisan effort under both President Bush and President Clinton led to an international agreement to ban chemical weapons.

Establishing enforceable international agreements and cooperation to combat biological and chemical weapons and terrorism is one part of the U.S. strategy for dealing with these threats. Research—aimed, for instance, at building the capacity to develop quickly antidotes and antibodies—is another. Given the magnitude of the danger, there is concern that the United States is spending too little on such research.

INCREASING THE EFFICIENCY
OF THE DEFENSE DEPARTMENT

No matter how much is spent on defense, it should be spent well. Recent attention has been focused on improving the Defense Department's procurement policies and on reorganization.

DEFENSE
PROCUREMENT

During the height of the Cold War, thousands of firms focused on supplying the research and weapons required for the expanding military. Producing for the military was in many ways different from producing for the civilian sector. Civilian aircraft had many potential buyers. The various aircraft manufacturers produced the plane that they thought best met the aviation needs of the world, and then tried to persuade each of the airlines that their aircraft was better than their rivals'. If an aircraft manufacturer produced an advanced military plane, there was usually only one customer, the Department of Defense. And usually the Department of Defense had only one supplier of that particular plane; it was simply too costly to have two or more firms producing exactly the same plane. While many of the procurement problems described below apply across all branches of government, some are particularly acute in the Defense Department, because of the unique nature of its purchases.

STANDARD PROCEDURES To ensure that it obtains the best price, the government usually resorts to competitive bidding: different contractors tell the government the price at which they are willing to deliver, say, one thousand tanks of a given specification, and the government purchases the tanks from the lowest bidder. Frequently, however, there are major **cost overruns**—that is, the costs exceed the producer's original estimate. Sometimes the contract calls for these costs to be shared by the government and the private contractor; such contracts are called **cost-sharing contracts.** Even when the contract does not explicitly call for sharing of cost overruns, the government may absorb all or a significant fraction of the additional costs. The contractor may claim that the cost overruns are a result of changes in the design specification; such changes almost always accompany the development of a new weapon, particularly when the development occurs over a period of several years, and it is often difficult to ascertain to what extent the cost overruns are in fact a result of the design changes. In other cases, the private contractor simply says that it cannot complete the contract without further funds; the government then has the choice of losing all that it has already spent or negotiating a settlement with the contractor. And even if the government were to sue the contractor for breach of contract, the delays in the development and deployment of the weapons could be very costly.

The prevalence of cost overruns means the public seldom has an accurate view of the cost of a ship, a defense system, a tank, and so on at the time a commitment is made to purchase them. It also means that the government seldom knows whether it has, in fact, let out the contract to the lowest-cost producer;[4] all that it knows is that it let out the contract to the lowest bidder.

What are the reasons for these cost overruns? In the case of new weapons, errors in estimating costs are common. But why should there be a bias in these errors? That is, why should there be a systematic tendency to underestimate the costs? Part of the reason has to do with the competitive bidding process: potential contractors know that they have to produce a low bid to win. The system of cost sharing (implicit or explicit) means that there is relatively little penalty associated with bidding too low. There is, however,

---

[4] Notice that at the time the cost overruns occur, what limited competition there was before the contract was let no longer exists: it would, in general, be costly or impossible for the government at that point to turn to other potential suppliers.

a penalty associated with bidding too high, particularly when other firms are bidding low (using, say, their most optimistic estimates of costs): the high-bidding firm will fail to get the contract.

The system of cost sharing has a further disadvantage in addition to reducing the penalty for underbidding: the winner of the contract has little incentive to be efficient. Indeed, some contracts are of a **cost-plus** form; that is, the government pays whatever it costs to develop the weapons plus, say, 10 percent. Such contracts provide incentives to be inefficient—the more the firm spends, the more it gets from the government.

Why does the government engage in cost sharing, with all its obvious disadvantages? Part of the reason for cost sharing is the uncertainty inherent in the development of a new weapons system. The best that a firm can do, as we have said, is to provide an estimate of these costs. If there were a **fixed-fee contract** (a contract where the contractor was paid a fixed amount, regardless of the eventual cost), the contractor would have to bear considerable risk; even if it were very efficient, there is some chance that it would encounter difficulties in the development of the system that would increase its costs way beyond the fixed fee it would receive, in which case it might incur an enormous loss. If firms (or their managers) are risk averse and insist on being compensated for bearing risks, they will all put in high bids, representing their estimate of the actual costs plus a fee for bearing the risk. The government is in a better position to bear the risk. By agreeing to a cost-sharing contract, it absorbs much of the risk, but at the same time reduces the incentives for efficiency.

Though this provides an important rationale for cost-sharing contracts, some critics of the Pentagon argue that other forces are at work when the government agrees to pay all or part of a cost overrun. A large number of military officers upon their retirement from the armed forces take up positions in private industry, and in particular with defense contractors. Critics say that this provides an incentive for these officers to be accommodating to the requests of defense contractors.

Supporters of the current system, though admitting that it is far from perfect, point out that there is a healthy level of competition among defense contractors and that this competition provides at least some limit to the extent of inefficiency. Any contractor that performed persistently worse than other firms would find itself having difficulty obtaining contracts.

EXCESSIVE MONITORING AND PROCUREMENT REFORM There are many who believe that the most important problem with defense contracting is not cost overruns, but the detailed procedures which are instituted to ensure that the government is not cheated. These require excessive monitoring and record keeping, and reduce the flexibility that firms need to produce in a cost-effective manner. Indeed, when the government buys exactly the same equipment that the private sector buys, such as a jet engine, as a result of government procurement procedures the government winds up paying substantially more—because it costs the firm substantially more to produce the item. In 1994, the Department of Defense reformed its procurement procedures, which had added substantially to its cost of doing business. It sought to make its procedures conform more closely to those standard in the private sector. Because with military downsizing, fewer firms would be able to produce exclusively for the military, fewer firms would be willing to go through the hassle required to conform to government procurement rules.

There were several aspects to procurement reform. One was the promotion of **dual-use technologies,** that is, technologies that could be used both by civilian and military customers. This would have two advantages. For many of the items, the larger market would reduce the cost of production and enhance the degree of competition. Another aspect to procurement reform was to emphasize "off-the-shelf" products—products that are available commercially. Thus, rather than buying made-to-order T-shirts, the Defense Department might choose among T-shirts already in the market. There is no compelling reason why defense T-shirts need to be designed differently from T-shirts used elsewhere.

DEFENSE CONVERSION

The end of the Cold War brought with it both a downsizing of the military and a restructuring. This process was referred to as **defense conversion.** Any change of this magnitude—a redeployment of even a couple of percent of GDP—puts strains on the economy. And strains on the economy get translated quickly into political pressures. While the major rationale for defense expenditures is protection of the United States, political support for the Department of Defense arises too from the fact that defense expenditures generate so many jobs. While a sound macroeconomic policy should be able to maintain the economy at or near full employment, individuals in defense-related jobs worry that defense cutbacks will cost them their job, and that even if they could get another job, it would not be as good as their current job.

These concerns are exemplified by the controversy over base closures. As the size of the military forces was reduced, fewer bases were required. But closing a base means a loss of jobs. Congressional representatives see maintaining jobs in their districts as one of their key responsibilities.

The politics of base closure were so intense that in 1988, Congress created the Secretary of Defense's Commission on Base Realignment and Closure, to recommend bases to be closed.[5] The commission depoliticized the process (and took the heat off Congress), because while Congress could veto the commission's entire recommendation, it could not remove individual bases from the list. The 1988 commission recommended that 86 facilities be closed, and the 1991 commission recommended that 34 bases be closed. The 1993 commission selected 130 facilities for closure. All recommendations were accepted by Congress.

The 1995 base closure recommendations, however, encountered more difficulty. The commission recommended closing a large number of bases

---

[5] Authorization for the 1988 commission expired and similar commissions were created, making recommendations in 1991 and 1993.

DOWNSIZING DEFENSE

• Defense conversion entails redeploying resources. There may be significant costs to redeployment.

• It is important that resources, such as bases, be redeployed efficiently.

• Though in the long run society benefits from redeployment, particular individuals and communities may be adversely affected. Markets fail to provide insurance against economic dislocation, and accordingly there may be grounds for government assistance.

in California, which was already hard hit by defense downsizing and faced an unemployment rate that was much higher than the national average. The administration put pressure for a revision of the original recommendations, and the amended list was passed by Congress. Critics worried, however, that the administration's interventions might constitute a step backward in the attempt to depoliticize base closures.

Defense downsizing led to high levels of unemployment and other serious adverse economic impacts on many communities that relied heavily on defense expenditures. Some have argued that the federal government has special responsibility to aid these communities. There is a market failure rationale for such aid: the inability to obtain insurance against events. In effect, by providing transitional help in the face of large shocks, society is providing a form of insurance not available through the market. Critics of such aid argue that this is simply part of capitalism: communities are buffeted by all sorts of shifts in demand. They ask, why should one kind of shift in demand—that arising from a change in the demand by government for defense services—warrant preferential treatment? In practice, the government has tried to soften the adverse effects, by slowing down the pace of transition and giving substantial advance warning.

TECHNOLOGY

The United States government (like governments in other countries) has long played an important role in the diffusion and development of new technologies. For example, a key factor in the remarkable increase in agricultural productivity in this century has been the Cooperative Agricultural Extension Service, established by an act of Congress in 1914. The nuclear age was a direct outgrowth of government research, largely conducted in government-run laboratories. Other marvels of the twentieth century, such as the jet engine and supercomputers, were largely by-products of defense R&D expenditures. Today, the federal government spends approximately

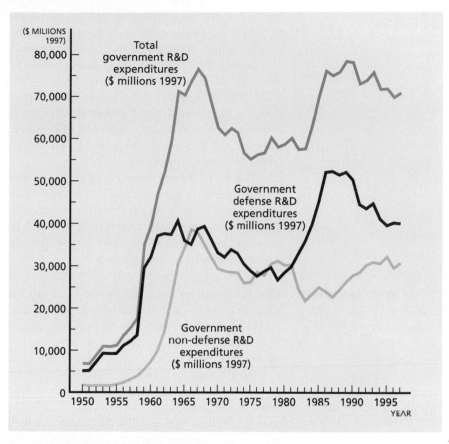

($ MILllONS 1997)

Total government R&D expenditures ($ millions 1997)

Government defense R&D expenditures ($ millions 1997)

Government non-defense R&D expenditures ($ millions 1997)

YEAR

FIGURE 13.3   **Government Expenditures on Research and Development, Fiscal Years 1950–1997** The figure shows defense, non-defense, and total federal expenditures on research and development, in 1997 dollars. The United States government spent $71 billion on research and development in 1997, much of it on defense projects.

SOURCE: Executive Office of the President, Office of Management and Budget, *Budget of the United States Government, Fiscal Year 1999*, Historical Tables, Table 9.8.

$71 billion a year in research (see Figure 13.3). While the government is currently increasing expenditures on non-defense R&D, defense R&D still accounts for 57 percent of total R&D expenditures—about the same as the average for the entire 1950–1993 period, but down from the peak of 84 percent in 1959. Moreover, combining public and private expenditures as a percentage of GDP, the United States spends substantially less on non-defense R&D (1.95 percent) than Japan (2.60 percent), Germany (2.25 percent), or France (2.05 percent).[6] It is perhaps not surprising that the United

[6] National Science Foundation, *Science and Engineering Indicators, 1998*, Appendix Table 4-44. The percentages noted are for 1994.

States has not been doing as well at innovating, as evidenced, for instance, by patent applications. In both Japan and Germany, the rate of patent applications, adjusted for population, is far higher than in the United States.

During the 1996 election, considerable concern was expressed at the slow rate of growth in the United States—the growth of productivity since 1973 has averaged slightly more than 1 percent, in contrast to the two decades after World War II, when it averaged slightly less than 3 percent. Although the U.S. economy achieved impressive rates of growth in 1998, only time will tell if this is the beginning of a stable departure from the long-run trend of slower growth.

There are three sources of growth in productivity: increases in capital, improvements in human capital (the quality of the labor force) through education and experience, and technological change. The major source of the slowdown in productivity growth since 1973 has been the slowdown in the pace of technological change—hence the concern with the underinvestment in research and development.

MARKET FAILURES

The slowdown by itself might not be a rationale for government intervention, at least from an economist's perspective. The question is, is there a market failure, a reason why the market, left to its own, would underinvest? The answer is yes: Knowledge is, in many respects, like a public good, and as we saw in Chapter 6, the private sector will underinvest in public goods.

Recall from that discussion that there are two critical properties of public goods: the undesirability of exclusion (the zero marginal cost of providing the good to an additional individual)[7] and the impossibility of exclusion. Research and development (or more accurately, knowledge, the product of research) has the first property, and often has the second as well. Giving information to additional individuals does not detract from the total amount of knowledge available.[8] But if knowledge were provided freely, it would not pay anyone to produce it. Thus either the government must provide for the production of knowledge, through direct support of R&D, or it must ensure that individuals or firms that produce knowledge are compensated for doing so.

INTELLECTUAL PROPERTY RIGHTS To enable individuals to reap rewards from their knowledge-creating activities, others must be excluded from using it, or at least from using it witout compensating the creator. The government does this by creating "property rights" in knowledge; that is, it grants a **patent,** which gives the discoverer of the knowledge exclusive use of the knowledge (including the right to license others to use it) for a limited period of time. A **copyright** gives

---

[7] The observation that knowledge had this property was made forcefully by Thomas Jefferson, who observed that knowledge was like a candle, which, even as it lights another candle, does not have its own light diminished.

[8] This fact should not be confused with the fact that the *return* that an individual can obtain from a particular piece of knowledge may depend on how many other people know that piece of information. A monopolist of a piece of information may be able to obtain a return, which he could not if the information were made freely available.

the author of a work the exclusive right to use and market her own writings. Patents and copyrights establish **intellectual property rights.** They ensure that inventors and authors can appropriate some of the fruits of their labor. The framers of the U.S. Constitution recognized the importance of intellectual property rights when they gave the newly established federal government the right to grant copyrights and patents to encourage creative activity.

Not all ideas and discoveries are patentable—mathematical theorems, for instance, are not, while algorithms may be—and even when a particular discovery is patentable, it is often possible to invent around the patent. Thus, while it is possible to patent a drug, it is often easy to devise a slight modification of the same drug, with the same medicinal properties. For this reason, and because to obtain a patent a firm must disclose a considerable amount of information, many firms prefer not to patent their discoveries. Instead, they rely on secrecy to maintain their market advantage. For instance, the formula for Coca-Cola is not patented: its discoverers chose instead to keep the formula in a bank vault.

In determining the life of a patent, the government faces a trade-off. By extending the life of the patent, it provides greater incentives for private firms to engage in R&D; but on the other hand, the knowledge produced will not be used efficiently for a longer period of time. Assume, for instance, that a firm has discovered a new, less expensive way of making a product— so much less expensive that the firm can undercut all its rivals. By patenting the discovery, the firm will be in a monopoly position. Less of the product will be produced than if the knowledge were freely disseminated.

The loss resulting from the patent can be seen in Figure 13.4, where we have drawn the market demand curve for a medicine. The cost of production

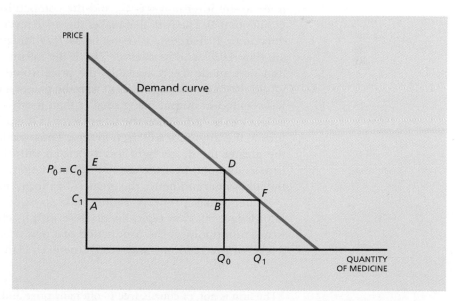

FIGURE 13.4 **Effects of Patents** A patent system results in a lower output than with free dissemination of knowledge. The deadweight loss is given by the triangle *BDF*.

THE SCOPE OF THE PATENT: CAN THE HUMAN BODY BE PATENTED?

Intellectual property rights enable inventors to appropriate some part of the fruits of their innovative activity. But there are important issues in defining intellectual property. For instance, the traditional life of a patent is seventeen years. The longer the life, the greater the returns to the innovator, but the longer the period over which the innovator exercises monopoly power, and therefore the longer the period during which the production of the innovation is restricted.

The *life* of the patent is not the only issue in defining intellectual property. An equally important issue is *scope*: how broad should the patent be. Consider recent advances in genetic engineering. Should the first person who develops a genetically engineered tomato be granted a patent for (a) all genetically engineered plants and animals; (b) all genetically engineered plants; (c) all genetically engineered tomatoes; (d) this particular variety of tomato? Controversy over the scope of a patent has recently been brought home forcefully by research on human genes. Decoding the millions of genes that make a human being is an immensely important task; it should, for instance, enable the development of drugs that can address innumerable diseases and health conditions. But for these purposes, it is not necessary to decode

---

prior to the invention was C_0, and the competitive equilibrium was thus (P_0, Q_0) at point D. The firm that makes the small invention has a lower cost of production C_1. It charges a price just below P_0, getting the entire market; its profits are thus $ABDE$, and its sales are Q_0.[9] If the information about the new innovation were made freely available, the price would fall to C_1 and the quantity would rise to Q_1. Giving the firm with the patent a monopoly on its knowledge has resulted in output being smaller than it otherwise would be, and a deadweight loss of BDF. When the patent expires the price will fall to C_1, but the return to the innovator will drop to zero. Thus, the longer the life of the patent, the greater the deadweight loss associated with the inefficiency of giving the firm a monopoly over the use of the information; but the greater the return to the innovators and hence the greater the incentives for innovation.

Intellectual property rights make possible the private provision of knowledge, but they typically interfere with its efficient utilization. Giving a firm a monopoly on the production of a new product will result in too small a level of production—and this is true even if there is a rationale in provid-

---

[9] The firm is not, of course, free to offer any price and quantity, since at any price at or above C_0 the firm loses its monopoly position. In other words, the firm maximizes its profits subject to the constraint that $P_1 < C_0$.

the entire gene; most of the relevant "information" is contained in only a fraction of the gene. Some firms claim that if they can decode that information, they should be granted a patent on the gene. Others find the entire idea of patenting a human gene repugnant.

Most of the important decisions on intellectual property are made in the courts, on a case-by-case basis. So far, the courts have not ruled on this important controversy.

Knowledge is one of the essential inputs in the production of further knowledge. Broadening the scope of patents can increase the cost of the "knowledge" input into follow-on research, and thus actually reduce the overall pace of innovation. The academic community has, in particular, been concerned that excessively broad patents could stifle their research.*

*The private sector has argued (following upon the ideas of Coase, discussed in Chapter 9) that property rights can never be excessively broad. It would always pay a firm to grant a license to a follow-on inventor who might make use of its innovation. But as we noted there, Coase's analysis assumed no transactions costs, perfect information, and competitive markets. In practice, these assumptions are not satisfied, and excessively broad patents can stifle innovation.

ing the monopoly. There is a trade-off between "dynamic efficiency"—providing firms with an incentive to innovate—and "static efficiency," which requires that firms produce up to the point where price equals marginal cost.

As we have noted, many discoveries are not protected by intellectual property rights, or are protected only imperfectly. The key lesson is that intellectual property rights, as important as they are, only partially solve the market failures associated with the production of knowledge. Other government interventions are required.

OTHER MECHANISMS FOR ENCOURAGING PRIVATE PRODUCTION OF KNOWLEDGE
Governments also encourage the private production of knowledge by subsidizing a critical input into R&D, scientific manpower, through its support of education programs (see Chapter 16), and through a tax credit, the **incremental research and experimentation tax credit** (R&E credit).[10]

[10] The credit has not been a permanent feature of the tax code, but has regularly been extended, with a few exceptions. (There was a one-year hiatus in the credit from July 1, 1995, to June 30, 1996.) There is concern that the incentive effects have been attenuated because companies can no longer rely on the credit. (The credit expired again on June 30, 1998.)

Firms that increase their research expenditure are allowed to deduct 20 percent of their incremental expenditures from their tax; the government pays, in effect, 20 percent of the marginal costs. The reason the credit is on incremental expenditures is to lower the *marginal* cost of research—the government does directly subsidize research that would otherwise have been undertaken anyway—and thus to maximize the "bang for the buck." The advantage of a tax credit over a direct subsidy is that the government does not have to choose among applicants: those who believe that their projects are worth undertaking put up their own money, matched by the government (on a one-to-four basis) at the margin. The disadvantage of a tax credit is that it does not distinguish research projects which have large externalities from those which have none. Indeed, there is even some question about whether some of what gets supported is real research—overhead and marketing research may be passed off as R&D expenditures.

GOVERNMENT DIRECT SUPPORT

Government supports research not only indirectly, such as through the patent system and tax credits, but directly. Such direct support is particularly important for *basic research.* Basic research adds to our underlying store of fundamental knowledge (as opposed to *applied research,* which is intended to result more immediately in a new product or manufacturing technique). The results of basic research are more likely to be inappropriable; even if they are appropriable, the social cost of restricting the utilization of this knowledge may be particularly high, since basic research is such an important input into the production of other ideas. As a result, it is generally agreed that some form of direct support for basic research is required if there is to be an efficient allocation of resources to it.

Far more controversial, however, is government support to applied research. Sometimes, governments pick out particular industries to encourage through supporting research in those areas. Such funding or other policies, such as protection from foreign imports, aimed at promoting particular industries are referred to as **industrial policies.** Advocates of these policies argue that there is no clear line between basic and applied research; that much of applied research has huge spillovers—externalities to others that are not appropriated by the innovator—and that hence, there will be underinvestment. While the transistor was invented in Bell Labs, and was of immediate benefit to AT&T, which paid for the research, the benefits to the world clearly extended far beyond.

Critics have argued that the government has a terrible record of picking winners, because of its lack of "profit motive," and that the government should not be in the business of directing the economy. Michael Boskin, chairman of the Council of Economic Advisers under President Bush, was quoted as saying, "It makes no difference whether the economy produces potato chips or computer chips."

Advocates of government support for technology reply that the government actually has a remarkably good record of picking winners—which is

KNOWLEDGE, PUBLIC GOODS, AND EXTERNALITIES

Knowledge is, to a large extent, a public good. Through patent protection (or other forms of intellectual property rights) inventors can appropriate some of the returns to their inventive activity. Still, there are likely to be externalities. Moreover, the appropriation interferes with the efficient diffusion and utilization of knowledge. This provides the rationale for government support. It is particularly cogent for basic research.

not to say that it has not supported its fair share of losers as well.[11] They argue that the objective of government support is not to push the economy in particular directions, but simply to identify areas where there appear to be large spillovers, so that without government support, there will be under-investment. Several examples could be cited. For instance, the telecommunications industry owes much to the federal government, from the first telegraph line between Baltimore and Washington in 1842 to the development of the Internet. In the nineteenth century, government support for agriculture research and its dissemination was key to the enormous increase in productivity in that sector—the core of the economy at that time; while in the twentieth century, government was central in high technology industries, from computers to bio-medicine.

In its recent technology programs, the government has tried to learn from its past mistakes: to improve incentives, it has focused on partnerships, in which the private sector puts up at least 50 percent of the costs; it has provided grants on a competitive basis, with evaluations by outside experts, and with projects in a wide variety of areas competing against each other. And it has instituted a system of ongoing review to terminate unsuccessful projects. (In the past, the reluctance to terminate such projects has been a major problem; congressional representatives from districts in which projects are located typically argue that success is just around the corner.) Ironically, while these reforms seem to have worked, they have also undermined sup-

---

[11] Government attempts at coal gasification and other synthetic fuel projects are usually cited as examples of these failures. Interest in industrial policies grew in the 1980s, when Japan's economic success was often contrasted with the problems facing the U.S. economy. Japan had long used industrial policies, for instance to encourage the development of the computer chip industry. The U.S. government provided support for the computer chip industry; it helped establish a consortium of U.S. producers, called Sematech, which it then subsidized. The industry has enjoyed a resurgence in the United States, to the point where the country once again dominates the world market. Government subsidies to Sematech have now ceased.

port for technology research programs: special interests no longer see them as cash cows and therefore devote little resources to lobbying for them.

REVIEW AND PRACTICE

SUMMARY

1   In determining "how much is enough" in defense expenditures, marginal analysis—looking at the incremental benefit from increased expenditures—is essential.

2   Alternative views of overall defense strategy are important determinants of defense needs. During the Cold War, attention was focused on deterrence; President Reagan initiated the Strategic Defense Initiative; more recently, debate has focused on the desirability of having a two-theatre capability. There is increasing concern over nuclear proliferation, and over the use by rogue states of chemical and biological warfare and terrorism.

3   The Defense Department has attempted to increase its efficiency by reforming its procurement policy, with greater reliance on performance standards and off-the-shelf purchases and on the development of dual-use technologies. Traditional procurement systems, including cost-plus contracts, may have contributed significantly to high costs by providing attenuated or perverse incentives.

4   Base closures and other reductions in defense spending will cause economic hardship in some areas. There is disagreement on what and how much the government should do to help affected communities. The absence of insurance markets insuring against these economic risks provides a rationale for government action.

5   The government has long had a role in the support of research and the development of technology. Knowledge has both of the properties of a public good, so that without some government intervention, there will be underinvestment in research.

6   The government encourages innovation by establishing intellectual property rights (through patents). While patents thus allow innovators to appropriate some of the returns to their innovation, and thus provide incentives for the *production* of knowledge, they interfere with its efficient *use*.

7   The government also provides direct support for research, especially basic research, and indirect support through tax credits and the support of education—producing the scientists who are the critical input into research. Government programs in support of technology are aimed at identifying areas where there are large spillovers. While such industrial policies have been controversial, the government has a credible record of picking winners. Recent government policies emphasize public-private

partnerships, with the private sector providing a significant fraction of the costs.

KEY CONCEPTS

Peace dividend	Dual-use technologies
Deterrence	Defense conversion
Strategic Defense Initiative (SDI)	Patent
Second strike capability	Copyright
Two-theatre capability	Intellectual property rights
Cost overrun	Incremental research and experimentation tax credit
Cost-sharing contracts	
Cost-plus contracts	Industrial policies
Fixed-fee contract	

QUESTIONS AND PROBLEMS

1 Assume the government has decided to install a missile system designed to provide a second strike capability with 100 missiles. It is now considering whether to increase the number to 110. Assume you are on the congressional committee that must approve the increased expenditure. List some of the questions you might ask to ascertain whether the increased expenditures are desirable.

2 Should military officers and Defense Department officials be proscribed from working for private defense contractors for a period of several years after termination of their government service?

3 In what ways is the purchase of a hammer or of labor services by the military different from the purchase of an MX missile system? How does this affect government procurement policies in these two areas?

4 Consider the following proposed system of bidding: The contract would be awarded to the lowest bidder at the price bid by the second-lowest bid. Why does such a system encourage bidders to bid honestly their true costs of production?

5 In some cases, the government runs duplicative projects, particularly at early stages of development. What do you think is the advantage of doing this? The disadvantage?

6 Consider the following proposal for reducing cost overruns. Two contractors would be given a contract to produce a tank of a given specification. Producer A would be reimbursed for the *actual* costs incurred by producer B, and vice versa. Explain why this system might induce each firm to produce efficiently. If the two firms were essentially identical, what

risk premium would they require in bidding on the contract? Under what conditions might the risk premium be large? What are other possible pitfalls in this system?

7   Imagine that Congress is considering a bill to reduce the current seventeen-year life of patents to eight years. What negative effects might this change have on the rate of innovation? What positive effect might it have for the economy?

8   Suppose that many years ago, one inventor received a patent for orange juice, and then another inventor came forward and requested a patent for lemonade. The first inventor maintained that the orange juice patent should be interpreted to cover all fruit juices, while the second inventor argued that the original patent included only one particular method of producing one kind of juice. What trade-offs does society face in setting rules for deciding cases like these?

9   Why might a company invest in research and development even if it does not believe it will be able to patent its discovery?

10 Some public goods are "local," that is, they provide services only to those living in a particular locality. What might be meant by a "global" public good? Why might knowledge be thought of as a global public good? What implications does this have for government policy in a small country? Can a country be a "free rider" in basic research?

11 In what sense is international security, including efforts to stymie nuclear proliferation, a global public good?

14 Social Insurance

FOCUS QUESTIONS

1 What is social insurance, and why does government provide it? What market failures in particular provide the rationale for social security?

2 What are the financial problems facing social security programs, and why do they seem so hard to remedy? What are the merits of various proposals for financial reforms?

3 What are major inequities and inefficiencies associated with the design of the social security system, and how might they be remedied?

Modern governments have long taken some responsibility for providing for the needy, but during the past fifty years this has come to be viewed as one of the primary functions of government. In the United States in 1997, social insurance and welfare expenditures represented more than one-third of the federal government's budget. Social security, however, differs from most government programs in that it has its own earmarked payroll tax. The revenues from this tax go into special trust funds that finance benefit payments. Social security was originally designed to be self-financing, that is, revenues from the payroll tax were intended to cover outlays.

Of the major social insurance programs, by far the largest is Old-Age, Survivors, and Disability Insurance (OASDI), enacted in 1935. This is usu-

TABLE 14.1

Expenditures in
Major Social
Insurance Programs

	BILLIONS OF 1997 DOLLARS		
	1962	1980	1997
Social Security (OASDI)	80.5	240.7	365.2
Old-Age and Survivors Insurance[a]	74.3	209.7	318.5
Disability insurance	6.3	30.9	46.7
Unemployment insurance	20.2	35.2	22.9
Medicare	—	62.5	190.0

[a] Most of the expenditures on Old-Age and Survivors Insurance go to provide retirement income, but there are also benefits for widows and for children.

SOURCES: Executive Office of the President, Office of Management and Budget, *Budget of the United States Government, Fiscal Year 1999*, Historical Tables, Table 3.2; U.S. Department of Health and Human Services, Social Security Administration, *Social Security Bulletin*, 1997 Annual Statistical Supplement, Tables 4.A1, 4.A2; *1998 Annual Report of the Board of Trustees of the Federal Old-Age and Survivors Insurance and Disability Insurance Trust Funds*, April 28, 1998 (real numbers calculated using consumer price index from *Economic Report of the President, 1998*).

ally referred to as **social security** and is intended to provide a basic standard of living to the aged, the disabled, and their survivors. As Table 14.1 indicates, in thirty-five years this program more than quadrupled in real terms, from $80.5 billion (in 1997 dollars) in 1962 to $365 billion dollars in 1997. Disability—technically, also included under social security—provides money to those no longer able to work. The second largest program, Medicare, provides medical care for the aged; it was discussed in detail in Chapter 12. Unemployment insurance, also enacted in 1935, is intended to provide income to individuals during short-term spells of unemployment (as its name suggests). Other social insurance programs include workers' compensation, which provides money to individuals who are injured on the job; disability benefits for veterans; retirement benefits for railroad workers; and funds for coal miners suffering from black lung.[1]

In many ways, social insurance programs provide insurance to individuals against particular risks that they face, just as private insurance does. Thus Medicare covers medical expenditures of the aged, just as a private health policy would. Social security is designed to replace a part of the income lost due to retirement or disability; private insurance policies exist that meet the same need. There is one important difference: With private insurance there is a close relationship between the payments of the individual, the risks he faces, and what he receives. Thus the premium for a private health insurance policy depends on factors affecting the individual's health condition, such as his age. The amount that an individual receives back from an **annuity** (a private insurance policy providing a certain income every year after the individual reaches, say, age 65) on average is effectively just what he puts

[1] Like many private employers, the federal and state governments provide additional retirement benefits to their civilian employees and military personnel, which should probably be viewed as deferred compensation rather than as social insurance programs.

in (plus accumulated interest). This is not true of social insurance. Social insurance programs provide insurance *and* redistribute income. Confusion between these two roles has been a major impediment in the evaluation and reform of social insurance programs.

The social security system has been expanded greatly in the half century since its enactment. Originally, it covered only a fraction of the working population, with agricultural workers, the self-employed, government employees, and employees of nonprofit institutions excluded. Today, the only employees not covered are federal employees hired before 1984 and a few categories of employees of state and local governments. The number of beneficiaries increased from 3.5 million in 1950 to 44 million in 1997. While the number of beneficiaries of OASDI increased more than tenfold over these years, in real terms the benefits increased fiftyfold, from $6.7 billion in 1950 (in 1997 dollars) to approximately $365 billion in 1997.[2] Note that a very large fraction of our social insurance system is aimed at the elderly, and that the "social security" program itself is only about half of total federal outlays for the elderly. (See Figure 14.1.)

This chapter discusses the major issues facing the social security (OASDI) insurance program.

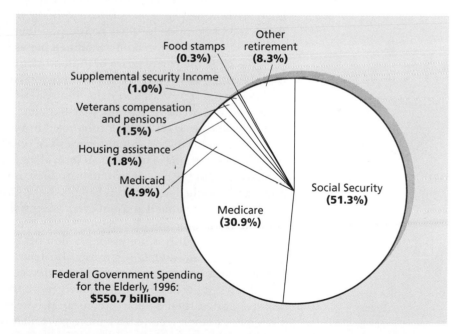

FIGURE 14.1 **Federal Outlays Benefiting the Elderly** About 82 percent of federal spending for the elderly is in the form of social security and Medicare benefits.

SOURCE: Congressional Budget Office, Unpublished Memo, "Estimated Federal Spending for the Elderly under Selected Programs, Fiscal Year 1980–1996," December 1996.

[2] See *Social Security Bulletin*, spring 1994, Tables 1.A1 and 1.B1.

THE SOCIAL SECURITY SYSTEM

OASDI is financed by a payroll tax that is paid partly by employees and partly by their employers. In 1997, the combined tax rate was 12.4 percent on the first $65,400 of income. In addition, there is a 2.9 percent tax on all income used to finance Medicare. (The inclusion of all income for the purposes of the Medicare tax was one of the changes instituted in 1993.) Both the maximum base and the tax rate have increased dramatically over time. Beginning at $3000 and 2 percent combined employer/employee tax in 1937, the base more than doubled by 1967, to $6600 with an 8.8 percent combined rate; doubled again by 1974 to a $13,200 base and an 11.7 percent combined rate; and doubled again in the next seven years to $29,700 with a 13.3 percent rate. Thus, in sixty years, the maximum tax payment on social security alone had increased by a factor of 135, from $60 to more than $8000.

According to the law, half the tax is paid by employees and half by their employers; but most economists believe that this is simply a legal fiction. The consequences of the tax are essentially the same as they would be if the individual were responsible for paying all of it. What difference should it make who mails the check to the government?[3]

A pension system in which each age group's pension is supported by its own contributions is called a **fully funded system.** Private pension systems normally are fully funded; while they are working, individuals contribute to a fund that is used to provide for their pensions in retirement. By contrast, the social security system is organized on a **modified pay-as-you-go basis.** In a pure pay-as-you-go system, the payroll taxes of those working today pay for the benefits received by the elderly today. The U.S. system is called a modified pay-as-you-go system because revenues and expenditures are not supposed to balance out each year, but over a seventy-five-year horizon. The balance between receipts and expenditures is added to or subtracted from the social security trust fund.

The benefits an individual receives are linked to her contributions by a complicated formula. The more an individual contributes, the more she gets back—just as in the case of private insurance. But in the case of private insurance, an individual who spends $10,000 to buy an annuity (a retirement policy that pays, say, a fixed amount every year) will get approximately ten times the benefit of someone who spends $1000. This is not the case with social security. Social security is not just a pension program; it is a redistribution program. Poorer individuals (or those who have made smaller contributions) get back proportionately more; and married couples in which only one individual worked get back proportionately more than do couples in which both worked and earned similar incomes. Moreover, since women live longer than men, women receive back more per dollar contributed than do men.

The system has changed dramatically over time. Figure 14.2 illustrates how the difference between the present discounted value of payments and

---

[3] Employers are only concerned with their total labor costs, including any employment taxes; employees are concerned only with their net after-tax income. The government's revenue is simply the difference between the two, and it makes little difference who the government says is paying the tax. For more extensive discussion, see Chapter 18.

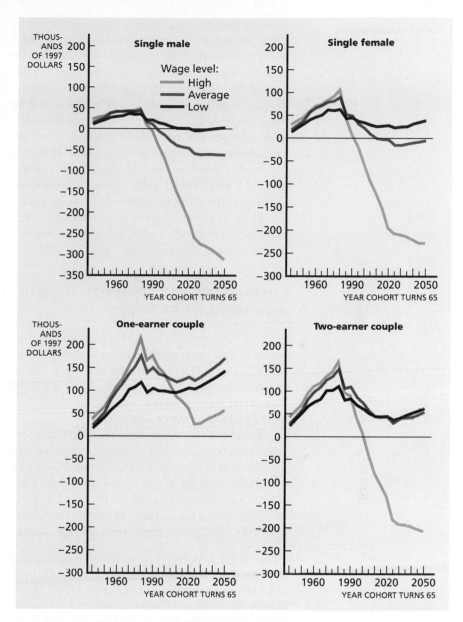

FIGURE 14.2   **Net Lifetime Social Security Transfer** In the initial years of social security, net transfers (the difference between benefits and contributions) increased significantly, but in recent years they have declined, and that trend is expected to continue. Net transfers have always been highest for one-earner couples. While net transfers used to be largest for high-wage workers, this is no longer true.

SOURCE: C. Eugene Steuerle and Jon M. Bakija. *Retooling Social Security for the 21st Century: Right & Wrong Approaches to Reform* (Washington, D.C.: The Urban Institute Press, 1994), pp. 109 and 287.

receipts has changed and is projected to change in coming years.[4] Until 1983, essentially all groups received more than they contributed—this was just a transfer from the younger generation to the older. Interestingly, *high-wage workers used to receive a larger transfer than did low-wage workers*: though the *ratio* of their benefits to payments was smaller, the absolute amount of the transfer was larger. This is still true for one-earner families, but for high-wage single individuals and high-wage two-earner families, benefits are less than receipts. For two-earner families, it will be a couple of decades before the transfer to low-wage workers equals that to middle-income workers.

It also used to be that the present discounted value of benefits increased if one retired early; today, those who retire early have their benefits reduced sufficiently so that there is no incentive to retire early.

Thus, the social security system redistributes income toward the poor, to one-earner families, and, on average, from the current working generation to present retirees.

SOCIAL SECURITY, PRIVATE INSURANCE, AND MARKET FAILURES

Prior to 1935, private markets provided life insurance but not retirement insurance. Few firms provided much in the way of pensions.

The Great Depression caused a crisis: there were many aged thrown out of work who had little prospect of being rehired and no means of support. The social security system was intended to ensure that all of the aged had at least a minimal level of support.

In subsequent years, however, there have been marked improvements in private markets. Pension coverage expanded rapidly in the 1950s when large manufacturers adopted pension plans. While in 1950 only 25 percent of nonagricultural workers in the private sector were covered by private pensions, by 1979, 55 percent were covered. In the early 1980s, pension coverage declined to 50 percent as the number of jobs in manufacturing declined and the poorly covered service sector grew, and coverage has remained at that low level.[5] The

---

[4] The figures depict the net transfer to someone *retiring* at the age of 65 in that year. They present the present discounted value of benefits minus the present discounted value of contributions, using a 2 percent real interest rate. They take into account chances of death and "typical" family structures. *If* individuals had taken the same money and invested it in the stock market, they would have received returns substantially in excess of the 2 percent interest rate postulated in the charts, so that for the high-income individuals, the net negative transfer is greatly understated (that is, the net benefits are much less than the net contributions). Note that because of the long time span over which contributions are made, it is possible that some individuals receive back more than they contribute (that is, they can get a positive return), but a return far less than they could have had had they invested the returns on their own.

[5] See: Senate Special Committee on Aging, *The Pension Gamble: Who Wins? Who Loses?*, 99th Congress, 1st sess., serial no. 99–5, June 14, 1985, pp. 85, 126; also U.S. Department of Labor, Social Security Administration, U.S. Small Business Administration, and Pension Benefit Guaranty Corporation, *Pension and Health Benefits of American Workers: New Findings from the April 1993 Current Population Survey*, May 1994; and House Committee on Ways and Means, *1998 Green Book*, May 19, 1998, p. 844.

HIGH TRANSACTIONS COSTS

government has taken steps to ensure the financial soundness of private pension programs.[6] But these private insurance policies are deficient in several respects.

To provide for their retirement, individuals can purchase annuities from private firms. Annuities pay a fixed amount every month from some age (usually 65 or 70) until the individual dies, no matter how long he or she lives. Under most private annuity programs, however, the expected rate of return does not appear to be very good—far lower than market rates of interest. This is partly because of high administrative costs (including in many cases substantial commissions for the salespeople). While administrative costs for social security are less than 1 percent of benefits paid, those of private pensions are almost 6 percent.[7]

The trade-offs between reducing costs and increasing the scope for individual choice are clear: it is administratively less expensive to provide a uniform retirement program for all individuals than to have a large number of competing programs available, among which the individuals can choose. So long, however, as the level of retirement benefits is relatively low, few individuals are being forced to save more for retirement than they would like; hence, there is no significant welfare loss from the provision of a reasonably low level of benefits. This argument does not hold, however, if the retirement benefits are substantial.

LACK OF INDEXING: THE INABILITY OF PRIVATE MARKETS TO INSURE SOCIAL RISKS

A major difference between private insurance policies and the social security program is that social security benefits are **indexed;** they increase with inflation. The closest private policies have come to indexed benefits are annuities whose benefits are linked with the performance of the stock market. When these insurance policies were introduced, it was thought that they would provide a hedge against inflation; the stock market would go up with prices in general. However, there have been long periods of time when stock prices have not kept up with inflation, and in general it is now recognized that stocks provide relatively poor protection against inflation.

---

[6] The government not only regulates private pensions but provides insurance to ensure that workers receive the promised pensions. A number of large defaults on the private pension schemes have threatened the financial viability of the federal insurance program. The program run by the U.S. Pension Guaranty Corporation had a deficit of $2.7 billion in 1992. In response, Congress passed the Retirement Protection Act of 1994. Currently, the program covers 42 million workers and retirees, and has a small surplus. See House Committee on Ways and Means, *1998 Green Book*, pp. 905, 909.

[7] See Department of Labor, *Pension and Health Benefits of American Workers*, Table A15; and *Annual Social Security Trustees Report 1998*, April 28, 1998, p. 2. Interestingly, when social security is compared to private insurance companies (including annuities) more generally, government looks even more favorable. Private insurance companies spend one dollar in administrative costs, dividends (profits), and taxes for every two dollars in benefits paid. See Charles T. Goodsell, *The Case for Bureaucracy* (Chatham, N.J.: Chatham House Publishers, 1983), p. 52.

The risks of inflation are an example of an important class of risks referred to as **social risks.** These are risks faced by society as a whole. It is difficult for any private insurance firm to bear such risks. Aside from exceptional circumstances, such as war, the deaths of different individuals are "independent" events. A firm that insures a large number of individuals can predict fairly accurately the number of individuals that will die each year. But if there is a war, the number may be much larger. Thus, most insurance policies exclude the coverage of death in a war. Similarly, if a firm insured against inflation, it would find that if the inflation rate increased much faster than it had expected, it would bear a loss on all of its policies; it might well find that it was not able to meet all these commitments at the same time. This is perhaps part of the reason why there is no market for insurance against inflation; in fact, there is no way that individuals can hedge against inflation by buying any private security or mix of securities.

Though the market cannot, or at least has not, provided insurance against inflation, the government can provide insurance against inflation. It can sell—and beginning in January 1997, actually has sold—bonds, the returns to which are guaranteed in real terms. Thus, while one of the great advantages of social security is that it provides retirees with some protection against inflation, this by itself does not provide a strong rationale for social security.

There are two major distinctions between the ability of the government and that of private firms to provide insurance for social risks. First, the government is in a position to meet its obligations by raising taxes. Second, the government can engage in risk sharing across generations. The costs of a war, for instance, can be shared by the current generation and future generations: through reducing investment during the period of war and through subsequently imposing taxes on the young for the benefit of the old, the costs of the war can effectively be shared by the generation that is working during the period of war and by subsequent generations. If the economy experiences a particularly bad episode of inflation in a given decade, it can transfer some of the burden of that onto younger, working generations.

ADVERSE SELECTION, DIFFERENTIAL RISKS, AND THE COST OF INSURANCE

A third major problem with private insurance arises from the fact that different individuals have different life expectancies. Consider life insurance, which provides a fixed payment to the insured person's survivors after his death. (Thus, life insurance is actually death or survivors' insurance.) A firm selling a life insurance policy does not want to insure people who are likely to die; if it knows that they are likely to die, it will insist on charging a high premium. For someone over the age of 65 or someone with a heart condition, the premium may be particularly high. On the other hand, for private insurance firms selling an annuity, the concern is just the opposite: they only want to insure people who are unhealthy, who are likely to die soon. Since women live longer than men, insurance companies in the past charged women lower life insurance premiums but higher premiums for annuities.

To the extent that differences in individuals' life expectancies can easily be identified, economic efficiency requires that private insurance firms charge premiums reflecting those differences. There are those who believe that this is unfair: someone who has bad health is unlucky enough; to charge him a higher premium for his life insurance adds insult to injury.

In practice, it is costly to identify good risks, and insurance firms spend considerable resources attempting to do so. Indeed, an insurance company's profits can be increased as much through better ways of identifying good risks from bad risks as they can be by improving the efficiency and quality of overall service provided. If private insurance firms cannot discriminate among individuals by levels of risk, quite another problem arises. In competitive equilibrium, the premiums must reflect the *average* risk of those who purchase the policy (for life insurance or an annuity, this corresponds to the average life expectancy). But this means that good risks are in effect subsidizing poor risks. With annuities, those who die young subsidize those who live a long time; with life insurance, those who live a long time subsidize those who die young. This means, in turn, that good risks, on average, get back less from the insurance company than they put in. To them, insurance is a bad gamble. But if some individuals know that they are low risk, but cannot demonstrate this to the insurance company, if they are not very risk averse, they will not buy insurance. When the best risks no longer purchase insurance, the premiums must increase. This process, by which only the worst risks purchase private insurance, is called *adverse selection*.[8] Adverse selection may provide part of the explanation for high premiums charged for annuities. The government, however, can force all individuals to purchase the insurance, and thus avoid the problem of adverse selection. In doing so, it is engaging in some redistribution; good risks are paying more, and bad risks are paying less, than they "should."

MORAL HAZARD AND SOCIAL SECURITY

There is another reason why private insurance firms often offer only limited insurance. Insurance may reduce the individual's incentive to avoid the insured-for event; we referred to this as *moral hazard* in Chapter 12.

Individuals, in contemplating making provisions for their eventual retirement, face two important sources of risk. The first is that they do not know how long they might live after retirement. An individual who did not buy an annuity would have to husband her resources carefully; she would have to worry about the possibility that she will live longer than average. In insuring this risk, no significant moral-hazard problem arises. But a moral hazard problem does arise in the second risk, for which social security provides insurance: individuals do not know how well they will be able to work at the age of 62 or 65 or 70. Some individuals are healthy and their skills have not become obsolete; they continue to work well beyond 70. Others are incapable of working; they become disabled. But many individuals are

---

[8] For a more extended analysis of the effects of adverse selection in insurance markets, see M. Rothschild and J. E. Stiglitz, "Equilibrium in Competitive Insurance Markets," *Quarterly Journal of Economics* 90 (1976): 629–50.

in an in-between state at 62 or 65; they are not medically disabled, but they are finding it increasingly difficult, or less enjoyable, or less productive, to work. When they are younger, individuals like to purchase insurance against the possibility that they will fall in this gray area, not so disabled as to qualify for a medical disability but not so well that they can easily continue working. Social security provides that insurance: it enables an individual who wishes to retire at 62 to do so. But the better the "insurance"—the larger the fraction of working income that social security replaces—the weaker the incentive to work; with full replacement, even an individual who is in perfect health and highly productive might be induced to retire. This is the central moral-hazard problem associated with social security.

The failure of the private market to provide complete insurance should not be viewed as a capricious consequence of rapacious insurance companies trying to exploit hapless consumers, but rather as a rational response to a critical economic problem, of providing at least some incentives to the insured. To the extent that this explains the limitations of insurance provided by the private market, there is no reason to believe that the government can do any better: the trade-offs between risk reduction and incentives remain the same. In other words, concerns about the moral hazard problem provide a limitation on the extent of insurance that can or should be provided, privately or publicly.[9]

RETIREMENT INSURANCE AS A MERIT GOOD

Even where there are good insurance markets, there remains a rationale for government action: If society believes that it cannot countenance an older individual suffering because he has failed to make adequate provision for his retirement years, and if a number of individuals fail to make adequate provision for their retirement on their own, there is an argument for *compelling* individuals to do so. Those who do make provision for their retirement may feel that it is unfair for them to bear the burden of those who could have made adequate provision for their retirement but lacked the foresight to do so. In this view, retirement insurance (and life insurance) are merit goods that a paternalistic government forces on the individual for his own good. But they are different from many other merit goods in that much of the cost of the individual's failure to purchase the good is borne by others. To the extent that this provides the rationale for social insurance, however, it suggests only that the government should require individuals to obtain insurance, not that the government should require individuals to purchase the insurance from the government itself. And it provides a rationale only for a certain "base level" of social security, just high enough that government feels no necessity to raise their consumption further, should they do no additional saving.

---

[9] This is a slight simplification. The trade-offs as viewed by a private insurance company may look markedly different than viewed by the government. For instance, the government should be aware that early retirement may result in a loss of tax revenues, a consideration that the private insurer would not care about.

MARKET FAILURES

High transactions costs

Incomplete insurance

- Inability of private markets to insure social risks: lack of indexing

- Adverse selection: possible explanation of imperfections in annuity markets

- Moral hazard

Retirement insurance as a merit good: moral hazard problem created in supporting those who fail to provide for themselves

SHOULD SOCIAL SECURITY BE REFORMED?

The previous discussion has clarified the many different roles that social security plays. It is a forced savings plan, ensuring that individuals put aside sufficient amounts so that they do not become public charges in their old age; it is a "community-rated" inflation-indexed annuity plan, in which all individuals who make the same contributions, regardless of their health conditions and life expectancy, get the same benefits, with the level of those benefits insured against inflation; and it is a redistribution program.[10] To its advocates, this mixture is one of its strengths; it may have done more to reduce poverty among the elderly than might have been politically acceptable in an *explicit* redistribution program. (Today, poverty among the elderly is lower than it has been since data began to be collected in the late 1950s.) To its critics, this mixture is one of its weaknesses: it leads to a lack of *transparency,* which should be the hallmark of democratic government. Just as there has been increasing demands for "truth in advertising"—that the consumer should have the information that allows him to know what he is purchasing—so too in the public sector. Taxpayers should know, for instance, to what extent their tax dollars or social security contributions are being used to redistribute income from one group to another. Lack of transparency may contribute to the difficulties in reforming social security, as myths and reality get confused together. For instance, the aged resist cuts in benefits, believing that they have already paid for those benefits through their social security contributions, even if the value of the benefits significantly exceeds the value of their contributions.

[10] It used to provide insurance against "early obsolescence": individuals who retired earlier, either because of health or because their job skills no longer were highly valued in the labor market, were, in effect, compensated by receiving a higher present discounted value of benefits (though lower annual benefits). In the future, this will no longer be the case, as early retirees will have monthly checks reduced accordingly.

Reform of social security is so difficult both because it performs this multiplicity of roles and because it addresses a multiplicity of market failures. For instance, *if* social security were solely a "forced savings plan," it is not obvious that individuals should be required to save through the government; a private savings mandate might do as well. Before turning to these reform issues, we first discuss the complaints against social security—why reform is needed.

From many perspectives, social security has been a success: while in the past, poverty among the elderly was viewed as a real social problem, today, not only are poverty rates among the elderly far lower, they are lower than in the population as a whole. The beneficiaries are not only the recipients but their children, who otherwise would have helped to support them or felt guilty about not doing so. In the past, the elderly frequently had no choice but to move into their children's home; now they have a choice, and increasingly, they exercise that choice by maintaining independent households.[11]

There are five major complaints against social security. First, it is contributing to the country's long-run fiscal crisis. Beginning around 2021, there will be a shortfall of revenues relative to expenditures, and the trust fund that has been set aside to meet the needs of the aging population will be drawn upon; it will be exhausted by 2032.[12] (See Figure 14.3.) As a result, confidence in the social security system has eroded. For instance, a recent poll of 18- to 34-year-olds showed that more believe in UFOs (46 percent) than that social security will exist by the time they retire (28 percent).[13]

Second, critics allege that social security discourages savings, and thus slows down the growth of the economy. Third, critics argue that it discourages work effort. Fourth, they complain that it gives a low rate of return—it is a bad investment. And fifth, there are a number of inequities in its design.

It is worth noting that there are *not* major complaints about either the efficiency of the Social Security Administration or its responsiveness to its "clients." Miraculously, it appears to be the one major government department which has managed a successful computerization. Its overall administrative costs are low compared to either public or private agencies engaged in similar activities. And a recent consumer satisfaction survey focusing on telephone service ranked the Social Security Administration among the top four "companies."

THE NATURE OF THE FISCAL CRISIS

The essential fiscal problem facing the social security system, in its modified pay-as-you-go basis, is that the system's financial viability depends on the ratio of the number of workers to the number of retirees. As Figure

[11] Indeed, as a result, the household poverty data probably understate the improvement in the economic status of the elderly. When they have their own household, the household income may fall below the poverty threshold, while when they were in their children's household, they may have been above the poverty threshold. To the extent that they have *chosen* to keep their own household, they are nonetheless better off, in spite of the fact that the poverty statistics would show an increase in the number of elderly living in households below the poverty line.

[12] The precise estimates vary from year to year. These numbers are from the *Annual Social Security Trustees Report 1998*, April 28, 1998, p. 4.

[13] Peter G. Peterson, *Will America Grow Up before It Grows Old?* (New York: Random House, 1996).

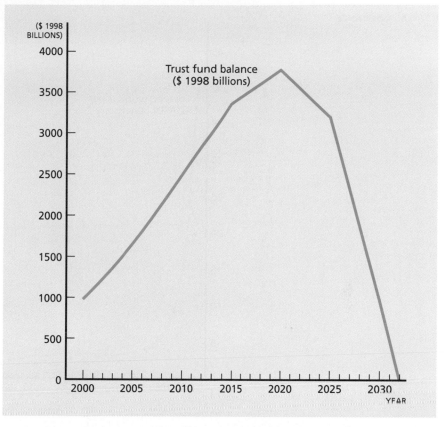

($ 1998
BILLIONS)

Trust fund balance
($ 1998 billions)

YEAR

FIGURE 14.3   **Social Security Trust Fund** After 2020, the social security trust fund is expected
to begin being depleted, and by 2032 it is expected to be completely exhausted.

SOURCE: Department of Health and Human Services, Social Security Administration, *1998 Annual
Report of the Board of Trustees of the Federal Old-Age and Survivors Insurance and Disability Insurance Trust Funds*, April 28, 1998, Table III.B3.F19 (intermediate projections).

14.4 shows, that number has decreased markedly, from more than 16 to 1
in 1950 to slightly more than 3 to 1 today; and it is anticipated to decrease
further to 2 to 1 in the next forty years. There are three reasons for the
change: earlier retirement ages,[14] increased longevity,[15] and slower popula-

[14] In 1940, the average age at which retirees began receiving social security was 68.8
for men and 68.1 for women. By 1991, those numbers had declined to 63.7 for men
and 63.7 for women. In 1950, 46 percent of males 65 and over worked; in 1991, only
16 percent did. Steuerle and Bakija, *Retooling Social Security for the 21st Century*, p. 43.
See House Committee on Ways and Means , *1998 Green Book*, for further information
about retirement ages.

[15] In 1940, the average remaining life expectancy for those surviving to age 65 was
12.7 years for men and 14.7 years for women. By 1990, these figures had increased to
15.3 for men and 19.6 for women. By 2050, they are expected to increase still further
to 18.0 for men and 22.4 for women. Steuerle and Bakija, p. 41.

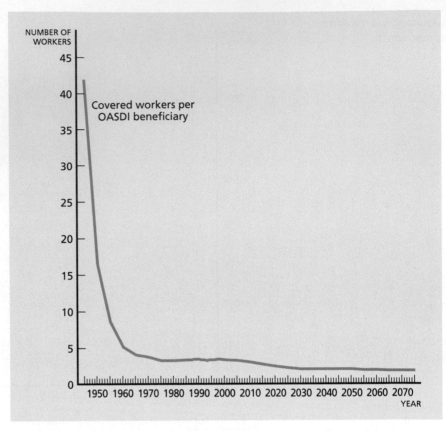

FIGURE 14.4   **Ratio of Covered Workers to OASDI Beneficiaries** Since the inception of OASDI, there has been a marked decline in the number of workers per OASDI beneficiary. The ratio is expected to decline well into the future.

SOURCE: Department of Health and Human Services, Social Security Administration, *1998 Annual Report of the Board of Trustees of the Federal Old-Age and Survivors Insurance and Disability Insurance Trust Funds*, April 28, 1998, Table II.F19 (intermediate projections).

tion growth.[16] The first two reasons translate into a larger population of retired people, and a slower population growth rate means that the ratio of the young to the old is lower than it used to be. The increased labor-force participation of women during the last three decades has somewhat offset these demographic trends, but in the decades ahead the underlying trends will dominate.

[16] Fertility rates (the average number of children born to a woman) after reaching a peak of 3.7 in 1957, have fallen to about 2. At these low fertility rates, population will (apart from immigration) start to decline. See U.S. Department of Health and Human Services, Social Security Administration, Office of the Actuary, *Social Security Area Population Projections: 1991*, February 1992, Table 3.

The second factor determining the viability of the system is the rate of increase of productivity. What matters is the income of those working relative to the benefits of the retirees. If incomes are rising rapidly, due to increased productivity, then there is more income available to support retirees. But the rate of productivity increase (and the associated rate of increase in incomes) has declined markedly—by more than half—since 1973,[17] exacerbating the fiscal problems.[18] Even if current signs of an upturn in productivity increase represent more than a short-run trend—it is too soon to tell—the upturn is too small to restore financial viability.

Social security is only one of several programs directed at the aged; others (Medicare, and the long-term-care part of Medicaid) were discussed in Chapter 12. They share in the problems we have just discussed: providing these programs for a growing aged population will impose increasing burdens on the working population. In the United States, the problem will be crystallized with the retirement of the baby boomers beginning sometime after the turn of the century. Most of the advanced industrialized countries face problems that are even more severe; and many of them—including Japan—will face the problem earlier.

Taken as a whole, these entitlement programs present an immense budgetary problem. Expenditures on them (as currently designed), as a percentage of GDP, are projected to more than double between 1997 and 2050, from 9 percent to about 20 percent. (See Figure 14.5.) Since, historically, the federal share of taxes in GDP has averaged around 19 to 20 percent, taxes would have to be increased substantially and/or other government programs would have to be cut back drastically in order to meet these expenditures.

Social security itself only contributes a small part of the problem: its expenditures are projected to grow from 4.7 percent of GDP to 6.3 percent. The social security problem is both smaller and easier to address. It is *just* a financial problem: either receipts (contributions) have to be increased or benefits reduced. The shortfall could be permanently corrected by a tax increase of around 3 percentage points, or a benefit decrease of a corresponding magnitude.[19]

[17] For the decades prior to 1973 the annual rate of increase of productivity averaged 2.9 percent; from 1973 through 1993 it averaged 1.1 percent. Since then, different statistics show either a slight increase or a slight decrease. See the *Economic Report of the President, 1997*.
[18] The problem has been made even worse by the increased inequality of incomes. Thus, even while average productivity and wages have increased, *median* real wages—which are much more relevant to the social security program—have not kept pace.
[19] There is some uncertainty about these numbers. The social security trustees estimate alternative scenarios, involving different rates of growth of production, population, etc. In the pessimistic scenario, the gap is twice as big. In the optimistic scenario, there is even a surplus under current arrangements.

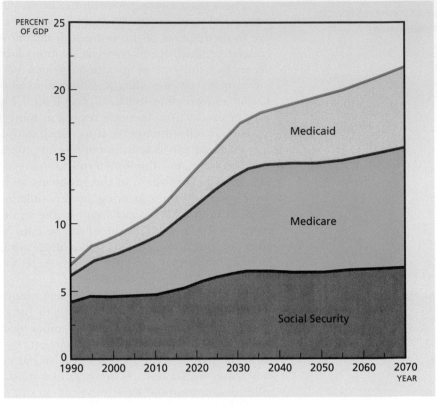

FIGURE 14.5   **Growth in Entitlement Spending** Social security, Medicare, and other entitlement spending are projected to increase to 20 percent or more of GDP, crowding out other government expenditures or necessitating major increases in taxation.

SOURCE: *Economic Report of the President, 1997*, Chart 3-4.

But Medicare and Medicaid's expenditures are increasing *both* because the number of aged are increasing *and* because the cost of delivering *the same set of benefits* is increasing. Thus, a major challenge facing those programs is to contain costs; this entails reforming the health care delivery system, a far more complicated issue. (See Chapter 12.)

There is particular concern that these programs, directed at the aged, are crowding out expenditures on children—investments in the country's future. As it is, the federal government now spends more than eleven times as much on each elderly person as it spends on each child.[20] And this is in

[20] The statistic, while widely quoted, may be somewhat misleading, since it includes federal social security payments, which can be thought of as benefits to which the individual has herself contributed, in the same way that she would have if she had purchased a retirement policy; only the *transfer* component should actually be included.

SOURCES OF FISCAL IMBALANCE

Decrease in population growth

Decrease in productivity growth

Decrease in retirement age

Increase in longevity

spite of the fact that children are far more likely to be in poverty than are the elderly.

SAVINGS The provision of social security reduces individuals' need to save for retirement. There is concern that this leads to lower aggregate savings, hence lower investment and growth in productivity. The magnitude of the effects on savings and its implications for growth and policy have been a subject of debate.

While Harvard professor (and former chairman of the Council of Economic Advisers) Martin Feldstein claims that social security may have led to a reduction in private savings in the United States of as much as 60 percent,[21] others argue that the effects are much smaller—and that the system may indeed have encouraged savings.[22] It allowed individuals to retire early, and as they thought about earlier retirement, they realized that they would need more than the amount provided by social security. This perspective is consistent with the marked growth of private pension plans, which occurred

[21] The original source for these arguments is Martin Feldstein, "Social Security, Induced Retirement, and Aggregate Capital Accumulation," *Journal of Political Economy* 82, no. 5 (1974): 905–26. In a more recent article, Feldstein attempted to answer his critics and show that his results were robust: "Social Security and Saving: New Time Series Evidence," *National Tax Journal* 49, no. 2 (June 1996): 151–64.

[22] There is considerable controversy concerning Feldstein's results, involving a number of technical issues. S. Danziger, R. Haveman, and R. Plotnick, in "How Income Transfers Affect Work, Savings, and Income Distribution" (*Journal of Economic Literature*, September 1981) conclude in their survey that the transfer programs (in which the effect of social security is dominant) " . . . have depressed annual private savings by 0 to 20 percent relative to their value without these programs, with the most likely estimate lying near the lower end of this range." Robert Barro has taken a more extreme view, and argued on theoretical grounds that the social security program should have no effect on savings, since parents simply adjust the bequests that they leave to their children in response to the social security program (providing larger bequests in response to the larger deficits). He has also attempted to provide empirical support for this proposition, though most economists remain skeptical. See R. J. Barro, *The Impact of Social Security on Private Savings* (Washington, D.C.: American Enterprise Institute, 1978).

after social security began, and which account for more than 60 percent of U.S. personal savings.[23]

In an open economy (in which the country can borrow from abroad), reduced savings need not be directly translated into reduced investment and thereby reduced productivity:[24] currently, it appears as if a $100 savings reduction will lead to an investment reduction of around $40 to $60. Thus, negative impacts on savings remain a source of concern.

The low savings rate in the United States is a problem that has probably contributed to the slow rate of productivity growth in recent decades. Though it is difficult to address the problem, and doing so would go well beyond a reform of social security, policy makers need to ask whether there are ways to reform social security that would enhance national savings. Recent changes in taxation—subjecting retirees with higher income to taxation on 85 percent of social security benefits—have the effect of reducing the net returns to savings, and thus the level of savings, for many individuals. One reform that would probably increase national savings would be fully funding social security, so that each generation puts aside funds for its own benefit. A more controversial reform, which some argue would increase savings, is privatization of social security. This topic is discussed later in the chapter.

LABOR SUPPLY

Social security also has an effect on labor supply: it induces individuals to retire earlier than they otherwise would. The large decline during recent decades in labor force participation of those over 65, which was noted above, has occurred at exactly the same time that there has been a large increase in social security benefits per recipient. (Between 1968 and 1976, real benefits were increased by 39 percent.) Michael Hurd of the State University of New York at Stony Brook and Michael Boskin of Stanford University argue that the decline in labor force participation was, indeed, due largely to the real increase in social security benefits.

Government programs have both income effects and substitution effects. Inefficiencies are associated with substitution effects. Both of these effects arise in the case of social security. The large transfer of resources to the elderly has an income effect; the elderly take some of this increased income in the form of extra leisure—early retirement. In addition there is a substitution effect, because social security changes the return to working.

There is, however, considerable controversy about the size, and even direction, of the substitution effect. As individuals work longer, their total contributions to social security increase, since they are taxed on their additional income. Their benefits per year are also increased. The question is, do the benefits increase *enough* to compensate for the increased payments?

---

[23] Bureau of Economic Analysis, *National Income and Product Accounts Annual Data*, Tables 2.1, 6.11B, 6.11C, and 8.18 for selected years.

[24] Even then, however, it leads to increased indebtedness to foreigners and thereby lower future standards of living.

At present the adjustment is not enough, but as a result of the reform act of 1983, by the year 2008, on average, there will be a full adjustment. And in recent years, there has been an effect encouraging workers to stay on: the magnitude of social security benefits depends on individuals' contributions in previous years. In 1937 their contributions were limited to the first $3000 of their income; in 1997 they were based on earnings up to $65,400. Thus the way social security benefits are calculated means that an individual with, say, a $40,000 income may now experience a significant increase in benefits by staying at work an additional year or two.

Eventually, however, for most individuals, the social security system will not act as much of a tax. Their increased contributions "buy" commensurately higher retirement income. The system acts as a tax only to the extent that individuals are forced to save more than they otherwise might, or that returns are lower than they might otherwise have obtained. Since most individuals do save beyond social security, it is not *forcing* them to save more than they would like. For poor individuals, the benefit formula generates returns to contributions that are beyond those that could be obtained elsewhere, and hence there is a positive substitution effect; while for rich individuals the opposite is true.

Note that there is a distortion of the labor-leisure choice whether individuals are subsidized or taxed. The fact that some individuals are subsidized and some are taxed does not result in the distortions' netting out: the total distortion is not simply related to the average value of the marginal subsidy or tax.

While for most individuals the substitution effects are probably small, there is one group—the elderly—for whom it is probably large, for two reasons. First, for those between 65 and 69, for every three dollars they earn above a certain amount, they lose one dollar of benefits, in effect a 33⅓ percent tax on earnings—besides having to pay income taxes on their additional earnings. As a result, a 66-year-old with a high income from investments could face an effective marginal tax rate of more than 60 percent on

EFFECTS OF SOCIAL SECURITY

Social security may have an adverse effect on savings:

- Reduces need for private savings for retirement.
- Reduced savings may result in lower investment and lower growth in productivity.

Social security may have an adverse effect on labor supply:

- The effect in general is probably small.
- The effect may be larger among older workers.

his wage income—and this does not include state and local income taxes.[25] Moreover, social security benefits are calculated on the basis of the individual's highest-earning thirty-five years; as a result, for many elderly individuals, especially those working part-time, benefits are completely unaffected by their additional earnings; for them, social security contributions are simply taxes.

THE RATE OF RETURN

The fourth complaint, voiced increasingly, is that social security does not provide a rate of return comparable to that obtained in private retirement accounts. The complaint was not heard in the past, because then benefits far exceeded contributions, as we have noted. But it has been heard since the 1983 reforms, as a semblance of fiscal responsibility was striven for. The complaint is, in one sense, not quite accurate. The return should be contrasted with a security with comparable risk properties—a U.S. government bond that is indexed against inflation. Though these bonds have not been around long enough to be sure what they will yield in the long run, especially if the United States encounters a period of high and variable inflation, it appears as if the returns are comparable (perhaps slightly higher) than would be obtained if the funds had been invested in such securities. The returns are substantially lower than obtained on the stock market when it is having a boom—as it did beginning in 1995, but substantially higher than obtained on the stock market when it is going through a slump—as it has periodically, as with the stock market crashes of 1929 and 1987. Investments in equity thus have greater returns, but also greater risks.[26]

But the question is really misplaced. The United States has a pay-as-you-go system; in a pay-as-you-go system, the long-run return (in equilibrium) is related to the rate of growth of the economy, which will typically be lower than the rate of return on capital.[27] The low rate of return is not

---

[25] Assume a 66-year-old earns $100 more, and is in the 40 percent marginal tax bracket, so after tax, he gets to keep only $60. He loses $33 in benefits. With 85 percent of social security benefits taxable, the "net" cost of this loss is only $22. Netting this from his $60, however, leaves him with only $38: in effect, he faces a 62 percent marginal tax rate.

[26] There is actually some controversy over this issue: a widely diversified portfolio of stock held for more than twenty-five years invested in *any* year since 1930 would have done better than a comparable investment in government securities. But this is no guarantee that this will be true in the future. Indeed, as investors have become aware of these differential returns, they have bid up the price of equities, reducing their returns.

[27] This can be seen in a stylized overlapping generations model, where each generation lives for two periods, working in the first. In the absence of growth, a tax on the young used to pay retirement benefits for the old generates a "return" of zero: each generation gets back exactly the amount that they have contributed. If population is growing at the rate n and wages are growing at the rate p, then for each dollar of contributions made when they are young, workers receive back $(1 + n)(1 + p)$ when they are old.

the result of a failure to invest well—or a result of high transactions costs
(indeed, transactions costs are remarkably low)—but simply the result of
having a pay-as-you-go system. Returns could be increased, but only by
switching out of the system; as we shall see later, doing so would entail a
sacrifice in consumption on the part of the generations involved in the
switch.

INEQUITIES It is in the nature of any insurance program that some individuals get back
more than they contribute in premiums, and some less. Buyers of fire insurance who do not have a fire "lose," and those whose house burns down gain.
In social security, those who live long get back far more than they contribute, while those who die before retirement get back less. This in itself is
not inequitable.

But within social security, those who make similar contributions get
back *on average* different amounts. That is, their *expected* paybacks differ because of differences in family status. To some, these differences are viewed
as inequitable: why should someone simply get more because he or she
chooses to get married?[28]

Of course, because there is a redistributive aspect of social security, for
some people benefits relative to contributions may be large. To most observers, this is not inequitable, so long as those receiving the redistribution
are in some sense "deserving." But in determining the magnitude of the redistribution, social security only looks at the individual's social security contributions, not his wealth or nonwage income.

REASONS FOR REFORM

Fiscal imbalance

Adverse effect on savings

Adverse effect on labor supply

Low (*perceived*) rate of return

Inequities—different actuarial benefits among those making similar
contributions; redistribution not based on overall assessment of need

---

[28] Since married men tend to live longer, even if there were no spousal benefits, the
actuarial benefits of married men would exceed those of single men making comparable contributions.

There are other examples of possible inequities: Because women live longer
than men, for comparable contributions women receive back more than men; because nonsmokers live longer than smokers, for comparable contributions they receive back more. Private insurance firms would adjust payments to reflect differences in life expectancies (where they are allowed to do so).

REFORMING SOCIAL SECURITY

There are two sets of proposals for reforming social security. A set of modest proposals entails reducing expenditures and increasing revenues to bring the program into fiscal balance, with only modest changes in its structure. A set of more drastic reforms entails significant structural changes, among them privatizing social security.

REDUCING EXPENDITURES

A number of proposals have been put forward for reducing expenditures without undermining the overall effectiveness of the program.

ADJUSTMENTS OF BENEFIT FORMULAE The formula for determining benefits could be adjusted in ways which would slightly reduce expenditures, and might even enhance efficiency and equity. For instance, as was noted earlier, currently benefits are based on the highest thirty-five years of contributions. Individuals who work longer—but whose income in those later working years is not among their best—receive no increase in benefits in return for their additional contributions. The formula could be adjusted in ways which do not affect benefits of most workers who have been full-time participants in the work force all of their lives, but which at the same time provide greater incentives for work and reduce benefits for those who are currently being encouraged to retire earlier because of the peculiar way that benefits are calculated.

ADJUSTING THE NORMAL RETIREMENT AGE The 1983 reforms increased the normal retirement age at a very gradual pace, to 67 by the year 2022. The argument for increasing the retirement age is that better overall health has led to increased longevity (contributing to the system's financial problem); on average, individuals should be able to remain in the labor force longer. (There is a certain irony that at the same time, the actual retirement age has been coming down.) However, there is a wide range of health conditions: a substantial number of elderly have sufficiently poor health that they must retire at 65 or 62. Increasing the "normal" retirement age still further—say, to 68—will reduce the benefits for these individuals, by 10 percent or more. This could impose severe hardship on many of these people, who often have few assets or other sources of income. Advocates of increasing the retirement age give two answers: If such individuals truly have to retire, then they should be covered by disability; and if reducing benefits imposes real hardship, they should become eligible for supplementary income benefits. Changing the retirement age may necessitate concomitant adjustments in the disability and supplementary income programs, but this is no reason not to make an adjustment in retirement age in line with changes in current conditions.

ADJUSTMENT OF THE COST OF LIVING INDEX Once an individual retires, his benefits increase with the rate of inflation, as measured by the consumer price index (CPI). But there is widespread agreement that for a variety of technical reasons, the CPI overstates increases in the cost of living. A commission appointed by the Senate Finance Committee and headed by Michael Boskin, who had been chairman of the Council of Economic Advisers under President Bush, reported in December 1996 that they believed that the CPI overstated inflation by 1.1 percent per year. Even a half-percent correction in the CPI would reduce the long-term social security deficit substantially, by as much as a third.

Some worry that the consumer price index, which is based on the cost of living on average, understates increases in the true cost of living of the elderly, especially because the elderly have higher medical costs. But the rise in medical costs recently has appeared to be contained; and those who have looked carefully at the quality improvements in medical care believe that medical costs represent one of the major areas of overstatement—adjusting for quality, health care costs may be increasing more slowly than prices in general, and might even be decreasing.

As in the case of changing the retirement age, it may be desirable to make concomitant adjustments in the disability and supplementary income programs at the same time that a CPI adjustment is made; but to the extent that the CPI adjustment accurately reflects changes in cost of living, the CPI adjustment is intended merely to ensure that inflation itself does not impose additional hardship on the aged. Inflation also should not be an excuse for providing unintended increases in real benefits. If there is a desire to increase real benefits—unlikely, given the financial stringency facing the system—then there should be an explicit decision to do so.

MEANS TESTING BENEFITS Social security is an unusual program: it redistributes income, but in doing so, does not look at the overall well-being of the recipient, but only on his (social security) wage income. A billionaire who worked little during his life—and so had low wages—would receive back far more than his social security contributions, an amount identical to that received by an unskilled worker with the same history. Thus, subjecting at least the redistributive component of social security to means testing would increase equity and reduce expenditures.

Opposition to means testing has, however, been strong; for it would make explicit the redistribution role of social security. Today, many if not most individuals think of social security more as a government-run retirement program, to which they make contributions (pay premiums), with benefits commensurate with the contributions. Making social security means tested would convert it into a welfare program; and social security advocates worry that in the long run, this will undermine support for the program.

INCREASING REVENUES The major proposal for increasing revenues is to subject social security payments to taxation. We noted earlier the anomalous nature of social security redistributions. There is a similar anomaly in the tax treatment of social security. The general principle of taxation is that taxes should be based on "ability to pay"; individuals with higher income should pay higher taxes. An important exception (which will be discussed more extensively in later chapters) is that much of retirement savings is tax-exempt; this is so partly to encourage individuals to save more for their retirement, or at least not to discourage them from saving. Individuals' own social security contributions are included in their income, and are subject to tax; but the contributions that employers make on behalf of their workers are not included in individuals' incomes, and accordingly are not taxed. At the same time, in the past none of social security benefits were taxed; today, for upper-income individuals, 85 percent of the benefits—representing roughly the employer's share of the contributions plus interest—is taxed. But there is no theoretical rationale for imposing the tax only on upper-income individuals. Two elderly individuals could have exactly the same retirement income, one derived exclusively from social security, the other derived largely from IRAs, but pay different taxes. From this perspective, subjecting social security income to treatment comparable to other forms of retirement savings would increase equity at the same time as it raised revenue.

SUMMARY These reforms could make a significant impact on social security's fiscal situation. By one calculation, simply raising social security retirement age, adjusting the cost-of-living increases, instituting means testing, and making more of social security benefits taxable could restore fiscal balance, at least through the year 2030.

STRUCTURAL REFORMS

Several minor structural reforms which would increase equity, increase efficiency, and improve social security's financial position have already been noted: changes in the benefit formula to make benefits increase with contributions; means testing at least the redistributive component of social security; and subjecting social security at least to taxation comparable to other forms of retirement savings.

The dependence of social security benefits (relative to contributions) on family status has also been strongly criticized. Currently, nonworking spouses receive substantial benefits, so the actuarial benefits of a married worker whose spouse does not work outside the home are substantially higher than those of a single worker who has made the same contributions. Similarly, the returns relative to contributions are lower for a family in which both husband and wife work. Advocates of this preferential treatment sometimes argue that spouses who remain at home to raise children work too, and therefore should receive retirement benefits. But that is not the issue; the issue is the magnitude of the benefits relative to social security contributions. Spousal benefits could be provided, but the monthly benefits would be adjusted to ensure that those who make comparable contributions receive comparable *actuarial* benefits. These inequities might have been overlooked in the past, when there was one predominant family structure, with a man working and his wife staying at home. Given today's varying patterns of family structures and work, there is increasing concern about these inequities.

There are two major proposed changes beyond these structural reforms. One entails social security investing its trust funds in equities. The other entails privatization of social security.

INVESTING TRUST FUNDS IN EQUITIES For at least the past seventy-five years, any-one who invested broadly in equities (stocks) and held them for twenty years or more would have done better than if she had invested a comparable amount in government bonds. For these long holding periods, stocks have earned substantially higher expected returns—some estimates put the differ-ence of average returns at 4 percent per year or higher—with no additional risk. If a fraction of the social security trust fund were invested in a broad base of equities, the financial position of social security would accordingly be improved. Simulation exercises based on the distribution of returns of equi-ties over the past seventy-five years show that, even if no other reforms were undertaken, the life of the trust fund could be substantially extended. Advo-cates of this proposal suggest further that the increased demand for equities will increase the price of equities, and hence lead to increased investment.

But critics raise three objections. First, they worry about risk. Another major stock market crash—such as that of 1987 or 1929—is always possible. (This objection can be raised even more forcefully against privatization pro-posals; at least with the trust fund, there is the possibility of smoothing any losses that occur over an extended period of time.) Second, critics worry that because today much of the deficit is "financed" by borrowing from so-cial security (the social security trust fund invests its holdings today solely in government debt), government borrowing costs will increase. Thus, while social security's financial position may be improved, that of the rest of the government will become worse. There are no reliable estimates of the ex-tent to which interest rates would rise—and therefore of the adverse bud-getary impacts. Many economists, however, believe that the worldwide de-mand for U.S. government securities is sufficiently thick that the interest rate effects of social security investing, say, 30 percent of its trust funds in equity would be modest, and far smaller than the increased revenues that the Social Security Administration would be receiving.

Third, there is concern that the resulting government ownership of equi-ties would affect the private equities market. Some worry about how the shares would be voted. But even after the trust fund had invested 30 percent of its funds in equities, studies suggest that government ownership would be under 5 percent of the market. If these were treated as effectively nonvoting shares, the effect on the functioning of the stock market would be insignificant.

PRIVATIZATION The boldest set of reforms, which has increasingly been the subject of discussion, is privatization. A few countries, such as Chile, have privatized their social security system. It is alleged that privatization will in-crease savings—and Chile's recent experience, where savings increased to more than 20 percent of GDP, supports that view.

But there are some reasons why Chile's experience cannot be extrapo-lated to the United States economy, and some cautionary aspects as well. Chile, like the United States, had a pay-as-you-go system; privatization re-quires funding the unfunded liability. For the United States, these un-funded liabilities amount to over $8 trillion.[29] Chile used the funds from pri-

[29] Peterson, *Will America Grow Up before It Grows Old?*, p. 18.

SOCIAL SECURITY ABROAD

Many countries have faced problems with their social security systems. For instance, in many European countries, expenditures on social security not only are much larger than in the United States, but have grown more rapidly. As a result, payroll taxes (earmarked, as in the United States, for social security) are high: for example, 28 percent in the Netherlands and 27 percent in Italy. There has been increasing concern within these countries about the incentive effects of such high tax rates (particularly when combined with high income tax rates).

In some countries, the social security system (at least before recent reforms) gave rise to far larger distortions as well as budgetary problems. In Uruguay, benefits were especially related to the last few years of an individual's working life; not surprisingly, large incomes were reported during those years.

In recent years, many countries have undertaken major reforms, privatizing at least part of their social security system. Chile's reforms have received perhaps the most attention. Chile used proceeds from privatizing its copper mines to fund the switch from a pay-as-you-go system to a fully funded system with individual accounts. After the reform, savings rates increased substantially. The individual accounts spurred the country's mutual funds industry. While great care was

vatization of one of its major industries, its copper mines. If the United States privatized, it would have to fund the unfunded liability in some other way. One suggestion would be a tax—a value added of around 2 percent, for seventy-five years, or a wage tax at a somewhat higher rate. Note however that if there were a willingness to pay higher taxes of this magnitude, then social security would face no significant financial problems and no drastic remedies such as privatization would need to be contemplated.

The two major motivations for the drive for privatization are that private investments provide a higher return, and that national savings would be increased. But as was noted earlier, the low return on social security is not because of high transactions costs, or poor investment strategies; it is mainly because of the pay-as-you-go structure. By switching to a fully funded system, later generations could achieve a higher return; but the temporary (seventy-five years!) tax to finance the transition would be equivalent to lowering the welfare (returns) of the intervening generations. We have also noted that the trust fund could be invested in equities, generating higher returns; and because of the greater potential for smoothing returns over longer periods of time, the associated risk might be considerably lower than the risks associated with private investments in equities.

taken to prevent abuses, transactions costs were still very high and the euphoria with the system faded in the mid-1990s, when share returns fell. Individuals finally realized that while in a growth market returns might exceed those that they had received under the former system, in a slump returns could even be negative. Individuals bore more risk under the privatized system.

These concerns heightened in the financial crisis afflicting less developed countries in 1997 and 1998, which saw stock prices in less developed countries collapse 30 percent, 50 percent, or more. Had workers invested a large part of their retirement savings in the stock market, they could have been left destitute. Government bailouts might follow, so that at least part of the improvement in the fiscal position as a result of privatization would prove to be a mirage. Advocates of privatization say there is an easy answer: individuals in LDCs should invest in stock markets in the more developed countries. But unless there are offsetting inflows from other countries, one of the other major advantages of privatization—an increase of funds available for productive investments—will also prove to be a mirage. And in any case, most less-developed countries may find it difficult to justify a government program that, in effect, provides capital from the poor countries to help the rich!

Indeed, while in the early days of Chile's privatized social security system there was considerable enthusiasm, as it coincided with a period of high stock returns, when the returns fell enthusiasm diminished considerably, as investors began to comprehend more fully the high transactions costs (especially associated with the high selling costs), and the high risk. The Advisory Council on Social Security, in its December 1996 report, suggested that even in the United States, the transactions costs would be substantial, upward of 100 basis points per year (that is, for every $100,000 investment, $1000 would go to Wall Street brokers and other investment agents)—substantially higher than the costs that the Social Security Administration would face even if it invested in equities.

In the long run, the savings rate under a fully funded social security or retirement system would be higher than under a pay-as-you-go system, though the differences are often exaggerated. This is because under a fully funded social security or retirement system, the elderly are dissaving, at the same time that the young are saving. Net national savings is only the difference between the two. If the economy is growing very slowly, then this difference is likely to be small, and so the contribution to net national savings from retirement savings will be small. The problem is, what will happen to savings in the transition to a fully funded system? If, instead of making a transition to a privatized system, one imposed the same 2 percent tax and used the proceeds to create a larger trust fund (government savings), then national savings in the short run would be increased a comparable amount. *The increased savings arises from switching from a pay-as-you-go to a fully funded system; it does not arise from the privatization of the system itself.*

The arguments for and against privatization—beyond the lower transactions costs of a public system, and the greater ability of a government program to engage in redistributions and to smooth risks within and across generations—are largely political. Would a public system really have the resolve to remain fully funded? While under privatization the government *could* engage in similar redistributions and risk sharing, but *would* it? But if the redistribution were undertaken only because it was hidden in the gizzards of a quite complicated benefit formula, would this be appropriate—isn't transparency one of the fundamental tenets of democratic decision-making?

To many, there is one fundamental political economy issue: Can the federal government make the relatively minor adjustments required to restore the program to long-run financial viability? If it cannot, the hard bud-

PRIVATIZATION OF SOCIAL SECURITY

Advantages	Disadvantages
Increase savings.	Same impact can be had by switching to a fully funded social security system.
Enforce hard budget constraint.	Restricts ability to engage in redistributions and risk sharing within and across generations.
Increase returns.	Higher transactions costs may actually lower returns.
	Transition requires taxes to fund unfunded liability, lowering welfare (returns) for transition generations.
	If individuals invest in excessively risky investments, they may become public charges in old age; avoiding this was one reason for introducing social security in first place.

get constraints imposed by privatization may be the only way out of the political morass in which problems are continually being passed from one generation to the next.

REVIEW AND PRACTICE

SUMMARY

1   Governments provide social insurance because markets failed to provide insurance against many of the most important risks facing individuals. Private insurance markets face problems of adverse selection, moral hazard, and high transactions costs, and of insuring against social risks.

2   Another important motivation for social security is a moral hazard problem: if the government provides substantial assistance for the aged who are destitute because they have made no provision for their old age, then individuals will have insufficient incentive to provide for their own old age.

3   The social security retirement program is a forced savings program, an insurance program, and a transfer program.

4   The social security program has an effect on labor supply (most notably through its effect on early retirements) and on capital formation (through its effect on savings). There is dispute about the significance of these effects.

5   Changes in birth rates and life expectancy, in labor force participation among the aged, and in the rate of growth of productivity all contributed to recent financial crises facing the social security system.

6   While in recent years several of the inequities in the social security program and features which contribute to inefficiencies have been corrected, several remain, including the differential treatment of families in different circumstances.

7   Restoring financial viability requires either changing benefits, such as by correcting the adjustment for increases in the cost of living, adjusting the benefit formulae, or means testing benefits; or increasing revenues, such as by subjecting social security benefits to taxation. Many of these reforms would increase equity and/or efficiency.

8   More drastic reforms include investing a portion of the social security trust fund in equities, and privatization.

KEY CONCEPTS

Social security	Modified pay-as-you-go basis
Annuity	Indexing
Fully funded system	Social risks

1   For each of the major aspects of the social security program
(retirement insurance, survivors insurance, disability insurance) describe
the market failures that gave rise to the program or that might be used to
justify its continuation. Assume you were asked to design a program that
was to address only one of the market failures. For as many market failures
as you can, describe an alternative program to the present system and
explain its advantages and disadvantages over the present one.

2   List the risks against which the social security program provides
insurance. In which of these instances do you think providing insurance
affects the likelihood of the insured-against event's occurring?

3   What are the theoretical reasons why social security might be expected
to decrease savings? Are there any theoretical reasons why social security
might be expected to increase savings? Why might a tax on interest income
lead to later retirements? Under what circumstances might such a tax be
desirable?

4   Discuss the equity and efficiency effects of the following recent and
proposed changes in the social security system and, where appropriate,
provide alternative reforms directed at the same objective:

  a   Changing the formula by which social security benefits are calculated
      to reflect total contributions, not just the contributions in a limited
      number of years.

  b   Tougher eligibility standards for disability payments.

  c   Increasing the eligibility age for social security benefits.

  d   Increasing benefits for those who retire later so that they receive the
      same expected present discounted value of benefits, regardless of age
      of retirement.

  e   Exempting those over the age of 65 from paying social security taxes.

  f   Lowering the cost of living adjustment for social security benefits.

5   To what extent could the purposes of the social security program be
served by a law requiring individuals to purchase retirement insurance from
a private firm? Discuss difficulties with such a proposal, and what kinds of
regulations might be required to avoid these difficulties.

6   Do you think social security benefits, unemployment benefits, or
disability payments should be treated like ordinary income for purposes of
the income tax?

7   Smokers do not live as long as nonsmokers. This means that the
expected present discounted value of social security benefits for smokers is
much smaller than that for nonsmokers. Is this unfair? What differences in
individual or family circumstances should the social security program
recognize?

8 If individuals are risk averse, why do they care more about large losses—that is, why are they willing to pay a larger amount in excess of the actuarial value of the losses for insurance? What does this imply for the design of social insurance?

9 Consider a 68-year-old individual facing a 39.6 percent marginal tax rate, with no wage income. Assume that if he earns a dollar, he loses 50 cents in social security benefits, and that 85 percent of his social security benefits are included in his taxable income. Calculate his total marginal tax rate.

If he lives in California and faces an 11 percent state income tax, what is his marginal tax rate?

Assume he is self-employed, and must pay an additional 15 percent self-employment tax (a social security tax), but that his social security payments do not increase at all. Half of the tax is deductible from his income for purposes of his income tax. What is his marginal tax rate now?

10 Consider a simple life-cycle model, in which individuals live for two periods; they work in the first, saving for the second. Let C_1 denote consumption in the first period, C_2 consumption in the second. Let r denote the interest rate, w the wage. Then

1 $C_2 = (w - C_1)(1 + r).$

Assume there is no growth, and savings are used to buy capital goods, which last for one year, so

2 $K = w - C_1,$

where K = capital stock. The gross output of the economy, Q, increases with the capital stock,

3 $Q = F(K),$

the interest rate is the marginal product of capital,

4 $1 + r = F'(K),$

and workers receive what is left over,

5 $wL = F - KF'(K),$

where L is the labor supply, which for convenience, we set equal to 1.

Individuals supply labor inelastically, but decide how much to consume by maximizing

$U(C_1, C_2),$

the two-period utility function, subject to (1).

Describe the market equilibrium. You may find the following graphical interpretation useful. Put C_2 on the vertical axis and C_1 on the horizontal. Plot the set of feasible combinations, using equations (1) through (5). For each K there is a value of the wage; for each value of consumption in the two periods there is a value of the marginal rate of substitution, the amount of consumption while working individuals are willing to trade off for more consumption in retirement. In equilibrium, the marginal rate of substitution equals the interest rate. Through any point on the feasibility locus, you can draw a line with slope equal to $1 + r$ (this just depends on K), and you can draw the indifference curve. The equilibrium point along the feasibility locus is the point where the two are tangent *at that point.*

Now explore how a pay-as-you-go social security system changes the equilibrium. Let T be the transfer from the younger generation to the older. Now

$$C_2 = (w - T - C_1)(1 + r) + T.$$

Show how the equilibrium may be affected, and why the capital stock may be smaller.

Welfare Programs and the Redistribution of Income

15

FOCUS QUESTIONS

1 What are the major welfare programs? How have they grown over time? To what extent did the growth of welfare programs account for the growth in the deficit in the 1980s?

2 What are the dimensions of the poverty problem in the United States? How has it changed over time?

3 What is the effect of welfare programs on labor supply? What other distortions are associated with welfare programs?

4 In what forms are welfare benefits received? What is the distinction between categorical and broad-based assistance? What are the efficiency and equity issues associated with each of these forms of assistance?

5 What has been the impetus for welfare reform? What have been the major reform proposals? What are the major components of the 1996 welfare reform bill, and what are the likely consequences?

All societies have made some provision for the poor and destitute. We call programs that transfer cash and consumption goods to the poor **public assistance** or **welfare** programs. The manner in which the very poor are taken care of has changed dramatically over time. In medieval Europe the church took responsibility, often establishing almshouses. In modern societies, governments play a

385

major role. In this century, there have been two dramatic changes in the manner in which government fulfills that role. The first was in 1935, when the federal government first took on a major responsibility for welfare under the **Aid to Families with Dependent Children (AFDC)** program. The second was on August 22, 1996, when President Clinton signed a historic bill, the Personal Responsibility and Work Opportunity Reconciliation Act of 1996, which even changed the name of the assistance program from AFDC to TANF, **Temporary Assistance for Needy Families.** This act culminated a movement for reforming the welfare system that had been the subject of increasing national attention.

In his presidential campaign four years earlier, Clinton had accompanied his promise to "end welfare as we know it" with the slogans "a hand up, not a hand out" and "making work pay." Welfare, it was felt, had created a kind of dependency; there was widespread agreement that the welfare system had to be restructured to help those on welfare get off welfare and become productive members of the labor force. This required economic incentives—it had to pay to work rather than to be on welfare. But it was felt that the carrot of increased income would not suffice: there had to be a stick—the termination of welfare payments after a fixed period of time (two to five years).

Though the antipathy to welfare was partly based on its seeming failure, it was also largely driven by a misperception. The federal deficit had become a major source of concern in the 1990s. There was a widespread impression that welfare was largely responsible, and that many on welfare were taking the system for a free ride. But in fact, total welfare expenditures have never amounted to a large fraction of total government expenditures. In 1996 total welfare expenditures were less than 10 percent of total federal government outlays, and welfare expenditures excluding Medicaid were only 4 percent of total outlays. Even complete elimination of welfare expenditures—a far more Draconian measure than anyone was proposing—would not have eliminated the deficit. Indeed, the magnitude of the spending cuts enacted under the new legislation did not significantly alter the status of the federal deficit.

Ironically, shortly after the passage of the bill, not only did the fiscal deficit cease to be an immediate problem—the federal government turned a large surplus, for the first time in three decades—but welfare rolls declined precipitously, partly because of the booming economy which had brought overall unemployment rates down to 4.3 percent, to levels which also had not been seen in three decades.

This chapter provides a brief review of the history of the U.S. welfare policy and programs, a summary of the major analytic issues, and a discussion of the 1996 welfare bill, explaining why it was so controversial and describing ongoing efforts at further reforms.

A BRIEF DESCRIPTION OF MAJOR U.S. WELFARE PROGRAMS

In the United States, while states and localities have long provided some form of general assistance to the needy, supplementing church and other voluntary programs, the federal government took on major responsibility in the New Deal in the 1930s. The Social Security Act of 1935 established Aid to Families with Dependent Children (AFDC) to provide assistance to families without a major breadwinner and **Supplemental Security Income (SSI)** to provide funds to aged and disabled individuals with low incomes (supplementing social security payments).

The next major expansion of federal welfare programs occurred when President Johnson declared a "War on Poverty" in the 1960s. As part of that war, a number of programs were introduced, including Medicaid, to provide medical assistance, which has subsequently become the largest assistance program in dollar terms. The following sections describe briefly the major programs.

AFDC AND TANF

Since 1935, AFDC had been the primary cash program in the U.S. welfare system. The program was a combination of federal and state programs. The states not only administered AFDC, but set benefit levels, and had some discretion over rules. The federal government provided a fraction of the funds, which varied from approximately one-half to three-fourths, depending on the state's per capita income. Programs in which federal outlays depend on state expenditures are called **matching programs.** The federal matching subsidy presumably resulted in the states' providing higher levels of benefits than they would have if they had had to pay the full (marginal) costs themselves. States were given considerable discretion in determining the level of expenditures. Not surprisingly, there was considerable variation in the level of benefits provided by the states, with the highest benefits, in Alaska, being more than seven times the lowest benefits, in Mississippi. Expenditures also varied greatly over time. While total expenditures (in real 1996 dollars) increased from $19 billion in 1970 to $22 billion in 1996, the total number of beneficiaries almost doubled in that period, from 7.4 million to 12.6 million, so that average benefits per family declined by almost half, from $734 to $374.[1]

Over time, the details of the federal program varied. Any **means-tested** program of assistance—that is, any program where benefits are targeted to those with low incomes—has to reduce benefits as income rises. Before 1979, welfare recipients' benefits were cut $67 for every increase of $100 in earned income beyond a certain minimal amount, an effective marginal tax rate of 67 percent. After 1979, the effective tax rate was raised to 100 percent, though some allowance was made for child care expenses.

Starting in 1997, TANF replaced AFDC. TANF represented a marked departure from the earlier system in two ways. First, it replaced the old sys-

---

[1] U.S. House of Representatives, Committee on Ways and Means, *Background Material and Data on Programs within the Jurisdiction of the Committee on Ways and Means: 1998 Green Book*, p. 413. This is a report published every few years by the House Ways and Means Committee which provides the most complete compilation on the welfare programs. It is generally referred to as simply the *Green Book* (reflecting the color of its cover). Much of the data for this chapter is drawn from the 1998 and 1996 reports, and in the references below, will be referred to simply as *1998 Green Book* or *1996 Green Book.*

tem of matching grants with **block grants,** a fixed amount of money, with states given considerable discretion in how that money could be spent (including discretion in determining the eligibility of needy families and the benefits and services those families receive). Secondly, TANF focused on moving individuals from welfare to work. The states were given broad flexibility in the design and operation of their welfare-to-work programs, but the use of TANF funds had to be consistent with federal priorities of strong work requirements, time limits to receiving assistance, a reduction in welfare dependency, and the encouragement of two-parent families.

THE EARNED INCOME TAX CREDIT

This program, known by its acronym, **EITC,** supplements the income of low-income families with children[2] by an amount which depends on their income and number of children. While in the 1980s this amount was small, and was intended to offset social security contributions, in 1993 the EITC was greatly expanded: a worker with two dependents could have his income supplemented by as much as 40 percent. Thus, a worker receiving $5 an hour has his wage increased, in effect, to $7 an hour. The maximum benefit in 1996 was $3556. Under the old AFDC program, these benefits were not counted as income for the purposes of determining benefit levels, so individuals were still better off as a result of working. If a worker receiving this maximum benefit earned an extra $100 of income, though his AFDC benefits would go down by approximately $100, his EITC payment would go up by $40, so that he faced an effective tax rate of "only" 60 percent. On the other hand, as income increases beyond $11,650, the benefit is reduced (by about 21 cents for each extra dollar earned); benefits are completely phased out when income reaches $28,495. TANF has no provision regarding treatment of earned and unearned income. States set their own income limits and make their own rules governing the treatment of earnings and other income, so the interaction between TANF and EITC may vary from state to state.

The number of families receiving EITC benefits grew from 6.2 million at its inception in 1975 to 18 million in 1996; the average credit per family grew from $200 to $1400, and the total expenditures grew from $1.25 billion to $25 billion.

FOOD STAMPS

TANF is the principal **cash welfare program.** Most assistance to the poor is directed at benefits **in-kind,** such as medical care, or to finance particular categories of expenditure, such as food and energy. Food stamps, first introduced in 1975 on a nationwide basis, are designed to assist poor individuals in buying food. The federal government bears essentially all the costs, and sets uniform benefit levels. The benefits depend on a measure of income, which allows a variety of adjustments, the most important of which is that housing expenditures are deductible. For each $100 increase in income net

[2] The 1993 law added a small credit (with a maximum of $306) for childless workers earning less than $9000 per year. (All EITC figures are indexed for inflation, so that currently, the maximum credit is somewhat greater.)

of housing expenditures, benefits are reduced by $30. Thus, the food stamp program imposes a 30 percent income tax and a 30 percent subsidy on housing. Though total benefits more than doubled between 1975 and 1996, because of the more than 50 percent increase in beneficiaries average monthly benefits increased only about 40 percent over those twenty-one years. In 1996, average monthly benefits per person were $73.30 and about $175 per household.[3] The welfare reform bill passed in 1996 left the basic structure of food stamps unchanged, but limited benefits of working-age adults without children. Such individuals cannot receive food stamps more than three months in a thirty-six-month period if they have not worked twenty hours a week, completed a job training program, or participated in a **workfare** program. (Workfare programs provide assistance in exchange for work.)

While food stamps are the most important "food" program, two others should be noted. Twenty-five million children receive free or subsidized lunches, and five million children receive free or subsidized breakfasts. These programs were started when, in the nationwide draft for World War II, the extent of malnutrition in poor children was first widely recognized; moreover, educators have long argued that inadequate nutrition adversely affected learning.

An additional 1.5 million pregnant women, infants, and children under 5 who are at risk of inadequate nutrition receive food support under the **Special Supplemental Nutrition Program for Women, Infants, and Children (WIC).** Inadequate nutrition at these points can have lifelong effects, particularly on a child's ability to learn. While the other programs described so far are **entitlement programs**—that is, anyone meeting the criteria are entitled to receive the benefits, and total federal expenditures thus depend simply on the number of individuals who are eligible and who decide to apply—the federal government provides a fixed amount of money to support the WIC program.

MEDICAID

Established in 1966, this program provides medical assistance to the poor, especially poor children; medical care to the disabled; and nursing home care to a large proportion of the aged. Medicaid is a federal-state government matching program, with the federal government paying between 50 and 83 percent of the costs, depending on the state's per capita income. The states were given considerable discretion in determining **eligibility** and coverage. The program recently covered approximately 36 million low-income individuals, including 18 million children.

Historically, families receiving benefits under AFDC were eligible for Medicaid. Though TANF families are not automatically eligible, states are still required to provide Medicaid to children and family members who would have been eligible for AFDC using the program's terms as of July 16, 1996 (making

[3] The gross monthly income eligibility limit is set at 130 percent of the poverty threshold (poverty line), a measure of the minimum subsistence level required for, say, a family of four. In 1996, the amount of the threshold for a family of four was $16,036.

adjustments for inflation). Eligibility for Medicaid is thus based on a **threshold test**: those with incomes above the threshold (essentially, the cutoff level of AFDC) are not eligible. Because many employers do not provide medical benefits to low-income workers, many of those on welfare find themselves in a bind: even if they would like to work, they lose eligibility for Medicaid benefits if they accept a job. This is particularly important for those with children requiring medical attention. As a result, they are reluctant to move off welfare. This situation is referred to as **welfare lock.** States can remove adults from Medicaid rolls if they refuse to comply with the work requirements of TANF.

A new program providing health care for children was also recently created. The **Children's Health Insurance Program (CHIP)** was passed as part of the Balanced Budget Act of 1997. CHIP is the largest single expansion of health insurance coverage for children in more than thirty years. This new initiative set aside $24 billion over five years for states to provide new health coverage for children with family income below 200 percent of the federal poverty threshold.

HOUSING

In 1996, 5.7 million households received a total of almost $26.1 billion of housing assistance in a myriad of programs. In constant dollars, outlays per housing unit have almost doubled over the past two decades, to $5490 in 1997. Originally, the government provided public housing for the poor. These programs were greatly criticized on several grounds. Costs were high for the quality of housing that was provided—the government seemed an inefficient producer and manager of housing. Worse, government housing projects isolated the poor; they became "warehouses of the poor." The government was unable to maintain them adequately, and they became infested with crime, drugs, and rats.

By the mid-1990s, the problems had become so manifest that the federal government set about tearing down the worst of these projects, ending "public housing as we know it." In one famous incident, the city of St. Louis leveled its Pruit-Igoe project with dynamite rather than trying to maintain the facility. By 1997, the number of occupied public housing units had declined 12 percent from the 1985 level.[4] In their place, several other programs designed to provide improved incentives and greater social integration were expanded. These programs include tax credits to builders for mixed-income housing; mortgage and rent subsidies; and "housing vouchers." Housing vouchers are like food stamps: they give the recipient a certain amount to be spent on housing.

OTHER PROGRAMS

There are many other means-tested programs. The **Low-Income Home Energy Assistance Program (LIHEAP)** is one. A variety of education programs exist, such as Head Start, which provides preschool education for children of low-income families, and Pell Grants, which help pay for college education for children in low-income families. Still other programs provide job training to unskilled and economically disadvantaged individuals.

[4] Department of Housing and Urban Development web page, "1997 Picture of Subsidized Households Quick Facts," [http://www.huduser.org/], and *Statistical Abstract of the United States, 1996,* Table 1203.

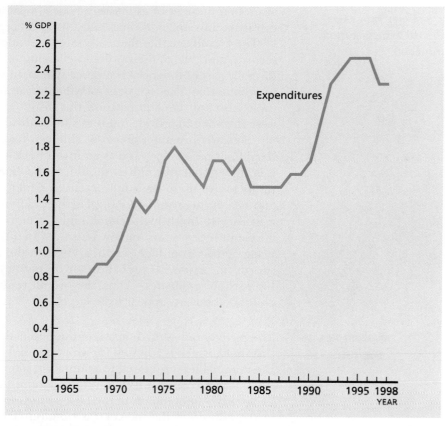

FIGURE 15.1   **Expenditures on Means-Tested Programs** Overall expenditures on means-
tested programs have increased significantly over the past quarter century.

SOURCE: Office of Management and Budget, *Budget of the U.S. Government, Fiscal Year 1999,
Historical Tables,* Table 8.2.

Figure 15.1 shows overall expenditures on means-tested programs.
Much of the increase is accounted for by Medicaid, which increased from
27 percent of welfare expenditures in 1975 to 47 percent in 1995.

RATIONALE FOR GOVERNMENT
WELFARE PROGRAMS

Chapters 3, 4, and 5 set forth the basic theoretical rationale for government
programs: Markets may produce efficient outcomes (ignoring the market
failures), but they do not necessarily produce a distribution of income that
is socially acceptable. Welfare programs focus on one aspect of the distribution of income: those at the very bottom.

Government programs are often thought of as **safety net** programs.
There is a view, for instance, that a civilized society cannot allow individuals
to starve, or to die as a result of inadequate health care. These programs are

also often thought of as a form of **social insurance.** Knowing that adversity can strike anyone, individuals may think, "There but for the grace of God go I." The knowledge that there is a safety net adds to their sense of economic security, and thus to their overall well-being. (The welfare programs are not formally part of the social insurance system, in which individuals pay explicit premiums to obtain, say, unemployment insurance, against the risk of losing their jobs; but they still perform this insurance function.) These programs were intended to provide funds to allow individuals to get back on their feet.

Similarly programs aimed at children have been justified both as a reflection of basic values and as an investment in the future. As a basic value, it is argued that all children should, to the extent possible, have the opportunity to live up to their full potential. Children with inadequate nutrition and health care cannot do this. Further, children growing up in poverty are less likely to finish high school, and are more likely to end up in a life of crime: in recent years, on any given day, a quarter of young males who do not graduate from high school are within the ambit of the criminal justice system (in prison, on probation, or on parole), in contrast to 4 percent of high school graduates.[5] Thus, the overall returns to society from reducing childhood poverty appear to be large.

**DIMENSIONS OF
THE PROBLEM**

The **poverty rate** is the fraction of the population whose income lies below a threshold, which is adjusted for inflation, and which is intended to measure the minimal level required to maintain a subsistence living standard. While there is some controversy about the measure (what does it really mean to be in poverty?), movements in the poverty measure do track what is happening at the bottom of the income distribution. The overall poverty rate, which was more than 22 percent in 1960, was reduced to a much lower level of about 12 percent in the 1970s. But since then the poverty rate has risen, reaching a recent peak of 15.1 in 1993, and averaging 14.5 percent throughout the 1990s. The primary reason for the increase in poverty since the 1970s has been reduction in the real wages of those at the bottom of the income distribution since that time. This in turn is largely the result of changes in technology, which have increased the premium put on high skills—the ratio of the wage of a college graduate to that of a high school graduate increased markedly.

Particularly disturbing is the rapid rise in the number of children in poverty. The poverty rate for children rose from 15 percent in 1970 to 20 percent in 1995. Much of this arose from an increase in the number of children being raised in households with single earners.

The problems of poverty in the United States are seen most strongly among the black population. In 1996 11.2 percent of whites lived below the poverty line, but 28.4 percent of blacks.[6] As a result, the infant mortality and

[5] *Economic Report of the President, 1996* (Washington, D.C.: Government Printing Office, 1996), p. 36.

[6] Leatha Lamison-White, U.S. Bureau of the Census, Current Population Reports, Series P60-198, *Poverty in the United States: 1996* (Washington, D.C.: U.S. Government Printing Office, 1997), pp. 3–4.

life expectancy rates for blacks compare unfavorably to those for whites. In 1996, whites experienced an infant mortality rate of 6 per 1000, whereas blacks had a rate of 14.2 per 1000; life expectancy in 1996 was 76.8 years for whites, but 70.3 for blacks.[7]

ANALYTIC ISSUES

Over the years, policy debates surrounding the welfare programs have focused on a set of incentive and equity issues: Do welfare programs discourage work? How can people most effectively be moved from welfare to work? Do noncash programs have other adverse incentive effects? On what grounds can they be justified? Do welfare programs contribute to the long-run welfare problem by causing dependency and encouraging out-of-wedlock births?

LABOR SUPPLY
Welfare programs use income as a basic criterion for determining eligibility. As income rises, benefits are reduced. If income rises above a threshold, a family may become ineligible for Medicaid benefits. Individuals care about their total income—what they earn plus what they receive from the government. The total net income of poor individuals thus rises far more slowly than their before-subsidy income—it is as if poor individuals face very high marginal tax rates. (Recall that the *marginal* tax is the extra tax an individual pays as a result of earning an extra dollar of income.) Thus, prior to the 1996 reforms, a very-low-income individual on welfare who earned an extra $100 would have AFDC benefits cut by $100 but have her EITC increased by $40. Her increased EITC payments, however, would reduce food stamps by about $10. Hence, her net income would increase only by $30—there was, in effect, a 70 percent tax rate. Such high tax rates discourage work—or at least discourage reporting the income earned from work.

Because the marginal return—the extra net income received from working an extra hour—is reduced, individuals on welfare have less incentive to work. A survey of recent studies shows a midpoint estimate of work reduction for AFDC and food stamp recipients of 30 percent attributable to AFDC and of 10 percent attributable to food stamps.[8,9] The main effect

---

[7] Stephanie J. Ventura et al., "Births and Deaths: United States, 1996," *Monthly Vital Statistics Report,* Preliminary data from the Centers for Disease Control and Prevention, vol. 46, no. 1, supplement 2, September 11, 1997, Table D, p. 5.

[8] R. Moffit, "Incentive Effects of the U.S. Welfare System: A Review," *Journal of Economic Literature,* March 1992, pp. 1–61. There is a wide range of estimates. See for instance J. Hausman's chapter, "Labor Supply," in *How Taxes Affect Economic Behavior,* ed. H. Aaron and J. Pechman (Washington, D.C.: Brookings Institution, 1981), pp. 27–72: Hausman obtains estimates thirty-seven times as large as those obtained by R. Moffit in "An Economic Model of Welfare Stigma," Rutgers University mimeo, 1980. For a more recent study, see Nada Eissa and Jeffrey Liebman, "Labor Supply Responses to the Earned Income Tax Credit," *Quarterly Journal of Economics* 111, no. 2 (May 1996): 603–37.

[9] These numbers may exaggerate the effects, because there may be a larger reduction in *reported* income and work, than in actual income and work.

seems to be a reduction in labor force participation (whether the recipient works or not); for those who work, there appears to be little effect on hours.[10]

The earned income tax credit was designed to provide greater incentives for individuals to participate in the labor force—it increased the overall return to working. (At the same time, for many individuals, it decreased the marginal return to working an additional hour, since benefits were cut as income rose.) One of the aims of TANF was to complement the "carrot" that the EITC provided for those with children to *participate* in the labor force. Eligibility for receiving welfare had strict time limits and work requirements.

Welfare programs that employ thresholds, like Medicaid, have even more dramatic adverse effects on work. The extra return to earning a dollar that pushes a family over the threshold is very negative. Loss of eligibility of medical benefits is cited as one of the main impediments to moving people from welfare to work, especially since many employers of low-wage workers do not provide health care benefits to their employees.

While many workers may not work because of the loss of benefits, many others work but do not report it. For instance, a welfare recipient may be employed as a household worker, performing services such as house cleaning or child care, but not report the income. Given the secretive nature of this behavior, economists remain uncertain about its prevalence, though a few studies have been conducted. One widely cited study in Chicago investigated fifty welfare mothers. All received non-AFDC income. Only four of the fifty reported this income, and not even these four reported all of it. The study found that unreported income came from various sources, including income from relatives or fathers (43 percent), off-the-book jobs (22 percent), salaried jobs (12 percent), and vice, such as prostitution (11 percent).[11]

DIAGRAMMATIC EXPOSITION We can use standard budget constraints and indifference curves to illustrate the adverse effects of welfare on work. In Figure 15.2, *BB* gives the before-tax budget constraint, showing how Alfred's consumption (after-tax income) increases as work increases (leisure decreases). The slope of the budget constraint is the wage: if Alfred's wage is $6.00 an hour, an extra hour of work increases consumption by $6. The indifference curves have the shape illustrated because Alfred does not like to work (or at least does not like the work available to him)—he prefers leisure. Alfred requires extra consumption to compensate him for working more, and since the more he works the less leisure he has, the more valuable leisure is to him at the margin; and since the more he works the higher his consumption, the less valuable his marginal increase in consumption. Accordingly, the extra consumption he requires to compensate him for an

[10] R. Moffit and A. Rangarajan, "The Work Incentives of AFDC Tax Rates: Reconciling Different Estimates," *Journal of Human Resources*, winter 1991, pp. 165–79.
[11] See Christopher Jencks, *Rethinking Social Policy* (Cambridge, Mass.: Harvard University Press, 1992).

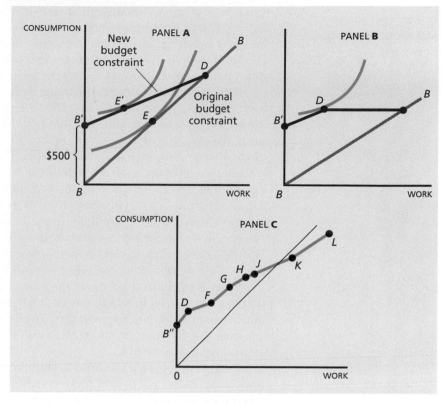

FIGURE 15.2   **Effect of Welfare Programs on Labor Supply** Welfare programs can adversely affect labor supply. Panel A: Stylized version of welfare program before 1979, when payments were reduced as the individual earned more. Both the income and substitution effects led to reduced work. Panel B: Stylized version of welfare program after 1979, when benefits were reduced dollar for dollar, beyond a certain minimal amount. No one worked beyond this level. Panel C: A simplified version of the current system, with TANF, EITC, and food stamps.

B"D—Basic level of income which an individual can earn (the "disregard") without having benefits affected. Individual pays social security taxes but no income taxes and receives EITC benefits.

DF—EITC increases return to work, but TANF and food stamp benefits are cut.

FG—At *F*, TANF benefits are eliminated; EITC continues to increase the return to working, but the reduction in food stamps reduces it.

GH—At *G*, the individual has to start paying income taxes. This reduces the return to working further.

HJ—At *H*, EITC benefits start to be cut. This reduces the return to working further.

JK—At *J*, food stamps are eliminated. This increases the return to working.

KL—At *K*, EITC benefits are eliminated. This increases the return to working further.

extra hour of work—the marginal rate of substitution—increases the more he works. That is why the indifference curve not only is upward-sloping, but becomes steeper as the individual works more. The original equilibrium is at point *E*, where the slope of the budget constraint equals the slope of the indifference curve: the wage equals the marginal rate of substitution.

B'DB is the new budget constraint under a welfare system in which Alfred gets a fixed payment—say, $500 per month, which diminishes the higher his income becomes. (At point *D*, the benefit is completely phased out.) We assume—as was the case prior to 1979—that for every $3 of income Alfred earns, he loses $1 of benefits. Thus, the new budget constraint is flatter; his after-tax wage is not $6.00 an hour but $4.00 an hour. The new equilibrium is at *E'*, with a lower level of work than before. Work is reduced for two reasons. First, because Alfred is better off, he takes some extra leisure. This is the income effect; normally, as incomes rise individuals consume more of any good. Second, because the return to working an extra hour is reduced, Alfred's incentives for working are reduced; this is the substitution effect. Both have the effect of reducing work.

Panel B of Figure 15.2 shows the budget constraint under a welfare system in which Alfred loses a dollar for each dollar he earns beyond a certain minimum amount. Not surprisingly, Alfred chooses to work only enough to generate that income; he would be foolish to work more than that, since he earns no marginal return.

Panel C of Figure 15.2 shows a simplified version of the current system, combining TANF, EITC, and food stamps. In this stylized version, there are seven segments to Alfred's budget constraint. There is a certain basic benefit, given by *OB''*. There is a certain minimal amount which the individual can earn without losing benefits. Thus, the slope of the budget constraint in the segment *B''D* is just the wage, $6.00 an hour augmented by the EITC but reduced by social security taxes. Beyond this point, benefits are reduced the more the individual works; but the EITC supplements his wage by 40 percent, so that his net tax rate is about 70 percent—the return per hour worked is $1.80. Thus, in the interval *DF*, the budget constraint is relatively flat. At *F*, TANF benefits are eliminated, but the individual still has food stamps, pays social security taxes, and receives the EITC. Thus, the slope of the budget constraint in the interval *FG* is much steeper than in *DF*. But then, at an only slightly higher income, Alfred starts paying income taxes. This is reflected in a flatter budget constraint in the interval *GH*. At a slightly higher income, EITC benefits start being cut (segment *HJ*). This greatly reduces the marginal return to working. Soon thereafter, eligibility for food stamps is exhausted. In the interval *JK*, the slope of the budget constraint is thus slightly steeper. Eventually, EITC benefits also are exhausted, and the individual has to pay social security and income taxes (segment *KL*).

From the budget constraint, one can see that, depending on the part of the budget constraint at which an individual is located, there can be a variety of effects on labor supply. In general, the marginal return to working is less than the wage—in some cases far less. This is the substitution effect; the large substitution effect implies that there are large distortions, and that

INCENTIVE EFFECTS OF WELFARE PROGRAMS

1 The EITC provides positive incentives to participate in the labor force.

2 Welfare programs provide disincentives to work longer hours; effectively there is a high marginal tax rate on working longer hours.

3 Benefits with thresholds—which suddenly disappear when incomes exceed a certain level—have particularly adverse incentive effects near the cutoff level.

labor supply will be reduced. In addition, for most of the poor individuals, their after-tax and transfer-payment income is greater than it would be without taxes and subsidies; the income effect too induces less work. The income and substitution effects thus reinforce each other.

CASH VERSUS IN-KIND REDISTRIBUTION

Over 70 percent of welfare benefits are not unrestricted cash, but are directed to the purchase of food, housing, energy, or medical care. Today, Medicaid alone accounts for half of all welfare expenditures. Two dollars out of every ten transferred through welfare are provided in the form of subsidized food, housing, and energy. The present system is criticized on three grounds:

1 It introduces inefficiencies in resource allocations when there are substitution effects; and when there are no substitution effects, the consequences are not different from those of a direct transfer of income.
2 It is inappropriate for the government to attempt to distort individuals' consumption decisions; that is to say, in-kind benefits are paternalistic.
3 It is administratively costly: each program has to be run separately; several different agencies have to determine the eligibility of each individual for each program. (Eligibility standards to determine who is qualified to receive aid under each program are based primarily on income, but adjustments for family size and other circumstances are generally made, and may differ markedly from program to program.)

The sections that follow discuss the first two criticisms in greater detail. The third criticism applies broadly to most focused welfare programs, whether they are directed at particular groups of individuals (**categorical programs**) or particular forms of assistance (in-kind benefits). While the eligibility standards for the various programs could clearly be coordinated and simplified, there will always remain significant administrative costs associated with such programs. The broader question, addressed below, is whether there are benefits from such noncash and categorical programs that justify these additional costs.

In-kind benefit programs often distort individuals' choices, typically because they reduce the cost of obtaining the good—and thus induce individuals to consume more of the good than they would otherwise. In some cases, the programs reduce the marginal cost of the good to zero—up to the limit provided by the government. Clearly, if the government is giving away a good, individuals will consume it (so long as it has a positive benefit), whether or not the value to them is less than the cost of production. Of course, one of the reasons for in-kind benefits is precisely to promote the consumption of certain goods. *Whether* government should do that is another matter, to which we shall turn shortly.

FOOD STAMPS The food stamp program provides an excellent illustration of how in-kind benefits can distort behavior, as we saw earlier in this chapter. Three aspects of behavior are affected:

1 Because (under the current system) an individual with a given income receives a fixed amount of food stamps, in principle the food stamps should have the same effect on behavior as would a comparable transfer of income, so long as the individual consumes at least as much in food as provided by the food stamps—which is the case for 85 to 90 percent of participating households.[12] For these households, it appears that food stamps have a slightly larger effect on consumption than one might have expected, with $100 of food stamps leading to an increase in food expenditures of between $20 and $45.[13]

2 Because the value of food stamps given decreases as an individual's income increases, the food stamp program has an adverse effect on labor supply.

3 Because the value of food stamps given increases the smaller the individual's income *net of housing expenditures,* the food stamp program encourages housing consumption. It is ironic that while the food stamp program is intended to encourage food consumption, its major effects may be to encourage housing consumption and to discourage work.

[12] Janet Currie, "Welfare and the Well-Being of Children: The Relative Effectiveness of Cash and In-Kind Transfers," in *Tax Policy and the Economy,* vol. 8, ed. James M. Poterba (Cambridge, Mass.: MIT Press for the National Bureau of Economic Research, 1994), pp. 1–43.

[13] Barbara Devaney and Thomas M. Fraker, "The Effect of Food Stamps on Food Expenditures," *American Journal of Agricultural Economics,* February 1989, pp. 99–104. These results contrast with estimates of 5 to 13 cents additional food expenditures for an additional dollar of cash, reported by Thomas M. Fraker in *The Effects of Food Stamps on Food Consumption: A Review of the Literature* (Alexandria, Va.: U.S. Department of Agriculture, Office of Analysis and Evaluation, Food and Nutrition Service, 1990), and are consistent with experimental findings that show that when individuals receive, instead of food stamps, the equivalent in cash, food consumption actually decreases, by between 18 and 28 cents for each dollar of food stamps cashed out. See Thomas M. Fraker, Alberto P. Martini, and James C. Ols, "The Effect of Food Stamp Cashout on Food Expenditures: An Assessment of the Findings from Four Demonstrations," *Journal of Human Resources* 30, no. 4 (fall 1995): 633–49.

MEDICAID AND THRESHOLDS All means-tested programs can have adverse effects on labor supply, as we have noted; but the effects of certain in-kind benefits can be particularly dramatic. These are programs where the government provides a certain benefit for free to those who are eligible, that is, for those whose income is below a certain threshold, and nothing for those above it. The most important program having this feature is Medicaid. There is an obvious administrative reason for such provisions: It makes it much easier to determine whether an individual qualifies for a program. An alternative would require the individual to face a fee schedule that depended on her income. Now, the doctor simply has to know whether the individual qualifies for the program. Under the alternative, either the doctor or the government would have to send poor individuals a bill for each service rendered that would depend on the individual's income.

Figure 15.3 shows the budget constraint for David, who consumes a fixed amount of medical care services. Labor is shown on the horizontal axis, and consumption (including Medicaid benefits) on the vertical. As David works beyond a certain level, his income, L^*, exceeds the threshold for Medicaid, and so his total consumption actually falls. Clearly, David will work an amount either just short of L^*, or considerably greater than L^*.

HOUSING Public housing programs raise a number of complicated issues associated with in-kind programs. Direct provision increases the quantity of housing supplied at any price, and thus benefits not only those who receive

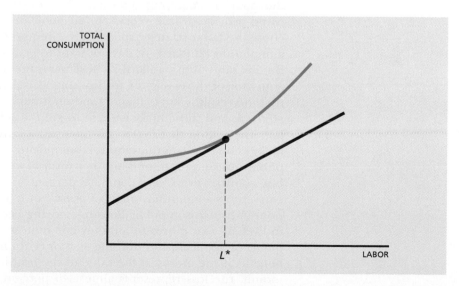

FIGURE 15.3 **Effect of Thresholds on Labor Supply** Programs like Medicaid, in which there is a given level of income above which individuals lose eligibility, discourage work.

public housing, but others, since it drives down the equilibrium rent. On the other hand, government has proven itself an inefficient producer of housing—with the costs per square foot considerably higher than in comparable privately provided housing. That is one of the motivations for vouchers and tax credits.

Tax credits also operate directly on the supply side. Those who produce low-income housing receive a subsidy through the tax system. More housing is supplied at each price, lowering the equilibrium price both for those living in subsidized housing and for others. Programs that require housing receiving such special tax treatment to be mixed-income—that is, that the apartment buildings not just have low-income units—have reduced the isolation of the poor. But these programs have also been criticized: much of the tax benefit goes to the brokers who package the deals. The "bang for the buck" may be relatively low.

Housing advocates, accordingly, have argued that money should be given directly to the poor, rather than to real estate developers. This is what housing vouchers do. They subsidize the rent which individuals pay. Figure 15.4 shows vouchers as shifting the demand curve for housing to the right. In the short run, when the supply is relatively inelastic, the main effect may be on equilibrium rents. Then those not receiving the vouchers are actually made worse off. In the long run, when the supply is relatively elastic (panel B), supply responds—just as it would if the government had directly provided the housing itself. Still, unless the long-run supply curve is horizontal, those not receiving the subsidy are hurt.

One particularly troublesome feature of the design of U.S. housing programs arises from the fact that there is a limited budget for assisting the poor in acquiring housing. The government faced a dilemma: It could provide a little subsidy to all poor, or a large subsidy to a few. It chose the latter strategy: specifically it required that public housing meet a minimum standard—it did not want to be accused of being a slumlord. But the minimum standard it chose was quite high. As a result, only about a quarter of those eligible for housing assistance get it. There is concern that the result is worse than a random lottery, with most poor people unaffected, and those lucky enough to get the subsidy receiving a big windfall. The reason that it is worse than just a lottery is that it inhibits those lucky enough to get the subsidy from moving from welfare to work. Thus, public housing represents another form of welfare lock. America is a mobile country; every year about 16 percent of Americans move from one community to another, often in search of a job, or a better job. But for poor individuals in public housing, moving becomes very unattractive. An individual who moves to another community goes to the bottom of the queue of applicants for housing assistance. In most cases, she will lose her benefits if she moves. If the value of the housing subsidy is, say, $300 per month, the loss represents almost 40 percent of the income of a minimum-wage worker. When combined with other costs of moving—and other taxes, implicit and explicit—moving to another community for work becomes decidedly unattractive.

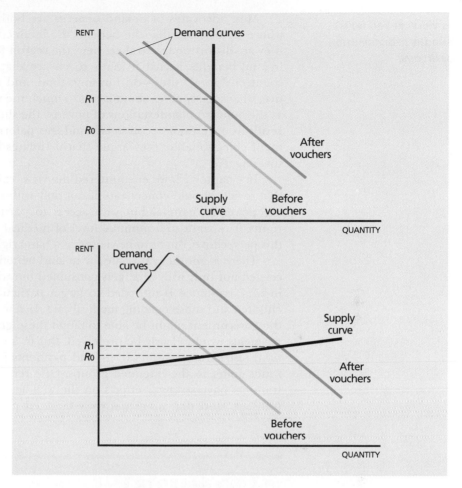

FIGURE 15.4 **Housing Market Equilibrium with Vouchers** Vouchers shift the demand curve to the right. Panel A: In the short run, supply is inelastic. The main effect is on price. Those not receiving the vouchers are worse off, as rents increase. Panel B: In the long run, supply is more elastic. But unless the long-run supply curve is perfectly horizontal, there will be some increase in rents.

ARE IN-KIND BENEFITS PATERNALISTIC?

We have noted that in-kind benefits are typically distortionary; that is, there is a substitution effect associated with them. Individuals would be better off if they were just given the same amount in cash; alternatively, the government could make them just as well off, and reduce its total expenditures. Ironically, the only circumstances in which in-kind benefits are not distortionary are when they have no substitution effect, only an income effect; then they simply increase administrative costs, but the effect on consumption of food (or whatever the benefit being provided) is the same as a cash benefit.

Most advocates of in-kind benefits are bothered more by those cases where it turns out that the benefits are ineffective than by those in which they are distortionary. In their view, the reason for government's providing in-kind benefits is that it wants to ensure that the money transferred is spent on "good" uses—on housing, food, and medicine. In this perspective, what society cares about is not so much the well-being of the recipients as the outward manifestations of poverty, the slums, malnutrition, etc., that result from it. Some economists find this paternalistic view of the government objectionable; they argue that it violates the principle of consumer sovereignty.

In Chapter 12, we encountered the view, called specific egalitarianism, that society should concern itself not only with the distribution of purchasing power in general but with access to particular goods, services, and rights. The right to a minimal level of medical care, food, and shelter, in this perspective, ought to be viewed as a basic right.

There is another rationale for in-kind benefits: The government is concerned not only with what gets consumed but with who consumes it. Some in-kind assistance is intended to target particular beneficiaries, especially children and those needing medical care. In a world of perfect information, the government might be able to target these groups; and in that case cash payments would clearly be preferred. But in a world of imperfect information, restricting transfers to in-kind payments increases the proportion of funds going to the intended groups. One recent study found that in-kind transfers have stronger effects on the well-being of children than do cash transfers, and that more narrowly targeted programs (like Medicaid and

IN-KIND BENEFITS

Arguments in favor:

• Targets aid where it is most needed

• Specific egalitarianism

Arguments against:

• High administrative costs

• Inefficient (distortionary: same gain in well-being of recipients could be achieved at lower costs)

• Rules exacerbate distortions: food stamp program encourages consumption of housing.

• Ineffective (often do not significantly increase expenditures on desired items, like food)

• Paternalistic

Head Start) have greater impacts than more broadly targeted programs (like food stamps).[14]

Finally, there are *political* arguments for in-kind benefits. Different congressional committees oversee each of the programs. Food stamps, for example, are under the jurisdiction of the congressional agricultural committees. One of the reasons why the committees supported expansion of the food stamp program was that they viewed the program as benefiting their special interest—the agricultural sector—just as the housing industry is one of the strongest advocates of housing programs. In this perspective, overall support for welfare benefits would be reduced if they were converted into cash payments.

CATEGORICAL VERSUS BROAD-BASED AID

Should aid be given to all poor, or only to the poor who fall into certain categories? A number of programs raise this question. For instance, the Supplemental Security Income Program transfers income only to the aged or disabled poor.

The most basic criticism of categorical aid programs (whether in-kind or cash) is their relatively high administrative costs, as noted in the discussion of in-kind benefits. The greater expense of these programs arises primarily from the costs associated with ascertaining eligibility. For instance, in recent years, administrative costs per beneficiary for the Supplemental Security Income Program have averaged five times more per beneficiary and nearly nine times more per dollar of benefit payments than administrative costs for the Old-Age and Survivors Insurance Program.[15]

EFFICIENCY AND EQUITY ISSUES Besides considerations of administrative costs, there are both efficiency and equity issues that arise in comparing categorical versus broad-based aid. Categorical aid may have the effect of inducing individuals to fall into the benefited category; it may have a distortionary effect. This is not true of social security: individuals do not become older faster simply to take advantage of the program. But there are allegations that AFDC has contributed to the breakup of families, since in most states eligibility could be affected by the presence of a man in the household.

The major advantage of categorical aid over broad-based programs is that under certain circumstances, it can provide more effective redistribution, with less loss in efficiency. It can enable the targeting of aid to the most needy, who, at the same time, will not have adverse incentive responses. We have repeatedly emphasized the trade-offs between equity and efficiency considerations in the design of redistribution programs. Providing a basic level of income through transfer payments that then de-

---

[14] Janet Currie, "Welfare and the Well-Being of Children." See also Charles Blackorby and David Donaldson, "Cash versus In-Kind, Self-Selection and Efficient Transfers," *American Economic Review*, September 1988, pp. 691–700.

[15] House Committee on Ways and Means, *1998 Green Book*, pp. 17, 81, 279, 317, various tables.

CATEGORICAL AID

Argument in favor:

• Targets aid where it is most needed, reducing overall distortionary effects and costs

Arguments against:

• Unfair to treat different poor differently

• Distortionary effects in meeting eligibility standards (effect of AFDC on family dissolutions)

• High administrative costs

cline as the individual's income increases from wages or other sources may discourage work. This will normally imply that a lower level of redistribution is more desirable for individuals whose response to incentives is large than for individuals whose response to wage incentives is small (e.g., those over 70).

There is an equity argument against categorical programs. Some believe that the government should not discriminate in favor of or against any particular groups. Two individuals who are equally poor should receive the same amount from the government, whether they are young or old. There should not be "favored" categories, such as single-parent households or the aged. Admittedly, older individuals may have more medical expenses, and one might want to adjust the transfers to take this into account; but this is already effectively done through Medicare.

IS MEANS TESTING OBJECTIONABLE IN ITS OWN RIGHT?
A far more fundamental set of questions is raised by means testing. Should benefits be targeted at the poor alone? Any program—like Medicare—that provides benefits for all individuals, irrespective of their income, has a disproportionate effect on the poor. One way to help the poor is to provide benefits to everyone in society. Such programs have several distinct advantages. First, they reduce the distortions associated with the phaseout of means-tested benefits. Second, means-tested programs are often viewed as demeaning. That is one reason why social security and Medicare were not means tested. Not all those who are eligible for public assistance participate. The administrative complexity may provide part of the explanation; but another reason may be that some of those eligible view means testing programs as demeaning. Finally, there is a political argument, which is sometimes put thus: "Means-tested programs are mean"—that is, because they lack political support, they tend to be stingy.

In recent years, as the government has faced increasing financial stringency, these arguments have been overwhelmed by the desire to target the limited funds to those most needy. Thus, there has been increasing support for making wealthier individuals pay a higher fraction of their Medicare costs.

OTHER DISTORTIONS So far, we have discussed how welfare programs can adversely affect labor supply, and how in-kind benefits can distort consumption decisions. Critics of welfare programs argue that they have even more fundamental effects on behavior: that they have contributed to family breakdown, increased teenage pregnancy, and concentrated welfare dependency in those states paying the highest benefits, as the poor migrate to those states.

It is clear that welfare has, or has had, features which might result in those behavioral effects. For instance, since welfare benefits typically depend on household income, the departure of a low-wage father may increase total "family" income by making the family eligible for assistance.[16] It is also true that a disproportionately large number of welfare recipients are unmarried teenagers.[17] But the causal link has been questioned. Out-of-wedlock births also increased dramatically among those not on welfare during the 1970s and 1980s (though they declined somewhat among both groups in the nineties), and the incidence of out-of-wedlock births does not seem to be higher in those states offering larger benefits. Indeed, in many states in which there has been a marked rise in such births, benefits come nowhere near covering the additional costs of a child. While there may be some effect, welfare benefits simply cannot account quantitatively for the magnitude of the change.[18] Indeed, studies have not found effects of welfare on illegitimacy large enough to explain the observed increases in female-headed families.[19] To

---

[16] According to one study, the combined AFDC and food stamp benefit for an AFDC family was higher than the reported income of 62 percent of black men aged 20 to 24 and of 29 percent of black men aged 25 to 34. See Frank Levy and Richard Michel, "Work for Welfare: How Much Good Will It Do?" *American Economic Review* 76 (May 1986): 399–404.

[17] In 1993, 55 percent of AFDC mothers were adolescents at the time of their first birth, and 47.5 percent of AFDC mothers were never married, whereas only 23.6 percent of non-AFDC mothers were never married. In 1996, 34 percent of never-married mothers reported receiving AFDC that year. Sources: House Ways and Means Committee, *1996 Green Book*, p. 516, and *1998 Green Book*, pp. 537, 540.

[18] One recent interesting theory attributes the increased incidence of out-of-wedlock birth to the increased availability of abortions. Previously, a significant fraction of marriages were shotgun marriages—as evidenced by the number of firstborn children arriving, say, seven months or less after marriage. This number has decreased dramatically; the availability of abortions has meant that men no longer feel the moral obligation to marry, since the woman has a choice. See George A. Akerlof, Janet L. Yellen, and Michael L. Katz, "An Analysis of Out-of-Wedlock Childbearing in the United States," *Quarterly Journal of Economics* 111, no. 2 (May 1996): 277–317.

[19] See Robert Moffit, "Incentive Effects of the U.S. Welfare System." David Ellwood of Harvard and Larry Summers, currently secretary of the treasury, found that variations in benefit levels across states were not associated with variations in divorce rates, illegitimacy, or percentages of children in families headed by single parents; see D. Ellwood and L. Summers, "Poverty in America: Is Welfare the Answer or the Problem," in *Fighting Poverty: What Works and What Doesn't*, ed. S. Danziger and D. Weinberg (Cambridge, Mass.: Harvard University Press, 1986), pp. 78–105.

be sure, poverty itself contributes to family breakdown and welfare dependency.[20]

Welfare programs' adverse effect on child support payments, or at least reported payments, has not been well studied, but may well be more significant. It makes little sense for the mother to expend any effort to collect, or to report having collected, funds from the father, when her benefits will be reduced dollar for dollar. Under the new welfare-reform law, states are encouraged to be more aggressive in seeking out these payments. Some states will require the mother to report the father. Efforts are being made to ensure coordination among the states, so deadbeat fathers cannot escape their obligations by crossing state lines.

While there has been extensive migration, especially from the South to northern urban areas, since AFDC was first adopted in the midst of the depression, there is debate about the extent to which that migration was induced by AFDC. Jobs were more available, pay was higher, and there was less racial and class discrimination. Although from an economist's perspective, if one is going to be unemployed, simply receiving checks, it makes sense to do so where the checks are largest, migration does not seem to be particularly sensitive to changes in welfare benefits. This may be because most welfare recipients plan to return to work; job opportunities and other factors, such as proximity to friends, dominate. These, plus the costs of moving, more than offset the differences in welfare benefits among the states.

WELFARE REFORM: INTEGRATION OF PROGRAMS

The chapter began by noting that some of the dissatisfaction with welfare programs was misplaced: though blamed for the increasing deficit, they really had little to do with it. But the discussion in the preceding section has uncovered several other complaints, about actual or perceived distortions in behavior induced by the system. In recent years, there have been major initiatives for reform—one aimed at simplifying and integrating the welfare programs, and another aimed at trying to "make work pay."

As we have seen, the current welfare system consists of a potpourri of programs. Some programs, such as TANF, originated to deal with particular problems. Others grew in part in response to special interest groups—for example, the **food stamp** program gave the agriculture industry an opportunity to increase the demand for their products, and thus the income of farmers.

Regardless of the origins of programs within the welfare system, their lack of integration has two negative effects. First, it greatly increases admin-

---

[20] See Janet Currie, "Welfare and the Well-Being of Children." According to Moffit, "The results show consistent evidence of the strong correlations between parental welfare receipt and later behavior of daughters. Daughters of welfare families are much more likely to participate in the welfare system themselves at a later date, and are more likely to have births in general and premarital births in particular." ("Incentive Effects of the U.S. Welfare System," p. 36.)

istrative costs and burdens. Each program has, for instance, a different eligibility form. The bureaucratic complexity discourages some who could really benefit from the programs from taking advantage of them. It is estimated that only about two-thirds of those eligible for AFDC received it, only 60 percent of those eligible for food stamps receive food stamps, and only 83 percent of those eligible for EITC actually collect it.[21]

The second negative effect of the lack of integration is that the programs interact in ways which increase the magnitude of the distortions. Each means-tested program has a phaseout, an interval of incomes over which benefits decline. The decline in benefits is equivalent to a tax. While legislators may be aware of this effect, as they consider each program in isolation they seldom think of the combined effects of all of these taxes. As we have seen, the combined effect may result in a total marginal tax rate well in excess of 60 percent. If all the programs were consolidated into a single cash program, not only would overall administrative costs be reduced, but attention would be paid to the combined effects.

At various times, there has been support for integrating all of the welfare programs together, and "cashing them out"—allowing those on welfare to spend the money however they wish. Such proposals amount to an expanded EITC. They are sometimes referred to as **negative income tax** proposals.

In this system, all individuals would be required to file a tax return, but just as only individuals above a critical threshold level would have to pay income taxes, those below that critical threshold level would receive a check from the government. Consider a tax regime in which everyone receives a check from the government of, say, $1000 per year but then pays to the government, say, one-third of each dollar that she earns. Those with an income of less than $3000 would receive something net from the government; those with an income greater than $3000 would pay to the government more than they receive. Those who favor this system argue that it is not only administratively simpler, but less demeaning than the present system, which forces individuals to present evidence to several agencies concerning their low income.

Advocates of a negative income tax, however, have argued for more than just the consolidation of current welfare programs and a conversion to cash benefits. They have argued for a change in the structure of total benefits, for two key reasons. First, the high marginal tax rates on the poor discourage work effort among people whose attachment to the labor force is already weak; second, the total benefits under the current system amount to less than what is required to remain out of poverty.

But this gives rise to one of the fundamental dilemmas in welfare policy. If we want to provide benefits which are large enough to ensure a minimal (say, poverty) level of income even for those who do not work, and if we want the "phaseout" to be slow—so that the implicit marginal tax rate is low—then the benefits must extend high up into the income distribution. For instance, if the minimal benefit for a family of three were $12,000, and the marginal tax rate (including the full social security contributions of ap-

---

[21] John K. Scholz, "Tax Policy and the Working Poor: The Earned Income Tax Credit," *Focus,* winter 1993–1994, pp. 1–12.

BASIC TRADE-OFF IN THE DESIGN OF NEGATIVE INCOME TAX

Higher benefits for the very poor entail either greater expenditures (raising tax rates, and reducing incentives for higher-income individuals) or faster phaseouts, implicitly entailing higher marginal tax rates for lower-income individuals.

proximately 15 percent) were kept to 30 percent, ignoring state taxes, then benefits would extend up to families with an $80,000 income; if the marginal tax rate were increased to 55 percent—more than one out of two dollars earned by the individual thus going to the government—benefits would still extend up to $40,000. The costs of such an arrangement would be prohibitive (especially given recent budget stringency). Thus, *either* initial benefits must be below the poverty level, *or* effective marginal tax rates must be very high.

THE WELFARE REFORM BILL OF 1996

As we have noted, the Personal Responsibility and Work Opportunity Reconciliation Act of 1996 marked a major departure from the past in two important ways. First, it replaced the AFDC system, in which the federal government paid a fraction of the costs, depending on the per capita income in the state, with the block grants of TANF. Second, it imposed a number of stringent requirements designed to encourage movement from welfare to work. Two beliefs underlay the reforms: that the programs were too costly (partly based on the misperception noted earlier concerning the size and growth of welfare programs and their role in the growing deficit); and that the programs had failed in their primary purpose—rather than being a safety net, for too many people, welfare had become a way of life.

BLOCK GRANTING While the states administered the AFDC program, many of its basic features were dictated by the federal government. One of the most important features of the 1996 welfare reform was to end the federal welfare entitlement. State matching grants—in which the federal government contributed, say, a dollar for every dollar spent by the state—were converted to block grants—fixed amounts of money—giving the states much more discretion in how they administered the funds. Critics worried, however, that converting to block grants would lead to reductions in expenditures. The 50 percent matching rate had effectively lowered the "price" of welfare. A state could get two dollars of welfare benefits for its citizens by spending only one dollar. Welfare, it was argued, was like any other good: lowering the price raised the quantity demanded; raising the price would lower the quantity demanded.

Critics worried further that there would be a "race to the bottom." Lowering a state's welfare benefits relative to those of neighboring states would provide incentives for those on welfare to move; each state would have an incentive to encourage those free riding on the welfare system to leave. The upshot of these incentives, critics argued, would be competition among the states to drive out those dependent on welfare.

Advocates of block grants argued that there was not strong evidence of a large elasticity of demand—that is, of a large responsiveness to price—so that fears of welfare cuts were exaggerated. Moreover, there were incentives to drive out welfare recipients under the old regime—the states still paid half of the cost of the benefits—though to be sure, these incentives would be enhanced if the states had to pay, at the margin, 100 percent of the benefits. Nonetheless, it was hard to see evidence of a race to the bottom; though there were differences in benefit levels among states, they were related more to the states' income and demographics. Moreover, advocates of block grants argued, the increased efficiency resulting from state control and the elimination of federal bureaucratic requirements would increase the benefit received per dollar spent—at least partially offsetting the fact that the federal government was no longer picking up 50 percent of the tab.

To address concerns that there would be an excessive reduction in welfare support, proponents of block grants agreed to a "maintenance-of-effort provision," under which states receiving the block grants would agree to continue spending at least 75 percent of the amount that they had previously spent on welfare. Advocates argued that with the greater efficiency resulting from the devolution of responsibility to the states, the effective level of welfare benefits would not be cut at all. But critics raised two objections: Advocates of block grants exaggerated the negative impact of federal regulations and bureaucracy, so that any major cut in expenditures would be felt. Moreover, with time, the adverse impact of block grants would worsen, particularly in states in which for one reason or another there was a marked increase in the welfare load (for instance, because of an economic downturn). If under the old regime, benefits would have expanded by only 15 percent, then a 75 percent maintenance-of-effort requirement would be equivalent to more than a one-third cut in benefits, relative to what they otherwise would have been.

Moreover, hidden in the 1996 bill were provisions that allowed funds spent on other social programs directed at the poor to be counted toward the maintenance-of-effort requirement, substantially lowering the effective maintenance-of-effort requirement.

**ANALYTICS
OF STATE RESPONSES
TO BLOCK GRANTS**

We can use some simple diagrams to illustrate why economists worried that converting from a matching system for welfare to a block grant would reduce overall support for welfare.

Figure 15.5 shows how the states might be anticipated to respond. *BB* gives a state's budget constraint between welfare and other expenditures before the federal program, and shows a hypothetical state indifference curve, depicting the trade-off between welfare and other expenditures. The state chooses point *E*, maximizing its (economic) welfare, subject to its budget constraint.

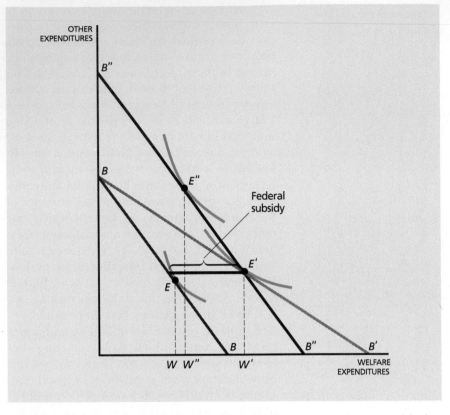

FIGURE 15.5   **Effect of Block Granting** Switching from a matching grant system to a block grant costing an equal amount of money is likely to reduce welfare expenditures.

BB' gives a state's budget constraint under the former system of federal matching funds. The state is induced to spend more on welfare both because of an income effect (the state is better off as a result of the federal subsidy) and because of a substitution effect (for each dollar of increased welfare expenditure, the state has to give up only 50 cents of non-welfare expenditures). The state now chooses point *E'*. The increased funding for welfare and the lower price both lead to more expenditure on welfare than before. There are positive income and substitution effects.

B"B" now gives the budget constraint when the federal subsidy is converted into a lump sum, not dependent on the amount spent. The state is better off, but unless the income effect is large, expenditures on welfare are decreased (though because of the income effect they remain higher than with no subsidy). The figure shows what has been the concern of critics of block granting: a large decrease in welfare expenditures. (Note, however, that as depicted the indifference curve in the new equilibrium is at a higher level, reflecting the general proposition that non-distorting subsidies are more efficient.)

TIME LIMITS

The 1996 welfare reform introduced time limits into the welfare programs. Federal rules stipulate that federal TANF funds may not be received by a family which includes an adult who has received sixty months of TANF funds previously. However, a state may exempt up to 20 percent of its caseload from the five-year limit based on hardship. States may continue to assist all families beyond five years if they choose, and those funds will be counted toward the states' maintenance-of-effort requirements. Many states adopted a shorter two-year period. Advocates of these time limits hoped not only that they would push people off the welfare rolls, but that they would discourage people from joining them in the first place. The prospect of re-entering the labor market five years down the road would motivate prospective welfare recipients to remain in the labor market, where they could maintain and expand their job skills. Moreover, since employers prefer to hire workers with current job experience, remaining in the labor force would enhance the long-run employment prospects of employees. Evidence supporting this theory came in the months immediately following the passage of the welfare reform bill, during which time welfare rolls decreased substantially, to 8.4 million recipients by June 1998, not only undoing the large increase that had occurred in the early 1990s, but putting the number well below the 1990 level of 11.46 million.[22] While improved economic conditions—the continuing decline in the unemployment rate to a three-decade low of just over 4 percent—explained a large part of the overall decline, the remaining decrease seems attributable, at least in part, to the 1996 welfare reform.[23]

MANDATORY WORK

In addition to time limits, the 1996 reform required states to impose work requirements. Adults had to engage in some form of work after a maximum of two years of TANF benefits, and to participate, unless the state opted out, in community service after two months. This work requirement does not apply to single parents of children under age 6 who cannot obtain child care. The work can be unsubsidized private employment, subsidized private employment, public employment, on-the-job training, community service, vocational education, or secondary education. To be considered working, the individual had to work for at least a weekly minimum average of twenty hours in 1997–98; rising to thirty hours after the year 2000.

THE WELFARE REFORM DEBATE OF 1996

The debate over the 1996 reform took up a wide range of questions about values, political judgments, and economic assumptions.

[22] House Ways and Means Committee, *1998 Green Book.*
[23] The Council of Economic Advisers concluded that the 20 percent decline in welfare caseload during the 1993–1996 period can be attributed to the stronger economy (40 percent), welfare reform policies (30 percent), and the other factors such as the earned income tax credit (the remainder). Council of Economic Advisers, *Explaining the Decline in Welfare Receipt, 1993 to 1996* (Washington, D.C.: Government Printing Office, May 1998).

WELFARE RECIPIENTS AND LABOR MARKETS Did welfare recipients have the fore-sight—without further training and education—to realize that it was in their best interest to remain in the labor market? A lack of such foresight would undermine the intended incentive effects of the time limit.

Did welfare recipients have the skills required to be effective members of the labor force, or were many simply unsuitable for participation in the labor force? Welfare advocates argued that more training funds were required. Indeed, they proposed that meaningful reform would cost more in the short run than simply continuing the old system; but the bill that passed made minimal provisions for training. Advocates of the reform bill countered that "soft skills," such as the basic ability to get up and go to work every morning, were most important, and that these skills were best acquired in the labor market.

Some in the policy debate worried that there were many welfare recipients who could not function effectively in the labor market. These advocates argued for large exceptions from the work requirement. More ardent welfare reformers objected that these large exceptions would undermine the whole reform effort. Those who really could not function in the labor market should be treated as disabled—and be subjected to the same disability standards as everyone else.

Was it unwillingness to work or a lack of jobs that led people to welfare? And could the labor market provide low-skill jobs in sufficient numbers? Most economists believed the labor market had the capacity to create jobs—after all, between 1993 and 1996, 11 million jobs had been created—and that it would create jobs that corresponded to the skills that were available. They also believed that, at least in many locations, the lack of participation in the labor force was not due to a shortage of jobs: indeed, immigrants, with few skills, managed to get low-skilled jobs ranging from work in fast-food restaurants to taxicab services. The problem was neither lack of jobs nor lack of training, but the lack of the soft skills noted earlier.

TIME LIMITS What would happen when the time limits expired? Should children suffer because their parents were unable, or unwilling, to work? One option, called workfare, would be for government to provide jobs in exchange for welfare. But this raises a host of issues: How much would workfare jobs pay? Would they undermine employment opportunities of other people participating in the work force? Would workfare jobs negate the incentive for welfare recipients to find regular employment?

SOCIAL WORKERS IN THE WELFARE SYSTEM In the absence of incentives, would the workers who ran the old welfare system—who critics said were more in the business of sending out checks than of getting welfare recipients to work—be transformed into job placement officers? Or, if welfare recipients were to be moved to work, would greater reliance have to be placed on private placement agencies?

Those who focused on the present system's failures were not sanguine about the ability of the welfare system to transform itself. Without adequate incentives, they saw current social workers as simply perpetuating, perhaps under some other guise, the current system. Not surprisingly, those who saw less of a necessity for reform adamantly opposed turning over social services to for-profit agencies. They were less concerned about the current system's inadequacies than about the potential of for-profit agencies to exploit the poor.

CHILD CARE Who would take care of the children while a welfare mother was working? The welfare reform bill made some provision for child care services, but far less than was required to cover child care expenses. On the other hand, lower-income mothers in working families were struggling to find adequate child care arrangements. Did it make sense to provide child care arrangements for former welfare recipients, but not for low-income mothers who had never been on welfare? In a time of severe budget stringency, few believed that child care costs could be provided to all low-income mothers. Indeed, in many cases the government would be paying child care costs that exceeded the earnings of those receiving the benefits. It was precisely this dilemma that resulted in the compromise where some, but limited, child care expenses were provided for welfare mothers.

In the end, the policy debate, the debate about consequences and values, was subsumed under the political debate: the strong desire of many Americans to see significant reforms, and the desire of the state governors to assume more control over their welfare system. The reductions in welfare rolls in the years immediately following passage of the 1996 reform bill provided considerable validation for the arguments underlying the reform. But two questions remained: What would happen if and when the economy went into a prolonged economic downturn? And what would happen to the "hard-core" welfare recipients, amounting to perhaps a quarter or more of the beneficiaries—those with few skills and little interest or ability to acquire them? Two contrasting pictures are painted for the future. One sees welfare mothers begging on the street, an image of America that harks back to the nineteenth century and across to less developed countries. Another sees welfare restored to its original intent of temporary help in times of adversity.

CONCLUDING REMARKS

The public assistance programs described in this chapter have almost surely helped reduce poverty in the United States. While in some instances they may have contributed to the vicious cycle of poverty, by removing incentives for recipients to be actively engaged in the labor force, more broadly they have been fighting a rising tide of inequality that has affected not only the United States, but many other countries as well. This long-term trend—in evidence now for more than two decades—is largely related to the increasing premium placed on skills in the labor market. Since President Johnson, there has been an increased emphasis on getting at poverty's root cause, by

EMPOWER-MENT ZONES

This chapter has looked at strategies to reduce poverty that focus on people—on transferring cash and in-kind benefits to low-income families. But poverty in the United States is concentrated geographically, and there is a place-based strategy designed to improve living conditions and job prospects in those areas, especially in America's inner cities.

Urban poverty feeds on itself. High crime rates, substance abuse, weak family structures, and poor schools combine to perpetuate poverty. In 1993, Congress funded a set of empowerment zones with the aim of focusing private and public efforts to improve life in these impoverished districts. Nine empowerment zones received tax benefits equivalent to $2 billion over five years, while another ninety-five communities received smaller benefits. A national competition was established to qualify for these funds.*

Each department of the federal government was charged with devising programs to help meet the needs of the empowerment zones. Thus, the Department of Justice proposed enhanced law enforcement programs, and the Department of Housing and Urban Development improved housing programs. The Department of Transportation was charged with ensuring that public transportation systems enabled those who lived in the zones to travel to places where there were jobs. A major focus of concern was job creation. Federal, state, and local communities were charged with finding ways

improving educational and job opportunities, beginning with programs such as Head Start, which focuses on preschool children, on through improved grade school and high school education, job training programs, and programs to facilitate the movement from school to work and to increase access to higher education. These education programs are discussed further in Chapter 16.

REVIEW AND PRACTICE

SUMMARY

1 Public assistance provides cash and in-kind benefits to the poor. Expenditures for in-kind transfers have grown rapidly in recent years, but cash assistance (as a percentage of government expenditures) has fallen. Increases in welfare programs played a relatively small role in the increase in the overall federal deficit during the 1980s and early 1990s.

to change regulations to facilitate the creation of new enterprises. A set of community development banks was to be created, which would help channel private money to these new enterprises. Tax credits would encourage the creation of jobs within the zones and the employment of people living in the zones in jobs both within and outside the zone. These job incentives were perhaps the most controversial part of the proposal. There was concern that employers outside the zones would not be induced to hire more workers from the zones; they would simply look through their list of existing workers, to see who was eligible. While some argued that the focus should be on job creation within the zones, others, pointing out that most of America does not live where it works, asked why the inner-city areas should be any different.

The empowerment zones are predicated on the belief that building up communities will require more than just economic development, but that economic development can occur most effectively if there is a broader array of support, both within the community and from all levels of government. It will take years to see whether the modicum of financial aid that the government provides will suffice to leverage the private sector activity which, in the end, must form the basis of the economic renewal of these communities.

*See Executive Office of the President, Office of Management and Budget, *Budget of the United States Government, Fiscal Year 1995, Analytical Perspectives*, Table 6-1.

2 The earned income tax credit, greatly expanded in 1993, increases the incentives for working (for participating in the labor force), though for those with incomes above a certain level, it decreases incentives to work longer hours.

3 Welfare benefits decrease as income increases; the decrease in benefits has the same effect as a marginal tax rate, discouraging work effort. Programs with more generous benefits for the very poor must either cost more or have faster phaseouts. Faster phaseouts are associated with higher marginal tax rates, and thus greater work disincentives. Eligibility thresholds have particularly adverse incentive effects.

4 The in-kind redistributive programs have several disadvantages:

   a They are administratively costly.

b In some cases, they have only an income effect (i.e., they have the same effect as a transfer of cash); in other cases, they have a substitution effect, and in those cases, the government could make the poor better off at less cost through a cash subsidy.

c The effect of many eligibility standards is to discourage work and, when compounded with payroll and state income taxes, can result in very high marginal tax rates.

d The structure of eligibility standards provides unintended results; for instance, the food stamp program subsidizes the consumption of housing.

e The programs are paternalistic.

5 Categorical programs have similar disadvantages:

a They are administratively costly.

b They are viewed by some as inequitable, since individuals with the same income may be treated differently.

c They are sometimes distortionary, as individuals attempt to qualify for subsidies.

However, when groups differ in their labor supply responses (or other responses) to government programs, the government may be able to obtain a higher degree of redistribution, for the same loss of inefficiency, by providing categorical aid.

6 The 1996 welfare reform ended the federal entitlement to welfare, converted the system of matching grants to the states to block grants, and put time limits on welfare. There is concern that switching to block grants will result in a "race to the bottom," a long-run decline in benefits. Though welfare rolls fell dramatically immediately following the passage of the bill, concern remains about "hard-core" welfare recipients who will be difficult to place in jobs and about what might happen in the event of another recession. Critics of the 1996 bill argue that it did not provide adequate assistance for training; advocates argue that what is required is not expensive training, but the acquisition of "soft skills"—good work habits—that are best acquired in the workplace.

7 The lack of integration of the various welfare programs results in high marginal tax rates, with strong adverse incentive effects. While there are proposals to "cash out" benefits and consolidate programs, given fiscal constraints, either benefits for those with little income will fall far below the poverty threshold, or generous initial benefits will have to be phased out quickly, resulting in high marginal tax rates.

Public assistance	Special Supplemental Nutrition Program for Women, Infants, and Children (WIC)
Welfare	
Aid to Families with Dependent Children (AFDC)	
	Eligibility requirements
Temporary Assistance to Needy Families (TANF)	Threshold test
	Welfare lock
Supplemental Security Income (SSI)	Children's Health Insurance Program (CHIP)
Matching programs	
Means tested	Low-Income Home Energy Assistance Program (LIHEAP)
Block grants	
Earned Income Tax Credit (EITC)	Safety net
Cash welfare program	Social insurance
In-kind benefits	Poverty rate
Workfare	Categorical programs
	Food stamps
	Negative income tax

QUESTIONS AND PROBLEMS

1 It has sometimes been suggested that the government should restrict the use of food stamps to "healthy" foods. Discuss the merits of this proposal. Assuming that it would be easy to distinguish between "healthy" and "unhealthy" foods, describe the effect of such a restriction on an individual's consumption of the two kinds of foods.

2 Consider a welfare program (such as housing) with an eligibility standard that requires that an individual's income be below some threshold level. Draw the individual's budget constraint with and without the subsidy (put labor on one axis, consumption on the other).

3 Consider a welfare program (such as food stamps) with benefits that decrease as an individual's income increases. Draw the individual's budget constraint with and without the subsidy. (Put hours of work on the horizontal axis, and income on the vertical axis.) Use the diagram to illustrate how work incentives are reduced and how a fixed dollar subsidy could lead the individual to the same level of utility at lower dollar cost.

4 There have been proposals for more extensive use of government subsidies to help poor individuals purchase private housing (just as the government's food stamp program helps them purchase food). Discuss the merits of private versus public provision of housing.

5 Several different proposals have been put forward concerning how housing subsidies should be provided. Discuss the merits of:

a The government's paying a given fraction of the family's housing expenditures, up to some maximum, with the percentage depending on the family's income

b The government's paying a fixed dollar amount of housing allowance, the amount depending on the family's income

In both cases, discuss the consequences for the family's expenditures on medicine; on food.

6 Assume you were particularly concerned with the welfare of children. How would this affect the kind of welfare programs you might support or how you might design your welfare programs?

7 **a** Draw the budget constraint of an individual facing a negative income tax with a constant marginal tax rate of, say, 30 percent, assuming the individual receives $1000 if he does not work (and has no other source of income). Assume that the basic "grant" is increased to $2000 and the marginal tax rate is increased to 45 percent. Draw the new budget constraint. Explain why 1) very poor individuals are likely to work less under the second regime; 2) middle- and upper-income individuals may work more or less.

If the government were particularly concerned about the lack of work incentives of the poor, but still wanted to provide a high level of basic support, it could have a marginal tax rate of, say, 30 percent, up to $30,000 of income, and then impose, say, a tax rate of 55 percent for higher incomes. Compare work effort in these two regimes. Who is likely to work harder? less hard? Why might you be more concerned with the reduced work effort of upper-income individuals compared to the increased work effort of lower-income individuals?

b The size of the earned income tax credit depends on family size. Explain why it might make sense for the increase in benefits with a third child to be less than the increase in benefits from a second child. (Families with no children get no benefits.) What incentives might such a structure have for families breaking up?

c Explain why, even taking into account social security taxes, two poor people can be made better off if they hire each other to look after their children. Would it pay them to hire each other to do nothing?

8 Several proposals have been made to encourage employers to hire former welfare recipients, but there has been concern that such subsidies will lead to welfare recipients' simply displacing other unskilled workers from their jobs.

a Using standard demand and supply diagrams, assume that former welfare recipients are identical to other unskilled labor, and that work requirements simply shift the supply curve of unskilled labor. What happens to employment and wages of unskilled workers?

b Now assume that there is a minimum wage which is above the equilibrium level of wages for unskilled workers. What happens to employment and wages of unskilled workers? What happens to the unemployment rate?

c Now assume that the government provides tax subsidies to employers who hire former welfare recipients. Will this affect the total number of unskilled workers hired? Will it affect *which* unskilled workers get hired?

d Now assume the government provides tax subsidies for the employment of *all* unskilled workers. What happens to employment, wages, and the unemployment rate?

e Now assume that welfare recipients are slightly less productive than other unskilled workers, say, because they have been out of the labor market; if they return to the labor market for a short period of time, say, six months, their productivity becomes equal to that of other unskilled workers. If there is a minimum wage, but no special tax provisions for welfare recipients, what will happen to employment of welfare recipients? What will be the consequences of a short-term subsidy for hiring former welfare recipients?

9 Calculate the slopes of different segments of the stylized budget constraint of Figure 15.2, panel C. What other shapes might the budget constraint take?

16 Education

FOCUS QUESTIONS

1 What are the reasons why government plays such a big role in education?

2 What are the key problems with education in the United States today?

3 What are the major proposed solutions?

4 What is the relationship between educational expenditures and outcomes?

5 What are vouchers, and the arguments for and against them?

6 What other initiatives are there for changing school governance?

7 Why is there controversy over school standards?

In the United States, education has long been recognized as a responsibility of government. The Land Ordinance of 1785, enacted even before the Constitution, set aside land in the newly established territories to fund public schools. While the locus of responsibility remains at the state and local levels—education is the single largest expenditure at those levels—today the federal government finances about 9 percent of all education expenditures, using these funds for specific purposes, such as providing education for the disadvantaged, encouraging the establishment of educational standards, promoting science education, and providing financial assistance to enable more people to attend college.

In U.S. national politics, bipartisan consensus on the importance of education is the norm. But major controversies exist over how best to attain a high-quality education system that provides equality of opportunity even to the poor. Most recently, during the budgetary stringency of the 1990s, President Bill Clinton kept education high among his budget priorities. In fact, it was one of the few areas in which real expenditures increased.

Two major economic issues—a slowdown in productivity and increasing inequality—have informed much of the recent concern about education in the United States. During the decades between World War II and the early 1970s, output per worker grew at a rate of 2.9 percent per year, but since that time the annual rate of productivity growth has averaged about 1.1 percent. Though explanations of this productivity slowdown remain uncertain, many economists and policy makers agree that improvements in human capital—the skills and experience of workers—may hold the key to improving productivity growth; and strong education is seen as critical to that goal.

The early 1970s also marked an important change in the pattern of income distribution in the United States. The fruits of economic growth were shared more equitably during the two decades prior to 1973 than during recent decades.[1] Much of this increase in inequality can be related to education. During the 1980s, the difference between the income of a college graduate and that of a high school graduate increased enormously[2] as the market placed a greater premium on skilled (educated) workers. Thus, providing better education and ensuring that a larger fraction of the population went to college were seen as ways of enhancing opportunity and reducing inequality. Not only would those receiving a college education enjoy higher incomes, but wages would rise in the market for unskilled labor as the number of unskilled laborers dropped.

For these reasons, and others, economists and policy makers have placed a high priority on strong education. But how strong is the education system in the United States? One of the most impressive achievements of the U.S. system has been the growth in college attendance throughout the latter half of the twentieth century. The GI Bill of Rights, which provided an opportunity for World War II veterans to attend college, transformed higher education from a privilege of the elite to an expectation of the broad middle class. That expectation carried through to another generation as

---

[1] One way of seeing this is to divide the country into quintiles by income, distinguishing the poorest fifth of the population from the next poorest fifth, and so on. Prior to 1973, all quintiles saw their incomes growing, and the poorest quintiles saw their incomes growing fastest. From 1973 through the early 1990s, the poorest quintile actually saw incomes declining, while the richest quintile enjoyed income growth. Since 1993 there has been a reversal of this trend, but the change is too small to have undone what occurred over the previous two decades. Source: *Economic Report of the President, 1997* (Washington, D.C.: Government Printing Office, 1997), Chart 5-1, p. 164, Chart 5-8, p. 178.
[2] Ibid., Chart 5-4, p. 169.

college enrollment rates soared in the 1970s and 1980s,[3] while high school dropout rates fell.[4]

Even so, in recent decades questions have been raised about the caliber of the U.S. education system. International comparisons inform some of these questions. For instance, one set of statistics suggested that in 1994 America had a smaller percentage of citizens with the equivalent of thirteen or more years of schooling than did France and Germany, and even than Singapore, which a few short years earlier had been classified as an underdeveloped country.[5] On a standardized math and science test administered around the world in 1994–1995, the United States ranked twenty-eighth in math—behind Singapore, South Korea, Bulgaria, Russia, and most of the developed countries—and seventeenth in science. Inequality in the United States may help explain such results. Students outside of America's poor urban schools achieve results comparable to their peers in other advanced countries, and though the median mathematics scores of American students ranked below those of France, Canada, and Spain, the best American students (in the ninety-ninth percentile) ranked above their peers from those countries.[6]

This brings us to a major issue in recent policy debates: education of the economically disadvantaged, particularly in America's inner cities and impoverished rural areas. Indigent students receive inadequate primary and secondary education, leaving them unprepared for colleges and universities. Without adequate skills, these people earn low wages, and are thus forced to continue to live in poor areas, continuing the cycle of poverty. The problem has been exacerbated by some other trends in the economy. During the 1980s, while real wages of the poorest declined, real tuition at public two- and four-year institutions of higher learning increased markedly, so that those indigent students who were qualified for higher education faced increasingly insurmountable financial hurdles. Thus, while the increased returns to education noted earlier did lead to an increase in college enrollments, children of more affluent families were better able to respond to these market signals, and the gap between enrollment rates of the disadvantaged and other Americans actually increased.

All of these issues have made education a critical concern for the U.S. public sector. This chapter describes the structure of the U.S. education system, explores the rationale for public finance and provision of education in the United States, and analyzes some of these current issues in U.S. education policy.

---

[3] *Economic Report of the President, 1996*, Chart 7-1, p. 193.

[4] The percentage of those under the age of 45 who had not completed high school was substantially lower than for the population as a whole—12 percent versus 18 percent. See *Statistical Abstract of the United States, 1996*, Table 243.

[5] *The Economist*, special issue, April 1997.

[6] *Economic Report of the President, 1996*, Chart 7-2, p. 195

THE STRUCTURE OF EDUCATION IN THE UNITED STATES

Traditionally, elementary and secondary school education has been the responsibility of local communities. They financed it (usually with property taxes), hired the teachers, and determined the curriculum. Figure 16.1 shows the trends in local, state, and federal spending on elementary and secondary education. From 1945 to 1972, the state percentage of education funds remained steady at 39 percent. During the mid-1970s, state expenditures began to increase at a faster rate than local expenditures, so that by the end of the decade, states actually paid for a higher percentage of total costs. More recently, in the 1990s, local spending increased more than state

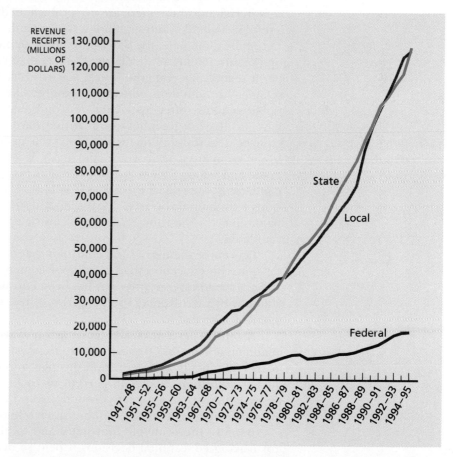

FIGURE 16.1   **Revenue Sources of Public Elementary and Secondary Schools** All sources of support have increased markedly in recent years.

SOURCE: U.S. Department of Education, National Center for Education Statistics, *Digest of Education Statistics, 1985–1986*, Table 69, p. 80.

spending, so that the two each contribute approximately 45 percent of total funds. Federal support for education, mostly for special programs such as aid to schools with a large number of disadvantaged children, increased in the 1960s and 1970s, and by 1980 represented almost 10 percent of total financing for public elementary and secondary schools. While federal support declined from that level to under 7 percent in the mid-1980s, by the mid-1990s it was restored almost to its former level (as a percentage of total expenditures).

There is, however, a great deal of variability, both in the federal government's role and in the states'. For example, while in recent years the federal government has provided approximately a sixth of the funds for primary and secondary schools in Mississippi, it has provided less than 4 percent of the funds in New Jersey and New Hampshire. On average, states provided slightly more than half of the nonfederal funds, but this varied, from almost 100 percent in Hawaii (where there are no local school districts), to slightly less than a third in Nebraska, and slightly less than a tenth in New Hampshire.

At the same time, the states have taken an increasingly active role in setting certain minimum standards. They set the number of days students must be in school per year; the lowest age at which children may drop out of school; the minimum education requirements for teachers employed in public schools (often specifying not only that the teachers, for instance, have a college degree, but also that they have taken a specified number of courses in education). States also play a role in determining curriculum. For example, many states require courses in American history in the eleventh grade and adopt certain approved lists of textbooks, from which the local community must select the books it will use. Several states have made provisions for state takeovers of local school districts when there is "academic bankruptcy"—when the local school districts fail to meet certain minimal standards.

One consequence of local control is that many rich communities spend far more on education than most poor communities. The range in educational expenditures per student has been enormous, even within individual states, with rich districts spending two, three, or more times the amount spent in poor districts.

About 90 percent of all elementary and secondary school students attend public schools. Of those who go to private schools, half go to Catholic parochial schools. Private institutions play a much more important role in higher education. About 38 percent of bachelor's, master's, and doctor's degrees are earned at private institutions, and more than 60 percent of first professional degrees are earned in private schools.[7]

Because the principle that states and localities should be responsible for making educational decisions is held so dear, the federal government has relied on a variety of indirect ways to try to influence states and locali-

[7] First professional degrees include those for medicine, dentistry, pharmacy, veterinary medicine, law, and theological professions. See *Digest of Education Statistics, 1997.*

ties. After the Soviet Union launched Sputnik, the first space satellite, in 1957, and thus appeared to be surpassing the United States in science, the U.S. federal government supported efforts to improve the science curriculum in elementary and secondary schools. In the early nineties, when it became apparent that many of those graduating from high school who did not go on to college were having a hard time entering the labor force, the federal government sponsored a school-to-work initiative. This encouraged the states to design apprenticeship-like programs (so successful in other countries, such as Germany) that would facilitate the movement from school to work. When, again in the early nineties, the federal government wanted to encourage higher standards in elementary and secondary schools, it did not impose national standards, but rather provided funding that helped the states establish standards for themselves, and several commissions were set up to help in the formation of national standards in the various disciplines.

FEDERAL TAX SUBSIDIES TO PRIVATE AND PUBLIC SCHOOLS

The personal income tax may have important effects on the demand for public and private education. Expenditures of state and local communities for education (as well as for other purposes) are implicitly subsidized by the federal government because state and local taxes (other than sales taxes) are deductible on federal income tax returns, and interest on state and local bonds is exempt from federal taxation. This means that if my community taxes me $1000 to support public schools, the cost to me is far less than $1000. If I am in the 31% marginal tax bracket (so that I pay 31 cents of each additional dollar of taxable income to the federal government), then by deducting $1000, my federal taxes are reduced by $310. The *net* cost to me of $1000 on public education is only $690. In contrast, if I spend $1000 on private education, it costs me $1000 that I could have spent elsewhere.[8]

The total value of tax expenditures specifically for education in 1998 was estimated to be approximately $14 billion, as Table 16.1 shows. Most of these expenditures arose from the deductibility of state and local taxes from federal income tax. Since the value of the tax deductions is greatest for higher-income individuals, this form of support for education is, in effect, *regressive*; that is, it benefits higher-income individuals and higher-income communities more than lower-income ones.

At the same time, the tax system serves to discourage private expenditures on education.[9] If I spend $1000 in tuition to send my child to a private school, not only do I pass up the already-paid-for public education, but the expenditure is not even tax deductible. Later, the return to the education, which occurs in the form of higher wages, is taxed. The tax system thus discourages private spending on education.

[8] This example assumes that I itemize my deductions rather than claiming the standard deduction. Only individuals with large deductible expenses (such as interest on a home mortgage) itemize. See Chapter 22 for a more detailed discussion.

[9] However, the tax deductibility of gifts to private schools (which are treated as charities) strongly encourages private education.

TABLE 16.1
Estimated Federal Tax
Expenditures for
Education, Fiscal Year
1998 (in millions of
dollars)

	REVENUE LOSS	
	CORPORATE	INDIVIDUAL
Exclusion of Scholarship and Fellowship Income		$ 850
Exclusion of Interest on State and Local Student Loans Bonds and Debt for Private Nonprofit Facilities	$465	710
Exclusion of Interest on Savings Bonds Transferred to Educational Institutions		10
Exclusion of Employer-Provided Educational Assistance		20
Parental Personal Exemption for Students Age 19 or Over		885
Deductibility of Charitable Contributions for Educational Purposes	200	1860
Deduction of Non-Business State and Local Taxes (Total =$30,995)		8679
Total	$665	$13,014

SOURCE: Calculated from Executive Office of the President, Office of Management and Budget, *Budget of the United States Government, Fiscal Year 1998, Analytical Perspectives,* Table 5-2. The expenditure resulting from the deductibility of state and local taxes assumes state and local jurisdictions spend 28 percent of revenues on education (calculated from *Statistical Abstract of the United States, 1997,* Table 478, on government finances for fiscal year 1994).

WHY IS EDUCATION PUBLICLY PROVIDED AND PUBLICLY FINANCED?

In the United States the public role in the provision of education has been so pervasive that it is generally taken for granted. In some other countries, however, while the government may provide funds to educational institutions, much of the education itself is provided by private, particularly religious, schools.

IS THERE A MARKET FAILURE? Education is not a pure public good. The marginal cost of educating an additional child is far from zero; indeed, the marginal and average costs are (at least for large school districts) approximately the same. And there is no technical difficulty in charging individuals for use of this service.

Those who seek to justify public education in terms of a market failure focus on the importance of externalities. It is often claimed, for instance, that there are important externalities associated with having an educated citizenry. A society in which everyone can read functions far more smoothly than a society in which few can read. But there is a large private return to being able to read, and even in the absence of government support, many individuals would learn this and other basic skills. Indeed, most individuals would go far beyond that. The question is, given the level of education that individuals would choose to undertake privately were there no government subsidy, would further increases in education generate any significant externalities? There is no agreement concerning the answer, but the case for government support based on these kinds of externalities—at least for advanced industrial economies like the United States—seems, at best, unproved.[10]

There may be other important externalities associated with education. Public education may have played an important role in integrating new immigrant groups into American culture. Public education may have been essential in making the melting pot work. The benefits of this accrued not only to individuals but to the nation as a whole.

There is another indirect form of externality to investments in science and technology education: people with these scarce skills are the key to technological progress; and typically innovators capture only a fraction of their overall contribution to the increase in productivity.

There may, however, be a reason why individuals do not invest as much in education as they would like, even to the point where the private return equals the cost of capital: They may lack access to funds to finance their education. Private lenders are not, for the most part, willing to lend to finance education; understandably, banks are concerned about getting repaid. Hence those lacking funds of their own (or funds from their families) would be denied access to higher education without some assistance from the government.

There is another reason why there may be underinvestment in education. At the elementary and secondary level, parents make decisions on behalf of their children. Though most parents may view expenditures on their children altruistically, investing in their children so long as the returns are sufficiently high, some parents may not. Under a system of privately financed education, the children of such parents might receive an insufficient education. Thus, a rationale for public support of primary and secondary education is provided on distributional grounds: there is a widespread belief that children's access to education should not depend on their parents' financial ability or their sense of altruism. Indeed, such distributional concerns provide the strongest motivation for a public role in education more generally—for the financing of elementary and secondary education and for the extensive financial support of higher education, especially with loan programs.

While these arguments provide a rationale for government financing of education, they do not provide an argument for government production. Why is it that at the elementary and secondary level, government produc-

---

[10] See, for instance, D. M. Windham, "Economic Analysis and the Public Support of Higher Education: The Divergence of Theory and Policy," in *Economic Dimensions of Education*, A Report of a Committee of the National Academy of Education, May 1979.

tion (public schools) dominates, while at the college level private education plays a far more important role? In many other countries, private elementary and secondary schools play a far more important role than they do in the United States. Later in this chapter we will examine the controversy over private schools.

THE FEDERAL ROLE The arguments discussed above explain why *some* governmental entity should provide financing for education. But they do not explain the level—local, state, or federal—at which the support should be provided. Increasingly, many arguments for a public role in education are arguments for a federal role. Largely this is because to the extent that there are externalities, given the huge migrations which occur throughout the country, those externalities need to be addressed at the federal level. Inadequate education is associated with a variety of social problems and antisocial behaviors. Those who grow up in one state and receive an inadequate education there have a good chance of practicing their antisocial behaviors in another state.

Moreover, distribution concerns can be addressed fully only at the national level, given the huge disparities in per capita incomes (and corresponding disparities in education expenditures per pupil) across states.[11] States that spend less on education per pupil tend to generate lower performance, as measured by earnings.[12]

ISSUES AND CONTROVERSIES IN EDUCATIONAL POLICY

Education has long been a source of political and intellectual debate. There are different perspectives on the basic impact of education on students, how education should be produced and financed, and whether the current system results in too much inequality. The following sections take up some of these issues and controversies.

EDUCATION OUTCOMES There are different perspectives on the outcomes of the education process. One view, implicit in the foregoing discussion, holds that education increases the skills of individuals, and thereby wages. Called the **human capital** view, this perspective sees investment in people as akin to capital investment. The greater the investment, the greater the productivity.[13] But there is controversy over why and to what extent the higher

[11] For instance, the state with the highest per capita income (Connecticut) had a per capita income almost twice that of the lowest (Mississippi) in 1996; expenditures per pupil in Connecticut were slightly more than twice that of Mississippi.
[12] David Card and Alan B. Krueger, "Does School Quality Matter? Returns to Education and the Characteristics of Public School in the United States," *Journal of Political Economy*, vol. 100, February 1992, pp. 1–40.
[13] See Gary Becker, *Human Capital: A Theoretical and Empirical Analysis with Special References to Education*, 2d ed. (New York: National Bureau of Economic Research, Columbia University Press, 1975).

wages earned by skilled workers reflect an increase in their productivity resulting from education.

One variant of the human capital view, emphasized by Samuel Bowles and Herb Gintis of the University of Massachusetts, focuses on the socializing role of education. Education teaches people how to perform well in the workplace, by teaching how to obey orders, follow directions, and work in teams. When successful, this socialization teaches punctuality and reliability. In this perspective, those who go to school longer learn more of these social skills, or, in any case, have demonstrated a greater ability or willingness to cope with the demands of the school system. These social abilities (or drives) make these individuals more valuable in the workplace.[14]

Another view of education, called the **screening** view, argues that one of the important functions of education is to identify the abilities of different individuals. Those who go to school longer get a higher wage and are observed to be more productive. This is not because the schools have increased their productivity, but rather because the schools have identified those individuals who are the most productive, or who have the necessary drive and ambition. The school system is viewed as a screening device, separating the very able and highly motivated from the less able and less motivated.[15]

In the screening perspective, the *social* returns to education are far less than the *private* returns. The private returns can be significant: those who go to college receive a substantially higher income than those who do not. But if all that was going on were the identification of who was more able and who less, the total production of society would be unaffected; the social returns would be zero. In fact, education also identifies differences in skills, enabling a better matching of individuals and jobs, and this does increase overall productivity: there can be significant social returns to screening. There is general agreement today that some of the returns to education are the result of increases in skills and some are a result of screening; the controversy arises over their relative importance.[16]

[14] Andrew Weiss, "Human Capital versus Signaling Explanations of Wages, *Journal of Economic Perspectives* 9, no. 4 (fall 1995): 133–54. Weiss studied closely low-skilled workers in a manufacturing plant. Long-run success depended not on any particular skill but on social characteristics like reliability (low levels of absenteeism) and punctuality.

[15] This view has been put forward by J. E. Stiglitz, "The Theory of Screening Education and the Distribution of Income," *American Economic Review* 65 (1975): 283–300; A. Michael Spence, "Job Market Signaling," *Quarterly Journal of Economics* 87 (1973): 355–74; and K. J. Arrow, "Higher Education as a Filter," *Journal of Public Economics* 2 (1973): 193–216.

[16] For instance, studies showing that wages do not depend closely on the subjects studied suggest that content (skill formation) matters little. Moreover, if skill formation were predominant, one would expect that the increase in returns would be a relatively steady process, so that the increment in wages per year would be the same; but in fact, the increase in wages from the completion of the fourth year of college is much greater than the increase in wages from the completion of the preceding three years.

The significance of the ways in which education differs from other commodities is posed most starkly by the controversy over whether increased educational expenditures lead to increased education performance. In the
production of a standard commodity, an increase in input would necessarily
lead to an increase in output. Earlier, we noted the low performance of
American students compared to those abroad, as indicated by certain test
scores. Figure 16.2 shows clearly that this is not because the United States is
spending less; in fact, on a per pupil basis it is spending more than almost
any other country. Similarly, expenditures per pupil have increased
markedly over the past fifteen years, with only a modicum of effect on test
scores. The weak link between expenditures and performance had been
demonstrated earlier, in a classic study by James Coleman and his co-

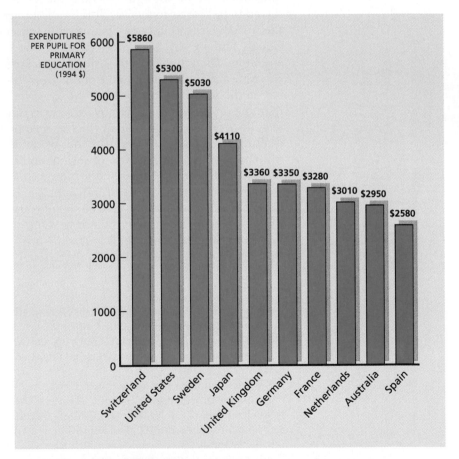

FIGURE 16.2   **Differences in Educational Expenditures among Countries** The United States
spends more per pupil on primary education than almost any other country.

Source: Organization for Economic Cooperation and Development, *Education at a Glance*, Education Indicators, 1997, Table B4.1.

authors.[17] Coleman's study spawned a huge literature, with his results still in dispute.[18]

Many economists believe that increased expenditures do make a difference—a greater difference than Coleman's earlier study suggested. A set of studies that looked at the performance of identical twins (so that natural differences were fully accounted for) showed that levels of education made a systematic difference in earnings. Another study compared states with different rules for when students could drop out of school; those who were forced to stay in school longer (controlling for other variables) seemed to do better.

The problem with interpreting the consequences of differences in expenditure levels is that much—and an increasing proportion—of education expenditures in the United States goes to purposes not directly related to teaching (such as administrative expenses) and to addressing the requirements of those with special needs. There are only limited data looking at, for instance, the consequences of smaller class sizes. The most famous experiment occurred in Tennessee, where students were randomly assigned to different class sizes; the results of that experiment, while not conclusive, support the view that smaller class size (entailing greater expenditures) does lead to improved student performance.[19]

Another set of critiques of Coleman's findings argues that the real output of educational expenditures is not supposed to be higher test scores but

---

[17] James S. Coleman et al., *Equality of Educational Opportunity* (Washington, D.C.: Department of Health, Education, and Welfare, 1966).

[18] See the recent survey by Eric A. Hanushek, "School Resources and Student Performance," in *Does Money Matter? The Effect of School Resources on Student Achievement and Adult Success,* ed. Gary Burtless (Washington, D.C.: Brookings Institution, 1996), pp. 43–73; and Hanushek's earlier article, "The Economics of Schooling: Production and Efficiency in Public Schools," *Journal of Economic Literature* 24, no. 3 (September 1986): 1141–77. See also Harold Wenglinsky, *When Money Matters: How Educational Expenditures Improve Student Performance and How They Don't* (Princeton, N.J.: Educational Testing Service, Policy Information Center, April 1997); and Alan B. Krueger, "Experimental Estimates of Educational Production Functions," *Quarterly Journal of Economics* 113 (May 1999).

[19] See E. Word et al., "Student/Teacher Achievement Ratio (STAR)—Tennessee's K-3 Class Size Study," Tennessee Department of Education. This study corroborates other findings. In an analysis of many studies, Gene Glass concluded that "small classes were very much better than large classes; large classes were hardly any better than very large classes." See G. V. Glass, *School Class Size: Research and Policy* (Beverly Hills, Calif.: Sage Publications, 1982), p. 47. In a review of eleven studies, Robert Slavin found that the largest (but still modest) effects of class size on test performance were observed in the study with the largest reduction in class size (from twenty-three to fifteen). See Robert E. Slavin, "School and Classroom Organization in Beginning Reading," in *Preventing Early School Failure: Research, Policy, and Practice,* ed. Slavin et al. (Boston: Allyn and Bacon, 1994), pp. 122–30. See also Karen Akerhielm, "Does Class Size Matter?" *Economics of Education Review* 13, no. 3 (September 1995): 229–41; and David Card and Alan Krueger, "School Resources and Student Outcomes," *Annals of the American Academy of Political and Social Science* 559 (September 1998): 39–53.

higher productivity, leading to higher wages. Several recent studies have established a clear link between expenditures and earnings.[20]

Those who believe that schools have relatively little impact on earnings believe that home background is critical. Even in that view, it is still possible that by increasing expenditures on the disadvantaged, public schools can help offset deficiencies in home background. This raises fundamental questions about the allocation of resources *within* schools: how much should go to helping the academically gifted, how much to the average student, and how much to those at the bottom? The country's technological leadership depends on having the best scientists in the world, and this argues for putting resources at the disposal of the scientifically gifted. On the other hand, without adequate skills, those at the bottom will see their wages fall behind, as they have been doing in the last two decades. (See Figure 16.3.) Increasing inequality is likely to give rise to increasing social problems in the decades ahead. Education advocates argue that we should spend more on both, but given the current overall limitations on expenditures, the issue is, should we direct more to the top or the bottom, or do we now have just about the right balance? The appendix to this chapter presents a framework for thinking about this issue.

SCHOOL VOUCHERS: CHOICE AND COMPETITION

Perhaps the most heated recent debate in the political sphere has concerned the question of school choice. Should parents be given more choice about where their children go to school? The simplest proposals for providing school choice entail vouchers: each child would be given a coupon—worth, say, $5000—to be used at the school of the parent's choice. Public schools would, under this proposal, have to compete directly with private schools; they would have to raise their revenue by persuading students to attend, just as private schools do. If parents valued the kinds of programs provided by the public schools, then the public schools would do well.

Implicit in much of the discussion favoring vouchers is a critique of the role of government in education: today it both finances education and produces it. Many believe, as we saw in Chapter 8, that, for a variety of reasons, the government is not an efficient producer, and that in the competition between schools, private schools would win out. Moreover, they say, when parents choose their children's school, they become more committed to that school and more involved in their children's education, and this contributes to school performance.

Interestingly, and contrary to the claims of critics, advocates of choice argue that private schools not only produce a higher-quality education at lower costs, but actually promote equality. In another famous study, the late James Coleman of the University of Chicago and his co-authors argued that America's public schools were actually more segregated, both racially and socioeconomically, than were its private schools. The segregation results because the public school system, especially at the primary level, is based on

[20] See, for example, Ronald Rizzuto and Paul Wachtel, "Further Evidence on the Returns to School Quality," *Journal of Human Resources*, spring 1980, pp. 240–54; and David Card and Alan B. Krueger, "Labor Market Effects of School Quality: Theory and Evidence," in Burtless, *Does Money Matter?* pp. 97–140.

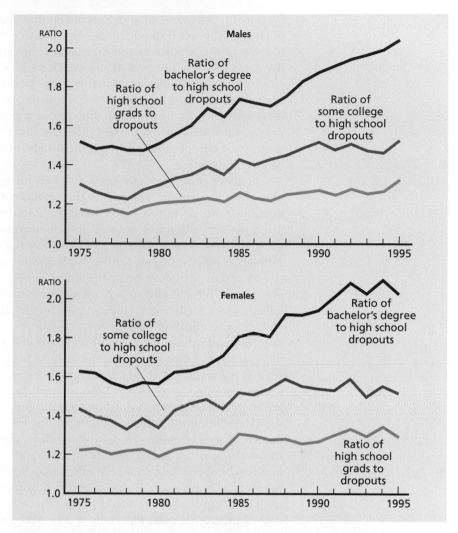

FIGURE 16.3 **Differences in Income across Levels of Education** These charts plot median incomes of men and women with higher levels of education relative to high school dropouts. Since 1975, the earnings of minimally educated men and women have fallen behind their better-educated peers.

SOURCES: *Digest of Education Statistics, 1991*, Table 357; *Digest of Education Statistics, 1997*, Table 378. The ratios are computed from median incomes of full-time workers aged 25 and older, in 1995 dollars.

neighborhood schools, and neighborhoods are in effect segregated. They also argue that private schools are more effective in educating disadvantaged students (for instance, as measured by test scores).[21]

[21] James Coleman, Thomas Hoffer, and Sally Kilgore, "Public and Private Schools: An Analysis of High School and Beyond" (U.S. Department of Education, National Center for Educational Statistics, November 1981).

Finally, advocates of vouchers argue that America already has a system of choice, but constrained choice. Those with enough resources can choose to move to the suburbs or put their kids in private school. It is the poor that the current system deprives of choice. There is competition, but only for the children of the affluent, not for the poor. America believes in competition. It may be natural for those in any industry to argue that competition in their sector would be less desirable, and the postulates of perfect competition may not be satisfied perfectly. Still, as a country we believe that the advantages of competition outweigh the disadvantages. Why should education be any different?

Voucher programs have been attacked on several grounds. Some economists argue that the conditions that make competition work in conventional markets do not exist in education. Parents, particularly less well educated parents, often are not well informed; they are ill prepared to judge the effectiveness of schools in providing key skills. Indeed, this information problem is a key rationale for the establishment of national standards.

Moreover, in many areas, the number of schools is limited; many parents are inclined to choose schools on the basis of convenience rather than educational excellence. Competition is further limited by the fact that once children are enrolled in a school, transferring is likely to be difficult; and the less standardized the curriculum, the more difficult adjustment will be.

Critics of choice argue that the alleged superior performance of private schools is a mirage. Part of the seemingly superior performance arises from a selection effect: those who chose to send their children to private schools are more committed to education, and it is this commitment, rather than what the schools do, which accounts for any measured differences in performance. Secondly, there is a discipline effect: private schools reject or expel those who are disruptive or who in other ways fail to perform adequately. Public schools cannot do this. While it may be true that today performance in private schools exceeds that of public schools for individuals of seemingly similar backgrounds, this would not be the case if there were a major expansion of private schools, especially if they were required to take all students, including those with discipline problems.

Moreover, say many critics of vouchers, the scheme would lead to a more socially and economically stratified society, with children of wealthy and well-educated parents going to one set of schools and children of poor and less well educated parents going to another. Though regulations to prevent racial discrimination might be easily enforced, regulations to ensure the absence of socioeconomic stratification would be difficult to implement.

Voucher schemes remain very much on the political agenda. In part this reflects the widespread dissatisfaction with American elementary and secondary education—though curiously, while most parents are critical of the state of education overall, they believe their own children are receiving a good education. The concerns over quality are especially strong in America's inner cities, which have high dropout rates.

In the 1996 election, the Republican presidential candidate, Robert Dole, proposed a national voucher plan, but budgetary constraints required it to be of limited scope. Teachers' unions have strongly opposed even a limited form of vouchers. While they marshall all the arguments given earlier for public education, and warn that vouchers will drain resources out of public schools, critics of the unions say their real motives are less public spirited: the unions have a stranglehold on public schools, and are weak or nonexistent in private schools; like any monopoly, these resist competition, fearing that it will weaken their bargaining power, in the same way that unions in other competitive sectors have been weakened.

Meanwhile, those seeking to introduce innovation and more competition *within* public schools have looked to alternatives to vouchers. One is "contracting out": the school district contracts outside managers to run their schools. The competition between management teams will, advocates claim, lead to higher performance. School districts can make more informed decisions concerning management teams than many parents can concerning schools. Several school districts are currently experimenting with such arrangements, and initial results look positive. In particular, the contracting firms have been willing to engage in heavy up-front investments, for instance in training and development of teaching materials, that public schools would have found hard to finance themselves.[22]

Still another initiative involves "charter schools," schools which are self-managed or managed directly by the children's parents, rather than by a larger school district. There is now a large number of such schools, and parents of children attending them generally are highly supportive. Supporters of the charter schools hope that their innovations will be imitated elsewhere, and that they will thereby spur an overall improvement in educa-

---

THE VOUCHER DEBATE

Pro	Con
• Competition promotes efficiency.	• Conditions that make competition work not satisfied.
• Choice promotes commitment.	• Will result in more social and economic stratification.
• Need not result in greater inequality: private schools currently doing as well as or better than public schools.	• Evidence on greater efficiency questionable: what will happen to problem children?

---

[22] For an extensive discussion of contracting out, see Paul T. Hill, Lawrence C. Pierce, and James W. Guthrie, *Reinventing Public Education: How Contracting Can Transform America's Schools*, (Chicago: University of Chicago Press, 1997).

VOUCHERS: THE SAN JOSE AND MILWAUKEE EXPERIMENTS

Education vouchers would seem to be an ideal subject for experimentation: a few communities could make vouchers available and see what happens. In fact, a few communities have done just that. One of the earliest experiments, involving choice only among public schools, occurred in San Jose, California. One study concluded, after examining the results of that experiment, that,

> . . . education vouchers stand little chance of succeeding in American elementary and secondary schools. [Parents eventually] learn about their alternatives and the rules governing choice. But there is still some question about the social consequences of parents' or students' program choices. Specifically, there is some concern that parents pick programs which reinforce their class-related social values, so that poor children have little opportunity to acquire the beliefs, attitudes, and social competencies necessary for social mobility to the middle class . . . *

One of the few experiments to provide vouchers that could be used in public or private schools was begun in Milwaukee in 1990. Curiously, as the experiment proceeded, both supporters and critics of vouchers claimed that the Milwaukee experiment confirmed their views concerning the effectiveness of vouchers.

Milwaukee provided a limited number of vouchers which parents could use to send their children to the school of their choice. In 1990, the first year of the voucher program, the number of vouchers was limited to 1 percent of the public school enrollment (approximately 950 students); the program was expanded to 1.5 percent in 1994.

---

tional quality. But critics are more skeptical. Currently, charter schools, like private schools, cater to those most committed to education, those most desirous of an alternative to the current public school system. But without wider scope for school choice, how will their impact be felt on public education more broadly? And there is concern that, should they become more widespread, unions will attempt to impose the same restrictions on them that face public schools more generally. In some places such attempts are already under way.

Other reforms emphasize the broader role of incentives, such as merit pay for teachers. How effective such incentives can be depends to a large extent on how well teacher performance can be measured.[23]

---

[23] There is a large and growing literature discussing these reforms. See, for instance, Eric Hanushek and Dale Jorgenson, eds., *Improving America's Schools, The Role of Incentives* (Washington, D.C.: National Research Council, 1996).

Critics pointed out that relatively few parents availed themselves of the opportunity. During 1990–1993, fewer than 600 parents applied each year, with an average of under 400 selected and 350 actually enrolled. To set this number in perspective, Milwaukee public school enrollment was 95,000, of which 42 percent came from families below the poverty level; any family with an income of up to 1.75 times the poverty level was eligible to apply. Even more telling, of those who elected to go to private schools, a large fraction transferred back into public schools within a year or so. By 1994, only 92 of the 354 enrolled in a choice school in 1990 remained in the program. There seemed to be little effective competition with—and therefore spur to—public schools, and little spur to the expansion or creation of new private schools.

Advocates pointed to the higher performance of those who did switch to private schools and remained there—compared to that of peers with similar backgrounds who had remained in public schools. Statisticians clashed over the extent to which these differences could be attributed to the special nature of the children who had elected to go to and remain with the private schools.[†]

*Gary Bridge, "Citizen Choice in Public Services; Voucher System," in *Alternatives for Delivering Public Services*, ed. E. S. Savas (Boulder, Colo.: Westview Press, 1977).

†Source: Cecilia Elena Rouse, "Private School Vouchers and Student Achievement: An Evaluation of the Milwaukee Parental Choice Program," *Quarterly Journal of Economics* 113, no. 2 (May 1998): 553–602.

SCHOOL DECENTRALIZATION

A widely discussed school reform, school decentralization aims to address problems associated with the control of schools by large educational bureaucracies.[24] Decentralization has been an issue in large urban school districts, where such bureaucracies have been seen as unresponsive to parents. The effect of decentralization is to shift authority to individual schools and their principals, giving greater influence to individual parents. Advocates argue that school decentralization creates stronger incentives for parents to monitor teachers and schools, to the benefit of school performance. Teachers too, the argument goes, have stronger incentives to perform better because they have greater influence in the educational process at their schools.

[24] For an extensive discussion of decentralization, see Jane Hannaway and Martin Carnoy, eds., *Decentralization and School Improvement* (San Francisco: Jossey-Bass, 1993).

Criticisms of decentralization have been far more muted than those of the voucher programs, and a number of important decentralization initiatives are already in place, including those in the country's two largest cities, New York and Chicago. However, there is concern that unless union rules and attitudes are changed, little headway will be made in fundamental reform. Another worry is that if there is too much discretion at the level of schools, too much inequality will be generated: some schools will be far better than others, and this seems unfair. Supporters of decentralization point out that this, of course, is already true. Thus, any attempt to improve quality will entail some temporary inequality, until the poorer schools are lifted to the level of the better schools. But it makes little sense to keep the best schools down simply to avoid a disparity.

PERFORMANCE STANDARDS AND GOALS 2000

Many believe that before decentralization, choice, or any other reform can be effective, clear performance measures for schools must be established. Without such measures, parents, teachers, and educational reformers cannot begin to determine if schools are performing well or poorly, and therefore have no basis for educational reforms.

Establishing clear performance goals was the aim of the Goals 2000 legislation passed by Congress in 1994. Under this legislation, task forces have been established to set national performance goals in each of the major subject areas.

While there is widespread support for the establishment of goals, the legislation encountered opposition, for several reasons. Some voiced a concern that certain skills are easier to test than others; and that teachers are likely to gear their teaching in response to the tests. For example, there are good ways of testing basic skills, like phonics, but testing creativity and what are called "higher order" cognitive (thinking) skills is far more difficult. One of the strong points of American education has been how it has encouraged creativity. Will the tests divert teachers' attention toward teaching basic skills, and away from encouraging creativity and thinking skills?

On the other hand, advocates claim that our schools are failing to teach basic skills to many youngsters, and getting them to do that would be a major advance.

Still others are worried about potential inequalities. Schools with disadvantaged children worry that they will be criticized for their poor performance, and they are not persuaded by reassurances that in being judged,

ENHANCING THE EFFICIENCY OF SCHOOLS

1 Choice and competition: school vouchers

2 Reorganization: decentralization

3 Performance standards: Goals 2000

account of the background of their students will be taken. There is also a concern that children from disadvantaged backgrounds will likely perform relatively poorly on these standardized tests, and that employers will likely use these tests as a simple and acceptable screen for determining whom to hire, putting already disadvantaged groups in an even worse position.

Most importantly, critics of Goals 2000 argue that parents already know that schools are not performing as well as they would like. They believe that without more fundamental changes in the organization of schools, information itself will do little but increase parents' sense of helplessness.

INEQUALITY

One of the underlying purposes of public provision (finance) of education is to promote equality of opportunity. But there is a major concern that today, the public school system does not come close to living up to that ideal.

The major reason for the shortfall is not hard to find. Education has remained primarily a local responsibility. The resources available in some communities, such as wealthy suburban communities or towns in which there is a large factory, are a multiple of those available in others. Demands for public services in general are greater in some communities than in others: urban communities typically require far higher expenditures for maintaining public safety than do rural communities. Finally, different communities have expressed different "preferences" for education. Communities with the same resources may spend different amounts.

The system of local funding has been tested in the nation's courts. A number of state supreme courts have found that relying on local property taxes to finance education violates provisions of state constitutions ensuring equal access to public education. At the federal level, in 1972 the U.S. Supreme Court ruled, in *San Antonio Independent School District v. Rodriguez*, that local funding in Texas did not violate the "equal protection clause" of the U.S. Constitution (the Fourteenth Amendment) even though it resulted in large variability in expenditures.

Such decisions raise several important questions. Should spending be required to be the same in every community within a state? Or should the provision of a minimal level of education in every community be the only requirement? Mandating equality would seem to preclude communities' spending more on their children. Several states have in fact put caps on the levels of expenditures, thereby attaining equality not only by raising the minimum level but by lowering the maximum. If only a minimum standard is required, how is it to be determined? Obviously, if the standard is set low enough, it will have no effect at all. If it is set too high, how will poorer communities find the funds? Higher standards necessitate a greater role for the state in financing education. If equality is insisted upon, what adjustments should be made for differences in the costs of education in different communities, and in the nature of the student bodies? Is equality of spending enough? Some communities might use more of their funds to develop better athletic facilities, others for basic-skills development, others for special educational programs. The result is different treatment of similar individuals who happen to reside in different communities. To ensure complete equality would require eliminating community control and establishing a centralized educational system within each state.

At issue are not only the basic trade-offs of equity and efficiency. Most people to some degree believe that every parent should have the right to make decisions concerning his or her child's education. With local control of education, parents at least feel that they can have some influence over the outcomes. Thus local autonomy of schools has become for many a principle in its own right; some individuals might still favor local control even if it could be shown that central control was both more equitable and more efficient. To others, the trade-off at issue is between the rights of parents (to decide about their children's education) and the rights of children (to equality of opportunity, regardless of who their parents are).

Both state and federal governments have responded to these concerns by attempting to increase equality while retaining at least some degree of local autonomy, especially by providing funds to communities with low incomes and with many disadvantaged children. New Jersey, for instance, has broadened its role in financing education (with poorer districts getting much more aid than better-off districts); set minimal educational standards that all districts must attain; and, in some cases, placed ceilings on the amount that higher-spending school districts can spend.

LIMITATIONS ON EQUALITY IMPOSED BY PARENTAL CHOICE Some attempts to attain greater equality, such as the ceilings on expenditures by richer school districts, have been criticized as misguided and self-defeating, since the underlying problem is not just the degree of inequality within public schools but the total extent of inequality in our society. So long as the government is not willing to prohibit individuals from going to private schools, any attempt to introduce too much equality into the public educational system will result in individuals' transferring to private schools.

In England there have been periodic proposals for the government actively to discourage the private schools, on the grounds that private education leads to social stratification (only the upper and upper-middle classes send their children to private schools). But in the United States, restrictions on private schools might well be unconstitutional; in any case, though there has been controversy about whether private schools should receive public support, no one has suggested that private schools be actively discouraged.

APPROACHES TO ENHANCING EQUALITY

• Provide minimum level of expenditures for all districts

• Cap expenditures of high-spending districts

• Federal and state financial assistance to low income communities and communities with large numbers of disadvantaged children

• Key issue: How to maintain local responsibility and autonomy while providing equality of opportunity

AID TO HIGHER EDUCATION

Interestingly, many of the controversies that plague elementary and secondary education have been resolved at the higher-education level. There has even been a voucher plan: The GI Bill of Rights, which spurred the growth of higher education in the United States after World War II, in effect gave veterans a voucher they could use at any university, public or private. Private schools, as we have already noted, play a large role at the college and university level, and there is a high level of decentralization. The federal role dates from the setting aside of land for a university in the Land Ordinance of 1785, to the founding of the land grant universities in 1862, to the extensive support of research universities through grants and contracts in the post–World War II era.

A fundamental difference between higher education and elementary and secondary education is that the students have reached an age at which they can make decisions for themselves. It is the students who should judge whether the returns to further education warrant further investment. From this perspective, government's key role should be to ensure access, so that students have the financial resources to go on to college. Currently, this is accomplished in five ways. First, states greatly subsidize higher education, typically charging, in their public colleges and universities, tuitions that are a fraction of the total costs. Second, the federal government provides grants, called Pell Grants, for students who meet eligibility criteria based on financial need. Third, the federal government sponsors loan programs for higher education, such as the Stafford Loan Program. Fourth, it supports a limited work-study program, called the Federal Work-Study Program; and fifth, it provides tuition tax deductions and credits.

The state subsidies have been widely criticized as being untargeted. Indeed, since enrollment rates typically are higher among the children of the affluent, on average it is the more affluent who benefit from such subsidies. Moreover, to the extent that the subsidies can be thought of as directed at the children themselves, rather than at the parents, lifetime incomes, even of children from poorer families, will be higher than the average income of the population. Therefore, critics say, government should focus its attention on loans or grants to children from poor families.

Federal tuition tax credits were introduced in 1997 (effective in 1998). These too have been criticized as untargeted: the money will not go to the very poor (who do not pay taxes in any case). Critics worry that the tuition tax credit—up to $1500 for each of the first two years of college—may simply induce colleges to raise tuitions, especially in states that charge very low tuition (below $1000) for their community colleges.[25] They worry that enrollment rates of the very poor may even go down, as poor people who cannot take advantage of the tuition tax credit find college less affordable, un-

---

[25] The credit is 100 percent of the first $1000 in tuition and 50 percent of the second $1000. Raising tuition from $500 to $1000 will thus cost the student nothing—what he pays will be unchanged, though what the federal government pays will increase substantially.

441

less states increase scholarship funds to offset any tuition increases. (Proponents argue that even if tuitions increase, the increased availability of funds for education will be helpful.)

Federal student loan programs date back to 1959, when the Federal Perkins Loan Program was started. Though today there is little controversy about the value of student loans, there has been recent debate over how best to provide them. The federal government now has two major loan programs: the Federal Family Education Loan Program, in which private institutions lend to students while the government bears the risk of default; and the William D. Ford Federal Direct Loan Program, in which the federal government lends directly to students. The latter began in 1994 at the request of the Clinton administration, which claimed that the federal government could administer the program more effectively and at lower cost than private sector institutions. Part of the rationale for the new program is that the division of risk bearing and administration under the existing program gave rise to insufficient incentives for screening and debt enforcement (collection) on the part of private institutions. Moreover, the government would be able to introduce more flexible loan instruments, including one in which the maximum amount repaid in any year was limited to 10 percent of the individual's income, with the repayment period stretched out for lower-income individuals. Initial reactions to the new program have been highly supportive, but the real test will take years, when the overall administration costs and repayment rates can be properly assessed.

With the expansion of student loans and Pell Grants between 1993 and 1997, the country came close to providing "guaranteed financial access" to higher education. Critics of the tax deduction and credit program argued that it would have cost far less and been far more effective in increasing enrollment rates, particularly among the disadvantaged, if the government had announced a broader policy of guaranteed financial access, a combination of loans, grants, and work to assure all Americans access to higher education.

REVIEW AND PRACTICE

SUMMARY

1   The past thirty-five years have seen changes in the structure of education in the United States, including an increase in the fraction of funds provided by states and the federal government. While direct federal expenditures for education are low relative to state and local spending, federal tax expenditures provide large implicit subsidies. In addition, federal involvement in guiding education policy is growing.

2   Education is not a pure public good, nor do externalities provide a persuasive justification for the role of the government. The major justification for public support of elementary and secondary education is the belief that the quality of education obtained should not depend

solely on the resources of the child's parents. Imperfections of capital markets provide the main justification for public support for higher education.

3 There are concerns about both the efficiency and equity of the U.S. educational system. Proposals to improve the efficiency of the system are: a) a voucher program to enable more choice and promote competition; b) decentralization reforms, to enable teachers and parents to exert more control over schools; c) charter schools to provide more scope for innovation; d) contracting out, to provide more competition for school management, without the disadvantage of social stratification that may arise from voucher plans; and e) national standards with clearer goals and performance measures, both for schools and teachers.

4 The heavy reliance on local finance for schools results in a great deal of inequality in expenditures. Reforms include providing more state aid. So long as parents have the option of sending children to private schools, only a limited degree of equality can be obtained through the public school systems.

5 Though education is not the only determinant of an individual's future wages, there is a systematic correlation between the level of education and wages. There is, however, controversy concerning the explanation of this correlation. Some claim that it is primarily due to the increased skills that children obtain at school (the human capital view), while others claim that it is due to the schools' identifying the very able and differentiating them from the less able (the screening view).

6 The poor performance of American students on standardized international exams is not due to a low level of overall expenditures. It is related in part to the high level of inequality in the United States, and in part to the large amount of expenditures going to administration and special programs. The overall link between expenditures and performance has been hotly debated.

7 The government has long played an active role in higher education, though its dominance is not as great as at the elementary and secondary school levels. Some believe that the effects of government aid to higher education are regressive, since those who benefit from college are likely to have higher incomes. They believe that direct subsidies should be replaced by loan programs.

8 The federal government has long played an important role in supporting higher education. Student loans and federal grant programs have made higher education accessible to most Americans. There is considerable controversy over the extent to which tuition tax credits will increase enrollments. Most agree, however, that such tax credits are not well targeted.

Human capital   School vouchers

Screening

1 a) Discuss the equity and efficiency arguments for raising tuition at state universities. To what extent do your answers depend on whether there is a good college loan program available? b) Discuss the equity and efficiency arguments for providing college loans at subsidized interest rates.

2 List some characteristics of our educational institutions or outcomes of our educational system that seem to be more consistent with the screening view of education than with the human capital view.

3 The property tax base per student is often as high in industrial centers as it is in the suburbs. Why might you still expect expenditure per pupil to be lower in industrial centers than in the suburbs?

4 Discuss the trade-offs involved in deciding upon the appropriate level and form of decentralization/centralization within education. Bear in mind that different aspects—finance, control of curriculum, control of hiring—can be decentralized to different extents; and that the issues of centralization and decentralization relate not only to the division of responsibility between the federal government, the state, and the local community, but also to the division of responsibility within the school district, between central office administrators, school principals, and teachers.

5 Discuss the trade-offs between parental choice and equality of opportunity. To what extent should the principle of consumer sovereignty extend to parental rights to choose the amount and form of education for their children?

6 Provide an economic analysis of the issue of tracking (putting students of similar abilities in the same classes). What evidence would you like to have to decide whether tracking is desirable? What are the trade-offs? (How does your answer depend on whether teachers find it easier to teach classes in which students have relatively similar abilities, and the extent to which less able students learn from having more able students inside the classroom?)

7 A community is considering how to allocate expenditures between education and other goods. Draw the budget constraint, putting "education" on the horizontal axis, and "other goods" on the vertical.

   a Contrast the budget constraint of a poor community with that of a richer community. Using indifference curves, explain why a poorer community is likely to spend less on education than a richer community.

b Show how the deductibility of property taxes—used to finance public education—affects the budget constraints of the two communities. How does it affect choices? If the price elasticity of the demand for education is unity (1), what should be the effect on the demand for education in a community in which the median voter is in the 33 percent marginal tax bracket? in the 15 percentage tax bracket?

c Assume now that the poor community is subsidized (and the rich community taxed) so that extra educational expenditures it gets from a 1 percent tax is the same as that of a rich community. Now draw the budget constraints. Will the poorer community continue to spend less on education than the richer community? What does your answer depend on?

d Whose indifference curve is relevant for the analysis? (Recall the discussion of median voters from Chapter 7.)

8 List the various concerns about inadequacies of the U.S. educational system. Evaluate various reform initiatives in terms of the extent to which they address these concerns.

a If you thought that the primary problem was education of the disadvantaged, what reforms would you emphasize?

b If you thought that the primary problem was the lack of an adequate supply of highly trained scientists and engineers, what reforms would you emphasize?

c If you thought that the primary problem was inadequate performance of elementary and secondary schools, which reforms would you emphasize?

d If you thought that the primary problem was the lack of enrollment in universities, what reforms would you emphasize?

9 Assume that spending more on the education of a student increases her productivity. Draw the relationship between productivity/wages (assuming that wages increase in tandem with productivity and that there are diminishing returns). Assume that more able students have, for each level of education, a higher level of productivity.

a Assume that one wanted to maximize total output for a given level of expenditure. How would you allocate educational expenditures? Would you necessarily spend more on the more able students?

b Assume that you wanted to reduce inequalities in income. How would this affect patterns of educational expenditure?

445

HOW SHOULD PUBLIC EDUCATIONAL FUNDS BE ALLOCATED?

Every school district faces the problem of allocating its educational budget. It can allocate more funds for special education, for remedial classes for the disadvantaged, or for accelerated classes for the gifted. As more funds are allocated to any one individual, there is some increase in that individual's productivity. This is the return to education.

If we wished to maximize national output, and if efficiency alone were our goal, we would allocate funds so that the increase in productivity from spending an extra dollar on one individual would be the same as the increase in productivity from spending an extra dollar on another. If very able individuals not only reach a higher level of productivity than others at each level of education but also benefit more from education, so that the *marginal* return to education is higher, such a policy entails spending a greater amount on the education of the able than on that of the less able. Some would say this is unfair; the government should ensure equality of expenditures in public education. But when educational expenditures are equalized, those who are more able—or who have home backgrounds that give them an advantage—will still be better off. Accordingly, some believe that government should engage in **compensatory education;** it should attempt to equalize not *input* (expenditure) but *output* (achievement). It should attempt to compensate for the background disadvantages facing some groups in our society. One of the major federal programs is directed specifically at encouraging local communities to provide such compensatory education.

As more and more funds (of a fixed budget) are allocated to the less able, and less and less to the more able, total output falls, since the marginal return to education (under our assumption) for the less able is smaller than for the more able. Thus there is a trade-off between efficiency and equality, as depicted in Figure 16.4A. What point one chooses on this locus depends on one's values, on how one is willing to trade off efficiency versus equality.

Some maintain, however, that the trade-off curve does not look like Figure 16.4A but like Figure 16.4B—that is, some movement toward compensatory education may actually increase national output. In this view, those who are advantaged have a higher output than the disadvantaged at each educational level, but the *marginal* return to further education for the more able is actually lower than for the less advantaged. This implies that we can get both more efficiency (higher output) and more equality with at least some degree of compensatory education. Unfortunately, there is little empirical evidence to support one view versus the other.

Note that the differences in the education-productivity relationship between one individual and another may result either from differences in innate ability or from differences in environment (home background). There is a longstanding controversy about the relative contribution of these two factors in explaining performance. In the case of two individuals with the same innate ability but different home backgrounds, the nature of the edu-

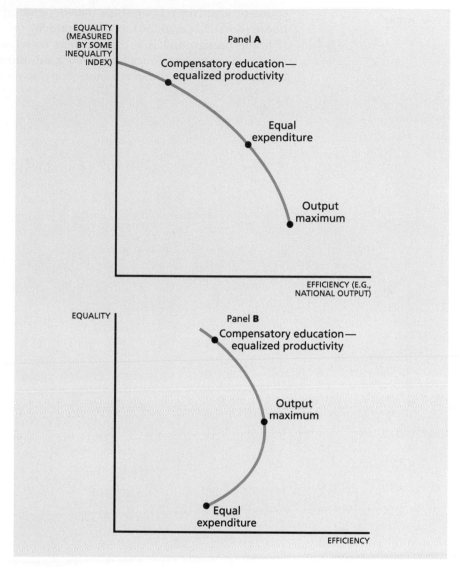

FIGURE 16.4 **Equity-Efficiency Trade-offs in Education Expenditures** Panel A. Poorer individuals with poorer home backgrounds have, at any level of educational expenditures, a lower marginal return to education. Accordingly, maximizing output requires spending more on richer individuals. By spending an equal amount, output is reduced but equality is increased. Compensatory education—equalizing productivity—requires spending even more on poorer individuals, reducing output but increasing equality. Panel B. Here, poorer individuals may have a lower level of income at any given level of educational expenditures, but a higher marginal return. Then output maximization (equalizing marginal returns) requires spending more on poorer individuals. Spending an equal amount on each will then lower equality and efficiency.

cation-productivity relationships may depend on whether education in the home (home background) is a **substitute** for or a **complement** to schooling. If home background is a complement to schooling, it means that it increases the return to education. If it is a substitute, the more education that occurs in the home, the smaller the return to formal education.

PART FIVE

TAXATION: THEORY

The next two parts are concerned with taxation. Part Five develops the general theory of taxation, and Part Six examines in some detail taxation in the United States.

First Chapter 17 sets out the general principles of taxation. Then Chapter 18 discusses who bears the burden of taxation. Chapter 19 analyzes the effects of taxation on economic efficiency, while Chapter 20 shows how equity and efficiency considerations may be balanced off against each other. Chapter 21 examines one of the most important problems of tax design: how to tax the returns to capital.

17 Introduction to Taxation

FOCUS QUESTIONS

1 What are the five key attributes that a good tax system should have?

2 What are the various ways in which tax systems affect economic efficiency?

3 What are the difficulties in determining what is a "fair" tax system?

Unlike most transfers of money from one individual to another, which are entered into voluntarily, taxation is compulsory. Chapter 6 showed that contributions to support public services need to be compulsory because of the free rider problem: unless support for public goods is made compulsory no one will have an incentive to contribute. The discussion showed how all individuals may be made better off by being compelled to contribute to the support of public goods.

Government's ability to compel individuals' support of public goods, however, may also enable it to compel individuals' support of special interest groups: it can force one group to give up its resources to another group. Such forced transfers have been likened to theft, with one major difference: Transfers through the government wear the mantle of legality and respectability conferred upon them by the political process. When the political process in a country becomes detached from the citizenry and is used to transfer resources to the groups in power, the distinction between taxation and theft becomes blurred at best.

These issues were of critical concern to the founders of the United States. The rebellion that became the Revolutionary War is often dated to the Boston Tea Party, which was motivated by the conviction that unjust taxes were being levied on the colonies. The slogan "Taxation without representation is tyranny" provided one of the central motifs of the revolution. Distinguishing between the legitimate and illegitimate uses of the power of taxation is a matter of continual contention.

BACKGROUND

Taxation is as old as organized government. The Bible says that a tithe (one-tenth) of the crops should be set aside for purposes of redistribution and for the support of the priesthood. It is not clear what the enforcement mechanism was then, and the Bible does not report on the extent of tax evasion. In the Middle Ages, individuals provided services directly to their feudal lords; these were effectively taxes but they were not monetized. The fact that vassals were forced to provide these services meant that they were, to some extent, slaves. Some have argued that the fact that modern taxes are **monetized**—individuals are compelled to provide not services (except in the special case of the draft) but money—should not obscure the underlying relationships. An individual who must give the government, say, one-fourth of his earnings is, effectively, working for the government one-fourth of the time.

There are, however, two critical distinctions between feudal levies and modern taxes. In the former case, individuals were not allowed to leave their manor without the permission of their lord; today individuals can choose where they wish to live, and therefore the jurisdiction that will impose taxes upon them. Second, while under the manorial system individuals were compelled to work, in modern taxation individuals are compelled only to share with the government what they receive from working (or what they receive from investing, or what they spend). They can choose to pay less if they are willing to work less and receive less for themselves.

In the United States, concern about the possible abuse of the power to tax led to certain constitutional restrictions on the kinds of taxes that could be imposed. For instance, because the agricultural South—then the major exporting region of the country—was afraid that the more populous North would impose export levies, forcing southerners to bear a disproportionate share of the costs of government, such levies were explicitly barred by the Constitution. Other provisions of the Constitution attempted to ensure that taxes would not be imposed in a discriminatory manner. For example, the uniformity clause says that taxes must be imposed in a uniform way, and the apportionment clause says that direct taxes must be apportioned among the states on the basis of population. Such constitutional restrictions were interpreted to imply that the government could not impose an income tax and it was not until a constitutional amendment was passed in 1913 that the federal government could impose such a tax.

The restrictions on taxation reflected the experiences of the American colonies with discriminatory taxes levied by the British government. The writers of the Constitution did not and probably could not have anticipated all of the forms of discriminatory taxation. Thus despite the safeguards that the founders of the republic attempted to provide through the Constitution, issues of taxation have been among the most divisive facing the country. For instance, in the early nineteenth century there was considerable controversy over tariffs.[1] Although they raised revenues, tariffs on industrial goods also served to protect the industrial North, and the South suffered by having to pay higher prices for the protected goods.

THE FORMS OF TAXATION

The variety of taxes governments have levied has been huge. At various times there have been taxes on windows, luxury boats, sales of securities, dividends, capital gains . . . and many more items. Taxes can be divided into two broad categories: *direct taxes* on individuals and corporations; and *indirect taxes* on a variety of goods and services.

In the United States, the three principal direct taxes at the federal level are the individual income tax; the payroll tax (a fixed percentage of wages up to some limit), used to finance social security; and the corporation income tax, a tax on the net income of corporations. Another important direct tax is the estate and gift tax, which is primarily a tax on bequests from one generation to the next. Because the individual income tax is levied both on wages and on capital income, it affects decisions about labor supply, retirement, education, and so forth, as well as decisions about savings and investment. At the state and local level, there is one other important direct tax, on property.

The principal indirect taxes at the federal level are customs duties, levied on imports of goods from abroad; and excise taxes, on goods like telephone service, air travel, and luxuries. Many states and local jurisdictions also impose a sales tax, a flat percentage tax on all retail sales of a broad category of goods. Some states exempt food from their sales tax, while others have a broader range of exemptions. Many foreign governments, rather than imposing a sales tax at the retail level, impose a value-added tax: at each stage of production, the value added is the difference between the value of the sales and the value of purchased (non-labor) inputs.

Figures 17.1 and 17.2 show the sources of revenues at the federal, state, and local levels in 1997. At the federal level, social security taxes and individual income taxes together account for over 80 percent of revenues, and the corporate income tax accounts for around 12 percent. All other taxes are small by comparison. At the state and local level, individual income and payroll taxes together make up just over one-fifth of revenues (22.6 percent); and property taxes, sales taxes, and transfers from the federal government each account for another fifth.

[1] Tariffs are taxes imposed on imported goods. By raising the prices of the imported goods, they enable domestic producers of similar goods to raise their prices as well. In this way tariffs "protect" domestic producers.

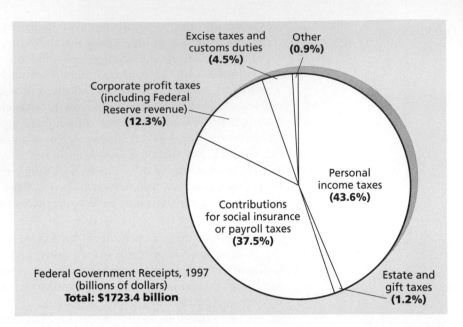

FIGURE 17.1 **Sources of Federal Revenue, 1997** The individual income tax and payroll taxes for social insurance account for the lion's share of federal revenues.

Source: U.S. Department of Commerce, Bureau of Economic Analysis, *Survey of Current Business*, May 1998, Table 3.2.

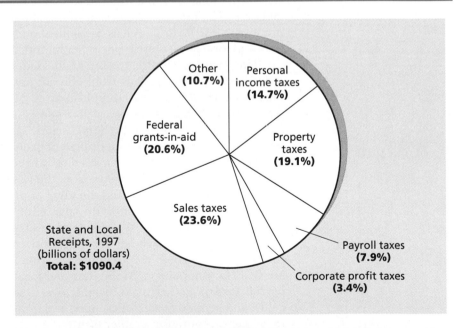

FIGURE 17.2 **Sources of State and Local Revenues, 1997** Sales taxes, property taxes, and federal grants contribute about equal amounts to state and local revenues. Income taxes are less important.

Source: *Survey of Current Business*, May 1998, Table 3.3.

The establishment of the income tax with the passage of the Sixteenth Amendment in 1913 marked a turning point in the structure of taxation in the United States. Prior to that, the principal sources of federal revenues were excise taxes and customs duties. During the twentieth century, these have dwindled in importance, and individual income taxes and social security payroll taxes have become the principal source of revenue to the federal government.

Figure 17.3 shows the changes in the relative importance of various taxes during the past century. In particular, we see: (a) a marked increase in the relative importance of taxes imposed directly on individuals and corporations and a steep drop in the importance of indirect taxes; and (b) within direct taxes, a sharp decrease since 1960 in the role of the corporate income tax and a marked increase in the role of payroll taxes.

There have also been marked trends at the state and local level, reflected in Figure 17.4: an increased reliance on income and sales taxes and a decreased reliance on property taxes.

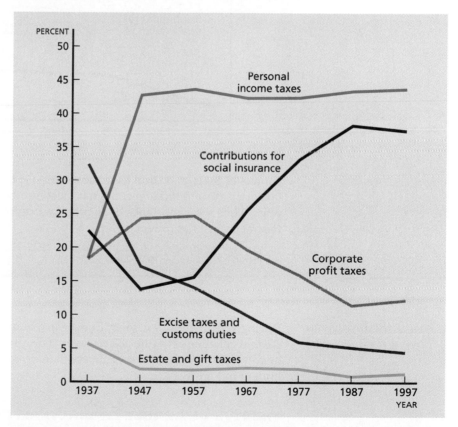

FIGURE 17.3   **Sources of Federal Revenue, 1933–1997** Customs and excise taxes, and the corporate income tax, have diminished in importance over time, while the dependence on payroll taxes for social insurance has grown.

Sources: U.S. Department of Commerce, Bureau of Economic Analysis, *National Income and Product Accounts of the United States: 1929–1982*; and *Survey of Current Business*, September 1988 and May 1998, Table 3.2.

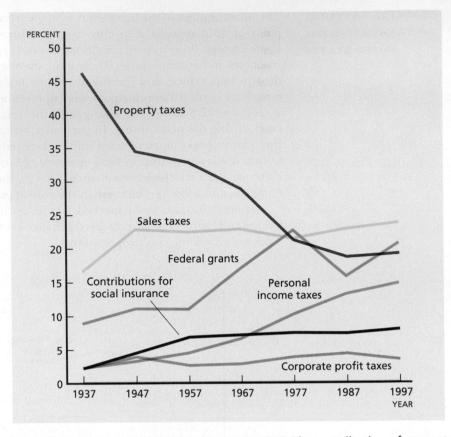

PERCENT

Property taxes

Sales taxes

Federal grants

Contributions for
social insurance

Personal
income taxes

Corporate profit taxes

1937 1947 1957 1967 1977 1987 1997
YEAR

FIGURE 17.4 **Sources of State and Local Revenues, 1933–1997** The contribution of property taxes to state and local revenues has fallen substantially over the last sixty years, while the importance of all other sources (particularly sales taxes and federal grants) has grown.

SOURCES: *National Income and Product Accounts, 1929–1982*; and *Survey of Current Business*, September 1988 and May 1998, Table 3.3.

**COMPARISONS WITH
OTHER COUNTRIES**

During recent decades, most European countries have switched to an increased reliance on value-added taxes. The United States relies much more heavily on the individual income tax than do other advanced countries, as is evident in Figure 17.5.

THE FIVE DESIRABLE CHARACTERISTICS OF ANY TAX SYSTEM

Taxes are inevitably painful. Not surprisingly, designing tax systems has always been a subject of considerable controversy. To put it most simply, most people would like to see their own taxes reduced. Quite ingenious arguments can be devised for why others should pay more. Governments, in de-

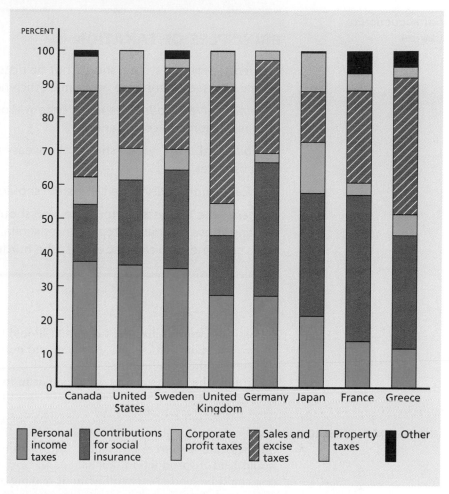

FIGURE 17.5 **Sources of Revenue for Selected Countries, 1995** Individual income taxes are
more important in the United States than in other countries, where sales taxes
and contributions for social insurance are larger. (Sales taxes include excise
taxes, customs taxes, value-added taxes, and general sales taxes.)

SOURCE: Organization for Economic Cooperation and Development, *Revenue Statistics
1965–1996* (Paris: 1997), Tables 11, 13, 15, 23, and 25.

ciding how best to raise the revenue they require, have looked for general
principles. There are five accepted properties of a "good" tax system:

1 Economic efficiency: the tax system should not interfere with the efficient
allocation of resources.

2 Administrative simplicity: the tax system ought to be easy and relatively in-
expensive to administer.

3 Flexibility: the tax system ought to be able to respond easily (in some
cases automatically) to changed economic circumstances.

PRINCIPLES OF TAXATION

Efficiency—the tax system should not be distortionary; if possible, it should be used to enhance economic efficiency.

Administrative simplicity—the tax system should have low costs of administration and compliance.

Flexibility—the tax system should allow easy adaptation to changed circumstances.

Political responsibility—the tax system should be transparent.

Fairness—the tax system should be, and should be seen to be, fair, treating those in similar circumstances similarly, and imposing higher taxes on those who can better bear the burden of taxation.

4 Political responsibility: the tax system should be designed so that individuals can ascertain what they are paying, and evaluate how accurately the system reflects their preferences.

5 Fairness: the tax system ought to be fair in its relative treatment of different individuals.

ECONOMIC EFFICIENCY

Recall that in the absence of market failures, the economy would automatically allocate resources efficiently. Information conveyed by market prices would lead to production, exchange, and product mix efficiency; and no one could be made better off without making anyone worse off. Most taxes change relative prices. As a result, the price signals are distorted, and the allocation of resources is altered.

A persistent concern is the extent to which the tax system discourages savings and work, and distorts other decisions relating to consumption and production. For instance, the large number of Arabian and other very expensive breeds of horses in the United States has been attributed to a peculiar loophole in the tax structure. The special treatment of gas and oil may have led to excessive drilling. Railroad boxcars were used for a while as a tax shelter, until a glut of these developed.

The history of taxation is dotted with other examples of distortionary effects. The result of the window tax imposed in Britain during the seventeenth century was that houses without windows were constructed. Modern England provides other examples. Three-wheel vehicles, though perhaps slightly less safe and not much less costly than four-wheel vehicles, were taxed more lightly than the latter. Hence many individuals chose them in preference to the more conventional four-wheel vehicles. Vans (station wagons without windows) were taxed more lightly than station wagons with windows, and again, many individuals were motivated to purchase these vehicles, though not by a preference for darkness in the rear of their vehicle. In the United States, the favorable depreciation treatment for movable walls[2] has encouraged the building of commercial office buildings with movable walls—even if there is no intention of ever moving them. While movable walls do provide greater flexibility, they typically provide less sound insulation. Thus, while we no longer have a window tax, modern tax laws nonetheless do affect construction patterns.

BEHAVIORAL EFFECTS OF TAXATION Most of the efficiency effects of taxation are far more subtle and difficult to assess. Income taxation may affect the length of time an individual stays in school by affecting the after-tax return to education, the choice of jobs (because for some jobs a larger fraction of the return comes in untaxed "benefits"), whether an individual enters the labor force or stays at home to take care of children, the number of hours a taxpayer works (when he or she has discretion over that), whether he or she takes a second job and the effort put into the job, the amount that the individual saves and the form savings take (the choice between bank accounts and the stock market), the age at which an individual retires, and whether he or she works part-time beyond the age of 65.

The effects of taxation are not limited to decisions concerning work, savings, education, and consumption. While the extent to which the tax system affects individuals' decisions to marry or divorce is open to question, there is little doubt that it affects the timing of these decisions. For instance, the United States tax code considers a couple married for the entire calendar year even if the wedding is held on December 31. So two working people who earn similar incomes, choosing between a December and January wedding date, are strongly encouraged by the income tax to choose January. The reverse is true for divorce.[3] Taxation affects risk taking, the allocation of resources to research and development, and the long-run rate of growth of the economy. It affects not only the level of investment in firms but the form of the investment (including the durability of machines). It affects the fraction of national savings that is allocated to housing, to other structures, and to equipment. It affects the rate at which our natural resources are depleted. There is hardly an important resource allocation decision in our economy that is unaffected in some way or another by taxation.

With tax rates at current levels, tax considerations are often of primary concern; it may seem more advantageous to allocate one's effort to reducing one's taxes than to designing better projects or producing more.

---

[2] Taxpayers are allowed to deduct from their income an amount that reflects the wearing out (or depreciation) of their plant or equipment. Movable walls are treated as equipment, and thus can be depreciated much more rapidly than fixed walls. As a result, the present discount value of the depreciation allowances are much higher.

[3] Married couples are taxed on the basis of their combined income. Because the income tax is progressive, the income of the lower-earning spouse is taxed at a higher rate than it would be if the individual were single. (See Chapter 22.)

FINANCIAL EFFECTS OF TAXATION Sometimes taxation affects a transaction's form more than its substance. For instance, apart from tax considerations, it may make little practical difference whether an employer gives an employee money to purchase a Blue Cross health insurance policy or purchases it for him. In tax terms, it makes a great deal of difference. In the former case the individual receives "income" upon which he is taxed; in the latter case the "benefit" is not taxed. Similarly, in real terms it makes little difference whether I save directly for my retirement or my employer takes some of my salary and invests it in a (fully funded) pension plan. But the tax implications are quite different, and as a result individuals are induced to save through the pension plan rather than directly. These financial effects may in turn, of course, have further real effects on the economy: because of the restrictions imposed on pension plans, they may invest their funds differently than the way an individual saving for his retirement might invest them. Typically, they cannot, for instance, invest in highly risky "below investment grade" securities. Moreover, some individuals may be "forced" to save through their pension plans more than they would voluntarily save on their own.

Similarly, since dividends, capital gains (increases in the price of an asset), and interest are all treated differently, the tax structure may have a significant effect on the *financial* structure of U.S. corporations—for instance, on firms' decisions whether to finance additional investments by borrowing or by issuing new shares. These financial decisions, in turn, have real consequences. A firm with a heavy debt burden is likely to be less willing to undertake risky projects than a firm which has raised most of its funds by issuing stock.

ORGANIZATIONAL EFFECTS OF TAXATION Taxes affect the way our economy is organized. Many of these organizational effects have real consequences for how resources get allocated—for instance, for how much risk taking occurs. Our tax laws differentiate between corporations, which have limited liability, and individuals and partnerships, which do not. Because with unlimited liability the losses which an investor can incur from a $100 investment are far greater than just the $100 she has invested, without limited liability enterprises often have a difficult time raising capital, and managers of enterprises with unlimited liability may act in a far more risk-averse manner. By tilting the tax system either for or against corporations, the tax system can either encourage or discourage economic activity from taking place within corporations, thereby changing the degree of risk taking in the economy.

Financial effects are often intertwined with organizational effects. The tax system may encourage or discourage banks relative to other financial institutions or arrangements; this may lead firms to raise more or less money through banks (rather than, say, on the stock or bond market). This can make a great deal of difference. Recent studies have shown, for instance, that firms that raise more of their money through banks exhibit less volatility in investment, partly because the bank is better able to monitor why the firm may be short of funds—whether, for instance, it is because of short-run cyclical effects or because of problems of mismanagement. Because banks can better identify the nature of the problem, they can respond effectively when there is a cyclical downturn, providing capital to good firms that are temporarily short of cash, withholding funds from firms that have more fundamental weaknesses. By contrast, firms that rely on capital markets (issuing bonds or new equities) to raise funds find life far more difficult in a downturn; they may find it virtually impossible or extremely expensive to raise funds at such times.

Another major economic organization within our society is the family. Tax laws affect both family formation and the distribution of well-being within a family. For instance, tax laws typically tax only payments from corporations to households (that is, to their employees). They do not tax consumption within corporations. Thus, tax laws encourage "inside the firm" consumption—large company cars, expensive company meals, and so forth. In those economies, such as the United States before World War II, where males typically worked outside the home and females within the home, such tax policies obviously had the effect of discriminating in favor of the spouse working outside the home.

GENERAL EQUILIBRIUM EFFECTS The imposition of a tax such as that on wages or on the return to capital alters the equilibrium of the economy. A tax on interest may reduce the supply of savings and, eventually, the stock of capital; this in turn may reduce the productivity of workers and their wages. We refer to these indirect repercussions of the tax as its **general equilibrium effects.**

General equilibrium effects have important distributional consequences, sometimes in a direction quite opposite to the intent of the legislation. A tax on capital may reduce the supply of capital, thereby increasing the return to capital; in some instances, the degree of inequality may actually be increased by such a tax.

ANNOUNCEMENT EFFECTS AND CAPITALIZATION The economy does not instantaneously adjust to a new tax. Often, the long-run distortions are much greater than the short-run distortions, as the economy is able to respond more fully to the new situation.

But some effects of the tax may be felt even before it is imposed, simply upon its announcement. An announcement concerning the future tax treatment of an asset has an immediate impact on the value of the asset. If, for instance, it is believed that a particular category of assets (say, housing) is about to be subjected to greater taxation (e.g., the interest deduction on mortgages is about to be eliminated), then the price of that category of assets may fall markedly. Owners of those assets at the time the announcement is made will, perhaps unfairly, bear the major burden of the tax.

It is these **announcement effects,** or *impact effects*, which may be quite significant, that have given rise to the saying that "an old tax is a good tax." Not only may the announcement effect present serious equity problems, but anticipation of it can affect the supply of assets. Discussions about eliminating the deduction of interest paid on home mortgages may lead individuals to anticipate significant capital loss, were they to invest in housing, and hence the demand for new housing may be seriously reduced.

ECONOMIC IMPACTS OF TAXATION

Behavioral effects

• Work, education, retirement

• Savings, investment, risk taking

• Energies devoted to avoiding taxes instead of creating wealth

• Marriage and divorce

Financial effects

• Fringe benefits

• Financial structure of firms

Organizational effects

• Corporations versus unincorporated enterprises

• Intertwined with financial effects (banks versus insurance versus other forms of finance)

General equilibrium effects

• Often important indirect effects, especially with broad-based taxes, such as on wages or interest

Announcement effects and capitalization

• Future taxes on an asset reflected ("capitalized") in the price of the asset at the time the tax is announced

---

DISTORTIONARY AND NONDISTORTIONARY TAXATION Any tax system influences behavior. After all, the government is taking money away from an individual, and we would expect him to respond, in some way, to this lower income. When we say that we want the tax system to be nondistortionary, clearly we do not mean that we want the individual not to react at all.

A tax is **nondistortionary** if, and only if, there is nothing an individual or firm can do to alter his tax liability. Economists call taxes that are nondistortionary **lump-sum taxes.** Distortions are associated with the individual's or firm's attempt to lower the tax liability. Virtually all taxes imposed in the United States are, in this sense, distortionary. A *head tax*—a tax one has to pay regardless of income or wealth—is a lump-sum tax. A tax that depends on nonalterable characteristics (age, sex) is also a lump-sum tax. Since individuals and firms cannot avoid them, lump-sum taxes do not lead to changes in behavior or the reallocation of resources, other than the income effect of reduced after-tax income.

Any tax on commodities is distortionary: an individual can change his tax liability simply by reducing his purchases of the commodity. Any tax on income is also distortionary: an individual can reduce his tax liability simply by working less or by saving less.

In Chapter 19 we shall see that distortionary taxes are inefficient in the sense that *if* the government could replace them with a lump-sum tax, it could raise more revenue, with the same effect on the welfare of individuals; or equivalently, the government could raise the same revenue and increase the welfare of individuals.

CORRECTIVE TAXATION So far, this discussion has emphasized the negative aspects of taxation: that a tax system should be designed so as not to interfere with economic efficiency. But recall that in the presence of market failures, the allocation of resources will not, in general, be efficient. Taxation can sometimes be used in a positive way, to correct some market failure. Recall the discussion in Chapter 9, which showed that taxation could sometimes be used to correct for externalities. **Corrective taxes** (as these taxes are called) both raise revenue and improve the efficiency of resource allocations. The United States has made limited use of corrective taxes. The tax imposed on the chemical industry, to pay for the costs of cleaning up and disposing of toxic wastes, can be thought of as a corrective tax. Those who view American energy consumption as excessive (because of the associated pollution) have argued for an energy tax, which would both raise revenue and reduce profligate energy consumption. These concerns have increased with the awareness of the dangers of global warming associated with the buildup of greenhouse gases (such as carbon dioxide) in the atmosphere, largely resulting from high energy usage.

TAXES AND ECONOMIC EFFICIENCY

All taxes affect behavior (reduce spending power); *distortions* are associated with actions an individual takes to avoid taxes, for example by working less, one's tax liability is reduced.

Lump-sum taxes are taxes that are fixed, and cannot be altered by any action that the individual can take.

Corrective taxation, by imposing taxes on activities, such as pollution, that generate negative externalities, simultaneously raises revenues and improves economic efficiency.

In the 1990s, corrective taxes gained increasing support, in two areas. The first was smoking. The recognition that smokers impose costs on others, including higher health costs, underlay the idea that a tax on cigarettes should help finance health care reforms, such as the provision of health insurance for poor children.

The second has to do with air pollution. Greenhouse gases lead to global warming, and are generated by the burning of fossil fuels. A carbon tax would "correct" this externality. President Clinton proposed a modification of such a tax (called the BTU tax, because it was a tax based on the amount of energy in a fuel) in his 1993 budget. Some forms of energy—burning of coal—give rise to far more greenhouse gases than others. (Hydroelectric power gives rise to none). Hence, the BTU tax was only an imperfect substitute for a "carbon" tax. But the industries which were high users of energy, as

ADMINISTRATIVE COSTS

Administering our tax system entails significant costs. There are direct costs—the cost of running the Internal Revenue Service—and indirect costs, borne by taxpayers. These indirect costs take on a variety of forms: the costs of time spent filling out tax forms, costs of record keeping, and the costs of services of accountants and tax lawyers. Joel Slemrod of the University of Michigan has estimated that the indirect costs are at least five times greater than the direct costs.

The administrative costs of running a tax system depend on a number of factors. First, they depend on what records would be kept in the absence of taxation. Businesses need to keep records for their own internal management purposes: the advent of high-speed computers has greatly reduced the costs of record keeping for large corporations. Thus, the tax system imposes a relatively small additional burden on large corporations for reporting wage income of their employees. At the other extreme, many small businesses and most households which hire domestic help find the additional record keeping and filings required by the income tax very burdensome. In 1993, the government allowed those with household employees to file their tax reports on their employees with their own individual income tax (though they still have to make separate filings with the Social Security Administration, for unemployment insurance, for state income taxes, and sometimes for local income taxes).

The record keeping required for capital gains taxation is particularly onerous because the records often have to be kept over a long period of time. Indeed, record keeping associated with taxation on owner-occupied housing was sufficiently onerous that few fully complied with the law; finally, in 1997, the tax laws were changed to exempt almost all capital gains from

well as the oil, coal, and gas industries, mounted a successful campaign against the tax, and Congress passed instead a 4.3 cent increase in the gasoline tax. This too can be viewed as a corrective tax—it helps correct for the externalities associated with auto pollution and congestion.

Such taxes are attractive because they raise revenues at the same time that they correct a market failure. Thus less revenues have to be raised through other, distortionary, methods. There is, accordingly, a "double dividend" associated with such a tax. The economy benefits from the reduced pollution *and* from the reduced reliance on taxes that distort production. The argument for corrective taxation is sometimes put another way: Why should society tax productive ("good") economic activities, like savings and hard work, rather than bad economic activities, like pollution?

owner-occupied housing from taxation.

A second factor that determines the administrative costs of a tax system is its complexity. Much of the cost of administering the income tax system comes from special provisions. For instance, the deductibility of certain categories of expenditures (medical, charity, interest) requires that records be kept on these expenditures.

Differentiation of rates across individuals (with some individuals paying a much higher rate than others) and across categories of income gives rise to attempts to "shift" income to members of one's family with lower tax rates, or to categories of income that are more lightly taxed. Attempts to restrict this shifting also account for much of the complexity of the current tax structure.

Third, taxing some categories of income may be more expensive than taxing others. It is widely believed that the administrative costs associated with imposing taxes on capital are much larger than those associated with taxing labor, partly because of the difficulty of differentiating between income and capital. For instance, payments to capital owners may be "income" (dividends) or "principal" (the repayment of previously invested funds); the dollars look the same. If the tax law treats these payments differently, taxpayers will be moved to characterize the dollars one way or the other. The government had to write elaborate rules which only partially address the problem.

Similarly, the administrative costs of raising taxes (per dollar of revenue raised) from small businesses may be much larger than from large corporations. Thus, the administrative costs of the value-added tax, in which a large fraction of the revenue is raised from large corporations responsible for a significant fraction of the economy's value added, is lower than a sales tax, which imposes taxes only at the final sale, in the myriad of retail outlets.

FLEXIBILITY

Changes in economic circumstances require changes in tax rates. For some tax structures these adjustments are easy; for some they require extensive political debate; for still others they occur automatically.

AUTOMATIC STABILIZATION For instance, as the economy goes into a recession, a reduction in tax revenues may be extremely desirable, to provide needed stimulus for the economy. When prices are stable, a progressive tax structure will provide "automatic" stabilization. When incomes drop, as a result of a recession, the average tax rate is reduced—individuals face lower tax rates because their incomes are lower. On the other hand, when income increases, the average tax rate increases. However, before tax brackets were indexed (that is, adjusted to take account of inflation) in 1981, during periods of *stagflation*—where the economy was in a recession but there was still inflation—the average tax rate increased, though a lower rate was needed to move the economy out of the recession. Indexing thus contributes to stabilization when prices rise during recessions. During periods of expansion and inflation, indexing reduces the built-in stabilizing effects of the income tax.

POLITICAL DIFFICULTIES OF ADJUSTING RATES When changing the tax rates is considered desirable, attempts to adjust the U.S. income tax often occasion intense political debate. Given the complexity of the tax code, which rates ought to be adjusted? Should all rates be increased proportionately, or are the rich or the poor already bearing a disproportionately large share of the tax burden, so that their taxes should be increased less than proportionately? Indeed, it is not even clear how to assess the fairness of a reform proposal. Is it fairer to reduce the taxes of individuals at different income levels by the same *dollar* amount, or by the same *percentage* amount? Should focus be on the average tax rates individuals pay, or on their marginal tax rates? Is a tax reform fair if it lowers the average rate faced by a one-earner family but increases the average rate on a two-earner family? Should the tax rate on capital be decreased, to encourage more savings, or increased, because capital owners are in a better position to bear the tax?

The political difficulty of adjusting the income tax rate should be contrasted, for instance, with that of the property tax. The property tax is beset by a number of administrative problems, not least of which is the difficulty of assessing the value of various pieces of property. Still, it has one advantage: Adjustments in the tax rates are made annually in a simple manner as the revenues required for the provision of local public services change.

SPEED OF ADJUSTMENTS Finally, an important aspect of the "flexibility" of a tax system for purposes of stabilizing the economy is timing: the speed with which changes in the tax code (once enacted) can be implemented, and the lags in the collection of funds. If fluctuations in the economy are rapid,

**POLITICAL
RESPONSIBILITY**

the lags may limit the efficacy of, say, the income tax, in stabilizing the economy. There is always the danger that with sufficiently long lags, taxes will be increased just when the economy needs a tax reduction and vice versa.

A widely embraced political value is that government should not try to take advantage of uninformed citizens. In the context of taxation, this view recommends taxes for which the burden of payment is clear. Such taxes are known as *transparent taxes*, and **transparency** has increasingly been recognized as an important characteristic of good government. Government policies are said to be *transparent* when they are subject to daylight—when it is clear who is benefiting and who is paying.[4] In this view, the individual income tax is a good tax.

Sometimes it seems as if the government deliberately misrepresents the true costs of the services it provides or who bears the costs. For instance, there is widespread agreement that there is no meaningful distinction between the part of the social security tax that is paid by the employer and the part paid by the employee. (According to law, half is paid by each.) The employer is concerned only with the total costs of her employee, the employee only with her take-home pay. No one's economic behavior should be affected if it were announced that the entire tax was to be borne by the employee, were employers to give an equivalent pay raise to their employees to cover the increased tax. Would workers' attitudes toward social security be altered if they thought they had to bear the entire costs?

In some cases there is an almost deliberate attempt to persuade individuals that the cost of government is less than it is. Just as businesses find that they can sell cars more easily if they describe the cost as "only $340 a month for a short 40 months" than if they describe it as "$13,600 paid over 3½ years," so, too, governments sometimes show a preference for tax systems in which individuals never fully reckon the cost of government. One of the arguments put forward for sales taxes is that they are less noticed than other taxes, such as income taxes. Individuals never calculate the *total* amount they pay to the government.

Jean-Baptiste Colbert, a finance minister to Louis XIV, wrote: "The art of taxation consists in so plucking the goose as to obtain the largest amount of feathers with the least possible amount of hissing."[5] From this perspective, the corporation tax may thus be viewed to be a good tax. Politicians can claim that it is anonymous corporations who pay it. From the perspective of transparency, the corporation tax is one of the worst, because who really pays the tax is not apparent. Taxes are paid by people, not by institutions: it is the shareholders, workers, and customers who ultimately bear the burden of the tax.

---

[4] The term has taken on a particular meaning in some recent discussions. The NGO (nongovernment organization) Transparency International focuses on identifying corrupt practices and corrupt governments. Their view is that it is lack of transparency that gives rise to much of the political corruption one sees.
[5] Cited in *Newsweek*, April 16, 1984, p. 69.

A politically responsible tax structure is also one in which changes in taxes come about as a result of legislation, and where the government must repeatedly come back to the citizenry for an appraisal of whether it is spending too much or too little. Steeply progressive tax rates (rates that rise as incomes rise) combined with a tax system that does not adjust for inflation result in government's tax revenues in *real* terms (as a share of, say, national income) rising in inflationary times, as they did between 1975 and 1980. These increases in taxes were never directly legislated: indeed, many would argue that Congress would have been unlikely to impose directly, say, a 10 percent increase in taxes in 1980, although inflation had exactly this effect.

FAIRNESS Most criticisms of tax systems begin with their unfairness. However, as we shall see, it is difficult to define precisely what is or is not fair. There are two distinct concepts of fairness: horizontal equity and vertical equity.

HORIZONTAL EQUITY A tax system is said to be *horizontally equitable* if individuals who are the same in all relevant respects are treated the same. The principle of **horizontal equity** is so important that it is, in effect, enshrined in the Constitution as the Fourteenth Amendment (the Equal Protection Clause). Thus a tax system that discriminates on the basis of race, color, or creed would, in the United States, generally be viewed to be horizontally inequitable (and unconstitutional). Although the underlying idea is clear enough, there are two fuzzy notions in our definition: What does it mean for two individuals to be identical in all relevant respects? And what does it mean for two individuals to be treated the same?

Consider twins who are identical in every respect except that one likes chocolate ice cream and only chocolate ice cream, while the other likes vanilla ice cream and only vanilla. For simplicity, we assume that chocolate and vanilla ice cream cost exactly the same amount. Is the tax system treating the two individuals in a horizontally equitable manner if it taxes vanilla and chocolate ice cream at different rates? One ends up paying more in taxes than the other, and in this sense the tax system appears to be unfair. But the twins faced the same "opportunity set." The chocolate lover could have bought vanilla ice cream if he had wanted (or vice versa). The tax system did not discriminate; it did not differentiate between individuals. This example is contrived so we could have two commodities that are "essentially" identical. In practice, there are many examples where the tax system treats differently individuals who differ in tastes—the higher taxes on hard liquor discriminate against those who prefer scotch relative to those who prefer wine or beer. Individuals who prefer to spend their vacations in their own vacation homes are treated preferentially compared to those who prefer to travel during their vacation.

If we say that the differences in taste are an important economic difference which the tax system may well take into account, then we can say that the principle of horizontal equity does not apply here. The twins are not identical in all relevant respects. Carried to this extreme, the principle soon becomes vacuous: no two individuals are ever identical. What are to be acceptable distinctions? Unfortunately, the principle of horizontal equity gives us little guidance on how to answer this question.

One's first intuition might be that all distinctions are inadmissible: age, sex, and marital status should all be irrelevant. In fact, at present we make distinctions on the basis of age (those over 65 are allowed an extra exemption) and marital status (two individuals with the same income who marry pay more in taxes than they did before marriage). Congress has felt that those distinctions are relevant.

Perhaps age and marital status are relevant because they affect individuals' ability to pay. But if these are admissible bases for differentiation, are there others? For instance, does variation in the economic costs associated with taxing different groups provide legitimate grounds for differentiation? In a later chapter we shall see that the inefficiencies arising out of a tax system depend on the magnitude of the responses to the tax. In households with two workers, the worker with the lower wage displays much more sensitivity to the wage rate than the higher-earning worker. While income taxes have almost no effect on the amount of labor supplied by the primary worker, they may have large effects on the secondary worker. Thus if the government were concerned with minimizing the inefficiencies arising out of the tax system, it would impose a lower tax on the secondary workers. Is this fair? Another example illustrating the difficulties is provided by health care expenditures. Should two individuals with the same income but different health care expenditures be treated the same? Does it make a difference whether the health care expenditures are "voluntary" (for instance, for a face-lift) or "necessary" (say, for heart bypass surgery)? Can the government tell which is which?

The following example illustrates the difficulty of even defining the meaning of equal treatment. Assume we could agree that a man and a woman who had received the same income over their working lives should be treated equally for purposes of social security. Should the total expected benefits be the same for the man as for the woman, or should the annual benefit be the same? On average, women live significantly longer than men, so these two rules give different results. If the woman receives the same annual benefit as the man (as is the case at present), the total expected value of her benefits will be much greater than the man's. Many would view this to be unfair.

VERTICAL EQUITY While the principle of horizontal equity says that individuals who are essentially identical should be treated the same, the principle of **vertical equity** says that some individuals are in a position to pay higher taxes than others, and that these individuals should do so. There are three problems: determining who, in principle, should pay at the higher rate; implementing this principle—that is, writing tax rules corresponding to this principle; and deciding, if someone is in a position to pay the higher rate, how much more he should pay than others.

INCOME AS A BASIS OF TAXATION Income is the most widely used basis of taxation; it is widely viewed by governments and policy makers as a good measure of ability to pay. Those who have a higher income have greater ability to pay and should therefore pay higher taxes. How much more is, as we have said, a more difficult question. There is a widely held view that those with a higher income not only should pay more taxes, but should pay a higher fraction of their income in taxes—that is, taxes should be progressive. But note that the rich can pay a smaller fraction of their income in taxes—taxes can be regressive—but still pay more in absolute terms.

Until the twentieth century, governments relied on indirect taxes—tariffs and customs duties and taxes on certain luxuries—to raise revenues. It was only when governments took on a wider role, with a greater need for income, that they resorted to broad-based taxes, and especially the income tax. In addition, the income tax seemed able to introduce a high degree of progressivity and to avoid the distortions associated with having a large number of taxes on different commodities. Economists and philosophers, however, have extensively criticized the income tax, and today, in much of the world, the income tax has become a less important source of revenue. It has been replaced, or supplemented, by the value-added tax, which is designed to tax only consumption, not savings or investment, and which is typically not progressive.[6]

CONSUMPTION AS A BASIS OF TAXATION One of the most forceful arguments against income as a fair basis of taxation is that income corresponds to the individual's contribution to society, the value of her economic output. Is it not fairer to tax individuals on the basis of what they take out of society rather than what they contribute—that is, on the basis of consumption rather than income?

Income and consumption differ by savings.[7] That is, income (Y) is either consumed (C) or saved (S);

$C + S = Y$, or
$C = Y - S$.

Thus a major issue is whether savings ought to be exempt from taxation. It can be shown that this is equivalent to the question of whether the return to savings (interest, dividends, and capital gains) ought to be exempt from taxation. The following example illustrates again the conflicting views of equity.

Consider another pair of identical twins, whom we shall refer to as Prudence and Imprudence. They both earn the same wages during their lifetimes. Prudence, however, saves 20 percent of her wages during her lifetime, accumulating a sizable nest egg for her retirement. Imprudence, on the other hand, always spends what she receives and, when she reaches retirement, applies for welfare. Under the present tax system, Prudence pays considerably higher taxes than Imprudence (since Prudence must pay taxes on the interest that she earns on her savings), while she receives fewer government benefits.

---

[6] Sometimes countries introduce some degree of progressivity by exempting, or taxing at lower rates, food and other commodities which play a larger role in the expenditure patterns of the poor; at the same time, some expenditures, like foreign travel, which loom larger in the expenditures of the rich, escape taxation as well.

[7] And by bequests and inheritances, which we could view as special forms of consumption and income.

Prudence views the present tax system as unfair, since their economic opportunity sets were, in fact, identical. Because their opportunity sets were identical, she believes they really have the same ability to pay, and should pay the same taxes. She asks, "Should the government force me to be my sister's keeper, if my sister does not choose to help herself?" Is it fair to punish Prudence with additional taxation and reward her high-living sister? Her sister replies that the past makes no difference: as they approach retirement their incomes differ. The fact is that Prudence's income is considerably in excess of Imprudence's and Prudence is therefore better able to pay for the support of the government (and her sister).

LIFETIME INCOME AS THE BASIS OF TAXATION The contrast between consumption and income as a basis of taxation may not be as stark as it has sometimes been portrayed. The real issue may be what is the appropriate time unit to use as the basis of taxation. Under a view that is growing in support, the appropriate basis of taxation should be lifetime income, not income in one year. Lifetime income is defined as the *present discounted value* of the individual's wage income.

Recall from Chapter 11 the discussion of the problem of adding up the benefits (and costs) of a project that occurred at different dates. We argued there that $1.00 in the next period was worth less than $1.00 in this period. If we receive $1.00 in this period, we could put it in the bank, and have $(1 + r)$ dollars in the next period, where r is the rate of interest. If r is 10 percent, we would have $1.10 in the next period. Thus, we should be indifferent between receiving $1.00 today or $1.10 in the next period. We say that the present discounted value of $1.10 in the next period is $1.00. That is, we discount future receipts because they are less valuable. If an individual lives for two periods, and receives a wage of w_0 in the first period and w_1 in the second, the present discounted value of his income, Y^* is

$$Y^* = w_0 + \frac{w_1}{1 + r}.$$

Of course, the present discounted value of an individual's consumption over his lifetime must be equal to the present discounted value of his income. That is, if c_0 is the individual's consumption in the first period of his life and c_1 is his consumption in the second,[8]

$$Y^* = c_0 + \frac{c_1}{1 + r}.$$

[8] To confirm this, assume that the individual consumed an amount that is less than his wage income in the first period. His savings would then be $(w_0 - c_0)$. Next period, he would have his wage income, plus his savings to consume, that is

$$c_1 = w_1 + (w_0 - c_0)(1 + r).$$

We can rearrange terms to write

$$c_1 + c_0(1 + r) = w_1 + w_0(1 + r).$$

Divide by $(1 + r)$ to obtain the desired result.

It thus becomes clear that if we believe that the correct basis of taxation is the individual's lifetime income, this is equivalent to believing that the correct basis of taxation is the individual's lifetime consumption.[9]

To say that taxes should be based on lifetime income or consumption means that if two individuals have the same lifetime income or consumption, then they should pay the same (present discounted value of) tax, regardless of the pattern of that income or consumption over their lifetime. *When* they pay that tax depends on how the tax is implemented.[10]

Note the one, strong implication of using lifetime income as a basis of taxation: Interest income should be exempt from taxation. A consumption tax is equivalent to a lifetime income tax, which in turn is equivalent to a tax on wages alone. While many see the first two as plausible bases for taxes, they find the third hard to accept—even after they see its equivalence to the others. Why should those who earn interest income be exempt from taxation?[11]

CRITICISMS OF INCOME AS A BASIS OF TAXATION Some have criticized the use of income as a basis for taxation, believing that neither income—lifetime or annual—nor consumption provides a fair basis of taxation. Their reasoning is illustrated by the following example. Consider Joe Smith and his twin brother, Jim, who have identical abilities and education. Joe decides to take a job as a high school teacher of economics. He teaches six hours a day and the rest of the time he spends fishing, swimming, and sailing. He is very happy. Not surprisingly, his pay is very low. Jim becomes an economic consultant. He works seventy hours a week and has no time for fishing, swimming, or sailing. Their economic opportunity sets, what they could have

---

[9] There are a couple of qualifications to this analysis. First, with bequests and inheritances, the present discounted value of an individual's consumption may either exceed or be less than his lifetime income. While for most individuals bequests and inheritances are relatively small—and thus could safely be ignored—for the very rich, they loom large. How they "should" be and are treated is discussed in Chapter 21.

This analysis also ignores uncertainty. While (ignoring bequests and inheritances) by definition, lifetime income equals lifetime consumption, an individual who faces larger uninsured risks (say, associated with a variable wage) is likely to be worse off than an individual with the same expected income but facing no risk; yet under the consumption (or lifetime income) tax they both pay the same taxes to the government. Is this fair? Is there any "fair" way to reflect such risks in the design of taxation? This issue so far has not received much attention.

[10] This is most easily seen in the case of proportional taxation. Then the tax can be imposed on wages (in which case it is paid as individuals earn their wage income) or on consumption (in which case it is paid as individuals consume goods).

The analysis has ignored the problems which arise if there is an imperfect capital market, such that there is no single interest rate at which individuals can borrow or lend.

[11] We said in note 11 that the equivalence only held if there are no inheritances. One might argue that interest received on inherited capital should receive different treatment. In fact, under current U.S. law, the return on a large fraction of an individual's savings over his lifetime (retirement savings, as well as investments in housing) are not taxed.

done, are identical. (Jim and Joe have the same earning ability.) Yet they have made different choices. One has a high income, one a low income. Is it fair that Jim should pay far higher taxes than Joe? Joe believes that it is not economic opportunities that provide the fair basis of taxation but the extent to which individuals have seized advantage of whatever opportunities society has offered—in short, actual income provides the appropriate basis of taxation. Jim believes that it is not actual income that should be relevant, but earning ability.

The problem is that even if one accepted Jim's argument, the government has no way of accurately assessing the individual's opportunity set. Wage rates may provide a better indicator than income, but even wages are affected by individuals' choices (for instance, how hard to work, or whether to accept a high-risk job). Moreover, in many jobs, wages are hard to measure and even harder to verify. We may know how much income an individual gets paid, but it is often difficult to know how many hours she has worked, especially in jobs where individuals do not punch a clock.

In practice, then, governments use income or consumption as the basis of taxation, even if they are flawed measures either of ability to pay or of an individual's well-being.

THE BENEFIT APPROACH We noted earlier that one argument for the use of consumption as the appropriate basis for taxation is that it seems fairer to tax individuals on the basis of what they take out of the economic system. Some economists have gone further and argued that individuals should contribute to the support of the government in proportion to the benefit they receive from public services. The principles of charging for public services should be analogous to those used for private services. And taxes can be viewed as simply the "charge" for the provision of public services.

In a few cases, the benefit approach is explicitly adopted: fees (taxes) are charged for the use of bridges and some toll roads. Financing roads with gasoline taxes can be thought of as a simple mechanism for relating benefits (road usage, as measured by gasoline consumption) to taxes.

For the most part, economists have not been attracted to the benefit approach to taxation, largely because it is impossible to identify the magnitude of the benefits received by different individuals. We all receive some benefit from defense expenditures, but how are the relative benefits to be apportioned among different individuals? For many categories of expenditures, assessment of benefits is essentially impossible. A second objection raised against benefit taxes when they are related to usage is that they are distortionary. Basing taxes on usage of a public facility (such as a bridge) may discourage its use and thus lead to an inefficient allocation of resources.

There are often equity-efficiency trade-offs involved in levying benefit taxes (in those cases where it is possible to do so). In the absence of benefit taxes, it is impossible to make those who benefit from a public facility such as a bridge bear the cost; if the bridge is financed out of general revenues, those who do not use the bridge (but contribute to it through taxes) are made worse off. It seems unfair to them that they should subsidize those who use the bridge.

ALTERNATIVE BASES OF TAXATION The principle of vertical equity says that those who are better off or have a greater ability to pay ought to contribute more than those less well off to support the government. The principle of horizontal equity says that those who are equally well off (who have equal ability to pay) should all contribute the same amount. Our discussion of both principles has focused on the difficulties of determining whether one individual is better off than another, or of determining whether one individual has a greater ability to pay than another. How should we adjust for the myriad differences in circumstances facing different individuals?

In each of the three following examples, present tax laws make some adjustments for differences in circumstances; there is, however, some controversy about whether the adjustments are appropriate.

The first example has to do with health. Clearly, an individual who is sick and has an income of $10,000 is different from an individual who is well and has the same income. Most of us would say that the individual who is sick is worse off (other things being equal) than the one who is well. Being sick or well is not always readily observable. Accordingly, it is difficult for the tax code to make adjustments for health status. But there is a surrogate: medical expenditures. Those who spend more on hospital bills are, on average, worse off than those who have no hospital bills. The current tax law does allow for the deduction of medical expenses in excess of 7½ percent of the individual's income.

The second example has to do with marriage. Individuals who are married differ from those who are not. Surveys by sociologists indicate that married men, for instance, are happier. Whether or not much credence should be placed in such evidence, the fact is that married men do live longer and are, on average, in better health. This would suggest that a married man with a given income is better off than an unmarried man with the same income. Does the principle of vertical equity imply that the married man should pay higher taxes? The present tax structure does discriminate against married individuals where the husband and the wife have similar incomes (though probably not for the reasons just given), while marriage may reduce the taxes of a man and woman who have very different incomes.

The third example has to do with the tax treatment of children. Consider two married couples with identical incomes. Both couples would like to have two children. One of the couples is infertile, the other is blessed with two children. Clearly, the couple with the two children is better off than the infertile couple. Even taking account of the extra costs of raising children, the fertile couple would not change places with the other. The principle that those who are better off should pay more taxes would suggest that this couple should pay more taxes; in fact, the tax law results in the couple with children paying lower taxes. The law seemingly looks not at their "well-being" but at their ability to pay, and recognizes that, having had the children, they face additional expenses which make them less able to pay taxes.

The analysis so far has shown that though the principles of vertical and horizontal equity seem, at first, to provide "reasonable" bases for designing a fair tax system, they are, in fact, of only limited help. The difficult questions—how we tell which of two individuals is better off or which has a greater ability to pay, and what we mean by equality of treatment—are left unanswered. Furthermore, the principle of vertical equity does not tell us how much more someone who is better off should contribute to the support of the government; all it tells us is that he should pay more.

Because of these difficulties, economists have looked for other principles by which to choose among alternative tax systems.

FAIRNESS

Horizontal equity: Individuals who are identical (or in essentially similar economic circumstances) should be treated the same, and pay the same taxes.

> *Key question:* What differences are relevant?

Vertical equity: Individuals who have greater ability to pay or who are better off or receive greater benefits from government services should pay more taxes.

> *Key questions:* What should be the basis of taxation?
>
> How is "ability to pay" or "benefits received" or "economic welfare" to be measured?
>
> How much more should those considered better off pay?

• Income is most often used as a basis of taxation, an indirect and imperfect measure of both ability to pay and economic well-being.

• Consumption may be "fairer"—it measures what one takes out of society rather than what one contributes.

• Lifetime consumption is equivalent to lifetime income. Lifetime income is a fairer basis than annual income (a better measure of overall ability to pay, or welfare).

• Lifetime consumption/income is a flawed measure of ability to pay; it unfairly disadvantages individual who chooses to work hard rather than enjoy leisure; it is not a real measure of one's opportunity set.

• Benefit taxation is hindered by difficulties of measuring benefits, especially for pure public goods.

• What are fair adjustments to income as the basis of taxation, taking into account differences in health, marital status, children?

GENERAL FRAMEWORK FOR CHOOSING AMONG TAX SYSTEMS

The concerns of equity and efficiency that we have raised about different bases of taxation may be integrated into a general framework, essentially an application of standard welfare economics. We first look at efficiency (taking into account both the distortions and the resources used to implement a tax, the administrative and compliance costs). We identify **Pareto efficient tax systems**—tax structures such that, given the tools and information available to the government, no one can be made better off without making someone else worse off. Then we choose among the possible Pareto efficient tax structures using a social welfare function, which summarizes society's attitudes toward the welfare of different individuals.

The advantage of this approach is that it separates efficiency considerations from value judgments. Almost all would agree that if a tax structure could be found in which everyone was better off (or some better off and no one else worse off), it should be adopted. On the other hand, often none of the alternative tax systems available dominates the others. In one tax system the poor may be better off, the rich worse off; but are the gains to the poor sufficiently large to justify the losses to the rich? The answer depends on value judgments, over which reasonable people may differ.

Recall from Chapter 5 that economists have made use of two special social welfare functions: the utilitarian (social welfare equals the sum of all individuals' utilities) and the Rawlsian (social welfare equals the utility of the worst-off individual). Either social welfare function makes it possible to say not only by how much taxes should increase with income but also, for instance, whether and under what circumstances a deduction for medical expenses should be allowed.[12] We now explore briefly what each of these two social welfare functions implies for tax design.

UTILITARIANISM

Traditionally, utilitarianism was thought to provide a rationale for progressive taxation, the taxation of rich individuals at higher rates than poor individuals. Under utilitarianism, taxes should be such that the marginal utility of income—the loss in utility from taking a dollar away from an individual—should be the same for all individuals.[13] If the marginal utility of income of Jim exceeds that of Joe, reducing Jim's tax by a dollar and increasing Joe's by a dollar increases total utility (social welfare), since the

---

[12] To make utilitarianism (or Rawlsianism) operational, one must make additional assumptions, as we noted in Chapter 5. It is conventionally assumed that all individuals have the same utility function (at each level of income all individuals benefit equally from an extra dollar), and that they exhibit diminishing returns (an extra dollar is worth less at progressively higher levels of income).

[13] Thus under utilitarianism taxes are not *directly* related to the benefits one receives from a tax, or to the level of economic welfare, but to the *marginal* benefit of a dollar of additional income.

gain in utility to Jim exceeds the loss to Joe. Since taking a dollar away from a rich person causes him less loss of welfare than taking a dollar away from a poor person, utilitarianism seemed to provide a basis for progressive taxation.

But this argument fails to take into account that individuals' income depends on their work (effort), and that raising taxes on those earning higher incomes may lead to a reduction in their work (effort). It is thus possible that raising the tax rate actually reduces the government's tax revenue, or that the marginal utility loss to the individual per dollar raised by the government may be very large. The earlier argument assumed, in other words, that income would not be affected by the imposition of taxes; it is now widely assumed that it generally will be. When it is, utilitarianism requires that we compare the loss in utility from an increase in a tax with the gain in revenue. We require that

$$\frac{\text{change in utility}}{\text{change in revenue}}$$

be the same for all individuals. If some group of individuals has a very elastic labor supply (that is, as tax rates are increased they greatly reduce their labor supply), an increase in the income tax rate on that group will yield relatively little revenue, so they should not be heavily taxed.

Utilitarianism was also once thought to provide a basis for the principle of horizontal equity. If everyone had the same utility function, individuals with the same income should be taxed the same. Assume that one individual faced a higher tax than another with the same income. Because of diminishing marginal utility, her marginal utility of income would be higher than the other's. Raising the tax on the individual with the *low* tax rate would cause her less loss in utility than the gain in utility from lowering the tax on the individual with the high tax rate. Again, this argument would be correct if income were unaffected. But it is affected, so the argument may no longer be valid.[14]

The argument that utilitarianism may imply horizontal *inequity* is perhaps best made by the story of the shipwrecked crew. The crew has enough food for all but one of its members to survive. Equality would thus imply that all individuals must die, clearly a worse situation (from a utilitarian point of view) than one in which only one dies.

---

[14] It can be shown that, under plausible conditions, utilitarianism requires that with distortionary taxes individuals who appear to be essentially identical should be treated differently. A formal exposition of the argument is presented in J. E. Stiglitz, "Utilitarianism and Horizontal Equity: The Case for Random Taxation," *Journal of Public Economics* 21 (1982): 257–94. See also Dagobert L. Brito et al., "Randomization in Optimal Tax Schedules," *Journal of Public Economics* 56, no. 2 (February 1995): 189–223.

Some economists and philosophers believe that the utilitarian approach is not sufficiently egalitarian, that it pays insufficient attention to inequality. In Chapter 5 we discussed the view of John Rawls that society should be concerned only with the welfare of the worst-off individual, that it ought to design the tax system (and other social policies) so as to maximize his welfare. The Rawlsian social welfare function, maximizing the welfare of the worst-off individual, has some simple and direct implications for tax policy: Increase the tax rates on all individuals (other than the worst-off individual) to the point where the tax revenues from them are maximized. This does not necessarily imply that very rich individuals should be taxed at 80 percent or 90 percent of their income, or even that marginal tax rates should always increase with income. It may turn out that those with very high incomes have labor supplies that are more sensitive to tax rates than middle-income individuals.

There are those who argue that not even the Rawlsian criterion is sufficiently egalitarian. Consider a change that makes the worst-off individual just slightly better off, but makes the richest 5 percent of the population much, much better off. Under Rawls, this is a desirable change—Rawls only pays attention to the worst-off individual. But some would argue that inequality itself is a social evil or gives rise to social evils. Differences in levels of wealth may give rise, for instance, to social tensions. Inequality of goods leads, in many political situations, to inequality in political power, and this may be used, eventually, to the advantage of the well-off at the expense of the poor.

Though economists have found the social welfare function extremely useful in thinking about the trade-offs in designing tax structures, the fundamental problems of the ability to pay and related principles remain (though often swept underneath the surface). *If* everyone were the same except for some attribute, such as their wage or inheritance, then it would be plausible

GENERAL FRAMEWORK FOR THINKING ABOUT TAXATION

Pareto efficient taxation: tax structures such that, given the revenue raised, no one can be made better off without making someone else worse off. Choice among Pareto efficient tax structures depends on values, reflected in the *social welfare function.*

Utilitarian social welfare function: chooses the Pareto efficient tax structure that maximizes the sum of utilities of individuals; marginal loss of utility per dollar of revenue raised must be the same for all individuals.

Rawlsian social welfare function: chooses the Pareto efficient tax structure that maximizes the utility of the worst-off individual.

to treat them the same; we could, under utilitarianism, simply add up their "utilities." But individuals *do* differ; some have a need for immediate gratification; others get more enjoyment from taking a longer-run perspective. The social welfare function approach may tell us that in choosing a tax structure, we should equate the change in utility to the change in revenue for all individuals. But it does not tell us how we can compare the utility of Spendthrift with that of his brother Scrooge.[15] And actually to design a tax structure requires making such judgments.

WHAT ECONOMISTS CAN CONTRIBUTE TO DISCUSSIONS OF FAIRNESS

Although economists (or philosophers) have not resolved the basic issues involved in the choice of bases for judging fairness, still much can be said. It is important, for instance, to be able to describe the full consequences of any tax, and these are seldom simply described by the amounts of tax each person pays directly. We can attempt to describe how various groups in the population are affected by different tax programs. In all tax systems there are certain groups that seem to pay less than their fair share—given any reasonable concept of fairness. We then need to ask, why are they treated differentially? It may be that to treat them fairly would necessitate introducing other, even worse inequities into the tax code. Tax systems must be based on *observable* variables, variables such as income or expenditures. As we noted earlier, many of the concepts involved in our more general philosophical discussions (e.g., welfare) are not directly measurable. Even income is not as well defined as might seem to be the case at first. Thus, many apparent inequities in our tax system are simply consequences of the inherent difficulty of translating what seem like well-defined concepts into the precise language required by any tax law.

In other cases, by considering carefully how different provisions of the tax code and changes in those provisions affect different groups, we can obtain some insight into why one group may claim that a set of provisions is unfair while another group claims that to change them is unfair. We can attempt to distinguish those cases where the term "fairness" is used simply to cover up a group's pursuit of self-interest from those cases where some reasonable ethical or philosophical position underlies individuals' claims.

REVIEW AND PRACTICE

SUMMARY

1 The five attributes that a good tax system should have are:
   Economic efficiency
   Administrative simplicity
   Flexibility
   Political responsiveness
   Fairness

[15] Recall the discussion in Chapter 5 on the problems of interpersonal utility comparisons.

2 Tax distortions arise when behavior is altered in an attempt to avoid or reduce taxes. With the exception of lump-sum taxes, all taxes create such distortions. Taxes affect decisions in all markets, including labor supply and savings decisions, and have impacts on financial and organization structures. Taxes on the future returns of an asset are typically capitalized in the value of the asset at the time the taxes are announced.

3 The two major aspects of fairness are horizontal equity and vertical equity.

4 A central question in applying the principle of horizontal equity (which requires that identical individuals pay identical taxes) is specifying criteria for grouping individuals as identical (for purposes of taxation).

5 The principle of vertical equity says that those who are more able to pay, or who have a higher welfare, or who receive greater benefits from government, should pay higher taxes. Income is the most commonly used measure of either ability to pay or economic welfare, but it is a flawed measure. Some argue that consumption provides a better basis. Taxing lifetime consumption is equivalent to taxing lifetime income, and both are widely viewed as superior to basing taxes on annual income. Hard questions are posed by what adjustments should be taken into account—for instance, for differences in health, marital status, or children.

6 Pareto efficient tax structures are those such that, given the tools and information available to the government, no one can be made better off without someone else being made worse off.

7 The utilitarian approach argues that the tax system chosen should maximize the sum of utilities. The Rawlsian approach argues that the tax system chosen should maximize the welfare of the worst-off individual.

KEY CONCEPTS

Monetized taxes	Corrective taxes
General equilibrium effects	Transparency
Announcement effects	Horizontal equity
Nondistortionary taxes	Vertical equity
Distortionary taxes	Benefit approach
Lump-sum taxes	Pareto efficient tax systems

QUESTIONS AND PROBLEMS

1 Discuss how your views concerning the tax treatment of children might be affected by whether you (a) lived in a highly congested country or in an underpopulated country; (b) viewed children as a consumption good (for

their parents), like other consumption goods. Discuss both efficiency and equity considerations.

2   With a progressive tax structure, it makes a great deal of difference whether husbands' and wives' incomes are added together or taxed separately. Discuss some of the equity and efficiency considerations that bear on the tax treatment of the family.

3   Does utilitarianism necessarily imply that tax structures should be progressive?

4   Consider an individual who has lost a leg but, with a new artificial leg, has the same earning power he had before. How should his taxes differ from a similar individual who has not lost his leg: (a) under utilitarianism; (b) under a Rawlsian social welfare function; (c) if you believed that ability to pay provided the appropriate basis for taxation?

5   The government has passed a number of pieces of legislation aimed at ensuring that firms do not take advantage of consumers' limited information. What might be meant by a "truth in taxation" law? What might be the advantages of and problems with such a law?

6   "Since the needs, other than medical, of the aged are typically not as great as those of younger individuals who have children to support, if the government provides free medical care to the aged, it should simultaneously subject the aged to higher income tax rates." Discuss the equity and efficiency consequences of doing this (consider alternative views of equity).

7   Suppose that the labor supply of married women is very sensitive to the after-tax wage (that is, it is very elastic), whereas the labor supply of men is not. The government proposes to reduce the tax on income earned by married women by 5 percent, and to raise by 15 percent the tax on earnings of married men. How would this tax change affect total tax revenues? How would it affect the distribution of income?

8   Consider a state debating how to finance emergency road and bridge improvements. Among the possibilities: increased fees on drivers' licenses, a personal property tax on motor vehicles, a tax on automobile parts (including tires), and higher taxes on cigarettes and liquor. Which of these taxes are benefit taxes, which are corrective taxes, which are both? Which of these taxes is least distortionary?

9   Issues of efficiency and fairness often get intertwined in complex ways. Use the perspectives on the principles of taxation provided in the text to discuss the appropriateness of (a) taxes on gasoline; (b) subsidies to public transportation; (c) the polluter pay principle, in which those who cause pollution have to pay for its cleanup (like dry-cleaning establishments having to clean up the toxic wastes resulting from the chemicals which they use).

18 Tax Incidence

FOCUS QUESTIONS

1 What is meant by the incidence of a tax? Why is it that those who ultimately bear the burden of a tax may differ markedly from those upon whom the tax is legally imposed?

2 What determines who bears the burden of taxes? How does it depend on the elasticity of demand and supply? On whether markets are competitive or not? Why might it differ between the short run and the long run?

3 Why are some taxes that appear to be markedly different really equivalent?

4 Who bears the burden of taxation in the United States?

When Congress or a state legislature enacts a new tax, the debate usually includes some opinions about who should pay for running the government or for the particular program being supported by the tax. For example, when Congress adopted the social security tax to pay for the social security system, it levied half the tax on the employer and half on the employee. It thought that both parties should share in the costs of the social security system.

But economic reality—for better or worse—does not always follow the laws passed by legislatures. Thus, economists distinguish between those who bear the **burden** of a tax and those on whom a tax is imposed or levied. The *tax burden* is the true economic weight of a tax. It is the difference between the individual's real income before and after the tax has been imposed, taking full account of how wages and prices may have adjusted. Economists use a more neutral word to describe the effects of taxation—they ask, what is the **incidence** of the tax? Who actually pays, in the sense that their real income is lowered? This chapter studies the incidence of various taxes.

The actual incidence of the tax may differ markedly from the intended incidence. Consider two taxes that are imposed on firms, the employer-paid portion of the social security tax and the corporation income tax. As a result of either tax, wages might fall or prices might rise. If wages fall, we say that the tax has been **shifted backward** (to a factor of production, labor): if wages fall by the full amount of the tax, we say that they have been fully shifted; if wages fall by less than the amount of the tax, we say they have been partially shifted. If prices rise, we say that the tax has been **shifted forward** (to consumers). Most economists believe that most of the employer-paid portion of the social security tax is shifted backward and that the effect of the tax officially levied on employers is essentially the same as that levied on workers. Thus, although the government levied only half of the tax on employees, they bear the full (or almost the full) burden of the tax in the form of lower wages.

There is considerable controversy over the incidence of the corporation income tax. While one reason why the tax is popular is that ostensibly firms and their shareholders pay the tax, most economists believe that a substantial portion of the tax is shifted. If firms raise their prices as a result of the tax, the tax is borne by consumers. If, as a result of the tax, demand for labor falls and wages fall, the tax if partially borne by workers, not investors. If the tax makes investing in the corporate sector less attractive, capital will move out of the sector, driving down the return to capital in the unincorporated sector. Thus, part of the burden of the corporate tax is on capital as a whole, not just capital in the corporate sector.

The study of tax incidence is one of the most important and difficult topics in the economics of the public sector. In the last chapter, we saw that one of the principles of a desirable tax system is that it should be *fair.* But fairness depends not on whom the tax is imposed, but on who actually pays the tax—on the incidence of the tax. If it were decided, for instance, that fairness dictated that owners of capital should pay higher taxes, but the tax was levied in such a way that the owners of capital could shift the tax onto consumers or workers, then the tax would not have achieved its goal. Economics, not Congress, often determines who actually bears the burden of a tax, though in designing the tax Congress can often affect the outcome: two taxes, both imposed on corporations but differently designed, can have markedly different consequences.

Just as two taxes that look similar, in that both are imposed on, say, corporations, can have markedly different effects, two taxes that look different, in that they are imposed in quite different ways, can have identical effects. Such taxes are said to be **equivalent.**

In Chapter 17 we saw that another principle of a desirable tax system, besides fairness, is transparency. This has two implications. First, it is preferable to impose taxes whose incidence is clear. Second, because most individuals do not understand incidence analysis, it is preferable to impose taxes in a manner which makes the apparent incidence of a tax correspond to the actual incidence. Thus, imposing half of the social security tax on the employer contributes to the lack of transparency, as it makes workers believe that the employer actually bears half the burden of the tax.

The incidence of a tax depends on a number of factors—most importantly, on whether the economy is competitive; and if it is competitive, on the shape of the demand and supply curves. This chapter is divided into five sections. The first and second analyze incidence in perfectly competitive markets and in markets in which there is imperfect or no competition. The third analyzes some important equivalent tax structures. In the fourth section, some other important determinants of incidence are discussed, examining a tax on capital in the corporate sector. In the final section, we discuss briefly the implications of our analysis for the overall incidence of taxation in the United States.

While this chapter focuses on the incidence of taxes, it should be clear that precisely the same issues arise in discussing subsidies and other benefits, such as those discussed in earlier chapters on government expenditures. If corn is subsidized, it may not be corn growers who really benefit: if the price of corn falls, the benefit is shifted forward to consumers; if the price of land on which corn is grown increases, the benefit is shifted backward to the owners of land. The principles elucidated here apply equally to the analysis of government benefit programs.

TAX INCIDENCE IN COMPETITIVE MARKETS

In this section, we will show that it makes no difference whether a tax on a commodity is legally imposed on the commodity's consumers or on its producers—it makes no difference whether producers of beer or its consumers "pay" the tax. What does make a difference is the shape of the demand and supply curves.

EFFECT OF TAX AT THE LEVEL OF A FIRM

Consider a commodity tax imposed at a fixed rate per unit of the good (so many cents per can of beer) which the firm must pay. Figure 18.1 illustrates the effect of the tax on the firm's production decision. In competitive markets, firms produce at the level where price equals marginal costs.[1] If the firm has to pay the tax, then its effective cost of production has been increased, *by the amount of the tax.* Accordingly, the amount it is willing to supply at the price p_0 is reduced.

The firm's supply curve gives the amount the firm is willing to supply at each price. Its supply curve is shifted, as illustrated in panel A of Figure 18.1. This is, of course, true for *every* firm. The *market* supply curve gives the

---

[1] At lower levels of output, increasing output increases revenues by more than the increased costs, so profits increase. The converse occurs at higher levels of output.

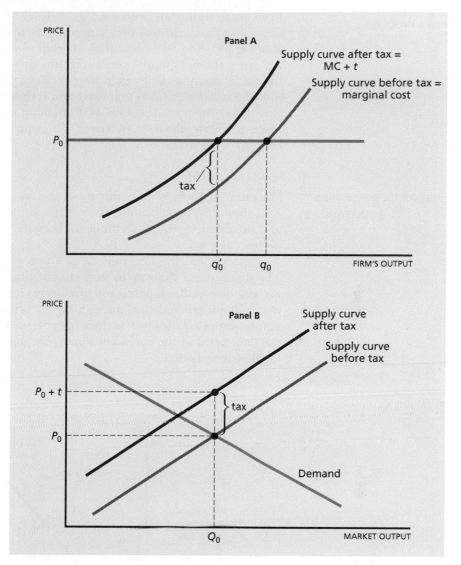

FIGURE 18.1   **The Effect of a Commodity Tax on Supply** Panel A shows the effect of a
commodity tax on the quantity supplied by a firm. At any price, p_0, the firm
will supply a lower quantity. The tax can be thought of as increasing the
marginal cost of production. Output supplied is reduced from q_0 to q_0'. Panel
B shows the effect of a commodity tax on the market supply curve and
equilibrium. At each price the market is willing to supply less (the supply curve
shifts to the left); or equivalently, the price required to elicit a given supply
out of the market is higher, by an amount exactly equal to the tax.

total amount that *all* firms are willing to supply at each price. It is simply the
"sum" of the supply curves of each firm. Equivalently, we can think of the
market supply curve as telling us what the market price must be in order for

firms to be willing to produce a given level of output. The market supply curve, like the individual firm supply curves, is shifted, as illustrated in panel B of Figure 18.1. The amount of the shift is easy to ascertain. If t is the tax rate, then the net amount received by the firm when the price is $p_0 + t$ after the tax is the same as it would have received when the price was just p_0 before the tax; the quantity that each firm is thus willing to supply at the price $p_0 + t$ after the tax is the same as it would have been willing to supply at the price p_0 before the tax. In effect, the supply curve is shifted up by the amount of the tax.

IMPACT ON MARKET EQUILIBRIUM

We can now easily see the impact of the tax on prices and output. Figure 18.2 shows the equilibrium before taxes, at the intersection of the demand and supply curve, where Q_0 bottles of beer are produced in equilibrium, at a price of $1 each.

Assume that the tax on each producer is 10 cents per bottle of beer. The supply curve shifts up by that amount, and the price rises. Although the tax was nominally imposed on producers, consumers are forced to pay a part of the increased cost, through higher prices. But notice that in this example, the price rises by less than 10 cents, to $1.05. Producers cannot shift the entire cost of the tax to consumers because as the price rises, the quantity demanded falls.

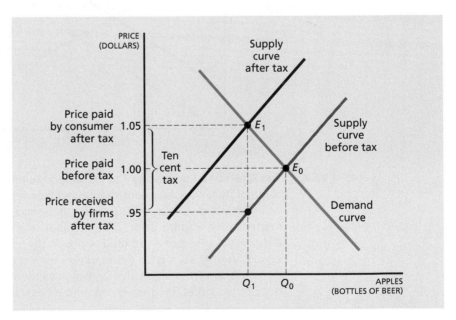

FIGURE 18.2 **Effect of Tax on Prices and Quantities** The tax shifts the supply curve up by the amount of tax. This lowers the quantity consumed and raises the price paid by consumers.

Each firm now receives the higher price of $1.05, and faces additional costs of 10 cents per bottle. The firms in Figure 18.2 produce less than before the tax, but more than they would have if consumers did not bear part of the additional cost.

DOES IT MATTER WHETHER THE TAX IS LEVIED ON CONSUMERS OR ON PRODUCERS?

Consider now what would happen if Congress passed a beer tax, but this time said that consumers would have to pay the tax. For each bottle of beer purchased, consumers would have to pay a 10-cent tax. What consumers care about, of course, is not who receives the money they pay, but simply the total cost of the beer—just as what producers care about is how much they receive. Return to Figure 18.2, which showed the effect of a 10-cent tax imposed on producers. At the new equilibrium output Q_1, producers receive, after tax, $.95 and consumers pay $1.05. In that situation, the producers mail the government a check for 10 cents for every bottle of beer. But nothing would change if consumers, or the retailers from whom they buy beer, had to send a check in for the same amount. Producers would then pay no *direct* attention to the tax. They would sell the beer to consumers for 95 cents, and at that price they would be willing to produce Q_1. Consumers would pay the producers 95 cents and pay the government 10 cents for a total price of $1.05. At the total price of $1.05, they are willing to purchase Q_1, so at Q_1, and a consumer price of $1.05 and a producer price of $.95, demand equals supply.

This situation is depicted diagrammatically in Figure 18.3. If we now interpret the price on the vertical axis to be the price received by the pro-

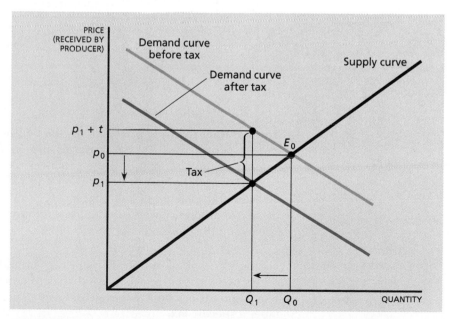

FIGURE 18.3 **Alternate Views of a Tax** The effects of a tax can be viewed as either a downward shift in the demand curve or an upward shift in the supply curve (compare with Figure 18.2).

THE INCIDENCE OF GOVERNMENT BENEFITS

The framework we have developed for analyzing the incidence of taxes can be used to analyze the incidence of a government program or subsidy. Consider a subsidy for beef. For simplicity, assume the government subsidizes beef at $1.00 a pound. In the short run, the supply curve is relatively inelastic, as depicted in the first figure below. That means there is a small quantity response, but a large price response: in the short run much of the benefit does go to farmers.

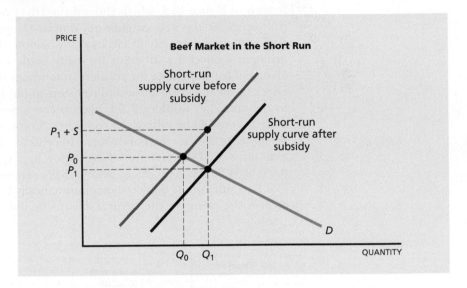

The ad valorem tax can be thought of as shifting down the demand ducer (rather than the price paid by the consumer), the tax on consumers can be represented by a downward shift in the demand curve, by the amount of the tax. That is, if the producer receives p_1, the consumer must pay $p_1 + t$, and the level of demand is Q_1, just as it would be if, in the before-tax situation, producers had charged $p_1 + t$. It should be apparent that it makes no difference whether Congress imposes the tax on the producers of beer or on the consumers of beer.

AD VALOREM VERSUS SPECIFIC TAXES

Not only does it make no difference on whom the tax is levied, it makes no difference whether the tax is levied as a given percentage of the price or as a fixed amount per unit output. The former is called an **ad valorem tax,** the latter a **specific tax.**

The ad valorem tax can be thought of as shifting down the demand curve, with the amount by which it is shifted down depending on the price, as illustrated in Figure 18.4. At a zero price (where the demand curve intersects the horizontal axis) there is no tax. The manufacturer receives a fixed

But in the long run, as entry occurs and producers can expand their facilities, the supply curve for beef becomes relatively flat; there is a large supply of acreage that can be used for pasture, and though it takes time to breed cattle, they can be bred, and the costs of breeding and feeding are roughly fixed. The figure below for the long-run beef market shows a horizontal supply curve combined with a downward-sloping demand curve, and the before-subsidy equilibrium at Q_0. The subsidy can be thought of as shifting the supply curve as depicted. The new equilibrium entails a larger quantity, but the price received by farmers remains unchanged. In the long run, all the benefit of the subsidy is received by meat consumers, none by farmers.

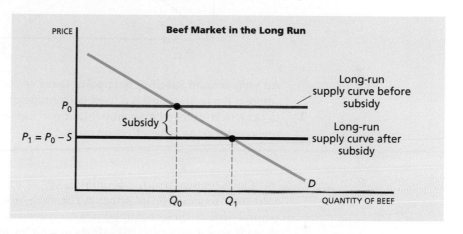

percentage of the price paid by the consumer, say 95 percent (if the ad valorem tax rate is 5 percent). E_1 is the after-tax equilibrium, at the intersection of the after-tax demand curve D_1D_1 and the supply curve. In the figure, the after-tax demand curve is also drawn for the case of a specific tax *which is of the same magnitude at the equilibrium E_1.* With the tax at the same level at the equilibrium, the demand curve is shifted down by the same amount at that level of output, and thus the equilibrium output, tax revenues, prices paid by consumers, and prices received by manufacturers are all the same.

In practice the two taxes often differ, because tax authorities cannot adjust appropriately for differences in qualities of goods. When the government levies a specific tax—say, so many cents per pack of cigarettes—the tax is the same regardless of the quality of the product. Thus, the tax is a higher percentage of the price for low-quality goods than it is for higher-quality goods. In effect, the specific tax discriminates against lower-quality goods. While in principle the government could adjust the specific tax rate to offset this bias, in fact it seldom does so.

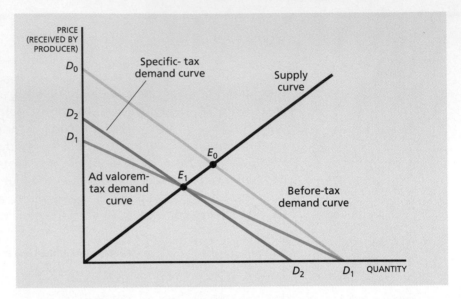

FIGURE 18.4   **Ad Valorem and Specific Commodity Taxes** In competitive markets, an ad valorem tax (a tax which is a fixed percentage of the price) and a specific tax (a tax which is a fixed amount per unit purchased) which raise the same revenue have the same effect on output.

On the other hand, it is often easier to monitor the quantity of a good sold than to monitor its price, particularly when firms sell more than one commodity. If these commodities are taxed at different ad valorem rates, there is an incentive to strike deals in which the higher-taxed commodity is underpriced on invoices, and the tax administrator may not be able to detect this. This kind of administrative problem has been the principal determinant of the form of taxation.

TAX INCIDENCE

The incidence of a tax describes who actually bears the tax. It does not depend on who writes the check to the government.

It makes no difference whether a commodity tax is levied on producers or consumers.

It makes no difference whether the social security tax (payroll tax) is paid half by the employer and half by the employee, or entirely paid by one or the other.

In a competitive market, the incidences of an ad valorem and an equivalent specific tax are identical.

The amount by which price rises—the extent to which consumers bear a tax—depends on the shape of the demand and supply curves, not on whom the tax is levied. In two limiting cases, the price rises by the full 10 cents, so the entire burden is borne by consumers. This occurs when the supply curve is perfectly horizontal, as in Figure 18.5, panel A, or when the demand curve is perfectly vertical (individuals insist on consuming a fixed amount of beer, regardless of price), as in panel B.

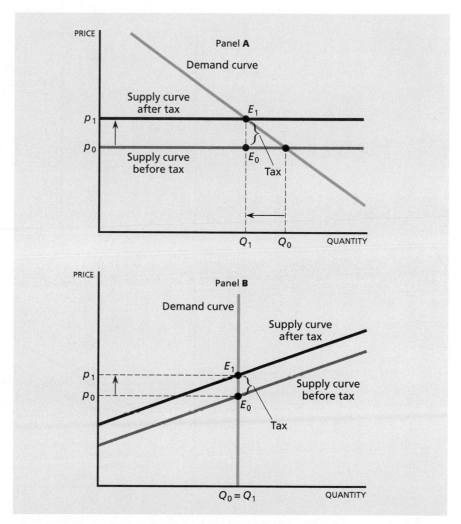

FIGURE 18.5   **Elasticity of Supply and Demand: Tax Borne by Consumers** (A) Perfectly elastic supply curve: With a perfectly elastic supply curve (horizontal supply curve), the price rises by the full amount of the tax; the entire burden of the tax is on consumers. (B) Perfectly inelastic demand: With a perfectly inelastic demand curve, the price rises by the full amount of the tax; the entire burden of the tax is on the consumers.

There are also two cases in which the price paid by consumers does not rise at all—that is, in which the tax is borne entirely by producers, as shown in panels A and B of Figure 18.6. This occurs when the supply curve is perfectly vertical—the amount supplied does not depend at all on price—or when the demand curve is perfectly horizontal.

More generally the steeper the demand curve or the flatter the supply curve, the more the tax will be borne by consumers; the flatter the de-

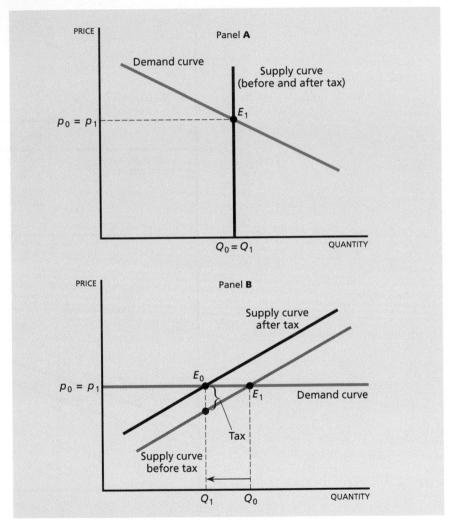

FIGURE 18.6   **Elasticity of Supply and Demand: Tax Borne by Producers** (A) Perfectly inelastic supply curve: With a perfectly inelastic supply curve, the price does not rise at all; the full burden of the tax is on producers. (B) Perfectly elastic demand: With a perfectly elastic (horizontal) demand curve, the price does not rise at all; the entire burden of the tax is on producers.

INCIDENCE IN COMPETITIVE MARKETS

In competitive markets, incidence depends on the elasticity of demand and supply.

A commodity tax is not borne at all by consumers if the demand curve is perfectly elastic, or by producers if the supply curve is perfectly elastic. It is borne completely by consumers if the demand curve is perfectly inelastic, or by producers if the supply curve is perfectly inelastic.

mand curve or the steeper the supply curve, the more the tax will be borne by producers. We measure the steepness of a demand curve by the **elasticity of demand;** the elasticity of demand gives the percentage change in the quantity of the good consumed due to a percentage change in its price. We thus say that the horizontal demand curve, where a small reduction in the price results in an enormous increase in demand, is infinitely elastic; and we say that the vertical demand curve, where demand does not change at all with a reduction in price, has zero elasticity.

Similarly, we measure the steepness of a supply curve by the **elasticity of supply;** the elasticity of supply gives the percentage change in the quantity of the good supplied due to a percentage change in its price. We thus say that a vertical supply curve, where the supply does not change at all with a change in price, has zero elasticity, while a horizontal supply curve has infinite elasticity.

The more elastic the demand curve and the less elastic the supply curve, the more the tax is borne by producers; the less elastic the demand curve and the more elastic the supply curve, the more the tax will be borne by consumers.

TAXATION OF FACTORS The basic principles we have just derived apply to all taxes in competitive markets, including taxes on factors of production.

TAX INCIDENCE AND THE DEMAND AND SUPPLY FOR LABOR Figure 18.7A depicts the market demand and supply curves for labor. It makes no difference whether a tax on labor is imposed on consumers (in this case, the firms which pay for the use of labor) or on producers (in this case, the individuals who are selling their labor services); the incidence of the tax is the same. The distinction made by Congress, that half of the social security tax should be paid by the employer and half by the employee, makes absolutely no difference for the effect of the tax. The consequences would have been the

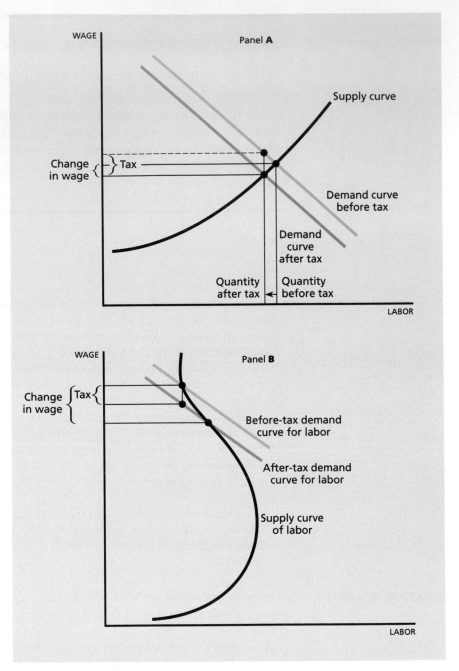

FIGURE 18.7   **Comparing the Effects of a Tax on the Demand for Labor** (A) The effect of a tax on labor is to shift the demand curve for labor down. A tax on labor will lead to a lower wage and a lower level of employment. (B) With a backward-bending supply schedule, the wage may fall by more than the amount of the tax.

same had Congress said that firms must pay the entire tax or that individuals must pay the entire tax.[2]

Who effectively pays the tax depends on the elasticity of demand and supply for labor. If, as is frequently claimed, the supply of labor is relatively inelastic (i.e., almost vertical), most of the burden of the tax falls on workers, regardless of the legal imposition of the tax.

Some economists believe that the supply curve of labor actually is backward-bending, as illustrated in Figure 18.7B. As the wage rises above a certain level, the supply of labor actually decreases. Individuals decide that, at the higher standards of living that they can attain with the higher wages, they prefer to work less. Thus, higher wages reduce the supply of labor rather than increase it. In this case, a tax on labor may result in a reduction in the wage rate that is greater than the tax itself, as the decrease in wages induces a larger labor supply, which drives down the wage further.

TAXATION OF INELASTIC FACTORS As we have noted, if the supply elasticity of labor or of a commodity is zero, the tax is borne fully by the supplier. The classic example of a commodity with a zero supply elasticity is unimproved land. The supply of land is fixed. Thus, if a tax is imposed on unimproved land, the total burden of the tax will fall on the landowners.

Unfortunately, it is difficult to distinguish the value of land from the value of improvements to it. In many parts of the United States, for instance, land in the wilderness, with no access to roads, sewers, or water, has almost no commercial value. It is difficult to ascertain how much of the value of land in urban areas is inherent in the land and how much is attributable to improvements. Because the supply elasticity of land improvements is large, a land tax may be largely shifted.

Another example of a factor in long-run inelastic supply is crude oil. Hence, a tax on oil is borne primarily by the owners of oil deposits. Since a disproportionate share of the world's oil is owned by those outside of the major consuming nations, the consuming nations have strong incentives to impose taxes on oil. Of course, owners of oil wells in the United States actively resist these taxes, and they are a sufficiently powerful lobby group to have done so quite successfully. In the United States, taxes on oil are far lower than those in most Western European nations.

---

[2] There may be a short-run difference. If Congress had imposed the entire tax on firms, it is unlikely that wages would have fallen immediately. In the short run, the labor market would not have been in equilibrium, and firms would have absorbed a large part of the social security tax.

There are also some differences arising out of the income tax. While the employee's contribution to social security is included in his income (upon which he must pay income tax), the employer's contribution to social security is not. Also, if the individual works for more than one employer and pays more than the maximum social security, he can claim a refund of the excess, but the employer is not entitled to any refund.

THE PHILADELPHIA WAGE TAX

Many cities, including Philadelphia, Pennsylvania, levy a wage tax. A careful look at the incidence of the tax suggests that the burden of the tax is largely upon landowners in Philadelphia. The supply curves for other factors, in particular for labor and capital, are relatively flat *in the long run*. Workers have a choice of working in Philadelphia or elsewhere. If their after-tax wage income is not commensurate with what they can receive elsewhere (taking into account the special amenities of Philadelphia), they will leave Philadelphia for employment elsewhere, and firms will not be able to recruit new workers. Thus, if a city such as Philadelphia imposes a wage tax, in the long run wages must rise to fully offset the tax. Similarly, owners of capital have a choice of investing in Philadelphia or elsewhere. If their return is not commensurate with what they receive elsewhere they will not invest in Philadelphia. Thus, after-tax wages and after-tax returns to capital are unaffected by the tax. Who then pays the tax?

TAXATION OF PERFECTLY ELASTIC FACTORS Just as taxes imposed on perfectly inelastic factors of production are borne totally by the factor, taxes on perfectly elastic factors are not borne at all by the taxed factor; they are entirely shifted. This simple observation has important implications for tax policy. The supply of capital to a small country is usually thought of as being highly elastic: just as a small firm must take the price it pays for capital as given, so too does a small country in an open, global market. The country cannot induce capital to flow in if it pays less than the market rate of interest; but at the market rate, it can obtain all the capital it could possibly absorb. Figure 18.8 plots the demand and supply of capital depending on the interest rate. With a tax on interest, the interest paid differs from the interest received. But the capital owner must receive the market rate, or she supplies nothing. The users of capital must make up the difference, paying $i + t$. In the figure, the vertical axis represents the interest rate re-

TAXATION OF FACTORS

The incidence of a tax on a factor in a competitive market depends on the elasticity of supply and demand for the factor.

The incidence of a tax on a factor whose supply is perfectly inelastic is borne completely by the factor.

A tax on a factor whose supply is perfectly elastic is completely shifted.

Only factors which are not mobile. Land, in particular, is not only not mobile; it is in inelastic supply. Thus land bears the brunt of the tax.

Pittsburgh, across the state, takes a different route from Philadelphia, taxing unimproved land directly, and at a much higher rate than it taxes improvements. Pittsburgh is the only major U.S. city that uses a graded property tax—where land and buildings are taxed at different rates. In 1979 and 1980, Pittsburgh restructured its property tax system so that land was taxed at more than five times the rate on buildings (or improvements).*

*For more discussion of the property tax in Pittsburgh and the economic effects of this property tax experiment, see Wallace E. Oates and Robert M. Schwab, "The Impact of Urban Land Taxation: The Pittsburgh Experience," *National Tax Journal* 50, no. 1 (March 1997): 1–21.

ceived, so the supply curve remains unchanged. The tax shifts the demand curve for capital down. At the new equilibrium, the interest rate received is unchanged. A tax on interest in this situation is fully shifted from capital owners to capital users.

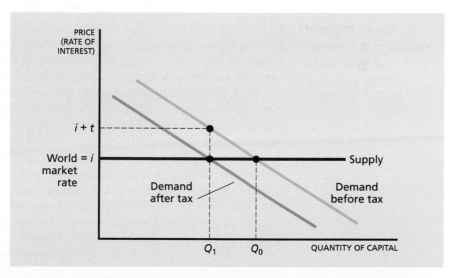

FIGURE 18.8 **Perfectly Elastically Supplied Factor** The incidence of a tax imposed on a perfectly elastically supplied factor is always fully shifted. The demand curve is shifted down by the amount of tax, leaving the price received by suppliers unchanged.

TAX INCIDENCE IN ENVIRONMENTS WITHOUT PERFECT COMPETITION

The effect of the imposition of a tax depends critically on the nature of the market. The analysis in the preceding section assumed that markets are competitive. But if markets are less than fully competitive—if, for instance, the industry consists of a monopoly, or of firms acting collusively, so that their combined behavior is similar to that of a monopoly—the effect of a tax could be markedly different.

In the absence of a tax, a monopolist will choose that level of output such that the cost of producing any additional output (the marginal cost) is just equal to the additional sales revenue he would receive (his marginal revenue). To maximize profits, the monopolist thus sets his **marginal cost** equal to his **marginal revenue.**

Figure 18.9 depicts the demand curve for aluminum, the marginal revenue curve, and the marginal cost of production. The marginal revenue curve lies below the demand curve. It represents the extra revenue the firm receives from selling an extra unit of output. The marginal revenue is the price the firm receives for that extra unit, minus the loss it sustains on the other units it sells, because as it attempts to sell more, it must lower the price.[3] The monopolist chooses Q_0 as his level of output, the quantity where the marginal cost and marginal revenue curves intersect. To find the price charged by the monopolist, we go up to the demand curve and locate price p_0.

A tax on aluminum can be viewed simply as an increase in the cost of production, which is to say a shift upward in the marginal cost curve. This will reduce output to Q_1 and increase the price to p_1.

RELATIONSHIP BETWEEN THE CHANGE IN THE PRICE AND THE TAX

In the case of a competitive industry, we showed that the consumer price increased by an amount that normally was less than the tax, and that the magnitude of the price increase depended on the demand and supply elasticities. The results for a monopolist are more complicated.

First, the steeper the marginal cost curve, the smaller the change in output and hence the smaller the increase in price. With a perfectly vertical marginal cost schedule, there is no change in output and no change in price; the tax is borne by producers. A supply (or marginal cost) curve is perfectly vertical if no increase in price calls forth an increase in supply. This result parallels that for competitive markets.

On the other hand, with a horizontal marginal cost schedule, as in Figure 18.9, the extent to which producers or consumers bear the tax depends on the *shape* of the demand curve. (Contrast this to competitive markets, where the consumer would bear the entire tax.) Panels A and B of Figure 18.9 illustrate two possibilities. With a linear demand curve, as in panel A,

---

[3] Recall that, in contrast, a perfectly competitive firm must take the market price as fixed, but can sell any amount of output at that price. Its marginal revenue is simply the market price.

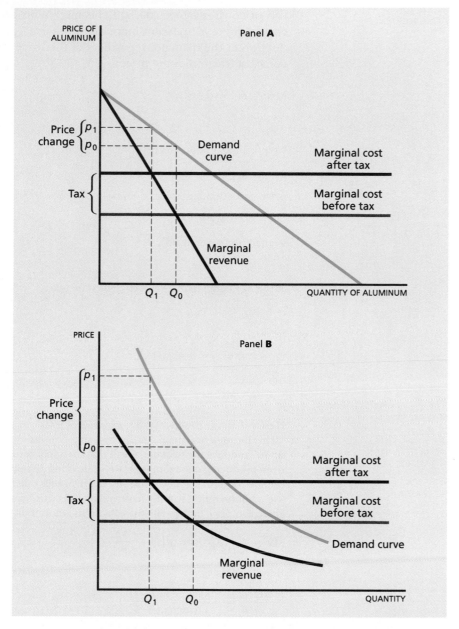

FIGURE 18.9 **Taxing a Monopoly** (A) With linear demand and horizontal marginal cost curves, the price paid by consumers rises by exactly half the tax; consumers and producers share the burden of the tax. (B) With constant elasticity demand curves, the price rises by more than the tax.

the price rises by exactly half the tax.[4] With a constant elasticity demand curve (where a 1 percent increase in the price results in, say, a 2 percent reduction in the demand, regardless of the price level), marginal revenue is a constant fraction of the price:[5]

$$MR = p(1 - 1/\eta^d),$$

---

[4] With a linear demand curve

$$p = a - bQ,$$

price and output are related linearly. Revenue, pQ, is given by

$$pQ = aQ - bQ^2,$$

so marginal revenue, MR, is

$$a - 2bQ.$$

This is set equal to marginal cost plus the tax:

$$a - 2bQ = MC + t$$

or

$$2a - 2bQ = 2p = a + MC + t$$

or

$$p = \frac{a + MC + t}{2}.$$

Hence if t increases by, say, \$2, p increases by \$1.

[5] This formula is general. In the case of a constant elasticity demand curve, η^d is constant. To derive the formula, recall that marginal revenue is the extra revenue received from producing one more unit. Revenue is just the price received per unit, p, times the number of units sold, Q. Thus, when a firm sells one more unit it receives p, but to sell the additional unit it must have reduced its price from its previous level. Denote the change in price by Δp. The firm loses this amount on all sales, Q. Thus the net gain is

$$MR = p + \Delta p \cdot Q = p\left(1 + \frac{\Delta p}{p} \cdot Q\right).$$

Recall too that

$$-\frac{\Delta Q/Q}{\Delta p/p} = -\frac{\text{change in } Q/Q}{\text{change in } p/p}$$

is just the percent change in quantity as a result of a percent change in price, which is just the elasticity of demand.

Here, the change in quantity is just 1, that is $\Delta Q = 1$, so we can rewrite

$$-\frac{\Delta p}{p} \cdot Q = -\frac{\Delta p}{p} \cdot \frac{Q}{\Delta Q} = -\frac{\Delta p/p}{\Delta Q/Q} = \text{elasticity of demand} = \eta^d.$$

So,

$$MR = p\left(1 - \frac{1}{\eta^d}\right).$$

where η^d is the elasticity of demand (a constant). Since the monopolist sets marginal revenue equal to marginal cost,

$$MR = MC$$

or

$$p\,(1 - 1/\eta^d) = MC$$

or

$$p = MC/(1 - 1/\eta^d).$$

A tax has the same effect as raising the marginal cost of production, that is

$$p = (MC + t)/(1 - 1/\eta^d).$$

Hence price increases by a multiple $[1/(1 - 1/\eta^d)]$ of the tax. If η^d is 2, then the increase in price is twice the tax.

AD VALOREM VERSUS SPECIFIC TAXES

There is another important difference between the taxation of competitive and monopolistic industries. In the case of competitive industries, the form in which the tax is levied makes no difference. We can choose between a specific tax, which is specified as a fixed amount per unit of output, and an ad valorem tax, which is specified as a percentage of the value of the output. All that matters for determining the effect of the tax is the magnitude of the difference (in equilibrium) between the price received by producers and the price paid by consumers, what we refer to as the wedge between the two.

In the case of monopolistic industries, however, ad valorem and specific taxes have quite different effects. We show in the appendix that for any given revenue raised by the government, the monopolist's output will be higher with an ad valorem tax than with a specific tax.

TAX INCIDENCE IN OLIGOPOLIES

Between the extremes of perfect competition and monopoly is the oligopoly market structure. In an **oligopoly,** such as the airline market and the rental car market, each producer interacts strategically with every other producer. If one producer changes its prices or output, the other producers may also change their prices or outputs, but these responses may be hard to predict.

There is no widely accepted theory of firm behavior in oligopoly, and so it is impossible to make any definite predictions about the incidence of taxation in this case. Some economists believe that oligopolists are not likely to raise the prices they charge consumers when taxes change. Each oligopolist may believe that if he raises his price, other firms will steal his market share. An opposite conclusion follows if each oligopolist expects that his competitors will match his price increase after a tax is imposed. In this case, all will raise their prices and thereby shift the burden of the tax to consumers.

Though economists have explored the incidence of taxes in an oligopoly under different specific behavioral assumptions, until they gain a better

TAX INCIDENCE IN MONOPOLIES OR IMPERFECTLY COMPETITIVE MARKETS

In monopolies or imperfectly competitive markets, tax incidence depends on the shape of the demand and supply curves; there may be more than 100 percent shifting.

In a monopoly, with constant marginal cost, and with constant elasticity demand curves, there will always be more than 100 percent shifting of specific commodity taxes. With linear demand curves, price rises by half of the tax.

understanding of oligopolistic behavior, there can be no general theory of the incidence of a tax in an oligopolistic market.

EQUIVALENT TAXES

In the discussion thus far, several instances have been pointed out where taxes appear to be different—a tax on employers to finance social security and a tax on employees; a tax on the producers of beer or a tax on beer consumers—but are really equivalent. There are many other examples of taxes that appear to be very different (and that from an administrative point of view *are* different) that are, from an economic point of view, equivalent.

INCOME TAX AND VALUE-ADDED TAX

An obvious example follows from the basic identity between national income (the total of what all the individuals in our society receive) and national output (the total of what they all produce). Since the value of income and the value of output must be the same, a uniform tax on income (a tax that taxes all sources of income at the same rate) and a uniform tax on output (a tax that taxes all outputs at the same rate) must be equivalent. A comprehensive uniform sales tax is a uniform tax on output and is thus equivalent to a uniform income tax.

The production of any commodity entails a large number of steps. The value of the final product represents the sum of the *value added* at each stage of production. We could impose the tax at the end of the production process, or at each stage along the way. A tax at the end of the production process is called a sales tax. A tax imposed at each stage of the production process is called a value-added tax. Thus, a uniform value-added tax and a comprehensive uniform sales tax are equivalent; and both are equivalent to a uniform income tax.

The value-added tax is used in most European countries, and there has been some discussion in the United States about introducing such a tax.

Since a uniform value-added tax is equivalent to a uniform (proportional) income tax, replacing our current income tax system with a value-added tax would be equivalent to replacing it with a proportional income tax system.

The value-added tax in Europe typically exempts investment goods. It is imposed only on consumption. Thus, the European form of the value-added tax is equivalent to a tax on consumption. Since consumption is equal to income minus savings, a consumption tax is equivalent to a tax on income in which savings are exempted.

EQUIVALENCE OF CONSUMPTION AND WAGE TAXES

Suppose that individuals receive no inheritances and leave no bequests. Then a uniform tax on wages and a uniform tax on consumption are equivalent. To put it another way, a consumption tax is equivalent to an income tax in which interest and other returns to capital have been exempted. (Our present tax system, in which part of the return to capital is tax exempt, can be viewed as somewhere between a consumption tax and an income tax.)

The equivalence may be seen most clearly by looking at the lifetime budget constraint of an individual (with no inheritances or bequests). For simplicity, we divide the life of the individual into two periods. Her wage income is w_1 in the first period and w_2 in the second. The individual has to decide how much to consume the first period of her life, while she is young, and how much while she is old. If she reduces her consumption today by a dollar and invests it, next period she will have $1 + r$ dollars, where r is the rate of interest. With a 10 percent interest rate, she will have $1.10. The budget constraint is a straight line, depicted in Figure 18.10.

Consider what happens to her budget constraint when a wage tax of 20 percent is imposed. The amount that she can consume shifts down. The slope of the budget constraint remains unchanged: it is still the case that by giving up $1 of consumption in the first period, she can get $1.10 next period.

Now consider what happens to her budget constraint when a 20 percent consumption tax is imposed. Just as before, the amount that she can consume shifts down, and the slope of the budget constraint remains unchanged. If the individual spends $1 today, she gets 20 percent fewer goods because of the tax; but when she spends $1 tomorrow, she also gets 20 percent fewer goods because of the tax. The trade-off between spending today and spending tomorrow remains unchanged. A wage tax and a consumption tax are equivalent.[6] Only the timing of the revenues to the government differs between the two taxes; this may be important if capital markets are imperfect.

There are, again, several ways that equivalent taxes can be imposed. We can impose a tax on wage income in each period, exempting all interest, dividends, and other returns on capital. Or we can tax consumption in each period, which can be calculated by having the individual report her total income minus total savings.

---

[6] If there are bequests and inheritances, a wage-plus-inheritance tax is equivalent to a consumption-plus-bequest tax. These equivalency relations require a perfect capital market but are true even if there is risk. See A. B. Atkinson and J. E. Stiglitz, *Lectures on Public Economics* (New York: McGraw-Hill, 1980), Lecture 3.

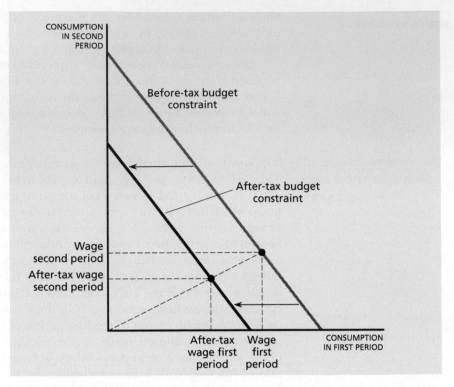

FIGURE 18.10   **Comparing the Effects of a Consumption Tax and Wage Tax** A consumption tax and a wage tax have exactly the same effect on the individual's budget constraint.

EQUIVALENCE OF LIFETIME CONSUMPTION AND LIFETIME INCOME TAXES

This analysis has one other important interpretation. Continuing with our example in which the life of an individual is divided into two periods, we can write the budget constraint[7] as:

$$C_1 + \frac{C_2}{1 + r} = w_1 + \frac{w_2}{1 + r}.$$

---

[7] This can be seen in a slightly different way. An individual's savings (borrowings) are the difference between wages and consumption in the first period:

$$w_1 - C_1.$$

Consumption in the second period is thus second-period wage income plus the savings with its interest (minus borrowings, with interest):

$$C_2 = w_2 + (1 + r)(w_1 - C_1).$$

Rearranging terms, we have

$$C_1(1 + r) + C_2 = (1 + r)w_1 + w_2.$$

Dividing by $(1 + r)$ we obtain the budget constraint in the form presented in the text.

EQUIVALENT TAXES

Two sets of taxes are equivalent if their incidence is exactly the same.

Income taxes and value-added taxes (without exemption for investment) are equivalent.

Consumption taxes and value-added taxes with an exemption for investment are equivalent.

Consumption and wage taxes are equivalent.

Lifetime income and consumption taxes (in the absence of bequests and inheritances) are equivalent.

The left-hand side of the equation is the present discounted value of the individual's consumption, and the right-hand side is the present discounted value of wage income. In the absence of bequests and inheritances, the present discounted value of consumption must equal the present discounted value of (wage) income. Thus, a lifetime consumption tax and a tax based on lifetime income are equivalent, as we saw in Chapter 17.

A CAVEAT ON EQUIVALENCE

The fact that two taxes are equivalent does not mean that there are no effects when one tax is switched to the other (or from some third tax to either of the two). Equivalence only means that the two taxes have exactly the same effects in the long run; in the short run—including the transition period as the tax is adopted—the effects may differ markedly. Take, for example, a switch from a lifetime income tax to a lifetime consumption tax. Leaving aside the problems of transition, the result would be that the elderly would face double taxation: in their youth, they paid taxes on wages, in their retirement, they pay taxes on their consumption. Or say a value-added tax is imposed. In the short run, prices consumers face rise, and more of the burden of the tax in the short run may be shifted to consumers than if the same revenues were raised by an income tax.

OTHER FACTORS AFFECTING TAX INCIDENCE

So far we have shown that what determines who bears the burden of any tax is not who Congress says should bear it, but certain properties of demand and supply curves, and the nature of the market—whether it is competitive or monopolistic or oligopolistic.

Several other important factors need to be taken into account in incidence analysis. First, there is an important distinction between a tax in a single industry and a tax affecting many industries. We considered above a tax on a small industry (beer). The presumption is that such a tax will not, for instance, have any significant effect on the wage rate. Though the reduction in the demand for beer will reduce the demand for labor in the beer industry, the assumption is that this industry is so small that workers released from their jobs can find employment elsewhere without any significant effect on the wage rate. We refer to this kind of analysis, where we assume that all prices and wages (other than those on which attention is explicitly focused) remain constant, as **partial equilibrium analysis.**

Unfortunately, many taxes affect many industries simultaneously. The corporate income tax affects all incorporated businesses. If, as a result of the tax, incorporated businesses reduce their demand for capital, the capital released cannot be absorbed by the rest of the economy (the unincorporated sector) without reducing the return to capital there. Thus, we cannot assume that what the corporate sector must pay to obtain capital is independent of the tax imposed on that sector. To analyze the impact of the corporation tax requires analyzing its effect on the equilibrium of the entire economy, not just the businesses on which the tax is imposed. Such an analysis is called a **general equilibrium analysis.** There are many instances where the general equilibrium impact of a tax may be markedly different from the partial equilibrium effect. For instance, if capital can be shifted relatively easily from the incorporated to the unincorporated sectors of the economy, the tax on corporate capital must be borne equally by capital in *both* sectors of the economy; they both must have the same after-tax return.

The overall incidence of the corporation income tax, like the tax on any factor, depends on the elasticity of demand and supply curves. While we will postpone until Chapter 23 a fuller discussion of the incidence of the corporation income tax, we can see why the general equilibrium impact may be markedly different from the apparent effect by considering the limiting case where the supply curve of capital is perfectly elastic. Savers insist on a return r^*, as depicted in Figure 18.11. Below r^*, they supply no capital; at r^*, they are willing to supply an arbitrarily large amount. That means that the *after*-tax return to capital—in both the corporate and the unincorporated sector—must be r^*, so the before-tax return in the corporate sector must be $r^* + t$. The tax simply raises the before-tax cost of capital in the corporate sector. This has two effects. First, it raises the price of the products produced in the corporate sector, reducing demand for them; demand is shifted to the unincorporated sector. And second, within the corporate sector, firms use more labor and less capital. In general, some of the tax is shifted to workers and some is shifted forward to consumers of the goods the corporate sector produces. But the magnitude of the effect on, say, workers, depends on, for instance, how easily firms in the corporate sector can substitute labor for capital and on the relative labor intensity of goods in the unincorporated and corporate sectors. If firms in the corporate sector can easily substitute labor for the more costly capital, and if goods in the

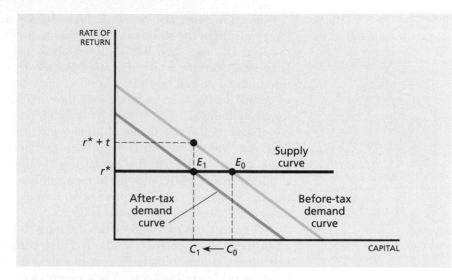

RATE OF RETURN

$r^* + t$

r^*

E_1 E_0

Supply curve

After-tax demand curve

Before-tax demand curve

$C_1 \leftarrow C_0$ CAPITAL

FIGURE 18.11   **Incidence of Tax on the Return to Capital in the Corporate Sector** With an infinite elasticity of supply of capital, providers of funds must obtain the same after-tax return as they did before the tax was imposed. The tax is fully shifted.

unincorporated sector are relatively labor intensive, then the general equilibrium effects may lead to an overall increase in the demand for labor, so that wages actually increase, if labor is inelastically supplied. In that case, the burden of the corporate income tax lies on consumers of the goods produced by the corporate sector. Workers and owners of capital may both be adversely affected by the price increase, but the *relative* impact may depend as much on consumption patterns as on anything else. If owners of capital largely consume services produced by the unincorporated sector, while workers consume more manufactured goods, then more of the burden of the tax may be borne by workers.

Three important points emerge from this analysis:

1 Corporations don't bear taxes, people do: shareholders, workers, consumers.
2 Because of general equilibrium responses, the impacts of corporation taxes are felt not just in the corporate sector, but throughout the economy.
3 The effects may vary depending on the period of analysis and on various assumptions about the structure of the economy. Can we assume that the overall stock of capital is fixed, or that capital can be shifted from one use to another with some degree of ease or difficulty? Can labor be easily substituted for capital? Can labor and capital move from one sector of the economy to another? The answers to such questions are critical to determining the effects of the tax.

A distinction must also be made between the incidence of the tax in the long run and in the short run. Many things are fixed in the short run that in the long run can vary. While capital presently being used in one industry (like steel) cannot easily be shifted for use into another, in the long run new investment can be shifted to other industries. Thus a tax on the return to capital in the steel industry may have markedly different effects in the long run than in the short run.

If savings are taxed, the short-run effect may be minimal. But in the long run, the tax may discourage savings, and this may reduce the capital stock. The reduction in the capital stock will reduce the demand for (and productivity of) labor, and this in turn will lead to a lowering of wages. As a result, the *long-run incidence* of a tax on savings (or capital) may be on workers, even if the *short-run incidence* is not.

The short run may differ from the long run also because of dynamics of adjustment. For instance, even in fairly competitive markets, firms frequently set prices initially by certain rules of thumb, which entail a given markup over variable costs. The long-run equilibrium in these industries has the markup adjust to the competitive level. In the short run, the market may be out of equilibrium.

The distinction between short-run and long-run effects is important, because governments and politicians are often shortsighted. They observe the immediate effect of a tax without realizing that the full consequences may not be those that they intended.

There are a number of factors which affect the disparity between the short-run and long-run effects, and between the partial and general equilibrium effects.

One of the most important is whether the economy is closed (does not trade with other countries) or open. If a small, open country like Switzerland imposed a tax on capital, the before-tax rate of return would have to adjust fully to offset the tax (or else investors would withdraw their funds from Switzerland and invest elsewhere); the tax would be borne by land and labor. Effectively, the supply schedule for capital is infinitely elastic. The same analysis applies, of course, to any state within the United States.

The final aspect of incidence analysis that needs to be discussed here is that it is almost never possible for the government to change only one policy at a time. There is a basic government budget constraint, which says that tax revenues plus the increase in the size of the deficit (increased borrowing) must equal government expenditures. If the government raises some tax rate, it must either lower another, reduce its borrowing, or increase its expenditure. Different combinations of policies will have different effects. We cannot simply ask the question, what would happen if the government increased income taxes? We need to specify whether the income tax is to be accompanied by a reduction in some other tax, by an increase in government expenditure, or by a reduction in government borrowing. (Often the accompanying change is taken to be

FACTORS AFFECTING INCIDENCE

Time span: short run versus long run

• Demand and supply curves are likely to be more elastic in the long run than in the short run.

Open versus closed economy

• Supply curves of factors are more elastic in an open economy.

Mix of policy changes

• Differential tax analysis: one tax is substituted for another, keeping revenue constant.

• Balanced budget analysis: expenditure is changed as tax revenues change.

• Balanced growth analysis: a mix of policies which leaves capital accumulation unaffected.

understood but not made explicit; e.g., if taxes are raised, there will be a smaller deficit.)

We call the analysis of a tax increase accompanied by a decrease in some other tax **differential tax incidence analysis;** we call the analysis of a tax increase accompanied by an increase in government expenditure a **balanced budget tax incidence analysis.** Such exercises have become particularly relevant in recent years as budgetary processes in the United States have been reformed in an attempt to control the deficit. Under what are called PAYGO rules, any increase in expenditure has to be matched by a decrease somewhere else, or by a new source of tax revenue.[8]

Sometimes we are interested in analyzing combinations of policies that leave some important economic variable unchanged. For example, a tax increase may lead to a reduction in output. We may want to distinguish the effects of a tax program on the level of output (and the effects that this

---

[8] Much of the focus on balanced budget incidence relates to macroeconomic consequences. Lower taxes or increased expenditures lead to higher levels of aggregate demand, unless offset by tighter monetary policy. Today, most analyses of tax and expenditure incidence assume that the monetary authorities will take offsetting actions to maintain the economy at full employment. These offsetting actions have, of course, distribution and other general equilibrium effects. Thus, a full analysis of the incidence of any set of tax or expenditure policies needs to take into account the consequences of the offsetting actions of the monetary authorities.

may have, say, on its distribution) from the direct effects of the tax itself; thus we may look at combinations of policies that leave the level of national output unaffected.

Similarly, many taxes have an effect on the level of capital accumulation. The fall in the capital stock in turn may lower wages. Again, one may want to distinguish the direct from the indirect effects of a tax resulting from its impact on capital accumulation. This is particularly the case if one believes that other instruments can be used to offset these indirect effects. If an inheritance tax reduces capital accumulation, for example, it may be possible to undo the effects by providing an investment tax credit. We may examine a set of policies whose effect is to leave capital accumulation unaffected; incidence analysis of this sort is called **balanced growth incidence analysis.**

INCIDENCE OF TAXES IN THE UNITED STATES

In this chapter, we have explained why the actual burden of taxes does not necessarily fall upon those upon whom the tax is imposed. Officially, the United States, like most advanced countries, has a **progressive** tax system, one in which the rich are supposed to pay a higher proportion of their income in taxes than the poor. The income tax imposes a 40 percent tax rate on the rich, while poor families receive as much as a 40 percent subsidy (through the earned income tax credit). But there is a general consensus that, overall, the U.S. tax system is far less progressive than the official tax code might suggest. (A tax system is said to be **regressive** if the poor pay a higher percentage of their income in taxes than do the rich.)[9]

There are three reasons for this view. First, the income tax itself is less progressive than appears, because it has certain specific design features which allow certain types of income or categories of individuals at least partially to escape taxation. For instance, capital gains are taxed at lower rates than other forms of income, and there are a variety of special provisions, discussed later, which lower the **effective rate** even more. Individuals can put away savings into tax-exempt accounts, and richer individuals tend to avail themselves of this opportunity more than poor individuals. There may be, as we shall see, good reasons for these and other provisions of the tax code, but their net effect is to reduce the progressivity of the tax system.

---

[9] The discussion below considers progressivity in terms of the ratio of annual taxes to annual income. A more appropriate measure would be lifetime taxes relative to lifetime income or consumption. The distinction is important. Changes in tax policy that may look regressive in the annual measure may not be so in terms of the more fundamental measure, as we shall see in later chapters.

Second, the income tax itself is only one of several taxes; many of the other taxes, such as state and local sales taxes[10] and the payroll tax, are less progressive, or even regressive.[11]

Third, the incidence of many taxes differs from those upon whom the tax is legislated; workers often bear the effect of taxes which are "intended" for others. As noted previously, there is a general consensus among economists that workers, not employers, bear the full burden of the employer share of the social security tax. There is also a general consensus that much of the corporation income tax is shifted, though there is disagreement both about the extent, and to whom it is shifted. As world capital markets have become more integrated, it becomes more likely that the tax is not borne by capital. Whether it is shifted forward to consumers or back to workers is less apparent; but in either case, its impact is less progressive than it would be if it were borne by the owners of corporations.

Precise estimates of the overall burden of the federal tax system clearly depend on assumptions concerning who bears the burden of various taxes, such as social security payroll taxes and the corporation income tax. Figure 18.12 looks at the effective federal individual income tax rates, while Figure 18.13 looks at the effective tax rates including all federal taxes, assuming that workers bear the full burden of payroll taxes (including those supposedly paid by employers) but that the corporation tax falls half on owners of capital, half on consumers. What is remarkable is that while the overall tax rates are clearly higher, the pattern is strikingly similar, with differences in tax rates from quintile to quintile being roughly comparable.

There is a high degree of progressivity at the bottom—the poorest 20 percent of the population paying approximately 8 percent of their income in taxes, half that of the next quintile. On the other hand, at the very top, progressivity is limited, with the top 1 percent paying only a few percentage points more in taxes than those in the top 10 percent. The data probably overstate the overall degree of progressivity of the U.S. tax system, since, as already noted, state and local taxes tend to be less progressive than federal taxes. Also, since only realized capital gains are included in income, the unrealized capital gains—which have been huge in recent years as a result of

---

[10] State and local sales taxes tend to be at fixed rates, but they are levied only on the purchases of certain goods. The fraction of income spent on those goods tends to be lower for richer individuals than for poor; in states where food is exempt, it is the middle-income individuals who pay the highest percentage of their income.

[11] The payroll tax is a fixed percentage of wage income, up to a cap. Thus, higher-wage individuals pay a tax on only a portion of their wage income; and since wealthier individuals, on average, derive a smaller fraction of their income from wages, payroll taxes are an even smaller percentage of total income for richer individuals. Interpreting whether the social security system is, as a result, regressive is, however, far more controversial, for we need to take into account not only the contributions, but also the benefits. Historically, as we saw in Chapter 14, richer individuals have gotten back far more in excess of what they contributed than did poorer individuals, but today, there is a close correspondence between contributions and payments, except for the poor, who receive back more than they contribute.

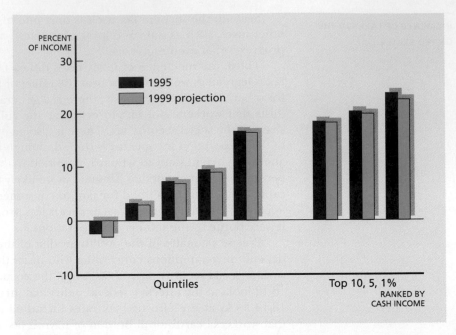

FIGURE 18.12 **Progressivity of Federal Individual Income Tax** Effective tax rates on the individual income tax (the ratio of tax payments to incomes) were far lower than the legislated rates, as a result of a variety of special provisions. Still, the tax schedule exhibited considerable progressivity.

the large increase in the value of the stock market and other assets—are not included. To include them would result in a lower effective tax rate among the richest Americans. The 1997 tax law, by providing still further special treatment of capital gains, reduced the progressivity of the tax system, undoing some of the increase in progressivity that was introduced in 1993, when marginal tax rates on upper-income individuals were raised from 28 percent to close to 40 percent. (Taken together, the 1993 and 1997 changes shifted the burden of taxation *among* high-income individuals, increasing the effective tax rates of those who received high salaries, and lowering the effective tax rates of those deriving income from, say, real estate speculation.)[12]

[12] The increased flows of international capital suggest that more of the burden of the corporate income tax may be borne by consumers and less by capital than is reflected in the figure. In that case, the overall degree of progressivity is less than depicted.

Since benefits are roughly commensurate with social security contributions, the *net* tax imposed by the social security system is only associated with its redistributions. Lower-income individuals receive somewhat more than they contribute, and higher-income individuals receive somewhat less. Figure 18.13 only looks at payroll taxes, not benefits.

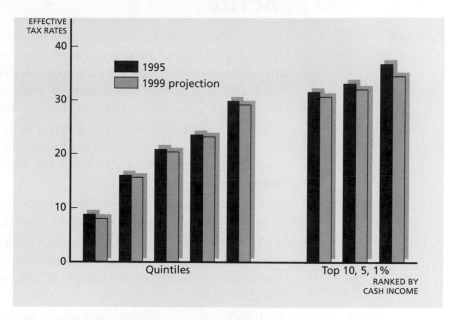

FIGURE 18.13 **Progressivity of Federal Tax Structure** When all taxes are included, effective tax rates are higher, and remain progressive.

The issue of incidence has played a major role in recent tax reforms. With each proposal, tables have been drawn up showing how effective tax rates would change. Since politicians find it hard to defend tax cuts for the very rich, a great deal of effort goes into trying to find alternative ways of characterizing the impact of a tax change. For instance, advocates of cutting capital gains tax rates—the main beneficiaries of which are the very rich—argue that such cuts will induce these individuals to sell more of their assets; and since capital gains are only taxed when the asset is sold, at least initially tax collections from the rich will go up—even if in the long run tax collections go down. Thus, advocates of capital gains tax cuts for upper-income individuals focused not on the cut in tax rates, but on the increases in tax payments in the initial years. More generally, controversies over incidence—for instance, over who really pays taxes such as the corporation income tax—play a key role in debates over whether particular reforms increase or decrease the progressivity of the tax system. At issue are matters of both theory and empirical analysis, and the impacts often depend on detailed provisions of the tax code. The following chapters of this book will elucidate many of the key issues in these debates.

REVIEW AND PRACTICE

SUMMARY

1   It makes no difference whether a tax is imposed on the suppliers of a factor or commodity or on the consumers. Instead, who bears the burden of the tax depends on the demand and supply elasticities, and on whether the market is competitive or noncompetitive. Taxes induce changes in relative prices, and it is this market response that determines who bears the tax.

2   In a competitive market, if the supply is completely inelastic or if demand is completely elastic, the tax is borne by producers. If the supply is completely elastic or demand is completely inelastic, the tax is entirely borne by consumers.

3   A tax on a monopolist may be shifted more than 100 percent—that is, the price paid by consumers may rise by more than the tax.

4   The general equilibrium incidence of a tax, taking into account repercussions in all industries, may differ from the partial equilibrium incidence. The incidence of a tax may be different in the long run than in the short run.

5   It is almost never possible for the government to change one policy at a time. Differential tax incidence focuses on how substituting one tax for another will affect the distribution of the tax burden.

6   A tax on output (a uniform sales tax), a proportional income tax, and a uniform value-added tax are all equivalent. A uniform tax on wages and a uniform tax on consumption are equivalent.

7   Empirical studies of who bears the burden of the set of taxes imposed in the United States show that the degree of progressivity of the tax structure depends on assumptions concerning the incidence of taxes on corporations and on payrolls. The current United States tax structure has some progressivity, though less than appears "on paper."

KEY CONCEPTS

Burden	Marginal revenue
Tax incidence	Oligopoly
Shifting backward	Partial equilibrium analysis
Shifting forward	General equilibrium analysis
Equivalent taxes	Differential tax incidence analysis
Ad valorem tax	Balanced budget tax incidence analysis
Specific tax	Balanced growth incidence analysis
Elasticity of demand	Progressive
Elasticity of supply	Regressive
Marginal cost	Effective tax rate

1   Consider a mineral that is in fixed supply, $Q^S = 4$. The demand for the mineral is given by $Q^D = 10 - 2p$, where p is the price per pound, and Q^D is the quantity demanded. The government imposes a tax of $2 per pound on the consumer,

   a   What is the price paid by the consumer before the tax is imposed, and in the post-tax equilibrium?

   b   What is the price received by producers?

   c   How much revenue is raised?

2   Consider a small town in which workers are highly mobile (i.e., they can be induced to leave the town if opportunities elsewhere improve slightly). What do you think the incidence of a tax on wages in that town would be, compared to the incidence in a town in which workers are immobile?

3   It is frequently asserted that taxes on cigarettes and beer are regressive, because poor individuals spend a larger fraction of their income on such items than do better-off individuals. How would your estimate of the degree of regressivity be affected if you thought these commodities were produced by: (a) competitive industries with inelastic supply schedules; (b) a monopoly with a linear demand schedule; (c) a monopoly facing a constant elasticity demand schedule?

4   It is often asserted that gasoline taxes used to finance highway construction and maintenance are fair because they make users of roads pay for them. Who do you think bears the burden of such taxes?

5   If you believed that a proportional consumption tax was the best tax, what are various ways in which you could levy it? Might there be differences in administrative costs associated with levying such a tax in different ways?

6   In what ways may the actual incidence of a government expenditure program differ from the legislated intent? Why might the effects be different in the short run than in the long run? Illustrate with examples drawn from Part Four of the book, or with a discussion of the effects of government farm programs. Similarly, discuss how the short-run and long-run effects of a regulatory program, such as rent control, may differ.

APPENDIX

COMPARISON OF THE EFFECTS OF AN AD VALOREM AND SPECIFIC COMMODITY TAX ON A MONOPOLIST

Suppose the government imposes a tax on the output of a monopolist. We asserted in the text that an ad valorem tax (a tax based on a fixed percentage of the value of sales) would reduce output less than a specific tax (a fixed tax on each unit sold) for any given revenue raised by the government.

The reason is that the ad valorem tax reduces marginal revenues by less than the tax, while the specific tax reduces marginal revenues by exactly the amount of the tax. Since a monopolist sets marginal revenue equal to marginal cost, if marginal revenue is reduced by less, output is reduced by less.

We can see this diagrammatically in Figure 18.14. Panel A illustrates the effect of a specific commodity tax. Earlier, we represented the effects of such a tax by an increase in the marginal cost. Alternatively, we can represent the effects of this tax as a *decrease* in the price received by the firm at any given quantity sold, that is, as a downward shift in the demand schedule. Both the demand and marginal revenue schedules shift down by the magnitude of the tax, t.

With an ad valorem tax, if an individual pays a price p for a commodity, the amount received by the producer is $p(1 - \hat{t})$, where $\hat{t}$ represents the ad valorem tax rate. Thus the tax paid is a function of the market price. If the price were zero, there would be no tax paid, as we saw in the text. The effect of the tax is to rotate the demand curve as in panel B, rather than to shift it down uniformly as in panel A. The ad valorem tax at rate $\hat{t}$ reduces revenue by a fixed percentage—to $(1 - \hat{t})pQ$—and therefore lowers marginal revenue by the same percentage, to $(1 - \hat{t})MR_{bt}$, that is to $1 - \hat{t}$ times the before-tax level. The marginal revenue schedule too is rotated around the point where it intersects the horizontal axis.

The important point is that the marginal revenue is reduced by $\hat{t} \times MR$, and since marginal revenue is less than the price, it is reduced by less than $\hat{t} \times p$, the tax revenue per unit of the product sold. By contrast, with the specific tax, marginal revenue is decreased by precisely the amount of the specific tax. Thus, for any given level of equilibrium output—for any given reduction in marginal revenue—the ad valorem tax raises more revenue, as shown in the figure; or equivalently, for any given tax revenue per unit ($t = \hat{t} \times p$) output will be higher with an ad valorem tax and so price will be lower and total government revenue will be higher.

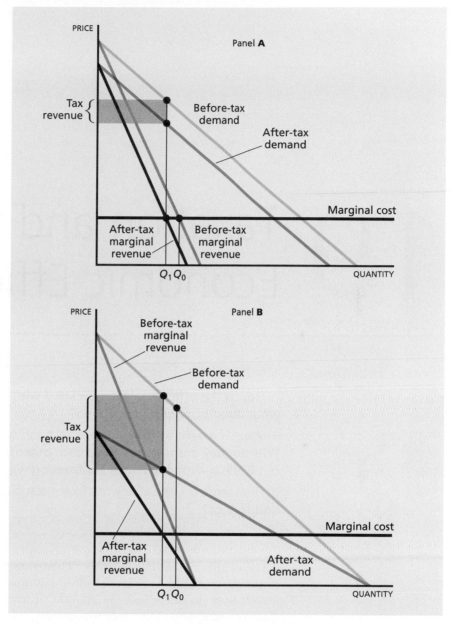

FIGURE 18.14 **Comparing the Effects of a Specific Tax and an Ad Valorem Tax on a Monopolist** (A) The effects of a specific commodity tax on a monopolist can be viewed either as a shift upward in the marginal cost schedule (as in the earlier diagrams) or, as here, a shift downward in the demand and marginal revenue schedules. (B) Analysis of the effects of an ad valorem tax on a monopolist. For any given level of output, Q_1, tax revenue is higher with an ad valorem tax than with a specific tax.

19 Taxation and Economic Efficiency

FOCUS QUESTIONS

1 How is the efficiency loss associated with taxation measured? On what does its magnitude depend?

2 What is meant by the income effect and substitution effects of a tax? Why do they normally reinforce each other for taxes on commodities, but work against each other for taxes on wages and interest?

3 How large are the efficiency losses associated with taxes on labor and savings?

All taxes affect economic behavior. They transfer resources from individuals to the government. As a result, individuals must alter their behavior in some way. If they do not adjust the amount of work they do, they must reduce their consumption. They may work more, enjoying less leisure; by working more, they need reduce their consumption less.

No matter how individuals adjust, an increase in taxes must make them worse off.[1] But some taxes reduce individuals' welfare less, for each dollar of

[1] This ignores, of course, the benefits that may accrue from the increased government expenditures that result from the increased taxes. In a sense, this chapter looks at the "costs" of government programs, that are associated with the taxes to finance them, while earlier chapters in the book looked at the benefits. An overall assessment requires balancing the two. Throughout this chapter we also ignore general equilibrium effects: before-tax wages and prices will be assumed to be unaffected by the imposition of a tax.

revenue raised, than do other taxes. Tax policy is concerned with designing tax structures which minimize welfare loss for any given amount of revenue raised—while still attaining the other objectives of tax policy discussed in Chapter 17. This chapter analyzes the determinants of welfare loss; Chapter 20 then uses the results to describe the basic principles of optimal taxation.

This chapter is divided into six sections. The first analyzes the effects of a tax on a consumption good, such as beer. After describing the effects qualitatively, the second section shows how the distortions can be quantified. The third section analyzes inefficiencies associated with taxes on producers. The fourth and fifth sections show how the same principles may be applied to taxes on the return to savings and on wages. The final section discusses various attempts to quantify the effects of taxation on labor supply.

EFFECT OF TAXES BORNE BY CONSUMERS

We begin the analysis with the simplest case, that of a tax borne fully by consumers. Assume that an individual's income is fixed, and he can choose between purchasing two commodities, soda and beer. His budget constraint is the line *SB* in Figure 19.1. This gives the various combinations of soda and beer that the individual can purchase. If he spent all his income on soda, he could purchase the amount *S*; if he spent all his income on beer, he could purchase the amount *B*.

Suppose that the government imposes a tax on beer. What will be the effect? (Throughout this section, we will assume that the consumer price rises by the full amount of the tax; that is, consumers bear the full burden of

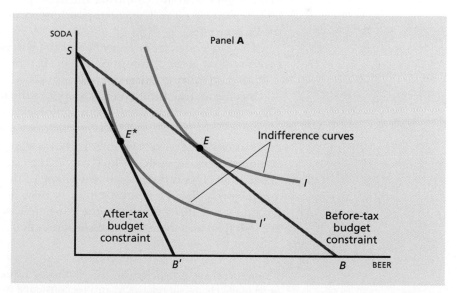

FIGURE 19.1   **Equilibrium After the Imposition of a Tax on Beer** The effect of the tax is to shift the budget constraint down and, thus, the equilibrium changes from *E* to *E**.

the tax. This will happen if the supply curves for beer and soda are infinitely elastic, as we showed in Chapter 18.) The tax on beer shifts the budget constraint in to SB'. The individual can still, if he wishes, spend all his income on soda, in which case he obtains S units of soda. But beer is now more expensive, so he can purchase less of it with his income.

Initially, the individual allocated his income by choosing point E on this budget constraint. This is the point of tangency between the budget constraint and the indifference curve. After the imposition of the tax, there is a new equilibrium, at point E^*. At E^*, the individual consumes less beer than at E.

SUBSTITUTION AND INCOME EFFECTS

The tax decreases the individual's consumption of beer, for two reasons. First, the tax—like any tax or loss of income—makes him worse off, by leaving him with less money to spend. Normally, when an individual is worse off, he consumes less of all goods. The amount by which his consumption of the taxed good is reduced because he is worse off is called the **income effect** of the tax. Second, the tax makes beer more expensive than other goods. When a good becomes relatively more expensive, individuals find substitutes for it. The extent to which consumption of the taxed good is reduced because of the increased *relative price* is the **substitution effect.**

Figure 19.2 shows how to decompose the movement from E to E^*—the reduction in beer consumption—into income and substitution effects. We first ask, how would consumption of beer have been reduced if we had taken away income from the individual, to put him on the new, lower indifference curve, but had not at the same time changed relative prices? This change is reflected in the budget constraint $\hat{S}\hat{B}$, which is parallel to the original budget constraint (implying the same prices), but tangent to the indifference curve I', at $\hat{E}$. The corresponding reduction in beer consumption is the income effect.

The movement from $\hat{E}$ to E^*, and the corresponding reduction in beer consumption, is the substitution effect. It represents the reduction in consumption *due solely to changes in relative prices.*

Income and substitution effects work in the same direction in the case of a beer tax: beer consumption drops continually as we move from E to $\hat{E}$ to E^*.

DETERMINING THE SIZE OF THE SUBSTITUTION EFFECT The magnitude of the substitution effect depends on how easy it is to substitute other goods for the taxed good. This is reflected in the shape of the indifference curves. If they are relatively flat, then substitution is easy, and the substitution effect is large.[2] Figure 19.2B illustrates the extreme case where indifference curves are L-shaped and there is no substitution effect.

---

[2] More precisely, it depends on the *elasticity of substitution,* which is defined as the percentage change in relative quantities consumed from a percentage change in relative prices. The L-shaped indifference curve of Figure 19.2B has a zero elasticity of substitution. The other extreme case is a straight-line indifference curve, in which case the elasticity of substitution is said to be infinite.

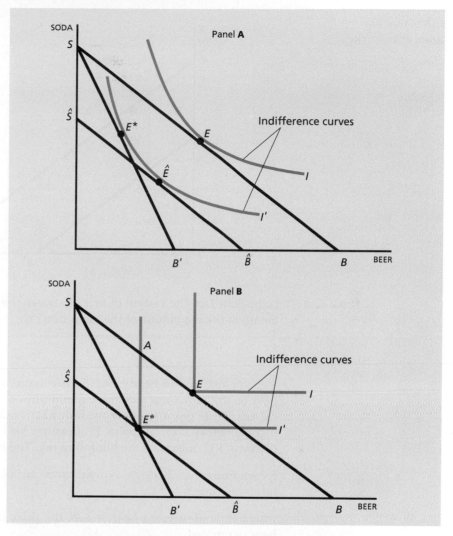

FIGURE 19.2 **Income and Substitution Effects of a Tax on Beer Consumption** Panel A
decomposes the movement from *E* to *E** into income and substitution effects.
The movement from *E* to *Ê* is the income effect, and the movement from *Ê* to
E* is the substituton effect. Panel B, where indifference curves are L-shaped,
represents the case in which there is no substitution effect.

QUANTIFYING THE DISTORTIONS

Any tax must have effects on consumption. After all, the purpose of a tax is
to transfer purchasing power from the individual to the government. Individuals have to reduce their consumption of something. An efficient tax minimizes the welfare loss per unit revenue raised. Chapter 17 introduced the
concept of a lump-sum tax, a tax which the individual must pay regardless on
what he does. Such a tax simply moves the budget constraint in a parallel

521

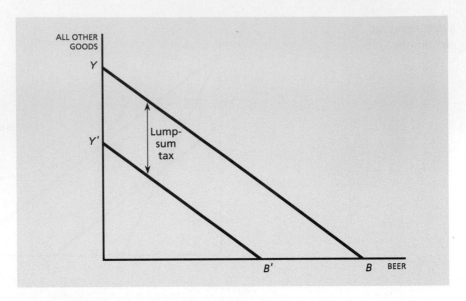

FIGURE 19.3   **Lump-Sum Tax** The vertical distance between the two budget constraints measures the magnitude of the lump-sum tax.

way, as illustrated in Figure 19.3. In the figure, we have put expenditures on beer on the horizontal axis and expenditures on all other goods on the vertical axis. Thus, point Y, where the individual consumes no beer, measures his income before tax; and point Y' measures his income after tax; the vertical distance, YY', measures the lump-sum tax. The budget constraint is

Expenditures on beer + expenditures on all other goods = income − lump-sum taxes,

where expenditures on beer = $p_B B$, the price of beer times the quantity of beer purchased.

We compare the effect of any tax—such as a tax on beer—with the effect of a lump-sum tax by asking: For the same revenue, how much worse off are individuals with the tax on beer than they would have been with the lump-sum tax? The extra loss in welfare is called the **deadweight loss.** Equivalently, we can ask: For the same effect on individual welfare, how much *extra* revenue would a lump-sum tax have raised, or how much *less* revenue does the beer tax raise? The difference in revenue is how we measure the deadweight loss of the tax.

Figure 19.4 contrasts the effect of a tax on beer with a lump-sum tax. The beer tax rotates the individual's budget constraint down, from YB to YB'. The income raised by the tax is the vertical distance between the before-tax budget constraint and the after-tax budget constraint. Clearly, when no beer is consumed (point Y), no revenue is raised. The more

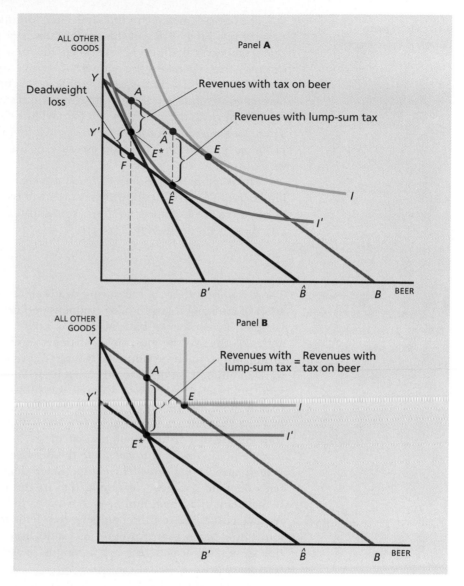

FIGURE 19.4   **Measuring the Deadweight Loss Using Indifference Curves** Individuals choose
the amount of beer to consume by the tangency between their indifference
curve and the budget constraint. The beer tax rotates the budget constraint.
The lump-sum tax moves the budget constraint down parallel. Panel A: The
extra revenue raised by the lump-sum tax is *E*F*. Panel B: When there is no
substitution effect, the beer tax has no deadweight loss; a lump-sum tax and a
tax on beer raise the same revenue.

beer that is consumed, the greater the tax revenue. The revenue raised
is *AE.**

The lump-sum tax with the same effect on utility moves the budget constraint from YB to $Y'\hat{B}$ and the equilibrium is now $\hat{E}$. The revenue raised is again the vertical difference between the new and the old budget constraints—this represents the amount of income that had to be taken away to leave the individual on the same indifference curve. Since the new and old budget constraints are parallel, that vertical distance $\hat{A}\hat{E}$ is exactly equal to AF. (The vertical distance between parallel lines is the same at any location.) Thus, *the lump-sum tax with the same effect on utility raises an additional revenue in the amount of $E*F$. $E*F$* is the measure of the deadweight loss associated with the tax.

The *magnitude of the deadweight loss depends on the substitution effect.* This is illustrated in Figure 19.4B, which is identical to 19.4A, except now indifference curves are L-shaped, so there is no substitution effect, and, it is apparent, there is no deadweight loss.

MEASURING DEADWEIGHT LOSS USING COMPENSATED DEMAND CURVES

There is another way of measuring deadweight loss, making use of the concepts of consumer surplus and compensated demand curves introduced in Chapter 5. Assume we have imposed a tax of 30 cents per bottle of beer, and, with the tax, the individual consumes ten bottles a week. We ask the individual how much he would be willing to give to the government if the tax were eliminated. In other words, what lump-sum tax would leave him at the same utility level he reached when he was subject to the 30-cent tax on beer? Clearly, he would be willing to pay at least 30 cents × 10 per week. Any extra revenue that such a tax would generate is the deadweight loss associated with the use of a distortionary tax system.

We now show how to calculate the deadweight loss using a consumer's *compensated demand curve.* The compensated demand curve gives the individual's demand for beer, assuming that as the price is lowered, income is being taken away from him in such a way as to leave him on the same indifference curve. We use the compensated demand curve because we wish to know how much more revenue we could have achieved with a nondistortionary tax, still leaving the individual just as well off as he was with the distortionary tax.

Assume initially the price of a bottle of beer is $1.50, including the 30-cent tax, and the individual consumes ten bottles a week. We then ask him how much extra he would be willing to pay to consume eleven bottles a week. He is willing to pay only $1.40. The total amount that the individual would be willing to pay us as a lump-sum tax if we lowered the tax from 30 cents to 20 cents (and lowered the price of beer from $1.50 to $1.40) is 10 cents × the 10 bottles he previously purchased, or $1.00 (the area *FGCD* in Figure 19.5A).

We now ask him to assume he is in a situation where we levied a $1.00 lump-sum tax and charged $1.40 each for eleven bottles of beer. How much *extra* would he be willing to pay for one extra bottle? Assume the individual said $1.30. We can now calculate the total lump-sum tax that an individual

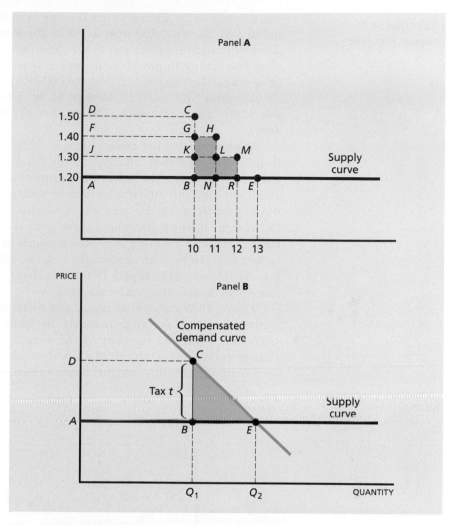

FIGURE 19.5   **Using Compensated Demand Curves to Measure Deadweight Loss**
Government revenue is area *ABCD*. Panel A shows how much the individual
would be willing to pay to have the price of beer reduced from $1.50 to $1.20
(keeping him at the same level of utility). The difference between this and the
tax revenue raised (the area *ABCD*) is the deadweight loss (the shaded area).
Panel B illustrates the case where the level of consumption can be varied in
very small increments.

would be willing to pay if the price were reduced from $1.50 to $1.30. He
would be willing to pay 20 cents a bottle for the first ten bottles (the area
JKCD) and 10 cents for the next (the area *GKLH*), for a total of $2.10.

Finally, we ask him to assume he is in a situation where we levied a
$2.10 lump-sum tax and charged $1.30 each for twelve bottles. How much

extra would he be willing to pay for one extra bottle? Assume the individual said $1.20. We could now calculate the total lump-sum tax that an individual would be willing to pay for the elimination of the 30-cent tax. He would be willing to pay 30 cents on the first ten bottles (the area *ABCD*), 20 cents on the next bottle (the area *BNHG*), 10 cents on the twelfth bottle (the area *NRML*), for a total of $3.30. The tax revenue from the tax was $3.00 (the area *ABCD*). The deadweight loss is 30 cents (the shaded area).

More generally, the amount that an individual would be willing to pay to have the price reduced by 1 cent is just 1 cent times the quantity consumed. As we lower the price, the quantity consumed increases. In Figure 19.5B the total the individual would be willing to pay to have the price reduced from *D* to *A* is the area *AECD*, which takes account of the change in the after-tax quantity consumed as the price is reduced. But of that, *ABCD* is the tax revenue (the tax *AD*—which equals *BC*—times the quantity consumed, *AB*). Hence the deadweight loss, the difference between the two, is just the triangle *BCE*. Figure 19.6 shows that as we double the tax rate, we more than double the deadweight loss.

Figure 19.7 shows that, for a given tax rate, the deadweight loss is greater the flatter (or more precisely, the more elastic) the demand curve. (Remember that the elasticity of the demand curve gives the percentage change in demand as a result of a 1 percent change in price.)

We now make these insights more precise.

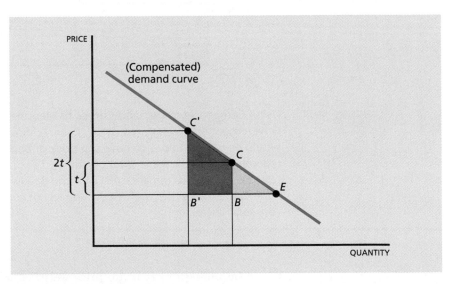

FIGURE 19.6   **Effect of an Increase in Tax Rate on the Deadweight Loss** A doubling of the tax rate more than doubles the deadweight loss. (The area *B′C′E* is four times the area *BCE*.)

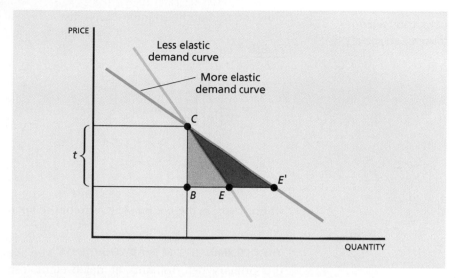

FIGURE 19.7 **Effect of an Increase in the (Compensated) Elasticity of Demand on
Deadweight Loss** An increase in the elasticity of the (compensated) demand
curve increases the deadweight loss. (*BEC* is deadweight loss from the less
elastic demand curve, *BE'C* from the more elastic demand curve.)

**CALCULATING THE
DEADWEIGHT LOSS**

Return to Figure 19.5, in which we used compensated demand curves to
measure deadweight loss. The height of the triangle, *BC*, is equal to the tax,
t. *BE* is the change in quantity as a result of the tax. Recall that the elasticity
of demand gives the percentage change in quantity as a result of a 1 percent
change in price, that is

$$\eta = \frac{\Delta Q/Q}{\Delta p/p}.$$

where the symbol ΔQ represents the change in quantity and the symbol Δp
represents the change in price. The symbol Δ is the (capital) Greek letter
"Delta" and is conventionally used to represent a change. The symbol η is
the Greek letter "eta" and is conventionally used to represent the elasticity
of demand. Rearranging, we can write the change in quantity as.

$$\Delta Q = \frac{\Delta p}{p} Q \eta.$$

This equation has the natural interpretation that the change in quantity will be
larger, the larger the change in price and the larger the elasticity of demand.
But the change in price is just the per unit tax, *t*. Thus, substituting, we obtain

$$BE = \frac{t}{p} Q \eta.$$

Now the area of the triangle BCE is just

$$\frac{t \cdot BE}{2} = \frac{1}{2}\frac{t^2}{p}Q\eta$$

$$= \frac{1}{2}\left[\frac{t}{p}\right]\left[\frac{t}{p}\right]pQ\eta$$

$$= \frac{1}{2}\hat{t}^2 pQ\eta,$$

where $\hat{t} \equiv \dfrac{t}{p}$ is the tax *rate*, the ratio of the tax to the price.

THE DETERMINANTS OF DEADWEIGHT LOSS The above formula identifies two of the primary determinants of deadweight loss. Deadweight loss increases with the *square* of the tax rate. High tax rates are far more distortionary than low tax rates.

And deadweight loss increases with the *elasticity of the compensated demand curve.*[3] The latter is precisely the substitution effect identified earlier as the critical determinant of deadweight loss. When indifference curves are very flat, the elasticity of the compensated demand curve is large—that is, a small percentage change in price leads to a large change in consumption. (Remember, the compensated demand curve simply describes a movement along an indifference curve, since, by definition, individuals are being compensated to keep them on the same indifference curve.) Many of the goods on which excise taxes are imposed have relatively low elasticities of demand,

---

DEADWEIGHT LOSS OF A TAX

The deadweight loss of a tax increases with the magnitude of the substitution effect (or the elasticity of the compensated demand curve) and increases with the *square* of the tax rate.

---

[3] Recall from Chapter 5 that the compensated demand curve is closely related to the ordinary demand curve. When price rises (say, as a result of the tax), individuals are worse off. If the individual previously purchased 100 bottles a beer a year, a 10-cent price increase makes him worse off; if we gave him $10, he would be fully compensated. The effect of a compensated price increase is just the ordinary direct effect, plus the effect of giving an individual an extra $10. If Bill spends only .1 percent of his income on beer, then the extra income induces an additional beer expenditure of 10 cents: there is little difference between the impact of a compensated and an uncompensated change.

so that the deadweight loss is relatively small. For instance, the 10 percent airline ticket tax is estimated to have a deadweight loss equal to 2.5 percent of the revenue raised (on the basis of an estimated .5 price elasticity of demand), an 8 percent beer tax generates a deadweight loss equal to 1.2 percent of the revenue raised (on the basis of an estimated price elasticity of .3), and a 15 percent cigarette tax is estimated to lead to a deadweight loss equal to 3 percent of the revenue raised (on the basis of a price elasticity of demand of .4).

EFFECT OF TAXES BORNE BY PRODUCERS

Up to now, this chapter has focused on the distortionary effects of a tax on a consumption good. We assumed that supply curves were horizontal, so the entire burden of the tax was on consumers.

But, at least in the short run, most supply curves are upward-sloping. This means that part of the burden of any tax on a consumption good will fall on producers. Will this cause an excess burden on producers, above and beyond the direct burden of the tax revenue? The answer is yes, except in the special case where the supply curve is vertical (that is, the elasticity of supply is zero).

Consider how a supply schedule (curve) is constructed. At each price, firms produce up to the point where price equals marginal cost. If the supply schedule is upward-sloping, the marginal cost rises as production rises. The area between the supply curve and price measures the **producer surplus,** which is just the difference between revenues and total variable costs. Changes in this area thus measure changes in profits.

Consider the example illustrated in panel A of Figure 19.8. What happens to profits as price increases from 1 to 4 and output increases from 1 to 4? The first unit of output costs $1; the next, $2; the third, $3; and the fourth, $4. If we pay the firm $4 for each unit, so it produces four units, the firm gets $3 more than marginal costs for producing the first unit, $2 more than marginal costs for producing the second unit, and $1 more than marginal costs for producing the third unit. The total profits are $3 + 2 + 1 = $6. Imposing a tax which lowers the price received by the producer to $3 lowers profit to $2 + $1 = $3. But if the tax is $1 per unit, tax collection will be $2, so the deadweight loss is $1.

This can be seen more generally in panel B of Figure 19.8. Assume initially the producer is receiving the price p. Then a tax is imposed that lowers the amount he receives to $p - t$. In the initial situation, his total profits are given by the area DBC.[4] Now, his profits are reduced to DGE. The change in his profits area is $EGBC$. But of this change, part accrues to the government as tax revenue—the rectangle $EGHC$. The tax on producers has resulted in

[4] More accurately, the shaded area measures the difference between revenues and total variable costs. To calculate profits, we need to subtract fixed costs. (Fixed costs are costs that are incurred as long as the firm operates; they do not depend on the scale of production.)

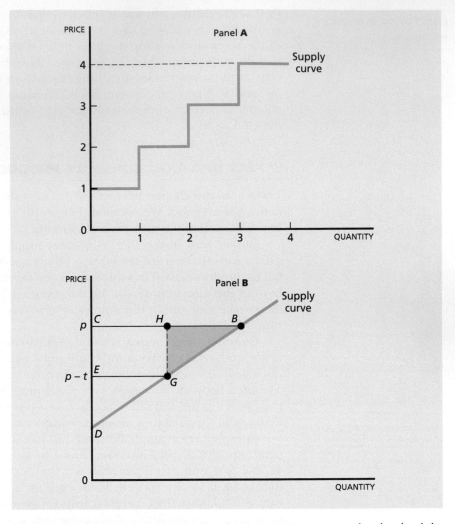

FIGURE 19.8 **The Deadweight Loss of a Tax on Production** *BGH* measures the deadweight
loss of a tax on production.

producers' profits being reduced by more than government revenue has increased. The difference between the two is the deadweight loss associated
with the tax. It is simply the shaded area *BGH*. To put it another way, the
government could have imposed a lump-sum tax on the firm, which left
price at *p* and which left the firm at the same level of profits as it had with a
price of *p* − *t*. That lump-sum tax would have generated higher revenues, by
the amount *BGH*, than the tax on the output of the firm.

It is clear that the steeper—the more inelastic—the supply schedule,
the smaller the deadweight loss. In particular, we can, as before, show that
for small taxes the deadweight loss increases with the square of the tax rate
and with the supply elasticity.

A similar analysis applies to taxes on goods that are used in production. For instance, assume we had a tax on some input, such as steel, into an industry (automobiles). We can ask what lump-sum tax we could impose on the industry that would have the same effect on profits as the tax on steel.[5] The difference in revenues raised by the lump-sum tax and the tax on steel is the deadweight loss from the tax. The magnitude of the deadweight loss will depend on the possibilities of substitution. If the firm cannot substitute any other input for steel (even partially), the tax on steel is no different from a tax on output. There is no distortionary effect on the input mix and, hence, no deadweight loss associated with a change in the input mix.

**EFFECTS OF TAXES
BORNE PARTLY BY
CONSUMERS, PARTLY
BY PRODUCERS**

It is straightforward to combine our analysis of producer deadweight loss with consumer deadweight loss. Figure 19.9 illustrates the case of a tax that is borne partly by producers (the price they receive falls from p to p_s) and partly by consumers (the price they pay rises from p to p_c). The change in market demand can be decomposed into two parts, just as before. The

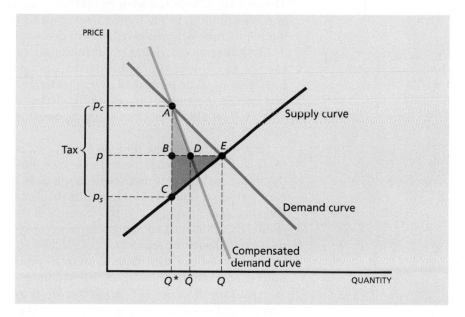

FIGURE 19.9   **Deadweight Loss from a Tax That Is Borne Partly by Consumers and Partly by Producers** The consumers' deadweight loss is the triangle *ABD;* the producers' is the triangle *BCE*. If the compensated and uncompensated demand schedules coincide, as they will if the demand curve is not sensitive to small changes in income, then the total deadweight loss is the big triangle *ACE*.

[5] This is not, of course, the only deadweight loss arising from the input tax. Since it increases the marginal cost of production, the input tax will result in an increase in the price consumers pay, and there will be a deadweight loss to consumers.

movement from Q to $\hat{Q}$ is the income effect of the tax; the movement from $\hat{Q}$ to Q^* is the substitution effect, as consumers substitute away from the taxed good along the compensated demand curve. That is, in the new equilibrium, at the price p_o, consumers are clearly worse off than they were at the original equilibrium price, p. If we ask how much they would have consumed, at the original (non-tax-distorted) price p, but at the new lower level of welfare, the answer is $\hat{Q}$, the point along the compensated demand schedule through A at the price p. The deadweight loss is associated with the movement along the compensated demand schedule, with the reduction of consumption from $\hat{Q}$ to Q^*, and is given by the triangle ABD.

What matters for producers, however, is the total change in quantity, from Q to Q^*, so their deadweight loss is the triangle BCE. The total deadweight loss is the sum of these two triangles, and depends, as before, on the elasticities of demand and supply.

TAXATION OF SAVINGS

The individual's allocation of her income between consumption this period and consumption in the future is very much like her decision about allocating her income between two different commodities.

By giving up one dollar of consumption today, the individual can obtain $(1 + r)$ of extra consumption dollars next period, where r is the interest rate. That is, if the individual saves the dollar and deposits it in a bank, she gets back at the end of the period her dollar plus the interest it has earned. Thus, $1/1 + r$ is the price of consumption tomorrow, relative to consumption today.

If the individual neither borrowed nor saved money, she would consume whatever her wages were in the two periods. We denote the wages in the initial period by w_0 and wages in the next by w_1. Suppose that w_0 and w_1 correspond to point W in Figure 19.10. By borrowing, the individual can consume more today, but at the expense of consuming less next period. By saving, the individual can consume more next period, but at the expense of consuming less this period.

The individual thus faces a budget constraint. She can either have $\bar{C}$ units of consumption today, or $(1 + r)\bar{C}$ units of consumption tomorrow, or any point on the straight line joining the two points, as depicted in Figure 19.10. The individual has a set of indifference curves between present consumption and future consumption, just as the individual has between beer and soda; each indifference curve gives those combinations of current and future consumption that leave her at the same level of utility. The individual is willing to consume less today in return for more future consumption. As her present consumption gets smaller and smaller, she becomes less willing to give up more; and as her future consumption gets larger and larger, the extra benefit she gets from each additional unit of future consumption gets smaller and smaller. Thus, the amount of increased consumption next period required to compensate the individual for a reduction by one unit in current consumption becomes larger and larger. That is why the indiffer-

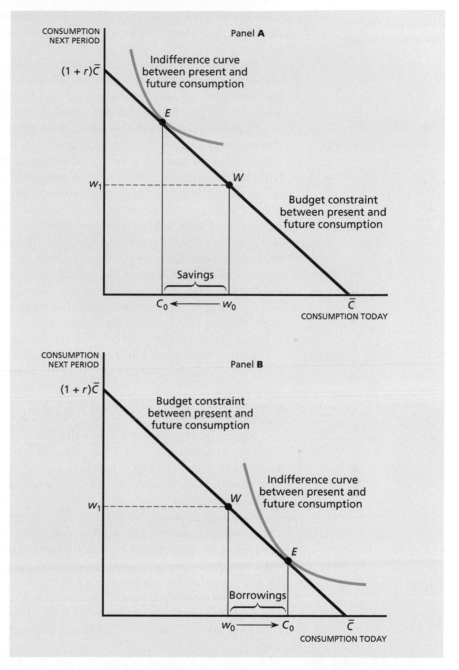

FIGURE 19.10 **Consumption, Savings, and Borrowings** The individual allocates her income between consumption this period and next period. In panel A the individual saves, while in panel B she borrows.

ence curve has the shape depicted. The individual chooses that point, denoted by E, on her budget constraint which is tangent to her indifference curve.

Panel A of Figure 19.10 illustrates a situation where the individual wishes to consume less than her wage income the first period and so saves the rest, while in panel B the individual wishes to consume more than her wage income the first period and so borrows the difference.

Consider now the effect of a tax, at the rate t, on interest income. (We assume that if interest income is negative—that is, the individual is a borrower—there is a negative tax; in other words, the borrower receives money from the government.) For a saver, someone whose first-period consumption is less than her (after-tax) first-period wage income, the tax has both an income effect and a substitution effect. Because the individual is worse off, she normally will reduce her consumption in both periods. Thus, the income effect leads to a lower current consumption. (Remember that savings is just the difference between after-tax wage income the first period and first-period consumption.) But because the individual receives a lower return from postponing consumption, the substitution effect discourages future consumption and encourages current consumption; it leads individuals to reduce their savings. The net effect on current consumption—and hence on savings—is ambiguous. If the substitution effect is large enough, savings are reduced.

If the substitution effect and the income effect were exactly to cancel each other, leaving savings unchanged, would this imply that the tax is nondistortionary? No, for the tax is distortionary so long as it causes the individual to substitute between current and future consumption along her indifference curve.

Figure 19.11 depicts the case where the income effect of the interest tax (the movement from E to $\hat{E}$) is just offset by the substitution effect (the movement from $\hat{E}$ to E^*). Therefore savings, $w_0 - C_0$, are the same before and after the tax. Nonetheless, there is a substantial distortion in second-period consumption.

We could contrast the effect of the interest income tax with a lump-sum tax, a tax that shifted the budget constraint down in a parallel manner. Again, it is straightforward to show that such a tax will, for any given effect on the individual's utility, raise more revenue (the deadweight loss is measured by E^*F), or that for any given level of revenue, individuals will be better off with the lump-sum tax than with the interest income tax. The magnitude of the distortion depends on the magnitude of the substitution effect, which in turn depends on how substitutable current and future consumption are.

Most empirical estimates suggest that the substitution effect slightly outweighs the income effect, so that an interest income tax has a slight negative effect on savings. While from one perspective this is good news—the tax system may not be reducing savings by much—from another perspective it is bad news: government is unlikely to encourage savings by much through tax incentives.

The fact that the net effect is small does not, of course, mean that the distortionary effect is small. That depends on the magnitude of the substitu-

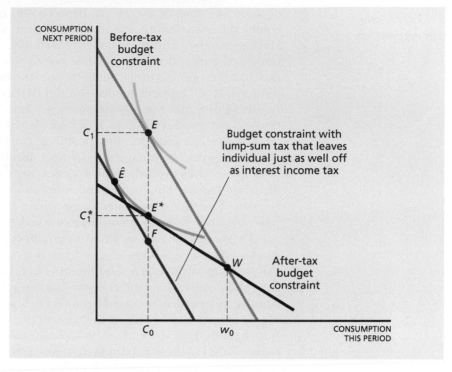

CONSUMPTION NEXT PERIOD

Before-tax budget constraint

C_1

E

Budget constraint with lump-sum tax that leaves individual just as well off as interest income tax

$\hat{E}$

C_1^*

E^*

F

W

After-tax budget constraint

C_0 w_0

CONSUMPTION THIS PERIOD

FIGURE 19.11 **Effect of Interest Income Tax** The income effect of the interest tax is just offset by the substitution effect in the first period. But there is still a deadweight loss of E^*F.

tion effect. But since most Americans save a relatively small fraction of their incremental income, the income effect is relatively small, implying that the substitution effect is also relatively small (since the two cancel out).

As we noted, distortionary effects increase with the square of the tax. Since much of saving is done by the rich, who face relatively high taxes, the deadweight loss may still be significant, even if the elasticity of substitution is small.

The precise magnitude of the deadweight loss remains a subject of controversy, with some economists arguing that the deadweight loss is actually quite large.

TAXATION OF LABOR INCOME

Exactly the same kind of analysis can be applied to labor supply decisions. There are, of course, many dimensions to labor supply—number of hours worked, effort exerted on the job, years of education (age of entry into the labor force), and age of retirement. The same principles apply to each. Here, we illustrate the analysis for the decision concerning the number of hours worked. As with the savings decision, we can model the labor supply decision in terms of the choice between two commodities. Here the two commodities are leisure and all consumption of goods and services. Figure 19.12 shows the individual's budget constraint, with hours of leisure on the horizontal axis and consumption (income)[6] on the vertical axis. The wage tax (like the beer tax) rotates the budget constraint. If the individual does not work at all, he faces no tax—he still has sixteen hours of leisure a day (ignoring the eight hours of sleep). At a 50 percent wage tax, his consumption—at any given level of work (leisure) is reduced by half. Again, there is an income effect and a substitution effect. The substitution effect, as before, makes him work less (enjoy more leisure). But the income effect makes him work more: when the individual is poorer, he "consumes" less of all "goods," including leisure. The income and substitution effects work in opposite directions. The figure illustrates a case where the two effects are essentially offsetting; there is no effect on hours worked.

The fact that the labor supply curve is relatively inelastic—that income and substitution effects are offsetting—does not mean that the income tax is not distortionary. It is, so long as there is a substitution effect. Indeed, Figure 19.13 shows a case where the income effect outweighs the substitution effect, so that the labor supply curve is backward-bending (at lower wages, individuals actually supply more labor). A tax in that case actually increases the labor supply. But, nonetheless, since there is a substitution effect, the tax is distortionary—that is, there is a deadweight loss associated with the tax.

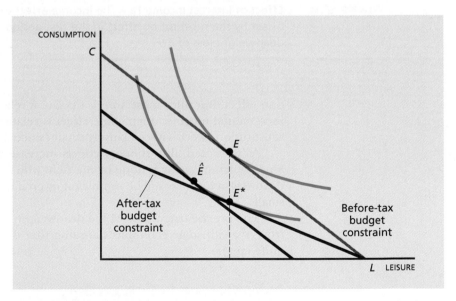

FIGURE 19.12 **Wage Taxation** Taxes on labor reduce the return to working. The substitution effect leads individuals to work less (enjoy more leisure), while the income effect leads individuals to work more. The two effects are offsetting.

---

[6] For purposes of this section, we assume there is no savings, so that consumption and income are identical.

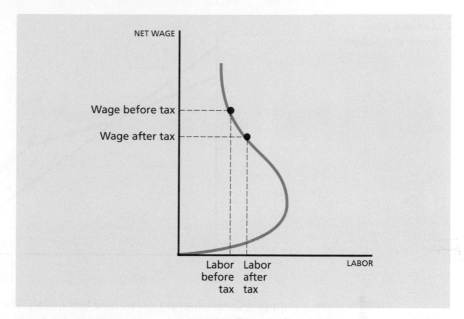

NET WAGE

Wage before tax

Wage after tax

Labor before tax Labor after tax

LABOR

FIGURE 19.13 **Backward-Bending Labor Supply Curve** If the income effect outweighs the substitution effect, the labor supply curve will be backward-bending; increases in wages will lead to less labor supply. Then a tax which reduces wages (net of taxes) may actually increase the labor supply. The tax still has a deadweight loss.

EFFECTS OF PROGRESSIVE TAXATION

So far in this chapter, we have focused on *proportional taxes*. The beer tax was a per unit tax, so that as consumption of beer increased, tax payments increased proportionally. Similarly for the interest income tax. Some wage taxes, such as the social security payroll tax, are proportional (up to some maximum), but other taxes, such as the individual income tax, are not.

EARNED INCOME TAX CREDIT Figure 19.14 shows the effect of taxes on the budget constraint facing a low-wage individual who receives a *wage subsidy* (under the earned income tax credit) up to some level, and faces a tax beyond a certain (higher) level.[7] In the interval *LA*, the new budget constraint is actually steeper than the before-tax budget constraint *LL*; in the interval *AB*, the new and old budget constraints are parallel; and in the interval *BC* the after-tax budget constraint is much flatter. For an individual who works little (chooses a point in the interval *LA*), the income and substitution effects work in opposite directions, with the income effect leading to less work (since the individual is better off) and the substitution effect to more work (since the return to working has increased). For an individual who works a moderate amount and chooses a point in the interval *AB*, there is only an income effect: he unambiguously works less than before the subsidy. For the hardworking individual, in the in-

[7] The analysis simplifies the full complexity of the tax law, by ignoring, for instance, both state and social security taxes.

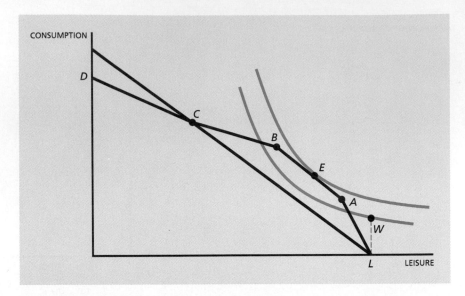

FIGURE 19.14 **Budget Constraint for Low-Income Individuals: The Effect of the Earned Income Tax Credit** Low-wage individuals who work little face positive incentives to work from the earned income tax credit. The tax credit affects both hours worked and labor force participation.

terval *BC*, the income and substitution effects are reinforcing: he is better off, and the return to working is lowered, so the reduction in work effort is even greater. Finally, in the interval *CD*, the individual's EITC benefit is completely exhausted and he now faces an income tax. Thus, he is worse off than he was in the absence of any tax/subsidy program. Now the income and substitution effects work in opposite directions. (Point *C*, where EITC is fully faced out, can occur to the left or the right of the before-tax budget constraint.)

PARTICIPATION VERSUS HOURS DECISIONS Even though for many individuals (those in the interval *BC*), marginal incentives to work are reduced by the EITC, *incentives to participate in the labor force are increased.* Assume, as an alternative to working, individuals can receive a fixed amount of welfare payments, represented in the figure by point *W* (where they enjoy full leisure). We have drawn the indifference curve through *W*.[8] It is clear that, with the earned income tax credit, the individual who would have been content simply to receive welfare now prefers to work.

Most economists believe that the participation decision is far more important than the hours decision. First, attachment to the labor force brings with it education, skills, and a sense of belonging to society which contributes to social stability. Second, for many jobs, discretion over the number of hours is far more limited than the discussion we have presented sug-

[8] In practice, under welfare individuals do not lose all benefits if they work, but rather face a high marginal tax rate. There is a flat budget constraint through *W*. We assume it is sufficiently flat that the individual chooses *W*.

gests.[9] There is either a workweek of five eight-hour-days, or, say, a work-week of five seven-hour-days. To be sure, over time, the number of hours worked does adjust in response to economic forces—the average number of hours worked declined markedly during the first half of the twentieth century, while more recently, as wages, particularly at the lower end of the income distribution, have failed to grow or even declined, hours worked have increased—the individual, in deciding to work, is not usually in a position to bargain about whether he should work thirty-five hours or thirty-seven hours.

HIGH-INCOME INDIVIDUALS Figure 19.15 analyzes the effect of taxation on high-income individuals in the 36 percent tax bracket. Someone in the 36 percent tax bracket faces a budget constraint with four segments, represent-

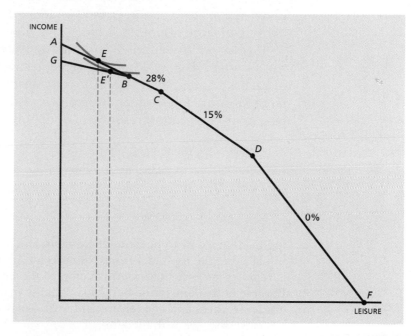

FIGURE 19.15   **Impact of 1993 Tax Change** In 1993, the tax rate on upper-income individuals was increased. The curve *ABCDF* depicts schematically the original budget constraint, with three marginal tax rates, at 0 percent, 15 percent, and 28 percent. After the change, there is a fourth segment, *BG*, at a tax rate of 36 percent. Originally, the high-income individual chooses point *E*. Afterward, he chooses *E'*. The income effect is small, since he only has to pay the higher tax on the excess of income over a very high threshold. The substitution effect is large relative to the income effect, so the individual works less (enjoys more leisure).

[9] This observation is consistent with a recent study of high-income physicians in Britain, which found that while self-employed physicians exhibited considerable sensitivity to the marginal tax rate, those who are employees have no discernible sensitivity. See Mark H. Showalter and Norman K. Thurston, "Taxes and Labor Supply of High-Income Physicians," *Journal of Public Economics* 66 (1997): 73–97.

In 1993, as the government faced ever-increasing deficits, some tax increases appeared imperative. The Clinton administration proposed that those who had benefited most from the economic expansion and the tax cuts of the 1980s should bear the brunt of these tax increases. Only the top 1.2 percent of taxpayers experienced rate increases. For example, married couples with incomes in excess of $140,000 had their income tax rates increased, from a marginal tax rate of approximately 28 percent to 36 or 39.6 percent.*

Critics, such as Professor Martin Feldstein of Harvard University, who was chairman of the Council of Economic Advisers under the Reagan administration, predicted that the tax increase would raise less revenue than both Congress and the administration had estimated, because of large responses in labor supply. As was illustrated in Figure 19.15, many of those facing tax increases were clustered near point B, the income level at which taxes were increased. For these individuals, as we have noted, there was little income effect from the tax but a large substitution effect, and therefore, Feldstein argued, there would be a large labor supply response. To support his theoretical arguments

* This ignores the Medicare tax, which was also raised.

ing the 0 percent, 15 percent, 28 percent, and 36 percent brackets. Assume initially that the top bracket was 28 percent. An increase in the top bracket is represented by a downward rotation of the budget constraint at point B. Because of the kink in the budget constraint, many individuals—with different preferences between leisure and work—may be clustered at the level of income associated with the kink.

For those near the kink, the income effect is small relative to the substitution effect, and hence their labor supply would have been expected to decrease, as depicted. (If the tax rate on all income had increased by the same percentage points, there would have been a large income effect; but for someone with an income just above the level at which the higher rate set in, the income effect was in fact negligible.)

SECONDARY LABOR FORCE PARTICIPANTS

Historically, in two-earner families with primary and secondary earners, the labor supply response of the secondary earner (typically the wife) has been markedly different from that of the primary earner. There are obvious reasons for this, particularly during the years in which there are small children at home. The *net* income—after subtracting out the costs of child care (which would not have to be paid if she did not work), costs of

he cited evidence that after the 1986 tax reform, which had reduced marginal rates for upper-income individuals, there had been a marked increase in income tax collections from upper-income individuals.

But, as is so often the case, reading the evidence is not easy. The 1986 tax reform also closed a number of loopholes which had allowed upper-income individuals to avoid taxation; and in the expansion of the economy which had begun in 1983, as the economy recovered from its worst recession since World War II, there was a strong trend of increased inequality—with earnings at the top growing far more rapidly than earnings in the middle. There was little direct evidence that upper-income individuals had worked either longer hours or harder as a result of the decrease in marginal tax rates.

As it turned out, the tax revenues raised on upper-income individuals in the years following 1993 were far higher than had been anticipated, and indeed these increased revenues were largely responsible for the elimination of the deficit in the late 1990s. And there was little evidence that the upper-income individuals had reduced their labor supply in the way Feldstein had predicted.

commuting, and so forth—may be far lower than the gross income. Thus, if in 1997 a woman earned $15,000 a year, and child care expenses amounted to $5000, the net income was just $10,000. The tax rate she faced is determined by *household* income, including that of her husband. If her husband earned more than $56,050 she faced a 28 percent (or higher) income tax on all of her income. (This ignores the payroll tax and state taxes.) But a 28 percent tax on her total income translates into a 42 percent tax on her net income. Her incentives to participate in the labor force are greatly reduced. Secondary workers have, accordingly, shown much more sensitivity in their labor force participation to changes in tax rates.

MEASURING THE EFFECTS OF TAXES ON LABOR SUPPLIED

The fact that theoretically the effect of a tax on wages is indeterminate makes it all the more important to attempt to determine empirically what its effects in fact have been. Research in this area has been extensive and has yielded important (but controversial) results. Two main methods have been employed to study these questions: statistical analyses using market data, and experiments.[10]

STATISTICAL TECHNIQUES USING MARKET DATA

The first method entails using statistical techniques to analyze how individuals in the past have responded to changes in their after-tax wages. In general, we do not have data on how particular individuals responded to changes in wages. Rather, we have data on how many hours individuals who earn different wages work. Those who earn higher wages seem to work more hours. From this we can calculate the "average" effect of wages on hours worked.

Up to now, we have simply described a *correlation*, an observed relationship between two economic variables. We now wish to use this to make an *inference*, a prediction or a statement about the effect of lowering take-home wages resulting from, say, the imposition of a tax. To make such an inference, we must make an assumption: that the reason individuals who receive higher wages are observed to work more is that they choose to work more because of the higher wage; in other words, that an individual who receives a higher wage is essentially like one who receives a lower wage; the only important difference is the difference in pay, and it is this difference that leads to a difference in the number of hours worked. There are, of course, other important differences, and more sophisticated statistical analyses attempt to take as many of these as possible (say, age or occupation or sex) into account; they attempt to see, among individuals of the same age, occupation, or sex (or who have other characteristics in common), whether those who receive higher wages work more.

The vast literature on labor supply suggests that estimated labor supply elasticities may depend on the precise statistical methods used as well as on the data employed.[11] There appears to be widespread agreement (though not unanimity) on the following:

• Labor supply of married males is fairly unresponsive to changes in the wage rate.[12]

---

[10] Earlier, several studies approached the problem using *qualitative* approaches, simply asking individuals whether taxes led them to work more or less. The different responses reflected the presence of income effects (leading to more work) and substitution effects (leading to less work). See D. M. Holland, "The Effect of Taxation on Effort: Some Results for Business Executives," *National Tax Association Proceedings of the Sixty-Second Annual Conference,* 1969; and George Break, "Income Taxes and Incentives to Work: An Empirical Study," *American Economic Review* 47 (1957): 529–49.

[11] For instance, Jim Heckman of the University of Chicago has argued that reporting errors may have obscured a larger decline in hours worked by men and may also account for much of the observed decline in real wages. This measurement error may also bias labor supply elasticities toward zero. See James J. Heckman, "What Has Been Learned about Labor Supply in the Past Twenty Years?" *American Economic Association Papers and Proceedings,* May 1993, pp. 116–21.

[12] For instance, one study estimated that the tax system (as of 1983) had resulted in only a 2.6 percent reduction in hours worked by married men. See Robert K. Triest, "The Effect of Income Taxation on Labor Supply in the United States," *Journal of Human Resources,* summer 1990, pp. 491–516. An earlier study, using similar data and model, had suggested a somewhat larger effect. See J. Hausman, "Labor Supply," in *How Taxes Affect Economic Behavior,* ed. H. J. Aaron and J. Pechman (Washington, D.C.: Brookings Institution, 1981), pp. 27–72.

• The compensated labor supply elasticity also appears to be small, though there appears to be more disagreement over this finding. (The uncompensated labor supply elasticity can be small either because of small offsetting substitution and income effects or because of large offsetting substitution and income effects.)[13]

• Labor supply elasticity of married females is larger, but more problematic to estimate.[14]

• Labor supply elasticity of female heads of household is somewhere in between that of married men and married women.

• The participation decision is more sensitive to the wage rate than are marginal hours of work.[15]

• Labor supply parameters estimated from market data tend to be larger than those estimated from experimental data (discussed in the next section).

Large changes in tax rates, of the kind that occurred in 1981, 1986, and 1993, provide natural tests of the effect of taxation on labor supply.

The 1993 tax changes have yet to be subjected to detailed analysis. But each of these changes was complex; different individuals faced different changes in tax rates, and a variety of loopholes were closed (or in some cases opened up). While the evidence is that the 1986 tax law led to an increase in taxable income faster than would have been predicted based on the assumption of fixed incomes,[16] there is controversy about the reason.

---

[13] Jerry Hausman of MIT, using a technique meant to capture the effects of the nonlinearities in the budget constraints described earlier, obtains much larger estimates than do others. See his "Labor Supply," cited above. His techniques have been criticized by Tom MaCurdy of Stanford, who claims that his technique "forces higher estimates of substitution effects or lower estimates of income effects than are obtained from other procedures. This . . . raises serious questions about the reliability of evidence cited by much of the literature to support recent tax reforms aimed at lowering marginal tax rates." See Thomas MaCurdy, "Work Disincentive Effects of Taxes: A Reexamination of Some Evidence," *American Economic Association Papers and Proceedings,* May 1992, pp. 243–49.

[14] See Thomas A. Mroz's widely cited study, "The Sensitivity of an Empirical Model of Married Women's Hours of Work to Economic and Statistical Assumptions" (*Econometrica,* July 1987, pp. 765–99). After noting that the estimated elasticity is sensitive to the specification of the model, Mroz concludes that when the correct specification is used, "factors such as wage rates, taxes and nonlabor incomes have a small impact on the labor supply behavior of working married women" (p. 795). His analysis only focused on working women, ignoring the participation decision.

[15] This could be either because of constraints imposed by the employer or because of the fixed costs of working.

Triest estimates that, despite the small responsiveness of hours worked, participation is so responsive that the U.S. (state and federal) tax system reduced total hours worked by wives by as much as 30 percent, depending on the specification employed. See "The Effect of Income Taxation on Labor Supply in the United States," cited in note 12.

[16] See Martin Feldstein, "The Effect of Marginal Tax Rates on Table Income: A Panel Study of the 1986 Tax Reform Act, *Journal of Political Economy* 1-3, no. 3 (1995): 551–72.

Did the changes, for instance, following the 1986 tax reform, reflect mostly the closing of loopholes? Or did they largely reflect underlying trends? Increasing inequality was placing a larger fraction of the nation's income in the hands of those facing higher tax rates.

Barry Bosworth and Gary Burtless of the Brookings Institution argued that the observed changes had little to do with changes in taxes, but mostly reflected underlying economic trends.[17] While it appears that after the tax cuts, labor supply was higher than it would have been had past trends continued (by 1989, for men, work effort was 6 percent above what it would have been had the 1967–1980 trend continued; and for women it was 5.4 percent higher), the interpretation of what went on is not so clear. If tax reform were the impetus for the growth in labor supply, we would expect higher-income workers (who experienced a greater change in marginal tax rates) to have increased their labor supply by proportionately more than lower-income workers (who were less affected by tax reform). Yet it was the lower-income individuals whose labor supply seems to have increased the most.[18] The fact that income tax revenues among the very rich continued to increase so robustly after 1993, in spite of the large increase in marginal tax rates, is consistent with the hypothesis that it was long-term trends and the closing of loopholes, not incentive effects on labor supply, that accounted for the increased tax revenues after the 1986 reform.

EXPERIMENTS

The second approach to obtaining a quantitative estimate of the magnitude of the labor supply responses to tax changes is an experimental one. We are interested in the question: What would happen to the labor supply if we raised or lowered tax rates (or changed the tax structure in some other way)? One approach is to say, "Let's change the tax structure and see what happens." This could be an expensive approach: the change might have a very negative effect on labor supply, but before the effects were recognized and the tax structure changed again, considerable damage (welfare loss) could have occurred.

But we can learn something by changing the tax structure for just a small portion of the population. Just as opinion polls can give fairly accurate estimates of how voters will vote in an election, simply by asking a small sample of the population (often fewer than 1000 individuals), so too the response of a small sample may give a fairly reliable indication of how other, similar individuals would respond facing the alternative tax structure. Opinion polls are careful to obtain a representative sample of views—they make sure that views of young and old, of the rich and poor, of skilled and unskilled workers, of married and unmarried individuals, and so on, are all

[17] Barry Bosworth and Gary Burtless, "Effects of Tax Reform on Labor Supply, Investment, and Saving," *Journal of Economic Perspectives,* winter 1992, pp. 3–25.

[18] Men in the lowest quintile increased hours worked by 31 percent, whereas those in the highest quintile increased hours worked by 3.2 percent; the corresponding numbers for women were 16.7 percent and 11.8 percent. (Bosworth and Burtless, "Effects of Tax Reform.")

represented; and in forming their estimate of how the population as a whole will vote, they weight the relative importance of the various groups in the population (when they are attempting to predict the outcome of elections, they assign weights corresponding to the known likelihood that members of different groups vote).

Between 1968 and 1982, a series of such experiments attempted to ascertain in particular the effects of changes in the tax structure and welfare system on the labor supplied by poorer individuals. Different individuals were confronted with different levels of guaranteed income and tax structures, making it possible, in principle, not only to estimate the overall effect of tax changes but to separate out the income effects from the substitution effects. The results were consistent with the view that the overall effect of taxes on labor supply is relatively small. The report on the first such experiment, conducted in New Jersey, described it as presenting "a picture of generally small absolute labor supply differentials between" those who were confronted with the alternative tax/welfare structures and those who faced the existing tax/welfare structure. "Only among wives, whose mean labor supply is quite small to begin with, are the differentials large in relative terms."[19] (In subsequent years, labor participation of wives has increased enormously, so that the aggregate effect of such adverse incentives is now far more significant.) The experiments yielded some further results concerning the possible effects of changes in the welfare/tax system. Providing more income to the poor resulted in their searching longer for a job when they became unemployed.

While the early experiments focused on the effect of alternative tax-subsidy schemes on labor supply (and related variables, like job search), later studies attempted to ascertain whether there were other effects as well. For instance, an experiment in Gary, Indiana, found a higher birth weight of babies—an indication of the health of the child—in families whose income had been increased. A large-scale experiment sponsored by the U.S. Department of Health, Education, and Welfare and conducted in Seattle, Washington, and Denver, Colorado, found that providing women with a guaranteed income, as the negative income tax does, might contribute to the breakup of families. However, the most generous negative income tax programs in the Seattle-Denver experiment had the *least* effect on family dissolution rates. It has been argued that income guarantees have two opposing effects on dissolution rates: On the one hand, they stabilize marriages by improving the family's ability to buy essential goods and services; on the other hand, they destabilize marriages by improving the economic viability of alternatives to marriage. Under this theory, the experimental results suggest that for low guaranteed income levels, the second effect (the "independence effect") dominates the first.

The experiments represented an important advance in the tools that are available to social scientists. At the same time, there are some important

[19] U.S. Department of Health, Education, and Welfare, *Summary Report: New Jersey Graduated Work Incentive Experiments* (Washington, D.C.: Government Printing Office, 1973).

545

limitations to the experimental approach that need to be borne in mind in evaluating the results.

First, there is a well-known phenomenon called the **Hawthorne effect,** which plagues all experimental work with individuals: When an individual is included in an experiment, and she knows her behavior is being examined, her behavior is often altered.

Second, there are problems associated with ensuring that the sample is representative. Since participation in the experiment is voluntary, there may be systematic biases associated with the kinds of individuals who refuse to participate.

Third, the response of individuals to short-run changes may differ from their responses to long-run changes. On the one hand, a temporary change in the tax structure that leads them to be better off has a smaller effect on lifetime income than a permanent change in the tax structure; hence the income effect may be understated. On the other hand, since the experiment discussed above often involved individuals facing a higher or lower marginal tax rate during the course of the experiment, the after-tax wage was temporarily reduced or increased; a temporary reduction in the wage may have different effects than a permanent reduction. In the absence of costs of adjustment there is a presumption that individuals will reduce their work (increase their leisure) more than they would with a permanent wage reduction. Thus an individual who was planning to take some time off from work (say, a woman thinking of having children in the near future) might have taken advantage of the temporary availability of a large subsidy combined with a high marginal tax rate. If this is true, the experiments overstate the effects relative to what they would be with a permanent change. On the other hand, costs of adjustment may be very high; an individual might be reluctant to quit his current job, knowing that he will want it back in three years' time (when the experiment is over), because he believes it will be difficult to get it back then. If these effects are important, the experiment may have understated not only the income effects but the substitution effects as well. Some of the more recent experiments have attempted to ascertain the magnitude of the biases in the estimates resulting from the fact that the change in tax structure/welfare payments was only temporary, by guaranteeing to the individual the same tax structure/welfare structure over a more extended period (up to twenty years).

A final important qualification on interpreting how accurately the experiments describe the extent to which labor supply is affected by changes in tax laws or welfare programs relates to the role of institutions in determining the length of the workweek. We commented earlier that, in the short run, institutional practices play an important role in restricting individuals' choices over the number of hours worked. But in the long run, these institutional practices themselves change, partly in response to changes in the economic environment. Thus many of the individuals in the experiment may have had only limited discretion over the number of hours they worked; but if everyone in society were confronted with the new tax/welfare payments structure, pressures might develop to alter these institutional practices to bring them more into conformity with individuals' preferences.

The high cost and ambiguous results of such experiments have meant that there have been few experiments of the scale and scope of the earlier studies. On the other hand, more care is placed in the design of pilot programs, so that stronger inferences can be made concerning what works and what does not work. There have been, for instance, a large number of studies of training programs and of programs designed to move people from welfare to work. Still, primary reliance has to be placed on "natural experiments," the experiments that occur as a result of, for example, different states' trying different programs. For instance, before the 1996 welfare reform, several states had experimented with time-limited welfare programs and welfare programs with work requirements. Such experiments suggested that the welfare reform would result in significantly reduced welfare dependency, a prediction borne out in the months after passage of the legislation—with the reduction in welfare roles far greater than could be explained by the declining unemployment rates.[20]

REVIEW AND PRACTICE

1   The imposition of a tax that is not a lump-sum tax introduces inefficiencies. The magnitude of the inefficiencies is measured by the deadweight loss, the difference in revenues that could be obtained from a lump-sum tax as compared to a distortionary tax, with the same effect on the level of welfare of consumers.

2   The effect of any tax can be decomposed into an income effect and a substitution effect. There is an income effect associated with a lump-sum tax, but no substitution effect. The greater the substitution effect, the greater the deadweight loss.

3   There is also a deadweight loss associated with the reduction in the price received by producers as a result of the imposition of a tax. The reduction in their profits exceeds the tax revenues they effectively pay to the government.

4   For a tax on a commodity, both the income effect and the substitution effect usually lead to a reduction in the level of consumption of that

[20] On negative income tax experiments, see Robins, "A Comparison of the Labor Supply Findings from the Four Negative Income Tax Experiments," *Journal of Human Resources* 20, no. 4 (fall 1985): 567–82; David Greenberg and Harlan Halsey, "Systematic Misreporting and Effects of Income Maintenance Experiments on Work Effort: Evidence from the Seattle-Denver Experiments," *Journal of Labor Economics* 1, no. 4 (October 1983): 380–407; and Robert G. Spiegelman and K. E. Yaeger, "The Seattle and Denver Income Maintenance Experiments: Overview," *Journal of Human Resources* 15, no. 4 (fall 1980): 463–79. On natural experiments of tax changes, see two articles in *Empirical Foundations of Household Taxation*, ed. Martin Feldstein and James Porteba (Chicago and London: University of Chicago Press, 1996): Nada Eissa, "Labor Supply and the Economic Recovery Tax Act of 1981" (pp. 5–32); and James J. Heckman, "Comment on Labour Supply and the Economic Recovery Tax Act of 1981" (pp. 32–38).

commodity. For an interest income tax as viewed by a saver, the income effect typically leads to an increase in savings and the substitution effect leads to a decrease in savings: the net effect is ambiguous. But even if the net effect is to leave savings unchanged, there is still a distortion associated with the interest income tax. For workers, the income and substitution effects of an increase in wages have opposite effects; thus higher wages may lead to either an increase or a decrease in labor supply.

5 Empirical evidence suggests that for males, the substitution and income effects of wage taxes virtually cancel, so that the total effect of the tax on the male labor supply is probably not large. For females, there may be a marked effect on labor force participation. On the other hand, even though the total effect may be small for males, the substitution effect, and hence the deadweight loss associated with the tax, may be significant.

KEY CONCEPTS

Income effect	Producer surplus
Substitution effect	Hawthorne effect

**QUESTIONS
AND PROBLEMS**

1   If savings do not respond to changes in the interest rate, does it mean that there is no deadweight loss associated with the taxation of interest?

2 What is the deadweight loss from the mineral tax in problem 1, Chapter 18? What is the relationship between deadweight loss and supply curves? Relate this to the discussion of lump-sum taxes.

3 Taxes and government expenditure programs affect a variety of other aspects of household behavior. Some economists, for instance, argue that they affect birth rates. What provisions of the tax system might affect the decision to have a child? What government expenditure programs?

4 Instead of representing the individual's decisions as a choice between consumption and leisure, they could be represented in terms of a choice between consumption and work. Draw the indifference curves, and identify the income and substitution effects resulting from a change in the tax rate on labor.

5 Compare the effects of a wage tax and a lump-sum tax raising the same revenue. In particular, show that the individual's utility is higher with the lump-sum tax than with the income tax.

6 Compare the effects of a proportional income tax and a progressive flat-rate income tax (i.e., one in which there is a lump-sum grant from the government of, say, $3000, and then a constant marginal tax rate on all income). In particular, show that if the two taxes raise the same revenue,

and all individuals have the same income, utility will be higher with the proportional tax.

7 Prior to 1981, the government imposed only a 67 percent (instead of a 100 percent) marginal tax rate on income earned by a mother receiving AFDC. Draw the budget constraint before 1981 and after 1981. Draw the indifference curve of someone who prefers to remain out of the labor force under both regimes. Draw the indifference curve of someone who worked before 1981 but chose not to work after 1981. Show how, for this person, lowering the tax rate will increase utility, reduce costs to the welfare system, and increase labor supply. Finally, draw the indifference curve of someone who worked both before and after 1981. Show how, for this person, the lower tax rate affects AFDC costs and affects labor supply. What can you say about government policy if there are some individuals of the first type, some of the second type, and some of the third type?

8 What would be the effect of a switch to taxing individuals on the basis of their own income (rather than family income) on labor force participation of wives?

9 Describe the income and substitution effects of an increase in the interest rate for a borrower. What does this imply for the effect of eliminating tax deductibility of interest payments?

20 Optimal Taxation

FOCUS QUESTIONS

1 What are the trade-offs involved in designing a progressive income tax system?

2 What should be the role of the taxation of commodities (such as luxuries) and savings in achieving greater equity in taxation?

3 If the government imposes taxes on different commodities, how should the tax rates be set so as to minimize the total deadweight loss?

In the previous chapter we observed that there may be a significant welfare loss (the *deadweight loss*) associated with any tax other than a lump-sum tax. Two questions immediately arise: Why, if this is the case, do we not just impose a lump-sum tax? And if we are to impose distortionary taxes, is there some way that they can be designed to minimize the deadweight loss? These questions have been at the center of theoretical research in taxation. The research has produced some remarkably simple and insightful answers, answers that may help to design better tax systems in the future.

The chapter is divided into four sections. The first section disposes of two fallacies that have long confused discussions of tax design. Next the basic principles of optimal taxation are described, and then applied to analyze the design of income tax structures. The final two sections analyze commodity taxation. The third section focuses on the effectiveness of taxing consumers' purchases of different commodities at different rates in achieving redistributive goals, and the fourth on the role of taxation of producers.

TWO FALLACIES OF OPTIMAL TAXATION

Before turning to the details of the analysis, we need to dispose of two fallacies which have misled discussions of tax design—one suggesting an overly simplified approach, the other that the world is so complex that nothing can be said.

THE FALLACY OF COUNTING DISTORTIONS

The first fallacy says we should simply have a tax on wage income. Additional taxes—taxes on commodities, such as cigarettes or alcohol, or taxes on savings—just add to the number of distortions and thus to economic inefficiency. One distortion is better than several distortions.

A tax on wage income would be optimal if there were no distortions associated with that tax; for then that tax would be equivalent to a lump-sum tax. But we showed in the previous chapter that an income tax distorts individuals' decisions to work, and it is not necessarily the case that one large distortion is better than several smaller distortions. Chapter 19 showed that the deadweight loss from a tax was proportional to the square of the tax rate. This suggests that it may be better to have a number of small taxes than a single large tax.

MISINTERPRETATIONS OF THE THEORY OF THE SECOND BEST

In earlier chapters we characterized Pareto efficient resource allocations. All of the required conditions are seldom satisfied. The **theory of the second best** is concerned with the design of government policy in situations where the economy is characterized by some important distortions that cannot be removed.[1] This is in contrast to "first-best" economies, where all the conditions for Pareto efficiency can be satisfied. Second-best considerations say that it may not be desirable to remove distortions in those sectors where they can be removed. The theory of the second best is often interpreted fallaciously as saying that as long as there are some distortions, economic theory has nothing to say. This is incorrect, as we shall shortly show. Economic theory can tell us under what circumstances two small distortions are preferable to one large one; when it is better to have inefficiencies in both consumption and production; and when it is better not to have inefficiencies in production. Second-best theory tells us that we cannot blindly apply the lessons of first-best economics. Finding out what we should do when some distortions exist is often a difficult task, but it is not impossible.

---

[1] Early formulations of the theory of the second best include those of James Meade, *Trade and Welfare: Mathematical Supplement* (Oxford: Oxford University Press, 1955), and R. G. Lipsey and K. Lancaster, "The General Theory of Second Best," *Review of Economic Studies* 24 (1956–1957): 11–32.

OPTIMAL AND PARETO EFFICIENT TAXATION

Chapter 3 introduced the concept of Pareto efficiency. Recall that a resource allocation was Pareto efficient if no one could be made better off without someone else's being made worse off. Similarly, in judging tax structures we again use the concept of Pareto efficiency: a **Pareto efficient tax structure** is one such that there exists no alternative tax structure which can make some individuals better off without making other individuals worse off.[2] If such an alternative tax system exists, then the current tax system is clearly inefficient.

There are many Pareto efficient tax structures, just as there are many Pareto efficient resource allocations without taxes. In each, no one can be made better off without someone else's being made worse off. They differ in distribution. In the two-person economy of Robinson Crusoe and Friday, Crusoe is better off in some Pareto efficient allocations, Friday is better off in others.

In Chapter 5, we learned how one can choose among Pareto efficient resource allocations using a social welfare function. So too in choosing among Pareto efficient tax structures: the **optimal tax system** is the set of taxes which maximizes social welfare. Clearly, different social welfare functions will generate different optimal tax structures. At a practical level, for instance, a social welfare function which reflects a greater concern for equality (such as a Rawlsian social welfare function) may imply that the optimal tax structure is more progressive, with the rich bearing a larger fraction of the burden for paying for public goods. One of the objectives of optimal tax theory is to determine whether there are some general properties of all Pareto efficient tax systems, that is, properties which hold regardless of the social welfare function.

LUMP-SUM TAXES

If all individuals were identical and were treated for tax purposes identically, a lump-sum tax would be the only efficient tax: any other tax would introduce distortions, so that the government could raise the same amount of revenue *and* make each individual better off. And if everyone were identical, there would be no reason to redistribute income. Both equity and efficiency would thus require that any revenue that the government needed be raised by imposing a uniform lump-sum tax on all individuals.

In the real world, things are more complicated. Individuals differ, governments wish to redistribute income, and in any case, there is a strong belief that individuals who can more easily pay taxes should pay more taxes than those who cannot easily pay. Even if the government wishes to make different people pay different taxes, it does not follow that it would have to impose distortionary taxes, like income or excise taxes.

---

[2] For a more detailed description of Pareto efficient tax structures, see J. E. Stiglitz, "Self-Selection and Pareto-Efficient Taxation," *Journal of Public Economics* 17 (1982): 213–40, and J. E. Stiglitz, "Pareto Efficient and Optimal Taxation and the New New Welfare Economics," in *Handbook of Public Economics*, ed. Alan J. Auerbach and Martin Feldstein (Amsterdam and New York: North Holland; distributed in Canada and U.S. by Elsevier Science Publishers, 1987), pp. 991–1042.

A Pareto efficient tax structure is one such that there exists no other tax structure which can make some individuals better off without making others worse off.

The optimal tax structure, given a particular social welfare function, is the Pareto efficient tax structure which maximizes that social welfare function.

Indeed, it can be argued that if the government had perfect information about the characteristics of each individual in our society, it would not impose distortionary taxes. If the government could ascertain who had greater abilities, and who therefore was in a better position to pay taxes, it would simply impose higher lump-sum taxes on those individuals.

But how can abilities be measured? Consider a family. Parents often believe that they have good information concerning the abilities of their children. A parent who has two children, one of whom has a great deal of ability but chooses to become a beachcomber, and the other of whom has limited ability that he uses to the fullest, is more likely to provide financial assistance to the latter than to the former; the assistance is not made on the basis of income—the beachcomber may in fact have a lower income than a hardworking but low-ability brother.

The government, however, is not in the position of the parent who can observe the ability and drive of his children. The government can base its tax only on *observable variables,* such as income and expenditure (and even these, as we shall see, are not easily observable). The choice facing the government is to have either a *uniform lump-sum tax,* one that individuals pay regardless of what they do or what their abilities are; or a tax that depends on easily measured variables, such as expenditures or income—and such a tax is inevitably distortionary. An income tax does not always succeed in taxing those whom we might think ought to be taxed—it treats equally the individual who has low ability but works extremely hard and the individual who is of high ability and takes it easy, provided the two have the same income. Still, most people believe that those who have a higher income ought to pay a higher share of government costs because those with a higher income are, *on average,* more able or have had better than average luck. Moreover, society may reasonably value the loss of income by the rich (implying, say, one less yacht) less than it values the loss of income to lower-income individuals.

The use of distortionary taxes is thus an inevitable consequence of our desire to redistribute income, in a world in which the government can observe the characteristics of individuals only imperfectly. Still, some tax systems are less distortionary than others.

Pareto efficient tax structures minimize distortions. For instance, one might ask, is it better to redistribute income just through a progressive income tax, or to supplement a progressive income tax with a tax on luxuries consumed by the rich? Before addressing that question, however, we ask a simpler one: Assuming there are no savings, so the only source of income is wages, and the only tax is an income tax, how progressive should the tax system be? That is, how much larger a portion of their income should rich people pay?

As always, economists focus on trade-offs. Here, the more progressive the tax, the larger the deadweight loss, the inefficiencies from the tax, but the less the degree of inequality. We can view much of the political debate concerning how progressive the tax structure should be as one involving differences in values, in how much deadweight loss one is willing to accept for a given decrease in inequality.

There may be disagreements not only about values but also about the empirical question of what the trade-offs are. Those who advocate more progressive taxes tend also to argue that the cost, in terms of the deadweight loss, of reducing inequality is relatively small. In Chapter 19 we showed that the magnitude of the deadweight loss from a tax was related to the substitution effect. If leisure and consumption goods are very substitutable, then the compensated labor supply schedule will be very elastic, and there will be a large deadweight loss from a tax on consumption or labor income. If consumption this period and consumption next period are very substitutable, then the savings schedule will be very elastic, and the deadweight loss associated with an interest income tax will be large. Those who believe that the deadweight losses are small are often referred to as *elasticity optimists*; they believe, for instance, that the (compensated) labor supply and savings elasticities are low, so that the distortions associated with high tax rates are low; while those who believe that the distortions are large are often referred to as *elasticity pessimists*, because they believe that the labor supply and savings elasticities are large.

WHY DOES MORE PROGRESSIVITY IMPLY MORE DEADWEIGHT LOSS?

The preceding section argued that as we use our tax system to attain greater equality, the deadweight loss increases. Panels A and B of Figure 20.1 illustrate this general proposition by contrasting two tax schedules. The first (in color) is a proportional income tax, in which the tax liability is the same percentage of income for all individuals, no matter how large or small their income. The second is a simple progressive income tax that imposes a tax at a flat rate on the difference between the individual's income and some critical level of income, $\hat{Y}$. Individuals whose income falls below the critical level receive a grant from the government equal to the tax rate times the shortfall between their income and the critical level. Notice from panel B that the marginal tax rate, the extra tax an individual pays or receives on an extra dollar of income, is constant for both tax systems. Therefore, both are called **flat-rate taxes.** But with the progressive tax, the *average* tax rate, the ratio of the total tax payments to the individual's income, increases with income. This is why we call the tax progressive.[3]

[3] Usage is not standardized. Some prefer to reserve the term *progressive* for tax structures where the *marginal* tax rate increases. Nothing important hinges on these semantic points. Notice that a flat-rate tax combined with a lump-sum tax is regressive, in the sense that the average tax rate decreases with income. For a more general discussion of the definition of progressive and regressive tax structures, see A. B. Atkinson and J. E. Stiglitz, *Lectures on Public Economics* (New York: McGraw-Hill, 1980), Chapter 2.

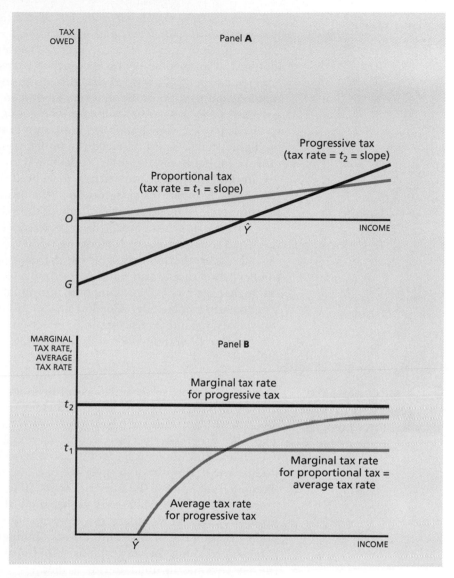

FIGURE 20.1   **Flat-Rate Income Tax Schedules** Panel A compares the tax schedule of a proportional flat-rate income tax with that of a progressive flat-rate income tax. Panel B compares average and marginal tax rates for these two taxes.

Because, as we have depicted it, the progressive flat tax provides for a payment to individuals whose income falls short of the critical level, we sometimes refer to that portion of the tax schedule below $\hat{Y}$ as a **negative income tax.**[4]

[4] In some tax systems, those with income above $\hat{Y}$ are taxed on the difference between their income and this exemption level, but those below the critical level neither pay taxes nor receive a rebate.

The progressive flat tax can be thought of as a combination of a uniform lump-sum grant to all individuals and a proportional income tax. Thus, in Figure 20.1A, a proportional tax at the rate t_2, combined with a grant of OG, is identical to an income tax on incomes in excess of $\hat{Y}$ ($\hat{Y}$ is the exemption level) at a rate of t_2, provided that those with incomes less than $\hat{Y}$ receive a rebate equal to t_2 times the difference between $\hat{Y}$ and their income. If the government is both to finance its public goods and other public expenditures *and* pay everyone a uniform lump-sum grant, the revenue raised must be higher than if it just financed the public goods, so the marginal tax rate must be higher than with just a proportional tax.

In the last chapter, we learned that the deadweight loss increases with the *marginal* tax rate: the magnitude of the deadweight loss is related to the substitution effect; and the magnitude of the substitution effect is related to the marginal tax rate. More progressive taxes have higher marginal tax rates, and thus greater deadweight loss.

Moreover, the more progressive the tax, the greater the *likelihood* of a smaller labor supply and national output necessitating on that account a still higher tax rate. All lower-income individuals are better off, so both substitution and income effects lead to smaller labor supply. For higher-income individuals, income and substitution effects are offsetting. Unless they have very backward-bending labor supply schedules, overall labor supply will be reduced.

A DIAGRAMMATIC ANALYSIS OF THE DEADWEIGHT LOSS OF PROGRESSIVE TAXATION

The fact that more progressive tax results in greater deadweight loss can be seen by looking at any individual, and comparing the revenues the government can obtain with two taxes which leave the individual just as well off. The more progressive tax has a higher marginal tax rate.

Figure 20.2 shows a budget constraint with a proportional tax and a budget constraint with a progressive tax, one which gives the individual a fixed income, even if she does not work. The marginal rate with the progressive tax is higher, but is set so that the individual is on the same indifference curve. We compare the total revenue. It is reflected in the distance between the before- and after-tax budget constraints. Since income is measured along the vertical axis (and hours along the horizontal axis), the tax revenue in dollar terms is measured as the vertical distance between the two budget constraints; for the proportional tax, by the distance $E'A'$, and for the progressive tax, by the distance EA. It is apparent that $E'A'$ is much larger than EA: for any given effect on utility, the progressive tax yields lower revenue.[5] It is less efficient than the proportional tax.

---

[5] The vertical distance between the indifference curve and the before-tax budget constraint is maximized at the point where the slope of the indifference curve is the same as the slope of the before-tax budget constraint. That is why a lump-sum tax, which does not alter the slope, maximizes revenue for any given impact on utility. Since at E' and E the slope of the indifference curve is flatter than the slope of the budget constraint, the vertical distance is larger the further "up" the indifference curve we move.

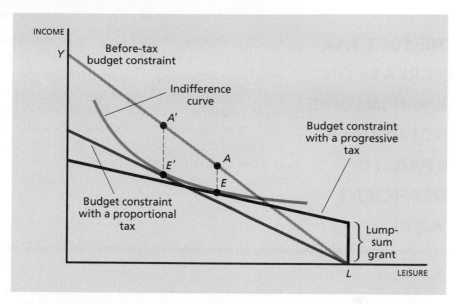

INCOME

Y

Before-tax
budget constraint

Indifference
curve

A'

Budget constraint
with a progressive
tax

E'

A

E

Budget constraint
with a proportional
tax

Lump-
sum
grant

L

LEISURE

FIGURE 20.2 **Comparing a Progressive and a Proportional Tax Which Have the Same Effect
on Utility** Tax revenue is higher with the proportional tax.

**CHOOSING AMONG
FLAT-RATE TAX
SCHEDULES**

The analysis has clarified the trade-offs faced as we increase the degree of progressivity. Poorer individuals gain, richer individuals lose. Like a leaky bucket, the dollar gains of the poor are less than the "dollar equivalent" losses of the rich, because of the deadweight losses associated with the tax. But the *social value* of the gains of the poor may well exceed the social value of the losses of the rich. Whether this is so depends, of course, on the social welfare function.

In Chapter 5 we introduced the concept of a Rawlsian social welfare function, where society is concerned about the welfare of the worst-off individuals. The worst-off individuals are those at the bottom of the income distribution, and their welfare is typically related directly to the size of the lump-sum grant. For a Rawlsian, the optimal tax structure is simply that which maximizes the lump-sum grant, that is, which maximizes the revenue that can be extracted from taxpayers. Such a tax rate may be quite high—one estimate[6] put the number at 80 percent, though others have estimated

---

[6] Nicholas H. Stern, "On the Specification of Models of Optimum Income Taxation," *Journal of Public Economics* 6 (1976): 123–62. He assumed that expenditures on public goods amount to 20 percent of national income. The results of the calculations are very sensitive to all the assumptions made, and in particular to assumptions concerning the compensated and uncompensated elasticities of labor supply. As we noted in Chapter 19, there is considerable controversy concerning their magnitude. Those who believe that the uncompensated elasticity is quite high believe that revenues that can be obtained from taxing the rich, to pay the lump-sum grant to the poor, peak out at much lower rates of taxation. Those who believe that the compensated elasticity is quite high believe that the deadweight loss from the progressive taxation is very high.

In 1993, Congress raised taxes on upper-income individuals. The tax increase clearly made them worse off. Critics claimed that it was a Pareto inefficient tax change (though the popular press did not use that vocabulary). The claim was made that these individuals would reduce their work effort—the substitution effect was larger than any income effect—so that tax revenues would be reduced. Thus, funds available to redistribute to the poor would actually be lowered. This did not happen. Instead, tax revenues for the rich increased faster than for others, and far faster than national income. To be sure,

lower rates. At 80 percent, the deadweight loss incurred by higher-income individuals is quite high. Other social welfare functions, which put more weight on middle- and upper-income individuals, accordingly suggest a lower optimal tax rate. One estimate[7] put the optimal tax with a utilitarian social welfare function—where all individuals are weighed equally—at 19 percent.

GENERAL EQUILIBRIUM EFFECTS

So far we have assumed that the income tax has no effect on before-tax incomes; that there is, in other words, no *shifting* of the income tax. Some economists, however, believe that there may be considerable shifting. In particular, it has been argued that the income tax system has increased the degree of before-tax inequality.

There are some who believe, first, that the wages and fees of managers and professionals adjust to the taxes, leaving their after-tax income relatively unchanged. Moreover, if as a result of the income tax, skilled workers supply less labor and investment is discouraged, unskilled laborers' productivity and, hence, their wage, will decline. At the present time, unfortunately, we do not know the quantitative significance of these effects. If they are important, it suggests that the benefits of progressivity are less than they seem when these effects are ignored.[8]

---

[7] Stern, "On the Specification of Models of Optimum Income Taxation."

[8] The importance of these general equilibrium effects in the design of optimal taxes was noted by Martin Feldstein, "On the Optimal Progressivity of the Income Tax," *Journal of Public Economics* 2 (1973): 357–76, using a simulation model. His results were corroborated and extended in subsequent theoretical work by N. Stern, "Optimum Taxation with Errors in Administration," *Journal of Public Economics* 17 (1982): 181–211; F. Allen, "Optimal Linear Income Taxation with General Equilibrium Effects on Wages," *Journal of Public Economics* 17 (1982): 135–43; J. E. Stiglitz, "Self-Selection and Pareto-Efficient Taxation." See also Laurence J. Kotlikoff and Lawrence H. Summers, "Tax Incidence," Chapter 16 in *Handbook of Public Economics*, vol.2, pp. 1043–92.

upper-income individuals are worse off than they would have been with lower taxes, but the taxes they paid increased. (Of course, it is possible that without the tax rate increase, incomes of the rich would have increased even more, enough so that tax revenues would have increased. But this would have required an implausibly large growth in their income, not commensurate with historical experience.) Thus, whether the tax change was desirable depends on the social welfare function, but it does not appear to have been Pareto inefficient.

RAISING BENEFITS FOR THE POOR The analysis also makes clear why it is so difficult to provide increased benefits for the poor. It is not "just" that financing those benefits requires raising taxes. There is a real problem in designing the "phaseout," that is, the rules stipulating how benefits get reduced as income increases. A rapid phaseout implies a high marginal tax rate (since benefits are reduced greatly for each extra dollar earned) over the phaseout income range, thus weakening work incentives. A slow phaseout reduces the magnitude of the disincentive effect, but, if the poorest are to receive the same benefit, raises the benefit levels of others, including lower-middle-income individuals, necessitating further tax increases. The objectives of *targeting* and *good incentives* are inevitably in conflict.

Consider the earned income tax credit (EITC), meant to supplement the wage income of poor families with dependent children. The idea behind the EITC was simple: reward the poor for working, thus encouraging them to work more and acquire more skills. In 1993, the EITC was greatly expanded and indexed, so that in 1997, the maximum benefit, for a family with two or more eligible children, of $3656 phased out over the range of $11,950 to $29,290, implying a marginal tax rate of 22 percent from the EITC. When the Clinton administration took office, it had hoped to expand the EITC so that all those working full-time would be out of poverty. But the overriding desire to reduce the deficit led to a lower maximum benefit than

BASIC TRADE-OFF IN TAX DESIGN

More progressive tax systems entail greater deadweight loss; more "equalitarian" social welfare functions (placing more weight on equality) will choose more progressive tax systems.

The simplicity of the flat-rate tax system has long attracted academic economists. In the early 1980s, Robert Hall and Alvin Rabuschka of Stanford University wrote a widely read book advocating the flat tax. In 1996, Malcolm Forbes ran a presidential primary campaign centered around the flat-rate tax. He proposed a high exemption level, and a low rate. Like the supply-siders of the 1980s, he believed the supply response to the lower tax rate would be a huge increase in national income. But most economists thought that the supply response would be far smaller, leaving a huge

was required to achieve this goal. Fiscal constraints forced a shorter phase-out range, thus leading to greater marginal disincentives.

NONLINEAR TAX STRUCTURES

The discussion so far has focused on the optimal flat-rate tax. In fact, the United States has had, for a long time, a highly nonlinear schedule, with marginal rates varying from zero to almost 40 percent. Nonlinear tax structures increase complexity and, for reasons that are explained more fully in Chapter 24, increase incentives and opportunities for tax avoidance. At the same time, they can reduce the total deadweight loss associated with attaining any set of revenue and distributive goals.

Earlier, we saw that the deadweight loss is related to the marginal tax rate and the elasticity of the (compensated) labor supply. The basic principles of efficient progressive income taxation are derived from that insight:

1 Impose high average tax rates with low marginal tax rates.
2 Make as few people as possible face high marginal tax rates.
3 Impose high marginal tax rates on those for whom the tax is least distorting.

Figure 20.3 compares two tax structures, a progressive flat-rate tax and a tax structure with high marginal tax rates at low incomes and very low marginal tax rates at very high incomes. *OB* is the lump-sum grant given to ssomeone who does not work and has no other source of income. This grant gets phased out as income rises. The high marginal tax rates (high phaseout rate) over the interval *BC* mean that at incomes beyond *C,* average rates can be higher while marginal rates are lower. For these middle- and upper-income individuals, this means the government is collecting more taxes with less distortion. The price is greater distortions for those with income in the range *BC.* The total deadweight loss will be low, however, if there are relatively few people in this interval, or if those in it have a relatively low labor supply elasticity. Even if they reduce their labor supply significantly, however, the total social loss may be relatively low if they are relatively unproductive.

deficit—estimated in the hundreds of billions per year. Raising the flat rate to eliminate the deficit made the proposal sound less attractive; but even then it would have represented a huge change in who bears the burden of taxation, with the rich facing markedly lowered burdens and the middle class facing higher burdens. As people examined the idea more closely, their enthusiasm for it languished, and so did Forbes's campaign. Still, the idea of a flat-rate tax is likely to be an active one on the political scene for years to come.

LOWERING TAX RATES FOR THE RICH Figure 20.4 shows why lowering the marginal tax rate for the highest income groups may be desirable. The figure depicts the budget constraint facing the highest income group, with individuals in the group choosing point E. The revenue raised is the amount EA. If, for those who have income above Y_A, we now lower the marginal tax rate to zero, the government still collects the same revenue; but with a lower marginal tax

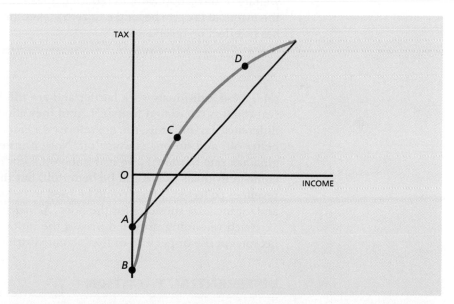

FIGURE 20.3   **Linear versus Nonlinear Tax Structures** Nonlinear tax structures may be able to increase the amount of redistribution without increasing the deadweight loss associated with the tax. The nonlinear schedule *ABCD* has a higher marginal tax rate among the very poor and low marginal tax rates at upper income ranges. On the other hand, higher earners face a higher average tax rate.

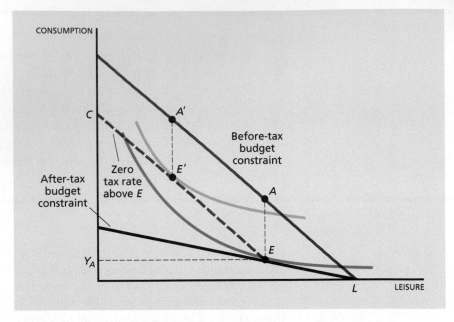

FIGURE 20.4 **Impact of Lowering Marginal Tax Rates for Upper-Income Individuals**
Lowering marginal tax rates for upper-income individuals may improve the welfare of this group without reducing government revenue. Here, lowering the marginal tax rate beyond E to zero makes the individual better off, but has no effect on revenue.

rate, these individuals work harder and are still better off. (The new budget constraint is the dotted line $EE'C$, and they choose point E', on a higher indifference curve.) Thus, the tax reform is a Pareto improvement: the rich are better off, and no one is worse off. Now, if instead of imposing a zero marginal tax rate beyond Y_A we had imposed a low marginal rate, the higher-income individuals would still be better off, but there would be additional tax revenues collected, which could be used to reduce taxes on the middle class and/or increase subsidies for the poor. *All individuals could be made better off.*

Such reasoning provided part of the rationale for the reduction in the tax rates at the upper end of the income distribution enacted in 1986.

DIFFERENTIAL TAXATION

The government imposes a huge array of taxes on various commodities, from airline tickets to tires to gasoline to perfume. Taxes that are imposed at different rates on different commodities are called **differential taxes.** Some of these taxes, such as the airline ticket tax, are designed as *benefit taxes*—that is, to make those who benefit from airline travel pay for the costs of the air traffic controller system and airports. Others, such as the taxes on gasoline, tobacco, and alcohol, are partially designed as "*corrective taxes*," to ameliorate some of the externalities they generate, such as traffic congestion and air pollution from automobiles. Finally, some, such as the tax on perfume, are *luxury taxes*, intended to increase the redistributive nature of our tax system.

In this section we address two key questions. First, if the government cannot impose an income tax to redistribute income—as is the case in many less-developed countries—what rates should it impose on different commodities? And second, if the government *can* impose an income tax to redistribute income, should it *also* impose taxes on different commodities at different rates? The two questions turn out to have markedly different answers.

RAMSEY TAXES

We begin with an even simpler question posed by the great Cambridge economist Frank Ramsey. Ramsey was not concerned with redistribution, only with efficiency. But he assumed that the government could not impose a lump-sum tax.[9] Hence, it had to raise revenues through commodity taxation. The question he asked was, what is the least distortionary pattern of taxes? Should, for instance, every commodity be taxed at the same rate—in which case the tax is just a tax on income? (Recall the discussion of equivalent taxes in Chapter 18.) That was the answer suggested by those who simply wanted to count distortions, for such a tax would have only one distortion. Ramsey showed not only that that was wrong, but that there was a simple formula for the optimal tax rate.

The commodity taxes that minimize the deadweight loss are called **Ramsey taxes.** Under certain simplifying conditions, Ramsey taxes are proportional to the sum of the reciprocals of the elasticities of demand and supply:

$$\frac{t}{p} = k(1/\eta_u^d + 1/\eta^s),$$

where k is a proportionality factor that depends on the total amount of revenue the government is attempting to raise, t is the per unit tax, p is the (after-tax) price, η_u^d is the compensated elasticity of demand, and η^s is the elasticity of supply. If the elasticity of supply is infinite (a horizontal supply schedule), the tax should simply be inversely proportional to the compensated elasticity of demand. Ramsey's result should not come as a surprise. In Chapter 19 we showed that the deadweight loss from a tax increased with the compensated elasticity of demand and with the elasticity of supply. (Recall Figure 18.8.)[10]

[9] F. Ramsey, "A Contribution to the Theory of Taxation," *Economic Journal* 37 (1927): 47–61. The question had been posed to him by his teacher, A. C. Pigou. See A. C. Pigou, *A Study in Public Finance,* 3rd ed. (London: Macmillan, 1947).

[10] If there is a tax rate t on corporate profits, the Ramsey formula is modified to:

$$\frac{t}{p} = k\left(1/\eta_u^d + \frac{(1-t)}{\eta^s}\right).$$

Hence, if corporate profits are taxed at 100 percent, the tax rate is simply inversely proportional to the elasticity of (compensated) demand.

Figure 20.5 shows the solution to the optimal commodity tax problem. Panel A depicts the deadweight loss as a function of the tax rate imposed on commodity i. Panel B shows the revenue raised as a function of the tax rate imposed on commodity i. From these two diagrams we can calculate, at each tax rate, the ratio of the increase in deadweight loss to the increase in

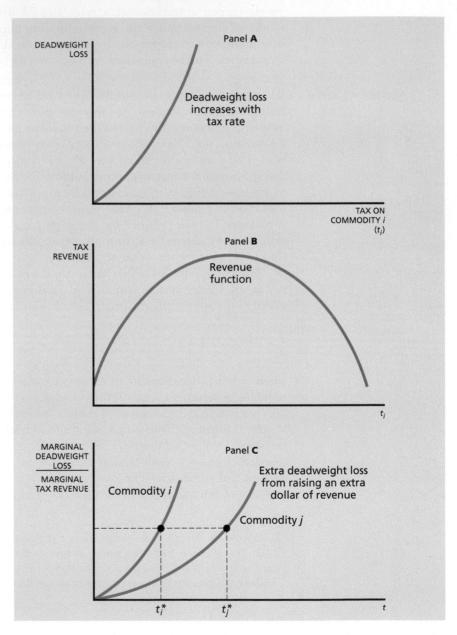

FIGURE 20.5　**Optimal Commodity Taxation** The marginal excess burden (deadweight loss) per marginal dollar raised must be the same for all commodities.

tax revenues from raising the tax a little bit—that is, the marginal dead-weight loss from raising an extra dollar of revenue from a tax on commodity i. Notice that we have drawn the curve not only so that excess burden increases as the revenue raised increases, but also so that the extra deadweight from raising an extra dollar of revenue increases with the tax rate (and thus with the revenue raised). This follows from the fact that the deadweight loss increases with the square of the tax rate.

A similar curve can be derived for commodity j, as shown in panel C. The tax rates should be set so that the increase in deadweight loss per extra dollar raised is the same for each commodity. If the increase in excess burden per extra dollar raised were greater for one commodity than for another, by adjusting tax rates so that one less dollar was raised on the first commodity and one more dollar was raised on the second commodity, total deadweight loss would be reduced.

In panel C, the marginal deadweight loss per marginal dollar of revenue raised is higher for commodity i than for commodity j at any given tax rate. To equate the marginal deadweight loss per marginal dollar of revenue raised we must impose a lower tax rate on i than on j. Ramsey's basic insight was to observe that *commodities with low elasticity of demand (or low elasticity of supply) have a lower marginal deadweight loss per marginal dollar of revenue raised, and thus should face higher marginal tax rates.*

OPTIMAL COMMODITY TAXATION WITH INTERDEPENDENT DEMANDS* The result we have just given requires that the compensated demand curves of each commodity are independent; that is, the demand for one commodity does not depend on the price of another. Another interpretation of Ramsey's result holds when supply curves are infinitely elastic, whether or not demand curves are interdependent: *The optimal tax structure is such that the percentage reduction in the compensated demand for each commodity is the same.*[11]

ALTERNATIVE INTERPRETATION: OPTIMAL COMMODITY TAX STRUCTURE WITH INTERDEPENDENT DEMANDS An income tax is distortionary because it induces individuals to make "incorrect" decisions concerning the amount of labor they wish to supply. Commodity taxation may help correct that distortion. If we tax commodities that are complements for leisure and subsidize commodities that are complements for work, we encourage individuals to work, and thus reduce the distortion caused by a uniform commodity tax (which is equivalent to just a wage tax). For instance, by taxing ski equipment and subsidizing commuter costs we induce individuals to work more and consume less leisure.[12]

---

* This subsection and the remaining subsections of this part of the chapter deal with more advanced topics and can be omitted.

[11] Note that if $\eta^s = \infty$, $t/p = k/\eta_u^d$; with horizontal supply curves, the percentage tax is inversely proportional to the compensated demand elasticity. The percentage change in output is equal to the percentage increase in price × percent change in demand from a percent change in price $= (k/\eta_u^d) \times \eta_u^d = k$—i.e., it is the same for all commodities.

[12] This interpretation was noted in W. J. Corlett and D. C. Hague, "Complementarity and the Excess Burden of Taxation," *Review of Economic Studies* 21 (1953): 21–30.

RAMSEY TAXES

In the absence of any income or profit taxes, and with all individuals identical, raising revenues so as to minimize deadweight loss requires imposing taxes in inverse relationship to the elasticity of demand and supply.

REDISTRIBUTION AND RAMSEY TAXES: COMMODITY TAXATION IN LDCs There is one very disturbing feature of Ramsey's analysis. The major reason why governments use distortionary rather than uniform lump-sum taxes is that they have certain redistributive goals that they cannot achieve otherwise. However, the early discussions of optimal taxation assumed that all individuals were identical (in which case the natural assumption would be that the government would employ uniform lump-sum taxation).

This was particularly vexing since the results described earlier suggest that high tax rates should be imposed on commodities with low price elasticities, such as food. These commodities often have low income elasticities, so that if a high tax is imposed on them the poor will bear a larger burden than the rich. But the original reason for employing commodity taxation was to shift more of the burden onto the rich than they would face, say, with a uniform lump-sum tax. Ramsey's analysis thus seemed to provide little guidance for any serious policy analysis and was, accordingly, largely dismissed.

Subsequent research has extended Ramsey's original analysis to include redistributive goals.[13] Not surprisingly, whether one wishes to tax income-elastic and price-elastic commodities, such as perfume, at a higher or lower rate than income-inelastic and price-inelastic commodities like food depends, in part, on the strength of one's concern for income redistribution.

Less developed countries typically place little reliance on income taxes, since they have difficulty monitoring income. Indeed, in many cases, they cannot even impose a tax on all commodities, but only on commodities that are imported or exported (since they have some control over what passes over their borders), and on commodities manufactured in the urban sector. Most LDCs have sufficient concern for redistribution that they tax luxuries at higher rates than basic necessities.

[13] See, in particular, Peter Diamond and James Mirrlees, "Optimal Taxation and Public Production, I: Production Efficiency and II: Tax Rules," *American Economic Review* 61 (1971): 8–27 and 261–78; P. Diamond, "A Many-Person Ramsey Tax Rule," *Journal of Public Economics* 4 (1975): 335–42; A. B. Atkinson and J. E. Stiglitz, "The Structure of Indirect Taxation and Economic Efficiency," *Journal of Public Economics* 1 (1972): 97–119; and A. B. Atkinson and J. E. Stiglitz, "The Design of Tax Structure: Direct versus Indirect Taxation," *Journal of Public Economics* 6 (1976): 55–75; reprinted in A. B. Atkinson (ed.), *Modern Public Finance*, vol 2. International Library of Critical Writings in Economics, no. 15 (Aldershot, U.K., and Brookfield, Vt.: Elgar, 1991), pp. 82–102.

DIFFERENTIAL COMMODITY TAXES IN ADVANCED COUNTRIES WITH PROGRESSIVE INCOME TAXES

All advanced industrialized countries, however, do have a progressive income tax. For them, the issue is markedly different from that posed by Ramsey. They ask: *If* there is an optimally designed income tax, does the marginal benefit of the extra redistribution which, say, a tax on luxuries provides exceed the marginal cost, in terms of the excess deadweight loss? The naïve answer to this question was rejected in the introduction to this chapter. Earlier discussions had suggested that introducing more distortions was bad, and that therefore differential commodity taxation was undesirable, but this fallacy was dismissed: one simply cannot count the number of distortions. Yet, remarkably enough, the conclusion of these earlier discussions was correct: If an income tax is well designed, adding differential commodity taxation is likely to increase the ability to redistribute income little, if at all. The objective of taxation is to redistribute income, or to impose the burden of taxation on those most able to afford it, and it turns out that the best way to do this, after all, is to focus taxation on what we are really interested in, namely income.[14]

INTEREST INCOME TAXATION AND COMMODITY TAXATION

In our earlier discussion we showed how a tax on interest income discourages future consumption. It changes the slope of the budget constraint in the same way that a tax on future consumption only would.

Thus an income tax that taxes interest can be viewed as a differential commodity tax in which future consumption is taxed more heavily than current consumption. The question whether it is desirable to tax interest income is then equivalent to the question whether it is desirable to tax future consumption at higher rates than current consumption.

Just as little may be gained by adding differential commodity taxation with a well-designed income tax, so little is gained from taxing consumption at different dates at different rates. This means, in effect, that interest income should be exempt from taxation. An income tax that exempts interest income is, of course, equivalent to a wage tax, and we showed in Chapter 18 that a wage tax was equivalent to a consumption tax (in the absence of bequests). This suggests that it may be optimal to have a consumption tax. We discuss this further in Chapter 25.

TAXES ON PRODUCERS

So far this chapter has focused on taxes on households, on their wage and interest income and their consumption. Many people believe that it is only fair that firms pay taxes too. Such reasoning is misguided: firms never bear the incidence of a tax, as we have seen, but individuals do, as shareholders, workers, or consumers. Figuring out the incidence of taxes on corporations is a complicated matter.

---

[14] Indeed, under standard assumptions, Pareto efficient taxation requires that there be no differential taxation of commodities. See Atkinson and Stiglitz, "The Design of Tax Structure."

But we can ask a more general question: Does Pareto efficient taxation imply that taxes should be imposed on production processes? The taxes described thus far interfere with one of the three conditions for Pareto efficiency discussed in Chapter 3, product mix efficiency: the marginal rate of transformation differs from the marginal rate of substitution.[15, 16] Do we want to maintain production efficiency, even if we cannot maintain product mix efficiency?

Many of our taxes also affect the production efficiency of the economy, which is to say that they result in the economy's not being on its production possibilities schedule. Production efficiency requires that the marginal rate of technical substitution between any two inputs be the same in all firms, and that the marginal rate of transformation between any two outputs (or between an input and an output) be the same in all firms. Productive efficiency is attained when all firms face the same prices for inputs and outputs. Thus, any tax on an input that is not uniform across all firms, or any tax on an output that is not uniform across all firms, results in the economy's not being productively efficient. For instance, the corporation income tax is widely viewed as a tax on capital inputs used in incorporated firms, because it raises the after-tax cost of capital in corporations above that in unincorporated businesses. Also, while gasoline that is used for most business purposes is taxed, gasoline used for farming is not. But these are only the most obvious examples.

Many production activities are performed in both the market and nonmarket sectors. Only activities performed in the market sector are taxed. Thus an individual driving himself to work is performing the same service that a taxicab driver who drives the individual to work performs. Yet there is a tax on the latter and not on the former. A person who bakes a loaf of bread at home is performing a service similar to that of a baker but is not taxed in the same way that the baker is taxed. There is thus a distortion between the marketed and nonmarketed sectors, and the economy is not productively efficient.

Any tax on *intermediate goods*—goods used to produce other goods—is distortionary. To see this most clearly, consider a firm that produces and uses computers in its own production plants; the cost of the computer is simply the cost of the factors of production (including the return to capital employed in the production). In a competitive economy this firm would be forced to sell the computers at its costs of production, so that the cost of any

[15] With a tax on wage income, the marginal rate of transformation, the wage, exceeds the marginal rate of substitution (the after-tax wage); with differential commodity taxes, relative producer prices (which equal the marginal rate of transformation) differ from relative consumer prices.

[16] We can also ask, if it is possible to charge individuals with different incomes different taxes on consumption, whether it is desirable to do so. In other words, is it desirable to maintain *exchange efficiency*? Under the conditions under which no differential commodity taxation is desirable, of course, there is exchange efficiency in the consumption of all goods; but when differential taxation is desirable, it is also in general desirable to have relative tax rates dependent on income.

other firm using a computer would be the same as the cost of the manufacturing firm in using it. But now, when a sales tax is imposed, the cost to the firm manufacturing the computer and using it is less than the cost to another firm using the computer in its production processes. There is thus an important distortion, and the economy is no longer productively efficient.

Should the government impose such distortionary taxes if it wishes to minimize the deadweight loss of the tax system? One naïve answer to this question is to say, of course not; the government should not introduce any additional distortions that it does not need to. This kind of argument is similar to the arguments we discussed earlier concerning differential commodity taxes. It makes no sense simply to count the number of distortions. Yet it turns out that under some circumstances, the conclusion of the naïve argument is correct.

If the government is able to tax away all profits in the private sector, and if there are no other restrictions on the ability of the government to impose taxes (other than the ability to impose lump-sum taxes), it is possible to show that productive efficiency is desirable. Hence, the government should impose no distortionary taxes on businesses. *Whatever the government could do with a distortionary tax on producers, it could do better with a direct tax on consumers that maintained the economy on the production possibilities schedule.*[17]

This analysis has some very strong implications. It suggests, in particular, the undesirability of import duties and of taxes on corporations that differ from taxes on unincorporated businesses.

There are many instances, however, when governments face difficulties in imposing taxes. For instance, governments cannot distinguish between final consumer use of a commodity and the use of the commodity by a business; thus, if a government is to impose a tax on consumers it must also impose a tax on business use. Whenever the government is not able to identify and tax away *all* pure profits in the private sector, and whenever there are other restrictions on the ability of the government to impose taxes, it may be desirable to impose distortionary taxes on producers.[18]

But the basic insight, suggesting that one look unfavorably on taxes that interfere with productive efficiency, is still a valuable one. Taxes on imports, for example, introduce an important inefficiency in the economy; at least in more developed countries, governments can impose a tax on the consumption of these goods rather than on just imports; and, *in general*, such consumption-based taxes are preferable.[19]

---

[17] This result was originally established in the important paper by Diamond and Mirrlees, "Optimal Taxation and Public Production, I: Production Efficiency." See also Alan J. Auerbach, "The Theory of Excess Burden and Optimal Taxation," Chapter 2 in *Handbook of Public Economics,* vol. 1, pp. 100–101.

[18] This result was established in J. E. Stiglitz and P. Dasgupta, "Differential Taxation, Public Goods and Economic Efficiency," *Review of Economic Studies* 39 (1971): 151–74.

[19] For a more extended discussion of the relationship between trade taxes and commodity taxes, see P. Dasgupta and J. E. Stiglitz, "Benefit-Cost Analysis and Trade Policies," *Journal of Political Economy* 82 (January–February 1974): 1–33.

Throughout this chapter, we have noted the dependence of the optimal tax results on the assumptions made concerning the set of available taxes. This was particularly true for commodity taxation. Whether there should be differential commodity taxation, and, if so, how the difference in rates should be chosen, depends on whether there is an income tax and if there is, on its structure. Ramsey showed that *in the absence of any income tax* (and assuming no redistributional objectives), different commodities should be taxed at different rates depending only on the elasticities of demand and supply. When there is an optimally chosen income tax, it may not be desirable to impose differential commodity taxes. When it is desirable to impose differential commodity taxes, they do not depend simply on the elasticities of demand.[20]

It should be emphasized, however, that the set of taxes that is feasible should itself be a subject for analysis: it depends, in particular, on what variables are easily observable and verifiable. In developing countries in which there are many barter transactions (trade not for cash) and in which the level of record keeping is low, it is difficult to enforce an income tax, and commodity taxes must be relied on to redistribute income and to ensure that the burden of taxation is equitably borne. But in the United States, the case for the use of redistributive commodity taxation is weak.

---

[20] The central question is whether the additional redistribution that might be obtained from differential commodity taxation is worth the extra deadweight loss.

When there is a flat-rate income tax, with the tax rate chosen optimally, the optimal tax rate on a commodity is simply inversely proportional to the elasticity of demand and proportional to a parameter that measures the extent to which the good is consumed relatively more by the rich (so that a tax on that good is progressive). In some simple cases, that distributional parameter itself is proportional to the price elasticity of demand; goods with low elasticities of demand (like food) have low deadweight losses but a tax on them is regressive. The two effects (efficiency, or deadweight loss, and distribution) are offsetting, and there should either be no differential taxation on different commodities, or it should depend on parameters other than the elasticity of demand.

In the more general case where an optimal income tax can be imposed that is not necessarily flat (that is, marginal rates can vary with income), a critical determinant of the commodity tax structure is how the marginal rate of substitution between two commodities depends on leisure; in the case where marginal rates of substitution among commodities do not depend at all on leisure, there should be no differential commodity taxation.

REVIEW AND PRACTICE

SUMMARY

1   Pareto efficient tax structures are such that there is no alternative that can make any individual better off without making some other individual(s) worse off. The nature of the Pareto efficient tax structure, in turn, depends on the information available to the government.

2   There are important trade-offs between distributional goals and efficiency in the design of tax structures. The optimal tax structure balances the gains from additional redistribution with the costs in terms of loss in efficiency.

3   The deadweight loss associated with the magnitude of the substitution effect suggests that it is desirable to have low marginal tax rates in those parts of the income distribution where there are a large number of individuals, which is to say in the middle income ranges. On the other hand, high marginal rates in such ranges enable the government to collect the same or greater revenue with a lower marginal tax rate from upper-income individuals. This reduces the deadweight loss per dollar of revenue raised from upper-income individuals.

4   Ramsey taxes minimize the deadweight loss associated with raising a given revenue through commodity taxes alone. In the simple case of independent demand and supply curves, the higher a good's supply and compensated demand elasticities, the lower the tax rate on a good.

5   Whether different commodities should be taxed at different rates depends on the taxes that are available to the government. If the government has imposed an optimal income tax, there may be little if any gain from the imposition of differential commodity taxes.

6   If there are no pure profits in the private sector (the economy is perfectly competitive, or the government can impose a 100 percent profits tax) and if there are no other restrictions on the ability of the government to impose taxes, then the government should not impose any taxes that interfere with the productive efficiency of the economy. When these stringent assumptions are removed, it may be desirable to introduce taxes that interfere with productive efficiency.

KEY CONCEPTS

Theory of the second best

Pareto efficient taxe structure

Optimal tax system

Flat-rate taxes

Negative income tax

Differential taxes

Ramsey tax

1 "If there are groups in the population who differ in their labor supply elasticity, they should be taxed at different rates." Justify this in terms of the theory of optimal taxation, and discuss its implications for the taxation of working spouses.

2 Earlier, we noted that consumption at different dates could be interpreted just like consumption of different commodities at the same date. What do the results on optimal taxation imply about the desirability of taxing interest income? (Hint: Recall that the price of consumption tomorrow relative to the price of consumption today is just $1/1 + r$, where r is the rate of interest.)

3 Explain why it might be desirable to have a regressive tax structure, even if the social welfare function is utilitarian, when general equilibrium effects of taxes are taken into account. Would it ever be desirable to impose a negative marginal tax rate on very high income individuals?

4 If you believed that those who were more productive in earning income also had a higher marginal utility of income (they were more efficient in consumption), what would that imply for the design of tax structures? Discuss the reasonableness of alternative assumptions.

5 Under what circumstances will an increase in the progressivity of the tax schedule increase the degree of before-tax inequality?

6 To what extent do you think that differences in views concerning how progressive our tax structure should be reflect differences in values, and to what extent do they reflect differences in judgments concerning the economic consequences of progressivity (deadweight loss, shifting)?

7 One argument sometimes made in favor of the use of commodity taxation rather than income taxation is that people do not accurately perceive the amount they pay in commodity taxes. They will object less to a 20 percent income tax supplemented by a 10 percent sales tax than to a 30 percent income tax. Do you think this is true? If it is, what do you think it implies about the design of tax policy?

8 Explain why the EITC may actually lower total work effort of the poor even if it increases labor force participation. (Hint: Focus separately on those below and above the maximum benefit level.)

APPENDIX A

DERIVING RAMSEY TAXES ON COMMODITIES

The formula for Ramsey taxation, given horizontal supply schedules, may be derived using calculus and certain standard results from microeconomic theory. We represent the individual's utility by her *indirect utility function*, giving her level of utility as a function of consumer prices (p_1, p_2, p_3, . . .)

and of income (I): $V = V(p_1, p_2, p_3, \ldots, I)$. A standard result[21] is that the change in utility from a change in price is just equal to the (negative of the) quantity consumed times the marginal utility of income $\frac{\partial V}{\partial I}$:

$$\frac{\partial V}{\partial p_i} = -Q_i \frac{\partial V}{\partial I}.$$

Let us now increase the per unit tax on, say, the first commodity (t_1) and reduce the per unit tax on the second commodity (t_2) in such a way as to leave utility unchanged. Since with horizontal supply curves producer prices are fixed, the change in the consumer price is just equal to the change in the tax: Then $dp_1 = dt_1 > 0$, $dp_2 = dt_2 < 0$. Clearly, to keep utility unchanged, the required change in the tax on the second commodity must satisfy $dV = \frac{\partial V}{\partial p_i} dt_1 + \frac{\partial V}{\partial p_2} dt_2 = 0$. We can substitute in the values of $\partial V/\partial p_1$ to obtain

$$\frac{dt_2}{dt_1} = -\frac{Q_1}{Q_2}.$$

Thus, if the quantity consumed of the first commodity is large (so the loss in welfare from the tax increase is large), the reduction in taxes on the second commodity must be large.

If the demand for each commodity depends only on its own price, then the change in revenue induced by an increase in the tax on the first commodity is just

$$\frac{\partial(t_1 Q_1)}{\partial t_1} = Q_1 + t_1 dQ/dp_1 = Q_1 \left(1 + \frac{t_1}{p_1} \frac{dQ_1}{dp_1} \frac{p_1}{Q_1}\right) = Q_1 \left(1 - \frac{t_1}{p_1} \eta_u^1\right),$$

where η_u^1 is the compensated demand elasticity for good 1. The term $t_1 \frac{dQ_1}{dp_1}$ represents the *loss* in revenue resulting from reduced sales in response to the changed price. The reason why it is the compensated demand elasticities that are relevant is that we are considering variations in two tax rates that, together, *leave the individual at the same level of welfare.*

Similarly, for each change in the tax on the second commodity, the change in revenue is given by

$$Q_2 \left(1 - \frac{t_2}{p_2} \eta_u^2\right).$$

[21] This result is known as Roy's Identity. For a proof, see H. Varian, *Microeconomic Analysis* Third Edition (New York: Norton, 1982), pp. 106–7, or A. Deaton and J. Muellbauer, *Economics and Consumer Behavior* (London: Cambridge University Press, 1980), pp. 37–41.

The total change in revenue is thus

$$\frac{dR}{dt_1} = Q_1\left(1 - \frac{t_1}{p_1}\eta_u^1\right) + \frac{dt_2}{dt_1}Q_2\left(1 - \frac{t_2}{p_2}\eta_u^2\right)$$

$$= Q_1\left[\left(1 - \frac{t_1}{p_1}\eta_u^1\right) - \left(1 - \frac{t_2}{p_2}\eta_u^2\right)\right] = Q_1\left[\frac{t_2}{p_2}\eta_u^2 - \frac{t_1}{p_1}\eta_u^1\right].$$

With an optimal tax structure, this must be zero, i.e., given that we are keeping the level of utility of the individual constant, revenues must be maximized. But this requires that

$$\frac{t_2}{p_2}\eta_u^2 - \frac{t_1}{p_1}\eta_u^1 = 0.$$

Generalizing this condition to all commodity taxes, $t_1, t_2, \ldots t_i, \ldots$, we know that $\frac{t_i}{p_i}\eta_u^i$ must be the same for all, that is, for all commodities. Let k be that value, so that

$$\frac{t_i}{p_i} = \frac{k}{\eta_u^i}.$$

This means that tax rates must be inversely proportional to compensated demand elasticities. This is the Ramsey rule.

APPENDIX B

DERIVATION OF RAMSEY FORMULA FOR LINEAR DEMAND SCHEDULE

Figure 20.6 illustrates a linear compensated demand schedule, $Q = a - b(p + t)$, with a fixed producer price (infinite elasticity supply schedule) and a tax t. The slope of the demand schedule is b. The deadweight loss

$$\text{DWL} = \tfrac{1}{2}bt^2,$$

so the marginal deadweight loss from increasing the tax is

$$\text{MDWL} = bt.$$

The revenue raised by the government is

$$R = tQ = at - b(pt + t^2),$$

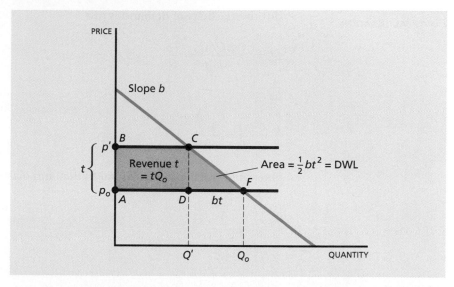

FIGURE 20.6 **Ramsey Pricing Calculation with Linear Demand Curves** With a linear demand schedule, the revenue raised by a tax at the rate t is the shaded square $ABCD$ (equals tQ'_o, where t is the tax rate and tQ'_o is the output after the tax. The deadweight loss is the triangle DCF, where DC equals the tax, t, and DF equals the change in output, which is just bt, where b is the slope of the demand curve. The total deadweight loss is just $\frac{1}{2} bt^2$. Ramsey looked at the extra deadweight loss associated with raising an extra dollar of revenues.

so the marginal revenue from increasing the tax is

$$MR = a - b\,(p + 2t).$$

The ratio of marginal revenue to marginal deadweight loss is

$$\frac{MR}{MDWL} = \frac{a - b(p + 2t)}{bt}$$

$$= \frac{Q}{bt} - 1$$

$$= k', \text{ the same for all commodities}$$

or

$$\frac{Q}{bt} = 1 + k' \equiv 1/k$$

or

$$t = k\,Q/b.$$

But the elasticity of demand is just

$$\eta_u^d = -\frac{\Delta Q/Q}{\Delta p/p} = \frac{bp}{Q}$$

so

$$\frac{t}{p} = \frac{kQ}{bp} = \frac{k}{\eta_u^d},$$

taxes are inversely proportional to demand elasticities.

21 Taxation of Capital

FOCUS QUESTIONS

1 What are the reasons why many argue that income from capital should be exempt from taxation?

2 What effect do capital taxes have on savings and investment? How can these effects be offset? Why are the effects different in a world with a global capital market?

3 What effect do taxes have on risk taking?

4 Why do depreciation, capital gains, and inflation pose problems for capital taxation? How are these problems addressed in our current tax system, and what are some of the resulting problems?

The previous chapter analyzed several of the central problems in tax design, including the trade-offs between redistribution and efficiency, their implication for the degree of progressivity of the tax system, and the role of commodity taxation in the design of an efficient tax system. But we made only passing reference to one of the most central problems in tax design: how to tax the returns to capital. Should income from capital—interest on bonds and savings accounts, dividends from stock, and the gains that come from selling assets at prices higher than original cost—be taxed at a higher or a lower rate than wage income?

Popular arguments have raged on all sides of this issue. "Capitalists are wealthier than working people," so, it is alleged, capital should be taxed more heavily.

On the other side: "Taxation of capital income represents double taxation—taxes have already been imposed when the principal (the original amount invested) was first earned." "Our economy depends on capital investment, and without incentives, there will be insufficient savings and investment." "Taxation of capital is distortionary; by eliminating capital taxation we eliminate one more government-imposed distortion."

The tax system has reflected many of the vagaries of popular discussions. Until 1981, the maximum tax rate on wage income was 50 percent, while the maximum tax rate on capital income was 70 percent. At the same time, certain forms of capital income were taxed at lower rates.

Yet many of these popular arguments—on both sides—are, if not fallacious, at least misleading. We have already explained what is wrong with arguments that just count the number of distortions. Even if capitalists are, on average, richer, it does not follow that capital income should be taxed more heavily, or even that it should be taxed at all. The issue is, *what is the appropriate basis for levying taxes?*

This chapter is divided into four sections. The first sets out the basic reasons for and against taxing income from capital. The middle sections discuss key efficiency and administrative issues: the impacts on savings and investment and on risk taking in both open and closed economies. The final section focuses on the complications for the taxation of capital posed by inflation, capital gains (the increase in the value of an asset over time), and depreciation (the decrease in value of an asset as it wears out or becomes obsolete).

At a practical level, corporations make the taxation of income from capital very complicated. The income of corporations, after paying wages, can largely be thought of as a return on capital. That return may be distributed to bondholders or shareholders or may be retained inside the firm. Eventually, of course, the owners of the company will receive the benefits of these retained earnings, in the form either of higher dividends or of an increased value of the shares in the corporation when they come to sell them. In principle, we could disregard the existence of corporations, that is, we could pretend that the firm distributed all of its profits to its shareholders, who then sent the company back a check (equal to the retained earnings) for reinvestment. The United States and most countries do not engage in such make-believe. They impose taxes on the income of corporations and on the income of individuals, when they receive their dividends or capital gains.

In this chapter, we attempt to ignore these complications by focusing on a simple economy in which individuals own their own firm, investing their savings in capital, facing decisions on how much to save and invest and what to invest in. The effects of taxes on capital are dependent on a number of the detailed provisions of the tax code, for instance, how the government treats assets as they wear out. We shall return to several of the themes in more detail in Chapters 22 and 23, where we look more closely at the individual and corporate income tax code in the United States. The issues raised in this chapter are of broader applicability, facing all countries as they think about the design of their tax system.

SHOULD CAPITAL BE TAXED?

Recent discussions of whether capital should be taxed have centered around three issues: equity, efficiency, and administrative complexity. Before beginning our detailed discussion, we need to review certain basic results on tax equivalence.

RELATIONSHIP BETWEEN CONSUMPTION TAXES, A WAGE TAX, AND EXEMPTING CAPITAL INCOME FROM TAXATION

In Chapter 18, we showed the equivalence between four tax structures: a proportional consumption tax, a proportional wage tax, an income tax with a tax exemption for income from capital, and a value-added tax, with an exemption for investment goods.[1] The equivalence is important, for it implies that the belief that capital should not be taxed is equivalent to the belief in a consumption tax or a wage tax. While the different taxes are equivalent, one way of describing a tax may make it look far less attractive than another way.

The equivalence is also important because it provides several alternative ways in which the same tax results can be implemented. Critics of consumption taxes often suggest that consumption is hard to measure. But consumption need not be measured directly: a prime example is the value-added tax with an exemption for investment, which is a very important tax in Europe.

EQUITY ISSUES

Both those who believe that capital should be taxed and those who believe it should not marshall equity arguments in their favor.

One of the most forceful arguments for basing taxes on consumption rather than on income was put forward more than seventy years ago by Irving Fisher, one of America's most distinguished economists. He argued that it was more appropriate to tax individuals on the basis of what they take out of society (their consumption) than on what they contribute to society (measured by their income).

Beyond this broad philosophical argument is the perspective that (ignoring inheritance), *taxing consumption is equivalent to taxing lifetime income,* as we saw in Chapter 18. Thus, with a consumption tax, two individuals with the same lifetime income have the same total tax burden. With an income tax, on the other hand, Imprudence, who puts nothing aside for the future, has a lower present discounted value of tax burden than does her sister Prudence, even though they have the same present discounted value of lifetime income. (Inequities are introduced if inheritances escape taxation, but under the current tax structure, at least for upper-income individuals, tax rates on inheritances are quite high.[2]) This argument supports excluding capital income from taxation, or equivalently, taxing consumption.

---

[1] Recall that this equivalence holds only if individuals receive no inheritances and leave no bequests.

[2] Though, historically, because of loopholes in the tax law, many bequests escaped taxation.

On the other hand, consumption taxes are often equated with sales taxes, and sales taxes are widely viewed as regressive. One reason for this is that sales taxes are imposed on only a portion of consumption, and the portion represents a smaller fraction of upper-income individuals' overall consumption than of lower-income individuals'. The consumption taxes under discussion here are levied on *all* consumption; and indeed, they can be levied at a progressive rate, so that the tax paid may go up more than proportionately with consumption. Progressive consumption taxes are thus also markedly different from value-added taxes, which are proportional.

Critics of a comprehensive consumption tax observe that since richer individuals save a larger fraction of their income than do poorer individuals, a proportional consumption tax is actually regressive, since the ratio of taxes to income for richer individuals is lower. But this ignores the basic issue of the appropriate tax base. If the *correct* tax base is consumption, then it makes no sense to compare tax payments with income; progressivity or regressivity should be judged by measuring tax payments relative to the appropriate tax base.

EFFICIENCY ARGUMENTS

There are three categories of efficiency arguments. One category focuses on the deadweight losses, using the kind of analysis introduced in Chapter 20. There, we showed that consumption at different dates could be treated like consumption of different commodities. And the basic argument that the most efficient way of obtaining redistributive goals is through a progressive wage income tax—with no differential commodity taxation—implies that there should be no differential taxation on consumption at different dates, which in turn implies that capital income should not be taxed.[3]

The second category of efficiency arguments focuses on the fact that we have a *hybrid system*, a mixture of a consumption tax and an income tax.

---

[3] The formal analysis makes a number of assumptions, such as that the only differences in individuals' income arise from differences in abilities; that relative wages are fixed; and that individuals' marginal rates of substitution between consumption early in life and later in life do not depend on how much they work. If these assumptions are only approximately satisfied, there will still be only little to gain from taxing interest income. In some cases, it will be desirable to impose an interest income subsidy, not an interest income tax. There are two circumstances under which a case for an interest income tax can be made: (a) If such a tax changes the before-tax distribution in a desirable way (if, for instance, decreasing the after-tax return to capital discourages savings, and if unskilled labor and capital are substitutes, the lower capital supply will increase the relative wages of the unskilled); since there is a deadweight loss in redistributing income, it is always desirable to incur some deadweight loss to change the before-tax distribution of income. (b) If individuals differ in their ability to invest, with some individuals obtaining a much higher return to their investments than others, then a wage tax alone (or equivalently, a consumption tax) will not be able to redistribute income efficiently. (The standard models assume that all individuals receive the same return on their capital.) Formally, if one attributes the extra return on capital to the individual's investing ability, then that extra return can be thought of as a return to labor. It is not possible, however, to make this distinction administratively.

Some forms of capital income, such as owner-occupied housing and retirement income, are essentially tax exempt. Others, such as capital gains, are taxed at a preferential rate. This hybrid may be less equitable, more distortionary, and more administratively complex than either a true income tax or a true consumption tax would be.

Popular discussions have not focused on these technical arguments of economists, but rather on a perception that the tax system discourages saving, investment, and risk taking, which are vital for a market economy. These potential effects have become of particular concern in recent years, as savings rates are so much lower in the United States than in Japan and Europe. Later sections of this chapter will address the validity of these concerns.

ADMINISTRATIVE PROBLEMS

Concern with the administrative complexity of our tax laws provides one of the strongest rationales for moving to a consumption base (exempting interest income). Much of the tax code's complexity arises from attempts to reduce opportunities for the avoidance of capital taxes. On the other hand, concern that consumption itself may be difficult to measure at one time provided an argument against a consumption tax. But one does not need actually to monitor an individual's purchases of goods in order to tax con-

---

ARGUMENTS FOR A CONSUMPTION-BASED TAX

Equity

• People should be taxed on what they take out of the system, not on what they contribute.

• Taxing life-cycle income (ignoring inheritances and bequests) is equivalent to taxing consumption: an income tax discriminates against those who prefer to consume later in life.

• A consumption-based tax can be made progressive.

Efficiency: A consumption tax lowers deadweight loss

• Eliminates discrimination against consumption later in life.

• Eliminates distortions arising from hybrid tax system, with some savings taxed differently from others.

Administrative Simplicity

• Much of the tax system's complexity arises from attempts to tax capital income and to reduce avoidance of capital income taxation.

---

sumption. Rather, all one needs to observe is an individual's cash flow. Since

Income = consumption + savings,

if one can measure income (total receipts, including gifts) and savings, one can infer the level of consumption. (The measurement of income for an income or consumption tax is identical.) The problem of measuring an individual's savings is not particularly difficult: one simple method calculates the total value of sales of securities during a year, less the total value of purchases during the same period.[4] The difference plus the individual's wage income is his cash flow and is equal to his consumption. Thus, the practical problems of implementing a consumption tax are at least no greater than those for implementing an income tax.

EFFECTS ON SAVINGS AND INVESTMENT

In Chapter 18, we discussed the ambiguous evidence concerning the effects of the interest income tax on savings. In this chapter, we assume that there is a negative effect on aggregate savings, and ask: What are the effects on the economy, and in particular on the level of investment and, eventually, on the capital stock? To the extent that a reduction in the level of savings gets translated into a reduction in the capital stock, output per worker will fall, and eventually there will be a reduction in standards of living.

EFFECTS OF REDUCED SAVINGS IN A CLOSED ECONOMY

Figure 21.1 illustrates the basic concern. There we have drawn a curve showing the demand for investment as a function of the interest rate and the supply of savings.[5] The intersection shows the initial equilibrium level of the interest rate, r_1, and investment, I_1. We now impose an interest income tax. The tax imposes a wedge between the return to investment and to savings, reducing the equilibrium level of investment to I_2. With lower levels of in-

---

[4] This understates the problem: not all asset sales and purchases are recorded, and there is some ambiguity between expenditures on assets and those on consumption. Particular problems arise in the transition; because there is no record of *current* asset holding, individuals could consume by selling currently owned assets. An individual might claim the purchase of a painting or a farm as an asset, not as an item of consumption. While these problems arise today, they might be exacerbated under a consumption tax. (Today, the problem is that an individual may sell a painting, failing to report the capital gain; under a consumption tax, he will claim that paintings that he really purchased for consumption purposes were purchased as investments.)

[5] This analysis makes one crucial simplification: There is only one asset (capital goods) which can be purchased with savings. In fact, there are other assets, including land and government bonds. Government tax policy affects the value of land. Tax policies which result in higher interest rates lead to lower land values; hence the magnitude of the decrease in capital is less than it would be in an economy with no land. If the value of land decreases, then more of savings can be directed into capital accumulation.

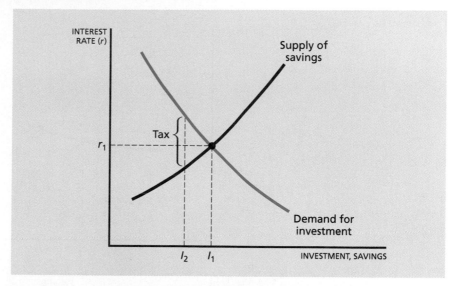

Supply of
savings

Tax

r_1

Demand for
investment

I_2 I_1 INVESTMENT, SAVINGS

FIGURE 21.1   **Effect of Tax on Interest Income on Equilibrium Investment in a Closed
Economy** A tax on the return to capital lowers the equilibrium level of
investment, and in the long run thus lowers the equilibrium capital stock.

vestment year after year, the economy's capital stock eventually is lowered
enough to affect adversely standards of living.

**THE DISTINCTION
BETWEEN SAVINGS
AND INVESTMENT**

In a closed economy, in equilibrium, savings must equal investment. Thus,
in equilibrium a policy which promotes savings must promote investment,
and conversely.

Some policies shift the supply of savings curve and some shift the demand for investment curve. For instance, an investment tax credit, in which
the government effectively pays part of the price of capital goods, shifts the
demand for investment curve up, as depicted in panel A of Figure 21.2. By
itself, this will lead to higher rates of interest and higher levels of investment.

Panel B shows how such policies can be used to offset (partially or totally) the effects of an interest income tax. In the new equilibrium, investment is the same.

Why, one might ask, impose a tax on savings and then simply offset its
effects by a subsidy to investment? The answer is that while investment may
be unaffected by this pair of policies, there may be significant other effects.
For instance, not all the return to savings is derived from investment in
plant and equipment in the United States; investors obtain returns from investments abroad and in real estate. Moreover, the investment subsidy only
affects new capital; taxes on the returns to capital affect old capital. As a result, the combination of a tax on the return to capital and a subsidy to new
investment has large redistribution effects, as the price of old capital falls
relative to new investments, and can raise substantial amounts of revenue.

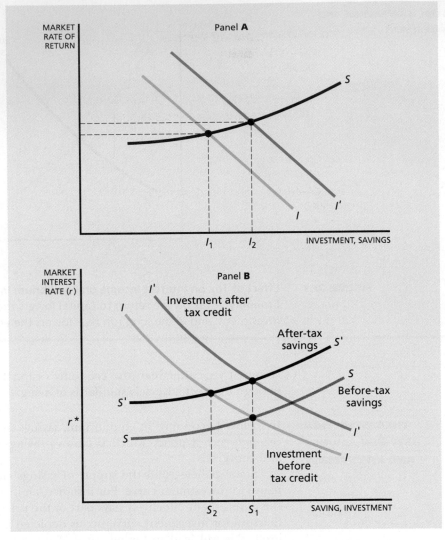

FIGURE 21.2 **Investment Tax Credits** Panel A: An investment tax credit shifts the demand curve for investment, and hence increases the equilibrium level of investment. Panel B: With an appropriately chosen rate, an investment tax credit can offset the effect of a tax on the return to capital, so that investment is left unchanged.

NATIONAL SAVINGS AND BUDGET NEUTRALITY

What matters for the nation's investment is, of course, not just the level of household or firm savings (private savings) but the level of national savings, which includes government savings—its budgetary surplus or deficit. Reducing the tax on the return to capital typically will lower government revenues, and hence increase the deficit, unless some other taxes are increased. Under plausible conditions, the increased deficit more than offsets the increased private savings, so that national savings—and hence investment—is actually reduced. If savings is relatively inelastic, then private savings will not be increased much, but the impact on the deficit can be considerable. Assume, for instance, that capital income amounted to 20 percent of GDP and that there was a 20 percent capital tax. Then the *short-run* effect of cutting in half the tax on capital income (ignoring any impact on interest rates) will be to lower government revenues by an amount equal to 2 percent of GDP—and thus the government deficit increases by an amount equal to 2 percent of GDP. If private savings currently equals 5 percent of GDP, and the interest elasticity is .1, then reducing the tax by 50 percent increases the return to capital by 12.5 percent, and increases savings by just over 1 percent, or .05 percent of GDP.[6] Hence national savings (private savings minus the government deficit) actually falls significantly.

On the other hand, if the government substitutes the decrease in the tax on capital income with an increase in the wage tax, in such a way as to leave the individual just as well off as before, then savings is unambiguously increased. This can be seen in Figure 21.3, where we have used a simplified model in which an individual lives two periods, denoted by C_1 and C_2, working in the first, and saving for her retirement in the second. BB is the individual's budget constraint before the interest income taxes, $B'B$ is her budget constraint after. E is the point chosen, and EF is the tax revenue (realized in the second period). DD is the budget constraint when a wage (or consumption) tax which leaves the individual just as well off is imposed. Now there is only a substitution effect, and the individual clearly consumes less; the incentive to save is increased. Thus private savings increases. Moreover, government revenue (in present value terms) is increased: the new tax revenue is $E'F'$, clearly greater than EF.[7] Thus the deficit is reduced. The magnitude of the increase in savings may, however, be relatively small, depending on the shapes of the indifference curves. Panel B shows the limiting case of L-shaped indifference curves, where private savings and government revenues are both unaffected.

These contrasting results emphasize how important it is to formulate the right question, being clear what is being held constant. Typically, the government is contemplating alternative ways of raising a given revenue. In that case, neither of the previous two formulations is quite correct. But the second provides a framework for arriving at the desired answer. Since a tax

---

[6] If we ignore the change in interest rates, after tax returns increase from $.8r$ to $.9r$, that is, by one-eighth. This induces an increase in private savings of 1.25 percent, or .0625 percent of GDP. The actual increase in private savings is somewhat greater: as the deficit increases, interest rates rise, and this elicits more savings, by an amount which depends on the interest elasticity of savings. Standard estimates suggest that approximately a third of the increased budgetary deficit might be offset by additional induced savings resulting from the higher interest rate, and hence the overall reduction in national savings might be only about one and a third percent of GDP—still a sizable sum. (When the induced flow of funds from abroad is also included in the analysis—as below—then the net impact on investment is reduced further, to approximately 2/3 of one percent of GDP.) If, on the other hand, the elasticity of savings is very large, increased private savings would more than offset the increased fiscal deficit.

[7] DD is parallel to BB (since there is no interest income tax). The distance between two parallel lines is the same everywhere. Thus, FG equals $E'F'$.

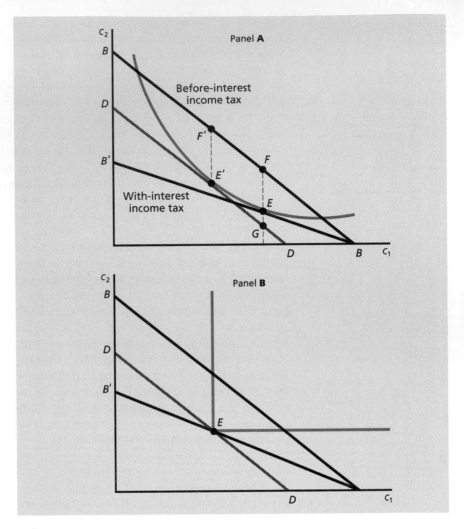

FIGURE 21.3   **Compensated Change in Tax** A reduction in the interest income tax compensated by an increase in a wage or consumption tax, in such a way as to leave the individual just as well off, leads to increased private savings and lower government deficits. Panel B shows the limiting case of L-shaped indifference curves, where neither savings nor government revenues are affected.

which generates equal utilities generates greater revenue with the consumption tax, the government could lower the tax rate. Thus, a consumption tax which raises the same revenue as an income tax generates a higher level of utility and national savings.[8]

[8] The timing of the government revenues may differ between the alternative regimes. The analysis compares taxes that generate the same present discounted value of revenues, using the before-tax interest rate.

But these effects may be greatly reduced in an open economy, where foreign savings can serve as a substitute for domestic savings. During the past three decades, a robust international capital market, allowing funds to flow from one country to another, has developed. In recent years, the United States has been borrowing hundreds of billions of dollars from Europe and Japan.[9] Slight increases in the U.S. rate of interest can draw into America large amounts of money. Many economists believe that as a result, the supply curve for funds to the United States is close to horizontal (see Figure 21.4).

Suppose that there are no taxes, and consider the limiting case where foreigners are willing to supply funds at an interest rate of r^*. That is, the supply of funds is infinitely elastic. The equilibrium interest rate would then be r^*, with S_1, being domestic savings, I_1 domestic investment, and the difference, $I_1 - S_1$, being financed by borrowing from abroad.

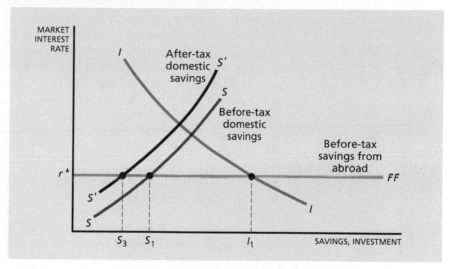

FIGURE 21.4   **Investment and Savings in an Open Economy** With well-developed international capital markets, foreign borrowing makes up the difference between domestic investment and domestic savings. If only the return to Americans is taxed, then investment will be unaffected, but domestic savings will be discouraged and borrowing from foreigners will rise.

[9] Between 1982 and 1986, the United States borrowed so heavily from abroad that it went from being the world's largest creditor nation to the largest debtor. The U.S. net international investment position—the excess of foreign assets owned by U.S. banks, multinational corporations, and individuals over and above the value of U.S. assets held by foreigners—stood at $147 billion in 1982 and at approximately *negative* $250 billion in 1986. (The main reasons for this change were the large federal deficits, discussed in Chapter 2.) By 1997 the net foreign indebtedness of the United States stood at $1322.5 billion. See Russell B. Scholl, "The International Investment Position of the United States," U.S. Department of Commerce, Bureau of Economic Analysis, *Survey of Current Business*, July 1998, pp. 24–34.

Now, a tax on the return to savings *by Americans* does nothing more than effectively shift the supply curve of savings up and to the left, as depicted in Figure 21.4. The level of investment remains unchanged, but now more of the investment is financed by savings from abroad. But while there is no effect on investment, and thus on the level of productivity in the United States, in the long run there is an adverse effect on standards of living. For in the long run, Americans will owe more money to foreigners; more of what is produced in America will have to be sent abroad to pay this indebtedness.

The real world is somewhere between the perfect global capital market just described and the closed capital market discussed in the previous section. Foreign capital is not a perfect substitute for domestic savings. Indeed, empirical studies show a high correlation between domestic savings and investment.[10]

As a result, changes in tax policy which affect domestic savings do affect domestic investment. Earlier, we looked at an example where capital income amounted to 20 percent of GDP, the capital income tax rate was 20 percent, the interest elasticity of savings was .1. We showed that a reduction of the tax by 50 percent would reduce national savings (at a fixed before-tax interest rate) by almost 2 percent of GDP. But this shift in the national savings "curve" itself leads to higher interest rates, which themselves lead to more domestic savings and increased flows of capital from abroad. Standard estimates suggest that the increased domestic savings would amount to about .7 percent of GDP, and the increased capital flows would also amount to about .7 percent of GDP. Since

Funds for investment = private savings − government deficit + capital flows from abroad = investment,

this means that investment will be reduced by only .7 percent, much less than if there were no capital flows from abroad.

IMPACT ON RISK TAKING

Without entrepreneurs undertaking risks, the capitalist economy would not have grown in the way that it has over the past two centuries, leading to immense increases in standards of living. No wonder, then, that there is alarm about any part of the tax system which might dampen entrepreneurial risk-taking. There is concern that taxes on capital discourage not only the overall level of savings and investment, but, in particular, the amount of risk taking.

[10] See, for example, Earl L. Grinols, "The Link between Domestic Investment and Domestic Savings in Open Economies: Evidence from Balanced Stochastic Growth," *Review of International Economics* 4, no. 2 (June 1996): 119–40. The correlation may be partly because domestic conditions that promote savings tend also to promote investment; it may be because much of investment is financed by firms themselves, so that when investment returns are high, they save more, or when their profits are high, so they can save more, they invest more.

Although some individuals enjoy taking risks on a regular basis, and almost all individuals enjoy taking small risks occasionally (as evidenced by the popularity of state lotteries and the gambling casinos of Atlantic City and Las Vegas), when it comes to managing their wealth, most individuals are more conservative. They are willing to take risks, but only if they receive, as compensation, a sufficiently high expected return over what they could have obtained in a safe investment. There is widespread concern that taxing the return to capital is effectively taxing the return to risk bearing, the risk premium that individuals receive for bearing additional risks, and thus discourages risk taking.

The fruits of risk taking undertaken by entrepreneurs are all around us: major inventions like the automobile, the airplane, and the computer were, in part, the result of investors and firms deciding to gamble their wealth on a new idea. These were the successes, and those undertaking the gamble earned huge rewards. For each of these successes, however, there were dozens of failures. But while the government takes away much of the fruits of success, it is often not as generous in helping to bear the costs of failure, a situation that exacerbates an already present market failure: the absence of insurance markets.[11] Normally, entrepreneurs can only partially divest themselves of the risks associated with their entrepreneurial activity. There is thus concern that even without the interference of the tax system, there would be too little (from a social perspective) investment in risk-taking activities.

WHY CAPITAL TAXATION WITH FULL LOSS DEDUCTIBILITY MAY INCREASE RISK TAKING

There is some controversy over the extent to which current taxes reduce risk taking. It is possible that they may actually increase it.

That the income tax might increase risk taking can be seen most easily by considering an extreme example. Assume that an individual has to decide between two assets: a safe asset yielding no return, and a risky asset that has a 50 percent chance of yielding a very large return and a 50 percent chance of yielding a negative return. The average return is positive, to compensate the individual for risk taking. The individual is conservative and so allocates a fraction of his wealth to the safe asset and the remainder to the risky asset.

We now impose a tax on the return to capital, but we allow a full deduction against other income for losses. The safe asset is unaffected. The risky

---

[11] There are several explanations for this market failure. For instance, investors typically have limited information concerning the potential risks and returns of investment projects, and it is costly to obtain more complete information. There is an infinite supply of charlatans willing to take money for harebrained schemes. Those most willing to sell shares in their projects are those who believe the market has overvalued them. See, for instance, Bruce Greenwald, Joseph E. Stiglitz, and Andrew Weiss, "Informational Imperfections in the Capital Market and Macroeconomic Fluctuations," *American Economic Review* 74 (2): 194–99; and Stewart C. Myers and Nicholas S. Majluf, "Corporate Financing and Investment Decisions When Firms Have Information That Investors Do Not Have," *Journal of Financial Economics* 13, no. 2 (June 1984): 187–221.

RISK TAKING AND THE 1993 TAX ACT

In the 1993 tax bill, the Clinton administration expressed strong concern for encouraging risk taking by new entrepreneurs. A special provision introduced by Senator Dale Bumpers of Arkansas permits investors to exclude 50 percent of gains held in new enterprises for at least five years. The amount of gain eligible for exclusion is the lesser of ten times what the taxpayer paid for the asset or $10 million.

asset has its return reduced by half, but the losses are also reduced by half. How does the individual respond to this? If he doubles the amount he previously invested in the risky asset, his after-tax income when the return is positive is the same, and his after-tax income when the return is negative is also the same. The tax has left him completely unaffected. Effectively, the government is sharing in the risks of the individual. By its willingness to share the risks—the losses as well as the gains—it is acting as a silent partner. And because the government is willing to share the risk, the individual is willing to increase his risk taking.[12]

The importance of the government's sharing in risk taking depends on how well the private market does. For securities that are actively traded on the stock market, the risks are widely spread throughout the economy. For smaller firms, however, the government may be able to provide risk-sharing opportunities that the market cannot provide.

This situation has one other interesting property: The tax yields on average a return to the government, but it has no effect on the welfare of the individual. The individual is unaffected because his after-tax position is the same as it was in the before-tax situation (whether the risky asset turns out to have a positive or negative return). This tax seems to do what no other tax seems capable of doing: it raises revenue (on average) without lowering welfare.

WHY CAPITAL TAXATION MAY REDUCE RISK TAKING

Before becoming too excited about the prospect of raising revenue without lowering welfare, one must keep several caveats in mind. First, with a progressive tax structure, returns to successful investments are taxed more heavily than losses from unsuccessful investments are subsidized. There is thus a built-in bias against risk taking.

[12] For an early discussion of the effect of taxation on risk taking, see E. D. Domar and R. A. Musgrave, "Proportional Income Taxation and Risk-Taking," *Quarterly Journal of Economics* 58 (1944): 388–422. The standard current view is presented in J. E. Stiglitz, "The Effects of Income, Wealth and Capital Gains Taxation on Risk Taking." *Quarterly Journal of Economics* 83 (1969): 262–83. See also A. B. Atkinson and J. E. Stiglitz, *Lectures on Public Economics* (New York: McGraw-Hill, 1980), Chapter 4; and A. Sandmo, "The Effects of Taxation on Savings and Risk-Taking," in *Handbook of Public Economics*, vol. 1, ed. A. Auerbach and M. Feldstein (Amsterdam: North Holland, 1985), pp. 293–309.

The provision was designed to encourage risk taking in new enterprises by engendering "patient capital." Now investors would have greater incentive to commit their funds for at least five years, and thus firms would enjoy an environment favorable to longer-run projects with higher risk. Many advocates of the provision believed Wall Street to be dominated by the pursuit of short-run gains, and saw the legislation as a way to correct the problem.

Second, in the current system, there are limitations on the magnitudes of the losses that can be offset. Thus the government, while sharing in the gains, shares in only some of the losses. Again, there is a bias against risk taking. The 1986 Tax Reform Act increased the severity of this limitation by providing that individuals cannot subtract losses from certain investment activities from their wage income in computing their income for tax purposes. (The limitation was imposed to reduce opportunities for tax avoidance through tax shelters. While the provision achieved that goal, it added greatly to the complexity of the tax code and worsened the tax laws' bias against risk taking.)

A final difficulty is that we have assumed that the safe rate of return is zero. If there is a significant positive return on safe assets, and if it is taxed, there will be a significant wealth effect associated with the capital income tax. That is, because the individual is worse off (he is, in a sense "less wealthy"), he is willing to take less risks; thus the wealth effect may lead to the reduction in the demand for risky assets. But this wealth effect would have occurred with a lump-sum tax as well—it is not a distortion, but simply a reflection of a lower willingness to take risks at lower levels of wealth.

Although the government in effect shares in the *financial* costs of investments, it does not share in the *effort* costs of entrepreneurs. The long hours put in by the innovators who contributed so much to the computer industry, such as Stephen Jobs, the founder of Apple Computers, are now legend. Most of the returns they obtained from this effort were in the form of gains on the sale of the companies that they started. There has been a real concern that high rates of taxation of capital gains will serve to discourage such risk taking and entrepreneurship. Concern about these adverse incentive effects of taxation was part of the motivation for the large reduction in capital gains tax rates in 1997. Others contend, however, that innovators are driven by other than monetary incentives, and that the tax on capital gains has only minimal effects. In this view, there was little incentive benefit from the reduction in capital gains tax rates. The real point of the reduction in capital gains taxes was to reduce the overall degree of progressivity of the tax system, since most capital gains accrue to the very rich.

CAPITAL TAXATION AND RISK TAKING

If the return on safe assets were zero and the government taxed gains and subsidized losses at the same rate, then capital taxation would encourage risk taking; the government would be, in effect, a silent partner. In practice, provisions for loss deductibility are limited, so that the net effect is to discourage risk taking. In addition, the wealth effect of capital taxation—it makes individuals poorer—may result in less risk taking, because poorer individuals are less willing to bear risks.

MEASURING CHANGES IN ASSET VALUES

Returns on capital come in two main forms—dividends and interest payments, and capital gains. An individual is better off when her assets increase in value, just as she would be better off if she received a dividend. If capital gains could be measured perfectly, there would be no reason to treat capital gains differently from any other return to capital. Indeed, for some assets—like holding gold—the only return is the capital gain. Thus, *if* the returns to capital are to be taxed, then it makes sense to tax the returns in whatever form they take, including capital gains. But by the same token, a decrease in the value of an asset constitutes a negative return, and that loss needs to be subtracted from the other returns (such as dividends) to ascertain the net return. The problem is that it is often difficult to measure either the increase or the decrease in the value of an asset. Tax codes throughout the world have dealt with this problem by, in effect, giving the taxpayer the benefit of the doubt: in the case of capital gains, the individual typically does not have to pay any tax until the gain is *recognized*, that is, until the asset is actually sold. For assets for which there are active markets—like widely traded stocks and bonds—it would in fact be easy to tax the capital gains on an annual basis, that is, simply by comparing the value of shares at the end of the year and to their value at the beginning of the year. The difference would constitute the capital gain. Such a system is called *marking-to-market*. However, for many assets, such as real estate, it is impossible to tell the value with any accuracy except when a deal is consummated; and there is a worry that treating some assets one way and others another way would not only be confusing, but also could create biases in the choice of assets.

In the case of depreciation, the taxpayer is allowed to deduct an estimate of the loss of value as a result of aging or obsolescence. The estimates are based on simple rules, which typically are overly generous, that is, they allow a larger loss of value in the early years of the asset, so that the present discounted value of the depreciation allowances is greater than it would be with "true" depreciation—that is, the decrease in value that would have occurred if there were a perfect competitive market for used capital.

We measure gains and losses in dollars, but the value of a dollar changes over time, as a result of inflation (see below).

CAPITAL GAINS

Because capital gains are taxed only upon realization, an individual who owns a security that has increased in value may be reluctant to sell it. She knows that if she sells it she will have to pay a tax. If she continues to hold the asset, she can postpone the tax until some later date. The present discounted value of her tax liabilities is reduced by the postponement of the tax. The individual is thus induced to hold on to her securities rather than to sell them. This distortion is referred to as the **locked-in effect.**

The consequences of this may easily be seen. Assume that an individual bought a security last month at $1, and that it suddenly rises to $101. She now expects that it will earn a return lower than the return she could obtain elsewhere. Assume, for instance, that she believes that there is another investment opportunity that could earn a return of 10 percent. In the absence of taxation, she would simply sell her security and buy the new investment.

Consider now what happens if she sells her security. She must immediately pay a capital gains tax.[13] Assuming she is in the 28 percent tax bracket, she must pay a tax of $28. She would thus have only $73 to reinvest.

Assume she believes she will need money in one year's time. Her after-tax yield in the new investment is $(1 - .20) \times 10\% = 8\%$. In one year's time she will thus have $73 \times 1.08 = \$78.84$. On the other hand, if she keeps her $101 in the old investment for one more year, and it increases in value at only 8 percent, she will have $101 \times 1.08 = \$109.08$. She must pay a capital gains tax of 20 percent on her gain (that is, her tax is $.20 \times \$108.08 = \$21.62$). Thus, after tax she has $87.46. She is better off with her money yielding a return of only 8 percent in her current asset than she would be if she sold her asset and purchased an asset yielding a much higher return of 10 percent.

CONSEQUENCES AND IMPORTANCE OF THE LOCKED-IN EFFECT There is considerable debate about the consequences and importance of this locked-in effect. Martin Feldstein, former chairman of the Council of Economic Advisers under President Reagan has claimed that the effect is so large that reducing the capital gains tax would lead individuals to sell securities that they previously had refused to sell, to such an extent that government revenues would actually increase.[14] But more recent estimates[15] suggest that a

[13] Her capital gains tax rate for short-term gains (less than 12 months) is equal to her personal income tax bracket; on long-term gains, the tax rate is 20 percent.

[14] M. S. Feldstein, J. Slemrod, and S. Yitzhaki, "The Effects of Taxing on Selling and Switching of Common Stock and the Realization of Capital Gains," *Quarterly Journal of Economics* 94 (1980): 777–91.

[15] See L. Burman and W. Randolph, "Measuring Permanent Responses to Capital Gains Tax Changes in Panel Data," *American Economic Review* 84, no. 4 (September 1994): 794–809.

The U.S. capital gains tax rate was reduced substantially in 1997: for high-income individuals, from 28 percent to 20 percent; for those in lower tax brackets, from 15 percent to 10 percent. A major issue in the debate was equity: The ownership of assets is much more concentrated than income. Thus a reduction in capital gains tax rates mainly benefits those at the very top.

permanent reduction in the capital gains tax rate would have little effect. This is in contrast to a temporary reduction. Clearly, if individuals believe that the tax during, say, the next two years will be substantially lower than subsequently, they will sell during this period; it is as if the government is having a sale. This effect is particularly pronounced if the tax reduction has been anticipated, for then individuals who might have sold their assets shortly before the lower tax takes effect decide that it is worthwhile postponing the sale for a short period.

Even if the locked-in effect is significant, however, there may be only a short-run revenue gain: the taxes that individuals pay now will not be paid later, so government revenues in the long run may be little changed. Moreover, because the reduction in the tax makes individuals better off, the tax may lead to an increase in current consumption and a decrease in aggregate savings at the same time that current government revenues are increased.

Interestingly, the 1997 tax changes were actually designed to encourage individuals to hold on to their assets longer. Under the legislation, assets held for more than twelve months are subjected to a rate of 20 percent (10 percent for those in the 15 percent income tax bracket); assets held for less than twelve months are subjected to a rate of 28 percent.

Even those who argue that there is a significant locked-in effect generally agree that it is largely the result of a special provision in the U.S. tax system which allows assets that are held until death to escape capital gains taxation. Thus, while younger people simply save on the *timing* of tax payments by postponing realization—and when interest rates are low, the resulting discounted value of tax savings is relatively low—for elderly individuals, the savings from postponing realizations may be very high, since they may be able to avoid the tax completely. The remedy for this problem is not, of course, to lower the capital gains tax rate, but to eliminate this special provision.[16]

[16] Technically, this provision is referred to as a "step-up in basis at death." An individual who inherits a security and then sells it is taxed on the increase in the value from the time he inherited it. By contrast, if someone gives a security to another as a gift, and then the recipient subsequently sells it, he is taxed on the capital gain *from the time the asset was originally purchased.* The cost to the U.S. Treasury from the "step-up in basis" is estimated at billions of dollars per year.

Various proposals were put forward to share more equitably the benefits from reducing capital gains taxes. For instance, it was proposed that up to $100,000 of capital gains be eligible for the special treatment in any year, or that individuals be allowed the special treatment on $1 million over their lifetime. These proposals were, however, rejected, and as a result, the overall progressivity of the income tax was substantially reduced.

EQUITY Those advocating special treatment of capital gains often point out that the tax is levied not on real capital gains—taking into account the effects of inflation—but on nominal capital gains. This, it is argued, is unfair. But unlike other forms of capital income, the tax is imposed only on realization, and this provides a significant benefit. One can ask, would an investor have been better off if the tax was levied on real capital gains, as they accrue, than under the current system? The answer depends on the period over which the asset was held: for many investors, the benefits of postponement more than offset the costs of taxing nominal income; this is especially true for investors who finance a significant part of their investments by borrowing.

There are further debates about the welfare consequences of the locked-in effect. Much of the discussion has focused on individuals' purchases of securities. Economic efficiency requires that each security be held by the individual who values it the most, who thinks that it will yield the highest return.[17] The locked-in effect means that an individual may retain a security even though there is someone else who values it more. This results in what is referred to as **exchange inefficiency.** Some economists believe, however, that the economic consequences of this should not be taken too seriously. They argue that the stock market is essentially a gambling casino for the rich and that though the locked-in effect may impair the efficiency of this gambling casino, it has few further repercussions for the economy. There is not, in their view, a very direct or strong relationship between the effect of the capital gains tax on the performance of the stock market and the decisions made by the managers and owners of firms concerning, for instance, investment and production.

The one area in which the capital gains tax may have a significant effect on the production efficiency of the economy is in smaller, owner-managed firms. There comes a point in the life cycle of such firms where the original

---

[17] We define economic efficiency in the usual sense of Pareto efficiency. In the presence of risk, however, there is some question about the appropriate way of measuring the welfare of each individual. The sense in which we use the term here is in terms of the individual's own expectations concerning the outcome, regardless of the objective reality of those expectations.

A favorite pastime of economists is to look for unintended distortions arising from seemingly innocuous tax provisions. One such example is the movable wall, which has become popular in the United States. There are markedly different depreciation rates for buildings and equipment—today, nonresidential buildings depreciate over thirty-nine years, equipment over five to ten years. The boundaries between the two are often not well defined. Clearly, a wall is part of a structure, and should be depreciated with

owner-manager's skills and talents become less appropriate for the development of the firm. In the absence of capital gains taxation, the original owner-manager might want to sell his firm to some other entrepreneurs; but the high cost imposed by the capital gains tax discourages him from doing so.

DEPRECIATION

Not all assets increase in value over time. Typically, machines become less valuable as they get older. This reduction in value is called **depreciation.** They suffer a capital loss. Conceptually, again, there is no problem in the tax treatment of depreciation: just as capital gains should be added to income, capital losses should be subtracted from it. The problem is an operational one: How do we measure the capital losses? The tax code provides for **depreciation allowances,** which are meant to be estimates of the decrease in value.

The reason that it is so important to make some provision for depreciation is illustrated by the following example. Consider a machine that lasts for, say, five years, after which it dies. The machine generates a revenue stream of $100 a year. The net income is clearly not $100 a year ($500 over the five years). Some account must be taken of the fact that each year, the machine is older, and that eventually it will wear out.

True economic depreciation is the actual decrease in the machine's market value. But because markets for most types of used machines are not well developed, the government has no easy way of ascertaining what the true decrease in market value is. Instead of using the true value of economic depreciation, the government uses simple procedures which are supposed to approximate actual depreciation, giving some benefit of the doubt to the investors. The procedures entail first estimating the average life of the machine: cars, for example, live on average for six years; commercial buildings for more than thirty years; office equipment for five or ten years. The depreciation allowances are then spread out over the life of the machine. The simplest procedure, called **straight-line depreciation,** allows the investor to deduct one-tenth of the purchase price for a ten-year machine, one-fifth for a five-year machine. (See Figure 21.5 on page 598.)

the rest of the structure. But when is a wall not a wall? If the wall is movable, it could be called equipment—after all, it could be moved from one building to another. To be part of the structure, it must be *attached*. There are, to be sure, other reasons for making walls detached from the structure: for example, it allows for more flexible use of space, in response to changing circumstances. But no doubt one of the determinants of the move to movable walls was the large tax advantage.

NEUTRAL TAXATION

To achieve neutrality in the choice of investment projects, the government has two options. One option we have already described: it would allow true economic depreciation allowances (or at least would attempt to devise rules that more closely approximate true economic depreciation).

The second method entails the government's allowing a 100 percent deduction for the cost of the investment. Then the government would be reducing the costs of the project by exactly the same amount that it is reducing the benefits (the returns that the investor receives). The government, in effect, would be entering as a silent partner into the enterprise. A project for which the present discounted value of returns exceeds the cost—which therefore would have been undertaken in the absence of the tax—would still be undertaken.

While the first method corresponds to a neutral capital income tax (i.e., one that does not distort the choice of investment projects), the second method corresponds to a neutral pure profits tax: the difference between the present discounted value of the returns to an investment project and its costs can be thought of as pure profits.[18]

In practice, many governments do not seek to achieve neutral taxation, but actually use the tax system to encourage investment in capital by **accelerated depreciation,** that is, by allowing depreciation even faster than straight-line depreciation. In Chapter 23, we shall look at some of the ways that this has been done in the United States.

INFLATION

Inflation presents several difficult problems in the definition of income from capital. One wants to tax *real* returns to capital, not nominal returns. If an individual owns an asset, and it increases in value by 10 percent, but prices in general have gone up by 10 percent, the individual is no better off. His **real capital gain** is zero, even though his **nominal capital gain** is positive.

[18] Some of the return may be attributed to managerial efforts, in which case the difference between the present discounted value of the returns and the *direct* costs (excluding those associated with management) is a mixture of pure profits and return to management and entrepreneurship.

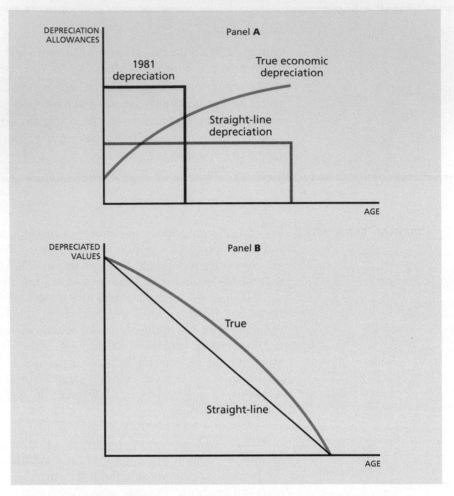

FIGURE 21.5 **Depreciation Schedules** Panel A: Straight-line depreciation entails the same depreciation allowance every year. For an asset with a constant stream of returns over a fixed life, true economic depreciation entails lower depreciation allowances in earlier years than in later years. Under the tax law in effect between 1981 and 1986, firms were allowed to use asset lifetimes that were much shorter than their true lifetimes. Panel B: Panel B shows the *depreciated value of the asset*, that is, the cost of the asset minus the sum of the depreciation allowances up to that date. This panel makes clear why "straight-line" depreciation has that name.

Similarly, consider an individual who puts $1000 in a savings account and receives $100 in interest. If the rate of inflation is 10 percent, the *real return* is zero. The $100 in interest is just enough to compensate him for the decrease in the real value of his savings account.

By the same token, inflation reduces the *real value* of the depreciation allowances, which are tied to the nominal price that the individual or the firm paid for the asset, and it does so much more for long-lived assets than for short-lived assets. In the late 1970s and early 1980s, the United States went through a period of high inflation, with annual rates of price increases exceeding 10 percent. (This was low by standards in other countries, where in extraordinary cases inflation rates have exceeded 100 percent *per month.*) It became clear that when inflation rates were high, our tax system did not treat returns to capital in a fair or efficient manner.

The tax system taxes nominal returns, not real returns. Thus, the first consequence of the presence of inflation is that individuals who have a small positive before-tax real return on capital find that they have a large negative after-tax real return.

Consider an individual in the 33 percent tax bracket, receiving a 12 percent return (say, in the form of interest) with an inflation rate of 10 percent. In periods of high inflation most of the return is just an adjustment for the decreased purchasing power of money. His real return is only 2 percent. (The real rate of return on an asset is the nominal return minus the rate of inflation.) But present tax laws do not take account of this. This individual would have to pay 33 percent of the nominal return to the government (ignoring state and local income taxes), leaving him a net after-tax return of 8 percent. With inflation, his real return is 8 percent − 10 percent = − 2 percent. He loses 2 percent of his ability to consume simply by postponing consumption by one year. One would expect that this would serve as a strong disincentive to savings.

Between 1974 and 1982 the price of stock was doing little more than keeping up with inflation (and in many cases not even doing that). But since the price level doubled, individuals found themselves paying a large capital gains tax if they sold their shares. Again, this seemed unfair.

There has been strong support for **indexing** tax brackets, that is, adjusting them to offset the effects of inflation, and since 1986 tax brackets, the standard deduction, and personal exemptions have all been indexed. As a result, the income levels at which taxpayers become subject to higher tax rates increase with the price level. Far more complicated than indexing the tax brackets, however, is designing the tax system so that only real returns to capital are taxed. Not only must capital gains be indexed, but so must interest payments, as well as interest receipts and depreciation. Thus, investors who have borrowed money would be able to deduct only their real interest payments, not their nominal interest payments. If capital gains were indexed but interest payments were not indexed, individuals would find it profitable in inflationary times to borrow to purchase capital assets that were increasing in value at the same rate as the rate of inflation.

The fact that much of capital gains are illusory—that is, they do not represent real increases in value—has been one of the motivations for the special treatment of long-term capital gains, such as the lower tax rates enacted in 1997. But as we noted earlier, the benefits of postponing taxes (capital gains are taxed only upon realization, not as they occur) have, at least in the past, more than offset the "unfair" taxation of inflation gains. More generally, taxing capital gains at a lower rate provides a very imperfect substitute for indexing: especially given the low inflation rates today, assets held for only a short period have almost no inflationary component, and thus the much lower rate at which they are taxed cannot be justified by inflation alone. Moreover, indexing capital gains, without indexing other forms of return or borrowing, creates large distortions.

Indeed, there has been some controversy over whether the tax system encouraged or discouraged investment in the inflationary period of the late 1970s. On the one hand, the fact that nominal interest payments were fully tax deductible while 60 percent of capital gains was tax-exempt created, in some cases, effective subsidies to capital. On the other hand, the fact that depreciation allowances were not indexed served to discourage investment.

It is apparent that our current tax system is not inflation-neutral; that as a result of inflation, in some circumstances, assets with a positive before-tax return have a negative after-tax return, discouraging investment, while in other cases, the tax system encourages investment.

What is required to obtain an inflation-neutral tax system is *full indexation*. Partial indexation of capital income (such as indexing capital gains but not debt) would exacerbate some of the distortions and would leave other distortions unchanged.[19]

In the debate leading up to the capital gains tax cut in 1997, the inequity associated with taxing nominal returns was emphasized by advocates of a reduction. But they failed to note the favorable treatment that results from the fact that capital gains are taxed only upon realization, and no one proposed full indexation, in particular allowing only real interest payments to be deductible, though a proposal to tax only real capital gains actually passed the House of Representatives. The lower tax rates that were enacted are, at best, a rough correction for the effects of inflation, which would have eroded the value of an asset held for twenty years far more than the value of one held for five.

KEY PROBLEMS IN IMPLEMENTING CAPITAL TAXES

• Measuring capital gains: increases in value

• Measuring depreciation: decreases in value as a result of machines wearing out or becoming obsolete

• Inflation: separating out real gains from inflationary gains

---

[19] There are other distortions in the tax system which may partially offset the distortions associated with the inappropriate treatment of inflation. For instance, the fact that failure to index depreciation results in excessively high taxation of especially long-lived assets is offset (with high inflation only partially; with very low inflation, more than completely) by the fact that depreciation formulae—even straight-line depreciation—typically are accelerated relative to true economic depreciation.

CAPITAL GAINS, DEPRECIATION, AND INFLATION

• Capital gains typically are taxed only upon the sale of the asset. This gives rise to the locked-in effect. The significance of the locked-in effect is, however, open to question.

• Most tax systems provide overly generous allowances for depreciation. Such provisions not only encourage investment, but also distort investment patterns, for instance favoring longer-term investments.

• The tax system taxes nominal, not real, returns. While there is now more indexing in the U.S. tax system than there used to be, returns to capital, including capital gains, are not indexed. Partial indexing—indexing capital gains but not debt—may be more distortionary than the current system. At the inflation rates that prevailed in the 1990s, the distortions associated with the failure to index taxation are small.

The decline in the inflation rate in the 1990s has taken much of the heat out of the issue. Moreover, there is a growing consensus that the way inflation is measured probably overstates the inflation rate, and possibly by a considerable amount (between 1 and 2 percentage points a year). Still, if the inflation rate again increases to the level attained in the 1970s, there will be a renewed concern about the distortions and inequities associated with the taxation of nominal returns to capital.

REVIEW AND PRACTICE

SUMMARY

1 There are both equity and efficiency reasons for arguing that income from capital should not be taxed. Some argue against the taxation of capital on the grounds that it involves heavy administrative costs; capital taxation accounts for much of the complexity of the tax code.

2 The taxation of the return to capital tends to reduce savings and investment. In a small open economy, in which only the returns to domestic investors are taxed, investment is unchanged but there is increased borrowing from abroad. In the U.S. economy today—a large open economy—taxation of savings does lead to some lowered investment, but less than would be the case if the United States could not borrow from abroad.

3 Investment tax credits can be used to encourage investment. Investment tax credits lead to a discrepancy between the price of new and old capital goods; a tax on savings offset by an investment tax credit can still have large redistribution effects.

4 A tax on capital with full loss offset provisions (so that the government in effect subsidizes losses at the same rate that it taxes gains) would—with a zero safe return to capital—typically increase risk taking; the government would be acting as a silent partner. Generally, loss offset provisions are very limited, so that the taxation of capital may reduce risk taking. With a positive return to the safe asset, a tax on capital typically makes individuals worse off, and at a lower level of welfare, they are less willing to undertake risk.

5 Capital gains—the increases in the value of assets over time—are just another form in which individuals receive a return to capital and should be taxed the same as other returns. There are, however, serious problems in the measurement of both capital gains and losses.

6 The fact that capital gains are taxed only when the asset is sold gives rise to the locked-in effect; individuals may retain an asset when, in the absence of taxation, they would have sold it. In the United States, however, the locked-in effect arises mainly because assets held until death completely escape capital gains taxation.

7 Because the actual decrease in the value of an asset as it wears out or becomes obsolete cannot be easily measured, governments use simple rules to estimate depreciation (called depreciation allowances). Even the simplest rules, such as taking off one-tenth the value of an asset each year for an asset that lasts ten years, tend to be excessively generous, that is, they provide allowances in early years that exceed true economic depreciation (the decrease in the value of the asset in a perfect competitive capital market). As a result, they introduce distortions, with longer-lived assets typically being favored. Tax neutrality requires either that depreciation allowances correspond to true economic depreciation, or that the total value of the asset be depreciated in the year of purchase (in which case the tax becomes a tax on pure profits, not a tax on the return to capital).

8 Ideally, the tax system would tax real returns, not nominal returns; there would be full indexing for inflation. But inflation is hard to measure. Partial indexing—indexing of capital gains but not of debt—may result in even greater distortions than no indexation.

KEY CONCEPTS

Net investment tax credit	Real capital gain
Locked-in effect	Straight-line depreciation
Depreciation	Accelerated depreciation
Depreciation allowances	Real versus nominal capital gain
True economic depreciation	Indexing

1   It is difficult to ascertain precisely the decline in the value of most assets as they grow older. An exception is automobiles. Assume that a new car costs $5000; that its value at the end of one year is $4000, at the end of two years $3000, at the end of three years $2000; and that it loses $250 in value for each of the following eight years. What is the true economic depreciation? What is the present discounted value of this, assuming a 5 percent after-tax interest rate? What will be the depreciation allowances under the current system? What is the present discounted value of these depreciation allowances? (Cars are treated as five-year assets.)

2   Supporters of accelerated depreciation in 1981 acknowledged that it favored heavy industry ("smokestack America") but argued that this was desirable. Why do economists tend to look askance at such arguments? Can you identify any major market failures? If it were decided to subsidize these industries, in what other ways might it be done?

3   The government has tried to encourage savings by allowing individuals to save a limited amount for their retirement, without facing taxes on interest. Assume individuals can put, say, $2000 a year in a retirement account (called an individual retirement account, or IRA), and that the interest would not be taxed. Draw the individual's budget constraint (between consumption today and consumption at retirement) with and without the IRA. Describe the income and substitution effects for (a) an individual who was planning to save a little; (b) an individual who was planning to save a great deal. In each case, what difference might it make if the individual has other assets, such as a savings account? Discuss the equity and efficiency consequences of changing the rules so that only amounts in excess of $2000 per year are afforded special tax treatment.

4   In the debate concerning repeal of the provision allowing capital gains on assets passed on to one's heirs to escape taxation, some have reasoned that death is not voluntary, and therefore one should not tax capital gains upon death. Evaluate.

5   Assume there are two "states of the world"; in the good state, a risky asset yields a high return; in the bad state, it yields a loss. The safe asset yields a zero return in both. Let C_g denote consumption in the good state, C_b in the bad. Draw a figure with consumption in the good state on the vertical axis and consumption in the bad on the horizontal axis. Draw a 45° line. In the figure, let S represent the individual's consumption in the two states if she invests only in the safe asset (consumption in the two states is the same), while R represents her consumption in the two states if she invests only in the risky asset (a higher consumption in the good state, a lower one in the bad). Explain why the line SR shows her consumption possibilities—her consumption in the two states depending on the proportion of her assets that she invests in the safe or risky asset. Now draw an indifference curve

showing the bundles of consumption in the two states among which she is indifferent. Mark the point of tangency between, the indifference curve tangent and the consumption possibilities curve with the letter E.

    a If E is halfway between S and R, what does this imply for how the individual allocates her portfolio?

    b Now assume a 50 percent tax is imposed, with full loss offset. What happens to point S? to point R? Draw the new consumption possibilities locus, and describe what happens to E, and to the portfolio allocation.

    c Assume now that losses are not deductible. What happens to point R? Draw the new consumption possibilities locus, and explain what happens to the portfolio allocation.

    d Assume now that there are no taxes, but the safe asset yields a positive return. Show what happens to point S. Now assume that there are taxes. What is the new point S? Use the diagram to analyze the impact of taxes on portfolio allocation with and without loss offsets.

6 In the text, we explained what happened to equilibrium investment in an open capital market, when a tax was imposed on the returns to capital received by Americans. Analyze what happens if a tax is imposed on the returns to capital whether received by Americans or by foreigners.

7 The text discussed the problems and distortions posed by inflation. In the late 1990s, the possibility of deflation has loomed large; some countries have actually seen falling prices. Describe the distortions and inequity associated with an unindexed tax system in the presence of deflation.

PART SIX

TAXATION IN THE UNITED STATES

These four chapters apply the general principles of taxation developed in Part Five to the analysis of taxation in the United States. Chapters 22 and 23 explain the major provisions of the personal and corporate income taxes, and their implications for both capital and labor, and discuss some of the major policy issues that have confronted the United States over the past fifteen years. Chapter 24 focuses on tax avoidance, while Chapter 25 looks back at the reforms of the 1980s and early '90s, and forward to the reforms of the future.

22 The Personal Income Tax

FOCUS QUESTIONS

1 What are the basic principles underlying the U.S. personal income tax?

2 What difference does it make whether taxes are levied on the individual or on the household?

3 What are the basic problems in implementing the income tax?

4 What equity and efficiency issues are associated with allowing deductibility of interest, state and local taxes, medical expenses, and child care expenses?

5 What special provisions pertain to the taxation of income from capital?

The personal (or individual) income tax is the single most important source of revenue for the federal government. It is also the tax that impinges most on our lives. So important is the personal income tax that tax changes have headed the political agenda no less than four times during the past two decades: in 1981, 1986, 1993, and 1997. Before evaluating these tax reforms, however, we must understand the basic structure of the U.S. income tax, the principles underlying it, and the major problems of administering it.

OUTLINE OF THE U.S. INCOME TAX

There are four steps in the calculation of an individual's tax liability. The first is to calculate *gross income*. One adds up the total of wages and salaries, dividends and interest received, net income from one's business, net rent (after expenses) from rental properties, and net gains from the sale of assets. Unemployment compensation is now taxed fully, and pensions are taxable to the extent that receipts exceed contributions upon which tax has already been paid. Alimony received is also included in income. Gambling earnings, reduced by gambling losses, are included. Illegal earnings (such as from drug dealing), from whatever source, are taxable, but not generally reported. But several sources of income are not taxable at all—among them child support, gifts and inheritances, interest on state and local bonds, some social security benefits, interest on life insurance, welfare, and veterans' benefits. None of these amounts is included in gross income. Benefits that employees receive from employers, such as health insurance and contributions to pension funds, are the most important exclusions from income for most individuals. Were these required to be reported, the amounts would be considerable. For instance, had individuals reported as income their employer-provided health insurance payments, tax revenues in fiscal year 1997 would have been $67 billion, or 4.1 percent higher. Tax savings from the exclusion of employer contributions for pensions amounted to another $71 billion. In recent years, the tax benefits associated with many other benefits, such as life insurance, have been reduced.

To get from gross income to **adjusted gross income** (AGI), one subtracts contributions to certain tax-exempt savings plans, alimony paid, and a few other items (see Table 22.1).

To get from adjusted gross income to **taxable income,** there are two alternatives. One can either itemize personal deductions—for large medical expenses and casualty losses, for mortgage interest, for state and local taxes other than sales taxes, for charitable contributions, and for moving and other job-related expenses—and then subtract the sum from adjusted gross income. Or one can take what is referred to as the **standard deduction,** which is a set amount for different categories of taxpayers.[1] The point of the standard deduction is to simplify tax reporting for the majority of taxpayers, who have a limited amount of deductions. Thus, an individual whose itemized deductions were less than the appropriate standard deduction would simply use the standard deduction.

Both those who itemize and those who take the standard deduction are entitled also to deduct one or more personal exemptions. A taxpayer is allowed personal exemptions for himself (and spouse, if filing jointly) and

---

[1] In 1997 the standard deductions were $6900 for a married couple filing jointly, $4150 for a single individual, $6050 for a head of household, and $3450 for spouses filing separately. These amounts increase with inflation (they are indexed), so that their real value remains fixed, though their nominal amounts change from year to year.

TABLE 22.1	Wages and salaries
Calculating Tax Liabilities	Interest income, dividends
	Net business income
	Net rental income
	+ Other income

GROSS INCOME

−IRA contributions (when eligible), and contributions by self-employed to pension plans

−Alimony

−½ of self-employment tax

−Part of health insurance premiums paid by self-employed for themselves and family

ADJUSTED GROSS INCOME

Alternative 1	Alternative 2: Itemized deductions
−Standard deduction	−Mortgage interest
	−State and local income and property taxes
	−Medical expenses in excess of 7.5% of adjusted gross income
	−Charitable contributions
	−Moving expenses (connected to relocation for employment)
	−Employee expenses (in excess of 2% of income)
	−Casualty losses
−Exemptions	−Exemptions

TAXABLE INCOME

× Tax rate

Tax liability

−Taxes previously withheld

−Tax credits (child care expense, foreign taxes paid, earned income tax credit, college tuition)

TAXES DUE

---

the family members he (or the couple filing jointly) supports.[2,3] Personal exemptions are phased out for high-income individuals.[4]

The exemptions do not, of course, represent the additional cost of support for an additional person, which are typically far greater. Rather, they

---

[2] In 1997 the amount was $2650 per exemption claimed.

[3] Difficulties in determining who should be allowed to take the exemption arise when individuals (such as children of divorced parents) are supported in part by more than one taxpayer, or earn part of their support themselves. Writing down rules on how such issues should be resolved contributes greatly to the length and complexity of the tax code.

[4] In 1997, the personal exemption became zero for married couples filing jointly with adjusted gross income exceeding $304,300 and for single individuals with AGI exceeding $243,700.

| TABLE 22.2 | SINGLE | | MARRIED FILING JOINTLY | | HEAD OF HOUSEHOLD | |
| Tax Rates, 1997 | | | | | | |
RATE	FROM	TO	FROM	TO	FROM	TO
15%	0	24650	0	41200	0	33050
28%	24650	59750	41200	99600	33050	85350
31%	59750	124650	99600	151750	85350	138200
36%	124650	271050	151750	271050	138200	271050
39.6%	over 271050		over 271050		over 271050	

are intended, combined with the standard deduction, to ensure that no taxes are imposed on the very poor. Historically, changes in the minimum income below which no tax is imposed have roughly followed the poverty level.

Subtracting itemized deductions or the standard deduction, and the personal exemption, from adjusted gross income gives us taxable income (see Table 22.1). The basic tax liability may then be calculated. Like the standard deduction, the tax will depend on whether the individual is single, married filing jointly with a spouse, married filing separately, or a head of household.

The extra tax that an individual must pay as a result of earning an extra dollar of income is called his **marginal tax rate.** The income tax is derived from five marginal tax rates. These are shown in Table 22.2, as applied in 1997 to different levels of income. For example, a single person with taxable income of $50,000 paid a tax of 15 percent on the first $24,650 and a tax of 28 percent on the remaining $25,350. The tax applied to the last dollar earned, the marginal tax rate, is 28 percent.

The true marginal tax rate is somewhat more complicated than Table 22.2 indicates, because personal exemptions and a portion of itemized deductions are phased out as adjusted gross income increases. The personal exemptions are reduced by 2 percent for each $2500 (or fraction thereof) of AGI over $181,800 for couples and over $121,200 for single persons. As a result of the phase-out of exemptions, the top true marginal rate is approximately 43 percent (rather than 39.6 percent), and in the 36 percent bracket of Table 22.2, the true marginal tax rate is 39 percent.[5] Note that once the exemptions are completely phased out, the marginal rate falls back to the level shown in Table 22.2. As a result, higher-income individuals may face lower marginal tax rates than lower-income individuals.

In addition, for high-income taxpayers, itemized deductions are reduced by 3 percent of the amount by which income exceeds $121,200 for

[5] The total value of exemptions for the family of four is $10,600. For each $2500 earned, the taxpayer loses $212 of exemptions. If he is in the 36 percent tax bracket, that means he pays an extra $76 tax, which is equivalent to a marginal tax rate of 3 percent. Thus, his marginal tax bracket is 39 percent.

families, $60,600 for individuals, up to a maximum reduction of 20 percent of the value of the deductions. Thus, if a $300,000 family of four has deductions of $30,000 it faces a marginal tax rate of approximately 44.1 percent.[6] On the other hand, a $400,000 family's marginal tax rate is still 39.6 percent, because its deductions have reached the maximum phaseout.

To determine the ultimate size of the tax bill, another set of adjustments have to be made. These involve **tax credits,** which are direct deductions from the taxes paid the government. Thus, if an individual would have owed $10,000 in taxes, but had tax credits for $900, he would send the government a check for only $9100. The 1997 Taxpayer Relief Act introduced a **child tax credit** amounting to $400 per child in 1998, and $500 thereafter (with the credit phasing out for families with incomes exceeding $110,000). The 1997 law also introduced a college tuition tax credit amounting to (up to) $1500 per year in the first two years of college for each child, and $1000 per year for each additional year of education per child.[7] There are two other important tax credits. The *earned income tax credit* (discussed in Chapter 15) allows a low-income family a credit of up to 40 percent of earnings; the **child care expense tax credit** allows a low-income family a credit of up to 30 percent of expenditures on child care.

There is one more complexity to the tax calculations: a capital gain, the increase in the value of an asset between the time it was purchased and the time it was sold, is taxed at a special rate. The 1997 law provided for tax rates of 20 percent on capital gains for upper-income individuals (above $55,000 for married, $32,000 for single), 10 percent for those with lower incomes, on gains on assets held more than twelve months.

**EFFECTIVE VERSUS
ACTUAL TAX RATES**

Because of all the deductions, credits, and special provisions, the actual tax paid by individuals is markedly lower than the "legislated" rate. The **effective tax rate** is defined as the ratio of tax payments to income. Effective tax rates increase with income, but because rich individuals typically have more opportunity to take advantage of the special provisions, the discrepancy between the "official" rate and the effective rate is larger for them. As a result the actual degree of progressivity (the extent to which the ratio of taxes to income increases as incomes increase) of the income tax is less than that suggested by the tax schedule. Table 22.3 shows how the effective tax rates have changed over time. The major tax reform in 1986 increased progressivity, lowering tax rates for the bottom four quintiles and raising the rate for the top quintile. The 1997 tax reform, by lowering taxes on capital gains—which mainly accrue to very high income individuals—is estimated to have decreased the degree of progressivity.

[6] The loss of deductions increases the effective marginal tax rate by $.03 \times 39.6 = 1.188$.

[7] The credit was 100 percent of the first $1000 in tuition, and 50 percent of the next $1000 in tuition.

TABLE 22.3

Average Effective Individual Income Tax Rates by Income Class and Tax Year (Income Class in Quintiles; Rate in Percent)

INCOME CLASS QUINTILES	1985	1988	1992	1995[a]	PROJECTED 1999[a]
Lowest	−0.2	−1.7	−2.8	−2.4	−3.0
Second	3.8	3.0	2.6	3.2	2.9
Third	6.7	6.4	6.3	7.2	6.8
Fourth	9.3	8.9	8.7	9.4	8.9
Highest	14.4	15.4	16.3	16.5	16.3
All families	10.7	11.0	11.5	11.3	11.1

[a] The 1995 and 1999 numbers are not perfectly comparable to the earlier numbers since the latter reflect the assignment of 100 percent of corporate taxes to capital, whereas the earlier numbers reflect a fifty-fifty assignment of corporate taxes to capital and labor.
SOURCES: Congressional Budget Office Memorandum, "Estimates of Federal Tax Liabilities for Individuals and Families by Income Category and Family Type for 1995 and 1999," May 1998; U.S. House of Representatives, Committee on Ways and Means, 1991 *Green Book*, Table 17.

When an individual earns an extra dollar his tax goes up. The amount by which his tax goes up—his effective marginal tax rate—depends, of course, on all the deductions, exemptions, and credits, which in turn depend in part on how he receives the money and how he spends it.

OTHER TAXES

This chapter focuses on the federal individual income tax, but it is important to remember that there are other taxes, and that behavior is affected by the net effect of all taxes together. Many states impose a state income tax. The marginal tax rate that an individual faces includes both the extra taxes he pays to the federal government and those he pays to the state government. In Chapter 14 we discussed the social security tax. Since for many individuals benefits increase with taxes, not all of the social security contributions should be viewed as a tax. But Medicare benefits do not depend on contributions, and thus Medicare "contributions" are taxes. Moreover, as we saw in Chapter 18, it makes little difference who actually sends the check to the government; both employer and employee contributions should be treated the same. Thus, the 2.9 percent Medicare tax (half paid by the employer) increases the marginal tax rate on an upper-income individual to as high as 47 percent, and when combined with state taxes, to 53 percent.[8]

For an individual's behavior, what is relevant is the impact of all the taxes and subsidies—with all their special provisions—together. For instance, what matters for labor supply is the net marginal tax rate—how

[8] If the individual lives in a state like California or New York that imposes a state income tax, marginal tax rates may run at 10 percent or higher, but the state income tax is deductible from the federal income tax. Taking all of this into account, the $300,000 family living in a state with a 10 percent state tax faces an effective marginal rate of approximately 53 percent (44.1 + 10 (1 − .396) + 2.9).

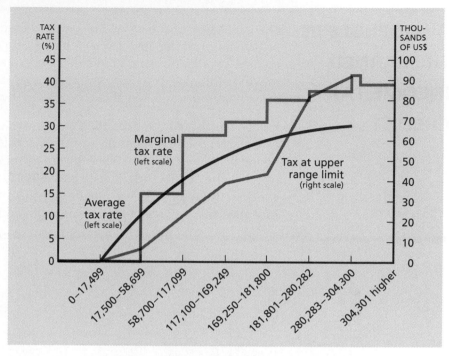

FIGURE 22.1 **Marginal and Average Tax Rates** Marginal tax rates change by jumps, as shown in the table, but average tax rates increase gradually.

SOURCE: Internal Revenue Service, Form 1040 (1997).

Note: Figure ignores EIIC; includes phase-out of deductions and exemptions.

much a taxpayer's consumption can go up if he earns an extra dollar. Even focusing only on the principal taxes—the basic income tax combined with the earned income tax credit and social security—yields a marginal tax rate that varies markedly with income. While the legislated marginal tax rate appears schematically in Figure 22.1, the actual marginal tax rate, taking into account various federal taxes (but ignoring state taxes) gives a far more complicated picture (see Figure 22.2). The earned income tax credit results in a −40 percent marginal tax rate for incomes below $9100, but then a positive marginal tax of 21 percent during the phaseout, between $11,950 and $29,290 (for a family of four).

The special provisions can have the effect of lowering the *average* effective rate at the same time as they raise the effective *marginal* rate. Table 22.4 illustrates how this can happen. It looks at an individual (in 1997) with two children and an initial income of $26,000 in the 15 percent bracket, with mortgage interest and medical, job, and child care expenses. Because of the deductions, initially the average rate is only .2 percent. After a $2001 salary increase, the average rate remains low, just over 3 percent, but the marginal tax rate is 42 percent—far higher than the legislated marginal tax rate of 15 percent.

A LOOPHOLE IN THE EARNED INCOME TAX CREDIT?

The expansion of the earned income tax credit was a major achievement of the 1993 tax law, benefiting over 19 million low-income families. It went a long way toward achieving the goal of making work pay, of ensuring that all those who work full-time, even at a minimum wage, are able to work their way out of poverty.

But one aspect of the expanded credit, while not yet seeming to have caused any problems, has given rise to considerable worry among economists. Very low income individuals receive a credit of 40 percent of what they earn. Thus, if they earn $8000, they receive a credit—a check in the mail from the government—of $3200. Consider the incentive this provides for two unemployed individuals. They hire

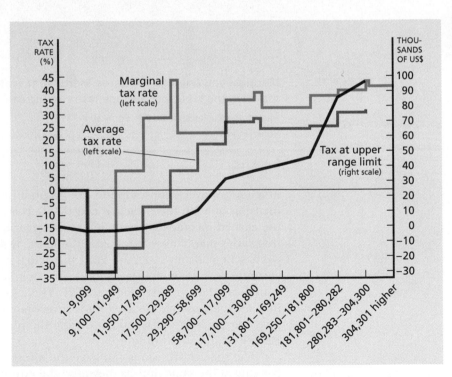

FIGURE 22.2   **Average and Marginal Tax Rates, Taking into Account Various Federal Taxes** The individual income tax is only one of the taxes people pay. As incomes rise, there are changes in payroll taxes, income taxes, and earned income tax credits, resulting in a complicated pattern of marginal tax rates.

SOURCE: Internal Revenue Service, Form 1040 (1997).

each other to clean their houses, paying each other $8000. They are honest folks, so they pay their social security contributions of 15 percent; each sends a check to the government of $1200. In return, they each receive back from the government a check for $3200, for a net gain of $2000. With a 40 percent subsidy rate, it is hard, in this scenario, to see why anyone does not report an income of at least the amount to make them eligible for the maximum earned income tax credit. While the transaction may *look* fraudulent, in fact the system encourages them actually to clean each other's house, to convert what would have been an activity simply inside the house into a "market" activity.

TABLE 22.4

Tax Laws Make Average Tax Rates Low, While Marginal Tax Rates Are High

CALCULATION OF TAXES		INITIALLY		AFTER $2001 RAISE
Adjusted gross income		26000		28001
Medical expenses	5000		5000	
Less 7.5% of AGI	1950		2100	
Equals deduction for medical expenses		3050		2900
Job expenses	750		750	
Less 2% of AGI	520		560	
Equals deduction for job expenses		230		190
Interest deduction	3000		3000	
Total deductions		6280		6090
Personal exemptions	2650 × 3	7950	2650 × 3	7950
Taxable income		11770		13961
Tax (15 percent)		1766		2094
Child care tax credit				
22% of $4800		1056		
20% of $4800				960
Earned income tax credit		688		266
Net tax liability		22		868
Average tax rate		0.1%		3.1%
Change in tax liability				846
Ratio of change in tax liability to change in income				42%
Legislated marginal tax rate				15%

615

PRINCIPLES BEHIND THE U.S. INCOME TAX

There are several basic principles underlying the U.S. tax system—though because the tax law is so complicated and has evolved so much over the decades since it was first introduced, not every provision is fully consistent with these principles.

THE INCOME-BASED PRINCIPLE AND THE HAIG-SIMONS DEFINITION

The current U.S. tax code rests on the premise that the appropriate basis for assessing tax liability is the household's income (net of expenses personally incurred on the job).

For the most part, economists have argued that a *comprehensive* definition of income should be used that includes not only cash income (net of expenses required to earn the income) but capital gains (whether the gain is realized or simply accrued). A number of other adjustments have to be made to convert "cash" income into the "comprehensive" income that, in principle, should form the basis of taxation. This comprehensive definition of income is referred to as the **Haig-Simons concept,** after two early-twentieth-century economists who advocated its use. They believed that such a comprehensive income measure most accurately reflects "ability to pay."

There are three major differences between how our present tax system measures income and the Haig-Simons concept of "comprehensive" income.

1 *Cash-basis market transactions.* For the most part, only **cash-basis** market transactions are taxed. The tax thus rests on a notion of income that is narrower than that which most economists would ideally like to see employed. Certain nonmarket (noncash) economic activities are excluded, though activities that appear to be identical and are marketed *are* subject to taxation. For instance, a housekeeper hired to clean house has her compensation taxed, while a spouse who performs exactly the same services in his or her home (and whose support by the spouse working outside the home can be thought of, at least partially, as compensation for the services performed) is not taxed. If an individual owns a house and rents it out, the net rental income is subject to taxation; if the individual lives in the house himself, no tax is due. The primary reason for this is the difficulty of determining appropriate values in the absence of market transactions; when there is a market transaction, there is an observable variable, the *transaction price*, which we can (and do) use to value the service.[9]

Some noncash transactions are listed in the tax code but are difficult to enforce. **Barter arrangements** (Sally Housepainter paints Joe Carpenter's house in return for his building her a new garage) are subject to tax. Also, when employers provide *in-kind payments* to their employees (such as making an automobile available for personal use), then, in principle, the employees are required to assess the value of these payments and report them on their 1040 forms. In fact, noncash payments often are not reported.

---

[9] Some countries (such as Sweden) have attempted to tax the imputed "rent" on owner-occupied houses, as if the individual rented the house to himself.

A major category of income that the tax system fails to trap is *unrealized capital gains*. Capital gains (the increase in the value of an asset) are taxed only when the asset is sold. Capital gains are taxed, in other words, only upon *realization*, rather than on an **accrual basis** (that is, as they actually occur from year to year).

To see why economists have argued that income should include capital gains, consider two individuals: one puts her $100 savings in a bank and earns 10 percent interest. Her income is $10. The other buys $100 worth of gold. During the course of the year, the price of gold rises by 10 percent. At the end of the year, he could sell his gold for $110. The capital gain increases the wealth of the individual just as the interest payments do; from an economic point of view, the two individuals appear to have an identical ability to pay. But their tax liabilities will differ: the individual who purchases gold only has to pay a tax on his capital gain when he sells the asset.

2 Equity-based adjustments. A second difference between our tax system's measure of income and true "comprehensive" income is that our tax system allows individuals who have large medical expenses or casualty losses to deduct a portion of those expenses from their income. The rationale here is fairness. These individuals are less able to pay taxes than someone with the same income, but without those expenses.

3 Incentive-based adjustments. Finally, the tax code is used to encourage certain activities, such as charitable contributions, by allowing tax credits or deductions for them. The tax code also allows the exclusion from income of most health insurance and life insurance premiums provided by employers to employees, presumably to encourage employers to provide these benefits.

Thus, while some capital income—such as owner-occupied housing—receives favorable treatment because of the absence of a cash market transaction, other capital income—such as money set aside in qualified retirement programs—receives favorable treatment because of a desire to encourage savings for retirement.

Those who advocate that consumption, not income, should be the basis of taxation argue that we should move away from the Haig-Simons attempt at a comprehensive definition of *income* toward a comprehensive definition of *consumption*. For consumption tax advocates, the failure of the current tax system is not that so much of capital income escapes taxation but that so much of capital income is taxed at all.

Our tax structure is based on the premise that those with higher incomes not only should pay more in taxes but should pay a larger fraction of their income. The effect of the differences between comprehensive income and the tax definition of income is to reduce significantly the effective degree of progressivity, as we have seen. To limit the extent to which individuals can avail themselves of these loopholes, Congress passed a **minimum tax,** the intent of which is to ensure that upper-income individuals pay a tax at least equal to 26 percent of their income (in excess of a basic exemption level).

While the 1986 tax reform pared back many of the special provisions, the 1997 reform brought back some of the old ones and introduced some new ones. The 1997 law provided something special for almost everyone: a child tax credit for those with young children; a tuition tax credit for those with college-age children; and lower taxes on capital gains, a provision of special benefit to the very wealthy. The result is that every income category saw its effective tax rates going down, by between .9 and 1.7 percentage points. But while the percentage point reduction for someone in, say, the $50,000 to $75,000 bracket was larger than for someone in the $100,000 to $200,000, the dollar value of the tax savings for the latter was obviously much, much greater. A millionaire would see his taxes going down $15,000, while someone with a $25,000 income would see his tax bill cut by $350.

Interestingly, the 1997 law undid what had been viewed as one of the major achievements of the 1986 tax reform, which had basically eliminated the preferential tax rates for capital gains. Indeed, prior to 1986, the value of these benefits and other tax loopholes that the rich had taken advantage of was so great that those with incomes over $1 million actually faced a lower effective tax rate than those with an income between $500,000 and $1 million.

THE FAMILY-BASED PRINCIPLE

The basic unit of taxation in the United States is not the individual but the family. Two individuals who decide to get married (and thus change their family status) will find that their tax liabilities are altered. The tax code attempts to make some limited adjustments for families in different circumstances. Families in which there is only one adult are taxed at a rate halfway between the rate of an individual and the rate of a two-adult family. Families with children are allowed exemptions for each child, as mentioned earlier. Families in which both parents work outside the home are allowed a credit for child care.

Although the tax system is basically family based, it is not completely so: while income of children under 14 is taxed at the family's marginal tax rate (that is, it is effectively included within the tax unit), income of children over 14 is not.[10] The United States is now one of the few countries still employing a family-based tax system. Other countries, such as Canada, have an individual-based system, where each individual is taxed on his or her own income.

Divorce presents problems for a family-based tax system: Which parent should claim a deduction for supporting the child, when both provide *some* support? How should the payments from one divorced parent to the other (alimony) be treated? (If the couple were still married, a transfer from one to the other would not affect taxes.) Under present provisions, alimony (but not child support) is deductible by the party paying it and taxable to the party receiving it.[11]

[10] Children over 14 can file their own tax return, so that their interest income and dividends are taxed at a lower rate than they would be if they were included in their parents' tax return.

[11] Thus with the progressive tax structure, if ex–husband and wife are in very different tax brackets, it pays to label payments that are really child support as alimony. Like everything else in modern life, getting divorced in a manner that minimizes tax liabilities requires care and thought.

UNIT OF TAXATION The unit of taxation makes a difference because of progressivity. In effect, our current tax system imposes a tax on marriages between couples of similar incomes and a subsidy on marriages between couples of disparate incomes. To see this, we contrast the effects of marriage on two different couples; the results are summarized in Table 22.5.

Abigail and Billy presently are living together but are not married; each earns $30,000, and they pay a total of $6960 in income taxes. Were they to get married, their joint tax liability would increase by $1068, to $8028. If they anticipate remaining married for, say, fifty years, and do not anticipate any change in their salaries (after adjusting for inflation) over that period, the present discounted cost to them of getting married would exceed (with a 5 percent real interest rate) $20,000. If Abigail and Billy have some doubts about whether to get married, this calculation might well resolve them. The increased tax payment resulting from getting married is sometimes referred to as the *marriage penalty*, or **marriage tax.**

By contrast, when Bradford marries his low-paid girlfriend, Amy, they find that their total tax liabilities are reduced by over $1080. For this couple, the tax system acts to encourage marriage. Assuming fifty years of marriage, and that their income ratios remain constant, the value of the government's subsidy to this couple's tying the knot is over $20,000.

Was it the intent of Congress, in enacting the tax code, to encourage marriages between individuals with very different incomes and to discourage marriages such as that between Abigail and Billy? Probably not.

But consider now what happens if we change the tax code to have all individuals pay on the basis of their own income. Now, individuals neither benefit from nor are penalized by marriage. This provision does eliminate the discrimination against those who choose to live together under the bonds of matrimony.

But now consider Amy and Bradford. They have the same family income as Abigail and Billy, but now their total tax liability is $9111.50 compared to that of Abigail and Billy, whose tax bill is only $6960. Not surprisingly, Bradford and Amy think this is unfair. Shouldn't the family's total tax burden depend simply on family income, not on how much each member of the family earns?

There is no tax arrangement that appears to be "fair" in all circumstances. But do the general theories of fairness we discussed in Chapter 17 provide any guidance? The ability-to-pay approach suggests that two families (with the same number of children and with both parents working) with the

TABLE 22.5	FILING STATUS		EARNINGS	TAX ON INDIVIDUAL	TOTAL TAX OF A&B
Tax Effect of Marriage, the 1997 Tax Law "Marriage Penalty"	Single	Abigail	30,000	3480	6960
		Billy	30,000	3480	
	Single	Amy	12,000	780	9111.50
		Bradford	48,000	8331.50	
	Married	A&B	60,000		8028

same income ought to pay the same taxes. Since the costs of two individuals living together are much lower than twice the costs of two individuals living singly, the ability-to-pay approach would suggest that whenever two individuals cohabit, they should be subjected to higher taxation than if they live singly. Unfortunately, the tax authorities cannot easily monitor cohabitation; so long as the vast majority of cohabitators are married, and so long as most married individuals live together, basing taxes on whether individuals are married (which is easier to ascertain) rather than on whether they cohabit (which is not easy to ascertain) does not create too many inequities. At the time the tax code was first adopted, it clearly reflected the vast majority of cases. Moreover, the inequities may not have been too large when most American households had a similar structure—with one wage earner. But today most women work outside the home, and there is a wide variety of household structures.

The utilitarian approach attempts to ascertain how the family circumstances in which individuals find themselves affect their marginal utility of income.

In both the utilitarian and the ability-to-pay approach, one might want to distinguish between families with two wage earners and those with one. Assume the families have the same total income. The current tax system treats them alike. Yet the family with both individuals working may have to purchase many services that the nonworking spouse provides free. Both those who believe in ability to pay and those who believe in utilitarianism might well argue that a family with two working individuals should pay a lower tax than a family with one worker.

Changes in the tax law in 1993 and 1997 affected the marriage penalty, for individuals at both ends of the income distribution. As of 1996, 42 percent of married couples paid a marriage tax, averaging $1750, while 51 percent received a marriage subsidy, averaging $1350. The marriage penalty for upper-income individuals can exceed $20,000: if two individuals, each with one child and a combined income of $300,000, marry, their taxes increase by $21,627. (This arises primarily because the entire income of the lower-earning spouse will now be taxed at the 39.6 percent rate.) Under the pre-1993 law, this couple would have been penalized only $6460.[12]

Because the marriage penalty seems so patently inconsistent with "American values," it has become a major focus of criticism, and advocates of tax cuts have repeatedly put forward proposals for its elimination or reduction. While nothing was done in the tax cuts adopted in 1997, Republican tax proposals since then have focused on the marriage penalty.

THE ADVANTAGES OF A FLAT-RATE TAX SCHEDULE There is one—and only one—way to avoid the inequities surrounding the choice of unit of taxation: impose a **flat-rate tax schedule.** If all individuals pay a proportional tax on income in excess of a basic exemption level (and if those with an income

[12] See Daniel R. Feenberg and Harvey S. Rosen, "Recent Developments in the Marriage Tax," National Bureau of Economic Research, Working Paper 4705, April 1994; and Congressional Budget Office, "For Better or for Worse: Marriage and the Federal Income Tax," June 1997, Table S-1, Table 4.

**THE ANNUAL MEASURE
OF INCOME PRINCIPLE**

below this exemption level receive a cash payment from the government), there is no penalty and no reward for marriage, and no reward for divorce.

The U.S. income tax is based on annual, not lifetime, income. Consequently two individuals with the same lifetime income may, over their lifetimes, pay quite different taxes. The individual who decides to postpone more of his consumption until retirement will, for instance, pay more in taxes than his less frugal brother. Or consider two individuals with the same (before-tax) present discounted value of income, one of whom is a late bloomer, earning most of her income in later life. The present discounted value of her tax payments will be lower.

Because of the progressivity of the tax structure, the use of an annual measure of income also affects differently those with stable incomes and those with fluctuating income. Middle-income families with variable income are adversely affected, while some upper-income individuals with variable income are better off. Consider a middle-income family of four whose average adjusted gross income is $58,700, but in half the years it has an income of $68,700, while in the other years it has an income of only $48,700. Using the 1997 tax law, in a good year the family will be taxed at a marginal rate of 28 percent; in a bad year it will be taxed at a marginal rate of 15 percent. Its total tax liability will be considerably greater than that of a family with a stable income of $58,700 which always faces a 15 percent marginal tax rate; the *average* additional annual tax payment of the family with a fluctuating income is $650.[13]

Prior to the 1986 Tax Reform Act, taxpayers were allowed to average income over periods when their income varied widely. By eliminating the privilege of income averaging, the tax reform aggravated the distortions produced by the annual basis of taxation. The main reason for dropping the averaging provisions is that they do cost the Treasury money; and as the government tried to maintain budget neutrality as it reformed the tax code—in a way which would have some degree of popularity—provisions like income averaging that made good tax policy sense, but did not have large political constituencies behind them, were sacrificed.

PRINCIPLES OF U.S. TAX SYSTEM

- Income-based
- Progressive
- Family-based
- Based on annual, not lifetime, income

---

[13] We assume that the family has no adjustments to income and takes the standard deduction. Then in the good year, the extra tax payment is .28 × $10,000. In the bad year, the reduced tax payment is .15 × $10,000. The total extra tax payment over a two-year period is thus $1300. Dividing by 2, we obtain the average annual extra payment.

PRACTICAL PROBLEMS IN IMPLEMENTING AN INCOME TAX SYSTEM

In translating the basic principles of the income tax into workable tax law, there are three extremely difficult problems: determining what "income" is; determining when somebody has received some income; and deciding what deductions from income to allow.

DETERMINING INCOME

For most wage earners, determining income for tax purposes is a simple matter: they add up their paychecks, interest, dividends, and so on. But for taxpayers who run their own business it is not. There are two central problems. The first has to do with determining depreciation (the loss in value of machines and buildings as they age) and adjusting the cost of inventories for inflation. The second problem is differentiating between consumption expenditures and legitimate business expenses.

The tax code recognizes that legitimate expenses required in order to earn a living ought to be deductible from an individual's income. The principle seems clear. Surely, a store owner who sells candy should not be taxed on the total value of his sales; his expenses—the rent for his store, the purchase of candy from the candy manufacturer, the salaries he pays his employees—should all be deducted from sales to calculate his gross income. But what about the candy he consumes while he is working? He may claim that his consumption of candy is a form of advertising; when customers see him chewing candy, they increase their purchases. But what of the candy that he consumes when no one is around? He may claim he is "testing" various samples, to ensure the quality of the candy he sells. One might suspect that neither of these explanations is the candy store owner's real motive for eating his candy. He simply likes candy.

Similarly, in many businesses there is very little difference between advertising and entertainment expenses. Taking clients to dinner is a method of persuading them to buy your product, just as putting an advertisement in the newspaper is an attempt to persuade customers to buy your product. On the other hand, there are other instances where "business entertainment" is purely a matter of having a good dinner partly at Uncle Sam's expense.

These examples illustrate the two central problems:

1 In many instances it is impossible to ascertain what are legitimate business expenses and what are not.
2 Even when the distinctions between legitimate and illegitimate business expenses are conceptually clear, performing the required monitoring is often impossible. Returning to our example, it is difficult to imagine the kinds of records that would be required to isolate the owner's consumption of candy (if we decided that consumption is not a legitimate business expense).

CONSEQUENCES OF ALTERNATIVE BUSINESS-EXPENSE RULES It is impossible to devise a system of distinguishing between legitimate and illegitimate expenditures in a way everyone would consider to be fair. Someone always either is unfairly burdened or benefits unfairly, no matter what rule is devised.

Either the government can allow a fairly generous treatment of expenses—for instance, for travel—in which case the individual who is really traveling for recreation purposes is unfairly receiving a tax benefit. Or the government can be fairly restrictive—for instance, by not allowing first-class travel and not allowing meal deductions above a certain amount—in which case the individual who has no recreational motive may be unfairly burdened. There is no way the tax code can be fair to both these individuals. Moreover, any rule induces economic distortions. If deductions for travel expenses are restricted, businesses requiring travel will be discouraged; if travel expenses are not restricted, businesses in which there is scope for hidden pleasure travel may be encouraged. The deductions are a form of tax-exempt income. Furthermore, if deductions for travel expenses are restricted, businesses may substitute less efficient communications methods for travel. This is because the relative after-tax price of travel will rise if travel expenses are not deductible, but other communication expenses (telephone, fax, etc.) are still deductible (see panel A of Figure 22.3).

In panel B of Figure 22.3, we consider a self-employed individual who is able to claim business entertainment as a deduction. The deductibility of these expenses shifts her budget constraint, the alternative combinations of "entertainment" and "other consumption goods" the individual can purchase. Her before-tax budget constraint is E_0C_0. With no deductibility, it is E_1C_1. When entertainment is deductible, it is E_0C_1. Entertainment becomes relatively less expensive; if the individual is in the 36 percent tax bracket, she has to give up only 64 cents' worth of other goods to get a dollar's worth of entertainment. Her consumption decisions are clearly distorted.

In the 1986 Tax Reform Act, Congress took an intermediate position: tax deductions for luxury cars were reduced, and only 80 percent of entertainment expenses and meals were deductible. In 1993, this was reduced further to 50 percent.

WHAT CONSTITUTES A BUSINESS? Not only is it difficult to determine what are legitimate business expenses, in some cases it is even difficult to determine what is a business. For instance, individuals who raise horses could be raising horses as a business. On the other hand, they could be keeping the horses simply for their own pleasure. If they buy a horse, keep it for several years, sell it, and take a loss, the loss is really not on a business activity or on an asset but on an ordinary pleasurable activity. One could argue that there is no reason why their capital loss should be deducted from their income tax. On the other hand, there are individuals who do earn their living raising horses—buying them at a lower price, feeding them, and then selling them at a higher price. Not to allow these individuals who are in the business of raising horses for profit to deduct their losses would seem to be grossly unfair. But it is virtually impossible to distinguish between the two situations.

The government attempts to combat this kind of tax avoidance by insisting that serious businesses make a profit. The rule of thumb is that an individual must make a profit in at least three years out of five; in the case of

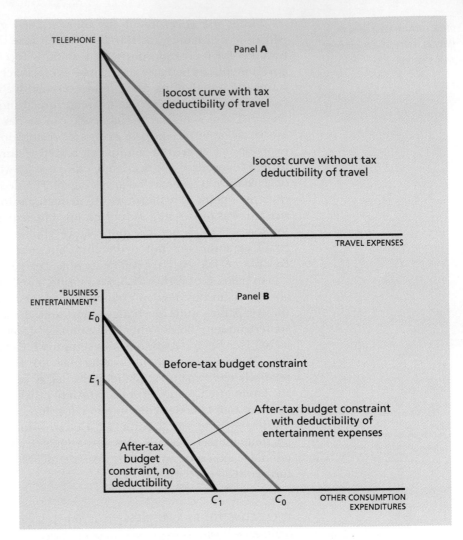

FIGURE 22.3 **Dilemmas of Tax Deductibility of Travel, Entertainment, and Related Expenditures** Panel A: If firms were denied the right to deduct travel expenses from income as a legitimate business expense, travel would become a relatively more expensive way of communicating than other forms of communication, such as telephone; thus production decisions would be distorted. (Isocost curves are similar to budget constraints. They give those combinations of inputs that together cost a given amount.) Panel B: For a self-employed individual who can claim a deduction for "business entertainment," the tax system reduces the cost of this form of consumption relative to other forms of consumption. There is a distortion (and hence a deadweight loss).

horse breeding, this rule is relaxed to at least two years out of seven. Such rules obviously do succeed in reducing the amount of tax avoidance. At the same time, of course, there are individuals who are seriously in business who make losses year after year. Setting up a business often takes three or four years in order to establish a reputation—and a profit.

EMPLOYEE BUSINESS DEDUCTIONS In principle, the "necessary costs" of working should be deductible. The difficulty is ascertaining what are necessary costs. Because of the impossibility of doing this on a case-by-case basis, the government has set up certain basic rules: some educational expenses are deductible, most are not. Moving expenses connected with a job are deductible, commuting expenses are not.

In drafting the 1986 Tax Reform Act, Congress in effect decided that the old law had resulted in too many individuals' claiming employee business expenses for what were actually ordinary consumption expenditures. Accordingly, they decided that only those taxpayers with large unreimbursed employee business expenses—exceeding 2 percent of adjusted gross income—could deduct them.

To the extent that expenses incurred as a result of going to work are not deductible, not only is an inequity created, but incentives to work are reduced. If a job requires clothing expenditures that the individual would not otherwise have incurred, for example, the net return to working is reduced. Say Bill earns $15,000 a year, and has work-related expenses which are not deductible of $5000, for a net income of $10,000. Because he has inherited a modest-sized fortune, he is in the 28 percent marginal tax bracket; and the government requires him to pay 28 percent of the total $15,000, that is, $4200, in taxes. This amounts to 42 percent of his net earned income of $10,000; the $5800 he receives yields a return below the minimum wage, and is hardly enough to motivate him to go to work.

CHILD CARE EXPENSES Child care expenses present a similar problem. In one sense they are voluntary—expenses resulting from a family's decision to have children. But having had children, they are expenses that can be avoided only by having one parent stay at home.

Present tax law allows a credit against child care expenses of up to $2400 for one child or $4800 for two children, paid to allow the taxpayer (and spouse, if they file jointly) to work or to look for work. The amount of the credit ranges from 30 percent of expenses for working parents with an adjusted gross income (AGI) under $10,000, to 20 percent of expenses for parents with AGI over $28,000. Therefore the maximum credit is .3 × $4800 = $1440. If a woman with a child goes to work and has to pay someone to take care of her child, the family's net income is just the difference between what she receives and what she must pay out. If she receives $15,000 and must pay out $5000 in child care expenses, the family's net income is only $10,000. Not allowing the deduction of these expenses creates strong distortions. Assume the woman is married, and as a result of her husband's income 31 percent of what she receives goes to the IRS. If she pays

$5000 for child care, the total increase in what the family can spend on other things (after taxes) is only $5350.[14] She may well be discouraged from taking the job. Allowing a credit of $480 (= .2 × $2400) goes only a little way toward fully alleviating the distortions or correcting the inequities. On the other hand, the child care tax credit creates a distortion itself. By lowering the price of child care, it encourages a greater consumption of child care.

This is an example of the more general problem arising from the fact that the income tax is based only on *market transactions*. Activity which occurs within the household—and is essentially identical to that purchased in the market—is not taxed.[15]

Both the inequities and the distortions arise from the inability to measure (and therefore to tax) the household services provided within the family. The failure to tax the "imputed" value of household services discriminates against the purchase of those services in the market; it encourages the production within the household.

Decisions concerning the tax treatment of child care expenditures not only have economic consequences; these decisions reflect, and have consequences for, social values and family structure. Family life when both parents work is different from that where one parent (usually the woman) remains at home. A tax system that penalizes women who enter the marketplace may be thought to reflect or perpetuate a particular set of attitudes concerning the role of women.

EMPLOYEE BENEFITS For many individuals, a significant fraction of their compensation comes in forms other than direct cash payment, especially in employee benefits. The most important of these is medical insurance. Some workers receive thousands of dollars' worth of medical and dental benefits that are exempt from taxation. Most economists believe that such benefits should be included within taxable income. Ironically, in 1993 and 1994, as Congress and the administration debated how to slow down the rising costs of medical care, even though it was recognized that these special provisions had the effect of encouraging health care expenditures, political pressures (both from unions, which had fought hard to achieve these benefits, and from the health care industry) kept the issue largely off the agenda.

SOME CONCLUSIONS There are three lessons to be learned from this discussion of the practical problems of defining "income" for tax purposes. First, what may seem like minor details of a tax law can have important conse-

---

[14] The additional amount the family has to spend will be further reduced by social security taxes and perhaps state and local income taxes.

[15] In spite of this, there is a strong trend for goods that used to be produced inside the household to be produced in the market. The reason why the distortion does not appear larger is that there are sufficient economies from market production that they overcome the tax distortion.

quences. Second, many (but by no means all) of the provisions of the tax code that seem unfair and distortionary are not the result of politicians' representing special interest groups, or of bureaucrats' incompetence. There are real difficulties in determining what is income and what are legitimate business expenses. Third, whatever rules are chosen will entail both some inequities and some inefficiencies. Designing the tax code necessitates weighing one inequity against another, one distortion against another. The objective of our discussion has been to clarify these trade-offs and to help explain the all-too-frequent situations where lawmakers discover that in the process of correcting one inequity or distortion, they have created a new one, as bad or worse than the first.

TIMING

The second important practical problem of implementing an income tax is determining when somebody has received some income. Again, for most wage income, there is no problem. But consider an author writing a book. Authors commonly are paid a royalty, a certain fraction of the revenues generated by sales of the book. Usually, the publisher provides an advance payment prior to the publication of the book in anticipation of future royalties. In principle, if the book fails to sell, the advance must be returned. Should the advance be treated as income to the author at the time she receives it? Or should it more properly be treated as a loan, which will be repaid with the proceeds of the book? In the latter case, the author would have to pay the tax when the book has been sold.

There are, in fact, many transactions that are, or can be made, to take on this form. Consider a contractor building a building. The contract is not fulfilled unless, and until, the building is completed. But he receives payments as the building progresses. Are these payments to be treated as loans (in which case the builder only records the income when the building is completed)? Similar issues arise in any long-term project (such as defense contracts to develop a new airplane).

People care about timing because a dollar today is worth more than a dollar tomorrow. The **present discounted** value of tax liabilities is reduced by postponing the tax.

On the other hand, these issues of timing are of less consequence for those who believe that consumption, and not income, is the appropriate basis of taxation. Timing is important because it allows individuals to escape, in effect, interest income taxation, which from this perspective should not be taxed in the first place.

**PERSONAL
DEDUCTIONS**

The third practical problem in implementing an income tax is deciding which deductions from income to allow. Thus, in arriving at taxable income from adjusted gross income, the government allows deductions that are designed to make a more equitable tax system and to encourage certain socially desirable activities. There are five important kinds of expenditures for which deductions are allowed: medical expenses, mortgage interest, state and local taxes except sales taxes, charitable contributions, and casualty losses.

627

MEDICAL EXPENSES The motivation for allowing medical expenditures to be deducted from income seems clear: Health problems lead to costly medical bills and often reduce the individual's earnings as well. An individual who is spending all of his income on doctors' bills simply to stay alive has a lesser ability to pay than an individual with the same income but no medical expenses. Ability to pay is measured best not by total income but by *discretionary* income, the amount in excess of the amount required to survive.

This argument has been criticized on two grounds. The first is that there are other categories of expenditures (such as food) that, at least at some level, are equally necessary. But differences in the necessary amount of food are likely to be smaller than differences in the necessary amount of medical expenditures. The second is that a significant fraction of medical expenses are discretionary (e.g., staying in a private room rather than a semiprivate room, having a television set in one's room, plastic surgery to stay young-looking, etc.), and the law does not distinguish between "necessary" and "discretionary" expenditures. Again, however, this is understandable, since the distinction, though clear in principle, is virtually impossible to make in practice. The tax rules now allow deductions for medical expenses only to the extent that they exceed 7.5 percent of adjusted gross income. This seems to reflect the judgment that significant inequities in ability to pay arise only with significant medical costs, and that these large medical costs are likely (though not always) to be nondiscretionary.

The provisions for deducting medical expenses effectively reduce the price of medical services. For someone in the 28 percent marginal tax bracket whose medical expenses exceed the 7.5 percent minimum, the private cost of an extra $100 of medical services is only $72. The distortions this introduces are obvious: to the extent that medical expenditures are discretionary, the individual has an incentive to spend too much on medical services (relative to other commodities). The amount by which the effective price of medical services is reduced depends on the individual's marginal tax bracket. For an individual in the 15 percent bracket, an extra $100 of medical services costs $85. Whenever individuals face different prices for the same commodity, there is inefficiency.[16]

Aside from the inefficiencies introduced by the medical expense deduction, this deduction has been objected to on grounds that it is unfair. The reduction in the tax liability as a result of, say, $1000 of medical expenses for an individual at a higher income level is greater than that for an individual at a lower income level. Thus if an individual in the 28 percent bracket incurs a $1000 medical expense (ignoring for the moment the provision limiting the amount that can be deducted), his tax liability is reduced by $280. On the other hand, an individual in the 15 percent bracket would

---

[16] There are further distortions associated with health expenditures. Employer-provided health insurance is not taxed, and self-employed individuals can also deduct health insurance premiums. This encourages the purchase of health insurance, and as we saw in Chapter 12, insurance, by lowering the cost of obtaining medical services, itself leads to excessive consumption of health services.

have his tax liability reduced by only $150. The *value* of the provisions for deductibility of expenses is thus much greater for the individual in the higher bracket.

The efficiency and equity arguments against deducting medical expenses (which apply to other categories of deductions as well) have led many economists to conclude that credits are preferable to deductions. With a tax credit, an individual with a $1000 medical expense would have his tax reduced by the same amount, regardless of his income. If there were a 20 percent tax credit, the government would in effect be paying 20 percent of medical expenditures. Not only does this seem fairer to many individuals, it also seems more efficient. Recall that one requirement for the Pareto efficiency of the economy is that all individuals' marginal rates of substitution between different commodities be the same. (This was called the *principle of exchange efficiency*.) This is ensured if all individuals face the same price for every commodity. With tax credits, since the government is in effect paying part of medical costs, individuals do not pay net (after tax) the true marginal cost of the medical services they obtain; but all individuals face the same effective price. With deductions, as we have noted, upper-income individuals face a lower price than lower-income individuals.

The above arguments are not completely persuasive. Recall that the motivation for allowing the deduction was to base taxes on some measure of ability to pay. It was believed that medical expenses reduce the individual's ability to pay. If this is true, gross income by itself does not provide an appropriate basis for judging ability to pay. Gross income, net of "involuntary" medical expenses, provides a better measure. Though we know we cannot separate out "voluntary" from "involuntary" medical expenses, we may believe it is better to take account of medical expenses than to ignore them; that is, we may believe that gross income, net of all medical expenses, is a better measure (though admittedly imperfect) than gross income alone.

It is, of course, true that the deductibility of medical expenses produces distortions, particularly for individuals in the 28 percent or 39 percent marginal brackets. As we discussed earlier, there is an important equity/efficiency trade-off. The fraction of medical expenses that should be tax deductible would presumably depend on the elasticity of demand for medical services. As we noted earlier, if the elasticity is low, the distortion is low, and there will be little gain in efficiency from making medical expenditures only partially deductible. On the other hand, if the elasticity of demand for medical expenditures is high, there are potentially great gains in efficiency, and then we may wish to have only a fraction of medical expenses deductible.

INTEREST The motivation for the tax deductibility of interest is simple: Income (as usually defined) includes wages plus net interest receipts—i.e., the difference between interest paid and interest received. If we believe that an individual who has positive net interest receipts has a higher ability to pay than someone with no interest receipts, and that an individual with negative net interest receipts has a lower ability to pay, interest paid should be tax deductible.

Those who believe that consumption is the appropriate basis of taxation argue that interest should not be taxed and that interest payments should not be tax deductible. Those who believe that income is the appropriate tax base, however, have been concerned about the inequities and inefficiencies to which interest deductibility gives rise. First, since some types of capital income receive favorable tax treatment, borrowing to finance favored types of investments provides one of the major classes of tax avoidance devices. Second, deductibilty of interest payments encourages borrowing, and thus discourages saving.

The 1986 Tax Reform Act took a compromise position. It continued the tax deductibility of mortgage interest (for up to two homes). But it eliminated the deductibility of all consumer interest. Money, however, is fungible; money borrowed allegedly for one purpose can be used for another. An individual who is buying a house and a car, and who was planning to borrow money to pay, say, 80 percent of the cost of each, can obviously borrow a little more against the house, using the additional funds to pay cash for the car. Banks make home equity loans, enabling an individual to borrow against the current market value of his or her house (which is often considerably more than the price at which it was purchased). These are treated as mortgages, and interest on these loans is tax deductible. The restriction on the deductibility of interest is thus likely to encourage this trend.

Congress was aware of this problem, and partially addressed it by limiting the size of the mortgage for which interest is deductible to the original purchase price plus borrowing for medical and educational purposes. How effective these provisions on the limitation of interest deductibility are is, however, questionable.[17]

STATE AND LOCAL TAXES State and local taxes (except sales taxes) are deductible. The primary motivation for this provision is the concern that without such a provision, the imposition of federal taxation would seriously impair the states' ability to raise revenues. Indeed, without such a provision, during World War II, when federal marginal tax rates reached as high as 94 percent, some individuals would have faced total marginal tax rates (combining federal and state taxes) in excess of 100 percent. Some individuals also have expressed a concern that without such a provision, there would effectively be double taxation of the same income. Whether such double taxation is inequitable is, however, another question. If the taxes are thought of as being associated with the benefits of living in a particular locale, it is not obvious that these expenditures should be treated any differently from expenditures on other goods and services.

[17] The provision limiting the size of the mortgage to the original purchase price plus borrowing for medical and educational purposes has an additional potential distortion: Individuals whose houses have increased in value will have an incentive to sell their house and buy a house of equivalent value. This is especially true as a result of the 1997 tax law, which allows the capital gain to go untaxed (up to $500,000 for a married couple).

Indeed, the deductibility of local taxes may give rise to an important source of distortions and inequities. Many services provided by local communities—garbage collection, sewage disposal, education, tennis courts—differ little from services that can be purchased privately. Such services provided by local communities are known as "local publicly provided goods": though all members of the community benefit from these goods, those outside it do not. Thus the deductibility of local taxes encourages the public provision of these goods and services (regardless of whether the services might be more efficiently provided privately) and encourages the consumption of those goods and services that can be provided through local communities.

Not all economists agree on the significance of these distortions or inequities. Although many goods provided by local communities are much like privately provided goods, many are basically public goods, little different from those associated with private charities (for which a deduction is allowed). For instance, the elderly do not benefit directly from the expenditures on education (though in some instances they may benefit indirectly, from the increased value of their house). In the voting models discussed in Chapter 7, the outcome of the political process depends critically on the median voter, the one who is such that half the voters want more public expenditures, and half less. In that case, what is critical is how the tax system affects the median voter. In most states and communities—but not all—the median voter does not itemize; that is, according to the median voter model, deductibility is essentially irrelevant. Still, many economists, and almost all politicians, were concerned that the elimination of the deductibility of state and local taxes would decrease the demand for state and local goods.

The 1986 Tax Reform Act represented a peculiar compromise. Sales taxes, which represent only 25 percent of all taxes collected at the state and local level, are no longer deductible; but all other taxes remain deductible. Moreover, states and localities may be induced, as a result of this provision, to switch from sales taxes to other sources of revenue. There is no convincing justification, other than political expediency, for this distinction in treatment between sales taxes and other taxes. Perhaps surprisingly, there has been less switching than one would have expected, partly because of the widespread antipathy to the income tax. In 1986 the sales to income tax ratio for state and local governments was 1.80; in 1997 the same ratio was 1.61, only a slight decrease.

CHARITY The deduction for gifts for charitable purposes—for education, religion, health, and welfare—is one of the more controversial provisions of the tax code. The motivation for allowing the deduction of these expenditures is clear. As we discussed at greater length in Chapter 6, there are insufficient private incentives for spending money on goods that generate benefits to others. Money spent to develop a polio vaccine may yield little direct benefit to the giver but may provide great benefits for mankind. Similarly, gifts to educational and other cultural institutions may contribute much to the welfare of society, but relatively few of the benefits accrue directly to the benefactors.

Opponents of the deduction for charity argue that:

1 Many of the expenditures are not really for public goods.
2 The public—i.e., the government—should determine directly how expenditures on public goods should be allocated.
3 The provision for deductibility of charitable gifts mainly benefits the rich and thus reduces the redistributive impact of our tax system.
4 Eliminating the provision of the deductibility of charitable gifts would have little effect on charitable giving.

It is difficult to assess the validity of these various claims. Many of the most important advances in medicine have been the outcome of research supported by private foundations. The Rockefeller Foundation's development of "miracle seeds" brought on a Green Revolution in developing countries that has greatly increased the availability of food in these countries. There is also some evidence that elimination of the deductibility of charitable donations would have a substantial effect on gift giving.[18]

Whether the deductibility provisions result in the tax system's being unfair is also not clear. To the extent that wealthy individuals create foundations that pay high salaries to their officers but spend little on true public goods, the provision for charitable donations may well be thought to be inequitable. But to the extent that the expenditures are really for public goods, the giver gets no more enjoyment out of the expenditure than do many other members of society. There is no more reason to include these expenditures in his or her income than in that of any other individual (who benefits equally by it).

If the appropriate basis of taxation is "income available for spending on private goods" (discretionary income), the appropriate tax treatment is to allow a full deduction (just as we argued earlier that the appropriate tax treatment of medical expenses was a deduction, not a credit). But the consequence of this is that the marginal cost of charity is less for those in the 28 percent or higher brackets than for those in the 15 percent bracket.

The charitable contribution has also sometimes been abused, with individuals giving away property (such as paintings), and assigning a value to the gift far in excess of the true value. Recent legislation has imposed severe penalties for those who get caught doing this.

The deductibility of charitable contributions raises basic questions concerning the manner in which decisions regarding the supply of public goods should be made. Critics claim that the tax deductibility of charitable contributions gives, in effect, undue power to the rich in deciding which

---

[18] See, for instance, Charles T. Clotfelter and Richard L. Schmalbeck, "The Impact of Fundamental Tax Reform on Nonprofit Organizations," in *Economic Effects of Fundamental Tax Reform*, ed. Henry J. Aaron and William G. Gale (Washington, D.C.: Brookings Institution Press, 1996), pp. 211–43; Gerald E. Auten, James M. Cilke, and William C. Randolph, "The Effects of Tax Reform on Charitable Contributions," *National Tax Journal* 45, no. 3 (September 1992): 267–90; and Yong S. Choe and Jinook Jeong, "Charitable Contributions by Low- and Middle-Income Taxpayers: Further Evidence with a New Method," *National Tax Journal* 46, no. 1 (March 1993): 33–39.

public goods should be provided. But political processes do not provide a very efficient mechanism for registering ordinary individuals' attitudes toward different public goods. Individuals vote for representatives and have little opportunity for expressing their views on the relative allocation, say, of educational and health expenditures.

On the other hand, the provision for charitable deductions has encouraged a system in which public goods are provided by a variety of institutions. Individuals can express their views about the importance of different categories of public goods in a variety of ways. If the government were the only source of funds for, say, health research, the views of that bureaucracy would exclusively determine the direction of health research; as it is, these decisions can be made independently in a variety of institutions. The arguments for the decentralization of decision making for public goods closely parallel those for the decentralization of decision making in other areas: having competing (or at least alternative) organizations providing similar services leads to greater efficiency, and it allows for diversification, so that the consequence of mistakes will be smaller.[19]

CASUALTY LOSSES Individuals are allowed to deduct losses from thefts, fire, accident, and other casualties that exceed 10 percent of their adjusted gross income. The motivation for these provisions is again clear. These losses reduce the individual's ability to pay; they represent "expenditures" that were not voluntary and from which the individual presumably got no enjoyment.

This provision has, however, some important consequences. In particular, it means that the government effectively provides a kind of insurance against these casualties. The magnitude of the insurance depends (as we noted in our discussion of the medical deduction) on the individual's marginal tax rate. Once individuals have suffered a loss, they are obviously much better off than if the government did not provide this kind of insurance. On the other hand, these provisions may seriously distort individuals' behavior. Insurance, in general, reduces individuals' incentives to avoid the losses in question. Thus, if the government pays 33 percent of the loss from theft, the individual may not make as much effort to avoid being robbed.

EDUCATION EXPENSES In 1997 two new tax credits were added for educational expenses: the Hope Scholarship credit, for tuition and related expenses incurred in the first two years of postsecondary education; and the lifetime learning credit, for tuition expenses incurred at any time. The Hope Scholarship credit is 100 percent of the first $1000 in expenses, and 50 percent of the next $1000. It is designed to make it possible for students in most states to go

---

[19] The provision for the deductibility of expenditures on religious charities has another motivation: Some argue that the constitutional prohibition against legislation interfering with the free exercise of religion prohibits taxation of religious organizations. Although this may provide a justification for exempting religious institutions directly from taxation, it does not seem to provide justification for deducting gifts to them for purposes of the income tax.

to a community college at almost no cost. The lifetime learning credit is 20 percent of up to $5000 in tuition ($10,000 beginning in 2002).[20] This was a tax credit designed to encourage college enrollment. It reflected a concern about growing wage inequality between those with secondary school education and those with college education, with real wages of unskilled workers actually declining between 1973 and 1993. College enrollment rates among children of poorer families have been markedly below those of children of the country's higher-income families. Without access to higher education, there is a vicious cycle perpetuating inequality, which seemed so much in contradiction to American ideals. Poor families lack the resources to send their children to college, so their children will have low incomes. The tuition tax credit represented an effort to enhance equality of educational opportunity.

The tuition tax credits were criticized on several grounds. First, critics argued that the much higher earnings of college graduates already provided sufficient private incentives to attend college. The major expansion of student loan programs enacted in 1993, combined with the increase in Pell Grants (tuition grants for children from lower-income families), had already largely eliminated the financial barrier to attending college. To the extent that any financial barrier remained, it was mainly among lower-income children; and for these, the tuition tax credit would be of little benefit—it would be far better to expand the Pell Grant program, and if necessary, the student loan program. Second, there was a concern that colleges and universities would respond by increasing tuition, and while that would benefit the university system, and ease pressure on state treasuries, it would not lead to much of an increase in student enrollment. It is too soon to tell whether the tuition tax credits will lead to either tuition increases or enrollment increases.

DEDUCTIONS VERSUS CREDITS

Adjustments to income for tax purposes can take the form of deductions or credits. A 20 percent tax credit is the same as a deduction for a person in the 20 percent tax bracket. By and large, most economists argue that *if an adjustment is to be made* it is preferable to use credits rather than deductions. Deductions give bigger benefits to those in high tax brackets, and are in that sense inequitable; and because deductions result in different individuals' facing different prices, they are distortionary. But as we have seen in the case of medical expenses, in some circumstances there can be an argument based on equity for deductions. If one believes that taxes should be based on ability to pay, and if ability to pay is best measured by income *net of expenditures on medical expenses*, then a deduction for medical expenses seems appropriate. If one believes that taxes should be based on private consumption—what one takes out of the economy—then expenditures on public goods (charity) should be subtracted.

[20] Both credits start to phase out at between $40,000 and $50,000 for single individuals and between $80,000 and $100,000 for married couples. (Eligibility is determined by the *modified* adjusted gross income, which excludes the deduction for contributions to IRAs, a deduction which is allowed in the calculation of adjusted gross income.)

IMPLEMENTATION PROBLEMS

- Determining income
- Timing
- Deductions

SPECIAL TREATMENT
OF CAPITAL INCOME

Among the most complicated provisions of the tax code are those that relate to savings and capital income. Some of the problems arise from the desire to encourage savings—in particular savings for retirement. But any preferential treatment of one category of income gives rise to problems as individuals seek to convert income into a form which receives preferential treatment. The tax authorities respond by imposing rules which hinder these conversions. Thus, many complexities of the tax code arise from attempts to reduce the scope for these tax avoidance activities. Some of the problems, however, are inherent in the attempt to tax the return on certain assets, most notably on housing.

HOUSING The most important investment for the majority of individuals is a home. The return to this asset—the housing service it provides—is not taxed in the United States.

In spite of the fact that the returns to housing (the housing services or imputed rent) are not taxed, money that individuals borrow to purchase houses (the interest on their mortgages) is tax deductible; indeed, since 1986 this has been the only form of consumer interest that is tax deductible.

Imputed rent on owner-occupied housing is not taxed because of the difficulty of ascertaining what the appropriate "rent" should be. But this is not an insurmountable problem: we "impute" the market value of houses for purposes of property taxes. Once property values are known, it is fairly easy to estimate what the appropriate rent should be. There is, perhaps, another reason: The tax laws reflect the values of our society, and the strong belief that it is good for individuals to own their own home (perhaps an extension of the Jeffersonian ideal that America should be a country of small landholders). Individuals who own their own home may be more likely to feel like members of the community and to participate as constructive citizens. Considerations such as these—as well as the lobbying of the new-home construction industry—were dominant in retaining the favorable treatment of housing under the 1986 Tax Reform Act.

In 1997, the favorable treatment of housing capital gains was extended: a family can make a gain of $500,000 every three years without incurring any tax liability. One of the reasons for this provision was that the tax on the capital gains in owner-occupied housing raised relatively little revenue (since it was not effectively enforced), but required extensive bookkeeping on the part of households.[21]

The favorable treatment of owner-occupied housing obviously has both equity and efficiency effects. It leads to an overinvestment in housing relative to other assets. And there has been a general presumption that it generates benefits to homeowners relative to renters. But how significant these effects are—and indeed, whether they even exist—has varied over time with tax rates and benefits. The reason is that the tax law also gives considerable benefits to renters, though indirectly: by providing accelerated depreciation, tax deduction of interest, and taxing capital gains only upon realization and at favorable rates the tax laws provide landlords with incentives to invest in rental housing; since this market is relatively competitive, in the long run, these benefits are passed on to renters. Thus, during the period 1981–1986, it appears that rental housing actually received more benefits than did owner-occupied housing, though since then, the traditional presumption appears to have been restored.[22] And the 1997 law, by effectively making capital gains in housing tax-exempt, exacerbated the incentives for overinvestment in owner-occupied housing.

SAVINGS FOR RETIREMENT

There are a variety of special provisions related to savings for retirement, including special treatment of pensions and IRAs (individual retirement accounts).

OLD-STYLE IRA ACCOUNTS The simplest of these to analyze is the old-style IRA accounts. Though they were disbanded in 1986, there is constant discussion of reintroducing them. In addition, self-employed individuals can still take advantage of what are called *Keogh accounts*, which are identical in design to the old-style IRA accounts. In computing their adjusted gross income, individuals were allowed to deduct contributions to these accounts of up to $2000 (or $2500 for an individual with a nonworking spouse) annually, and neither the contribution nor the interest income was taxed until it was withdrawn.

The implications for savings can be seen by looking at what happens if one puts $100 aside for retirement. If Abigail saves $100, her current tax is reduced by $100 \times t$, so her consumption falls by $(1 - t)100$. Upon retirement,

---

[21] Households were taxed on their capital gain, the difference between what they received when they sold their house, and what they paid for it, *plus any expenditures on home improvements.* Thus, in principle, they needed to keep detailed records over a long period of time. Investments in owner-occupied housing have long benefited from another special provision: Capital gains can be "rolled over." That is, if an individual sells a house, making a capital gain, but reinvests the proceeds in a larger house, the capital gain is postponed. He can continue to use the rollover provision, until he dies; then the special provisions relating to taxation of capital gains at death mean that the capital gain completely escapes taxation.

[22] See M. King and D. Fullerton, *The Taxation of Income from Capital* (Chicago: University of Chicago Press, 1984).

her consumption will increase. Assume the interest return is r (say, 20 percent). When she cashes in her investment, she must pay a tax on the total amount, that is $t \times (1 + r)$ 100. Her consumption next period thus goes up by $(1 - t)(1 + r)$ 100. The ratio of the change in consumption next period to the change in consumption this period is $1 + r$. *Allowing individuals to deduct savings from their income (but then taxing the entire amount, principal plus interest, upon retirement) is equivalent to exempting interest from taxation.* For those who save little, the preferential tax treatment has an ambiguous effect: an income effect which reduces savings (increases consumption) and a substitution effect which increases savings. But for those who save a lot, the preferential tax treatment unambiguously reduces savings, since there is only an income effect; for those with savings beyond $2000, there is no marginal incentive.

There is a further criticism: Individuals who already have assets do not have to save at all, to receive the tax benefit. All they need to do is to transfer savings from other accounts into an IRA account. For these individuals, there clearly is no marginal incentive effect, other than on the form of savings. (See Figure 22.4.)

NEW-STYLE IRAS The 1986 tax law limited the deductibility of contributions to IRAs to lower-income individuals and to individuals not covered by employer-sponsored plans. The 1997 law then expanded the IRAs slightly,

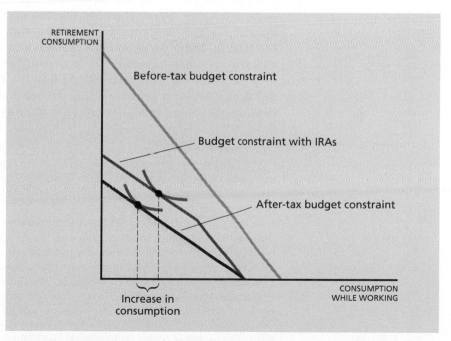

FIGURE 22.4   **The Effect of IRAs on Savings** For individuals who save more than the limit, IRAs simply have an income effect and no substitution effect; they actually reduce savings.

and provided more flexibility of withdrawal. However, anyone with an income below around $160,000 may make non-deductible contributions to an IRA and still defer the tax on the interest income. But we saw earlier that the old-style IRAs were equivalent simply to allowing an exemption from interest, with one important difference: the timing of tax payments to the government. With the new-style IRAs, individuals pay more taxes now and less taxes later, though the present discounted value is the same. With the government facing major budgetary constraints, the "ruse" of moving tax receipts earlier was irresistible. Note that doing so has no effect on the long-run budgetary position of the government, since it will be receiving less taxes later.[23]

The 1997 tax law greatly expanded the flexibility of the non-deductible IRAs through the Roth IRA, which became available in 1998. After a five-year holding period, distributions from a Roth IRA are tax free for those over 59½ and first-time home buyers using the funds to purchase a house.[24] Even with an ordinary IRA, under the 1997 provisions there is no penalty for early withdrawal of up to $10,000 for a first-time home buyer and for higher-education costs.[25]

PENSIONS Savings that firms put aside for individuals for their retirement typically are not taxed until the individual receives the money. At the same time, the firm can deduct the amount it has set aside, just as it would if it had paid the money directly to the individual. Clearly there is a tax preference. There are two reasons for allowing the preference. First, it may be difficult for the individual (or the tax authorities) to know how to value the benefit under a *defined benefit scheme*, where the employer specifies retirement benefits. Typically, these depend on how long the worker stays with the company, and what his pay is in the final years that he works for the firm. (Under a *defined contribution* scheme, there is no problem; the firm simply sets aside a given amount of money into an account with the

---

[23] The value to the government may differ, if the discount rates used by the government and by the investor differ. Since typically the government can borrow at lower rates than the private sector, the cost of postponement to it is less than the value of postponement to the private sector.

In recent years, however, the government has focused on reducing the deficit in the short run, and thus the backloaded IRAs have gained in favor. There have even been cynical inducements to encourage individuals to convert old-style IRAs (where taxes are not paid when money is put into the account, but when the money is withdrawn from the account) into new-style IRAs, with the "bribe" of greater flexibility in withdrawal. When the individual made the conversion, she would have to pay the accrued tax liability, so that current revenues would be enhanced.

[24] Individuals may contribute up to $2000 per year to a Roth IRA; eligibility phases out between $95,000 and $110,000 for an individual and between $150,000 and $160,000 for a married couple.

[25] The 1997 law also raised the limits on deductible IRAs: For single individuals, the phaseout range is $30,000 to $40,000; for married persons filing jointly, it is $50,000 to $60,000.

individual's name on it; it is as if the individual himself had received the money and put it into an IRA account.) The second reason may be more important: Government wanted to encourage employers to put aside money for their employees' retirement, so that there would be fewer destitute old people—fewer people to be a burden on the state in their old age.

INTEREST ON STATE AND MUNICIPAL BONDS

Interest on state and municipal bonds is tax-exempt. These may include bonds used by municipalities to finance schools and by states to finance roads; industrial revenue bonds, which raise funds that are re-lent to businesses located in the town; and community-issued bonds which raise funds to be re-lent for mortgages for lower- and middle-income individuals. Some states have set up special agencies to borrow funds to finance dormitories at private as well as state universities, to build sports complexes, and to construct hospitals.

The original motivation for the interest exemption was a concern about the constitutionality of taxing interest on state and local bonds. But the expansion of this provision to include bonds issued by municipalities for money to re-lend to private individuals was clearly viewed as a form of federal subsidy to the localities. Many municipalities took up this federal subsidy with such enthusiasm that severe curbs have been imposed on the issuance of tax-exempt bonds.

The tax-exempt bonds are an inefficient way of aiding states and localities: the cost to the U.S. Treasury exceeds the benefits to the states and localities. The reason is that the interest rate on the bonds adjusts to make the marginal buyer of the bonds indifferent between buying taxable or tax-exempt bonds. Currently, there are sufficiently few individuals in the 39.6 percent tax bracket that the marginal buyer is at a much lower tax bracket. If the marginal buyer is in the 28 percent bracket, and if a taxable bond yields 10 percent, a tax-exempt bond (of the same risk) would yield 7.2 percent. It is this lower cost of capital which makes the tax-exempt status of value to states and localities. But many of the bonds are purchased by individuals in the 39.6 percent tax bracket. If these individuals switch from a taxed to a tax-exempt bond, their tax payment goes down by 39.6 percent. If someone had $1 million to invest, she would have received $100,000 in interest and paid $40,000 in taxes, leaving her $60,000. Now she buys $1 million of tax-exempts. She receives $72,000 in interest; she is $12,000 better off. The community issuing the bond saves $28,000 in interest; it is better off than if the bonds had been taxable. The Treasury is worse off by $40,000. Almost a third of this amount goes not to benefit the community, but to benefit upper-income taxpayers.[26]

[26] One proposal for addressing this problem is to create "tax credit" bonds, where taxpayers would receive a credit at a particular rate for interest received from state and local bonds. These could be designed so that the interest paid by states and localities would be the same as with current tax-exempt bonds. Higher-income individuals, however, would not receive a windfall benefit as they do currently.

In Chapter 21 we saw that returns to capital could accrue in the form of capital gains, increases in the value of an asset, and that these were typically treated differently than other returns. As we noted, the preferential treatment is in part a consequence of the difficulty of measuring the increase in value on an accrual basis—that is, as it occurs. As a result, capital gains are typically taxed only upon realization—that is, when the asset is sold (as opposed to "marking to market," that is, taxing the increase in market value on a year-to-year basis). To be sure, there are assets, such as publicly traded stocks, for which it is easy to ascertain the market value; but taxing those differently from assets such as real estate would itself introduce a distortion.

While the taxation of capital gains upon realization is a natural outcome of the difficulty of measuring capital gains, the other forms of preferential treatment are largely a result of political pressures by wealthy individuals who receive much of their income in the form of capital gains. To be sure, they often argue that such preferential treatment is fair (otherwise they pay taxes on the spurious increases in value attributed to inflation), or that it increases efficiency by spurring risk taking and entrepreneurship.

The two main arguments for preferential treatment—that it is unfair to tax nominal, instead of real, returns, and that it is important to encourage risk taking—are arguments for special treatment of all returns to capital, or returns to investments in risky ventures; they are not arguments for the preferential treatment of capital gains alone, regardless of the asset in which they are invested. Moreover, we saw in Chapter 21 that the equity argument itself was dubious—once the benefits of taxation upon realization are taken into account, and once it is noted that nominal (not real) interest payments on borrowing to finance the debt are deductible.

Whether the preferential treatment of capital gains leads to more risky investments remains a subject of controversy. The 1993 tax law attempted to target capital gains tax relief at new enterprises, which typically are quite risky; the 1997 capital gains tax cut, by contrast, was across-the-board, and applied as much to capital gains on unproductive investments, like gold, as it did on high-risk new-technology ventures.

A further objection to the preferential treatment of capital gains—and one of the reasons why the preferential treatment was eliminated in 1986—was that it gives rise to a host of tax avoidance schemes, as taxpayers work to convert ordinary income into capital gains. While the scope for such schemes was greatly reduced in 1986, there is considerable worry that with the reintroduction of large preferences, they will re-emerge (see Chapter 21).

There was intense debate over lowering the capital gains tax rates in 1997. Critics pointed out that much of the benefit would accrue to investments that had already been made. Since the investments had been made, incentive did not matter. The lower taxes were just a windfall gain, giving these investors a far higher return than they had expected when they made their investments. Moreover, since wealth ownership is far more concentrated even than income, the benefits of the tax cut accrue disproportionately to the very rich. The reason why, in the end, the capital gains tax cut was so attractive was that the short-run budgetary cost is low. In the first few years, many individuals who have been "locked in" sell their asset, and have to pay capital gains taxes (though at reduced rates); this is especially true if they worry that later capital gains taxes may rise. But while the short-run budgetary cost may be low (or in some estimates, revenues may actually increase), in the long run there are adverse effects. The tax revenues today are partly at the expense of revenues that would have been realized in the future, when the asset would in any case have been sold.

CONCLUDING COMMENTS

We ask much of our income tax: It should be simple, fair, easy to collect, and should encourage economic efficiency. The tax is much maligned. It does not achieve any of its goals perfectly. It is the product of compromises: economic compromises between competing objectives as well as political compromises. Were equity considerations of less concern, a far less complex and less distortionary tax system would be easy to design. Yet, compared with the tax systems in many other countries, there is less tax avoidance and greater compliance in the U.S. tax system, and perhaps even fewer distortions. Still, there remain demands for reform of the tax system. The directions that these reforms might take will be discussed in Chapter 25. First, however, we will take a look at the other major tax, the corporate income tax, and will study some of the ways in which people avoid—legally—paying taxes under our current tax system.

SPECIAL TREATMENT OF CAPITAL INCOME

The U.S. tax system provides special treatment—lower rates or postponed taxes—to a large fraction of the total returns to capital. There are special provisions relating to:

- Housing
- Savings for retirement
- Pensions
- Capital gains

The preferential treatment distorts the allocation of resources and often introduces important inequities.

REVIEW AND PRACTICE

SUMMARY

1   The U.S. income tax system is based on the principle that taxes should be related progressively to the family's cash (marketed) annual income. The tax code discriminates in favor of nonmarket transactions and against those with fluctuating income.

2   There are problems in implementing an income tax system, both in defining income and in determining the time at which the tax should be imposed. A principal difficulty encountered in defining income is distinguishing activities that are motivated by business considerations from ordinary consumption activities.

3   Many of the problems associated with designing a workable income tax system arise from the unobservability of (or costs of observing) the essential variables, for example, of knowing whether some medical procedure was really "necessary."

4   The tax code allows a number of adjustments to income and personal deductions, motivated both by equity and by incentive considerations. But regardless of their motivations, the deductions have both incentive and equity effects that need to be taken into account. For instance, the medical deduction effectively lowers the price of medical care, and it lowers it more for high-income individuals.

5   The basic unit of taxation in the United States (unlike most other countries) is the family. The tax system has a number of provisions that are intended to ensure that those in different family situations face equitable taxation. There is a limited tax credit for child care expenses, and different rate schedules for married couples and single individuals. Still, the current system imposes a marriage penalty on individuals with similar incomes, and a marriage subsidy on individuals with very dissimilar incomes.

6   The tax bills of 1986, 1993, and 1997 all affected the degree of progressivity of the federal tax code. The 1986 act reduced progressivity and eliminated many of the special provisions. While deductibility of sales taxes was eliminated, state property and income taxes remain deductible, as is mortgage interest. Employee benefits, including medical benefits, are not taxed. The 1993 act substantially increased progressivity, by greatly increasing tax rates on upper-income individuals (from 28 percent to almost 40 percent). The 1997 act gave substantial benefits to the very rich, by enacting large cuts in capital gains, but at the same time it provided a child tax credit. The net effect of these changes is that upper-income salaried workers are worse off, upper-income individuals who live off of capital are better off, and middle-income individuals with children are better off. In addition, the simplification of the tax code, the great achievement of the 1986 bill, has been reversed, as numerous special provisions have been introduced, for example for education and capital gains.

Adjusted gross income

Taxable income

Standard deduction

Marginal tax rate

Tax credits

Child tax credit

Child care expense tax credit

Effective tax rate

Haig-Simons income

Cash basis

Barter arrangements

Accrual basis

Marriage tax

Flat-rate tax schedule

QUESTIONS AND PROBLEMS

1 For each provision of the tax code listed below, which provides the best explanation: incentives, horizontal equity, vertical equity, administrative reasons, or special interest groups?

    a Deductibility of mortgage interest

    b Deductibility of casualty losses

    c Deductibility of medical expenses

    d Deductibility of charitable contributions

    e Child care tax credit

    f Credit on taxes paid to foreign governments

    g Tuition tax credit/deduction

Which of these provisions can be justified as a response to a market failure? Compare this response—the use of the tax system—with alternative responses (such as direct government expenditures).

2 Discuss the arguments for and against using a tax credit rather than a deduction for: medical expenses, charitable contributions, and child care expenses.

3 If you were asked to write the regulations concerning the deductibility of business expenses, how would you treat the following items, and why? Discuss the inequities and inefficiencies associated with alternative possible rules.

    a Educational expenses required to maintain one's current job

    b Educational expenses incurred to obtain a better job

    c Moving expenses arising from a reassignment by one's present employer

    d Moving expenses incurred in obtaining a new job

    e Business suit worn by an individual who does not wear suits except for business

    f Business lunches costing more than $25

g Expensive cars

h Commuting costs

i Car expenses of a traveling sales representative

j Subsidized cafeteria lunches

4 Under the old tax law money that scientists received from winning the Nobel Prize (or similar prizes) was not taxable. Now it is. Which treatment do you think is appropriate? Under both the old and the new tax law, money received by lottery winners (as well as gambling receipts) is taxable, while the losses are not deductible. Is this fair? What distortions does this introduce?

5 Consider a divorced individual who earns $26,000, has two children, pays $4800 in child care expenses, $2000 in mortgage interest payments, and $4500 in medical expenses. Medical expenses in excess of 7.5 percent of one's income are deductible. When the individual's income is $26,000 she gets a 22 percent child care expense credit; when her income is $28,001 her credit is only 20 percent. Her base marginal tax rate is 15 percent. What is her actual marginal tax rate?

6 Explain why federal tuition tax credits might lead states to increase the tuition they charge. Many states currently charge a tuition in state community colleges that is substantially below $1500, the level of the federal credit. What might one expect to happen in those states?

7 In the debate over the tuition tax credit, one administration economist pointed out that in Georgia, which had provided these scholarships for its students, tuition had not increased after the credit had been provided. Why might a federal tuition tax credit or deduction be expected to have a different impact than a credit or deduction provided by the state for state universities?

23 The Corporation Income Tax

FOCUS QUESTIONS

1 What is the corporation tax a tax on, and who bears the burden—stockholders, workers, or consumers?

2 How does the corporation tax affect economic efficiency?

3 How does the corporation tax affect financial decisions—debt, dividends, and mergers?

4 Should there be a tax on corporations?

The corporation income tax has been the subject of considerable controversy, with some (such as Bill Clinton during the 1992 presidential campaign) arguing that corporations were escaping their fair share of taxes, while others (such as President Reagan, in an offhand remark in 1983) suggesting that corporations should not be taxed at all. There is even controversy about who actually pays the corporation income tax—its incidence; as we shall see, many economists believe that the tax is actually borne largely by consumers and workers, not by the owners of the corporation. Indeed, one of the reasons why the tax has remained so controversial is this widespread debate about who bears the tax. Economists agree on one thing (which is not well understood by others): *The corporation does not bear the tax.* People—shareholders, customers, workers—bear taxes. The question is, which people?

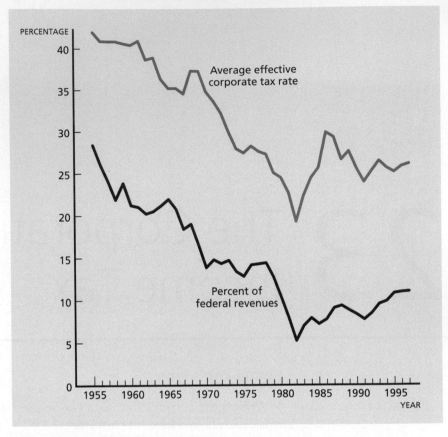

FIGURE 23.1 **Federal Corporate Income Tax: Effective Rate and Share of Total Federal Receipts** From 1955 through 1982, the average effective tax rate of the corporate income tax and its share of federal receipts declined steadily. Even though the rate and share of federal revenues have increased slightly since then, both numbers are still considerably below levels in the period 1955 to 1970.

SOURCES: U.S. Department of Commerce, Bureau of Economic Analysis, *National Income and Product Accounts, 1929–1994*, Tables 3.2, 6.17B, 6.17C; *Survey of Current Business*, August 1998, Tables 3.2, 6.17C.

After declining in importance as a source of federal revenue for almost three decades, average effective tax rates and the share of total federal receipts increased after 1983 (see Figure 23.1). Changes in aggregate revenues may not, however, convey much information about changes in the economic impact of the corporate tax. The corporate tax causes important distortions in the allocation and overall level of investment. The nature and magnitude of the distortion relate, in part, to specific provisions of the tax, such as the differences in tax treatment of interest payments and dividends, and the allowances for depreciation.

This chapter first describes the U.S. corporate income tax, then analyzes alternative interpretations of the tax—different theories ascribing the burden of the tax to different groups. The analysis includes not only how the tax affects economic efficiency, but also how it affects financial decisions. The chapter concludes with a discussion of the most fundamental issue: Should there be a tax on corporations?

THE BASIC FEATURES OF THE CORPORATION INCOME TAX

The corporation income tax applies only to *incorporated* businesses. The essential difference between an incorporated business and an unincorporated business is the liability of investors for the debts of the corporation. Corporations have limited liability; that is, investors can lose only the amount of money they have invested in the firm. In contrast, if an unincorporated business has debts it cannot pay, the creditors can attempt to recover their losses from the owners. Because of the protection provided to investors by the corporate form of organization, almost all large firms in the United States are incorporated.

The corporate tax is essentially a flat-rate tax, currently at 35 percent. As a concession to small business, the average tax rates for corporations with taxable incomes below $18.3 million are somewhat lower, as shown in Table 23.1. The tax base is corporate taxable income. In general, taxable income is defined in the tax law to be gross revenues less wages, materials, interest paid, and depreciation allowances. Dividend payments, however, are not deductible. Thus, when Congress legislates more generous depreciation allowances, as it did in 1981, a corporation's taxable income is reduced and so is its tax.

As with the individual income tax, after the tax liability is calculated, a firm's tax is reduced by *tax credits*. Before its repeal in 1986, the most important corporate tax credit was for new investment. Firms still obtain a credit for a portion of their research and development expenditures and for most taxes paid to foreign governments.

In the discussion that follows, we shall see that the impact of the corporation income tax depends on several features of the tax code—the fact that

TABLE 23.1	TAXABLE INCOME	MARGINAL RATE	AVERAGE RATE
Marginal and Average Tax Rates on Corporate Taxable Income	$0–50,000	15%	15%
	$50,000–75,000	25%	15%–18.3%
	$75,000–100,000	34%	18.3%–22.25%
	$100,000–335,000	39%	22.25%–34%
	$335,000–10,000,000	34%	34%
	$10,000,000–15,000,000	35%	34%–34.3%
	$15,000,000–18,333,333	38%	34.3%–35%
	Over $18,333,333	35%	35%

interest payments are tax deductible but dividend payments are not; the fact that depreciation allowances are typically more generous than true economic depreciation; and the fact that the government taxes profits but does not provide a symmetric treatment for losses[1]—and on the relative rates at which individual incomes and corporations are taxed. And we shall see that the impacts of the tax extend beyond whether investments in corporations are favored over investments in the noncorporate sector; they extend to how production in the economy is organized, the kinds of investments that are made, and how investments are financed.

THE INCIDENCE OF THE CORPORATION INCOME TAX AND ITS EFFECT ON EFFICIENCY

There are several different views on the effects of the corporation income tax. The popularity of the tax is attributable in part to the fact that its incidence is unclear. Politicians like to give the impression to voters that someone else pays the corporate tax. But the reality is that households, workers, consumers, and investors pay the tax, just as they pay any other tax. The question is how the burden is shared among these groups. Under some plausible conditions, for instance, the corporate income tax is effectively borne by workers and consumers, and not by investors at all; in other cases, it is borne not just by investors in the corporate sector, but by all investors.

THE CORPORATION INCOME TAX AS A TAX ON INCOME FROM CAPITAL IN THE CORPORATE SECTOR

One of the earliest views of the corporation income tax, and still one of the most prevalent, is that it is a tax on the return to capital in the corporate sector. With wage payments and purchases of other inputs tax deductible, what remains is profits and the return on capital. In a perfectly competitive economy, there would presumably be no pure profits, so the tax is *just* a tax on the return to capital.

Assume, for instance, that the firm did not finance any of its investment by borrowing (or that interest was not tax deductible). The corporation income tax reduces the after-tax return to capital in the corporate sector. *This is the short-run effect.* But typically, as we saw in Chapter 18, matters do not stop here. In an ingenious model, Arnold Harberger, then of the University of Chicago and now of UCLA, traced out the longer-run effects assuming that the overall supply of capital was fixed but that capital was perfectly mobile between the corporate and the unincorporated sectors. With a lower return to capital in the corporate sector, capital shifts out of that sector and into the unincorporated sector. Firms in the corporate sector substitute labor for cap-

---

[1] That is, the government is like a silent partner, which shares profits but not losses. The government does allow a firm to carry forward losses for a limited number of years. But because the benefits are not received until some time in the future, they are worth less. A loss of $100 today used to offset a profit next year is worth only approximately $85 if the firm pays a 15 percent interest rate, $70 if the firm has to wait two years before taking advantage of it.

ital, and thus labor shifts from the unincorporated sector into the corporate sector. Goods in the corporate sector become more expensive (the tax is like a cost of production). When matters are fully equilibrated, the after-tax return on capital is the same in the corporate and the unincorporated sectors: thus, to the extent that capital bears a cost, it is borne equally by those in all sectors of the economy. Consumers bear some of the cost in the form of higher prices. Workers, too, may bear some of the cost; if, for instance, the corporate sector is far more labor intensive than the unincorporated sector, the reduced demand for the output of the corporate sector reduces the overall demand for labor; this effect is reinforced if capital is easily substituted for labor in the unincorporated sector, for then firms in that sector may substitute capital for labor as the cost of capital falls. While the precise manner in which the burden is shared by consumers, owners of capital, and workers depends in complicated ways on demand elasticities, on elasticities of substitution (which measure how easy it is to substitute capital for labor), and on labor intensities in the two sectors, the fundamental point is that the long-run effect can be markedly different from the short-run effect.

John Shoven of Stanford University has solved explicitly for the effect of the corporation tax in the intermediate run, comparing the present equilibrium with what it would have been in the absence of the distortionary corporate tax on the return to capital. He estimated that the deadweight loss from the corporation income tax was roughly 12 percent of the tax revenue it generated.

He also estimated the extent to which the burden of the corporate tax was shifted from capital owners to consumers and workers. The share of the burden borne by owners of capital is measured by the change in the income of capital divided by total corporate tax revenues. If the burden exceeds 100 percent, then the income of capital is reduced by *more than* the tax. The corporate sector is relatively capital intensive (that is, a lot more capital is used for each worker than in the unincorporated sector). Hence a shift in demand toward the unincorporated sector indirectly reduces the demand for capital and, thus, the returns to capital. The smaller the elasticity of substitution in the unincorporated sector, the greater the extent to which the return to capital must be lowered to absorb all the capital that is released as a result of the change in the composition of demand. This explains why Shoven calculated that capital bears 162 percent of the burden of the tax in the case where the elasticity of substitution in the unincorporated sector is very low relative to that in the corporate sector and where the consumer demand elasticities are low.

Without knowing the precise value of the demand elasticities and elasticities of substitution, we cannot even tell whether capital bears more or less than 100 percent of the burden. No wonder, then, that there is no agreement about the extent to which the corporate tax is, effectively, a tax on capital or a tax on consumers!

**SHIFTING OF THE
CORPORATE TAX IN
THE LONG RUN**

The Harberger model has been important in focusing attention on the *general equilibrium* effects of taxes—in emphasizing that a tax imposed on capital in one sector has ramifications throughout the economy; that with perfect capital mobility, the tax must be borne equally by capital in both sectors of the economy; and that the general equilibrium incidence may be quite different from the direct impact, in some cases with capital bearing more than 100 percent of the tax.

But the Harberger model has been extensively criticized on two grounds. First, its assumption that the capital stock is fixed but that capital can be fully shifted between sectors seems peculiar. By contrast, if one assumes that the capital stock itself is variable, quite different (and sometimes simpler) results emerge. For instance, for a small country facing a perfectly elastic supply of capital at the international interest rate r^*,[2] the after-tax return remains unaffected by the tax. Thus, a) the tax increases the cost of production in the corporate sector; b) production thus shifts to the unincorporated sector; and c) as this happens, whether the demand for labor falls or increases depends (in part) on whether the unincorporated sector is less or more labor intensive than the corporate sector. Accordingly, owners of capital bear none of the tax, consumers of the goods produced by the corporate sector always bear some of the tax, and workers may or may not be adversely affected.

The second objection is more difficult to deal with. It is that the tax itself is not just a tax on the return to capital. Interest is tax deductible, and there are typically accelerated depreciation allowances. Obviously, more favorable tax provisions, such as accelerated depreciation, lower the cost of using capital, and thus encourage its usage. In the paragraphs below, we derive some detailed formulae relating the after-tax cost of using capital, called, not surprisingly, *the user cost of capital*, showing how a variety of tax provisions affect the costs of using capital. Not only is the effective tax rate often markedly lower than the official tax rate, but under some plausible assumptions capital is actually subsidized *at the margin*.

USER COST OF CAPITAL The magnitude of the effective tax on capital in the corporate sector depends on several provisions of the tax code—on investment tax credits, depreciation allowances, and the fraction of investment which is financed by debt (which is tax deductible).

Suppose the cost of a machine is p. If a firm rented the machine for a year, in a competitive capital market, the owner would charge rp in interest, where r is the interest rate, and δp in depreciation, where δ is the percentage reduction in the value of the machine as it has grown older. (Recall our discussion of depreciation from Chapter 21: as machines get older, they become less valuable both because they wear out and because they become obsolete. δ summarizes both effects.)[3] If R is the yield of the machine, the firm will rent the machine so long as

$$R > (r + \delta)p.$$

The effect of a tax imposed at the rate t on the corporation depends on what is deductible. If the firm were actually renting the machine, the full

[2] Similar results obtain if the supply of savings within a country is highly elastic.

[3] Changes in prices may, at times, result in capital gains on machines, in which case this too would be reflected in the rental price.

rental price would be deductible. If rental rates and depreciation charges $(r + \delta)p$ remained unchanged, then both sides of the inequality would be multiplied by $(1 - t)$. The tax would induce no distortions, because the firm would still rent the machine if $R > (r + \delta)p$, just as it does in the absence of the tax.

Now suppose that the firm buys its own machine, as is usually the case. The interest on the money the firm borrows to buy the machine is deductible. Assume a fraction α is financed by borrowing (for buildings, firms often borrow 80 percent or more of the costs; for machines, they often can borrow only a third). Then the interest deduction is $\alpha r p$.

δp is the true economic depreciation. But in Chapter 21, we pointed out that typically, firms are allowed more generous depreciation allowances. The 1981 tax law provided for greatly accelerated depreciation, and although these provisions were scaled back in 1986, depreciation still is at a greater rate than true economic depreciation. Let a denote the extent of acceleration, that is, the tax deduction for depreciation is $a\delta p$, with $a > 1$.

Finally, the government has, from time to time, provided an investment tax credit. If a machine costs \$100 million, a 5 percent investment tax credit means that the firm's taxes are reduced by \$5 million. It is as if the government has paid 5 percent of the cost, or the price has been reduced by 5 percent. Let c denote the tax credit rate, which effectively just reduces the price. Thus, the annual after-tax cost of capital is now

$$(r + \delta)p(1 - c) - t(\alpha r + a\delta)p(1 - c) =$$
$$(r + \delta)p(1 - t) - p\{c[r(1 - \alpha t) + \delta(c - at)] - t[(1 - \alpha)r + (1 - a)\delta]\}.$$

The first term is the annual cost, after accounting for the investment tax credit. The second term is the value of the income tax deductions.

Recall that after taxes, the machine yields $R(1 - t)$. If the cost is multiplied by the same factor, then the tax will have no effect on the firm's decision whether or not to buy the machine. But the above expression may be more or less than gross costs times $(1 - t)$, depending on whether the term in curly brackets is negative or positive. If the investment is totally debt-financed ($\alpha = 1$), there is no accelerated depreciation ($a = 1$), and there is no investment tax credit ($c = 0$), the cost of capital is reduced by exactly the same amount as the return is reduced; there is no distortion. Today there is no investment tax credit; for a firm financing 80 percent of its investment with debt, the benefits of accelerated depreciation exceed the tax on equity if

$$(a - 1)\,\delta > .2r.$$

The benefits of accelerated depreciation are typically greater for long-lived assets. The corporation income tax can lead to overinvestment in long-lived assets at the same time that it leads to underinvestment in short-lived assets.

USER COST OF CAPITAL

• The tax system affects how much it costs a firm to use capital.

• With accelerated depreciation and full deductibility of interest payments, investment may actually be encouraged relative to a no-tax situation.

• Investment is discouraged in assets which are financed by equity and those in which the benefits of accelerated depreciation are limited (such as short-lived assets).

THE CORPORATION TAX FOR A FIRM WITHOUT BORROWING CONSTRAINTS

The preceding analysis treated the firm as if it had a fixed debt-to-equity ratio, that is, it could only finance a certain fraction of its investment, α, with debt. In fact, one of the important decisions firms face is how to finance new investments they wish to undertake, and for most firms borrowing is an option. What, then, is the effect of the deductibility of interest payments on such decisions? We answer this question by assuming that depreciation allowances correctly reflect the decrease in the value of aging plant and equipment, thereby isolating the implications of the deductibility of interest payments.

If there is no accelerated depreciation and no investment tax credit, if a firm finances all of its investment with debt, there is no distortion. Returns are reduced by $(1-t)$, but the cost of capital is reduced proportionately. In economic decision-making, what matters is how returns and costs are affected *at the margin*. At the margin, firms in well-functioning capital markets can choose to finance additional investment out of borrowing. If they do, then their marginal costs are reduced by $(1-t)$, by the same proportion that their returns are. Investment decisions are thus unaffected by the corporate tax. Consider, for example, the simplest case of an infinitely lived asset (there is no depreciation). If the firm borrows to buy such an asset costing p dollars, its before-tax cost is rp, but its after-tax cost is $r(1-t)p$. When the firm asks itself, is it worth, at the margin, borrowing a little bit more to invest a little bit more, its answer is the same after the tax is imposed as before.[4] Thus, in the standard theory of the firm (sometimes called the *neoclassical theory*), where the firm faces no borrowing constraints, at the margin, it can be thought of as borrowing to finance investment, and with the marginal investment debt financed, and with debt tax deductible, the corporation income tax causes no distortion in investment.

---

[4] Equivalently, a firm with outstanding debt that is not currently borrowing from the market but that is doing some investment can ask itself: Is it worth investing a little bit less, and using the extra funds to repay some of our outstanding debt obligations?

In practice, much of investment is financed by debt at the margin. Typically, firms first use retained earnings (earnings less what they distribute as dividends) to finance investment, and investment beyond that amount is financed by borrowing.

THE INCIDENCE OF THE CORPORATION INCOME TAX WITH CREDIT-CONSTRAINED FIRMS

The model presented earlier in this chapter assumed, as we have noted, that at the margin, investments were financed the same way that they were on average. We have just seen that if firms are not credit constrained, at the margin, investment can be thought of as financed by borrowing, in which case there is no distortion.

But many firms are credit constrained. In that case, the impact of the corporation tax may be markedly different. If a firm can neither borrow nor issue equity, and if it is investing all of its retained earnings, taxes reduce the funds available for investing, and thus reduce investment. Note that in this case the impact of the corporate income tax depends on the total amount by which the funds available for investment are reduced, that is, it depends completely on *average* tax rates, not marginal tax rates, as in the earlier analysis.

There is a typical life cycle to the firm. Newly established firms sell shares to raise capital; it is often the only source of capital they can obtain—banks find long-term loans too risky, and these firms are too small to issue long-term bonds. Firms are reluctant to make long-term investments based on short-term loans. The original entrepreneur usually takes his return largely in the form of stock ownership (rather than wage payments). Thus the corporation income tax, which exempts interest payments, can be viewed effectively as a tax on these new, credit-constrained, entrepreneurial firms; it has adverse effects on the investment of new firms that cannot raise funds by borrowing additional amounts.[5]

If this view is correct, the long-run effects of the tax are not so much those associated with the reallocation of resources between the corporate and noncorporate sectors. Rather, they have to do with the degree of innovativeness of the corporate sector and the rate of technical progress. The magnitude of these effects depends on the elasticity of supply of entrepreneurship and risk taking. It was precisely these concerns that led President Clinton, in his 1993 tax bill, to include provisions for preferential treatment of very long term capital gains in new firms.

This analysis[6] makes clear that the impact of the corporation income tax depends critically both on the special features of the tax (such as the tax deductibility of interest) and the situation of the corporation (whether it is

---

[5] In addition, we noted in Chapter 21 that the imperfect risk-sharing (limitations on loss offset provisions) discourages risk taking, which is particularly important for these new enterprises.

[6] These alternative views of the corporation income tax were put forward in J. E. Stiglitz, "Taxation, Corporate Financial Policy, and the Cost of Capital," *Journal of Public Economics*, February 1973, pp. 1–34, and "The Corporation Income Tax," *Journal of Public Economics*, April–May 1976, pp. 303–11.

CORPORATION INCOME TAX WITH AND WITHOUT CREDIT CONSTRAINTS

• If firms can borrow to finance investment at the margin, then a corporation income tax with true economic depreciation does not distort investment.

• In effect, the corporation tax can thus be viewed as a tax on credit-constrained firms, such as new firms which cannot easily borrow.

• In these cases, the distortion may be more closely related to the average tax rate than to the marginal tax rate.

or is not credit constrained).[7] Many empirical studies of the effects of the corporation income tax simply assume that it increases the marginal cost of capital to the firm—the amount it would cost the firm to invest an additional dollar—by an amount equal to the average tax payments per unit of capital. That is, they assume that the marginal and average costs of capital are the same. We have seen that if firms can finance their marginal investment by borrowing (and if depreciation allowances are equal to true economic depreciation), there may be no marginal distortion caused by the tax system, and the marginal cost of capital may differ markedly from the average cost. Regardless of whether one holds the view that the marginal cost of capital is equal to (or less than) the marginal cost of funds raised by borrowing, there is no justification for the hypothesis that marginal and average costs of capital are the same.

THE CORPORATION TAX AS A TAX ON MONOPOLY PROFITS

When there are monopolies, there are monopoly profits. Pure profits, sometimes called *excess profits*, are total revenues less total costs, including a normal return on capital. (In long-run equilibrium, with competition, and with constant returns to scale, there are no pure profits.) That part of the corporate income tax corresponding to a tax on pure monopoly profits is,

---

[7] From this perspective, it makes little difference whether the firm actually cannot borrow or has to pay what it views as an exorbitant marginal interest rate. There is a large recent literature showing the prevalence of credit rationing, as well as providing theoretical rationale for its existence. See J. E. Stiglitz and A. Weiss, "Credit Rationing in Markets with Imperfect Information," *American Economic Review* 71, no. 3 (June 1981): 393–410; also see Thomas Hellman and Joseph Stiglitz, "A Unifying Theory of Credit and Equity Rationing in Markets with Adverse Selection," *European Economic Review* (forthcoming); Glenn Hubbard, ed., *Asymmetric Information, Corporate Finance, and Investment:* A National Bureau of Economic Research Project Report (Chicago and London: University of Chicago Press, 1990); and Jeremy Edwards et al., eds., *Recent Developments in Corporate Finance* (New York and Melbourne: Cambridge University Press, 1986).

in effect, a lump-sum tax on monopolists. The reason for this is simple. A monopolist maximizes his profits, π. If there is a tax at the rate t on his profits, his after-tax profits are $(1 - t)\pi$. But whatever the firm does to maximize π is exactly what he does to maximize $(1 - t)\pi$.

Whether the distortionary effects of the corporation income tax are greater (per dollar raised) with monopoly or competition is uncertain. On one hand, to the extent that the tax is partly a pure profits tax, it is nondistortionary. On the other hand, to the extent that it acts as an excise tax—a tax on what is produced in the corporate sector—and, because of monopoly, production of the sector is already lower than the socially optimal level, the tax causes a greater distortion.[8]

If a good is produced by a monopolist, the price may rise by more than the tax payments per unit output. As we saw in Chapter 18, under monopoly, with a demand curve of constant elasticity (that is, a 1 percent change in price has the same percentage effect on demand, regardless of the level of output), price is just a fixed markup over the marginal costs of production—including taxes. If the markup is, say, 20 percent, then if marginal costs increase by $1 from the imposition of the corporation tax, price will increase by $1.20.

Thus, if the corporate sector consists of a large number of industries, each controlled by a monopolist, the tax is largely shifted onto consumers, with the observed increase in prices being greater than the tax payments to government.

To predict how firms will be affected by—and respond to—the corporate income tax, we need a model of firm behavior. That is, we need to make assumptions about how firms act and what they try to achieve. The analysis so far has assumed that firms maximize their after-tax returns. There are a number of aspects of firms' behavior that seem hard to reconcile with this view. For instance, later we shall show that firms should not pay dividends; there are better (from a tax perspective) ways of distributing funds from the corporate to the household sector. The fact that firms have continued to distribute as much of their earnings as they have is called the "dividend paradox." Firms' dividend policy is not the only inexplicable aspect of corporate behavior.

---

[8] We noted in Chapter 19 that the deadweight loss of a tax increases with the square of the tax. The effect of monopoly is similar to that of a tax. Indeed, if the demand curve has a constant elasticity of, say, 2, monopoly has the same effect on output and consumer prices as a 50 percent tax on the output of a competitive industry. Imposing a 10 percent tax on the output of the monopoly thus has the incremental deadweight loss associated with increasing the tax on a competitive industry from 50 percent to 70 percent (taking into account the fact that the monopoly price rises by twice the magnitude of the tax when there is a constant elasticity demand curve with elasticity of 2). This is substantially larger than the incremental deadweight loss from increasing the tax from 0 percent to 10 percent on the output of competitive industry.

Accelerated depreciation provides another "tax paradox." At times, the government has given firms and individuals the right to depreciate their assets at an accelerated rate. Again, the total nominal depreciation allowances are unaffected (they equal the cost of the machine, minus its salvage value, if any). But more rapid depreciation reduces reported income and, hence, taxes, in the early years of the asset. All firms should want to take advantage of this opportunity; yet firms were very slow to do so. This is true even though firms can make it clear to their shareholders that *reported* earnings are lower than they otherwise would be because the firm has made use of accelerated depreciation; indeed, one might have thought that shareholders would take such a report as a positive signal of good management, and the absence of such a report as a negative signal.

Firms have a choice of how to treat their inventories. Assume a firm that is selling steel beams bought some steel at $40 a ton and some at $100 a ton, a few months later, as a result of rapid inflation in the industry. Both kinds of steel beams are in its inventory. When it sells some steel beams for, say, $110 a ton, does it say its cost of purchase was $40 or $100? The Internal Revenue Service allows the firm to choose what to say, so long as it does so in a consistent manner. It can say either that it is always selling the item most recently acquired (this is called the *last-in, first-out system*, or LIFO) or that it is selling the first item acquired (*first-in, first-out*, or FIFO). In inflationary periods LIFO has a decided advantage over FIFO. Current tax liabilities are lower (though future tax liabilities are increased by the same amount). But the general principle that a dollar today is worth more than a dollar tomorrow implies that firms are better off with lower current tax liabilities. Yet, amazingly, firms were very slow to switch to LIFO, and even today, many firms continue to use FIFO.

EXPLANATIONS FOR TAX PARADOXES Two explanations are offered for such seeming irrationalities. One is that managers of the firms have considerable discretion in managing their firms, sometimes pursuing their own interests at the expense of shareholders' interests. In particular, they may not pursue value-maximizing strategies. They may, for instance, wish to maximize the rate of growth of the firm; they may do this either because they believe that the larger their firm and the faster its rate of growth, the larger their salary; or simply because they enjoy the excitement that accompanies expansion and the personal recognition that it affords. In this view, the discipline of the marketplace simply isn't strong enough to ensure that managers act in a profit- or value-maximizing manner. Firms which, rather than maximizing profits, pursue the interests of managers are called **managerial firms.** The second explanation is that firms (or their managers) are rational but that shareholders are irrational. Shareholders do not understand how the tax system (or corporations) work. It is unlikely that they would notice a firm's switch to the LIFO system, but they would see the firm's current reported profits decline, and they would believe that the firm was not doing as well as it was. As a result, the price of the firm's shares would decline. Managers, whose compensation often depends partly on the market value of the firm, thus prefer to keep shareholders "happy" by engaging in policies that do not minimize the firm's tax liabilities. Both explanations probably are partially correct.

These theories of firm/managerial behavior are important for several reasons. For instance, they yield quite different predictions concerning the effects of changes in corporate taxes on firms' behavior and government revenue. Consider a simple change, such as allowing more-rapid accelerated depreciation. Standard theories might predict a strong investment response, with a concomitant reduction in revenues to the Treasury. But if managers are worried that the accelerated depreciation will make this year's profit statements look bad, many firms may fail to avail themselves of the tax advantages—with less loss of revenue to the government but also less stimulation of investment.

Increasing recognition of the differences in interests between managers and investors (and other stakeholders in the firm) has led to calls for tax policies directed at better aligning those interests. For instance, the view that managers succeed in getting the board of directors (which they arrange to be elected) to vote themselves outlandish salaries resulted in the Clinton administration's proposing and Congress's adopting a tax on salaries of top management in publicly owned corporations in excess of $1 million *that were not based on performance criteria.* (The ratio of the salaries of top managers to that of the average worker in the United States is reportedly more than five times that in Japan, and considerably larger than in virtually all other advanced countries.)

THE CORPORATE VEIL More generally, our analysis of firm behavior is predicated on the assumption that individuals can understand what is going on inside the firm: that they are indifferent, for instance, when choosing between owning 10 shares in a firm with 1000 shares or 9 shares out of 900 shares in the same firm; that if the firm reduces its debt obligations by $1000, the market will see that the net worth of the firm is now $1000 greater, and its share prices will correspondingly increase; that if the firm invests $1 million of retained earnings, and a shareholder owns 1 percent, it is as if the shareholder herself has invested $10,000 directly. We assume, in other words, that individuals can see through the **corporate veil** to what is really going on.

It is important to realize that all investors need not be well informed about firms' savings and investment for the corporate veil to be pierced. All that is required is that enough investors realize that a firm that has saved and invested $1 million should have a market value $1 million larger than it was before for the stock price to rise by the requisite amount. Uninformed shareholders may not know why the firm's shares have increased in value. All they know is that they have.

Whether shareholders see through the corporate veil has important consequences both for the behavior of the firm and for the economy. At the level of the firm, shareholders' seeing through the corporate veil means that in the absence of taxation, they would be completely indifferent about how the firm financed itself.[9]

At the level of the economy, the nature of the corporate veil is important because of its implications for aggregate savings. Currently, in the United States, most private savings is done not by individuals directly but by corporations.[10] The question is, does increased corporate savings lead to lower household savings? If individuals see through the corporate veil, they treat the savings done by corporations fully as if it had been done on their own account. So long as there are enough informed investors to bid up the price of shares to reflect the new investment, even uninformed investors act as if they saw through the corporate veil; for they respond to the increase in wealth resulting from the increased share prices by increasing current consumption (decreasing savings). In this view, then, the division of savings between household savings and corporate savings is purely an artifact of our current tax laws, which encourage savings within the firm. It is *as if* the corporation distributed all of its profits to its shareholders and then they decided how much to save. If the corporate veil is perfectly pierced, then, the corporate tax has less effect on the aggregate level of savings than on its allocation: some firms with high cash flows but lower marginal returns on investments may be induced to retain their funds and invest them internally, while if the funds had been recycled back to the shareholders, they would have found their way to higher return opportunities. But in a world with perfect or near perfect information—a world in which it was easy to pierce the corporate veil—even these distortions would not exist, for the firm with high cash flows would seek out the highest *marginal* return investment opportunities; it would not limit itself to investing in itself.

There is both macro- and micro-evidence (that is, evidence both at the level of the economy and at the level of the firm) that individuals do not see perfectly through the corporate veil. We have already referred to several puzzling aspects of corporate behavior that seem inconsistent with the hypothesis that individuals do see through the corporate veil.

Moreover, stock prices are highly volatile. Many economists believe that they reflect true capital values only imperfectly. More importantly, house-

---

[9] If the firm borrowed more, shareholders would treat the indebtedness as if the firm had borrowed on their behalf. If a shareholder did not like that amount of indebtedness, he could simply reduce the level of debt he had on his own account (or he could buy offsetting corporate bonds). If the firm invested its retained earnings, shareholders would treat the investment as if they had made it themselves directly in the firm. In this view, then, in the absence of taxation, whether firms paid dividends or retained earnings would make no difference. Accordingly, if taxes give preferential treatment to retained earnings and debt finance (as we shall show shortly that they do), then those tax considerations determine how the firm finances itself. See F. Modigliani and M. H. Miller, "The Cost of Capital, Corporation Finance, and the Theory of Investment," *American Economic Review* 48 (1958): 261–97; and J. E. Stiglitz, "On the Irrelevance of Corporation Financial Policy," *American Economic Review* 64 (1974): 851–66.

[10] In 1997, personal savings (226.7 billion) accounted for over 19 percent of gross private savings (1164.2 billion); corporate savings was about three times that amount (695.1 billion). *Survey of Current Business*, July 1998, Table 5.1.

MANAGERIAL FIRMS

• Firms may be run in the interests of managers and not be profit- or value-maximizing.

• A number of tax paradoxes—behavior that is hard to reconcile with profit or value maximization—are consistent with the managerial theory. These tax paradoxes include:

The dividend paradox—firms pay dividends when there are other ways in which profits could be distributed from the corporate to the household sector which would incur lower taxes.

Firms' frequent failure to take advantage of accelerated depreciation or other tax preferences.

• Shareholders may not be able to see completely through the corporate veil; accordingly they may react more to reported current profits (which may go down when a firm takes advantage of a tax preference) than to the long-run impact on the firm.

holds, at least in the short run, do not pay much attention to the day-to-day variations in the market value of their securities; they do not act as if they viewed these fluctuations as meaningful changes in their wealth, requiring an appropriate response in consumption levels. Still, in the long run any policy that led systematically to increased corporate savings would *eventually* have an impact on household savings, if only because such a policy would have a systematic effect on the value of corporations and, through this, on the shareholders' views of their net worth.

DEPRECIATION

We have seen in this chapter how detailed provisions of the tax code can make a large difference in its effect. The distortionary effect of the corporation income tax may be completely eliminated, for instance, if interest can be deducted, and if firms can borrow at the margin to finance their investment.

An equally important provision of the tax relates to depreciation. We saw in Chapter 21 why it was necessary to make some allowance for the depreciation of an asset; as it wore out or became obsolete, it became less valuable; the reduction in the value needs to be subtracted from income. True economic depreciation represents the true reduction in the value of the asset. But because it is typically difficult to find accurate estimates of this decrease in value, governments typically allow an estimate which is more generous (that is, the present discounted value of depreciation allowances exceed what they would be under true economic depreciation). The standard method is to estimate the lifetime of the asset, say ten years, and to allow one-tenth of the value of the asset to be subtracted every year. This, as we noted, is called *straight-line depreciation.*

Many governments have used still more generous depreciation allowances to encourage greater investment. With **accelerated depreciation,** firms and individuals are allowed to take more depreciation in the early years of the asset's life. The simplest way this can be done is to use a life span that is shorter than actual—say, three years, for an asset that will actually last five years. With a $100 asset, this would mean taking $33 over the first three years of the asset (and nothing thereafter), whereas with straight-line depreciation, using the true lifetime, the depreciation allowance would be $20 each year.

The value of accelerated depreciation can be enormous. This is illustrated in Table 23.2. There, we consider an asset that has a five-year lifetime and costs $100 but that the government allows to be depreciated in three years. The asset is assumed to yield a constant amount each year ($24) and to have no salvage value after five years. The interest rate is assumed to be 10 percent. At that interest rate, the present discounted value of the annual return equals its cost. In the first column of the table, we show the true economic depreciation, and in the second column the present discounted value of these depreciation allowances (as viewed at the time of purchase). The third and fourth columns show straight-line depreciation, and the fifth and sixth columns show one form of accelerated depreciation. It is clear that there is a very large subsidy— over 10 percent when compared to true economic depreciation. At higher discount rates, and for longer-lived projects, the benefit is even greater. Note that in this example, the difference between true economic depreciation and straight-line—with the true life of the asset—is relatively small (though straight-line depreciation still has a present discounted value of depreciation allowances that is greater than true economic depreciation).

Far more disturbing, however, is the fact that the magnitude of the subsidy varies greatly from one asset to another. Accelerated depreciation rules typically provide a major subsidy for long-lived assets. As a result, not only are some assets favored over others, but industries that use the favored assets gain at the expense of those that use the less favored assets.

Using a shorter-than-true life span for an asset is only one of several ways that governments have provided accelerated depreciation. The U.S.

TABLE 23.2
Comparison of True Economic Depreciation, Straight-Line Depreciation, and Accelerated Depreciation

YEAR	DISCOUNT FACTOR (10% INTEREST RATE)	1 TRUE ECONOMIC DEPRECIATION	2 PRESENT VALUE	3 STRAIGHT LINE	4 PRESENT VALUE	5 ACCELERATED DEPRECIATION	6 PRESENT VALUE
1	1	16	16	20	20	33.3	33.3
2	$1/(1.10) = .909$	18	16.36	20	18.18	33.3	30.3
3	$1/(1.10)^2 = .826$	20	16.52	20	16.52	33.3	27.6
4	$1/(1.10)^3 = .751$	22	16.52	20	15.02	7	5.3
5	$1/(1.10)^4 = .683$	24	16.39	20	13.65		
			81.79		83.37		91.2

government, for instance, offers another alternative, called *double declining balance*. Consider a five-year asset purchased on January 1. Instead of allowing 20 percent each year, an allowance of 40 percent is made. Then the next year, an allowance of 40 percent of the "declining balance"—which amounts to 60 percent of the original value. Thus the depreciation allowance the second year is 24 percent. The next year, 40 percent of the balance of 36 percent is taken, that is, 14.4 percent. For the remaining two years, straight-line depreciation is used *over the remaining* 21.6 percent of value, that is, 10.8 percent is taken each year.

The 1981 tax law for the first time introduced life spans that deliberately had no relationship with actual life spans. For instance, commercial buildings could be depreciated over fifteen years. The tax savings gave rise to a boon in commercial building, leading to a glut which took almost two decades to work itself out.

The vastly accelerated depreciation allowances for equipment were intended to revitalize "smokestack America," America's heavy industry. Most economists believed that there was no special reason to give preference to heavy industry over other sectors of the economy. While the accelerated depreciation was a major windfall for these industries, in fact there was little evidence that the tax provisions played a significant role in accelerating investment in that sector. Because of the concern that the accelerated depreciation allowances were highly distortionary, they were repealed a short five years after they were introduced.

One's view of the overall impact of the corporation tax needs to integrate the combined effects of both interest deductibility and accelerated depreciation. If firms can borrow to finance investment at the margin, and if there were true economic depreciation, then we have seen that the corporation income tax is nondistortionary. But if, as is the case, there is accelerated depreciation, then there will be overinvestment. On the other hand, for firms that are badly credit constrained, what drives investment is not incentives but resources, and high average tax rates can thus lead to underinvestment. The net impact of the corporation income tax is thus to shift investment away from new entrepreneurial, credit-constrained firms to old, established firms that have good access to credit markets.

COMBINED EFFECTS OF INDIVIDUAL AND CORPORATE INCOME TAX

To assess fully the effects of the corporation income tax, we must see how it interacts with the individual income tax. This in turn requires us looking more carefully at the relationship between the corporate and household sector.

In Figure 23.2 we have drawn a schematic picture of the relationship between the corporate and the household sector. Funds flow from the corporate sector to the household sector in the form of dividends, interest, and share repurchases. Funds flow from the household sector to the corporate sector in the form of new bonds and new equities. Funds flow within the household sector as individuals purchase shares and bonds from each other. And funds flow within the corporate sector as corporations purchase one another and are merged.

The tax authorities treat interest, dividends, and capital gains differently. Interest and dividends are taxed identically at the individual level, but payments from the corporation to the individual that are labeled "interest" are deductible from corporate income, while those labeled "dividends" are not. Therefore corporate earnings that are transferred to individuals in the form of dividends are taxed twice—once in the form of the corporate tax and again by way of the individual income tax. Earnings transferred in the form of interest are taxed only once. If the firm buys back shares, the individual shareholder is only taxed on the difference between the price at which he purchased the share and the price at which the firm buys it back. While there are legal constraints that prohibit a firm from regularly buying back a pro rata share of its stock from each of its stockholders in lieu of paying dividends, firms can simply buy back shares on the open market.[11]

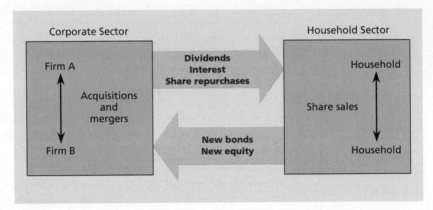

FIGURE 23.2   **Flow of Funds between and within Household and Corporate Sectors** Funds flow from the corporate sector to the household sector, from the household sector to the corporate sector, and within each of the two sectors.

---

[11] Note that if the firm bought back 5 percent of each individual's shares, the fraction of the firm that each owned would remain the same. This transaction is substantively the same as an equivalent cash dividend.

Note too that if the firm buys back the shares on the open market, the advantages of the share repurchase are even greater. Each individual could have sold back 5 percent of his shares; the fact that an individual chooses to sell back a different amount means that he is better off than if he were "forced" to sell back 5 percent of his shares. Individuals who bought the shares at a higher price may be more willing to sell their shares, since in doing so they encounter a smaller tax liability than those who bought the shares at a lower price. Thus, the transfer of funds from the corporate to the household sector will entail an even smaller tax liability than if the firm repurchased 5 percent of each shareholder's shares.

The fact that our tax code does not tax all transactions at the same rate, and taxes transfers in the form of dividends from the corporate sector to the household sector without allowing any deduction from corporate income, as it does for interest, has two basic implications:

1 Avoid transferring income (after paying interest) from the corporate to the household sector whenever possible.

2 When income must be transferred, do it in a form so that it is eligible for capital gains treatment.

The incentive for firms to retain earnings—not to transfer income from the corporate to the household sector—is of concern for several reasons. Managers of firms should have to persuade potential investors of the merits of their managerial skills and investment projects; with large amounts of funds retained within the firms—and a large tax wedge associated with redistributing money back to households—less discipline is required of managers, and with less discipline required of them, they may not do as effective a job either in managing their funds or in reinvesting their proceeds.

THE DIVIDEND PARADOX

Corporations often seem to engage in financial transactions that are not consistent with the above principles. Dividends provide one important example. The puzzle of why firms pay dividends, when funds could be distributed from the corporate to the household sector in ways that encountered lower tax liabilities such as share repurchases is called, as we have noted, the **dividend paradox.**[12]

A number of possible explanations have been put forward, most of which are not very convincing. One is that dividends serve as a "signal" concerning the firm's net worth. Though this may be true, buying back shares should be an equally effective signal.[13]

---

[12] The dividend paradox was discussed in J. E. Stiglitz, "Taxation, Corporate Financial Policy, and the Cost of Capital." Subsequent studies include J. Poterba and L. H. Summers, "Dividend Taxes, Corporate Investment, and 'Q'," *Journal of Public Economics*, 1983, pp. 135–67; A. Auerbach, "Wealth Maximization and the Cost of Capital," *Quarterly Journal of Economics*, August 1979, pp. 433–66; D. Bradford, "The Incidence and Allocation Effect of a Tax on Corporate Distributions," *Journal of Public Economics* 15 (1981): 1–22; and M. King, *Public Policy and the Corporation* (London: Chapman and Hall, 1977).

[13] There is considerable evidence, for instance, that the buyback of shares does serve as a signal; firms that buy back their shares see a marked increase in their market value. See, for instance, P. Asquith and D. Mullins, "Equity Issues and Offering Dilution," *Journal of Financial Economics* 15, no. 1–2 (January/February 1986): 61–89; Bruce Greenwald, J. E. Stiglitz, and Andrew Weiss, "Informational Imperfections in the Capital Market and Macroeconomic Fluctuations," *American Economic Review* 74, no. 2 (May 1984): 194–99; Stewart Myer and Nicholas Majluf, "Corporate Financing and Investment Decisions When Firms Have Information That Investors Do Not Have," *Journal of Financial Economics* 13, no. 2 (June 1984): 187–221.

Though many owners of stock are tax-exempt (and thus indifferent to whether the firm issues dividends or buys back shares), individual shareholders who pay taxes should prefer share buybacks.[14]

The tax advantages of distributing funds from the corporate to the household sector through share repurchases (as opposed to dividends) can be obtained in other ways. When one firm buys another for cash, the receipts by the owners of the acquired firm are subject to capital gains taxation.

Though many firms have persisted in policies that appear not to minimize total tax liabilities, in recent decades there has been increasing sensitivity to tax concerns.

During the ten years preceding the Tax Reform Act of 1986, mergers, acquisitions, and share repurchases increased enormously. While in the early 1970s payments for mergers, acquisitions, and share repurchases amounted to approximately 15 percent of dividends, by 1984 they exceeded dividends, and in 1985 they amounted to almost 50 percent more than total dividends. The cost to the Treasury in forgone tax revenues exceeded $25 billion in 1985.[15] Many economists believe that these activities were tax induced; that corporations had gradually come to recognize the advantages of distributing funds to the household sector in ways that subjected them to capital gains taxation.[16]

The 1986 Tax Reform Act not only reduced the tax advantages of capital gains by taxing them at full rates, but also repealed several provisions that resulted in capital gains taxes' being avoided when a firm was liquidated (either when it was sold to another firm, or when its assets were sold, with the proceeds distributed to the shareholders). The effect of these tax changes appears to have been dramatic: Share repurchases, which in 1980 had amounted to only 10 percent of dividends, had increased to 57 percent by 1985, but by 1990 had dropped back to 34 percent.[17] With the marked in-

[14] There are financial transactions that are even more puzzling than just paying dividends. For instance, when a firm simultaneously pays dividends and issues new shares, it unnecessarily increases tax payments. If the funds had been left in the corporate sector, the tax on the dividends could have been avoided. Even if some shareholders wanted the cash that the dividend provided, they would have been better off by selling an equivalent amount of their shares (to the individuals who would have bought the new share issues).

[15] From J. Shoven, "New Developments in Corporate Finance and Tax Avoidance: Some Evidence," in L. Summers, ed., *Tax Policy and the Economy*, National Bureau of Economic Research, 1987.

[16] But many economists argue that though there may have been tax benefits, these mergers and acquisitions had other motivations. See M. Jensen, "The Take-over Controversy," *Journal of Economic Perspectives*, winter 1988.

[17] From U.S. Department of the Treasury, *Report of the Department of the Treasury on Integration of the Individual and the Corporate Tax Systems: Taxing Business Income Once*, January 1992. Shoven and Bagwell report a huge increase in the percent of cash distributions through either acquisitions or share buybacks during the decade beginning in 1977, from slightly more than 20 percent to over 58 percent. See Laurie S. Bagwell and John B. Shoven, "Cash Distributions to Shareholders," *Journal of Economic Perspectives*, summer 1989, pp. 129–40.

crease in preferential treatment of capital gains from the tax laws of 1993 and 1997, we can expect to see a rise once again.

DOES THE CORPORATE
TAX BIAS FIRMS
TOWARD DEBT
FINANCE?

We have seen that debt is tax deductible. In the absence of taxation—and in the absence of imperfections in capital markets and information—firms would be indifferent over whether they financed themselves through debt or through equity. This basic idea, developed by Nobel Prize winners Merton Miller and Franco Modigliani, is sometimes explained by an analogy to milk: The market value of milk consists of the value of the cream and the value of the "skim" milk. One can repackage the product, skimming off some of the cream, to form 2 percent milk, but the overall value remains the same. Debt and equity represent different ways of packaging the return to an investment. Equity owners get whatever is left over after the claims of debtors are satisfied. With more debt, the amount left over for equity owners is reduced, and the variability of this residual may be greater; but the total amount that will go from the corporation to the households is the same, and hence the market value will be the same.

Taxes change this, because the amounts sent to households in the form of interest payments are deductible from the corporation tax, but the amounts sent to households in the form of dividends are not. But offsetting this advantage of debt, there is an advantage to equity: the amounts retained by firms, which increase the market value of the firm, receive preferential treatment—they are taxed only when the individual sells her shares, and then at preferential rates. If the individual holds on to her shares until her death, they escape taxation completely. Moreover, by financing new investment out of retained earnings, the corporation avoids the tax on the "round trip" that would be involved in first distributing money to shareholders (even if it manages to do so in a way which receives favorable capital gains treatment). Clearly, whether the firm is better off retaining less and borrowing more depends on the relative tax advantages of the interest deductibility and capital gains. As the rates at which corporate profits, dividends, and capital gains have been taxed have changed, the balance has shifted back and forth; overall the preferences do not appear to be very strong. There continues to be a slight preference for firms to finance as much of the investment as they can out of retained earnings. This is in fact the typical pattern, with investments in excess of retained earnings financed by borrowing, so long as the debt-to-equity ratio does not get too large and so long as the enterprise is not credit rationed. Risky new enterprises often have to resort to issuing new equity to raise the capital they require to grow.

But preferences for equity are sufficiently weak that it does not pay firms to restructure—that is, to borrow money to repurchase shares or issue dividends. Doing so would increase their debt/equity ratio—and thus increase the fraction of their gross income that they distribute in a tax-deductible manner. But there is a tax cost of restructuring: In the process of repurchasing shares or issuing dividends, an individual income tax liability is incurred, which otherwise would not have been, and the magnitude of this typically is greater than the (present discounted value of the) savings from the fact that interest payments are tax deductible.

Individuals in different individual income tax brackets might, however, argue for alternative policies. Low-income individuals and tax-exempt organizations would prefer that the firm pursue a high-debt strategy, since they incur no (or few) additional taxes upon restructuring, but the corporation saves money. The fact that different individuals would like the firm to pursue different strategies suggests that different firms should have different clientele. It is not apparent to what extent they in fact do, perhaps because these tax effects are not as important as other considerations.

If Modigliani and Miller were correct, the distortions in how a firm financed itself would be of little import, but in fact, for a variety of reasons, how a firm finances itself does make a difference. For instance, firms that are heavily debt financed may be particularly vulnerable to the threat of bankruptcy in the event of an economic downturn. By encouraging heavy debt finance, the tax laws may exacerbate the economy's fluctuations.

DISTORTIONS IN ORGANIZATIONAL FORM ARISING BECAUSE SOME FIRMS DO NOT HAVE TAXABLE INCOME

We have seen that the desire to distribute earnings in a form which receives preferential treatment may partially account for share repurchases, mergers, and acquisitions. Another aspect of the tax system has perhaps an even larger impact on organizational design: the limitations on loss offsets. Many firms have profits so small that they cannot fully take advantage of depreciation allowances; and still other firms have losses.

Debt financing or economic losses on past investments may lower taxable income to the point where companies cannot use all their depreciation deductions and tax credits.

Consider a firm with large depreciation allowances, say, because of accelerated depreciation on some new assets, which at the same time is making losses in a variety of other lines. If its taxable income is negative, the depreciation allowances have no value; when the tax is already zero, it cannot be reduced further.

Assume that the firm still will be doing poorly when the returns to the investment occur. Then, since the returns will not be taxed—there will be losses in other parts of the firm to offset the returns on this productive investment—the tax system may cause no distortion. But most firms that are doing badly and are investing anticipate doing better in the future; this implies that while the firm is not able to take advantage today of the depreciation allowances, it will have to pay taxes in the future on the returns to that investment, just like any other firm. Thus the tax system causes a strong distortion *against* investment in firms that are currently not doing well, and helps to perpetuate their weak position.

TAX-INDUCED MERGERS The market always attempts to find ways of dealing with inefficiencies created by the tax system. One way is for a firm with losses to merge with a firm with profits. This is referred to as a **tax-induced merger.** Many economists are concerned about the long-run consequences of these mergers. Such mergers may limit competition in the economy. More importantly, the mergers may not be based on underlying economic considerations, such as economies of scope or synergies between the parts of the merged firms. Managerial talents may be stretched, so that overall performance may be decreased. Moreover, it is believed that the vitality of a capitalist economy depends on there being a large variety of firms, each with its own strengths and thus in a position to take advantage of different situations. Some have made the analogy between firms and species of animals. Just as it may be advantageous to preserve a rich genetic pool, to be drawn upon in a variety of circumstances, so too may it be desirable to have a diversity of firms in the economy. The provisions of the tax code that encourage mergers (mergers that, apart from taxes, would not be undertaken) should, in this view, be altered.

Would it pay an individual who owns a business to incorporate? If she incorporates, she could pay out all of her "profits" in the form of wages, thus avoiding the corporate income tax. Or she could choose to retain her earnings. On her retained earnings, she would have to pay the corporate income tax. And if she reinvested the funds, she would have to pay the corporate income tax on the earnings from those investments. When she finally wished to get the funds, she would have to pay taxes on the distribution; if she managed it well, she might succeed in getting those distributions taxed at the favorable capital gains tax rate (and if she left her firm to her children, who then sold the firm, taxes might be avoided all together). Clearly, whether incorporation pays de-

COMBINED EFFECTS OF INDIVIDUAL AND CORPORATE TAXATION

• The effects of taxation depend on the interaction of the individual and corporate tax systems.

• While debt financing receives preferential treatment under the corporate income tax, capital gains receive preferential treatment under the individual income tax. Whether overall debt or equity is tax preferred depends on the tax bracket of the individual.

• Distributing money from the corporate to the household sector in the form of dividends rather than share repurchases or through mergers and acquisitions (in which case the distributions would receive capital gains treatment) lowers overall tax.

• Even if it pays a firm to borrow to finance new investment beyond that which it could finance through retained earnings, it may not pay a firm to restructure itself, for example, through borrowing to buy back shares, to increase its debt/equity ratio.

• Whether corporations overall are tax preferred depends on the tax bracket of individuals, and on the extent to which capital gains receive preferential treatment.

pends on the relative tax rates on corporations and individuals. For an individual at the maximum individual income tax bracket of 39.6 percent and the corporation tax at 35 percent, there is a slight preference for incorporation, especially if funds are retained within the firm long enough and when they are finally distributed, receive favorable capital gains treatment.

But more generally, income earned within a corporation is effectively double taxed, once within the firm, and again when it is distributed to households. There is little evidence, however, that this has a marked effect in discouraging incorporation.

CALCULATING EFFECTIVE TAX RATES

We have seen that the full effect of taxation on investment in a particular asset, in a particular industry, depends on a myriad of features of both the individual and corporate income tax, including the tax treatment of capital gains, losses, dividends, and interest, whether firms are or are not credit constrained, whether they are profit-maximizing or managers take decisions in their own interests. There are further issues we have not discussed here, such as property and state income taxes, and how those tax payments are treated under the individual and corporate income tax. Needless to say, calculating the marginal tax rate associated with an additional unit of investment is not easy. What is clear, however, is that the effective marginal tax rate typically differs markedly from the average tax rate, as well as from the marginal tax rate stated in legislation.

There have been several attempts at a full calculation of the effective marginal tax rate, taking into account all of the marginal taxes—corporate, property, and personal—that are paid as a result of a new investment. Perhaps the most thorough recent study of overall effective marginal tax rates on investment is that of Don Fullerton and Yolanda Henderson.[18] They asked: If an individual invests a dollar more in an asset that yields a before-tax return of, say, 10 percent, what will his after-tax return be, after paying property taxes, capital gains taxes, corporation taxes, taxes on dividends, interest, and so on? Alternatively, what before-tax rate of return is required if the individual is to obtain, say, an after-tax return of 10 percent? The striking result of their study was that for firms that could finance their *marginal* investment by debt, the effective marginal tax rates (for equipment, structures, public utilities, inventories, and land) were all very negative, so much so that, for instance under the 1981 tax law, corporate equipment yielding a before-tax return of −10 percent would yield an after-tax return of +10 percent. If, for some reason, firms could not finance their marginal investment by debt, then they faced positive effective marginal tax rates. Still, the overall effective marginal tax rate on capital appeared to be lower than on most wage income. Another surprising result of their analysis was that owner-occupied housing—which has often been thought to be "tax preferred," since there

---

[18] D. Fullerton and Y. K. Henderson, "Incentive Effects of Taxes on Income from Capital: Alternative Policies in the 1980s," in *The Legacy of Reaganomics: Prospects for Long-Term Growth*, ed. C. R. Hulten and I. V. Sawhill (Washington, D.C.: The Urban Institute Press, 1984).

are no taxes paid on the "imputed rent"—actually is taxed more heavily than other residential structures. The Fullerton-Henderson study was based on the highly distorted 1981 tax law; subsequent reforms, especially those enacted in 1986, substantially increased effective marginal tax rates in the corporate sector and on non-owner-occupied residential structures. These reforms, however, have not succeeded in creating a true "level" playing field.

DISTORTIONS FROM THE CORPORATION TAX

Corporation tax distorts level of investment.

- May result in underinvestment, especially for credit-constrained firms.

- With accelerated depreciation, firms that can finance marginal investment by borrowing may invest too much.

Corporation tax results in distortions in the kinds of investments that are made.

- Encourages long-lived versus short-lived capital goods.

- Encourages investment in assets that can be collateralized (more debt-financed), compared to those (like R&D) that cannot.

- Encourages investment in industries, like real estate, that have higher debt-to-equity ratios, or industries that have more long-lived assets.

Corporation tax may alter form of financing.

- Net effect depends on combined effects of corporate and individual income taxes.

- Deductibility of interest encourages debt financing.

- Preferential treatment of capital gains encourages financing through retained earnings.

Corporation tax may affect the organization of production.

- May discourage incorporation (with limited liability).

- Under current circumstances, net impact may be small.

Enterprises having easy access to credit may be preferred (face lower cost of capital) to those which are credit constrained.

Enterprises with profits may be preferred to those without profits.

- May give rise to leasing and tax-induced mergers.

Monopolies may be affected differently from firms in competitive markets.

THE CORPORATION TAX AS ECONOMIC POLICY

The distortions discussed in this chapter represent largely unintended consequences of the corporation tax. But the corporation tax has also been used as a tool of economic policy. One of the purposes for which taxes on capital have been used is economic stabilization: to encourage investment in economic downturns and to slow investment when it appears that the economy is overheating. This was the original motivation for the introduction of the investment tax credit. (See box above.)

While changes in tax rates and credits are sometimes used to stabilize the economy, without these adjustments, the corporate income tax would probably exacerbate business fluctuations. A significant part of economic fluctuations is due to variability in investments in small and medium-size enterprises[19] which typically have limited access to capital markets, especially in periods of economic downturn. In a recession, they face a shortage of funds, and are forced to cut back on investments. The corporate profits tax reduces the funds that they have available for reinvestment, and thus exacerbates the decline in investment. Some have suggested that

[19] Steven Fazzari, Glenn Hubbard, and Bruce Peterson, "Investment Financing Decisions, and Tax Policy," *American Economic Review* 78, no. 2 (May 1988): 200–205.

(as other decisions) is *marginal* cost, not average cost. By lowering the marginal cost of investing, the incremental investment tax credit might have provided a strong stimulus to the economy, at a fraction of the costs of a full investment tax credit (since the incremental investment would have been but a small fraction of total investment).

If firms had known that such a tax credit would be levied, it might have had distortionary effects, as firms reduced their levels of investment before the credit went into effect so as to make more of their investment eligible for the credit. But since the credit was explicitly made temporary, and the base from which increments were to be measured was investment in previous years, there was no point for firms to try to "game" their investment strategies.

Unfortunately, most firms saw little payoff in the proposal; they were more concerned with receiving money than with getting incentives, and the whole proposal was designed to minimize the amount of money transferred to the corporate sector while providing strong incentives. Without strong corporate backing, the proposal died in Congress.

if the government were more evenhanded in its risk sharing—sharing not only profits in good times, but losses in bad times—it would help stabilize investment. Under current law, firms are allowed to carry forward losses (that is, they can deduct losses incurred in 1999 from the profits that they earn in the year 2000), but no interest is paid, and the promise of future tax breaks does little to help them over the cash flow problems that they face today.

Besides stabilization, the most common policy use of the corporation tax is to promote investments in some industries (which means, in a full-employment economy, at the expense of investments in other industries). For instance, the favorable depreciation allowances enacted in 1981 were designed to help restore America's heavy industries. The special tax preferences afforded to the oil and gas industry are another example. Most economists believe that there is no economic justification for these special provisions; they are the result of political pressures from special interest groups.

Capital taxation, both within incorporated and unincorporated enterprises, is in fact subject to a myriad of special provisions, so much so that by one estimate 80 percent of capital income receives some kind of preferential treatment.[20]

[20] See E. Steuerle, "Is Income from Capital Subject to Individual Income Taxation?" *Public Finance Quarterly*, July 1982, pp. 283–303; and Jane Gravelle, *The Economic Effects of Taxing Capital Income* (Cambridge and London: MIT Press, 1994).

TAXATION OF MULTINATIONALS

Today, most major companies operate in many countries. Some of these are American companies, like Ford and General Motors, that have subsidiaries around the world. Others, like Toyota, Nestlé, and Phillips, are foreign companies which not only ship goods to the United States, but also actually produce here. Moreover, foreign companies have many shareholders who are American, just as many American companies have many shareholders who are foreign. The largest single shareholder in the largest U.S. bank is a Saudi Arabian. Some American companies are more than 50 percent foreign owned. All that it means to be "American" is that the company's official "home" is in the United States; it is incorporated here. It does not mean that the company is owned by Americans; or even that most of its production is here.

Indeed, production increasingly is occurring on a global scale, with parts gathered from all over the world. A label on a computer or car, "MADE IN USA" or "Made in Korea" may mean only that that was the place where it was assembled. The fraction of "value added" or the fraction of total labor costs occurring in that country may be relatively small.

This presents real problems for tax authorities. What is the "income" on which the corporation tax should be levied? There is a naïve answer: The tax should be levied on that part of the income attributed to economic activity in the country. The problem is how that is to be ascertained. Assume that USAComputer assembles a computer in the United States, using parts made by its factories in Hong Kong, Singapore, Taiwan, Malaysia, and Korea. If USAComputer had bought those parts from an unrelated supplier, calculating U.S. income would be easy. We would simply subtract from its gross sales its wages and other costs of production here as well as the costs of all the parts purchased abroad. But USAComputer owns its own factories, and does not sell its parts to anyone. There is no market price. To calculate its tax liability, it must make up a price, called a *transfer price*; this is an estimate of what the market price would have been, had it purchased the item in an arm's-length transaction with a third party.

If corporate tax rates in the United States are higher than in the countries where it produces its parts (which is typically the case), then USAComputer has a strong incentive to try to increase its profits there and to decrease its profits here, by claiming a high transfer price. With a high transfer price, U.S. profits are low. The company may claim that the high price is warranted by the high quality, a result of the high skills of the workers in its manufacturing plants. The IRS may claim that these components are little different from those produced by other producers, which sell for pennies in the open market. Alternatively, it might claim that most of the value of the parts is a result of research conducted in USAComputer labs in the United States, and accordingly that the value added by the parts manufacturer abroad is small. It should be clear that even with relatively intense scrutiny by the IRS, manufacturers have considerable discretion to shift profits from one country to another through transfer pricing; and that preventing more such shifting from occurring requires enormous diligence, and costs, by the IRS.

Moreover, in some cases, the corporation is put into a seemingly impossible situation, with, say, Japanese tax authorities—who would like more of the income attributed to activity in their country—arguing that the firm is using too low a transfer price while the United States claims that the firm is using too high a transfer price.

The huge costs and potential for disputes associated with the transfer price system has led to arguments for a *unitary* tax system, in which taxes are levied on a proportion of a firm's *worldwide* income. The portion is set by a formula, which looks at the fraction of employment, assets, and sales occurring within the country. Similar systems are used by states within the United States for levying state corporation taxes; indeed, given the close intertwining of production across state lines, trying to use a transfer price system within the United States would probably be close to impossible. As more and more production occurs within multinational firms, the problems of levying the corporation tax using a transfer price system are likely to become more and more apparent.

With global corporations, taxes can affect where production occurs and where and how funds are raised. The United States, in setting its tax regime, must worry about how its tax regime interacts with those of other countries. For instance, if it sets tax rates too high, firms may be induced to shift their production abroad.

SHOULD THERE BE A CORPORATION INCOME TAX?

The rationale for the corporation income tax has never been completely clear. Some believe that corporations, like individuals, ought to pay taxes. But most economists find this argument unpersuasive, since it is not the corporation that pays the tax, but people: those who work for the corporation, those who supply capital to it, and those who buy the goods produced by it.

While politicians often justify the corporate tax in terms of its progressive effects, it is possible that the tax has no significant redistributive effect. This is hard to determine because of the difficulties of ascertaining who really bears the corporate tax burden. The tax can be viewed as a tax on the corporate form of organization (on limited liability). Is there any reason why the government should wish to discourage this form of organization, or to penalize those who derive income from it?

**INTEGRATION
OF THE CORPORATE
AND INDIVIDUAL
INCOME TAX**

In fact, because the advantages of incorporation are so great, the tax may not have a significant effect in discouraging incorporation. There are nevertheless concerns about equity, and about the wider range of distortions in the form of finance that result from the interaction of the corporate and individual income tax. This has led to proposals for integrating the individual and corporate income tax systems. A simple form of integration would impute the earnings of a corporation to shareholders; corporations would be treated (for tax purposes) as if they were partnerships, in which profits were credited to the "account" of each shareholder. For the most part, such proposals have received at best a lukewarm reception, both from corporate executives and from shareholders. Shareholders worry that they would face tax liabilities, even though they have received no checks from the corporation. (They could, of course, simply sell some of their shares.) Corporate executives worry that they would be under pressure to distribute more of the company's profits, thus reducing their degree of discretion. Indeed, so concerned have corporate managers been with these pressures that they did not even support proposals put forward to make dividend distributions tax deductible.

Equally important, most forms of integration would reduce revenues, and in the budget stringency of recent years government officials have preferred to retain the corporate income tax in its current form, with its ambiguous incidence. If tax cuts are to be made, politicians have chosen to grant them in forms which seem to yield higher political payoffs—such as child care or education tax credits.

WHY IS THERE A CORPORATE INCOME TAX AT ALL?

Some critics of the corporate income tax have gone so far as to question why there is any corporate income tax at all. With full integration of corporate and individual income taxes, there would in effect be no corporate income tax. But short of full integration, without a corporate income tax, funds retained within the firm would escape bearing taxation until the funds were distributed. And for corporate holdings passed on to heirs, taxation could be completely avoided. In effect, the return to capital earned within a corporation would escape taxation. A corporation income tax is a necessary part of an individual *income* tax system. As we have seen, its distortionary effects may be limited so long as its rates are similar to those of the individual income tax.

By the same token, with a *consumption*-based tax system, there would be no rationale for a corporation income tax.

REVIEW AND PRACTICE

SUMMARY

1 The corporation tax is often viewed as a tax on capital in the corporate sector. The effective tax rate depends on a variety of details, including depreciation allowances and the fraction of debt financing. In the long run, if savings is fairly elastic or if capital is mobile internationally, most of the burden of the tax rests on consumers and workers.

2 If the supply of capital in the economy is fixed and the economy is competitive, the effect of the tax is to shift capital out of the corporate sector into the noncorporate sector, because after-tax returns in both must be the same. After-tax returns to capital may be lowered by even more than the tax.

3 Under our present tax system, interest payments are tax deductible. This means that if marginal investment can be thought of as being financed through debt, a corporation tax with true economic depreciation causes no distortion in the investment of the firm. With accelerated depreciation,

investment in the corporate sector is encouraged. The tax is best viewed as a tax on credit-constrained firms, which include many new firms; hence it can be viewed as a tax on entrepreneurship.

4   There is no reason to believe that firms finance new investments in the same way as they financed their previous investments, so that taxes may affect the marginal cost of capital differently from how they affect the average cost of capital.

5   If the corporate sector is noncompetitive, the tax is partially a tax on monopoly profits, and to that extent it is nondistortionary. But the tax may also be a tax on the return to corporate capital, and to that extent it may increase consumer prices by more than the increase in the costs of production resulting from the tax. There may appear to be more than 100 percent shifting.

6   In assessing the impact of the corporation income tax, one needs to consider the effect of the corporation tax simultaneously with the effect of the individual income tax. The total (corporate plus individual) tax liability associated with a marginal investment depends on how that investment is financed, whether through debt or through equity. The tax structure may affect how firms raise capital.

7   The fact that firms pay dividends when there are other ways of distributing income to shareholders which result in lower total tax payments is called the dividend paradox. It is only one example of paradoxical behavior by firms, where they do not seem to minimize their tax liabilities.

8   The corporation tax falls unevenly on different forms of corporate investment, thereby biasing investment decisions toward certain favored assets or industries and against others that are not so favored.

9   Many economists believe that the corporation and individual income taxes should be integrated.

10 With the growth of multinational firms, there are serious problems in administering a corporate income tax, in particular in ascertaining how much income (profit) should be attributed to each country. There are two approaches, the arm's-length transfer pricing approach and the unitary approach.

KEY CONCEPTS

Tax base

Managerial firms

Corporate veil

Accelerated depreciation

Dividend paradox

Debt

Tax-induced mergers

Integration of corporate and
   individual income tax

1 Discuss some of the controversies concerning who bears the burden of the corporation income tax. To what extent are differences in views accounted for by differences in assumptions concerning the nature of the tax?

2 Is it possible for: (a) the price of output of the corporate sector to rise by more than the tax revenues collected (per unit of output); (b) the after-tax rate of return in the corporate sector to increase, after the imposition of the corporate income tax? Give conditions under which either of these may occur.

3 Discuss the problems that arise when the corporation tax rate exceeds the highest personal income tax rates by a substantial amount.

4 Many firms pay their top executives with stock options, which give them the right to purchase shares in the company at a fixed price. When the firm does well, the value of the stocks increases, and hence the value of the option increases. Moreover, the income they obtain this way receives capital gains treatment. Some critics of stock options claim that similar incentive effects can be obtained by tying executives' pay to the performance of the stock, but that paying executives directly has overall favorable tax consequences, once all taxes—including corporate taxes, the taxes paid by executives, and the taxes of shareholders—are taken into account. Discuss. (When the company pays executives directly, the wages are deductible from the firm's income subject to the corporate income tax; the "costs" of stock options are not deductible.)

5 There have been proposals to allow firms interest on the losses they carry forward on their tax returns from one year to the next. That is, if a firm has a loss this year of $100,000, and the interest rate is 10 percent, it can deduct $110,000 from its income next year (assuming that it is positive). Why might such a proposal be desirable? Would it completely resolve the problems that it is intended to address?

6 Why do economists place so much emphasis on the difference between average taxes and marginal tax rates? Under what circumstances might these two differ significantly? Are there any circumstances in which you might be particularly concerned about what the average tax rate is?

7 Compare the taxes an individual would pay if he had a million dollars to invest in a machine which lasts one period only, yielding a gross return of $1.2 million, if he incorporates and if he does not. Assume that if he incorporates he (a) lends the company the million dollars to buy the machine; or (b) invests the money as equity. Also, assume that if he incorporates and provides capital to the firm in the form of equity, he (a) pays out the net profits as dividends; or (b) manages to distribute the funds in a way that gets favorable capital gains treatment; or (c) dies next year, before the profits have been distributed, and leaves the firm—with its

cash position of $200,000—to his son, who manages to sell the firm for $200,000. Assume that he can subtract the full million dollars as depreciation, and that interest is tax deductible.

8   Compare the present discounted value of taxes an individual who is the sole owner of a corporation that has $1 million in profits would pay under the following two scenarios: (a) She pays out the profits to herself, invests them in a bond yielding 10 percent, which she holds for seven years. (b) She retains the profits inside the corporation, invests in an asset yielding 10 percent; after seven years, she sells the asset (which has retained its original value), and distributes the proceeds to herself. (For simplicity, look at two cases, one in which the individual is in the 40 percent marginal tax bracket and pays a 20 percent capital gains tax rate; in the other the individual is in the 15 percent marginal tax bracket and pays a 10 percent capital gains tax rate.)

24 A Student's Guide to Tax Avoidance

FOCUS QUESTIONS

1 What are the two major principles of tax avoidance?

2 How do tax shelters work, and who gains and who loses from their distortionary effects?

3 In what ways have recent tax reforms affected the opportunities for tax avoidance?

There is a widespread belief that the rich are able to avoid paying much of the taxes that they would otherwise owe by taking advantage of loopholes in the tax law. Although tax laws change, there is a constant duel between the government and the tax lawyers, with the tax lawyers developing new loopholes almost as fast as old ones are closed.

From the public policy point of view, it is imperative to understand the nature of tax loopholes, for two reasons. First, the total impact of the tax law depends as much on these special provisions as it does on the law's overall design. Enacting a progressive tax structure may make little difference if the loopholes provide a method by which the rich can avoid paying high tax rates. Second, distortions in the patterns of investment and savings caused by these special provisions may be more significant than distortions in the level of savings and investment caused by uniform capital taxation.

We are concerned here with **tax avoidance,** as opposed to **tax evasion.** Tax evasion is illegal; tax avoidance entails taking full advantage of the provisions of the tax code to reduce one's tax obligations. Tax evasion includes not reporting all of one's income. Tax avoidance entails compliance with the tax laws, but recognizing that they tax different forms of income differently. Provisions of the tax code that allow an individual to "escape" paying taxes—or to reduce tax obligations—are called **loopholes.** But there are often disagreements about what constitutes a loophole. Consider, for example, a provision that encourages expansion of the oil industry. Critics, especially those who view the provision as unwarranted, a result of the influence of a special interest group, will label the provision a "loophole" because it reduces taxes of investors in the oil industry, while advocates will describe it as a *tax expenditure*, a reflection of a deliberate government decision to use tax incentives to encourage this vital industry. Like beauty, loopholes often are in the eyes of the beholder![1]

In 1986, during the administration of Ronald Reagan, the U.S. tax system was substantially reformed, and one of the explicit aims of the reform was to make tax avoidance more difficult. Changes in tax laws in 1993 and 1997 introduced a variety of new special provisions. Advocates claimed that these changes would encourage education and investments (especially investment in innovative small businesses); critics claimed that they reopened old—and opened some new—opportunities for tax avoidance.

PRINCIPLES OF TAX AVOIDANCE

There are two basic principles involved in income tax avoidance. The first is postponement of taxes. The second is taking advantage of differences in the tax rates for different types of income, and for income to different individuals, by shifting income from high-taxed categories to lower-taxed categories.

POSTPONEMENT
OF TAXES

A dollar today is worth more than a dollar next year. Accordingly, if one has a choice, it is always better to postpone one's taxes (assuming, of course, that tax rates do not rise). There are several major methods of postponing taxes.

ACCOUNTING TRICKS Accounting devices can be used to postpone the recognition of income. For instance, one way to postpone the capital gains tax on the sale of an asset is to postpone the date at which the transfer of the asset finally occurs. When an individual buys a business (or any other large asset), the seller often lends the buyer part of the purchase price, which the buyer repays over several years. When does the sale of the asset actually occur and, hence, when must the seller pay capital gains tax? Is it when "control" of the asset is transferred, or when the buyer pays off the loan? The answer depends at least in part on how the sale is "designed." If title is not transferred until all funds are received, the later payments may be deemed payment of

[1] There are some loopholes that are put inadvertently into the tax law, as a result of errors in writing legislation. Some of these are corrected in the "technical corrections acts" which are passed a year or so after the passage of every major tax act. The fact that such errors occur with such regularity is testimony to the complexity of the tax system, the difficulty of making precise legal definitions in a complex economy.

part of the purchase price rather than debt repayment. In this case, the seller will be able to postpone the capital gains tax. (Such transactions are called **installment purchases.**)

In construction projects and defense contracts, payments made prior to the completion of the contract are sometimes viewed as "loans" to the contractor, rather than payment for the project. This allows the recipient to defer payment of income taxes until the project is complete and the debt is paid off.[2] Almost half of the projected increase in corporate tax revenues under the 1986 reform act was due to changes in accounting rules, including those related to construction and defense contracts. In fact, many of these accounting gains did not materialize.

CAPITAL GAINS AND THE POSTPONEMENT OF TAXES Capital gains on an asset, as we have observed, are taxed only upon realization, that is, when the asset is sold. If one buys a capital asset and its value goes up, one can postpone paying the tax simply by not selling the asset. If one would like to sell part of the asset in order to buy, say, some consumer goods, it may be better to borrow, using the asset as collateral. This method has a further advantage: If one postpones the sale until death, no capital gains tax is due (even by one's heirs).[3] Standard estimates suggest that the ability to postpone the capital gains tax alone reduces the effective tax rate by 25 percent.

SHIFTING AND TAX ARBITRAGE

The second major strategy for avoiding taxes is based on the fact that income that accrues to different individuals is taxed at different rates, or that different kinds of income are taxed at different rates.

INCOME SHIFTING Under a tax structure with increasing marginal rates, a taxpayer at a high marginal rate will always want to "shift" income to a taxpayer with a low marginal rate. In particular, it pays parents to shift income-producing assets to their children. The 1986 Tax Reform Act tried to limit

---

[2] In this case, the tax advantages are related primarily to the differences in tax rates for the two sides of the transaction. Say one firm hires another to perform a task. If the first firm treats the payment to the second as a loan, it cannot take a business deduction, while the second firm does not record the receipt as income. If the first firm is in a lower tax bracket than the second, then the present discounted value of the *total* taxes of the two is decreased by postponing the tax; the two parties can split the gain between themselves. If an individual is purchasing, say, a home, then his payments to the contractor are not tax deductible, so there is an unambiguous gain from postponement. These examples illustrate a general principle: In assessing the tax impact of any particular arrangement, one has to look at how all the parties to the transaction are affected.

[3] The relevant provision is called a "step-up of basis." Capital gains taxes are due on the difference between the sale price and the acquisition price (called the *basis*). When an individual dies, his or her heirs take as the basis (the price at which they in effect acquired the asset) the price at the date *they* acquired the asset, not the price at the date their benefactor acquired the asset. Curiously, if a parent gives (rather than wills) an asset to his or her child, then the "basis" is not "stepped up," but remains the value at which the asset was originally acquired.

such shifting by taxing those under age 14 at the marginal tax rate of the parent (if it is higher).

There are several important points to note about **income shifting.** *First, typically it requires the transfer of an asset, such as stocks, bonds, real estate, or a share in the parents' business.* Working parents cannot simply ask their employer to make out their paychecks in their children's names.

Second, income shifting works simply because of the fact that marginal tax rates increase with income. With a flat-rate tax structure, in which the marginal rate is constant (the individual is taxed, at a fixed rate, on the excess of his or her income over some exemption level), there is no incentive for income shifting, provided that the exemption level for a family is proportional to the number of individuals in the family. Thus, the 1986 tax law reduced the incentive to shift income, while the 1993 law increased it. With a 40 percent tax rate, shifting $1000 from a parent to a 15-year-old child saves $400.[4]

Third, there is a limit to the tax savings an individual can achieve through income shifting. Consider a self-employed family of two adults and two children, and total family taxable income of $220,000. By shifting $60,000 to the 15-year-old son, the parents can reduce total family taxes by $7997,[5] a substantial amount, but still a relatively small percentage of their total tax liability.[6]

Fourth, the government has attempted to limit income shifting, with only partial success. Consider the problems posed by divorce: How should income from an ex-husband to his ex-wife and their children be treated? Under current law, alimony is excluded from the income of the payer and included in the income of the recipient. Therefore, characterizing payments from an ex-spouse as alimony (rather than as a property settlement or child support) may have significant tax advantages, if the payer has a higher income than the recipient.

While income shifting among members of a family represents a highly visible way in which upper-income families reduce their total tax liability, more important—in terms of lost tax revenue—are two other forms of shifting: (a) shifting of income among corporations; and (b) shifting income into a form that takes advantage of the preferential treatment afforded capital gains.

CORPORATE SHIFTING Corporations are allowed to deduct depreciation allowances, and at times there have been large investment tax credits. But if a firm has no income, a depreciation allowance is of no value. Consider a firm

---

[4] One quirk in the tax law which encourages tax shifting for those who own businesses is that a parent who hires a child does not have to pay social security taxes on the child's behalf. Though the provision was motivated by a concern for small businesses, the tax shifting advantages are significant.

[5] The total tax is minimized by transferring income until the marginal tax rates of the parents and son are equal. (Once marginal tax rates are equal, there are no further benefits from shifting income from one party to the other; this limits the amount of tax savings.) For couples filing jointly, the marginal tax rate on income over $151,750 (in 1997) is 36 percent. Of the $60,000 shifted to the son, $24,650 is taxed at the 15 percent rate, saving $5176.50; $35,100 is taxed at 28 percent, saving $2808; and $250 is taxed at 31 percent, saving $12.50.

[6] With income of $220,000, the tax would be $63,268.50 and hence the reduction in taxes would be just 13 percent.

SHORTING AGAINST THE BOX

Most stock brokerages permit clients to borrow shares of stock. An investor may sell borrowed shares today, and later buy the same shares on the market so that they may be returned to the lender. Selling borrowed shares is called *short selling*. If the value of the borrowed shares falls between the time they are sold and the time they are purchased again and returned, the investor may realize a profit. (Of course, if the share value rises, big losses may be racked up.) A related tax avoidance scheme, called *shorting against the box*, emerged from the favorable capital gains treatment that results when individuals leave assets to their heirs.

Shorting against the box worked like this: Suppose a wealthy individual owned 2000 shares of Microsoft that were trading at $100

that has been making losses that needs some cars or trucks. If it purchased the vehicles itself, the depreciation allowance would have no immediate value, since it is not, in any case, paying any taxes. But if another firm buys the vehicle and then leases it to the firm, the firm buying the vehicle gets to deduct the depreciation allowances. With strong competition among lessors (those buying the vehicles), most of the benefits will be received by the lessee (those using the vehicle). That is, the price at which the lessor rents the vehicle will reflect the tax breaks. This example serves to illustrate yet again an important general principle of taxation: It is often difficult to tell who really receives the benefit from a tax break. It may not be the person who enjoys the deduction.

CAPITAL GAINS The 1997 tax law substantially lowered the tax rate on capital gains (for upper-income individuals, from 28 to 20 percent, compared to a tax rate on ordinary income of close to 40 percent). Consider a $1 million asset which is expected to rise in value by 10 percent (and pays no dividend or other returns). If the interest rate is 10 percent without taxation, the individual would be just indifferent to buying the asset. If the individual can borrow to buy the asset, however, the interest may be tax deductible; at a 40 percent marginal tax rate, the after-tax interest cost is only 6 percent (or $60,000). But the capital gain is taxed at only 20 percent, so the after-tax value of the capital gain is $.8 \times \$100,000$, or $80,000. He makes a pure gain of $20,000 after tax. The same reasoning makes clear that it will now pay him to buy assets which even, in the absence of taxation, would entail losses. The entire profit is due to "tax arbitrage," discussed below.

TAX ARBITRAGE Arbitrage involves taking advantage of price differences for the same commodity. If gold is selling for $350 an ounce in New York, and $375 in Zurich, and the cost of shipping gold between the two is $20, someone can buy gold in New York and ship it to Zurich for a sure profit. **Tax ar-**

per share. She could raise $50,000 in cash by selling 500 shares, but assuming the shares were purchased at less than their current price, she would have to pay a capital gains tax. But if she sold short 500 shares—borrowing 500 shares from her brokerage firm and selling them on the market—while at the same time promising 500 of the shares she owned to be returned to the brokerage firm by her heirs after her death—putting them in the brokerage's "box," as they say on Wall Street—she could raise the same $50,000, and avoid the capital gains tax. In this way, the wealthy codger had her cake and ate it too: she got the cash, bore no risk, but avoided taxes as if she postponed selling the shares until after death.

This particular loophole was closed in 1997.

---

bitrage entails taking advantage of the different rates at which different kinds of income or different individuals are taxed.

Strictly speaking, the term "arbitrage" refers to situations where there is a sure gain—i.e., there is no risk assumed. Though in theory the tax code provides many opportunities for riskless tax arbitrage, in practice most tax avoidance activities involve the assumption of some risk. This is partly because of the general provision in the tax code that a set of transactions undertaken solely to avoid taxes will not be granted the favorable tax treatment. There are many situations where individuals must show that they are "at risk" to obtain the favorable tax treatment. But the risks that have to be borne are minimal.

The term "arbitrage" is also applied to situations where different individuals face different tax rates, and a set of riskless transactions are designed so that both are better off as a result of the reduction in their joint tax liabilities.

Still another form of arbitrage occurs when individuals borrow to put money into a tax-exempt bond or an IRA account. If an individual borrows, ostensibly to buy a house, then the interest payments are tax deductible. The government does not ask, does he *need* to borrow the funds; it only traces where the dollars actually went. It might pay someone with $100,000 in his bank account to borrow $100,000 more, to buy a house, and put the extra money into tax-exempt bonds. If he receives, say, 4 percent interest on the tax-exempt bond, even if he has to pay 6 percent interest to the mortgage company, if his combined federal and state marginal tax rate is 50 percent, then he will have an extra $1000 to spend every year. (The net cost, after tax, of his mortgage interest is only 3 percent, or $3000, and he receives $4000 on his tax-exempt bonds.)

Tax authorities have tried to limit tax arbitrages, by restricting the ability to borrow to buy tax-exempt bonds or to put money into an IRA. But such restriction is difficult in practice: individuals do not borrow to buy a municipal bond, but take out a larger mortgage on their house, so that they have more cash on hand to purchase a tax-exempt bond a few months later on.

PRINCIPLES OF TAX AVOIDANCE

Postponement of Taxes

    Taking advantage of the time value of money

Tax arbitrage

    Taking advantage of differences in tax treatments and rates

TAX SHELTERS

Investment schemes that reduce one's tax liabilities are called **tax shelters.** A tax shelter exists when deductions from one income source (e.g., oil and gas or real estate) can be offset against income from another source (e.g., salaries and wages).

There are a wide variety of tax shelters, but exploration of gas and oil is perhaps the most notorious. This tax shelter is based on a number of special, favorable tax provisions for the gas and oil industries. In Chapter 21, we discussed depreciation allowances. These are provided to take account of the fact that as a machine is used, it becomes less valuable (it wears out and becomes obsolete). Similarly, as oil is extracted from a well, the well becomes less valuable. To compensate for this, the government provides *depletion allowances*. These are related not directly to the change in the value of the asset, but to the value of the oil extracted. The level of depletion allowances has varied over time, at one time reaching 27½ percent of the value of the oil sold. The correspondence between the depletion allowance and the change in the value of the well is even weaker than that between the depreciation allowance for a machine and "true economic depreciation." For instance, over the life of the well, the depletion allowance may exceed the purchase price of the asset. Moreover, when an oil well (or lease) is sold, a capital loss can be taken against the original purchase price without accounting for the depletion allowances taken in the interim. It is as if the government allows two tax deductions for the decrease in the value of the asset.

The taxpayer can use these deductions to shelter other income from taxation.

**WHO GAINS FROM
TAX SHELTERS**

Consider an oil industry tax shelter. There are five possible beneficiaries. The benefit could accrue to the "intended" beneficiary, the oil industry. Or it could be shifted forward to consumers, in the form of cheaper oil; or shifted back, to the owners of the land under which there is oil. Or the benefits could accrue to the Wall Street firms that put together tax shelter deals. Or the benefits could be completely dissipated in excessive transactions costs.

If there were no transactions costs, the theory of incidence presented in Chapter 18 would tell us that who benefits depends on elasticity of demand and supply curves. Panel A of Figure 24.1 shows the case of a highly elastic supply curve. This might be more appropriate for subsidies to cattle. The special tax treatment can be thought of as lowering the cost of production, shifting the supply curve down (that is, the price required for the market to be willing to supply a given level of output is lowered). Because of the highly elastic supply curve, the market price is lowered by almost the full amount

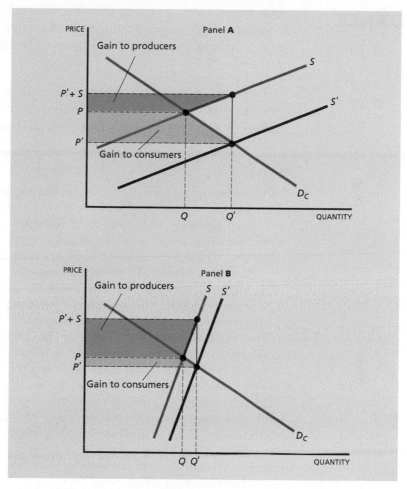

FIGURE 24.1 **Impact of Subsidies** Panel A: When supply is elastic, a shift in the supply curve (caused by favorable tax treatment for the supplier) brings about significant changes in equilibrium prices and quantities. The industry is able to produce more, but much of the gain accrues to consumers, in the form of a lower price. Panel B: When supply is inelastic, an increase in the subsidy leads to relatively small changes in equilibrium quantities and prices. Because the equilibrium price does not fall by much, producers are able to retain much of the gain from the subsidy. If the goal of the subsidy is to increase output, the policy is successful in case A; if the goal is to transfer money to producers, the policy is effective in case B.

THE
ECONOMICS
OF TAX
AVOIDANCE

For individuals with complicated tax situations, there are often gray areas, issues where there is ambiguity about the proper tax treatment. A wall is part of a structure of a building, and as such needs to be depreciated over the life of a building (a commercial building has an assumed life of thirty-nine years). But a *portable wall* is like equipment, and can typically be depreciated as if it were "equipment," not a building, and can be depreciated over ten years. How portable does a wall have to be to be "equipment" rather than "structure"?

Individuals, corporations, and their accountants engage in a risk analysis: they balance the risk of being caught taking an "aggressive" stance (that is, interpreting the tax law in the most favorable way,

of the subsidy: it is consumers, not producers, who benefit from the subsidy in this case. The fact that consumers are better off, however, is not an unmitigated blessing. They benefit by less than the amount of the subsidy; there is a deadweight loss. Because the supply curve is elastic, there is a large distortionary effect, and a large deadweight loss.

Panel B of Figure 24.1 shows the case of a highly inelastic supply curve. This might be more appropriate to special tax provisions for oil and gas, where the supply (in the long run) is relatively inelastic. Then, prices paid by consumers remain relatively unchanged. At first blush, it looks as if the industry is better off—by the full magnitude of the tax benefits. But because producing oil is more attractive, oil producers compete more actively for leases of land under which there is oil. It is these owners of land—of the inelastic factors required to produce oil—who get the benefit of the subsidy. (Of course, many oil producers also are large owners of oil-producing land, and to that extent they benefit directly.) With an inelastic supply curve, the distortionary effect is small, but from a social point of view, the subsidy is "wasted." The usual argument for a producer subsidy is to maintain or augment the size of an industry; with inelastic supply, there is no supply effect, just a redistribution effect.

In neither case would we expect to see the returns to investment in the subsidized industry (in the long run) higher than normal. Capital flows in until its rate of return (taking into account the subsidy) is the same as elsewhere. Thus capital in the affected industry does not receive much of the benefit. Evidence supports these theoretical predictions: the returns in heavily subsidized industries, like gas and oil, are no higher than returns elsewhere, adjusted for risk.

This analysis ignores transactions costs. Putting together and marketing tax deals costs money. If some firms have specialized talents in doing this, then they receive much of the benefits, in the form of payments for their specialized skills, which the tax law has made more valuable. In the short

from their own perspective) with the consequences. Typically, so long as there are *reasonable* grounds for a taxpayer's position, no penalty is levied, even if the IRS rules against the taxpayer. Hence, apart from the costs of hassle, it pays firms to take an aggressive stance. And corporations typically have large legal staffs to handle tax issues; the "battle" with the IRS is not viewed as hassle, but simply as a part of doing business.

On the other hand, the IRS can and does impose penalties for actions it views as unreasonable. Accountants often face a delicate balance in trying to decide how hard to push their clients' tax interest. The boundary between the reasonable and unreasonable is often blurry.

run, much of the benefit of tax shelters accrues to such firms, because there are always some firms that are quicker to recognize the full opportunities afforded by tax laws. In the long run, however, the "tricks" of the trade disseminate, more firms learn how to put together the tax shelters, and even the profits of the Wall Street promoters get competed away. Effectively, the value of the tax shelter is dissipated in transactions costs, including the costs of marketing the tax shelter.

MIDDLE-CLASS TAX SHELTERS While loopholes and tax shelters are typically thought of as provisions of the tax code which reduce tax liabilities for the rich, in fact there are a variety of provisions in the tax code which reduce taxes for middle-income taxpayers. The most important are employer-provided health benefits (worth an estimated $67,050 million in 1997), mortgage deductions (worth an estimated $49,060 million in 1997), and the deductibility of state and local income and property taxes (worth an estimated $47,635 million in 1997). Each of these provisions results in economic distortions: for instance, mortgage deductibility results in higher expenditure on housing. It also biases individuals to buy their homes rather than rent. As always, there is some ambiguity about the motivations of these provisions: Is the provision mainly a response to the efforts of the real estate lobby, to provide a subsidy which benefits them at the expense of other sectors of the economy? Or is the provision part of a social policy which encourages home ownership, in the belief that home ownership contributes to the stability of society?

TAX REFORM AND TAX AVOIDANCE

There have been four major tax reforms in the 1980s and 1990s. The first, in 1981, opened up a wide variety of tax loopholes. The market responded with enthusiasm, and the tax shelter industry boomed, giving rise to a demand for tax reform. While the 1986 tax reform represented

WHO GAINS AND LOSES FROM TAX SHELTERS?

When producers receive favorable tax treatment, the extent to which output increases or price falls depends on elasticity of demand and supply curves. Elasticity of supply is likely to be larger in the long run than in the short run.

Short-run beneficiaries:

• Owners of factors which are specific to industry at time preferential treatment is introduced (announced).

• Those who market tax shelters.

Long-run beneficiaries:

• Consumers (lower prices as industry expands)

Losers from tax shelters:

• Taxpayers

• Economy—misallocation of resources

the most serious attempt at reducing tax avoidance, the two subsequent tax reforms, in 1993 and 1997, opened up new opportunities for tax avoidance at the same time they markedly increased incentives for tax avoidance.

THE 1986 TAX REFORM   One of the major objectives of the 1986 tax reform was to design a tax system that was, and appeared to be, more fair. This meant that something had to be done about tax shelters. Three approaches were considered by the Treasury Department. The first was eliminating the provisions, such as the favorable treatment of capital gains and the special treatment of the gas and oil industry, that gave rise to tax shelters. The second was limiting the extent to which losses on one category of income could be used to offset income in other categories. The third was imposing a more effective minimum tax. After careful consideration, the Treasury in formulating its original proposals decided on the first approach—to go after the basic source of the problem—and clearly rejected the second. Unfortunately, when Congress took up the matter, members found it politically difficult to attack many of the shelters directly, though one change, the full taxation of capital gains, reduced the value of many tax shelters. Because Congress left many of the loopholes in place, it had to turn to the second and third methods of attacking tax shelters.

The most important way Congress did this was to divide income into three categories: ordinary (earned) income, investment income, and passive income. Income generated by tax shelters (in which the individual did not take an active role) was categorized as passive income. So was most real estate income. Losses in one category could not be used to offset income in another. Thus interest expenses on one investment could be used to offset income from another investment, but net losses on investments as a whole could not be used to offset ordinary income. Nor could losses on real estate be used to offset ordinary income.

The Treasury had rejected this approach to controlling tax shelters for two reasons. First, one of the original objectives of tax reform had been to *simplify* the tax code. Distinguishing between passive, investment, and ordinary income requires a host of definitions, regulations, and court cases that inevitably make the tax code even more complicated. Secondly, there was, and is, concern that these provisions are of only limited effectiveness. Though they limit the extent to which tax loopholes can be used to avoid taxation of wage income, they do not effectively limit the extent to which individuals (particularly the rich) can avoid taxation of capital income. They increase the transactions costs of tax avoidance. Real estate projects that generate taxable income are bundled together with real estate projects that generate taxable losses. Taxes on real estate can thus continue to be avoided.

MINIMUM TAX ON INDIVIDUALS

The 1986 tax act also attempted to reduce tax avoidance activities by imposing a somewhat stiffer minimum tax. The minimum tax on individuals is levied on a much broader definition of income; for instance, state and local income and property taxes are not deductible, and depreciation allowances are far less generous. The rules allowing individuals to take tax shelter losses are even more stringent than under the ordinary income tax. The alternative minimum tax rate was increased both in 1986 and 1993. Today it stands at 26 percent for "AMT taxable income" (the taxable income defined under the alternative minimum tax rules) of $175,000 or less (for a married couple), and a 28 percent rate on income in excess of that threshold.

The 1986 tax law substantially reduced the demand for tax shelters and the opportunities for tax avoidance by narrowing the gap between regular rates and the minimum tax rates, by lowering the top marginal tax rates, by restricting the ability to use losses on one type of income to offset gains on another, and by taxing capital gains at full rates.

THE 1993 AND 1997 TAX ACTS

The effects of the 1993 law were more ambiguous. The alternative minimum tax rates were increased, but so were the regular rates, with an increase in the absolute gap for upper-income individuals; and new ways of tax avoidance were introduced. The 1997 act unambiguously made matters worse: still further avenues of tax avoidance were introduced; a gap between the rates at which capital gains and ordinary income were taxed was introduced for all taxpayers, not just upper-income individuals; and the gap for upper-income individuals was increased.

EQUITY, EFFICIENCY, AND TAX REFORM

This chapter has not attempted to provide an exhaustive list of loopholes, tax avoidance devices, and tax shelters. These change rapidly; at a given moment some of the loopholes will have been closed and others opened up. The principles involved, however, remain the same.

Different industries have very strong incentives for attempting to garner special treatment for themselves. Often there is some small justification for the special treatment. This special treatment opens up a loophole, which can usually be put into one of the categories that we have described in this chapter. It is important to remember that the benefits of these tax shelters usually do not accrue to the investor attempting to take advantage of them. In a competitive market investors compete sufficiently vigorously to take advantage of the special tax preferences that the after-tax return—which, after all, is what the individual is really concerned with—is driven down to the after-tax return on other, less advantaged investments.

The major beneficiaries are the owners of the assets in the industry at the time that the loophole is opened up. The tax advantages are capitalized in the value of their assets; that is, if they sell their assets, they will receive a higher price for them; the buyer of the asset will pay a sufficiently high price that his or her after-tax return will be the same as it would be on any other asset.

Just as the imposition of such a tax benefit causes an inequity, a windfall capital gain for the current owners, the removal of the tax benefit causes an inequity, a windfall capital loss for the current owners. If the assets in the industry are owned by the same individuals when the benefit is granted as when it is withdrawn, the two cancel each other. But frequently, the removal of the special treatment occurs several years later, and it is often different individuals who will be affected by the removal of the special treatment. Closing the loophole is likely to be inequitable. This makes reforms—eliminating the distorting tax preferences—all the more difficult.

However great the magnitude of the inefficiencies and inequities introduced by the various tax loopholes and tax shelters, and regardless of whether such opportunities for tax avoidance can be justified as advancing (even successfully) some important social objective, loopholes and tax shelters have one very negative consequence: They erode confidence in the tax system, because they give rise to the impression that the system is unfair, with some individuals able to avoid bearing their proper share of the tax burden. These concerns have been one of the major motivations for the tax reforms which are the subject of the next chapter.

REVIEW AND PRACTICE

SUMMARY

1 There are two major principles underlying most of the devices by which individuals can legally attempt to reduce their tax liabilities: tax deferral, and income shifting, from high-taxed individuals and categories to lower-taxed individuals and categories (tax arbitrage).

2 Income shifting occurs under progressive taxes, where a family, by transferring assets to children, reduces its total family tax liability.

3 Tax deferral is based on the concept that a dollar today is worth more than a dollar tomorrow, so that taxes paid in the future are less costly than taxes paid today.

4 Tax loopholes have distortionary effects, and the benefits often do not accrue to those that they seem to be benefiting. The tax benefits of industry-specific loopholes (such as those relating to oil and gas) accrue to the owners of the inelastic factors in the industry (the land under which the hydrocarbon deposits lie), not to elastic factors (labor and capital).

5 The Tax Reform Act of 1986 attempted to restrict tax loopholes, not by eliminating them, but by imposing a more effective minimum tax; by dividing income into three categories (ordinary income, investment income, and passive income) and stipulating that losses attributable to one category cannot be used to offset income in another; and by taxing capital gains at the same rate as ordinary income. The 1993 and 1997 tax acts increased opportunities and demand for tax shelters by introducing new tax shelters; by increasing the top marginal tax rate; and by opening up a gap between the rates at which ordinary income and capital gains are taxed. These effects were partially offset by an increase in the alternative minimum tax rate.

KEY CONCEPTS

Tax avoidance

Tax evasion

Loopholes

Income shifting

Tax arbitrage

Tax shelters

QUESTIONS AND PROBLEMS

1 A tax avoidance device that became popular in the late 1970s and early 1980s was the zero coupon bond. This was a bond that paid no interest. When the interest rate was 7 percent, a ten-year bond promising to pay $100 in 1990 would sell for $50 when issued. The government required the individual to *impute* the receipt of interest—to assume that one-tenth of the $50 gain that occurred between 1980 and 1990 occurred in each year; at the same time, the issuer of the bond could impute the payment of interest. If the two (the issuer of the bond and the purchaser) were in the same tax bracket, what would be the consequences of these imputed interest payments and receipts? If they were in different tax brackets?

2 Another popularly used tax avoidance device before 1981 was a *straddle*, in which an individual would at the same time sign one contract to buy a commodity (like wheat) at some future date, and another contract to sell

the same commodity at a date shortly earlier or later. Thus, when she had a gain on the first contract, she generally would have a loss on the second. What she gained on one, she lost on the other. Can you think how you could use a straddle to postpone taxes? (Hint: Consider the consequences of selling one of the securities on December 31, the other on January 1.) Prior to 1986, long-term capital gains were taxed much more lightly than short-term capital gains. Can you think how you could use straddles to take advantage of this difference?

3   Describe the tax savings for someone in the 28 percent marginal tax bracket who owns a business with $10,000 in "profits" if he incorporates, giving his child (over 14) a 50 percent interest in the business. Assume his child has no other income and, as a dependent, cannot claim a personal exemption and can take only a standard deduction.

4   Citizen groups that monitor taxes paid by different corporations often complain about the low average tax rates that some corporations, especially those engaged in extensive leasing, pay. Is this allegation "fair"? Who may really benefit from such leasing?

5   Some have argued that leasing agreements among firms with different tax situations may enhance economic efficiency. Explain.

6   Who benefits from the fact that state and municipal bonds are tax-exempt—the buyer of the bond, or the municipality that issues them?

   a   Assume that there are so many individuals in the top income bracket that all of the bonds are purchased by them. What is your answer then?

   b   Assume that the government allows wealthy individuals to borrow to buy tax-exempt bonds. How does that affect your answer as to who benefits?

7   Explain how an individual can engage in tax arbitrage by borrowing: a) To put money into an IRA. b) To buy a tax-exempt bond.

8   Insurance policies often are a combination of a savings program and life insurance. The individual pays the company, say, $1000 a year; $100 of that goes to cover the risk of his dying during the year, and the remainder goes into a savings program. The return on the amount in the savings program accumulates free of tax—just like an IRA. Explain how insurance can be used as a tax avoidance device.

25 Reform of the Tax System

1 What have been the major impetuses for tax reforms during the last two decades?

2 How successful was the 1986 Tax Reform Act in lowering marginal tax rates, providing a level investment playing field, closing loopholes, and simplifying the tax code?

3 How did tax changes in 1981, 1986, 1993, and 1997 change the degree of progressivity of the tax code?

4 What are some of the basic trade-offs in the design of tax reform?

5 What are likely to be the major directions of tax reform in coming decades?

The past two decades have witnessed a succession of tax reforms. Each reform, promising a new era, in part undid the excesses of the previous reform. One reform reduced progressivity, the next increased it. One reform provided more investment tax incentives; the next tried to "level the playing field"; the next tried to tilt it again in a slightly different direction. Each reform was introduced with grand rhetoric. For instance, President

Reagan, in transmitting his tax reform to Congress on May 29, 1985, wrote:

> We face an historic challenge: to change our present tax system into a model of fairness, simplicity, efficiency, and compassion, to remove the obstacle to growth and unlock the door to a future of unparalleled innovation and achievement.
>
> For too long our tax code has been a source of ridicule and resentment, violating our Nation's most fundamental principles of justice and fair play. While most Americans labor under excessively high tax rates that discourage work and cut drastically into savings, many are able to exploit the tangled mess of loopholes that has grown up around our tax code to avoid paying their fair share—and sometimes paying any taxes at all. . . .

But by the time each reform had wended its way through Congress, it was but a pale shadow of the original.

Tax reforms have undergone enormous vicissitudes. In 1981, a whole variety of special provisions were introduced to encourage particular investments; the reforms of 1986 stripped these away, as well as a number of other special provisions that had accumulated over the years. Then in 1993, and even more so in 1997, a variety of new special provisions were introduced. In between, for instance in 1982 and 1990, there were other tax changes. While the tax acts each have more or less grandiose names—the Economic Recovery Tax Act of 1981 (ERTA), the Tax Reform Act of 1986 (TRA86), the Omnibus Budget Reconciliation Act of 1993 (OBRA93), and the Taxpayer Relief Act of 1997 (TRA97)—we shall refer to these simply as the 1981, 1986, 1993, and 1997 tax acts or reforms.

The rhetoric behind each tax reform—even those that went in opposite directions—was much the same: each promised a fairer, simpler tax code that would promote economic growth and efficiency. But there was debate about what "fairer" meant, and what changes would most effectively promote economic growth or increase equity. The issues are intertwined: the complexities of the tax code provide scope for tax avoidance, which is viewed to be unfair and which introduces distortions into the economy.

In this chapter, we first review the major themes of tax reforms over the past two decades, and assess each of the major tax reforms in terms of those themes. The second part of the chapter discusses likely themes of tax reforms as we approach the twenty-first century.

MAJOR IMPETUSES FOR TAX REFORM

Increased fairness

Improved efficiency

Reduced complexity/administrative costs

FAIRNESS

In Chapter 17, we noted that fairness, like beauty, is in the eye of the be-holder: most taxpayers feel that they pay more than their fair share of taxes; few taxpayers feel that they pay too little.

The fairness debate has focused around both issues highlighted in Chapter 17: Do individuals in similar economic circumstances (similar ability to pay) pay markedly different taxes—the issue of horizontal equity; and do richer individuals pay their "fair share," or do they manage to escape taxation by taking advantage of loopholes—the issue of vertical equity?

HORIZONTAL EQUITY ISSUES

A fair tax system imposes similar taxes on those in similar economic circumstances. Critics of the current tax system argue that it is unfair, because it both makes distinctions which it should not make, and occasionally does not make distinctions which it should.

In Chapter 22 we noted the variety of deductions and credits—for instance, for mortgage interest, for state and local income taxes, and for college tuition. As a result, homeowners may be favored over renters;[1] residents of states with income taxes are favored over residents of states that use sales taxes as the main instrument for raising revenues; and taxpayers with children going to college are favored over those without children going to college. *Base-broadening reforms seek to eliminate these special provisions, and in doing so, to increase the fairness (and efficiency) of the tax system.*

HOUSEHOLD STRUCTURE There is also an active debate about whether the tax system is fair in its treatment of those with nontraditional household structures. These concerns have grown as the diversity in household structures in the United States has increased. Under the current tax system, as we noted in Chapter 17, when two people with similar incomes marry, they may face a "marriage penalty," that is, their taxes rise simply as a result of their getting married; while when two people with dissimilar incomes marry, they may face a "marriage subsidy": that is, their taxes fall simply as a result of their getting married. There are deductions and credits for children. Is it fair, some ask, to give favorable treatment to a household who chooses to have, or is blessed with, children; while imposing higher tax rates on those who choose not to, or cannot, have children? Critics of these deductions and credits view a decision to have a child as a consumption decision little different from the decision to buy a car or a home, and argue that the government should not favor one form of consumption over another. Others, however, argue that the cost of an additional child is far greater than the tax deductions and credits, and so those with more children are less able to pay—and the tax code does not adequately reflect this difference in ability to pay.

---

[1] Though as we noted in Chapter 21, the magnitude of the advantage may not be as great as appears at first blush, because in competitive markets, the tax advantages of accelerated depreciation lead to lower rents.

There is also a debate about whether the tax code is fair to families in which both parents work. While the child care credit recognizes the additional expenses arising when both parents work, the credit goes only partway in reflecting the additional costs.

These issues—particularly the marriage tax—have drawn increasing attention from tax reformers, especially to the extent that they suggest conflicts between the tax code and basic American values. (Is the tax code anti-family? anti-children? against women taking an active role in the labor market?)

FAIRNESS IN CAPITAL TAXATION Some view any capital taxation as unfair. Two individuals with similar lifetime budget constraints will face different lifetime taxes, with the individual who chooses to consume more of his income later in life paying higher taxes than the one who chooses a more profligate lifestyle in his younger years. Moreover, much of the return to capital simply reflects inflation; it is not a real return. Why should someone who sees the real value of his wealth decreasing pay a tax, simply because the nominal value has increased?

Moreover, the failure to integrate the corporate and personal income taxes means that income in the corporate sector may be "double taxed," once within the corporation and a second time when the profits are distributed to the household sector.

On the other hand, the fact that a number of special provisions allow much of capital income to escape taxation is viewed by some as unfair. Critics claim the tax system is unfair both in the way it discriminates between owners of different kinds of assets and in the way it discriminates between capital income and wage income. For instance, capital gains are taxed only upon realization, and as we have noted, the value of this postponement may exceed the value of the taxes on the illusory increase in values as a result of inflation. Then, too, because of the "step-up in basis at death" (see Chapter 21), a considerable fraction of capital gains totally escapes taxation.

Not surprisingly, given the disparity in views concerning the fairness of the current system of taxation of capital income, there is a disparity of views concerning desirable reforms. Some argue for eliminating all taxes on capital income (those who see all taxation of capital income as unfair); others argue for closing "capital income loopholes," especially the favorable treatment of capital gains, including the step-up of basis. Most economists argue for better integration of the corporate and individual income tax; practical problems aside, there seems little justification for additional taxation of income generated in the corporate sector.

VERTICAL EQUITY

Even if it is accepted that the rich should pay a larger fraction of their income in taxes, the question remains, how much larger? As Figure 25.1 shows, historically, the rich have not paid a much higher percentage than those with average income. While the 1986 tax act was intended to close loopholes and lower rates, it was not intended to change the overall degree of progressivity. A major objective of the 1993 tax act was to redress that im-

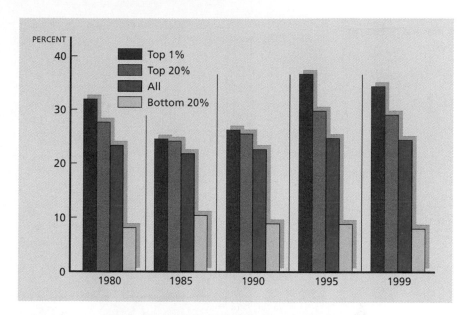

FIGURE 25.1   **Comparison of Federal Income Taxes Paid** Historically, families in the upper range of the income distribution have not paid a substantially larger percentage of income taxes compared to all families.

Sources: House Committee on Ways and Means, *Overview of Entitlement Programs, 1993 Green Book*, July 1993, p. 1513; R. Kasten and E. Toder, "CBO's Methodology for Distributional Analysis," paper for American Enterprise Institute Conference on Distributional Analysis for Making Tax Policy, December 1993; Congressional Budget Office, "Estimates of Federal Tax Liabilities for Individuals and Families by Income Category and Family Type for 1995 and 1999."

balance in a limited and partial way, by increasing the tax rates on the upper 2 percent of families. Some of the increased progressivity of 1993 was reversed in 1997 with the reduction in capital gains tax rates, much of the benefits of which accrue to the wealthy.

Similarly, while there is consensus that the poor should pay a smaller fraction of their income in taxes than the average family, the question is, how much smaller? One view is that those with incomes below the poverty line—the minimum income required to attain a basic standard of living—should pay no taxes. This was perhaps the original intent of the personal exemptions, but because they were not indexed until 1985, for long periods of our nation's history, we have in fact imposed taxes on those below the poverty threshold. (See Figure 25.2.) The 1986 tax reform removed most of those below poverty from the tax rolls—and in doing so greatly saved on administrative costs.

But the 1993 tax act went one step further. It not only reduced taxes on the poor; it actually increased subsidies available to the working poor who, often in spite of full-time work, remained below the poverty level. As a result, the goal of ensuring that all families with one full-time earner would be out of poverty was almost attained.

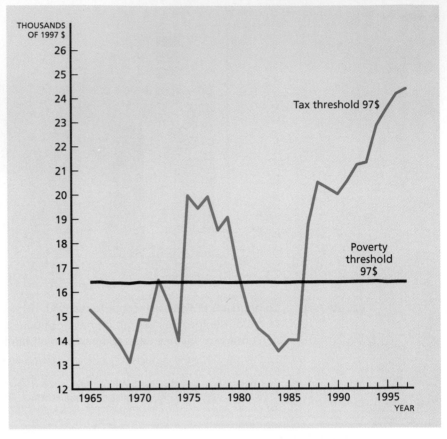

FIGURE 25.2 **The Poverty Level and the Income Tax Threshold for a Family of Four** The
figure compares the level of income below which a family is considered to live
in poverty, with the level of income at which a family begins to pay federal
income tax. The tax threshold (below which the family pays no taxes) depends
on the levels of the personal exemption, standard deduction, and earned
income tax credit. It dipped below the poverty level after 1980, but was
dramatically increased by the 1986 Tax Reform Act.

SOURCES: U.S. Bureau of the Census, Current Population Survey, accessed at the U.S. Census Bureau
web site (http://www.census.gov); *1998 Economic Report of the President* (Washington, D.C.: Government Printing Office), Table B-60; Internal Revenue Service, Form 1040, various years.

EFFICIENCY

Issues of equity are always contentious: as we have noted, fairness, like
beauty, is often in the eye of the beholder. There is, however, more consensus on what is meant by efficiency. Thus the Reagan administration did not
argue for lowering marginal tax rates on the rich on grounds of equity, that
they were paying too much. Such an argument probably would have fallen
on deaf ears. Rather, it based its contention on grounds of *efficiency:* that the
high marginal tax rates were causing large economic distortions, and that

the country as a whole was suffering from the reduced labor supply and savings. Indeed, advocates of the 1981 and 1986 reductions in top marginal tax rates went so far as to argue that the supply effects resulting from the lowering of tax rates, combined with reduced incentives to avoid and evade taxes, would be so large as to *increase* tax revenues.

Tax reform became a major issue again in the presidential campaign of 1996, with Senator Bob Dole arguing for a 15 percent across-the-board reduction in tax rates, claiming that such a reduction would stimulate the economy.

The debate has been plagued by a number of confusions. First, today most economists believe that in the long run, the overall level of unemployment is largely determined by monetary policy; looser monetary policy generates more investment and more jobs, and the Federal Reserve Board, which is in charge of monetary policy, seeks to keep unemployment as low as it can, without the tightness in the labor market giving rise to inflation pressures. Thus, tax policy has little to do with jobs, and job creation, except in circumstances when the economy is in a downturn.

Tax policy can affect the rate of growth and overall level of national income in several ways. It can encourage greater labor force participation, and can encourage individuals to work longer hours. Doing this will increase the level of national income, and in the short run, while participation rates and hours increase, the rate of growth. It can encourage greater savings and investment; and through this, greater productivity. Again, in the long run this will increase the level of national income, and in the short run, while productivity is increasing, it will increase the rate of growth. Finally, tax policy may be able to affect investments in research and development, and the *rate* of productivity increase, and in doing so, it can affect the rate of growth over the long run.

The point that tax rates can be so high that reductions in tax rates can increase tax revenues was popularized by economist Arthur Laffer. The so-called Laffer curve is depicted in Figure 25.3. If tax rates were set at 100 per-

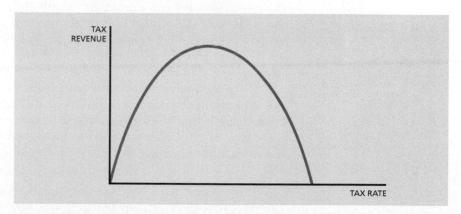

FIGURE 25.3 **The Laffer Curve** Raising tax rates beyond some level may reduce incentives enough to reduce output and tax revenues. There is, then, a tax rate at which tax revenues are maximized.

MARGINAL TAX RATES AND THE 1986 TAX REFORM

The 1986 tax reform was heralded as a major structural reform in our tax system, a "second American Revolution," to use President Reagan's rhetoric when he introduced it. In fact, the changes in marginal tax rates were far more modest, and some taxpayers (4 percent) actually experienced a marginal tax rate increase of more than 10 percent.* Only 11.3 percent experienced a marginal tax rate decrease of more than 10 percent (see figure). Much of the reduction in marginal tax rates simply reversed the bracket creep resulting from inflation that had occurred during the 1970s. Indeed, for a married couple with two children with an income in 1985 real dollars of $40,000, the marginal tax rate in 1988 of 28 percent was the same as in 1985, and still considerably above that in 1970 and 1960. For such a family, the big reduction in marginal rates occurred under the 1981 act.

Because the change in the marginal rate for so many individuals was so small, it is not surprising that it is estimated that the effects on labor supply and savings have been negligible.[†]

* For instance, the 1986 tax reform abolished the provision by which 10 percent of earnings of working spouses was deductible (up to $3000).

† See Hausman and Poterba, "Household Behavior and the Tax Reform Act of 1986," and Aaron, "Lessons for Tax Reform."

cent, clearly individuals would have no incentive to work, so that tax revenues would be zero. The question of how high tax rates have to be before tax revenues start to decline is an empirical one, about which economists disagree. There is a consensus that, overall, the lowering of tax rates in 1981 did what most economists outside the Reagan administration predicted it would—it lowered tax revenues; and the lowering of marginal tax rates in 1986 had at most a negligible effect on savings (which remained abysmally low) and on labor supply.

There is evidence that tax revenues from the very rich did increase after the 1981 and 1986 tax reforms, but there is disagreement about the reason.[2] Some believe that the rich recognized—correctly, as it turned out—that these low tax rates were too good to be permanent, and took advantage of the lower rates to realize, for instance, capital gains. Thus some of the in-

[2] See, for instance, Barry Bosworth and Gary Burtless, "Effects of Tax Reform on Labor Supply, Investment, and Saving," *Journal of Economic Perspectives*, winter 1992, pp. 3–25; and Lawrence Lindsey, *The Growth Experiment: How the New Tax Policy Is Transforming the U.S. Economy* (New York: Basic Books, 1990), and "Individual Taxpayer Response to Tax Cuts: 1982–1984, With Implications for Revenue Maximizing Tax Rate," *Journal of Public Economics* 33 (1987): 173–206.

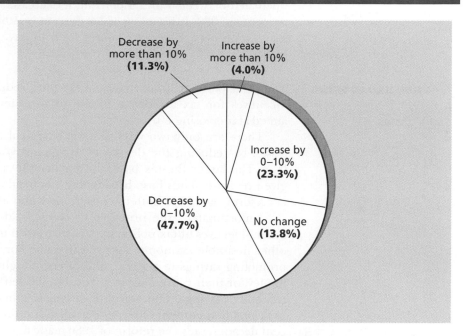

Marginal Tax Rate Changes from the 1986 Tax Reform Only a quarter of the population had a marginal tax rate change of more than 10 percent.

SOURCE: J. Hausman and J. Poterba, "Household Behavior and the Tax Reform Act of 1986," *Journal of Economic Perspectives*, summer 1987, pp. 101–20.

creased tax revenues were at the expense of tax revenues that would have been received later. Some believe that the increased reported income of the rich was the result not of increased incentives provided by the tax bill, but of reduced opportunities for tax avoidance, the closing of loopholes combined with the increased alternative minimum tax. Some argue that it was not just the opportunities for tax avoidance that were decreased in 1986, but the incentives as well (see Chapter 24).

Some believe that the increased income of the rich was largely a continuation of the movement toward greater inequality that has characterized the economy since 1973, and especially since 1980. The rich were getting richer, and the poor poorer; the tax system should no more get credit for making the rich richer than for making the poor poorer. The fact that tax revenues failed to increase in 1981 reinforced skepticism about the relevance of the Laffer curve; in the 1996 election, the view that the tax reduction would lead to increased government revenues received little popular support—and even less support among economists.

The effects of the 1993 tax act provide some insight into these still unresolved issues. Taxes on the very rich increased substantially, and yet their incomes and their tax payments continued to rise, at a pace even faster than that of the economy as a whole. While in the 1970s the personal savings rate fluctuated between 7 and 9 percent, it decreased through the 1980s, to 4.8 percent in 1989. It hit a low of 3.8 percent in 1994, but later rebounded to 4.5 to 5 percent. The tax changes seem to have had little effect on these trends.[3]

BASE BROADENING

The principle that lower marginal tax rates reduce deadweight losses and incentives for tax avoidance is one of the fundamentals of tax reforms aimed at increasing efficiency.

There are only two ways to lower marginal tax rates, without revenue losses: by reducing the degree of progressivity, or by broadening the tax base. The larger the tax base, the smaller the tax rate required to raise a given revenue. Thus **base broadening** has been another principal tenet of tax reform, agreed to both by conservatives and liberals.

Unfortunately, the principle of base broadening often conflicts with other objectives of tax policy, in particular, with using tax policy to promote other desirable economic and social goals. For example, the objective of promoting savings in general, and of encouraging individuals to put aside money for their retirement in particular, has led to special tax treatment of retirement savings. The objective of encouraging home ownership has led to favorable treatment of owner-occupied housing. Of the tax reforms of recent decades, only the reform of 1986 made a serious attempt at base broadening. Other tax reforms actually narrowed the tax base as they attempted to pursue other objectives.

This was most notable in the 1981, 1993, and 1997 tax acts. The 1981 act granted very favorable depreciation rates and investment tax credits to plant and equipment, in an unsuccessful attempt to encourage "smokestack America." The 1993 tax bill similarly narrowed the tax base by providing special treatment for investments in new small businesses. The 1997 tax act introduced still further special provisions to encourage education and savings.

Whether these special provisions actually increase overall economic efficiency, or whether they increase distortions, remains a subject of debate. If markets work well, providing preferential treatment simply decreases economic efficiency. The preferential treatments granted in 1981 were not based on any theory of market failures. The excess investments that they helped lead to in commercial real estate certainly corroborate the view that they distorted investment patterns. The 1986 tax reform took up as one of its mottoes "leveling the playing field," undoing the distortions introduced into the tax code a scant five years earlier. The 1993 act attempted to focus attention on what the economists in the Clinton administration saw as a market failure, the difficulty small businesses have obtaining capital.

[3] The 1986 tax reform has been extensively studied to ascertain its effects. See, for instance, Henry J. Aaron, "Lessons for Tax Reform," in *Do Taxes Matter: The Impact of the Tax Reform Act of 1986*, ed. J. Slemrod (Cambridge, Mass.: MIT Press, 1990), pp. 321–31.

The 1997 act was based on the notion that in today's world, people need a higher level of education: fourteen years of school needs to become the norm, rather than twelve. But critics argued that the tax proposals were not needed, and were likely ineffective, and possibly counterproductive. Given the high returns to education, individuals have an incentive to pursue additional years of schooling; the only possible "market failure" was access to credit, and the student loan programs—including major reforms enacted in 1993—went a long way to improving access to credit on a flexible basis. To the extent that this remained a problem, reforms should have focused on improving the loan program. The one group in the population for whom financial resources might be a barrier were the very poor; but tax reforms—aimed at middle-class parents—did nothing for them; again, critics claimed that the money could have been better spent on expanding Pell Grants (the government program for this group). Finally, some worried that the financial assistance provided through the tax system to middle-class students would only encourage colleges to increase tuition; the higher tuition would actually reduce affordability to poor students, for whom the tax breaks meant little.

The 1986 tax reform, for all its rhetoric, did not get very far in base broadening. Table 25.1 looks at three categories of potential base-broadening. While the deductibility of state and local sales taxes was removed, the far more important provision of deductibility of income and property taxes was retained; the reform simply encouraged states to shift to these forms of taxation. While deductibility of interest on consumer credit was eliminated, the more important deductibility of mortgage payments was kept; individuals were simply encouraged to take home equity loans (loans in which the equity in their house is used as collateral). While the medical expense deduction was modified (only expenses in excess of 7.5 percent of income were deductible), the far more important exclusion of employer contributions for medical insurance premiums and medical care was retained.

Because the 1986 tax act did not achieve much base-broadening, it also failed to lower marginal tax rates much (see Table 25.2). The distortions associated with the income tax are largely related to these marginal tax rates.

TABLE 25.1 Comparison of Tax Expenditures Retained and Dropped by the 1986 Tax Reform Act	
State and local tax deductions	
Sales tax (dropped)	$ 5.5 billion
Income and property tax (kept)	27.8
Interest deduction	
For consumer credit (dropped)	$17.6 billion
For mortgage interest on owner-occupied homes (kept)	26.9
Health care provisions	
Medical expense deduction (modified)	$ 3.8 billion
Exclusion of employer contributions for medical insurance premiums and medical care (kept)	23.5

TABLE 25.2

Marginal Tax Rates
over Four Decades

FILING STATUS	ADJUSTED GROSS INCOME (1997$)	MARGINAL TAX RATE (PERCENT)						
		1960	1970	1980	1985	1988	1994	1998
Single	$25,000	20	23	19	18	15	15	15
Married filing jointly (2 children)	$40,000	20	20	21	18	15	15	15
Married filing jointly (2 children)	$65,000	26	26	32	28	28	28	28
Married filing jointly (2 children)	$275,000	59	54	64	50	33	39	39

The 1993 tax reforms significantly increased marginal tax rates on the upper 2 percent of taxpayers, from 28 percent to approximately 40 percent, but left the marginal tax rates for the remainder essentially unchanged. The 1997 bill lowered the rate on one form of income, capital gains, but left rates on wages, dividends, and interest rates unchanged.

The increased progressivity (combined with other tax changes) has increased the marriage penalty and the marginal tax rates facing secondary wage earners (especially in upper-middle-income families). Again, with labor force participation rates reaching an all-time high as this book goes to press, any adverse effects appear to be limited. Critics say that participation rates have been increasing because of declining real wages, especially at the bottom of the income distribution (a backward-bending supply curve), but participation rates have increased throughout the economy, including in upper-income households. These increased participation rates clearly reflect social trends (attitudes toward women working and more households headed by single women). The debate is over whether participation rates would have been even higher with lower tax rates.

SIMPLIFYING THE TAX CODE AND REDUCING ADMINISTRATIVE COSTS

A third major impetus for tax reform has simply been that the tax code has grown too complicated. Complexity increases administrative costs, both for the taxpayer and for the government; it reduces compliance; it opens up opportunities for tax avoidance; and it contributes to the sense that the tax laws are inequitable.

ASSESSING COMPLEXITY

There are many indicators of the complexity of the tax system. There are more than 100 different forms. Of the 199 volumes comprising the Code of Federal Regulations (describing all general and permanent laws in force in the United States), the Internal Revenue Code is responsible for 20. Of these, 13 volumes, filling 8583 pages, are devoted to the individual and corporate income taxes.

Although the 1996 presidential primaries focused on the need to simplify the tax code, the 1997 tax act did little to achieve that simplification. Indeed, it increased complexity by adding new capital gains tax brackets (and thus requiring an additional worksheet for the calculation of taxes due), two new IRAs with new benefits and costs as compared to the existing two IRAs, and two different education tax credits with different rules to be mastered.

The complexity is reflected in the difficulties that even the Internal Revenue Service has in accurately assessing tax liabilities. Ralph Nader's Tax Reform Research Group created a tax schedule for a fictional couple that they sent to twenty-two IRS offices. The tax liabilities assessed by the different offices differed markedly, from a high refund of $811.96 to a tax underpayment of $52.14. IRS studies have shown that commercial firms which fill out tax returns for individuals with low incomes make errors on 82 percent of the returns. And people trained and employed by the IRS computed the wrong tax 72 percent of the time when handling relatively simple tax problems.[4] Efforts by the IRS to improve its record have been partially successful, but even so, the error rate remains high.

Another indication of the complexity of the code—the difficulty that individuals have of knowing whether they are or are not complying with the law—is that when individuals go to court to challenge the IRS, they often win: the IRS recovers only about one-third of what it claims.[5] Instances where one court has ruled one way and another court has ruled a different way on the same issue make the plight of the taxpayer even more difficult. For example, as we noted in Chapter 22, commuting costs are not, in general, deductible. A federal appeals court in New York ruled, however, that airplane pilots could deduct the costs of using their automobiles to transport their heavy paraphernalia (and themselves) between their homes and the airport. But a tax court in Florida, not bound by a decision in New York, ruled the other way.[6]

To collect its taxes, the federal government relies on a combination of voluntary compliance coupled with the threat of stiff fines and prosecution for outright fraud. To assist individuals whose sense of moral responsibility might be too weak to induce them to report all of their income, the

---

[4] *Consumer Reports*, March 1976. The IRS claims it is doing a better job recently. In 1992, an estimated 89 percent of 75 million inquiries were handled correctly, according to the *Internal Revenue Service Annual Report: 1992*, May 1993.

A more recent study (but based on 1979 data) confirms the high error rate of professional tax preparers. Only 25 percent of lawyer/CPA-prepared returns were correct. See Brian Erard, "Taxation with Representation: An Analysis of the Role of Tax Practitioners in Tax Compliance," *Journal of Public Economics* 52, no. 2 (September 1993): 163–197.

[5] *Business Week*, April 16, 1984. The IRS has a much better record when it brings criminal charges.

[6] Ibid.

government requires employers to report the wages they pay to their workers and firms to report the dividends and interest they pay to shareholders and bondholders. The government has only limited facilities, however, for checking on cash transactions, and the ability to avoid taxes by using cash has encouraged the growth of unreported transactions, referred to as the **underground economy.** Though precise estimates of the size of the underground economy are hard to come by, some observers believe that it may involve up to one-quarter of the work force and 15 percent of GNP. It includes unreported income not only of criminals, but also that of some

TABLE 25.3

Gross Tax Gap from Individual Income That Escapes the Tax Net (Tax Year 1992, Billions of 1997 Dollars)

TYPE OF INCOME	UNDERREPORTING TAX GAP	NET MISREPORTED AMOUNT	NET MISREPORTED PERCENTAGE
Wage income	3.7	27.5	0.9
Interest income	1.0	4.1	2.3
Dividends	1.5	7.0	7.8
State tax refunds	<0.06	0.1	0.8
Capital gains	2.9	10.8	7.2
Pensions and annuities	2.1	9.8	4.0
Social security benefits	0.2	1.1	4.2
Unemployment compensation	0.3	2.6	6.9
Rents and royalties	4.2	22.2	17.2
Alimony	0.1	0.3	13.3
Non-farm proprietor income	19.3	85.1	32.3
Farm income	3.9	20.5	32.2
Partnership and small business income	4.1	19.7	7.5
Sales of business property	0.8	4.5	28.0
Informal supplier income	14.1	68.2	81.4
Other income	8.7	41.1	24.9
Offsets to income			
Adjustments	0.2	0.8	2.0
Deductions	5.8	22.8	4.4
Exemptions	3.3	24.5	4.5
Tax credits	7.1	7.1	40.2
Total	**$83.4**	**$379.7**	n.a.

SOURCE: Internal Revenue Service, Federal Tax Compliance Research: *Individual Income Tax Gap Estimates for 1985, 1988, and 1992*, Publication 1415 (Rev. 4-96) (Washington, D.C.: 1996), Table 3.

Note: The source table provides a low and a high estimate to give a range for the underreported income. The high estimates are reported above.

waiters, baby-sitters, domestic help, carpenters, gardeners, and others.[7] The estimated income tax owed on unreported cash transactions, or resulting from overstated deductions or unjustified tax credits, is now $125 billion.

Other major sources of noncompliance are capital gains, small business income, rents, and farm income. Currently, somewhat less than half of capital gains, around half of small business income, and 60 percent of rents go unreported. Most dramatically, in one recent year, when $3 billion should have been reported on income taxes as farm income, the returns showed a loss of $10 billion.[8]

Unreported illegal income, though not so important as some of the sources of tax evasion given in Table 25.3, is still an important source of tax evasion.[9] (Al Capone, the 1920s mobster, was convicted for failing to report his illegal income when other charges would not stick.)

In recent years, the government has been auditing less, but increasing the efficiency of its audits; a higher fraction of those audited have had to pay more in taxes.

REDUCING TAX AVOIDANCE

Tax avoidance—taking advantage of all the loopholes in the tax structure—results in significant erosion of the tax base. In the previous chapter we discussed the principles of tax avoidance as well as some of the more important tax shelters. In the early 1980s tax avoidance had become rampant, fostering a general public impression that the tax system was not working. This provided the impetus for many of the reforms introduced in 1986. Though these reforms managed to reduce the degree of tax avoidance through tax shelters, they came at the price of increasing the complexity of the tax code.

---

[7] By its nature it is difficult to obtain accurate measures of the underground economy. While there is a wide range of estimates, they average between 6 and 7 percent of GNP, involving 17 percent of the work force. See Harry I. Greenfield, *Invisible, Outlawed and Untaxed: America's Underground Economy* (Westport, Conn.: Praeger, 1993), and Gregory K. Schoepfle, Jorge F. Perez-Lopez, and Eric Griego, "The Underground Economy in the United States," U.S. Department of Labor Occasional Paper on the Informal Sector, no. 2, September 1992.

[8] It is obviously easy for those who receive payments in cash simply not to report cash income. Other noncompliance problems arise from reporting as expenses items that are really not business expenses. While today, sales of stocks and bonds are reported to the IRS, other asset sales typically are not, and the IRS does not receive independent information about the basis (the purchase price).

Estimates of noncompliance are obtained through detailed and thorough audits of a relatively small number of taxpayers. The costs of such audits (both to the government and the taxpayer) are great, and do not justify the extra revenue raised. The purpose of these audits is to provide the IRS general information concerning compliance.

[9] It is estimated that Americans spend almost $60 billion on illegal drugs. See Executive Office of the President, Office of National Drug Control Policy, *What American Users Spend on Illegal Drugs, 1988–1995*, fall 1997, Table A, p. 3.

REDUCING ADMINISTRATIVE COSTS

We have seen that the complexity of the tax system results in problems of compliance and in perceptions of inequities. But it also contributes greatly to the costs of collecting taxes. The brunt of the administrative costs of the U.S. income tax system is borne by the taxpayers, and the costs are not only the direct costs of filling out the tax returns but the indirect costs of record keeping required to comply with the tax laws.

The tax laws are so complex that 44 percent of all taxpayers use tax preparers. One recent study estimated that the average household devoted 27.4 hours during the tax year to compliance with the federal tax laws, with an average total resource cost per household of $457.80.[10]

The IRS's own resources devoted to tax collection grew enormously from 1960 to the early 1990s. In constant dollars, IRS operating costs almost quadrupled between 1960 and 1993, and they stood at more than $7.2 billion in 1997. The IRS had only 51,000 employees in 1960, or .28 per thousand people. By 1997 the number of employees was 102,000, or .38 per thousand people, down from a 1993 level of 113,000 employees or .44 per thousand people. The cost of collecting $100 in taxes was 40 cents in 1960, 60 cents in 1993, and 44 cents in 1997.[11]

SOURCES OF COMPLEXITY

Whenever government taxes some income at different rates than other income (or does not tax some income, or provides a tax deduction or credit for some item), taxpayers have an incentive to ensure that income is received in a form that receives favorable treatment. The greater the tax consequences—the higher the tax rates and the greater the differences in tax treatments—the greater the incentives. Making clear distinctions and definitions in tax law is much harder in practice than in theory. Questions which might seem to be merely philosophical—"What is a family?" "When is a wall a 'structure' and when is it 'equipment'?" "What is interest?" "How do we distinguish between repayment of principal and interest?"—take on real importance when money is at stake.

While some areas of preferential treatment are the consequence of lobbying by special interest groups, many are the result of basic social and economic policy. The government wants to encourage savings for retirement. It considers it to be inequitable for someone with heavy medical expenses to pay the same tax as someone without these expenditures. It wants to encourage home ownership. Just as we saw earlier a trade-off between base broadening and the pursuit of these other objectives, so too is there a trade-off between these other objectives and complexity.

Much of the complexity arises out of an attempt to reduce tax avoidance—particularly in the area of taxation of returns to capital, but in other areas as well. When is an individual really a farmer, so that losses should be

[10] See Marsha Blumenthal and Joel Slemrod, "The Compliance Cost of the U.S. Individual Income Tax System: A Second Look after Tax Reform," *National Tax Journal* 45, no. 2 (June 1992): 185–202.

[11] U.S. Department of Treasury, Internal Revenue Service, *1997 Annual Data Book*, Publication 55B, Table 28.

tax deductible? When is farming simply a tax avoidance scheme? When is it a "consumption" activity, in which case losses should no more be deductible than expenditures on food or clothing? Even if the taxpayer knew his own motives clearly, the tax authorities cannot tell what motivated someone to buy a farm. Rules designed to distinguish real farmers from those who claim to be farmers for reasons of tax avoidance add to the complexity for everyone involved.

The complexity of the tax system has led to increasing dissatisfaction with it and with the IRS which administers it. Many are convinced that there are a myriad of loopholes which others can take advantage of, but they cannot—the tax system is fundamentally unfair. The seeming complexity induces anxiety, compounded in some cases by a fear of Gestapo techniques of the IRS. Horror stories fill the newspapers—small underpayments cascading through penalties and fines to massive obligations, with the IRS attaching bank accounts and putting liens on houses. In some cases, the IRS appears to have been misguided—given the millions of tax forms that have to be reviewed every year, such mistakes are inevitable—but worse, unresponsive to attempts to redress the mistakes. The crescendo of complaints against the IRS reached such an intensity that the Clinton administration reluctantly acceded to major administrative reforms in 1997, which gave taxpayers more rights in their struggle against the IRS. More of the burden of proof—that the taxpayer owed the government money—was placed on the IRS.

Some of the complaints against the IRS are based on perception as much as on reality. For example, a large fraction of the population fills out a simplified tax schedule (1040 A or EZ), which in principle should take a relatively short time to complete (a listing of a couple of W-2 wage statements, and a few statements of interest payments). But a large and increasing number of those filling out even these simplified returns turn to professional tax preparers.

The more fundamental problem is that the IRS has been unable to keep pace with the technological revolution in the rest of the economy. In principle, with W-2's and interest and dividend payments submitted directly to the IRS (with an increasing fraction submitted electronically), the IRS should be able to perform the tax calculations for all taxpayers not itemizing deductions; all they need to provide is information about their family status. Even most itemized deductions could be handled by the IRS (especially state and local income taxes and mortgage payments). In fact, however, the IRS's computerization program has been a massive disaster, with billions spent without obtaining a truly functioning system.

THE 1986 TAX REFORM

The 1986 tax reform had as one of its major objectives simplification of the tax code. In this, by most accounts, it failed. The major simplification that the supporters of the reform pointed to, the reduction in the number of tax brackets, was a superficial one. Looking up in the tax table the tax that is due, once one's taxable income has been calculated, is an easy task, regardless of the number of brackets.

In fact, the new distinctions introduced in the tax law between various categories of income made the tax law more complicated. As we said in

Chapter 24, distinguishing between passive, investment, and ordinary income has required a host of definitions, regulations, and court cases. Indeed, the 1986 tax law did not even result in any simplification of tax forms; some forms became more complicated, and several new forms were introduced.

TAX SIMPLIFICATION

A major impetus of tax reform has been tax simplification.

The U.S. tax structure is highly complex. The complexity:

• Gives rise to high costs of compliance.

• Opens up opportunities for tax avoidance, and inequities.

• Is caused partly by government's attempt to reduce tax avoidance, partly by attempts to achieve social and economic objectives through the tax system.

Leveling the playing field; reducing investment distortions: C−. Major distortions, such as for owner-occupied housing, remained. The major achievement was reversing the huge distortions introduced in 1981.

Improving economic efficiency; improving savings incentives: C−. The slight lowering of marginal tax rates improved matters, though the effect was somewhat offset by taxing capital gains at full rates; eliminating deductibility of IRA contributions for middle-class individuals reduced saving incentives.

Base broadening: D. The steps taken were far smaller than the steps not taken.

Simplification: F. The strategy chosen for closing loopholes increased complexity.

Transparency: F. Though this is one of the attributes of a good tax system discussed in Chapter 17, it was never one of the announced objectives of the 1986 tax reform. As part of the tax reform, corporation income taxes were increased. We have seen that the corporation income tax is among the least transparent of our taxes, since no one really knows what its incidence is. The 1986 tax reform act increased corporate taxes.

The 1993 and 1997 tax bills offered no progress toward a simpler tax code. Indeed, because both of these bills introduced important new elements of preferences, they served significantly to further complicate the tax system.

TRANSITION ISSUES AND THE POLITICS OF TAX REFORM

Changes in tax laws always entail problems; indeed, there is a maxim that "old taxes are good taxes." Each new tax law requires a myriad of court cases to determine how each provision of the new law is to be interpreted. Until these interpretations are clear, there is uncertainty, and uncertainty has its own economic costs.

The most difficult problems are those associated with capital (investments). As we saw earlier, tax provisions are, to a large extent, capitalized—reflected in the value of assets. Accordingly, changes in tax laws result in changes in capital values. Eliminating the special provisions for commercial real estimate might drastically reduce the demand for such real estate. In the short run, prices would fall. Owners would suffer a capital loss. At the lower prices, construction would stop. In the long run, prices of buildings would be restored, as the excess supply dried up. In the meanwhile, how-ever, both owners of commercial real estate and construction firms would suffer. This is precisely what happened in the aftermath of the 1986 tax reform.

Such changes raise fundamental equity issues as well as political prob-lems. Is it unfair to change rules? As we have noted before, investments are made with certain expectations concerning taxes. Changing taxes provides windfall gains to some and windfall losses to others, even when the taxes do not *directly* affect the investment in question. A tax benefit for owner-occu-pied housing reduces the demand for rental housing, and accordingly has adverse effects on the price of multifamily rental properties.

While equity issues are of concern, they clearly cannot dominate eco-nomic policy making: otherwise, one could never abolish any provision of a special interest group, no matter how distortionary. Those who are hurt by a new tax law often get much more concerned about the inequities than those who benefit; they lobby Congress for special transition rules. In the final days of the passage of every tax bill, a host of special provisions, worth billions of dollars, are adopted to the benefit of certain companies, particu-larly companies in the congressional districts of the bill's proponents. To some, this is just a reflection of the politics of taxation. To others, it is just a way to enhance the likelihood that the tax reform is a Pareto improve-ment—many of the special provisions are nothing but the side payments re-quired to compensate the losers. To still others, the special provisions sym-bolize the defeat of the principles of tax reform.

The problems presented by transition lead to two general maxims: Try to make tax reforms relatively seldom; and try to implement reforms gradu-ally, especially those reforms which have adverse effects on capital values.[12] The frequent revision of the tax code over the past two decades runs counter to the first maxim.

When President Reagan sent Congress his original proposal for tax re-form, he made it clear that his objective was to change the *structure* of the in-come tax, not the level of taxation. Thus he insisted that it be **revenue-neu-tral** (that is, that it raise the same amount of revenue as was being raised under the existing laws). Indeed, he even insisted that the overall degree of progressivity (the percentage of taxes paid by those in different income cat-egories) not be substantially changed. The concern was that nothing would come of an open-ended discussion, in which all of the structural issues were up for debate. He wished the discussion to focus on particular inefficiencies and inadequacies of the tax code.

---

[12] Concern about these equity effects often leads to provisions, called "grandfather-ing," which extend preferential treatment to those currently receiving the benefit, but not to others. While grandfathering thus reduces one sense of inequity—that arising out of unanticipated changes in tax treatment—it introduces a new source of inequity, between those who have access to the preferential treatment and those who do not.

To a large extent, tax reforms change the burden of taxation; there are many losers and winners. The fact that there are so many losers makes reform difficult.

Most economists, however, believe that important tax reforms are not "zero-sum" (that is, they believe they are more than just redistributing income); more is at stake than just how the economic pie is to be divided. By improving economic efficiency, by eliminating distortions, reforms increase the size of the economic pie. The problem, however, is that those who worry that the tax law change will hurt them feel the loss far more intensely than those who might gain; those who reform advocates say will gain are often skeptical that the gains will actually be realized.

In the discussions of the 1986 tax reform, to make the increase in the size of the pie look even bigger, corporation income taxes were increased so that individual income taxes could, overall, be reduced. Since most people do not accurately see the burden imposed upon them by the corporation tax, this enabled more individuals to see themselves as net winners.

Any tax bill is viewed as an opportunity by special interest groups to get favorable treatment. Congress has tried to reduce this pressure, by requiring that any congressperson who proposes an amendment granting tax relief has to specify how the offsetting extra revenue would be raised, that is, which taxes would be increased, or which loopholes would be eliminated.

TRANSITION ISSUES

Transitions give rise to equity issues—changes in asset values, windfall gains to some, losses to others.

There are efficiency costs associated with adjusting to new tax laws.

General principle: Try to avoid frequent tax law changes, and make changes that affect capital asset values gradually. (U.S. has had frequent changes.)

Politics of tax reform:

• Revenue-neutral taxes have as many winners as losers.

• Losers often feel losses more acutely.

• Not zero-sum—majority could be better off.

• Gimmicks are often required to garner enough support.

• To reduce scope of conflict, reforms often focus on revenue-neutral and distribution-neutral tax changes.

TAX REFORMS FOR THE
TWENTY-FIRST CENTURY

Considerable dissatisfaction with the tax system remains. Two groups of reforms have been under discussion recently: minor reforms in the current tax system, and major new reforms.

REFORMS WITHIN THE CURRENT FRAMEWORK

Recent reforms have struggled to achieve a balance among competing objectives.

1 High marginal tax rates increase deadweight loss, reduce tax compliance, and increase incentives for tax avoidance. Low marginal tax rates reduce progressivity.

2 Base broadening allows the reduction of tax rates. Preferential treatment of certain categories of income and expenditures introduces complexity, inequity, and opportunities for tax avoidance. To the extent that preferential treatment is introduced to enhance equity or to promote socially desirable objectives, eliminating preferential treatment reduces the tax system's instrumentality for achieving objectives other than raising revenues.

TAX REFORM IN THE 1990s In the 1990s, there has been increasing reliance on tax policy as an instrument for pursuing economic and social goals, simply because of the strong resistance to new taxes and increased direct expenditures. Tax expenditures appear to be more a politically acceptable means than direct expenditures, even if they are less well targeted and introduce more economic distortions.

PROMOTING VALUES THROUGH THE TAX SYSTEM Rather than focusing on base broadening, the reforms of 1993 and 1997 focused on using the tax system to express values—even when the provisions themselves have limited economic impact.

A number of reforms have focused on *family values*—encouraging adoptions, the child credit that was introduced in 1997, the expanded child care credit proposed in 1998, and the proposed reduction of the marriage penalty. Some want to encourage more women to participate in the labor force, by expanding the child care credit; others want to encourage mothers to stay home and take care of their own children, by reducing the child care credit. Other reforms, such as the tuition tax credit introduced in 1997, have focused on encouraging education.

PROMOTING SAVINGS AND INVESTMENT Still other reforms have focused on encouraging savings—especially the expansion in IRAs (individual retirement accounts) and the preferential treatment of capital gains. But while some reformers would like to extend the preferential treatment of the return to savings, taxing only consumption or wage income, others want to eliminate the preferences currently extended.

TAX SIMPLIFICATION A number of reforms concern simplifying the tax system. This was one of the motivations for the provision which exempted up to $500,000 in capital gains on owner-occupied housing. (The provision's political appeal did not go unnoticed by its advocates in both parties, however; the fact that the provision may have exacerbated the distortions of the tax system, by further encouraging investment in housing, was not of much concern.)

One way of reducing the taxpayers' burden would be for the government to assume responsibility for calculating taxes for the three-fourths of individuals who have simple tax forms—only wage income, interest, dividends, and capital gains on stocks. Many of the reforms which would broaden the tax base by eliminating special provisions would also help simplify the tax system. On the other hand, recent reforms that have tried to use the tax system to advance social and economic policies have moved in the opposite direction.

MAJOR NEW REFORMS

Most of the major reforms currently being debated embody the themes of simplification, base broadening, and promoting savings and investment.

THE FLAT-RATE TAX We noted that some of the complexities of the tax system arise from its progressivity. This has led to a proposal to have a single, flat rate. Individuals would pay a given percentage of their income above a certain threshold level. The proposal, while discussed by economists for a long time, entered the political arena in 1996 when it was advocated by presidential candidate Steve Forbes in the Republican primaries. Under flat-rate proposals, rates at the upper end would be lowered, necessitating an increase in rates elsewhere (unless one believed that the tax rates at upper incomes were so high that they could be reduced without reducing tax revenues). As a result, these proposals have not been well received.

One of the main advantages of the flat-rate tax proposal is the ease with which it can be administered. Since everyone pays the same marginal tax rate, it makes no difference whether the tax is collected at the level of the individual (who receives the income) or the level of the business (say, as she pays wages). Because flat-rate tax proposals typically eliminate all special provisions, individuals could fill out the tax on the back of a postcard. Note, however, that this simplification has little to do with the single rate, but rather with the elimination of special provisions.

CONSUMPTION TAXES Most of the major tax reforms propose to tax consumption only. This is true of the flat-rate proposals just discussed and the value-added tax proposal discussed in the next section. As we saw in earlier chapters (21 and 24), there are strong arguments for taxing consumption only: much of the complexity of the tax code arises from the attempt to tax interest; a consumption tax imposes the same tax on individuals with the same lifetime incomes, while the income tax discriminates against individuals who prefer to consume later in life; it seems more appropriate to tax

715

what individuals take out of society (their consumption) rather than what they contribute (measured by their income); and switching to a consumption tax would encourage savings, which remain abysmally low in the United States.

Critics of these proposals argue that given the insensitivity of savings to interest rates, switching to a consumption tax will not promote savings. Advocates point out that they are concerned with *switching* from an income tax to a consumption tax, and that what matters thus is not the interest elasticity, but the *compensated* interest elasticity, of savings—taking into account that as the tax on interest income falls, other taxes would have to increase.[13]

Advocates of the consumption tax believe that it would be easy to administer the tax. The simplest procedures focus on cash flow: an individual would be taxed on net cash flow (income) minus net additions to savings:

Consumption = income − savings.

Since individuals' purchases and sales of assets, like stocks, are already recorded, little extra work would be required. Critics worry that there are many other assets for which purchases and sales are not so easily monitored, and say that the transition into the system would be complicated by the fact that individuals have large amounts of assets already in their possession. Sales of these assets used to finance consumption might be hard to detect. Others argue that since the income with which these assets were purchased was already taxed once, it would be unfair to tax the consumption derived from their sale.

Politically, however, the major objection to adopting a consumption tax has been that to achieve the same degree of progressivity as under the current income tax system, marginal tax rates on consumption would have to be very high—many individuals would have to face marginal tax rates of 40 percent or more. Thus, while support for the idea went so far that two senators, Senators Nunn and Domenici, introduced a bill providing for a consumption tax, the high marginal tax rates foreseen have so far prevented the proposal from receiving great popular attention.

THE VALUE-ADDED TAX A **value-added tax** (VAT) is imposed at each stage of production on the difference between a firm's sales and its purchases from other firms, that is, on the value added by the firm. The VAT has become a

---

[13] The uncompensated interest elasticity of savings is low because of the offsetting income and substitution effects; a lower interest income tax means that individuals are better off, and this increases their consumption (reduces savings). But if at the same time that the interest income tax is reduced, other taxes (such as wage taxes) are increased, the income effect is eliminated, or at least reduced, so that the predominant effect is the substitution effect. The substitution effect unambiguously leads to more savings.

major source of revenue in most European countries, with rates as high as 20 percent.

There are several ways of calculating a country's output. One way focuses on sales of final output; another, on adding up the value added at each stage of production; a third, on adding up the incomes of all individuals. All three are equivalent, and all three form bases of levying taxes. A sales tax imposed on final sales, a value-added tax, and an income tax can, in this sense, all be made equivalent, though there may be marked differences in the costs of administering the different taxes. The advantage of the value-added tax is that most of value added occurs within large corporations. A tax on final sales puts a large burden on retailers, many of which are small businesses. As a result, there is a high degree of compliance with the VAT.

A major advantage of the VAT is its relative simplicity. But critics point out that it is a proportional tax, and thus less equitable than a progressive consumption or income tax. Though some degree of progressivity can be obtained by taxing different goods at different rates (for instance, exempting food), doing so reduces the tax's simplicity and introduces distortions—negating the great advantages of the VAT.

COMBINING THE VAT WITH OTHER FORMS OF TAXES Most proponents of the VAT do not advocate that it should replace the income tax—in Europe, both are used. Rather, they believe that it can be used to reduce substantially the revenues to be collected from the income tax, and hence the high marginal tax rates; since much of tax avoidance is related to the level of marginal rates, advocates believe that it will decrease the distortions and increase the equity of the tax system. Critics point out that the total distortion of the tax system is related to the sum of the (marginal) tax on income and the value-added tax, and that unless this is reduced, the deadweight loss associated with the tax will not be reduced. Moreover, they say, the gains in compliance costs from the reduction in the marginal tax rate will be more than offset by the additional administrative costs associated with collecting the value-added tax. Finally, there is concern that because the value-added tax is collected in a piecemeal way, individuals will not be conscious of the full scale of the taxes they pay, and this will lead politicians to increase the overall tax burden. For those who would like to see a larger public sector, this is an advantage; but for those who would like to see a smaller public sector, it is a disadvantage.

Advocates of a combined approach argue that it could be used to greatly reduce administrative and compliance costs, while retaining a fair degree of progressivity. For instance, a 10 percent VAT combined with a $100,000 standard deduction and income tax rates adjusted downward to reflect the VAT payments could generate approximately the same revenue as the current tax system, and have about the same degree of progressivity, but eliminate the necessity of filling out individual income tax forms for 96 percent of Americans. It would also virtually eliminate the distortions associated with the special provisions of the tax code (since almost all taxpayers would take advantage of the $100,000 standard deduc-

ORDINARY INCOME VERSUS CAPITAL GAINS

When capital gains are taxed at lower rates than ordinary income, individuals have an incentive to try to characterize income as a capital gain rather than as ordinary income. For instance, if a bond is issued paying an interest rate lower than the prevailing market rate of interest, the bond will sell at a discount; thus, if the market rate of interest is 10 percent, a bond promising to pay $100 in a year plus 5 percent interest will sell for approximately $95.

tion), without engaging in the political fights associated with their outright elimination.[14]

INTEGRATING STATE AND LOCAL INCOME TAXES Critics of all of these reforms point out that not much savings will occur unless there are commensurate reforms in state and local income taxes. While the distortions associated with unreformed state taxes are likely to be small (simply because state tax rates tend to be low), the administrative costs will remain high; the time to fill out complex tax forms does not in general depend on the tax rates, so unless states reform, households and firms will continue to waste huge amounts of time filling out complex tax forms. Traditionally, state and local authorities have followed the leadership of the federal government, but there are some notable exceptions. California has its own depreciation formula, for instance, necessitating firms in California performing two different sets of calculations.

ENERGY AND ENVIRONMENTAL TAXES

Another major reform is to shift more of the burden of taxation onto items that society wants to discourage and away from areas that should be encouraged. Thus, taxes on cigarettes and alcohol (sometimes called "sin taxes") and on gasoline and other goods that pollute the environment would be increased, and taxes on work and savings would be reduced. Taxes designed to address externalities, like pollution, are called *corrective* or *Pigouvian* taxes (after the famous Cambridge economist who advocated such taxes three quarters of a century ago). Such taxes not only raise revenues, they help align private incentives with social returns, and in that sense actually work to improve the overall efficiency of the economy.

[14] Under the current system, the very poor pay no tax, while with the VAT, they do. The effects of this could be offset by a broadened earned income tax credit; but doing so would reduce some of the simplification provided by the VAT system. On the other hand, with improved computerization the IRS could determine an individual's eligibility for benefits, provided that the individual only provided the requisite household data and certified that nonwage earnings did not exceed a threshold level.

Such a bond will yield the owner a 10 percent return—5 percent interest plus 5 percent capital gain. The 5 percent capital gain is nothing but disguised interest. In recent years, tax laws have attempted to stop this form of tax gimmickry by subjecting *original issue discounts* (that is, discounts which occur at the time the bonds are issued) to ordinary income taxation, not the preferential capital gains rates.

To be sure, such taxes may have adverse effects on GDP (the measure of national output), *as conventionally measured*, since conventional measures do not include environmental benefits like clean air or water. But there is a general consensus that standards of living, and especially health, are improved when smog does not cloud the skies three hundred days a year.

RECENT TAX REFORMS AND REFORM PROPOSALS

Conflicting objectives:

Increasing progressivity

Lowering marginal tax rates to reduce distortions

Simplification

Use of tax code to achieve broad range of objectives

Reforms under current framework:

Some of base broadening/simplification of 1986 undone by tax reforms of 1990s

Taxes used to:

• Promote values (family values)

• Promote savings and investment

• Promote education

Major reforms proposed:

Flat tax

Consumption tax

Value-added tax

Energy taxes (taxing "bads")

Though IRAs are designed to encourage savings, there is considerable controversy about whether they actually do. As they are currently designed, there is typically a maximum contribution ($2000), so that the marginal return to savings is unaffected for anyone saving more than the threshold level. Anyone with assets in her portfolio (such as a non-IRA savings account) can simply transfer those assets into her IRA account. The tax provision encourages people to transfer their assets, not to save more.

The most important of such taxes are those that affect energy consumption in general and the use of coal and other hydrocarbons in particular. With the accumulation of scientific evidence concerning the potential of global warming from greenhouse gas concentrations, there has been a concerted international effort, spearheaded by the signing of the Climate Convention in Rio de Janeiro in 1992, to reduce greenhouse gas emissions. These are much greater (per unit energy generated) from coal than from oil, which in turn has greater emissions than natural gas. A tax on greenhouse gas emissions would discourage the use of coal and oil, and thus reduce greenhouse gas emissions. In practice, the emissions cannot themselves be directly measured, but a **carbon tax,** which would set the tax rates on coal, oil, and natural gas in relationship to their carbon content (which determines emissions), would have much the same effect. Carbon taxes have received considerable attention in Europe, and have been instituted in Denmark, Finland, and the Netherlands. In 1993 a carbon tax was considered briefly by the U.S. government, but opposition from coal-producing states quickly forced the consideration of an alternative energy tax, called the **BTU tax.** A BTU (British thermal unit) is the standard way of measuring energy output. The BTU tax was designed to be a tax on energy consumption; reducing energy consumption would reduce greenhouse gas emissions, though not so efficiently as the more targeted carbon tax. The BTU tax actually proposed by the Clinton administration in February 1993 was a hybrid between a straight energy tax and a carbon tax, with rates on coal adjusted slightly higher and on natural gas slightly lower.

Not surprisingly, opposition from both energy-producing companies and high-energy-using firms (such as aluminum smelters) combined to defeat the tax, leaving in its place a slight expansion of the gasoline tax. While this tax has some environmental benefits, they are far smaller than those of the original proposals.

Other categories of environmental taxes which are currently under discussion, and which, in the long run, have some chance of success, focus on pesticide use and recycling. A major source of water pollution today is from pesticides and fertilizers used by farmers (what are called *non-point sources* of pollution). Unlike pollution generated by large factories, these are very hard to control directly. One way effectively to control this form of pollution is to make it more expensive to use the pollutants—by taxing them.

Moreover, the special provisions result in lowered government tax revenue—and thus lower government savings. Unless private savings increases by a greater amount than the losses in taxes, national savings will actually be reduced.

In spite of this, there is some evidence that IRAs may encourage savings, perhaps because banks and mutual funds have used the lure of the IRA to help advertise the virtues of savings.

The failure to reuse resources contributes to excessive waste. It costs money to recycle. But it also costs money to dispose of wastes. There is increasing concern about the social costs of waste disposal. Nobody wants a dump site in their backyard, partly because of the danger of toxic substances. As a result, communities have found it harder and harder to find places to dispose of waste. Increased fees for disposing of waste will encourage greater recycling. But there is concern that monitoring disposal is extremely difficult, and as fees for legal disposal increase there will be increased use of illegal means of disposal.

Another way of increasing recycling is to increase the cost of new versus recycled materials. For instance, a tax on virgin pulp (pulp from newly cut-down trees) will encourage more use of recycled pulp in manufacturing paper. The bottle recycling tax is now perhaps the most well known tax designed to encourage recycling.

Currently, the United States uses a variety of regulations to encourage good environmental policies in general and energy efficiency in particular. Most notable are the CAFE (corporate average fuel economy) standards, designed to increase the energy efficiency of cars. By switching from regulation to taxes, two benefits may be realized: (1) Economic efficiency may be enhanced, and (2) revenues will be raised, reducing the burden that must be imposed in the form of distortionary taxation. This notion of the *double dividend* to be realized through environmental taxation has gained considerable attention from economists and policy makers.[15]

[15] See, for instance, Lawrence H. Goulder, "Environmental Taxation and the 'Double Dividend': A Reader's Guide," *International Tax and Public Finance* 2, no. 2 (August 1995): 157–83; Wallace E. Oates, "Green Taxes: Can We Protect the Environment and Improve the Tax System at the Same Time?" *Southern Economic Journal* 61, no. 4 (April 1995): 915–22; Carlo Carraro, Marzio Galeotti, and Massimo Gallo, "Environmental Taxation and Unemployment: Some Evidence on the 'Double Dividend Hypothesis' in Europe," *Journal of Public Economics* 62, no. 1–2 (October 1996): 141–81; and A. Lans Bovenberg and Lawrence H. Goulder, "Optimal Environmental Taxation in the Presence of Other Taxes: General-Equilibrium Analyses," *American Economic Review* 86, no. 4 (September 1996): 985–1000.

REVIEW AND PRACTICE

SUMMARY

1 High administrative costs and low levels of compliance; the complexity of the tax code; the perceived inequities of the tax structure; and the large distortions associated with high marginal tax rates all have contributed to the impetus for tax reforms.

2 Many of the problems of the income tax system have arisen because too much has been asked of it. It was supposed to provide economic incentives (e.g., to invest, to save, to buy health insurance, to support state and local governments), and to redistribute income, as well as to raise revenue.

3 The 1986 Tax Reform Act decreased the highest marginal tax rate, removed those in poverty from the tax rolls, and made tax avoidance more difficult. Most Americans did not, however, face greatly reduced marginal tax rates, and for the most part the reductions simply reversed the effects of inflation of the 1970s.

4 The 1986 tax law did not simplify the tax code. It left some important loopholes. It did not substantially broaden the tax base. To the extent that it "leveled the playing field" for investments, it did so primarily by eliminating the special investment incentives that had been introduced in 1981.

5 The 1993 tax bill increased progressivity, by increasing marginal tax rates on the highest-income individuals and by substantially increasing the earned income tax credit. As a result, the goal of ensuring that all families with one full-time earner would be out of poverty was almost attained. The 1997 tax reform reduced progressivity, by restoring preferential treatment of capital gains, most of which accrue to the very wealthy.

6 The 1993 and 1997 tax laws introduced special provisions for investments in small and new businesses, expanded IRAs, introduced new tax credits for education, and increased the child care credit.

7 In the current political climate, tax laws are being used to encourage specific activities (such as education) through tax expenditures—since increases in direct expenditures are hard to obtain—and as an expression of values, such as encouraging families (by eliminating the marriage penalty and encouraging adoption).

8 Other major thrusts of tax reform under the current system include those to promote savings and to simplify some of the provisions contributing to tax complexity.

9 More major reforms include the flat tax, the value-added tax, basing taxes on consumption rather than income, and taxing energy (carbon) usage or other activities detrimental to the environment.

QUESTIONS AND PROBLEMS

1 There is a widespread view that a consumption tax would hurt the poor. Is this necessarily the case?

2 The adoption of a *consumption tax* would have a significant effect on the market value of certain assets. Which assets are likely to decrease in value? Which to increase in value? Should the government do anything to compensate the losers or to tax the gainers?

3 There is a widespread view that the appropriate basis for taxation is an individual's lifetime consumption (or lifetime income). Discuss the inequities and inefficiencies that would arise from a consumption tax which had increasing marginal tax rates but no provisions for averaging years of low consumption with years of high consumption. Would these problems also arise under a flat-rate consumption tax?

4 In Chapter 22 we discussed the problems associated with choosing the appropriate unit for taxation (family versus individual). How would these problems be affected by the adoption of a consumption tax? a flat-rate income tax?

5 Many economists and politicians have argued that moving from an income tax to a consumption tax would be unfair unless a wealth tax or an inheritance tax were enacted at the same time. Explain the arguments on both sides of this issue.

6 Explain why the repeal of the investment tax credit might have increased the value of existing capital goods.

7 Assume that contributions to an IRA account in excess of 10 percent of income are tax deductible. Use a two-period diagram to show the budget constraint. Explain why this form of IRA account is more likely to increase savings than the traditional form.

8 Assume that the supply of oil is inelastic. What is the effect of a tax by all countries on oil? Does it reduce oil consumption? Assume that only Switzerland imposes a tax on oil. What happens to world oil consumption? To Swiss oil consumption?

9 Consider a two-period model, in which oil (still in inelastic supply) can be used either this period or next period. In equilibrium, the price next period must by higher than the price this period, if an owner of oil is to be

willing not to sell it this period. Explain why if the interest rate is 10 percent, the price must be 10 percent higher. (The principle that price must rise at the rate of interest is called *Hotelling's principle*, after Harold Hotelling, a distinguished professor of statistics at Columbia and North Carolina State, who first enunciated it almost three-quarters of a century ago.) What are the consequences of imposing a tax on oil at the same rate in both periods?

10 Using the median voter model discussed in Chapter 7, discuss what might be the consequences of eliminating the deductibility of all state and local taxes for the level of expenditures at the state and local level. How does your answer depend on whether the median voter itemizes his deductions?

PART SEVEN

FURTHER ISSUES

The United States has a federal system of government, with some activities being undertaken at the state and local level, others at the national level. Chapter 26 explains the rationale for a federal system and some of the important interactions between the federal government and state and local governments. It also explores the role of competition among communities in ensuring that the correct levels and kinds of public goods are produced and that they are produced efficiently.

Chapter 27 briefly describes expenditures and taxes at the state and local levels. It focuses particularly on the incidence of taxes and expenditure programs in situations where capital and labor are highly mobile.

Chapter 28 addresses a major issue of the past two decades: America's budget deficit, which soared during the 1980s and was only brought under control in the later 1990s. The chapter analyzes the impact of the deficit, as well as taxation and government expenditures, on economic growth and stability.

26 Fiscal Federalism

FOCUS QUESTIONS

1 How are the responsibilities for providing public goods and services shared between the federal government and the states?

2 What are the economic principles that ought to govern the assignment of responsibilities? When can there be efficient decentralization of decision making concerning the provision and financing of public services?

3 What role should the federal government undertake in redistributing income from rich states to poor states? How does the federal government subsidize states now, and how effective are these subsidies?

The Constitution of the United States stipulates that those powers not expressly delegated to the federal government—such as providing for the national defense, printing money, and running the post office—rest with the states. For a long time, the prevailing view was that this seems to leave responsibility for the provision of most public services (such as education, police and fire protection, roads and highways) with the states. But the Constitution is a flexible document, and court interpretations of it have essentially freed the federal government to provide many other services.

There has been an ongoing debate about **fiscal federalism,** the division of economic responsibilities between the federal government and the states and localities. Federalism, of course, spans issues that go beyond economics. For example, in the 1960s, '70s, and '80s, civil rights advocates urged a more active role for the federal government, and those who resisted emphasized "states rights." This chapter focuses on economic issues such as, for example, what goods and services should be provided locally or nationally. This issue has surfaced periodically; in 1982, President Reagan in his State of the Union message called for a "New Federalism" giving states increased authority in welfare, with the federal government taking on more of the burden of paying for Medicaid. Critics argued that the New Federalism was a ploy for justifying cutbacks in federal assistance to states and localities, as a way of reducing the size of the federal government. Indeed, between 1980 and 1986, federal grants decreased from 3.3 percent of GDP to 2.6 percent. During the mid- and late 1990s, with a Republican majority in Congress, there were renewed demands for state control of federal programs that helped fuel the welfare reform of 1996.

This chapter briefly describes the broad division of responsibilities, then focuses on the central economic issues in fiscal federalism. It concludes with a few brief remarks about the underlying politics and philosophy in the debate.

THE DIVISION OF RESPONSIBILITIES

The relationships between the federal government and the states and localities are complex, and are not well described by a simple look at expenditures. There are two key issues: Who makes the decisions about the programs, and who pays for them? In some cases, the federal government pays for a program, and gives broad discretion to the states as to how to carry out the mandate. In other cases, the federal government essentially dictates all the terms—the states simply administer the program.

For instance, in the food stamp program, eligibility standards and amounts are determined federally; the states just administer the program. In some cases, the federal government gives a **matching grant;** the state determines the level of expenditure (within limits), and the federal government pays a fraction of the costs (which may depend on the per capita income of the state). In other cases, the federal government provides a **block grant**—a fixed amount of money. The state then bears the full costs of any expenditures above that amount. The federal government used to provide block grants that could be used for any purpose—this was called **general revenue-sharing.** (The government was sharing its revenues with the states, based on the presumption that the federal government could raise revenues more easily.) Today it no longer does this, but there are efforts to convert matching grants for specific purposes (like welfare) into block grants for those purposes. In 1996, the AFDC (Aid to Families with Dependent Children) program was replaced with a block grant program, TANF (Temporary Assistance for Needy Families), but the food stamp program remained federally financed, and the Medicaid program continued under a matching system.

Figure 26.1 shows the fraction of government expenditures for various categories financed at the federal level. (Bear in mind that expenditures give only a partial view of the role of each level of government in each activity.) States and localities retain responsibility for water and sanitation (sewers), education, and public safety (police and fire protection); and they bear a significant fraction of the costs for transportation (public roads). On the other hand, the federal government bears major responsibility for health, social security, and urban development. These patterns can be seen slightly differently in Figure 26.2, which shows how states and localities spend their money. Education is the single largest expenditure.

Just as there is a division of responsibility between the federal government, on the one hand, and state and local governments on the other, so there is a division of responsibility between state governments and local governments. The division is a complicated one, involving financing, regula-

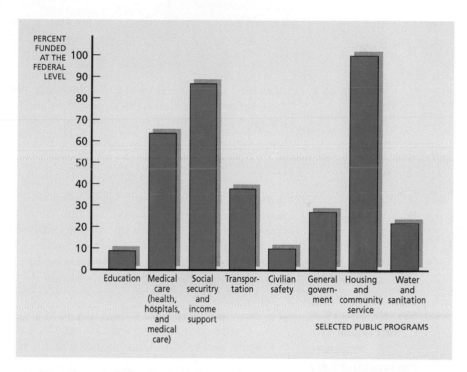

FIGURE 26.1 **Fraction of Government Expenditures for Selected Categories Financed at the Federal Level, 1997** The federal government finances most public-sector spending on social security, income support, and housing, but state and local governments finance most public-sector spending on education, police, and water and sanitation. Responsibility for transportation financing is almost evenly divided between the federal government and state and local governments.

Source: U.S. Department of Commerce, Bureau of Economic Analysis, *Survey of Current Business*, October 1998, Tables 3.16 and 3.17, pp. 7 and 9.

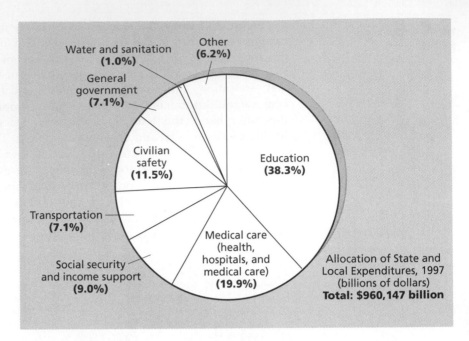

FIGURE 26.2   **Allocation of State and Local Expenditures in 1997 (Total expenditures of $960 billion)** Education is the largest state and local expenditure, followed by medical care, civilian safety, and income support programs.

SOURCE: *Survey of Current Business*, October 1998, Table 3.17, p. 9.

tion, and administration. Thus elementary and secondary schools are almost all run by local communities, but half of the financing comes from the states, which also impose a variety of regulations. While almost 60 percent of highway expenditures occur at the state level, almost all of sewage expenditures and expenditures on firefighting occur at the local level, along with almost three-quarters of police expenditures.[1]

OTHER INTERACTION BETWEEN THE FEDERAL GOVERNMENT AND THE STATE AND LOCAL GOVERNMENTS

The federal government affects the states and localities in a variety of other ways, besides providing grants. Its regulations and the federal tax code affect states and localities, just as they affect private businesses.

REGULATION The Constitution restricts the laws that states can pass. The states cannot enact legislation that deprives an individual of the right to a trial, no matter how heinous a crime he or she may have committed, nor can states bar an individual from holding a job on racial or religious grounds. Many Supreme Court decisions in recent years have countered state actions that are in violation of the Constitution.

[1] American Council on Intergovernmental Relations, *Significant Features of Fiscal Federalism*, vol. 2, October 1997, Tables 24 and 75.

State and local agencies may also be subject to the same pollution and environmental regulations that apply to private firms and individuals. In some cases the federal government has mandated that state and local governments provide certain services (such as access facilities for the handicapped) without providing the requisite funds. Not surprisingly, the states and local communities have complained that if the federal government attaches such importance to these services, it should also finance them (see box).

INCENTIVES Sometimes the federal government imposes its will through eligibility requirements for grants. For instance, until December 1995 transportation funds were made contingent upon maintaining speed limits of 55 miles per hour in urban areas and 65 in non-urban areas; educational funds are still made contingent upon having adequate affirmative action programs.

TAX EXPENDITURES One of the important ways that the federal government affects state and local expenditures is through the tax expenditures associated with the personal and corporate income taxes. These expenditures were estimated at almost $70 billion in 1997. For instance, interest on state bonds is not subject to federal taxation, and state and local income taxes are deductible from individual federal income taxes. As we shall see, this not only can be thought of as a subsidy to states and localities, but provides an incentive for greater expenditures at the state and local level.

THE SIZE OF FINANCIAL TRANSFERS

Chapter 2 emphasized that the magnitude of governmental expenditures does not provide a complete picture of government's role in the economy. Similarly, the magnitude of federal transfers to states and localities does not show the extent to which state and local government expenditures are affected by federal activities. Still, several features of these transfers are worth noting. First, they grew immensely between 1929, when they amounted to just 1.3 percent of state and local government revenues, and 1972, when they amounted to a fifth. While there have been some fluctuations in the level since then, by the mid-1990s they still represented just over a fifth. Second, federal aid appears to be more important at the state level than at the local level, accounting for slightly more than 20 percent of state revenues and slightly more than 3 percent of local revenues.

But these figures are deceptive. Much of the money granted to states is passed through to local governments. Transfers from state to local governments account for about 35 percent of local revenues.[2] Similarly, 47 percent of federal money transferred to state and local governments is passed on to individuals, primarily through TANF and Medicaid expenditures. Medicaid reimbursements account for a growing proportion of federal aid to states.

[2] *Significant Features of Fiscal Federalism,* vol. 2, October 1997, Tables 14 and 33.

UNFUNDED MANDATES

By 1994, the issue of unfunded mandates had been festering for a long time. Even pieces of legislation for which there was widespread support imposed financial burdens on states and localities that they found difficult to meet. For instance, the Americans With Disabilities Act required that states and municipalities ensure access to public buildings and public transportation by the handicapped. The reauthorization of the Clean Water Act brought the issue to a head. Communities realized that they would have to pay millions for new sewage-treatment facilities.

Critics of unfunded mandates argued that just as Congress had committed itself not to pass additional expenditures unless it could finance them, so too it should commit itself not to pass additional mandates on states and communities unless it paid for them. The unfunded mandates issue was also seized upon by those who wanted to cut back government activities in general: they saw it as one way of

---

In 1973, they accounted for 11 percent of federal grants; in 1997, Medicaid accounted for 41 percent of transfers to state and local governments.[3]

And even these Medicaid statistics are misleading. During the late 1980s and early 1990s, states learned how to use the Medicaid program as a form of general revenue-sharing. To see how the "scam" worked, assume some hospital increased its charges by $1000, with the state picking up $500 and the federal government picking up $500. The hospital could then rebate, say, $800 to the state. The hospital was better off—it had $200 more to spend. The state was better off; it had $300 to spend. Only the federal government was worse off. Expenditures for health care for the poor had gone up, but not because services had gone up, or because more resources had been devoted to the poor.

PRINCIPLES OF FISCAL FEDERALISM

In the previous section, we described the various activities that are undertaken at each level of government, the division of responsibilities. To a large extent, this division of responsibilities evolved over time. The Constitution, which more than two hundred years ago set forth the framework within which the division of responsibilities occurs, was written well before the development of the modern theory of public finance, before notions of public goods even existed.

---

[3] Executive Office of the President, Office of Management and Budget, *Budget of the United States Government, Fiscal Year 1999, Analytic Perspectives* (Washington, D.C.: Government Printing Office), Table 9-3. Slightly different data are contained in *Survey of Current Business*, October 1998, Table 3.16.

ensuring, for instance, that no new environmental legislation could be passed. It was precisely this aspect that made the unfunded mandates issue so alarming.

Economists pointed out that some of these "mandates," such as those involved in the Clean Water Act, did not ask localities to assume an "unfair" burden; they only mandated that localities not impose an externality on other communities. By failing to treat sewage adequately, some communities were imposing costs on other communities.

The compromise adopted by Congress in 1995 required that legislation which imposed costs on communities be accompanied with an estimate of the magnitude of those costs. Then, at least, Congress could judge whether those costs were reasonable, and whether the benefits of the legislation were commensurate with those costs.

But with the development of the modern theory of public finance, we can ask, what principles should guide the assignment of responsibilities? Are some assignments more likely to lead to efficiency, or to decisions about the level or kind of public goods being produced that are more in accord with the preferences of citizens? This section sets forth some of the key principles.

NATIONAL PUBLIC GOODS VERSUS LOCAL PUBLIC GOODS

For some kinds of goods there is a strong presumption for federal provision. These are national public goods, whose benefits accrue to everyone in the nation. In contrast, the benefits of **local public goods** accrue to residents of a particular community. National defense is a national public good; traffic lights and fire protection are local public goods.

Just as most goods publicly provided at the national level are not pure public goods, most goods publicly provided at the local level are not pure public goods. For some goods, such as public libraries, exclusion is easy but undesirable, since the cost of providing access to an additional individual is almost zero. Some goods which local governments provide—for example, education and public hospitals—are essentially private goods; exclusion is easy and the costs of providing services to additional individuals are significant. (See Chapter 6.) By the same token, some local public goods are not purely local; some of the benefits could accrue some of the time to those living in other communities.

The argument that if there is to be an efficient supply of public goods they must be provided publicly implies, by extension, that if there is to be an efficient supply of *national* public goods, they must be provided at the national level. If it were left up to each community to provide for national public

733

INTER-NATIONAL PUBLIC GOODS

Just as there are some public goods whose benefits accrue only to those living inside a particular community, there are some public goods whose benefits accrue to people living all over the world. And just as there will be an undersupply of national public goods if the provision is left to local communities, there is likely to be an undersupply of international public goods if the provision is left to national governments.

There are at least four important categories of such international public goods. The first, the global environment—the earth's atmosphere and the oceans that surround the continents—is perhaps the most obvious. Though increases in greenhouse gases are likely to affect different countries differently, the overall concentration of greenhouse gases is the result of the cumulative actions of all of the individual countries. The second, international security, can potentially affect almost everyone in the world, as it did during the two world wars of the

goods, there would be free rider problems, just as there would be if the provision of national public goods were left up to individual households and firms.

DO LOCAL COMMUNITIES PROVIDE LOCAL PUBLIC GOODS EFFICIENTLY?

While there is a presumption that the federal government should provide national public goods, the question remains, should the provision of local public goods be left up to states and localities?

In a remarkable article written more than forty years ago, Charles Tiebout of the University of Washington argued that one could think in terms of local communities' competing with each other to supply local public goods to citizens—efficiently, in the quantities and forms they want—just as firms compete to supply conventional private goods.[4] He argued that just

---

LOCAL, NATIONAL, AND INTERNATIONAL PUBLIC GOODS

National public goods: public goods whose benefits accrue to everyone in the nation

Local public goods: public goods whose benefits are limited to those living in a locality

International public goods: public goods whose benefits are global in nature

---

[4] See C. Tiebout, "A Pure Theory of Local Expenditure," *Journal of Political Economy* 64 (1956): 416–24.

twentieth century. The third is knowledge. The marginal cost of an additional person *anywhere in the world* having a bit of knowledge is zero—it does not subtract from what others know (though it may reduce the economic rents that they can obtain from the knowledge, and the marginal cost of *tranmission* of knowledge is not zero). And, at least for many types of knowledge, exclusion is difficult if not impossible. The fourth is international economic stability. An economic crisis in one country can spread to other countries, just as a disease in one person can infect others. (In fact, economists refer to the process as *contagion*.) Thus, maintaining international economic stability and containing the impact of crises is viewed as an international public good of first-order importance, and the international community has set up international financial institutions—the International Monetary Fund and the World Bank—to provide assistance in the event of a crisis.

as competition among private firms leads to the efficient provision of private goods, so too compctition among local communities leads to efficiency in the provision of local public goods. This hypothesis is called the **Tiebout hypothesis.** The following paragraphs explore the Tiebout hypothesis—including its limitations—in greater depth.

TIEBOUT HYPOTHESIS

Chapter 3 discussed the rationale for government activities. The fundamental theorem of welfare economics—Adam Smith's "invisible hand"—implies that in the absence of a market failure, such as public goods, the economy will be Pareto efficient. Individuals, each acting in their own self-interest, will make decisions that lead to Pareto efficiency. Competition among producers leads them to supply the goods individuals want at the lowest possible cost.

An analogous argument can be made for the provision of local public goods and services by state and local governments, as distinct from the federal government. Compctition among communities, it is argued, will result in communities' supplying the goods and services individuals want and producing these goods in an efficient manner.

Tiebout was originally concerned with the problem of *preference revelation* discussed in Chapter 7: While individuals reveal their preferences for private goods simply by buying goods, how are they to reveal their preferences for public goods? When individuals vote, they choose candidates who reflect their overall values, but they cannot express in detail their views about particular categories of expenditures. Only limited use of referenda is made in most states. And even if individuals were asked to vote directly on expenditures for particular programs, the resulting equilibrium would not, in general, be Pareto efficient.

Tiebout argued that individuals could "vote with their feet," that their choice of communities revealed their preferences toward locally provided public goods in the same way as their choices of products reveal their preferences for private goods. Moreover, just as there are incentives for firms to find out what commodities individuals prefer and to produce those commodities efficiently, so are there incentives for communities to find out what kinds of community-provided goods individuals prefer, and to provide them efficiently. This is seen most strongly in the case of community developers. In recent years these developers, recognizing that many individuals would like more security and more communal facilities (swimming pools, tennis courts) than are provided by the typical city, have formed large developments providing these services. Because these communities meet the needs of the individuals better than the available alternatives, individuals are willing to pay higher rents (or spend more to purchase homes in these communities). This gives developers a return for their efforts to ascertain what individuals want and to meet these desires.

More generally, communities that provide the services individuals like and provide them efficiently will experience an influx of individuals; communities that fail to do so will experience an outflux. Such migration (with its consequent effect on property values) provides essentially the same kind of signal to city managers that the market provides to a firm's managers (a firm that fails to provide a commodity individuals like will find its sales declining; a firm that succeeds will find its sales increasing). Politicians, sometimes under pressure from the electorate, respond to these signals in much the same way as a firm's managers respond to market signals.

The analogy is an instructive one. Under certain assumptions, the separate decisions of each community lead to a Pareto efficient allocation, just as the separate decisions of firms and individuals concerning private goods lead to Pareto efficiency.

But these assumptions generally do not hold. And even were they to hold, the inequality in the distribution of welfare across communities might be unacceptably large.

The qualifications to the Tiebout hypothesis closely parallel those we discussed in Part 2, concerning the circumstances in which market allocations might not be Pareto efficient or, even if efficient, might not be desirable.[5] The two most fundamental qualifications are the presence of market failures and dissatisfaction with the distribution of income.

---

[5] Since Tiebout, an extensive literature has developed evaluating the conditions under which the result is valid. See, in particular, J. E. Stiglitz, "Public Goods in Open Economies with Heterogeneous Individuals," in *Locational Analysis of Public Facilities,* ed. J. F. Thisse and H. G. Zoller (New York: Elsevier–North Holland, 1983) and "Theory of Local Public Goods," in *The Economics of Public Services,* ed. M. Feldstein and R. Inman (New York: Macmillan, 1977), pp. 274–333; T. Bewley, "A Critique of Tiebout's Theory of Local Public Expenditures," *Econometrica* 49 (1981): 713–40; and G. R. Zodrow and P. Mieszkowski, "Pigou, Tiebout, Property Taxation, and the Underprovision of Local Public Goods," *Journal of Urban Economics* 19 (1986): 356–70.

TIEBOUT HYPOTHESIS

Competition among communities ensures efficiency in the supply of local public goods, just as competition among firms ensures efficiency in the supply of private goods

Limitations:

- "Market failures"

  Externalities: decisions of community have effects on others

  Imperfect competition: limited number of communities

- Tax competition may simply lead to lower taxes on businesses

- Redistribution—With free migration and local competition, there will be no or, at most, limited redistribution at local level

---

MARKET FAILURES

The most important "market failures" have to do with externalities and imperfect competition.

EXTERNALITIES The actions of one community may have marked effects on other communities. If a community constructs a smelly sewage plant or allows the development of an industrial area at its boundary, in a location such that the winds blow the bad odors over the neighboring communities, an important externality results. We sometimes refer to these externalities as "spillovers." Not all spillovers are negative. Some economists believe that there are important public benefits from having an educated citizenry, and that they provide some justification for public support of education. To the extent that this is true, and to the extent that individuals move away from the community that provided them with a free education, there are spillovers from a local community's public education system.

Migration and location inefficiencies may be thought of as a particularly important class of externalities. Individuals who move into a community bring both benefits and costs; they may increase the tax base, but they also may lead to increased demands on public services, and increased congestion (for instance, of roads and parks). Since in many cases they neither pay for these costs nor are compensated for the benefits they confer, there are likely to be inefficiencies in location decisions. Many countries have become increasingly concerned about what they view as excessive concentration of population in the major cities (London, Paris, Mexico City), and have developed decentralization policies to attain what they consider a more efficient pattern of location.

COMPETITION AND PROFIT MAXIMIZATION A central assumption underlying the results concerning the efficiency of market economies is that there are many profit-maximizing firms. The Tiebout hypothesis similarly assumes the existence of many competing communities.[6] In most areas there is only a limited number of competing communities; there is, in effect, only limited competition. Moreover, communities do not decide which goods and services to provide on the basis of any simple profit-maximization criterion, but by a political process along the lines discussed in Chapter 7. The kinds of inefficiencies to which this may give rise will be described in the next chapter. Here we simply note that limited competition provides an explanation for why we should be skeptical about the Tiebout hypothesis.

TAX COMPETITION Tiebout's model suggests that competition among communities is not only healthy, but necessary to attain Pareto optimality. But there is another view of competition among communities which is far more negative. This view sees different communities competing to attract businesses, with the associated tax base and employment opportunities. Gains in one community are partly at the expense of losses in other communities. But more generally, the competition to attract businesses results in lower taxes for businesses: in the end, businesses are the ultimate beneficiaries. In this perspective, it would appear preferable for communities to agree not to compete.

Earlier, we pointed out that the incidence of taxes imposed by local communities had to be on immobile factors. The mobile factors could move to escape taxation. Capital (and businesses more generally) is mobile, and the competition to attract businesses through tax concessions is just a reflection of this reality. If communities agreed to give no tax concessions, competition would almost surely take other, probably more wasteful, forms, such as providing enhanced public facilities, such as roads, for the businesses. (If even this were somehow stopped, communities which had higher tax rates because they had a lower tax base would find it impossible to attract businesses.) From this perspective, then, trying to stop tax competition is like trying to stop competition elsewhere in the economy. Not only are such attempts likely to be ineffective, but to the extent they are effective, they are likely to lead to other problems, including inefficiencies.

As in other areas, complete collusion, were it successful, could have real effects. If all communities were able to agree not to compete for business, and agreed, say, to impose a uniform tax on business, then the communities

---

[6] Indeed, there must be so many that all residents within each community who have the same skills also have the same tastes for public goods. Another implication is that (provided voters are rational) there would be complete unanimity in voting. Obviously, neither of these conditions is satisfied. See R. W. Eberts and T. J. Gronberg, "Jurisdictional Homogeneity and the Tiebout Hypothesis," *Journal of Urban Economics* 10 (1981): 227–39; and H. Pack and J. Pack, "Metropolitan Fragmentation and Local Public Expenditure," *National Tax Journal* 31 (1978): 349–62.

would gain at the expense of businesses. Such a tax would be equivalent to a federally imposed tax.[7] The debate on tax competition illustrates the marked advantages the federal government has in imposing taxes.

REDISTRIBUTION

Redistribution—the second basic qualification to the Tiebout hypothesis—may be a more important explanation of the role of the federal government than the market failures we have just described. There is concern about the distribution of income both among individuals and across communities.

INEQUALITY AMONG INDIVIDUALS Should the extent of redistribution—the level of welfare payments—be a local or national decision? Is "redistribution" a local public good? Assume individuals in some community believe strongly that no individual should live in a slum, and so they provide a good public housing program, while individuals in some other community have different ethical concerns. Is there any reason why individuals in the first community should attempt to impose their ethical beliefs on the second, by attempting to make minimal housing standards a national rather than a local issue?

The answer is yes. The reason is that, with relatively free migration, the extent of redistribution that is feasible at the local level is very limited. Any community that decides to provide better housing for the poor, or better medical care, might find itself faced with an influx of the poor. Communities have an incentive to try to appear unattractive to the poor, so that they will move on to the next community. Some communities, for instance, do this by passing zoning laws that require multi-acre lots.[8] Others do it by limiting the provision of certain public services which are particularly valued by the poor and for which the wealthier have good private substitutes, such as bus services.

Indeed, if there were perfect competition among communities, the efforts to provide local public services at least cost to the taxpayers would result in taxpayers' paying taxes only commensurate with the benefits they themselves received. A community that had no welfare program and succeeded in excluding most of the poor would be able to provide public services (education, sewage treatment, libraries, etc.) at lower tax rates than a community that had an ambitious welfare program (public housing, good medical care, etc.) and educational programs aimed at disadvantaged children. The fact that competition is frequently limited, migration is slow, and that decisions concerning public services are made politically means that there often are local (and state) redistribution programs. But these remain limited.

INEQUALITY ACROSS COMMUNITIES We have already noted that there are marked differences among the states in per capita income. For a poor community to provide the same level of services as a rich one requires that it levy

---

[7] There remains the problem of tax competition among countries.
[8] Courts have recently restricted the use of zoning as an exclusionary device.

much higher tax rates. And indeed, we see enormous variation in per capita expenditures and tax rates across the United States. Per capita expenditures at the state level in 1996 varied from $2175 in Texas and $2191 in Missouri, to $8438 in Alaska, $4420 in Hawaii, and $4044 in New York (with an average for the country of $2854).[9] Total state and local taxes paid in New York were 12.7 percent of the income of a typical $50,000 family of four and 15 percent of a $100,000 family, but in Las Vegas were only 4.5 percent of the income of comparable families, and in Los Angeles were 8.1 percent of the income of a $50,000 family and 11 percent of the income of a $100,000 family.[10]

But why should we be more concerned with the inequality associated with locally provided public goods (and tax rates) than we are with inequality in general? Is there any reason why there should be specific federal programs directed at reducing this particular kind of inequality? If we want more redistribution, why not simply impose a more progressive federal tax, letting individuals then choose how to spend their money? If they wish to live in communities that spend more or less on local public goods, why not let them? The issues are analogous to those that arose in earlier chapters concerning whether the government should have specific policies directed at decreasing the extent of inequality of access to specific goods, such as medicine, food, and housing. The concept of *specific egalitarianism* was introduced—the view that the consumption of certain commodities should not depend on one's (or one's parents') income or wealth. Education, the most important locally and publicly provided good, is one of those goods for which the strongest argument for equality of access can be made.

Several arguments, however, can be made against providing programs aimed at reducing inequality in the provision of local public services.

1 *Consumer sovereignty.* The first is the standard "consumer sovereignty" argument: individuals should be allowed to choose the goods they prefer. The federal government should not force its preferences—for food, housing, or education—on local communities. Programs aimed at reducing inequality in the provision of local public goods (to the extent that they are effective) distort consumption patterns; they may result in greater consumption of "local public goods" and less consumption of private goods than a redistributive program providing cash to individuals. Categorical grants (again, to the extent that they are effective) cause a distortion in the mix of locally provided goods; they may, for instance, result in more education and urban redevelopment and less frequent sewage collection. Whenever there are such distortions there is a deadweight loss.

This consumer sovereignty argument, though relevant, is somewhat less forceful for some locally provided goods than for others. For instance, decisions concerning elementary and secondary school education are made not by the individual but by his or her parents; and decisions concerning local public goods are made by a political process, which need not yield efficient outcomes, as we saw in Chapter 7.

---

[9] *Statistical Abstract of the United States, 1998,* Table 516.
[10] *Statistical Abstract of the United States, 1998,* Table 520.

2 *The difficulty of targeting communities for redistribution.* A second argument against programs aimed at redistributing income across communities (localities, states) is that such programs are not well targeted. Most communities contain a mix of poor and rich individuals. A program aimed at redistributing resources to a community whose average income is low may simply result in a lowering of the tax rate; the program's main beneficiaries will thus be the rich individuals within the poor communities. On the other hand, certain specific programs, such as the school lunch program, may be more effective in redistributing income to *children* than programs aimed at redistributing income among families.

3 *Location inefficiencies.* A third argument is that programs redistributing income across communities result in location inefficiencies. They distort the decisions of individuals about where to live and the decisions of businesses about where to locate.

The United States is a very mobile society. We move often, and frequently quite far. There have been large migrations from the rural South to the urban North, and from the Snow Belt to the Sun Belt. A variety of reasons induce individuals to move, but economic considerations are among the more important. These include not only an individual's opportunities for employment and the wages he receives, but the taxes that are imposed and the public goods that are provided. As demands and technologies change, economic efficiency requires that individuals move to where they can be more productive. This will necessitate that some localities, and indeed even some regions, experience declining populations, while others experience rapidly rising populations. Federal aid aimed at redistributing income from one locality to another may interfere with the efficient allocation of labor and capital. The level of taxes and public services provided by one community will not correctly reflect the economic potential of that community. The inefficiencies to which this gives rise may be small in the short run but may become large in the long run. Individuals will be encouraged to stay where they are rather than move to more productive localities. Indeed, it might be better to use the same funds to subsidize emigration out of the unproductive areas. Similarly, with new highway systems, it may no longer be efficient to have the larger agglomerations of population associated with inner cities. Thus, aid to central cities may serve to perpetuate these inefficient patterns of location.[11]

Note that these inefficiencies arise from attempts to redistribute income among communities. If our basic concern is with inequality among individuals, redistribution should be aimed at individuals, not at regions or localities.

In addition, specific redistributive programs, if they are not well designed, may give rise to large distortions. A program aimed at remedying measured housing shortages among the very poor, by providing federal subsidies, may encourage communities to undertake actions that exacerbate

[11] On the other hand, the aid may compensate for positive externalities produced by the inner cities.

these shortages (such as rent control). A program to bail out cities that have borrowed excessively and appear to be in danger of defaulting on their bonds may encourage other communities to borrow more than they otherwise would, knowing that if they get into trouble the federal government is there to rescue them.

OTHER ARGUMENTS FOR LOCAL PROVISION

While the concept of local public goods provides the central argument for the provision of certain public goods locally, several other arguments have been put forward for assigning greater responsibility for the provision of collective goods to the local level—even when the goods are not pure local public goods, or even when doing so may limit the scope for redistribution. These arguments have played an important role in recent political debates in the United States. One is that by delegating more responsibility to local communities, there can be more adaptation to the circumstances and preferences of those who benefit from the good. Moreover, there is more likely to be active involvement of citizens, say, in schools, when they are the responsibility of local communities; and this involvement leads to higher-quality public services.

Moreover, at the local level, individuals see more clearly the link between benefits and costs (what they have to pay in taxes); when people sense clearly the link between government benefits and taxes, they are less likely to ask for benefits that are not worth the costs, and are more likely to demand efficiency in the provision of benefits. Moreover, there can be more experimentation, which provides information that is particularly valuable in designing programs in areas such as welfare, where there is a general sense of major need for improvement.

Besides these analytic arguments, some may push for delegating more responsibility to states and localities because they believe that the political process will result in decisions that are different—and more to their liking—than if made at the national level. For instance, many believe that assigning states and localities more of the responsibility for decisions concerning welfare programs will result in a more effective containment of costs.

PRODUCTION VERSUS FINANCE

Many of the arguments typically made for local provision of public goods—that local communities are more responsive to the needs and preferences of those who actually receive the goods, that local communities have greater incentives for efficiency, and that devolving responsibility to local communities provides greater opportunities for experimentation—are mainly arguments for local *control*—local decision-making—rather than local *finance*. But there are good reasons for concern about separating finance from control. If voters of the country as a whole believe that their tax dollars should be used to finance welfare expenditures for the poor, they want to be sure that their money actually goes for this purpose, and not to finance suburban swimming pools. Some controls on expenditure are necessary. The issue is one of degree: how much control? By imposing more controls, there may be greater assurance that the money is used in the way intended; but there is a cost—more bureaucracy, less adaptability to local circumstances, and less experimentation. In the case of the welfare program, prior to the 1996 reforms, there was a consensus that more local autonomy was needed, and the federal government granted the vast majority of states **waivers** of federal rules to allow them to introduce specific experiments.

When responsibility for decision making devolves downward from the federal government, there is a question of how far downward: to the states, to subunits of the states (like cities or counties), or directly to individuals? Many of the arguments for devolving responsibility suggest that the lower the level, the better. A housing program is more likely to be responsive to local needs if responsibility is given to the city or neighborhood, rather than to the state. Many argue, why involve intermediary levels of government at all? Why not simply give poor individuals housing vouchers—certificates that they can use to buy housing anywhere—giving them the decision-making responsibility over the kind of housing they want?

Assigning responsibility for decision making to local communities does not mean that they actually have to do the production themselves. Just as the federal government can produce goods and services directly or purchase them from private firms, the same is true at the local level. Typically, local communities are involved in the production of most of the goods and services which they provide—from police and fire protection to schools. But there are some areas—most notably, garbage collection—in which many communities contract out to private providers. (In still other localities, garbage collection is treated as a private good, with the community taking on no role at all.) The discussion of public versus private production at the local level parallels that at the national level (see Chapter 8). More recently, states and localities have been exploring new possibilities for contracting out—including prisons and administrative services. In 1997, Texas requested permission to use a private firm to process welfare claims. The federal government denied the application: even though there had been considerable devolution of responsibility for the welfare programs to the states, the federal government worried that a private contractor would have incentives that would lead to decisions about who was or was not eligible for welfare which were not consistent with the intent of the welfare legislation.

EFFECTIVENESS OF FEDERAL CATEGORICAL AID TO LOCAL COMMUNITIES

The intention of federal categorical aid to local communities is to encourage local spending on particular public services. Aid to bilingual education, to vocational education, and to school libraries is intended to result in an increase in expenditures in each of these categories. How effective is this aid? Do federal funds just substitute for local funds, or do they actually result in more expenditures for the intended purpose?

From a theoretical perspective, the issue is precisely the same as one that we discussed in Chapter 10. How effective is categorical aid to individuals in encouraging expenditures, say, on food or housing? The answer depends on whether there is a substitution effect or just an income effect.

We wish to compare three types of federal aid to local communities—a block grant not tied to any specific use, a block grant tied to a specific purpose, and matching aid for a specific purpose.

Figure 26.3 shows the budget constraint of the community. (We simplify by assuming all individuals within the community are identical, so that we can ignore questions concerning differences in tastes.) The community would choose point E, the tangency between the budget constraint and the indifference curve of the representative individual. Now assume that the federal government provides a block grant to the community. This shifts out the budget constraint, to line $B'B'$. There is now a new equilibrium, E^*. It entails a higher level of expenditure on local publicly provided goods and a higher level of per capita consumption of private goods. That is, the federal aid has in fact resulted in lowering the tax rate imposed on individuals. The federal money has partially substituted for local community money; the community, because it is better off, spends more on publicly provided goods as well as privately provided goods.

Now assume, however, that there are two different publicly provided goods, garbage collection and education, on which the community can spend funds. We represent the allocation decision of the community between the two goods by the same kind of diagrammatic devices we have

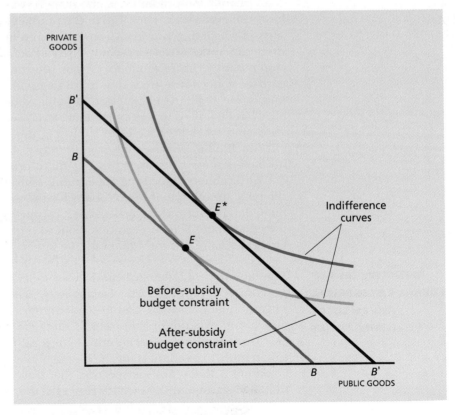

FIGURE 26.3   **Effect of Block Grants** A lump-sum transfer to a community will result in an increase in public expenditures, but by an amount less than the transfer; local taxes will go down.

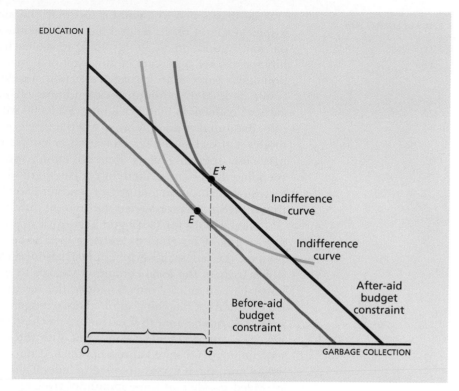

EDUCATION

E*

Indifference
curve

E

Indifference
curve

After-aid
budget
constraint

Before-aid
budget
constraint

O   G   GARBAGE COLLECTION

FIGURE 26.4   **Effects of Nonmatching Categorical Aid** It makes no difference whether the federal government stipulates that the funds be used for garbage collection or education, so long as the size of its grant is less than the total desired expenditure. (If the government stipulates that its funds be used for garbage collection, then so long as the government gives less than the amount *OG*, the stipulation has no effect.)

used to represent the allocation between private and publicly provided goods.[12] The community has a budget constraint; it needs to divide its total budget between the two goods, as represented by Figure 26.4. The community also has indifference curves between the two goods. The initial equilibrium is represented in Figure 26.4 by *E*. Now with the federal aid, the budget constraint has moved out, and the new equilibrium is *E**. Does it make any difference whether the government specifies that the funds be allocated to one public good or the other? Not usually. So long as the amount of fed-

[12] This kind of analysis assumes that we can separate the allocation decision among publicly provided goods from the allocation decision between private and public goods. This kind of separation is possible only under a fairly stringent mathematical condition on preferences known as *separability*, where we assume that the marginal rate of substitution between public goods 1 and 2 does not depend on the level of consumption of other goods.

eral aid that is tied to a good is less than the amount that the community wishes to spend on it, federal aid will substitute for local support for this particular good, on an almost dollar-for-dollar basis. That is, if the community spends, say, 5 percent of any additional increase in its wealth on education and 5 percent on garbage collection, a federal grant of $1 million will result in $50,000 additional expenditure on education and $50,000 on garbage collection. The remaining $900,000 will be used to lower the tax rate. But it makes no difference whether the government stipulates that the money it gives be used for education or not, so long as the community was previously spending more than $1 million on education. If it were not spending this amount, then, of course, there would be a slightly greater effect on its education budget; expenditure would increase by the amount that the federal aid exceeded the amount previously expended.[13]

These results for block grant categorical aid need to be contrasted with a government program of *matching* local expenditures (e.g., on libraries). Suppose the federal government matches local expenditures on a dollar-for-dollar basis. If the local community wishes to buy a book that costs $10, it costs the community only $5, since the federal government provides the other $5 with a matching grant. This arrangement obviously creates a considerable inducement to spend more on these services, as illustrated in Figure 26.5. The new budget constraint, with the subsidy for local government expenditures, is rotated around point B. If the community were to decide to spend nothing, it would not receive federal aid. For every dollar of privately provided goods that the community gives up, it can obtain twice as many publicly provided goods as previously. Thus the budget constraint is much flatter. This outward shift in the budget constraint has an income effect, as before; but now there is, in addition, a substitution effect. Since publicly provided goods are less expensive, the community will wish to spend more. The equilibrium will change from E to E^*.

Figure 26.5 also shows the community's budget constraint with a block grant that provides the community with the same welfare as the matching grant. (This budget constraint is clearly parallel to the before-subsidy budget constraint, and the new equilibrium at E^{**} is on the same indifference curve as E^*.) Two things should be noted: The equilibrium level of public expenditure on the public good is lower than with the matching grant, and the cost to the federal government is lower. There is a deadweight loss associated with the matching grant (of DE^*, in terms of privately provided goods).

If the matching funds are provided for a particular good, the federal aid will have a marked effect on the composition of the community's budget. It will encourage those goods whose prices are lowered (perhaps partly at the expense of other publicly provided goods, whose *relative* prices can now be viewed as being higher). By the same token, it should be clear that for any given level of federal grants, if the object of the federal government is to encourage the provision of particular goods, a system of matching

---

[13] A full analysis of this problem requires a three-dimensional diagram, with education, garbage collection, and private goods on the three axes.

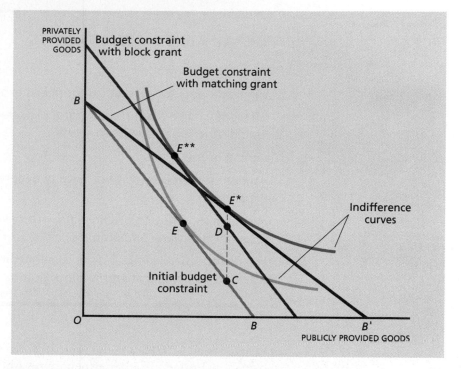

FIGURE 26.5 **The Effect of Matching Grants** Matching grants effectively lower the price of local public goods and result in an increase in the level of consumption of local public goods. With a 50 percent matching grant, to get $1 of public goods, the community need give up only 50 cents' worth of private goods. A block grant of *CD* gives the same level of utility as the matching grant of amount *CE**.

grants is far more effective than block grants—a lump-sum subsidy—whether restricted or not.

THEORY AND PRACTICE Evidence on actual government behavior supports our prediction that matching grants are more stimulative for local governmental spending than block grants. However, it does not support our prediction that nonmatching grants for specific purposes have the same effects as a lump-sum increase in private income; the evidence suggests that categorical programs do have an effect on government budgets.[14] This has been referred to as the **flypaper effect:** money sticks where it hits.[15] Several explana-

[14] See E. M. Gramlich, "Intergovernmental Grants: A Review of the Empirical Literature," in *The Political Economy of Fiscal Federalism* , ed. W. E. Oates (Lexington, Mass.: Lexington Books, 1977).
[15] P. N. Courant, E. M. Gramlich, and D. L. Rubinfeld, "The Stimulative Effect of Intergovernmental Grants: Or Why Money Sticks Where It Hits," in *Fiscal Federalism and Grants-in-Aid,* ed. P. Mieszkowski and W. Oakland (Washington, D. C.: Urban Institute, 1979), pp. 5–21.

FEDERAL AID TO COMMUNITIES

Block categorical grants

Fixed amounts for certain categories of expenditures

Effect much like a lump sum grant, provided grant is less than would otherwise have been spent

Matching grants

Amount received by state or locality depends on level of expenditure

Has both substitution and income effect—and therefore likely larger effect than comparable size block grant

Has distortionary effect—same level of community welfare can be attained at lower cost with a block grant

tions have been offered. One argument is that voters do not perceive the true marginal price of public expenditures when nonmatching grants are made; marginal costs exceed average costs, and voters are more aware of the latter than the former. Another explanation is that, at least in the short run, government bureaucrats have considerable discretion over their budgets. If they receive additional funds, the voters do not immediately know about it; and even if they did, they do not have the means to force the bureaucrats to pass the money back to them. A third argument has it that federal administrators can ensure that the money is spent in an incremental manner; they have enough discretion to withdraw funds if they believe that the federal funds are simply being used to substitute for state funds.

THE FEDERAL TAX SYSTEM AND LOCAL EXPENDITURES

The federal government affects local expenditures not only directly, through its aid programs, but indirectly, through the federal tax system. Two provisions of the income tax code have an important effect on local communities. The first is that interest on state and local bonds is completely exempt from taxation by the federal government. This means that if an individual faces a 36 percent marginal tax rate, a 6.4 return on a tax-exempt local government bond is equivalent to a 10 percent return on any other bond. After taxes, a 10 percent return yields 10% (1–.36) = 6.4 percent. This tax exemption for state and local bonds obviously lowers the cost to state and local authorities of borrowing funds.

The second provision is that state and local income and property taxes are deductible from the federal income tax. That is, if an individual has an income of $40,000 and pays $1000 in property taxes, she can deduct that amount from her income—that is, she has to pay taxes on only $39,000.

This means that if the individual is in the 36 percent tax bracket, the property tax reduces her net income (what she can spend to buy consumption goods) by only $640. Of the $1000 in property taxes, the federal government is, effectively, paying over one-third.

These tax benefits increase the level of expenditure on local public goods, encourage expenditures on capital projects, and induce some communities to finance their investments by debt.

Consider an idealized community in which all individuals are in the 36 percent tax bracket. If the community increases expenditures per family on education by $1000 and raises income and property taxes to finance the increased expenditures, the after-federal income tax cost to the individual is only $640. It is as if there is a federal matching grant for local public goods. The budget constraint facing the individual is identical to that depicted in Figure 26.5.

In most states, communities can borrow only to finance capital projects. If this restriction is binding (as it frequently is), the tax exemption of interest on local bonds implies that the effective cost of capital goods is lowered relative to that of current services (labor and materials); this results in a bias toward capital projects.

INEFFICIENCY OF TAX BENEFITS TO LOCAL COMMUNITIES There are four reasons why providing aid to local communities through the federal income tax system may be inefficient. We have just discussed the first: aid provides a large incentive for the public provision of goods, regardless of the efficiency with which the local communities are able to deliver these goods and services.

The second reason we discussed in Chapter 21: A significant fraction of the benefits of interest exemption accrue not to the communities but to wealthy taxpayers.

The third reason why tax exemption may not be an efficient way of subsidizing local communities is that because of competition among communities, some of the benefits may accrue to industries within the communities rather than to the communities themselves. Local communities can issue tax-exempt bonds to help finance some of the capital costs required to provide the infrastructure to attract firms. But if one community does this, other communities respond, either by trying to attract firms to their community or by trying to prevent firms from leaving. The net effect is that the level of public goods provided to businesses may be higher than it would be otherwise. If only one community provided the higher level of public goods, it would be reflected in the price firms were willing to pay for land in that community. But when all communities increase the level of public goods they provide, it may leave the total demand for land and hence the level of rents relatively unaffected.

The fourth consideration in an evaluation of federal tax and interest provisions is the inequities they create for individuals with different tastes and incomes. We have already noted that these provisions represent a considerable subsidy to the public provision of goods. Individuals who have a relatively strong preference for goods that tend to be publicly provided at the local level benefit by such measures, at the expense of those who have a weak preference for those commodities.

Since the magnitude of the reduction in effective costs of publicly provided goods depends on individuals' marginal tax rates, those who face a higher tax rate—usually wealthier individuals—receive a larger subsidy, and a larger reduction in their effective price of publicly provided goods. (To some extent, the "taste" effect and the pure income effect offset each other. Though they may receive a larger subsidy for each dollar spent by their local government, communities with wealthy individuals may actually spend less on at least certain categories of goods: for example, wealthier individuals are more likely to send their children to private schools.)

As persuasive as these arguments are to most economists, the political support for deductibility of state and local income and property taxes and preferential treatment of interest on state and local bonds remains strong enough that major changes in these deductions are unlikely in the foreseeable future.

REVIEW AND PRACTICE

SUMMARY

1 The federal government regulates and subsidizes states and localities. It subsidizes them through both matching and block grants for specific purposes. In the past, it also provided general revenue-sharing. In matching grants, the amount received by states and localities depends on the amount they spend. Indirect aid is provided by the exemption from taxation of interest on state and local bonds and the tax deductibility of state and local income and property taxes.

2 The arguments favoring local over federal provision of public goods are that local governments will be more responsive to the community's needs and preferences and have greater incentives to provide services efficiently.

3 Local public goods are public goods whose benefits are limited to those living in a particular locality. The Tiebout hypothesis postulates that competition among communities results in an efficient provision of local public goods. The reasons why federal intervention may be required include market failures (externalities, particularly those associated with choice of location, and limited competition) and redistribution (the limited ability to redistribute income at the local level).

4 There are marked disparities in income per capita and in the provision of local public services across states and localities. Whether government policy should be directed at reducing inequalities across communities (rather than inequalities across individuals) is debatable.

5 Matching grants are more effective in encouraging expenditures in the direction desired, but there is a deadweight loss associated with their use. Though traditional theoretical arguments suggest that block grants, even

for specific purposes, should have just income effects, and thus be equivalent to equal direct grants to the members of the community, the empirical evidence suggests the presence of a flypaper effect.

6 Tax subsidies (including the tax exemption of interest on local and state bonds) lead to increased expenditures on publicly provided goods and increased capital investment by state and local governments.

7 Tax subsidies are an inefficient way of subsidizing state and local communities. Some of the benefit accrues to wealthy investors rather than to the communities; some of the benefit is passed along to businesses (and not to the residents of the communities); and the tax subsidies discriminate in favor of high-income individuals and individuals who have a strong preference for publicly provided goods.

KEY CONCEPTS

Fiscal federalism	Local public goods
Matching grants	Tiebout hypothesis
Block grants	Waivers
General revenue-sharing	Flypaper effect

QUESTIONS AND PROBLEMS

1 Discuss the advantages and disadvantages of state versus national determination of eligibility standards and benefits for: food stamps; Medicaid; unemployment insurance; Temporary Assistance for Needy Families; and old-age and survivors insurance.

2 In President Reagan's State of the Union message in 1982, he proposed a trade with the states: in return for their taking over responsibility for the full costs of food stamps and Aid to Families with Dependent Children, the federal government would take over responsibility for Medicaid. In addition, he proposed phasing out most categorical grant programs (possibly substituting increases in block grants). (The proposal was never adopted.) Evaluate these proposals using the analysis of this chapter.

3 If the income elasticity of demand for education is 1, what will be the effect on expenditures on education of a small block grant of $100,000 if presently the community spends 5 percent of its total resources on education?

4 Many matching grant programs specify that the federal government matches on a dollar-for-dollar basis local expenditures up to some particular maximum. Draw the budget constraint between private goods and local public goods facing a community of identical individuals. Discuss the effect of such a matching program on communities that do not go to the maximum. Discuss the effect on communities that go beyond the maximum.

5 What would you expect to be the effects on spending on education if the federal income tax deduction for state and local taxes were eliminated? Show diagrammatically why you might expect such a change to increase the relative importance of private education.

6 Consider a community in which everyone is at the 36 percent marginal tax bracket. By how much would educational expenditures be reduced by the elimination of the tax deductibility of state and local taxes, if the price elasticity of demand for education is 1?

7 On the basis of the discussions in Chapters 9 and 10, discuss the relative merits of regulation versus matching grants as devices to elicit desired behavior on the part of state and local governments.

8 Recall from Chapter 7 the median voter theory. Consider a state that imposed a proportional income tax on everyone, but assume that the median voter did not itemize his deductions, so that his federal income tax payments did not depend on his state taxes. How, according to the theory, would expenditures in such a state differ from those in a state with similar average incomes but in which the median voter did itemize his deductions, so that increased state and local taxes reduced his federal tax payments?

9 The tax reform of 1986 eliminated tax deductibility of state sales taxes, but retained it for state income taxes. What implications should this have had for how states raised revenues? In fact, the share of individual and corporate income taxes in total state revenues today is lower than it was in 1980. How might you explain this?

10 Concern about *fungibility* of funds—of states not using money in the way intended—has led Congress in some instances to impose *maintenance-of-effort* requirements. Thus, in the 1996 welfare reform, to be eligible for the grant, states would have to continue to spend at least 75 percent of the amount that they had previously spent.[16]

   a Show what this does to the budget constraint of the community.

   b How effective are such restrictions likely to be over time, as incomes grow?

   c How might a state attempt to get around this requirement by reclassifying expenditures?

11 In the past, the federal government provided general revenue-sharing. The argument for general revenue-sharing was that the federal government was in a better position to collect tax revenues. States may, however, simply

---

[16] If a state fails to meet work participation rates, the spending level rises to 80 percent. *Source:* House Committee on Ways and Means, *Overview of Entitlement Programs, 1996 Green Book,* p. 1333.

impose a tax which is based on the individual's federal income tax; that is, they could impose a tax which is, say, 20 percent of the federal tax payment. Provided that the federal government shares its information about where individuals live and what taxes they have paid, there would then be little incremental cost of tax collection, either to individuals or the state. Why might the federal government nonetheless be in a better position to collect tax revenues than the states?

27 State and Local Taxes and Expenditures

FOCUS QUESTIONS

1 What is the incidence of various taxes imposed at the state and local levels?

2 What is the incidence of various benefits provided by states and localities?

3 To the extent that voters are aware of the true incidence of local taxes and benefits, how does the incidence affect the equilibrium level of expenditures and taxation? How does the answer depend on whether the median voter is an owner or a renter?

4 What are the special problems arising from multi-jurisdictional taxation?

Chapter 2 noted the changing pattern of taxation at the state and local levels: the decreased importance of property taxes and the increased importance of sales and income taxes. Does this changing pattern of financing result in a change in who bears the burden of state and local taxes, or only a change in the manner in which they are collected? The first part of this chapter considers the incidence of state and local taxes. The parallel issue of who benefits from the goods and services provided by local governments—the incidence of these expenditures—is then addressed. Finally, having analyzed these incidences, we discuss how the level and composition of public expenditures are determined locally.

TAX INCIDENCE APPLIED TO LOCAL PUBLIC FINANCE

In Chapter 18 we developed the basic principles of incidence analysis. There we showed that the incidence of a tax on a commodity or a factor depends on the elasticity of demand and supply for that commodity or factor.

The limiting case is where the supply schedule has an infinite elasticity—that is, where the supply schedule is completely horizontal. Then the incidence of the tax lies entirely on the buyer. The price he pays goes up by the amount of the tax. The amount received by the seller is unaffected.

The implications of this for local taxes can easily be derived. In the long run most factors are mobile; that is, they can easily move from community to community. This is particularly true of capital. Investors will invest in a community only if they can obtain at least the same return that they could obtain elsewhere. Mobility translates to elasticity; as a result, mobile factors will not bear the burden of local taxes.

LOCAL CAPITAL TAXES

A community that increases the taxes it imposes on capital will find that it attracts fewer investors. Though it may not be possible for those with fixed capital equipment—such as steel mills—to remove their capital, new investments will be reduced until the before-tax return to capital is driven up. The process will continue until the after-tax return is equal to what it is elsewhere.

Thus, in the long run, the burden of the local tax on capital is not felt by the owners of capital. It is felt by the landowners and by the labor that remains. Because there is less capital, the productivity of land and labor (and hence their income) will be reduced.

If as a result of the tax on capital the productivity of workers is decreased, wages will be lowered. But then, in the long run, workers will emigrate; if labor is perfectly mobile, workers will continue to emigrate until their (after-tax) income is the same as it is elsewhere. This leaves land as the only factor that cannot emigrate. With less capital and less labor, the return to land is less: in the long run, the full burden of the tax is borne by landowners.

This assumes that labor is perfectly mobile. Of course, in the short run, workers will not instantaneously migrate in response to a small change in the wage rate. Indeed, many individuals have strong preferences for living in the community in which they grew up or in which they have formed strong ties. These laborers are only partially mobile. They will bear some part of the burden of the tax on capital. Their wages will be reduced as a result of the outflow of capital.

Dramatic consequences may result if these considerations are ignored. Occasionally states have attempted to impose special taxes on particular industries. Some industries are especially "footloose." These industries will move out if higher taxes are imposed on them. They will shop for states and communities that offer the best deal.

THE PROPERTY TAX

Though its role has diminished, the property tax still accounts for 21 percent of state and local revenues. In some states, such as New Hampshire, it accounts for more than 60 percent of state and local revenues.[1]

The property tax is generally a tax on land and capital—buildings and equipment. The incidence of the two parts is markedly different. Land is inelastically supplied, so that the incidence of the tax is on landowners; the tax is fully reflected in a decrease in land values. In the long run, the supply of buildings is elastic: investors can decide where to invest, and do so on the basis of after-tax returns, taking into account any property taxes. Thus, the before-tax return must increase. The property tax thus distorts investment decisions. If the tax were levied uniformly on all forms of capital, it would affect only the use of capital relative to other factors of production (such as labor). But in practice, different kinds of capital are taxed differentially; some kinds of capital—such as working capital and the value of a firm's reputation—are essentially untaxed.

In the nineteenth century, the property tax got a terrible reputation for being administered in an arbitrary and capricious manner. For many types of property, there are not well-developed markets and transactions occur infrequently enough that precisely assessing a property's current value is difficult. County assessors have the task of judging the market value. In the past, businesses (and other friends of the assessor) often succeeded in persuading the assessor to give them low assessments. Today, though controversies over assessments remain, there are procedures (such as appeals of assessments) which seem to have reduced the inequities considerably.

Failure to adjust the property tax to changes in economic circumstances has been blamed for contributing to urban blight. In inner-city areas, many buildings have been abandoned, as property owners claim that they do not generate enough revenue to pay taxes. Evidently, the property tax exceeds 100 percent of the market value of the asset (otherwise, the property would presumably not be abandoned).

INCOME, WAGE, AND SALES TAXES

Similar principles apply to the taxation of labor. In a small community, if individuals had no particular attachment to the community, the long-run labor supply schedule would be perfectly elastic. A tax on labor would simply increase the before-tax wage and leave the after-tax wage unchanged. Again, the incidence of a wage tax is borne not by workers but by landowners. It is just an indirect—and inefficient—tax on land.

Uniform sales taxes on consumption and investment goods are, as we noted in Chapter 18, simply equivalent to proportional income taxes. They

---

[1] See Federation of Tax Administrators web page: www.taxadmin.org/fta/rate/slsource.html.

have effects that are analogous to wage taxes.[2] They are borne by land (and by workers with limited labor mobility).

DISTORTIONS

The fact that all local taxes are borne by the same, immobile factors does not mean that the taxes all have the same consequences. While a direct tax on land is nondistortionary, all the other ways of raising revenue induce distortions. The property tax (which is partly a tax on land, partly a tax on capital) raises the cost of capital to the community and induces a bias against capital. A wage tax or a sales tax raises the cost of labor and thus induces a bias against the use of labor; a sales tax may induce individuals to do their shopping across state borders. The higher sales tax in New York City, for example, induces many individuals to do their shopping in New Jersey; and when Washington, D.C., imposed a higher gasoline tax than neighboring Virginia and Maryland, drivers were induced to buy their gasoline outside the city. High state income taxes may induce individuals to live in one state and commute to another to avoid the high taxes that would be levied on their income.[3] For example, since New Hampshire imposes no income tax, many people find it advantageous to live there and commute to Massachusetts, which has an income tax. The tax is inefficient, both because it raises the cost of using labor in Massachusetts and because it induces unnecessary expenditures on commuting costs.

LIMITATIONS ON THE ABILITY TO REDISTRIBUTE INCOME

The fact that taxes are borne by immobile factors means that the extent of redistribution that is feasible at the local level is very limited. Assume, for instance, that some community decides doctors are too wealthy. The local government, accordingly, imposes a licensing tax on doctors in an attempt to redistribute income from this wealthy class of individuals to others. Doctors, in making their decision about where to set up practice, will look at their prospects in different communities. When they discover that after-tax income is lower in this community than elsewhere, they will be discouraged from setting up practice in this community. If the tax is not too high, doctors who are already established will not leave; the costs of moving exceed the losses from the tax. The fact that its doctors do not leave may fool the community into thinking that it has been successful in extracting some additional tax out of doctors; in the short run, it may be right. But gradually, as fewer doctors move into the community, the scarcity of doctors will become felt, and their wages will be bid up. Wages will continue to be bid up until the after-tax wages of

---

[2] Income taxes are taxes on wages plus income from capital. These taxes have a particularly distortionary effect on location decisions of wealthy individuals: they may choose not to live and work in a location where their productivity is highest because the net return (taking into account the additional taxes they must pay on their capital income) is lower. (Of course, many rich individuals have multiple homes. They *claim* as their principal residence the state with the lowest tax rate. This is particularly relevant for retired individuals for whom there is no work record against which to check such claims.)

[3] In such situations, they typically must pay taxes on any interest income they receive only to the state in which they reside.

doctors is equal to what they could have earned elsewhere. In the long run, doctors do not bear the burden of the tax (although they do in the short run). In the long run, the community as a whole bears the burden of the tax, in the form of less medical services and higher prices for doctors.

The same principle holds for any factor that is mobile in the long run. A number of states have suffered under the false impression that they could in fact succeed in taxing capital at higher rates than it is taxed elsewhere without either offering better public services or ultimately seeing an erosion of their capital base. Some states have attempted to include income of international enterprises operating outside the state (or country) in the tax base on which they levy a corporate profits tax. If the above analysis is correct, such attempts cannot, in the long run, be successful. These communities are often misled into believing that they can do this, because capital does not emigrate instantaneously.[4]

RENT CONTROL

Similarly, a number of communities have been under the impression that they could reduce the return to landlords, who were viewed to be exploiting the poorer renters. They have imposed **rent control** laws, whose effect has been to lower the rents paid by renters below what they otherwise would be. Again, in the short run, such measures may indeed be successful. In the long run, however, landlords make decisions about the construction of additional apartments and the renovation and maintenance of existing apartments. If the return is lowered below the return they can obtain on capital invested in other sectors of the economy, there is no reason for them to continue to invest in housing. Consequently, the rental market will dry up. In the long run, renters will be worse off than if the government had not imposed rent control; some renters will not be able to obtain a rental apartment at any price. (Not surprisingly, this will result in a demand for the public provision of housing for those dependent on rental markets, necessitating that the community subsidize the renters through general revenues rather than having the owners of rental apartments bear the burden alone.)

CAPITALIZATION

Consider two communities that are identical in every respect except that the taxes are higher in one than in the other (say, because of less efficiency in the provision of public services). Clearly, if the price of housing in the two communities were the same, everyone would prefer to live in the community with the lower tax rate. This cannot, of course, be an equilibrium. Individuals care about the total cost of living in the community. In equilibrium

---

[4] On the other hand, it may not be the case that, in equilibrium, the after-tax return in all communities will be exactly the same. Notions of loyalty may lead individuals to invest in their own country or community, even when they could obtain a higher return elsewhere.

Differences in information may also lead individuals to prefer investing in their own country and this reduces the mobility of capital.

INCIDENCE OF STATE AND LOCAL TAXES

Immobile factors bear all local taxes.

  Capital is likely to be very mobile.

  Skilled labor is likely to be relatively mobile.

  Land is immobile.

Application of general principle—factors in elastic supply do not bear much of the brunt of taxation; with perfect mobility, supply elasticity is infinite.

Limits ability to redistribute income locally.

---

the total cost of living—the sum of taxes plus annual housing costs—in the two communities must be the same. This means that the community with the higher tax rates will find that the prices of its houses (land) are reduced proportionately (recalling our assumption that no extra services are provided with the taxes). We say that the taxes are **capitalized** in house prices.

  The term "capitalized" is used here to refer to the fact that the price will reflect not only current taxes but all future taxes. To calculate the effect of a constant tax of, say, $1000 per year on the house price, recall that a dollar next year is worth less than a dollar this year. If we got a dollar this year we could have invested it in a money market fund or bank and obtained a return of, say, 10 percent, so at the end of the year we could have $1.10. Thus getting a dollar today is worth (is equivalent to) $1.10 tomorrow. More generally, a dollar today is worth $1 + r$ next year, where r is the rate of interest (i.e., a dollar next year is worth $1/1 + r$ today).[5] Thus, the value of T taxes this year, next year, the year after, and so on is

$$T + \frac{T}{1 + r} + \frac{T}{(1 + r)^2} + \frac{T}{(1 + r)^3} \cdots$$

This is the present discounted value of the tax liabilities. If the amount by which a house's price is reduced is given by the present discounted value of these tax liabilities, we say that the tax liabilities are fully capitalized in the value of the house. If two houses are identical except for their tax liabilities, and if the house prices differ by less than this amount, we say that the taxes are **partially capitalized** in the less expensive house.

---

[5] By the same reasoning, a dollar the year after next is equivalent to $\$1/1 + r = \$1/1.10 = \$.91$ next year; but this means that, since a dollar next year is worth $\$1/1 + r = \$1/1.10$ today, a dollar the year after next is worth $\$1/(1.10 \times 1.10) = \$.83$ this year—i.e., $\$1(1 + r)^2$. See Chapter 11 for a more extensive discussion of present discounted value.

INCENTIVES FOR PENSION SCHEMES

The fact that certain fiscal variables may not be fully capitalized has some important implications. There are incentives for communities to take advantage of this. Someone living in a community who thinks there is a reasonable chance that he will move out in ten years or so might vote for a large, unfunded pension scheme for public employees—that is, a pension scheme which fails to set aside the funds that will be needed to pay the promised pensions, but relies instead on future taxes. A generous pension allows the community to attract workers while paying lower current wages. In effect, future house owners in the town will be forced to pay for current services. The future buyer of a house is being deceived in much the same way that the manufacturer of a product which does not fully disclose some important characteristics of its commodity may attempt to deceive a purchaser. An important characteristic of a house (or any piece of property) is the future tax liabilities that are associated with it, and to know these, one must know the debt and unfunded pension liabilities of the community. Whether the appropriate way to deal with this is through disclosure laws (each community being required to notify all potential purchasers of a house of the debt obligations of the community prior to the completion of any sale) or through restrictions (not allowing unfunded pension schemes) is a debatable question.

CHOICE OF DEBT VERSUS TAX FINANCING

More generally, the extent of capitalization has implications for the decision whether to finance local public expenditures by debt or taxes. With full capitalization, a dollar increase in the local debt would simply decrease the net market value of the community by a dollar. Since house buyers can choose to live in this community or in some other community, their assumption of the debt of the community is a voluntary action. Therefore they will have to be compensated for it, through a corresponding decrease in the price of a house. This is true no matter how far in the future the debt is to be repaid. It does not have to be repaid during the period in which the next owner owns the house.

Assume, for example, that the debt is to be repaid in forty years, and each individual lives in the house for only ten years. The person who buys the house at the time that the debt is to be repaid clearly will pay less for the house, taking into account the increased tax liability associated with paying off the debt. But the preceding purchaser knows that the person to whom he will sell the house will be willing to pay less for it, and hence he will be willing to pay less for it (by the amount of the tax liability). Similarly, the previous purchaser knows that the price at which he can sell it will be lower by the amount of the increased debt, and so he too will be willing to pay less for it, and so on.

With full capitalization, current owners pay for current services—whether directly, through taxes, or indirectly, through the expectation of a lower price on their house resulting from a higher debt used to finance the public services. Which of these two methods is preferable turns out to depend on the treatment of local taxes and interest on local debt by the federal government, a question that was discussed in the previous chapter.[6]

---

[6] In the presence of credit rationing (limited availability of mortgages), the lower price of a house may increase its salability. The fact that communities may borrow more easily than individuals provides an argument for communities to borrow as much as they can.

Assume that taxes are increased on apartment buildings. If the amenities the community provides are unchanged, the rents will remain unchanged: the rents individuals are willing to pay depend on the services provided by the community and the landlord, rather than on the costs to the landlord of those services. In the short run, the market value of the apartment will thus decrease. But this will make investing in apartments in the community less attractive; the supply of apartments will be reduced (as old apartments deteriorate) or in any case will not keep up with population growth. This will result in an increase in rents. Eventually, rents will increase to the point where the after-tax return on the apartment is the same as investors could obtain from investments in any other community. Thus, although the tax is imposed legally on buildings, in the long run it is land and immobile individuals (who must pay higher rents) who bear the tax.

The same reasoning which leads us to conclude that the incidence of any tax resides with the owners of land (or other partially immobile factors) implies that the incidence of any benefits resides with the owners of land (or partially immobile factors). Any public good that makes a community more desirable to live in drives up the rents and hence increases the value of property in the community. In the short run, some of the benefits may be enjoyed by owners of buildings; but the increased rent on their buildings leads to increased investment in housing (new apartment buildings, replacing small, old apartment buildings with larger ones, etc.), and this drives down their return.[7] Ultimately the value of the public good is reflected in the price of land.

Similarly, some public goods make it more attractive to work in a given community. This will reduce the wage a firm must pay to recruit a worker. But again, the ultimate beneficiaries are the landowners.

To see the link between the wages individuals receive and the level of public services provided, consider what happens if a city decides to spend more on its symphony orchestra, which provides free concerts in the parks in the summer. This makes the city a more attractive place in which to live and work. A worker who enjoys the symphony, contemplating a job offer in this city, will accept the job at a slightly lower wage than she would accept in a community that is identical in every respect except its level of expenditure on its symphony orchestra. Thus, to the extent that workers in the city (regardless of where they choose to live) value the amenities it provides, wages in the city will be lower; firms will find it attractive to locate there. As they move into this city, the price of land will be bid up. Equilibrium is attained when the price of land is bid up just enough to compensate for the lower wages, so that investors receive the same return to their capital that they receive from investing it elsewhere. The ultimate beneficiaries of the

---

[7] Current owners of buildings have an incentive to maintain their higher return by restricting further investments, by zoning. The higher returns they enjoy should be viewed not as a return to capital but as a return to the property rights the zoning board has created.

provision of better public goods are not the residents in the city but the landowners.

This analysis assumes, of course, that labor is highly mobile, so that when the city provides a more attractive public good, there is sufficient migration to decrease wages and increase rents. If labor is not very mobile (and in the short run it may well not be), wages will not fall to fully reflect the increased amenities, and some of the benefits of the increased provision of local public goods will accrue to the current residents. Note that some current residents may be hurt by the provision of the symphony. Those who do not enjoy music may find that their rents are increased or wages reduced nonetheless.

The city's provision of the symphony orchestra does have important spillovers to other communities. In particular, firms located in the suburbs will find that they too can hire workers at a lower wage than they previously could, since music lovers will find accepting a job in a community near the city more attractive than accepting a job in an otherwise identical community without easy access to a symphony. This increases the value of the firms' land as well. Bedroom suburbs will also find that the demand for their housing has increased.

ABSOLUTE VERSUS RELATIVE CAPITALIZATION

We have discussed how if a community increases its level of expenditure on a public good, the differential expenditure will be reflected in the prices of the land in the community. There is, however, an important difference between the effects of a single community's increasing its expenditure on a public good and all communities' increasing their expenditures on that public good. If all communities increase their expenditures on a public good, the relative attractiveness of living in one community versus another is, of course, unchanged. Thus, in general, rentals will remain unchanged.[8]

This is an example of a phenomenon we noted in earlier chapters. The effects of a change in one community (a change in a tax on one commodity) may be quite different from the effects of a change in all communities (a change in the tax rate on all commodities).

THE USE OF CHANGES IN LAND RENTS TO MEASURE BENEFITS

Changes in rents have often been used to measure the value of certain public services. In studies of the economic effects of American railroads in the nineteenth century, one commonly employed way of measuring the benefits is to measure the change in land rents after construction of the railroad. Again, one has to be careful to distinguish partial from general equilibrium effects. Making one small plot of land more accessible will increase the demand for that plot of land, and the change in the rent will provide an accurate estimate of the reduction of the transportation costs of getting to that piece of land. However, changing the accessibility of a mass of

[8] There are exceptions. If the communities provide a public good that makes land more desirable, all individuals will attempt to rent or purchase more land, and this will increase the value of land. The opposite will be true if communities provide a public good that makes owning land less desirable. Thus, since public parks are, in part at least, a substitute for backyards, it is conceivable that if all communities spend more on providing public parks, rents and land prices would actually decrease.

land—as the railroad in fact did—has general equilibrium effects; the change in land rents will not correctly assess the value of such a change.[9]

Land values reflect the valuation of marginal individuals, those who are indifferent about choosing between living in this community and living somewhere else. When there is a sufficiently large number of communities, the valuation of these marginal individuals provides a good measure of the valuation of the entire community, but not otherwise.[10]

TESTING THE CAPITALIZATION HYPOTHESIS

The question of the degree to which the benefits provided by public goods and taxes are reflected in property values has been extensively studied.

If some communities are more efficient in providing public goods than others, so that they can provide the same level of public goods with lower taxes, property values in the low-tax communities should be higher. If all communities are equally efficient and maximize their property values, differences in taxes will be matched with differences in benefits. In this case, there will be no systematic relationship between property values and expenditures. This is the result obtained by Jan Brueckner of the University of Illinois, in his study based on fifty-four Massachusetts communities.[11]

CAPITALIZATION OF TAXES AND LOCAL PUBLIC GOODS

Future benefits and taxes are reflected in today's price of land.

• Implies that unfunded local public pension schemes (e.g., for police) depress land values.

• Implies that there is no difference between debt and tax financing—current owners pay cost of current consumption expenditures.

• Investment values can be affected in the short run, but in the long run, returns on investment must be equalized across communities.

A tax in one community on capital has a markedly different effect from a tax by all communities.

---

[9] There is a second limitation on the use of land rents to measure the value of such changes: they provide a good measure only in the case where there are no inframarginal individuals—no individuals who are enjoying a consumer surplus from living in the community.

[10] R. Arnott and J. E. Stiglitz, "Aggregate Land Rents, Expenditure on Public Goods and Optimal City Size," *Quarterly Journal of Economics* 93 (1979): 472–500, and "Aggregate Land Rents and Aggregate Transport Costs," *Economic Journal* 91 (1981): 331–47; and D. Starrett, "Principles of Optimal Location in a Large Homogeneous Area," *Journal of Economic Theory* 9 (1974): 418–48.

[11] J. K. Brueckner, "A Test for the Allocative Efficiency in the Local Public Sector," *Journal of Public Economics* 19 (1982): 311–31.

On the other hand, there is evidence that the value of amenities (such as clean air) for which there are not corresponding taxes is capitalized in property values.

PUBLIC CHOICE AT THE LOCAL LEVEL

In Chapter 7, which described how public choices are made, we showed that with majority voting, the allocation of public goods reflects the preferences of the median voter.[12] This voter assesses the costs and benefits to him of the expenditure of an extra dollar on public goods. We then assessed the efficiency of the majority voting equilibrium.

The issues at the local level are identical; in both cases we need to focus on the incidence of the benefits and costs associated with any increase in expenditure and taxation. We need to distinguish between the effects on renters and on landowners, under assumptions of perfect and imperfect mobility (with a large or small number of competing communities). It is useful to distinguish between two types of communities: one in which everyone is a renter and there is a separate group of landlords; and the other in which everyone owns their own home. In the real world, of course, communities are mixed; there are a few cities, like New York City, in which most people are renters, while in most of America, a majority are homeowners. Because renters and homeowners may be affected quite differently by local taxes and expenditures, they may vote for quite different policies.

We begin with a discussion of a world in which (essentially) everyone is a renter. With perfect mobility and a large number of competing communities, any improvement in the amenities provided by a community will be fully reflected in rents; hence marginal renters will be indifferent with respect to the public services provided. Moreover, since their rents are affected only by the services that are provided, not by the tax rates, renters will be completely unconcerned about the efficiency with which public services are provided, that is, with their cost. Thus, if there is perfect mobility and a large number of competing communities, there will be little concern about efficiency or about the public services provided in a community in which voters are mostly renters.

Under these same assumptions, landowners as a group will want public services to be increased so long as they lead to increases in rents exceeding increases in taxes. Thus in a landowner-controlled community, in equilibrium an extra $1000 spent on public goods should just increase aggregate rents by $1000. But the increased rents represent renters' marginal evaluation of the services provided by the community. As a result, a landowner-controlled community will provide an efficient level of public services. Moreover, since if the community can provide the same services at less cost, the after-tax receipts of landowners will be increased, landowner-controlled communities have every incentive to ensure that public services are provided in an efficient manner. Thus, if the level of expenditures is chosen to maximize property values, and if there is effective competition among communities, the resulting allocation of resources will be Pareto efficient.

[12] Assuming, of course, that a majority voting equilibrium exists.

All of this changes if there are relatively few communities competing against each other. Consider a metropolitan region in which there are two towns, A and B. A has high taxes and a high level of local public goods; B has low taxes and a low level of public goods. Those who have a strong preference for public goods (relative to private goods) live in A; those who have a strong preference for private goods live in B. The individual who is indifferent with respect to living in the two communities we call the *marginal* individual; the extra public goods he receives in A just compensate him for the extra taxes or rent he has to pay. All other individuals are called **infra-marginal.** For those who live in A, for instance, the extra benefits more than offset the extra taxes they have to pay. Were A to increase its taxes slightly without altering its benefits, they would still not wish to move to B.

Assume that there are houses for half the region's population in A, and half in B. All housing is rented. If B decides to provide fewer public goods, rents in B will have to adjust so that the marginal individual is still indifferent with respect to living in A or living in B. But of all the individuals who live in B, the marginal individual is the one with the strongest preference for public goods: the rents will fall in B to just compensate him for the lower level of public goods. If the rents decrease enough to make the marginal individual remain indifferent, the other individuals in B are actually better off. Rents fall by more than enough to keep the inframarginal persons, including the median voter, satisfied. Therefore, the median renter in B will have an incentive to vote for a very low level of expen-

---

PUBLIC CHOICE AT THE LOCAL LEVEL

• Renters and landowners can be affected markedly differently by changes in local taxes and expenditures, which will be reflected in how they vote.

• In a world with perfect mobility and strong competition among many communities, rents will reflect the value of services provided and taxes will be borne by landowners (the immobile factor). Hence, renters will be indifferent to the quality of publicly provided services and the efficiency with which they are delivered.

• In such a world, landowners' property values will fully reflect increases in efficiency and services provided, and hence landowners will have an incentive to provide an efficient level of services and to have those services provided efficiently.

• In a world with imperfect competition among communities, if communities are controlled by renters, there will be excessive diversity of benefits (e.g., in levels of expenditures), while if communities are controlled by landowners, there will be insufficient diversity.

PROPOSITION 13

In many states, voters have been worried about increased levels of expenditures at the state and local levels. They worry that politicians have strong incentives to initiate new policies (that is why they were elected). The politicians receive credit for additional programs, while the taxpayer bears the cost. The process of voting for legislators and city council members does not, in this perspective, provide an adequate check, since in most elections there is a host of other issues, such as abortion, the death penalty, and so forth, that frequently overshadow narrow budgetary issues. Accordingly, it is argued, voters must provide a direct limit on taxes and expenditures.

The question of imposing such limits was put on the ballot in a referendum in California in 1978 as Proposition 13 and was approved by 64 percent of those voting. The proposition restricted increases in property taxes. There was another problem that motivated its success: Many property owners found that their tax bills were increasing as their property values skyrocketed with rising real estate prices. They were what has since come to be called "house poor." They had considerable wealth, but not the income (cash flow) to pay taxes on their house. The property tax was forcing them to move. This seemed inequitable, particularly to the elderly. Thus, Proposition 13 allowed increases in assessments only upon sale.

In the years since passage, the problems posed by Proposition 13 have become increasing apparent. While addressing one inequity, it increased others. Owners of identical homes now frequently pay markedly different taxes: the owner of a house that was sold last year may pay ten or more times the tax paid by the owner of an identical house that has not been sold for fifteen years. Because some were paying only low taxes, the taxes on others had to be increased. These

diture on public goods, lower than is Pareto efficient. The same reasoning shows that the median renter in community A will have an incentive to vote for a very high level of expenditure on public goods, higher than is Pareto efficient.

Landowners have exactly the opposite bias. They are concerned only with the effect of increased expenditure on land values (rents). If the increased rents exceed the increased expenditures, they are worth undertaking. In community A, the increased rents from an increased expenditure reflect the marginal individual's evaluation; this is the individual who has the weakest preference for public goods. Thus the gain to others (the inframarginal renters) exceeds the gain to the marginal renter; but the landowners will pay no attention to this. As a result, they will vote for too little expendi-

inequities were sufficiently great that many thought that fundamental constitutional issues were raised, but in a court case (*Amador Valley Joint Union High School et al. v. State Board of Equalization et al.*), the Supreme Court of California sustained the law.*

Proposition 13 also induced some important economic inefficiencies. It significantly increased the cost of moving. An elderly couple living in a large house—well beyond the size required for their family—would decide to stay in the house; were they to move to a smaller house, their tax payments would actually go up. Thus, the housing stock was inefficiently allocated.

Finally, Proposition 13 contributed to a marked deterioration in the quality of public services in California. In some sense, this was its intention: to limit the growth of public expenditures. But Proposition 13 was a blunt instrument. It could not ensure that the limited amount of money went to the most beneficial areas. Thus, even though most voters believe strongly in the value of education, educational expenditures were among the hardest hit. While per pupil expenditures in the years preceding passage of Proposition 13 were higher than the national average, by the mid-1990s, California ranked thirty-third in spending and its expenditures were less than 90 percent of the national average.[†]

* In 1986, the U.S. Supreme Court ruled in *Allegheny Pittsburgh Coal Co. v. County Commission of Webster County* that non-uniform assessment of property violates the equal protection clause of the Fourteenth Amendment. Many suspected that Proposition 13 was vulnerable on similar grounds. See Frederick D. Stocker, ed., *Proposition 13, A Ten-Year Retrospective* (Cambridge, Mass.: Lincoln Institute of Land Policy, 1991) and Roger L. Kemp, *Coping with Proposition 13* (Lexington, Mass.: Lexington Books, 1980).

[†] The low level of expenditures may also have been adversely affected by court decisions (including *Serrano v. Priest*, 1971), which also restricted the ability of wealthy districts to spend more on their schools.

ture on public goods. By the same reasoning, in community B, landowners will vote for too high an expenditure on public goods.

Thus, just as we saw in Chapter 7 that the majority voting equilibrium did not provide a Pareto efficient level of expenditures on public goods in an isolated community, such is also the case when there is only a small number of communities. When there is limited competition, there may be systematic biases in the patterns of allocation, and marked differences between communities in which renters dominate (in which case differences among communities may be excessive) and those in which landowners dominate (in which case diversification among communities may be insufficient). However, if the number of communities is very large, and if they all recognize that capital and labor (of different skills) are perfectly mobile, then they will compete effectively against each other, providing an efficient supply of public goods corresponding to the preferences of the individuals in the different communities, and providing them in an efficient manner. While, under these circumstances, renters will be indifferent to what the government does, landowners will not be.[13]

PROBLEMS OF MULTI-JURISDICTIONAL TAXATION

In the previous chapter we discussed the problems of fiscal federalism, of the relationship between the federal government and the states. There is a second, related set of problems posed by federalism: the relationship between the states themselves.

One aspect of that relationship has been stressed in this and the previous chapter: competition. We saw that while Tiebout competition helps ensure economic efficiency, tax competition sometimes ensures that businesses escape much of the burden of taxation. The issue has recently become a source of acute concern, as some states have offered large tax breaks for businesses that establish new plants in their jurisdiction. As states bid for the plants, the tax breaks get larger. Plants may in fact be built where they would have been built anyway—but the shareholders gain by paying lower taxes regardless of where the businesses settle, and other taxpayers are left bearing a larger tax burden.

The fact that America is such an integrated economy, with free mobility of goods and people among jurisdictions, raises a host of practical problems in taxation. Just as businesses make decisions about where to locate partly based on tax considerations, those individuals who can, make choices on where to live partly based on tax considerations. A retired person with a large capital income or a writer with large royalties might chose to make New Hampshire her "official" residence, because there is no income tax in that state. If her income were $500,000, California, for instance, would in effect impose a charge in excess of $50,000 a year for the right to make that state her official residence. Tax considerations might affect whether a high-income individual working in New York City would choose to live in New York, New Jersey, or Connecticut.

---

[13] There are, clearly, a number of communities within most metropolitan areas. But are there enough to ensure that the resulting equilibrium is "close" to Pareto efficient? There is no agreement among economists about the answer to this.

The case where there is a sufficiently large number of communities to ensure efficiency has some further peculiar implications. There would be unanimity among all voters about what the local government should do. All individuals of any skill type within the community would be identical. These implications are sufficiently counter to what is observed in most situations to suggest to many economists that models assuming limited competition are closer to the mark.

State sales taxes clearly induce some cross-border shopping and shipping, though in many states with sales taxes, one is supposed to pay taxes on goods purchased in other states.

The corporation tax, imposed by many states, represents the greatest challenge. There is a fundamental problem in levying such a tax: determining how much of the corporation's income should be attributed to economic activity occurring within the state. States increasingly have come to use what is called the **unitary tax system,** relying on simple formulae. A fraction of the corporation's worldwide income is attributed to activities within the state, depending on the fraction of the corporation's assets, sales, and employment within the jurisdiction.

So long as differences among states in the levels and forms of taxation remain limited, the multi-jurisdictional tax problems, though conceptually important, will not be too severe. There remain, however, incentives for some states to use tax policy more actively, to increase their tax base and to attract people and businesses. To the extent that those states most inclined to do so are poorer states—such as New Hampshire—more in need of the revenue, the resulting distortions are offset by the distributional gains. Still, the same distributional outcomes could be obtained more efficiently with a more active federal policy of redistribution.

REVIEW AND PRACTICE

1 If capital and labor are mobile, the incidence of any tax lies on land, the immobile factor. If labor is only partially mobile, some of the burden may lie upon it.

2 Local taxes that are imposed on mobile factors—sales taxes (which are equivalent to income taxes), wage taxes, corporation income taxes, property taxes on buildings—induce distortions.

3 Improved public services provided by the government are reflected in rents paid. In a perfectly competitive environment (with a large number of communities with similar individuals), the benefits of improved government services accrue solely to landowners.

4 Future benefits and taxes may be capitalized in current land values.

5 The effect of an increase in benefits on land rents (values) will depend on whether one community alone increases its benefits or all communities increase their benefits.

6 If the level of expenditures is chosen to maximize property values, and there is effective competition among communities, the resulting allocation of resources is Pareto efficient.

7 If there is limited competition, however, the resulting equilibrium is not Pareto efficient; there is a tendency for too little diversification in the services provided by the different landowner-controlled communities.

8 In contrast, when renters control the community, there is a tendency (under the same circumstances) for excessive diversification. Communities that spend a great deal on public goods spend too much; communities that spend little spend too little.

9 Moreover, there is no incentive for renters to be concerned with the efficiency with which the government delivers its services.

10 In an economy with many tax jurisdictions, two further problems arise. First, tax competition sometimes results in businesses' escaping much of the burden of taxation, as some states use tax policy to increase their tax base and attract people and businesses. Second, there are often difficult problems of deciding how much income should be attributed to economic activity occurring within the jurisdiction; differential tax rates among jurisdictions may result in distorted locational decisions.

KEY CONCEPTS

Rent control

Capitalized

Partially capitalized

Inframarginal

Unitary tax system

QUESTIONS AND PROBLEMS

1 Explain why the property tax may lead to lower expenditures on capital (buildings) per unit of land.

2 Many firms have employees, plants, and sales in more than one state. In imposing state corporation income taxes, states use a rule for allocating a fraction of a firm's total profits to their state. Does it make a difference what rule is used? Discuss the consequences of alternative rules.

3 Many of the issues of state and local taxation are similar to issues that arise in international contexts. Many countries, for instance, have imposed taxes on capital owned by foreigners. Discuss the incidence of such taxes. Does it pay to subsidize capital owned by foreigners?

4 Discuss the incidence of a city wage tax.

5 Many cities have passed rent control legislation. Discuss carefully who benefits and loses from such legislation, in the short run and in the long run. Discuss the political economy of such legislation.

6 Henry George, a famous nineteenth-century American economist, proposed that only land be taxed (not buildings). Would this be unfair to landowners? Would it distort resource allocations, making land more expensive relative to buildings?

7 Who are the main beneficiaries of tax-exempt industrial development bonds (which enable communities to borrow funds to re-lend to firms

constructing new plants within the city):

   a   Workers in the town?

   b   Landowners in the town?

   c   The industries that move into the town?

Give your assumptions. Does it make a difference whether only one community provides these bonds or all communities provide them?

8   Who benefited from the construction of the subway system in Washington, D.C.:

   a   Owners of land near the subway line at the time the route was announced?

   b   Owners of land near the subway line at the time the subway was completed?

   c   Renters of apartments near the subway line at the time the route was announced?

   d   Renters of apartments near the subway line after the subway was completed?

   e   Renters of apartments not near the subway line?

In each case, give your assumptions.

9   In 1993, a major dispute broke out between California and the United Kingdom involving taxation of the income of Barclay's Bank, one of the major British banks. California imposed a tax that allocated a fraction of Barclay's income to its activities in California, and taxed that accordingly; Barclay's said that the formula used resulted in far too high a fraction. The U.K. government supported Barclay's position and threatened economic retaliation. The United States in its international negotiations over the years had criticized other countries using what are called unitary tax systems, in which simple formulae allocate income on the basis of a formula, as described in the text. It argued for using the transfer price system, in which an attempt is made to estimate the value of the goods and services that a company's plant in one country receives from and delivers to the company's facilities in other countries. (It attempts to "price" these transfers.) With the worldwide integration of economic production, such systems appear to be increasingly cumbersome; no state within the United States attempts to use a transfer price system. What do you think the U.S. government should have done in the Barclay's case?

28 Deficit Finance

FOCUS QUESTIONS

1 What gave rise to the fiscal deficit? And why was it so difficult to reduce?

2 What are the central economic issues in the debate about how deficits should be reduced?

3 What are the procedural reforms that have been proposed to ensure that deficits do not emerge in the future, and what are the problems with these reforms?

4 What are the long-term problems facing the United States and other industrialized countries that if not adequately addressed are likely to result in a deficit problem emerging in the future, even if the deficit is reduced now?

When the federal government spends more than it receives in taxes and other revenues in any given year, it has a budget deficit, commonly referred to as the **fiscal deficit.** The U.S. fiscal deficit ballooned during the 1980s and emerged from being a problem that interested mainly economists and political pundits into the national spotlight. By the 1992 presidential election, public opinion polls were persistently ranking the huge deficits among the central problems facing the country. The increased deficits led to increasing debt, and an increasing burden on the government simply to pay interest on the debt. To many economists, the higher deficits threatened the long term well-being of the economy; but regardless of one's view of the deficit's economic consequences, the attempt to reduce the deficit had fundamental effects on every aspect of government operations. Federal employment was cut back to levels of the early 1960s, and as a percentage of civilian employment, to levels not seen since the early 1930s.

Two major steps to bring the deficit under control were undertaken, in 1990 and 1993, both entailing controlling expenditures and raising revenues. After reaching 4.9 percent of GDP in 1992, the deficit as a share of GDP shrank rapidly in the ensuing years, to a negligible .5 percent of GDP in 1997. In August 1997, Congress passed and the President signed a five-year budget agreement that promised to eliminate the deficit by 2002. By 1998, the reforms of 1990 and 1993—combined with a booming economy and strong economic growth—had turned the deficit into a $70 billion surplus, with even larger surplusses looming over the horizon. But there was a general consensus that the hard problems had been bypassed. The increasing expenditures on entitlements, especially for the aged, would almost surely lead to mounting deficits in the early part of the twenty-first century, unless taxes were increased substantially and/or there were substantial reforms in these programs.

This chapter represents a bridge between the two branches of economics, macroeconomics, which is concerned with national aggregates like output, employment, and inflation, and microeconomics, which is concerned with the individual decisions of households and firms. Today, courses in the economics of the public sector focus on how taxes and expenditures affect these decisions and thus the *structure* of the economy—what goods get produced, how they get produced, and for whom they get produced—while courses in macroeconomics focus on how government affects the *level of* economic activity. In reality, the two subjects are intimately connected; the deficit has affected both macroeconomic and microeconomic policies. It has, for instance, reduced the ability of the government to use traditional fiscal policy (reductions in taxes or increases in expenditure) to stimulate the economy; and it has hampered government's ability to increase public investments, such as in infrastructure (like roads), human capital (education), and research to promote economic growth.

This chapter reviews the origins of the deficit problem, the solutions of the early 1990s, and the debate about the consequences of deficits.

THE U.S. DEFICIT PROBLEM
SINCE THE 1980s

The U.S. deficit problem began around 1981, when taxes were cut but expenditures were not cut commensurately. Figure 28.1 shows what happened. The real deficit peaked at more than $290 billion in 1992. The deficit as a percentage of GDP rose to a peacetime record of 6.1 percent in 1983, hovered between 3 and 5 percent for most of the remainder of the decade, gradually decreased from 4.7 percent in 1992, and finally turned into a surplus in 1998.

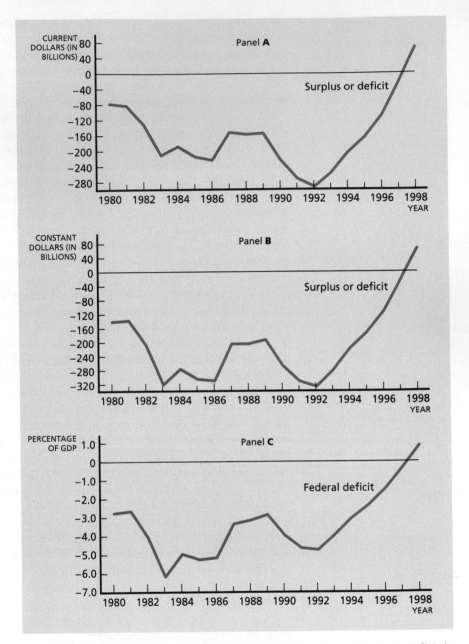

FIGURE 28.1 **Budget Deficits in the United States, 1980–1998** The federal budget deficit is represented here in three series of data. Panel A shows the nominal deficit; panel B shows the real deficit in 1997 dollars; and panel C shows the federal deficit as a percentage of GDP.

Source: *Economic Report of the President, 1999* (Washington, D.C.: Government Printing Office), Tables B-1, B-3, and B-80.

SOURCES OF THE DEFICIT PROBLEM A good way to pose the question of what caused the soaring budget deficit is to ask: What changed between the 1970s (and earlier decades) and the 1980s? There are five main answers to this question.

REDUCED FEDERAL TAXES During the 1970s, federal taxes usually collected between 18 and 19 percent of GDP. In 1980 and 1981 that percentage climbed to 20 percent. (Remember, 1 percent of a multitrillion-dollar economy will be tens of billions of dollars.) Tax cuts enacted early in the Reagan presidency pushed the federal tax take back down to its historical range of 18–19 percent of GDP. The slight increase in taxes in 1993 did not alter this basic picture.

HIGHER DEFENSE SPENDING Federal defense spending fell during the 1970s, as the Vietnam War came to an end, from 8.4 percent of GDP in 1970 to 4.9 percent of GDP in 1979. In 1979, though, after the Soviet Union invaded Afghanistan, President Carter called for a large defense buildup. After Ronald Reagan was elected President in 1980, he followed through on these plans. From 1983 to 1988, defense spending exceeded 6 percent of GDP. With the end of the Cold War, there has been a reduction in defense spending to under 4 percent of GDP. Though the threat of small wars in various parts of the world has kept the "peace dividend" smaller than many had hoped, the reduction in defense spending as a percentage of GDP played an important part in the deficit reductions after 1993.

HIGHER SOCIAL SPENDING ON THE ELDERLY As the elderly population in the United States has grown, not only absolutely but as a proportion of the population, federal expenditures on programs like social security and Medicare (providing health care to the aged) have expanded dramatically. These programs averaged 5.0 percent of GDP in the 1970s, but increased to over 6 percent of GDP by 1980 and close to 7 percent by 1982. Though they have increased only slightly since then (as a percentage of GDP), they are expected to increase substantially in the early part of the next century.

INCREASING HEALTH CARE EXPENDITURES Through Medicare and Medicaid (the government program providing health care to the poor), the government has assumed an increasing share of total health care expenditures, to the point where today the federal government alone pays 30 percent of all health care expenditures. Health care expenditures themselves have soared. Through the 1980s and early 1990s these expenditures were increasing at close to 12 percent per year, doubling every six years. A number of initiatives undertaken during the Bush and Clinton administrations brought the rate of increase down to between 8 percent and 10 percent, a number still far higher than the rate of income growth. By the late 1990s, there were signs that health care costs were beginning once again to rise at a more rapid rate.

MEASURING
BUDGET
DEFICITS:
WHAT'S
LARGE,
WHAT'S REAL,
AND WHAT'S
RIGHT?

The deficits of the 1980s and early 1990s were huge. At its peak in 1992 the dollar figure was $290 billion. But are dollar amounts the right way to measure the size and importance of deficits? Shouldn't we take into consideration the effects of inflation and the growth of the overall economy?

Robert Eisner of Northwestern University argues for focusing on the overall increase in the *real* debt—that is, the debt adjusted for changes in the price level. With total debt outstanding to the public of approximately $3.6 trillion, an inflation rate of 3 percent implies a reduction of the real value of the debt of $108 billion per year. This decrease in the real value of the outstanding debt should, in Eisner's view, be subtracted from any increase in debt due to the deficit. In fiscal 1996, this inflation-adjusted deficit was only $9 billion, compared to the measured deficit of $117 billion.

According to this definition, the Carter administration actually ran an inflation-adjusted surplus due to the effects of inflation on the value of the debt. By contrast, the relatively low rates of inflation during the Reagan and Bush administrations were not enough to offset the large deficits due to expenditures' far exceeding revenues.

The *full-employment* or *structural* deficit takes into account the level of economic activity in the economy. It asks, what would the deficit have been if the economy had been operating at full employment? For instance, in 1991, as the economy was in recession, the deficit was officially $269 billion—the largest in history up to that point—but the structural deficit was $191 billion, still large by any standards, but $78 billion less than the actual deficit. The Reagan years look particularly bad from this perspective, since, except during wars, the economy had never previously run large structural deficits.

In recent years, as well as in the years immediately following World Wars I and II, the U.S. government was saddled with a huge debt. The interest payments on this inherited debt made it particularly difficult

HIGHER INTEREST PAYMENTS Like other borrowers, the federal government pays interest. During the 1970s, federal interest payments were about 1.5 percent of GDP. But from 1983 to 1990 they exceeded 3 percent of GDP. The main reason was the increasing deficit. If the debt in 1995 had been the same as it had been at the start of the Reagan era in 1981 (after adjusting for inflation), the government would have been running a balanced budget, rather than a deficit of $160 billion. Deficits, through interest payments,

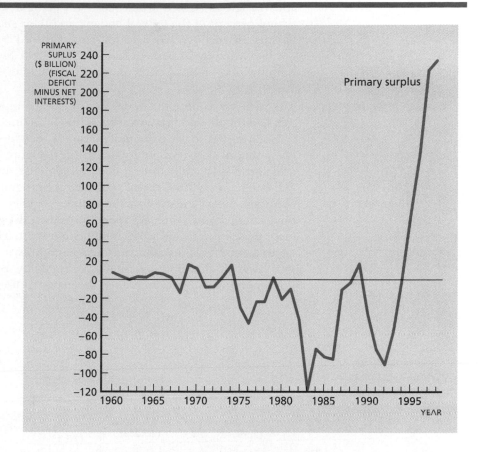

to attain a balanced budget. The *primary deficit* takes into account what the deficit would have been had there been no inherited debt; that is, it subtracts interest payments from the deficit. If the government is running a primary surplus, it means that revenues more than cover current expenditures. The government began running a primary surplus for only the second time since 1979 in 1995 (see figure).

SOURCE: *Economic Report of the President, 1996,* Table B-76.

feed on themselves. The lower interest rates in the late 1990s contributed to eliminating the deficit.

FACTORS NOT CONTRIBUTING TO THE DEFICIT PROBLEM

In a sense, any expenditure can be thought of as contributing to the deficit problem—reducing that expenditure, other things equal, would reduce the deficit. But some factors are blamed for the deficit problem undeservedly. For instance, polls suggest that many Americans believe welfare payments and foreign assistance are at fault. Yet general welfare payments are less than 4 percent of the federal budget, and their share of the federal budget has decreased in recent decades. Under the AFDC program, real benefits per family fell by 55 percent from 1970 to 1993. Similarly foreign assistance is minuscule—about 1 percent of the federal budget.

TAMING THE DEFICIT

The deficit was brought under control beginning around 1993. Why was this so difficult, and how was success finally attained?

The answer to the first question can be seen by looking once again at the composition of government expenditures (Figure 28.2). Expenditures typically are divided into three categories: defense, non-defense discretionary, and entitlements. **Entitlement programs** are programs like social security and Medicare, where the government defines eligibility criteria for certain benefits ("entitlements"); actual expenditures then depend on how many people meet those criteria and what those benefits cost. The government does not, on an annual basis, actually control expenditures; it can only change expenditure levels by changing the criteria for eligibility. By contrast, for the **discretionary programs,** government sets the expenditure levels on an annual basis.

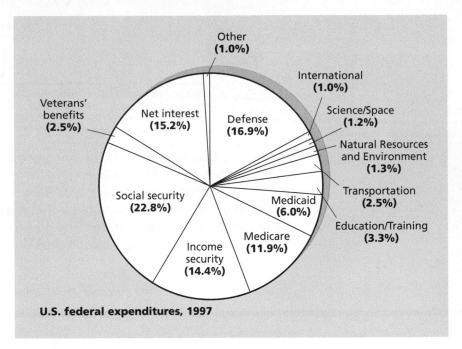

U.S. federal expenditures, 1997

FIGURE 28.2   **The Challenge of Reducing Federal Spending** A large portion of federal spending is devoted to three areas: defense, entitlement programs, and interest payments. To reduce federal spending significantly, large cuts must be made in at least some of these categories, since other areas of spending are simply not large enough to make much difference.

SOURCE: *Economic Report of the President, 1998*, Table B-81.

Thus, on an annual basis, government does not have direct control over 60 percent of its expenditures (interest, social security, Medicare, Medicaid, and other entitlements). Of the remainder, almost half goes to defense. Given President Reagan's commitments not to raise taxes, to increase defense expenditures, and not to cut social security, there simply was insufficient scope for cutting other expenditures to bring the budget into balance. Eliminating the deficit would have required cutting other categories of expenditure in half—beyond the level which seemed acceptable.

Three factors played a role in eventually taming the deficit in the 1990s: increased taxes on high-income individuals, limiting the growth of expenditures, and a strong economy. Each factor is estimated to have contributed approximately a third of the overall deficit reduction, but the factors are in fact intertwined, with some economists believing that the higher economic growth (which generated additional tax revenue) was at least partially due to the tax increases and expenditure reductions that were undertaken in 1993.[1]

The link between growth and deficits is a simple one: If the government has to borrow more money, interest rates rise. Figure 28.3 shows the de-

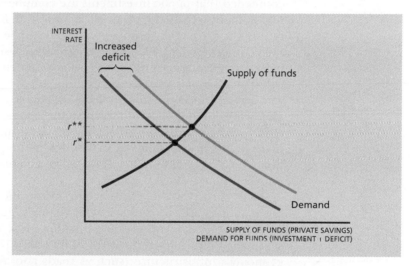

FIGURE 28.3 **Demand and Supply Curves for Funds (Capital)** An increased deficit increases the demand for funds, leading to a higher interest rate and lower investment.

[1] Economic recovery—the reduction of the unemployment rate from 7.8 percent of GDP to 4.9 percent of GDP—by itself would have generated additional revenues equal to approximately 1.2 percent of GDP. By what is known as *Okun's law* (after the chairman of the Council of Economic Advisers under President Johnson, who first "discovered" this empirical regularity), each percentage reduction in the unemployment rate gives rise to a 2 to 3 percent increase in output. Assuming the lower number, each percent increase in output in turn gives rise to an increase in tax revenues of approximately .2 percent of GDP. Deficit reduction itself may have contributed to an expansion of the economy by an amount that exceeded what would have been predicted by Okun's law, by encouraging increased investment: investment in equipment, for instance, increased by more than 45 percent during the period 1993–1997.

mand and supply for funds (capital). Increased government borrowing shifts the demand curve to the right, leading to higher interest rates. At higher interest rates, firms are willing to invest less. With less investment, there is less growth. We say that government borrowing has **crowded out** private investment.

The budget debates of the 1990s were complicated by the fact that while everyone agreed that deficits adversely affected growth, many also argued that the way the deficit was reduced could also affect growth. Conservatives claimed that raising taxes to reduce the deficit would have even more adverse effects on growth: deficits might be bad, but increased taxes were even worse. They argued that taxes on capital gains and interest reduce savings; lower savings lead to higher interest rates; and higher interest rates lead to less investment. As we saw in Chapter 18, the econometric evidence does not provide much support for this position, since savings do not seem to be very responsive to interest rates.

On the other hand, some economists claimed that reducing public investments would slow economic growth, especially in the long run. They contended that public investments are **complements** to private investment, that is, they increase the productivity of private investment so that at any interest rate, the level of private investment will be higher. In this view, for instance, a more educated labor force makes investments in the United States more attractive; government-supported research leads to findings that provide the basis of profitable innovations by the private sector. While those who saw a limited role for government agreed, they argued that there was plenty of room for expenditure cuts, for instance in entitlement programs, that would not adversely affect investments; and that the productivity of many public investments was so low that cutting back on them would have little effect on growth. As evidence, they cited studies showing low returns on many job training programs.

The thrust of the Clinton administration's budgets was to redirect more public expenditures toward investment and to increase the effectiveness of public expenditures by spending more money on those programs that had shown high returns. By 1993, there was real concern about the economy's infrastructure (such as roads and airports). During the previous twelve years, public expenditures on infrastructure as a percentage of GDP had sunk in half from what they were in the 1960s. The ratio of public capital to private capital had dropped by almost a third from 1965 to 1988. By 1993, the Department of Transportation estimated that almost 20 percent of the nation's highways had poor or mediocre pavement and almost 20 percent of the bridges were structurally deficient. The percentage of the federal budget devoted to all types of public investment (including research and education) fell from 35 percent in 1963 to 17 percent in 1992.

The Clinton administration made significant inroads in increasing public investment only in one area—education. Given the concern about the size of the deficit, an unwillingness to raise taxes, and an inability or unwillingness to cut back the major areas of non-investment expenditures—the entitlement programs (though the rate of increase of Medicare and Medicaid was reduced)—there was little scope for increasing investments. To achieve its deficit reduction targets, it decided to maintain—and even increase slightly—expenditures on education, but to cut back in real terms most other areas of non-defense non-entitlement expenditures, including investments. And while there was a serious attempt to avoid the mistakes of the past which, for instance, had led to training programs with low rates of return, many of the new programs were unproven, so that the magnitude of the returns would only be clear over time. Those who believe that the long-run growth prospects of the American economy depend on innovation, and that innovation must be based on a strong science and engineering foundation, were particularly disturbed at proposed cutbacks in support of research of between 20 percent and 30 percent. They argued that the marginal return from these expenditures is not only high, but higher than many other forms of investment (including some education and training programs).

Within the research budget, there was also controversy. Most scientists questioned the returns of the high levels of investment in space—they argued that money spent on the space station could be far better spent elsewhere. NASA (the National Aeronautics and Space Administration) had done a fantastic job of ensuring strong political support for its projects (for instance, by ensuring that contractors and subcontractors were located in a large number of congressional districts)—far better than the basic research community had done, though there was bipartisan agreement that basic research should be supported. Basic research is like a public good: the marginal cost of an additional individual's enjoying the benefits of the knowledge is low, and the cost of exclusion is often high. But the Clinton administration argued that the government should also support the development of new technology. There were substantial spillovers from many new technologies that were not captured by the inventor, as evidenced by the laser and the transistor, two innovations which had a huge range of benefits to the economy, extending well beyond what had been originally contemplated. Conservatives argued that these areas should be left to the private sector; the government should not be in the business of deciding which industries to promote, even by supporting research. They contended that the government had a bad track record of picking winners, and that such support was prone to influence by special interest groups.

The reality probably lay between the two extreme positions: While there were many examples of misguided government research programs, government had long played a central—and successful—role in promoting technology. The first telegraph line, between Baltimore and Washington, was financed by the federal government in 1842, as was the Internet. The rapid increase in productivity in agriculture during the nineteenth and twentieth centuries was based on government-funded research, and on the government-run extension services which widely disseminated the newfound knowledge. In one way or another, much of modern technology has been supported by the government, often as part of defense efforts. In the 1990s with the slowing down of defense expenditures, key questions facing policy makers were: Would more explicit governmental support of technology be required for the country to maintain its technological leadership? And were there ways, such as requiring more equity participation by private firms in government-supported technology research programs, to increase the success rate of government-supported projects? Under the exigency of the budget constraints, what had been a major initiative, to expand investments in new technology, got pared back—though the programs survived at lower levels of support.

CONSEQUENCES OF GOVERNMENT DEFICITS

When the government runs a deficit, it must borrow to pay the difference between its expenditures and its revenues. When it runs a deficit year after year, it must borrow year after year. The cumulated value of these borrowings is the *federal debt*—what the government owes. Figure 28.4 shows the federal debt. The immediate consequence of rising federal debt is that the government has to pay out more and more in interest—one of the factors that we identified earlier as itself contributing to the deficit.

Economists have traditionally argued that government borrowing, just like individual borrowing, may be justified relative to the purpose for which the money is used. It makes sense to borrow to buy a house that you will live in for many years, or a car that you will drive for several years. In that way, you spread out paying for the item as you use it. It makes economic sense to borrow money for an educational degree that will lead to a higher-paying job in the future. But if you are paying this year for your vacation from two years ago, maybe you should cut up your credit cards!

Countries are in a similar situation. Borrowing to finance a road, school, or industrial project that will be used for many years may be quite appropriate. Borrowing to pay for projects that are never completed (or perhaps are never even started), or borrowing to finance this year's government salaries, poses real problems. Many governments have taken on more debt than they could comfortably pay off, forcing them to raise taxes sharply and reduce living standards. Others have simply failed to repay, jeopardizing their ability to borrow in the future.

Financing government expenditures by borrowing rather than by raising taxes results in higher levels of consumption in the short run (since disposable income is higher). When the economy is at full employment, higher consumption implies there is less room for investment. To maintain the economy at full employment without inflation, the Federal Reserve Board has to increase interest rates. Deficit financing leads to lower investment, and thus, in the long run, to lower output and consumption.

Reducing the deficit has the opposite effect: it allows interest rates to fall, stimulating investment, and thus promoting economic growth and better future living standards.

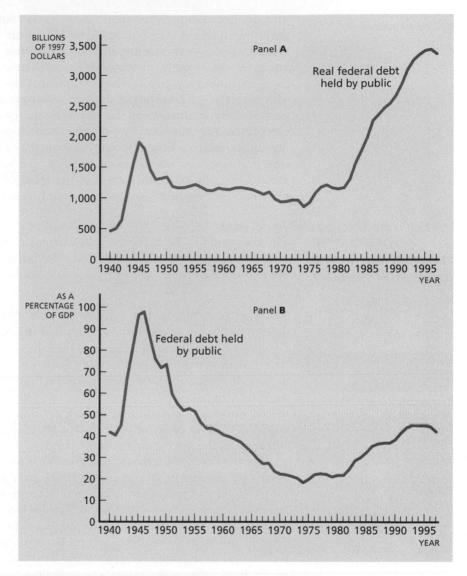

FIGURE 28.4   **The Federal Debt** The debt represents the accumulation of previous deficits. Panel A shows the federal debt (in real dollars) soaring enormously in the 1980s; by the early 1990s it had far exceeded the previous record set in World War II. Panel B shows the debt as a percentage of GDP. While the real debt continued to increase in the mid-1990s, as a percentage of GDP it had finally begun to stabilize.

**HOW DEFICITS AFFECT
FUTURE GENERATIONS**

By borrowing, the government places the burden of reduced consumption on future generations. It does this in two ways. Future output is lowered as a result of lower investment, as we have seen. But beyond this, some of the burden of current expenditures is put onto future generations. To see how this is done, consider the financing of World War II. This was done partly through borrowing rather than raising taxes. Suppose that the bonds the government issued were purchased by 40-year-old workers. Then thirty years later, as these workers entered retirement, the government paid off the bonds by raising taxes on those who were then in the labor force. In effect, the government was transferring funds from these younger workers to those who were the workers during the war, who were now 70 and retired. Thus, part of the cost of the war was borne by the generation who entered the work force after the war. The lifetime consumption of those who were 40 during the war was little affected. They might otherwise have put their savings into stocks or bonds issued by firms; the war (to the extent it was financed by debt, or bonds) affected the form of their savings, but not the total amount they had to spend over their lifetime.

ALTERNATIVE PERSPECTIVES ON THE BURDEN OF THE DEBT

The discussion so far represents the current dominant views. Some economists believe that these views overstate the burden of the debt. Four different reasons are given.

THE "DEBT DOES NOT MATTER BECAUSE WE OWE IT TO OURSELVES" ARGUMENT It used to be argued in the United States that the fiscal deficit does not matter because we simply owe the money to ourselves. The budget deficit was compared to the effect of one brother's borrowing from another on the total welfare of the family. One member of the family may be better off, another worse off, but the indebtedness does not matter much to the family as a whole. Financing government expenditures by debt, it was argued, could lead to a transfer of resources between generations, but this transfer would still keep all the buying power in the hands of U.S. citizens.

We now recognize that this argument is wrong on three counts. First, even if we owe the money to ourselves, the debt affects investment and thus future wages and productivity, as noted. Second, today we do not in fact owe the money to ourselves. The United States is borrowing abroad and becoming indebted to foreigners. The consequences of the country's spending beyond its means are no different from the consequences of a family's spending beyond its means. Eventually it has to pay the price of its consumption binge. In the case of a national consumption binge, it is future generations who have to pay the price.

Third, simply to pay interest on the debt requires high levels of taxes, and taxes introduce distortions into the economy, discouraging work and savings. (There is some disagreement among economists about the quantitative significance of these effects.)

RICARDIAN EQUIVALENCE: BEQUESTS OFFSET THE DEBT A more recent argument says that in the face of increased deficits, individuals save more. Robert Barro of Harvard University, developing an argument made (and later rejected) by David Ricardo, one of the nineteenth century's greatest economists, believes that individuals' concern for their children is so great that they increase their bequests when they see government deficits threatening their offspring with future indebtedness.[2] To be able to be more generous in their bequests, they increase their household savings by exactly the amount of the increase in the deficit: national savings does not change. The increased government dissaving is fully offset. This view is called **Ricardian equivalence** because it contends that taxation and deficits are equivalent means of financing expenditures.

The evidence does not support Barro's theoretical contention. Increased government deficits may lead to slightly higher household savings, but far less than necessary to offset fully the deficit increases. In the late 1980s and early 1990s, when the deficit was running at more than 5 percent of GDP, the household savings rate was only 3 to 4 percent. If Barro's theory were correct, then in the absence of the government deficit, household savings rates would have been an implausibly low number, between minus 1 and minus 2 percent.

Statistical evidence from a variety of countries confirms the experience in the United States that private savings does not fully offset government borrowing. And this is not surprising: individuals are not as rational as Barro assumes (fully taking into account public liabilities in current decision-making), nor as altruistic (setting aside an additional dollar of bequests for their heirs every time public indebtedness increases by a dollar). In many cases, they face borrowing constraints—they would like to consume more than they do, but cannot finance their additional consumption. If the government increases their disposable income, by lowering taxes, they spend most of this increased income, even if the government has increased public indebtedness at the same time.[3]

CONSEQUENCES OF GOVERNMENT DEFICITS

1 Some of the burden of current expenditures is shifted to future generations directly.

2 Issuing bonds may decrease investment and thus make future generations worse off indirectly.

3 Foreign indebtedness may increase, reducing future standards of living.

4 Government dissaving is not offset by private savings.

---

[2] R. Barro, "Are Government Bonds Net Wealth?" *Journal of Political Economy* 82 (1974): 1095–1117. Subsequent research has both generalized his result and shown how stringent the assumptions are under which it is valid. See, for instance, J. E. Stiglitz, "On the Relevance or Irrelevance of Public Financial Policy," in *The Economics of Public Debt*, ed., K. J. Arrow and M. J. Boskin (New York: Macmillan Press, 1988), pp. 41–76.

[3] For further discussions, see the Symposium in the *Journal of Economic Perspectives* 3, no. 2 (spring 1989).

The Congressional Budget Office (CBO) has long had a reputation for being nonpartisan. The director of the CBO at the time that President Clinton was introducing his managed health care reforms was Bob Reischauer, a Democrat; yet because he said that the evidence on the extent to which managed care would reduce health care costs was not clear, he refused to credit the programs with much savings. The nonpartisan nature of the CBO was reaffirmed when, under the new director, June O'Neill, appointed when the Republicans gained control of the House and Senate, the CBO refused to credit the Republican managed health care reforms with as much savings as they would have liked.

On other issues, however, critics worried that the CBO might be departing from its traditional nonpartisanship. Consider the question of how much interest rates would fall as a result of eliminating the deficit. Presumably, as government expenditures decreased, interest rates would fall, as the Federal Reserve Board took actions to ensure that the economy remained at full employment. Granted, how much interest rates would fall was problematic, since it depended on the interest elasticity of investment (the percentage increase in investment resulting from a 1 percent decrease in the interest rate), of which economists had

UNDERUTILIZATION OF RESOURCES: DEFICITS MAY ACTUALLY HELP If the economy is operating at less than full employment, then under traditional macroeconomic theories, deficits (either as a result of increased government expenditures or decreased taxes) can stimulate the economy. Interest rates may not rise, or rise very much, so that investment (and hence growth) will not be adversely affected. In effect, when the economy is not fully utilizing its resources, output today *and* output in the future can both be increased. This is especially true if the increased deficit arises from increased government expenditures on investments.

OPEN ECONOMY: AVOIDING CROWDING OUT For a small open economy in a world in which capital flows freely, the interest rate which its firms have to pay is determined internationally, and will be little affected by the size of its deficit. Thus, the level of investment—and thus the rate of growth in its GDP—may not be adversely affected by deficits. But to finance the investment plus an increased deficit, the country will have to borrow more abroad than it would with a smaller deficit. Its citizens will have to pay foreigners interest on these borrowings, and thus the net income of its citizens (what they have to spend, after paying foreigners for the use of their capital—its gross national product) will be lower. The country will, in this sense, be worse off even though the actual level of output is unaffected.

markedly different estimates. Still, CBO director O'Neill concluded that interest rates would fall by approximately 1.7 percentage points. But the CBO refused to give the Clinton deficit reduction package any credit for interest rate reduction, since in its estimates the Clinton budget deficit reduction package did not fully achieve a balanced budget. Critics of the CBO argued that the expenditure cuts were sufficiently severe that there should have been some interest rate reductions— roughly in proportion to the reductions in the expenditures.

Other critics pointed out that, apart from interest rate reductions, even the CBO's estimate of the magnitude of the deficit was problematic. It was more conservative than not only the Clinton administration's estimate but also the consensus of business forecasters. Moreover, its estimate of the rate of increase of health care costs failed to incorporate recent changes in trends in those variables, and was higher than those of the career actuaries who had for years collected the data and provided the estimates. But supporters of the CBO pointed out that in using those numbers, the CBO was simply continuing to use numbers similar to those that it had used under Democratic leadership; if there was a fault, it was not with partisan leadership, but with the longstanding methods of the CBO.

The United States is a large economy, and when it borrows more, there is an effect on international interest rates. It is estimated that if the United States runs a $100 billion additional deficit, slightly more than a third of that is financed by increased foreign borrowing, somewhat less than a third from increased domestic savings responding to the higher interest rates, and the rest by reduced investment—the deficits do partially crowd out private investment.

IMPROVING THE BUDGETARY PROCESS

The persistence of the deficit led many to argue that there should be a change in the way budgets are adopted. In this section, we consider two such changes. One of these has already been implemented; the other remains under discussion.

BUDGET ENFORCEMENT ACT AND SCORING

In 1990 Congress passed the Budget Enforcement Act, designed to reduce the likelihood of runaway deficits. Whenever Congress passes a new program, it is required to levy new taxes to pay for it, or to find offsetting expenditure cuts. The Congressional Budget Office (CBO)—ostensibly a nonpartisan group of professionals—"scores" the program, that is, it calculates how much it will cost. Inevitably, there are issues of judgment involved. Thus, in recent debates on health care reform, the CBO argued that managed care would, in the short run, result in only limited savings. Had it scored managed care as generating large savings, it might have been far easier to adopt health care reforms.

CAPITAL BUDGETS

Businesses emphasize the distinction between expenditures to buy machines—capital expenditures—and other expenditures. Investments enhance the firm's ability to produce in the future. We argued earlier that there was a marked difference between borrowing to make an investment and borrowing to buy a vacation. Government accounting systems do not make a distinction, though businesses do. Not only do businesses distinguish between the kinds of expenditure in their annual reports, but they maintain capital accounts which show their assets (including machines) and liabilities.

Some have argued that government should have a capital budget, which would identify expenditures on investments. While some countries have done so, the United States has not, partially because of the political problems of defining investments. Most capital budgets include only investments in physical objects, like roads; and education advocates have worried that such a capital budget would divert resources away from human capital formation—from education and research. Similarly, health care advocates argue that providing good health care for children is an investment in their future, raising their productivity and lowering future expenditures on medical care.

OTHER STRATEGIES

Two other suggestions for improving the budgetary process have been widely discussed. One, the **line item veto,** gives the President the right to veto particular expenditures within a budget bill. It went into effect in January 1997. Previously, Presidents could only accept or reject an entire bill. They were loath to veto a large bill for, say, national defense, simply because of some small wasteful expenditure that went to benefit the constituents of some congressional representative. The other suggestion is a constitutional amendment, called the **balanced budget amendment,** requiring Congress to adopt a balanced budget. Such an amendment has come within a few votes of passing several times. Advocates say it would (by definition) force fiscal responsibility; the government would have to come up with a balanced budget. Critics point out the severe problems of implementation: What would happen if Congress failed to comply, for instance because revenues fell short because of an economic recession? Balancing the budget on the basis of prospective expenditures and revenues would require someone to make estimates. Who should do that, and how would one ensure that it was done in a nonpolitical way? Many economists criticize the balanced budget amendment because it takes away one of the main tools of economic stabilization. It would make it more difficult to maintain the economy at full employment, putting almost all of the responsibility on monetary policy. Those who are less confident of the ability of monetary policy to counter quickly a severe recession are particularly worried about such an amendment. Some of the proposals—though not the ones that have come close to passage by Congress—have included escape clauses in the event of a recession.

THE LONG-TERM PROBLEM: ENTITLEMENTS AND THE AGED

Even though the United States has been able to eliminate its deficit, the long-term problem persists: entitlement expenditures for Medicare and social security are likely to soar in the coming decades. The reasons are twofold. First, the number of elderly in the U.S. population will increase dramatically, vastly increasing the number of eligible recipients for social security and Medicare. Second, health care costs for the elderly may continue to increase. Chapters 12 and 14 have described both of these trends, and outlined some of the policies which might address them.

At root, the problem is that the political process tends to focus on pressing concerns, not those that might or even probably will occur in the future. There is a chance that health care costs might grow much more slowly than anticipated, or that productivity might increase faster than anticipated (thus increasing tax revenues, without increasing tax rates). But there is also a chance that health care costs might rise more rapidly than is currently anticipated, or that productivity might increase more slowly than anticipated. Thus most economists believe that we should base our actions today on the best available information—and this information strongly suggests a soaring deficit in the future. If anything, uncertainty should make us more cautious. Postponing undertaking actions may necessitate taking more drastic and painful actions in the future.

How the government responds to this challenge, how it brings the entitlement programs under control, and what the consequences will be for other programs if these programs are not dramatically changed, are the most important issues facing the economics of the public sector in the coming decades.

REVIEW AND PRACTICE

1 The early 1980s were marked by a surge in the size of federal budget deficits. There are five main causes for the increase: lower taxes, higher defense spending, higher spending on support for the elderly, higher health care expenditures, and higher interest payments.

2 Reagan's commitment not to cut social security, not to raise taxes, and to increase defense expenditures made it virtually impossible to bring the deficits under control in the 1980s. Non-defense discretionary expenditures would have had to have been cut in half to achieve a balanced budget.

3 The deficit was finally brought under control in the late 1990s, through increased taxes, reduced expenditures, especially on defense, and a strong

economy. But the problems of growing entitlement expenditures, especially associated with programs for the aged, were not addressed, and unless they are, either taxes will have to be increased or the deficit will balloon early in the twenty-first century.

4 Government borrowing can burden future generations economically in several ways. First, future generations may have to bear the burden of paying off the borrowing; there is a transfer from one generation to another. Second, government borrowing can crowd out investment, which will reduce future output and wages. Third, when money is borrowed from foreign investors, then Americans as a whole must pay some of their national income each year to foreigners just for interest, resulting in lower standards of living.

5 Government dissavings (deficits) have not been offset by private savings, as Ricardian equivalence would have suggested; and it is not true that "the debt does not matter, because we only owe it to ourselves."

6 How the deficit is reduced may have an important effect on economic growth. Some economists worry that reducing the deficit by increasing taxes will reduce savings, but most econometric evidence suggests that this effect is small. Other economists worry that reducing the deficit by decreasing public investments will hurt economic growth, both because such investments have high returns and because they lead to increased private investment.

KEY CONCEPTS

Fiscal deficit	Crowding out	Line item veto
Entitlement programs	Complements	Balanced budget amendment
Discretionary programs	Ricardian equivalence	

QUESTIONS AND PROBLEMS

1 True or false: "Government borrowing can transfer resources from future generations to the present, but it cannot affect the overall wealth of the country." Discuss.

2 In an open economy, there are three sources of funds to finance investment: private savings (S_p), government savings (the difference between government revenues and expenditures, S_g), and foreign borrowing, B:

$$I = S_p + S_g + B.$$

a Suppose a certain country has private savings of 6 percent of GDP, foreign borrowing of 1 percent of GDP, and a balanced budget. What is its level of investment?

b Suppose now that the government runs a deficit of 3 percent of GDP, and investment and private savings remain unchanged. What must happen to foreign borrowing?

c Suppose now that the government runs a deficit of 3 percent of GDP, and this increases the interest rate. If this in turn leads to increased private savings, to 7 percent of GDP, and reduced investment from 7 percent to 6 percent of GDP, what happens to foreign borrowing?

3 In a closed economy, private savings plus government savings must equal investment:

$$I = S_p + S_g.$$

a Draw a savings-investment diagram to show the effect of an increased budget deficit.

b Assume that the increased government deficit is the result of increased government investment, and that the government investment increases the returns on private investment, so that at each interest rate there is increased private investment. Show the effect of the deficit on investment and interest rates now.

c Assume that Ricardian equivalence holds. What happens to national savings when the government increases the deficit? What happens to private savings?

d Ricardian equivalence focuses on the impact of future tax liabilities associated with increased deficits on private savings. What implications does the logic of Ricardian equivalence have for the consequences of additional public investment? In particular, what will be the impact on private savings of an increased deficit used to finance public investment which has a very high return, which will be realized only in the lives of the next generation?

4 Consider a small open economy with a perfectly elastic supply of savings at interest rate r^*, which is below the interest rate which would have prevailed in the economy if it could not have borrowed, and a normal investment curve. Show the market equilibrium, including the magnitude of foreign borrowing.

a Now show the effect of an increased budget deficit.

b Show the effect of an increased budget deficit which originates as a result of increased public investment, in which the public investment is a complement to private investment.

5 The real value of the debt (in 1995 dollars) in 1995 was $3.6 trillion and in 1980 was $1.3 trillion. Assume that 50 percent of this buildup in the debt would have gone into investment, so that the capital stock would have been

$1.15 trillion larger in 1995. Assume that the capital stock in 1995 was $15 trillion. By how much lower was GDP in 1995 as a result of the displaced investment, if an increase in the capital stock by 1 percent leads to a .2 percent increase in GDP?

6 One proposal to contain the deficits is a balanced budget amendment to the Constitution, that would require the government to maintain a balanced budget every year.

   a Explain why if the economy goes into a downturn, this would either force the government to raise taxes or reduce expenditures.

   b What would be the consequences of raising taxes or reducing expenditures under these circumstances?

   c How might you design a balanced budget amendment that would not force the government to cut back expenditures or raise taxes in an economic downturn?

   d Explain why if interest rates are increased to dampen the economy, the balanced budget amendment might force the government to cut back other expenditures (or raise taxes). More generally, describe the interaction between monetary and fiscal policy under a balanced budget amendment.

7 Should expenditures on health care for children be considered an "investment" in a capital budget? What other expenditures might legitimately be classified as "investment"?

8 Assume the government sells some of the land it currently rents out for grazing. Should the revenues received be counted as reducing the deficit? How would the transaction be treated under a capital budget?

9 Why does the way government achieves deficit reduction make a difference for economic growth?

   a Assuming that the government raises taxes on interest income, what is the total impact on national savings, taking into account both deficit reduction and changes in private savings? What is the impact on investment? (Hint: How does your answer depend on the interest elasticity of savings?)

   b Assuming that the government raises taxes on wage income, what is the impact on GDP in the short run? (Hint: How does your answer depend on the elasticity of labor supply?) What is the impact on the deficit and on investment?

   c Assume that the government reduces expenditures on investments in technology and education, which yield a return of 15 percent, while the marginal return on private investment is 7 percent. What is the impact on growth?

10 Throughout the text we have emphasized how different government actions affect various groups in the population differently.

    a Assume the government is considering whether to finance a war by borrowing or by taxes. Describe how different groups are affected by the two alternatives.

    b Assume the government is considering whether to reduce the deficit by increasing capital gains taxes or by increasing payroll taxes. Describe how different groups are affected by the alternatives.

REFERENCES

Aaron, H. J., "Lessons for Tax Reform," in J. Slemrod, (ed.), *Do Taxes Matter: The Impact of the Tax Reform Act of 1986* (Cambridge, Mass.: MIT Press, 1990), pp. 321–31.

Akerhielm, K., "Does Class Size Matter?" *Economics of Education Review* 13, no. 3 (September 1995): 229–41.

Akerlof, G., "The Market for Lemons: Qualitative Uncertainty and the Market Mechanism," *Quarterly Journal of Economics* 84 (1970): 488–500.

Akerlof, G., Yellen, J., and Katz, M., "An Analysis of Out-of-Wedlock Childbearing in the United States," *Quarterly Journal of Economics* 111, no. 2 (May 1996): 277–317.

Allen, F., "Optimal Linear Income Taxation with General Equilibrium Effects on Wages," *Journal of Public Economics* 17 (1982): 135–43.

Arnott, R., and Stiglitz, J. E., "Aggregate Land Rents, Expenditure on Public Goods and Optimal City Size," *Quarterly Journal of Economics* 93 (1979): 472–500.

Arnott, R., and Stiglitz, J. E., "Aggregate Land Rents and Aggregate Transport Costs," *Economic Journal* 91 (1981): 331–47.

Arrow, K. J., *Social Choice and Individual Values* (New York: Wiley, 1963).

Arrow, K. J., "Uncertainty and Welfare Economics of Medical Care," *American Economic Review* 53 (1963): 941–73.

Arrow, K. J., "Higher Education as a Filter," *Journal of Public Economics* 2 (1973): 193–216.

Arrow, K. J., et al., "Is There a Role for Benefit-Cost Analysis in Environmental, Health, and Safety Regulation," *Environment and Development Economics* 2, no. 2 (May 1997): 196–201.

Asquith, P., and Mullins, D., "Equity Issues and Offering Dilution," *Journal of Financial Economics*, 15, no. 1–2 (Jan-Feb. 1986): 61–89.

Atkinson, A. B., and Stiglitz, J. E., "The Structure of Indirect Taxation and Economic Efficiency," *Journal of Public Economics* (1972): 97–119.

Atkinson, A. B., and Stiglitz, J. E., "The Design of Tax Structure: Direct versus Indirect Taxation," *Journal of Public Economics* 6 (1976): 55–75.

Atkinson, A. B., and Stiglitz, J. E., *Lectures in Public Economics* (New York: McGraw-Hill, 1980).

Auerbach, A. J., "Wealth Maximization and the Cost of Capital," *Quarterly Journal of Economics* (August 1979): 433–66.

Auerbach, A. J., "The Theory of Excess Burden and Optimal Taxation," in Alan J. Auerbach and Martin Feldstein (eds.), *Handbook of Public Economics,* vol. 1 (New York: Elsevier, 1987), pp. 100–101.

Auten, G. E., Cilke, J. M., and Randolph, W. C., "The Effects of Tax Reform on Charitable Contributions," *National Tax Journal* 45, no. 3 (September 1992): 267–90.

Bagwell, L. S., and Shoven, J. B., "Cash Distributions to Shareholders," *Journal of Economic Perspectives* (summer 1989): 129–40.

Barro, R., "Are Government Bonds Net Wealth?" *Journal of Political Economy* 82, (1974): 1095–1117.

Barro, R. J., *The Impact of Social Security on Private Savings* (Washington, D.C.: American Enterprise Institute, 1978).

Baumol, W.J., "Contestable Markets: An Uprising in the Theory of Industry Structure," *American Economic Review* 72 (1982): 1–15.

Baumol, W.J., Panzar, J., and Willig, R., *Contestable Markets and the Theory of Industrial Organization* (New York: Harcourt Brace Jovanovich, 1982).

Becker, G., *Human Capital: A Theoretical and Empirical Analysis with Special References to Education* (New York: National Bureau of Economic Research, Columbia University Press, 2d ed., 1975).

Bewley, T., "A Critique of Tiebout's Theory of Local Public Expenditures," *Econometrica* 49 (1981): 713–40.

Blackorby, C., and Donaldson, D., "Cash versus In-Kind, Self-Selection and Efficient Transfers," *American Economic Review* (September 1988): 691–700.

Blumenthal, M., and Slemrod, J., "The Compliance Cost of the U.S. Individual Income Tax System: A Second Look after Tax Reform," *National Tax Journal* 45, no. 2 (June 1992): 185–202.

Bosworth, B., and Burtless, G., "Effects of Tax Reform on Labor Supply, Investment, and Saving," *Journal of Economic Perspectives* (winter 1992): 3–25.

Boteux, M., "On the Management of Public Monopolies Subject to Budgetary Constraints," *Journal of Economic Theory* 3 (1971): 219–40.

Bovenberg, A. L., and Goulder, L. H., "Optimal Environmental Taxation in the Presence of Other Taxes: General-Equilibrium Analyses," *American Economic Review* 86, no. 4 (September 1996): 985–1000.

Bradford, D., "The Incidence and Allocation Effect of a Tax on Corporate Distributions," *Journal of Public Economics* 15 (1981): 1–22.

Break, G., "Income Taxes and Incentives to Work: An Empirical Study," *American Economic Review* 47 (1957): 529–49.

Breyer, S. G., *Breaking the Vicious Circle: Toward Effective Risk Regulation* (Cambridge, Mass.: Harvard University Press, 1993), p. 12.

Brito, D. L., et al., "Randomization in Optimal Tax Schedules," *Journal of Public Economics* 56, no. 2 (February 1995): 189–223.

Brueckner, J. K., "A Test for the Allocative Efficiency in the Local Public Sector," *Journal of Public Economics* 19 (1982): 311–31.

Burman, L., and Randolph, W., "Measuring Permanent Responses to capital Gains Tax Changes in Panel Data," *American Economic Review* 84, no.1 (September 1994): 794–809.

Card, D., and Krueger, A., "Does School Quality Matter? Returns to Education and the Characteristics of Public School in the United States," *Journal of Political Economy*, vol. 100 (February 1992): 1–40.

Card, D., and Krueger, A., "Labor Market Effects of School Quality: Theory and Evidence," in Gary Burtless (ed.), *Does Money Matter: The Effect of School Resource on Student Achievement and Adult Success* (Washington, D.C.: Brookings Institution, 1996), pp. 97–140.

Card, D., and Krueger, A., "School Resources and Student Outcomes," *Annals of the American Academy of Political and Social Science* 559, no. (September 1998): 39–53.

Carraro, C., Galeotti, M, and Gallo, M., "Environmental Taxation and Unemployment: Some Evidence on the 'Double Dividend Hypothesis' in Europe," *Journal of Public Economics* 62, no. 1–2 (October 1996): 141–81.

Choe, Y. S., and Jeong, J., "Charitable Contributions by Low- and Middle-Income Taxpayers: Further Evidence with a New Method," *National Tax Journal* 46, no. 1 (March 1993): 33–39.

Clotfelter, C. T., and Schmalbeck, R. L., "The Impact of Fundamental Tax Reform on Nonprofit Organizations," in Henry J. Aaron and William G. Gale (eds.), *Economic Effects of Fundamental Tax Reform* (Washington, D.C.: Brookings Institution Press, 1996), pp. 211–43.

Coase, R. H., "The Problem of Social Cost," *Journal of Law and Economics* 3 (1960): 1–44.

Coleman, J., et al., *Equality of Educational Opportunity* (Washington, D.C.: Department of Health, Education, and Welfare, 1966).

Common, M., Reid, I., and Blaney, R., "Do Existence Values for Cost-Benefit Analysis Exist?" *Journal of Environmental and Resource Economics* 9, no. 2 (1997): 225–38.

Corlett, W. J., and Hague, D. C., "Complementarity and the Excess Burden of Taxation," *Review of Economic Studies* 21 (1953): 21–30.

Courant, P. N., Gramlich, E. M., and Rubinfeld, D. L., "The Stimulative Effect of Intergovernmental Grants: Or Why Money Sticks Where It Hits," in P. Mieszkowski and W. Oakland (eds.), *Fiscal Federalism and Grants-in-Aid* (Washington, D. C.: Urban Institute, 1979), pp. 5–21.

Cropper, M. L., and Oates, W. E., "Environmental Economics: A Survey," *Journal of Economic Literature* 30 (June 1992): 675–740.

Currie, J., "Welfare and the Well-Being of Children: The Relative Effectiveness of Cash and In-Kind Transfers," in James M. Poterba (ed.), *Tax Policy and the Economy*, vol. 8 (Cambridge, Mass.: MIT Press for the National Bureau of Economic Research, 1994), pp. 1–43.

Cutler, D., "A Guide to Health Care Reform," *Journal of Economic Perspectives* 8, no. 3 (summer 1994): 13–29.

Danzinger, S., Haveman, R., and Plotnick, R., "How Income Transfers Affect Work, Savings, and Income Distribution," *Journal of Economic Literature* (September 1981).

Dasgupta, P., and Stiglitz, J. E., "Differential Taxation, Public Goods and Economics Efficiency," *Review of Economics Studies* 39 (1971): 151–74.

Dasgupta, P., and Stiglitz, J. E., "Benefit-Cost Analysis and Trade Policies," *Journal of Political Economy* 82 (January-February 1974): 1–33.

DeBrock, L., and Arnold, R. J., "Utilization Control in HMOs," *Quarterly Review of Economics and Finance* 32, no. 3 (autumn 1992).

Devaney, B. and Fraker, T., "The Effect of Food Stamps on Food Expenditures," *American Journal of Agricultural Economics* (February 1989): 99–104.

Diamond, P., "A Many-Person Ramsey Tax Rule," *Journal of Public Economics* 4 (1975): 335–42.

Diamond, P., and Mirrlees, J., "Optimal Taxation and Public Production," *American Economic Review* 61 (1971): 261–78.

Domar, E. D., and Musgrave, R. A., "Proportional Income Taxation and Risk-Taking," *Quarterly Journal of Economics* 58 (1944): 388–422.

Duffield, J., "Nonmarket Valuation and the Courts: The Case of Exxon *Valdez,*" *Contemporary Economic Policy* 15, no. 4 (October 1997): 98–110.

Dumez, H., and Jeunemaitre, A., "Privatization in France: 1983–1993," in Vincent Wright (ed.), *Industrial Privatization in Western Europe: Pressures, Problems, and Paradoxes* (London and New York: Pinter Publishers, 1994), pp. 83–105, 194.

Eberts, R. W., and Gronberg, T. J., "Jurisdictional Homogeneity and the Tiebout Hypothesis," *Journal of Urban Economics* 10 (1981): 227–39.

Edwards, J., et al. (eds.), *Recent Developments in Corporate Finance* (New York and Melbourne: Cambridge University Press, 1986).

Eissa, N., "Labor Supply and the Economic Recovery Tax Act of 1981" in Martin Feldstein and James Poterba (eds.), *Empirical Foundations of Household Taxation* (Chicago and London: University of Chicago Press, 1996), pp. 5–32.

Eissa, N., and Liebman, J., "Labor Supply Responses to the Earned Income Tax Credit," *Quarterly Journal of Economics* 111, no. 2 (May 1996): 603–37.

Ellwood, D., and Summers, L., "Poverty in America: Is Welfare the Answer or the Problem," in S. Danziger and D. Weinberg (eds.), *Fighting Poverty: What Works and What Doesn't* (Cambridge, Mass.: Harvard University Press, 1986), pp. 78–105.

Erard, B., "Taxation with Representation: An Analysis of the Role of Tax Practitioners in Tax Compliance," *Journal of Public Economics* 52, no. 2 (September 1993): 163–197.

Fazzari, S., Hubbard, G., and Peterson, B., "Investment Financing Decisions and Tax Policy," *American Economic Review* 78, no. 2 (May 1988): 200–205.

Feenberg, D. R., and Rosen, H. S., "Recent Developments in the Marriage Tax," National Bureau of Economic Research, Working Paper 4705, April 1994.

Feldstein, M., "Distributional Equity and the Optimal Structure of Public Prices," *American Economic Review* 62 (1973): 32–36.

Feldstein, M., "On the Optimal Progressivity of the Income Tax," *Journal of Public Economics* 2 (1973): 357–76.

Feldstein, M., "Social Security, Induced Retirement, and Aggregate Capital Accumulation," *Journal of Political Economy* 82, no. 5 (1974): 905–26.

Feldstein, M., "The Effect of Marginal Tax Rates on Table Income: A Panel Study of the 1986 Tax Reform Act, *Journal of Political Economy* 1–3, no. 3 (1995): 551–72.

Feldstein, M., "Social Security and Saving: New Time Series Evidence," *National Tax Journal* 49, no. 2 (June 1996): 151–64.

Feldstein, M., Slemrod, J., and Yitzhake, S., "The Effects of Taxing on Selling and Switching of Common Stock and the Realization of Capital Gains," *Quarterly Journal of Economics* 94 (1980): 777–91.

Foley, D. K., "Resource Allocation and the Public Sector," *Yale Economic Essays* 7 (1967): 45–98.

Fraker, T., *The Effects of Food Stamps on Food Consumption: A Review of the Literature* (Alexandria, Va.: U.S. Department of Agriculture, Office of Analysis and Evaluation, Food and Nutrition Service, 1990).

Fraker, T., Martini, A., and Ols, J., "The Effect of Food Stamp Cashout on Food Expenditures: An Assessment of the Findings from Four Demonstrations," *Journal of Human Resources* 30, no. 4 (Fall 1995): 633–49.

Friedman, M., *Capitalism and Freedom* (Chicago: University of Chicago Press, 1962).

Fuchs, V., *Who Shall Live? Health Economics and Social Choice* (New York: Basic Books, 1975).

Fuchs, V., "The Supply of Surgeons and the Demand for Operations," in V. Fuchs (ed.), *The Health Economy* (London and Cambridge: Harvard University Press, 1986), pp. 126–147.

Fullerton, D., and Henderson, Y. K., "Incentive Effects of Taxes on Income from Capital: Alternative Policies in the 1980s," in C. R. Hulten and I. V. Sawhill (eds.), *The Legacy of Reaganomics: Prospects for Long-Term Growth* (Washington, D.C.: The Urban Institute Press, 1984).

Goodsell, Charles T., *The Case for Bureaucracy* (Chatham, N.J.: Chatham House Publishers, 1983).

Goulder, L. H., "Environmental Taxation and the Double Dividend: A Reader's Guide," *International Tax and Public Finance* 2 (August 1995): 157–83.

Gramlich, E. M., "Intergovernmental Grants: A Review of the Empirical Literature," in W. E. Oates (ed.), *The Political Economy of Fiscal Federalism* (Lexington, Mass.: Lexington Books, 1977).

Gravelle, J., *The Economic Effects of Taxing Capital Income* (Cambridge and London: MIT Press, 1994).

Greenberg, D., and Halsey, H., "Systematic Misreporting and Effects of Income Maintenance Experiments on Work Effort: Evidence from the Seattle–Denver Experiments," *Journal of Labor Economics* 1, no. 4 (October 1983): 380–407.

Greenfield, H. I., *Invisible, Outlawed and Untaxed: America's Underground Economy* (Westport, Conn.: Praeger, 1993).

Greenwald, B., and Stiglitz, J. E., "Externalities in Economies with Imperfect Information and Incomplete Markets," *Quarterly Journal of Economics* (May 1986): 229–264.

Greenwald, B., Stiglitz, J. E., and Weiss, A., "Informational Imperfections in the Capital Market and Macroeconomic Fluctuations," *American Economic Review* 74 (2): 194–99.

Grinols, E. L., "The Link Between Domestic Investment and Domestic Savings in Open Economies: Evidence from Balanced Stochastic Growth," *Review of International Economics* 4, no. 2 (June 1996): 119–40.

Guislain, P. *The Privatization Challenge: A Strategic, Legal, and Institutional Analysis of International Experience* (Washington, D.C.: World Bank, 1997).

Hannaway, J., and Carnoy, M. (eds.), *Decentralization and School Improvement* (San Francisco: Josscy-Bass, 1993).

Hanushek, E. A., "The Economics of Schooling: Production and Efficiency in Public Schools," *Journal of Economic Literature* 24, no. 3 (September 1986): 1141–77.

Hanushek, E. A., "School Resources and Student Performance," in Gary Burtless (ed.), *Does Money Matter: The Effect of School Resource on Student Achievement and Adult Success* (Washington, D.C.: Brookings Institution, 1996), pp. 43–73.

Hanushek, E., and Jorgenson, D. (eds.), *Improving America's Schools: The Role of Incentives* (Washington, D.C.: National Research Council, 1996).

Harberger, A., "Taxation, Resource Allocation and Welfare," in J. Due (ed.), *The Role of Direct and Indirect Taxes in the Federal Revenue System* (Princeton, N.J.: Princeton University Press, 1964), reprinted in A. Harberger, *Taxation and Welfare* (Chicago: University of Chicago Press, 1974).

Hausman, J., "Labor Supply," in H. Aaron and J. Pechman (eds.), *How Taxes Affect Economic Behavior* (Washington, D.C.: Brookings Institution, 1981), pp. 27–72.

Hausman, J., "Exact Consumer's Surplus and Deadweight Loss," *American Economic Review* 71 (1981): 662–76.

Hayward, N., and Kuper, G., "The National Economy and Productivity in Government," *Public Administration Review* 38 (1978).

Heckman, J. J., "What Has Been Learned about Labor Supply in the Past Twenty Years?" *American Economic Association Papers and Proceedings* (May 1993): 116–121.

Heckman, J. J., "Comment on Labour Supply and the Economic Recovery Tax Act of 1981" in M. Feldstein and J. Poterba (eds.), *Empirical Foundations of Household Taxation* (Chicago and London: University of Chicago Press, 1996), pp. 32–38.

Hill, P., Pierce, L., and Guthrie, J., *Reinventing Public Education: How Contracting Can Transform America's Schools* (Chicago: University of Chicago Press, 1997).

Hirschman, A. O., *Shifting Involvements: Private Interest and Public Action* (Princeton, N.J.: Princeton University Press, 1982).

Hitch, C. J., *Decision Making for Defense* (Berkeley: University of California Press, 1966), pp. 50–51.

Holland, D. M., "The Effect of Taxation on Effort: Some Results for Business Executives," *National Tax Association Proceedings of the Sixty-Second Annual Conference*, 1969.

Hotelling, H., "Stability in Competition," *Economic Journal* 39 (March 1929): 41–57.

Hubbard, G. (ed.), *Asymmetric Information, Corporate Finance, and Investment: A National Bureau of Economic Research Project Report* (Chicago and London: University of Chicago Press, 1990).

Jencks, C., *Rethinking Social Policy* (Cambridge, Mass.: Harvard University Press, 1992).

King, M., *Public Policy and the Corporation* (London: Chapman and Hall, 1977).

King, M., and Fullerton, D., *The Taxation of Income from Capital* (Chicago: University of Chicago Press, 1984).

Kotlikoff, L. J., and Summers, L. H., "Tax Incidence," chapter 16 in A. J. Auerbach and M. Feldstein (eds.), *The Handbook of Public Economics*, vol. 2 (New York: Elsevier, 1987), pp. 1043–1092.

Kramer, G., "On a Class of Equilibrium Conditions for Majority Rule," *Econometrica* 41 (1973): 285–97.

Krueger, Alan B. "Experimental Estimates of Educational Production Functions," *Quarterly Journal of Economics* 63 (May 1999).

Lau, L. J., Sheshinski, E., and Stiglitz, J. E., "Efficiency in the Optimum Supply of Public Goods," *Econometrica* 46 (1978): 269–84.

Levy, F., and Michel, R., "Work for Welfare: How Much Good Will It Do?" *American Economic Review* 76 (May 1986): 399–404.

Lindahl, E., "*Positive Lösung, Die Gerechtigkeit der Besteuerung*," translated as "Just Taxation—A Positive Solution" in R. A. Musgrave and A. T. Peacock (eds.), *Classics in the Theory of Public Finance* (New York: St. Martin's Press, 1958).

Lindsey, L., "Individual Taxpayer Response to Tax Cuts: 1982–1984, With Implications for Revenue Maximizing Tax Rate," *Journal of Public Economics* 33 (1987): 173–206.

Lindsey, L., *The Growth Experiment: How the New Tax Policy Is Transforming the U.S. Economy* (New York: Basic Books, 1990).

Lipsey, R. G., and Lancaster, K., "The General Theory of Second Best," *Review of Economic Studies* 24 (1956–1957): 11–32.

McClure, W., "Buying Right: The Consequences of Glut," *Business and Health* (September 1985): 43–46.

Meade, J., *Trade and Welfare: Mathematical Supplement* (Oxford: Oxford University Press, 1955).

Megginson, W. L., et al., "The Financial and Operating Performance of Newly Privatized Firms: An International Empirical Analysis," *Journal of Finance* 49, no. 2 (1994).

Modigliani, F., and Miller, M. H., "The Cost of Capital, Corporation Finance, and the Theory of Investment," *American Economic Review* 48 (1958): 261–97.

Moffit, R., "Incentive Effects of the U.S. Welfare System: A Review," *Journal of Economic Literature* (March 1992): 1–61.

Moffit, R., and Rangarajan, A., "The Work Incentives of AFDC Tax Rates: Reconciling Different Estimates," *Journal of Human Resources* (winter 1991): 165–79.

Mroz, T. A., "The Sensitivity of an Empirical Model of Married Women's Hours of Work to Economic and Statistical Assumptions" *Econometrica* (July 1987): 765–99.

Myers, S. C., and Majluf, N. S., "Corporate Financing and Investment Decisions When Firms Have Information That Investors Do Not Have," *Journal of Financial Economics* 13, no. 2 (June 1984): 187–221.

Newhouse, J. P., *Free for All? Lessons from the RAND Health Insurance Experiment* (Cambridge and London: Harvard University Press, 1993), p. 120.

Nozick, R., *Anarchy, State, and Utopia* (Oxford: Basil Blackwell, 1974).

Oates, W. A., "Green Taxes: Can We Protect the Environment and Improve the Tax System at the Same Time?" *Southern Economic Journal* 61, no. 4 (April 1995): 915–22.

Pack, H., and Pack, J., "Metropolitan Fragmentation and Local Public Expenditure," *National Tax Journal* 31 (1978): 349–62.

Pechman, J., *Federal Tax Policy*, 5th ed. (Washington D.C.: Brookings Institution, 1987).

Peltzman, S., "Pricing in Public and Private Enterprises: Electric Utilities in the United States," *Journal of Law and Economics* 14, no. 1 (April 1971): 109–47.

Peterson, Peter G., *Will America Grow Up before It Grows Old?* (New York: Random House, 1996).

Phelps, C. E., and Parente, S. T., "Priority Setting for Medical Technology and Medical Practice Assessment," *Medical Care* 28, no. 8 (August 1990): 702–23.

Pigou, A. C., *The Economics of Welfare* (London: Macmillan, 1918).

Pigou, A. C., *A Study in Public Finance*, 3rd ed. (London: Macmillan, 1947).

Portney, P. R., The Contingent Valuation Debate: Why Economists Should Care," *Journal of Economic Perspectives* 8, no. 4 (fall 1994): 3–17.

Poterba, J., and Summers, L. H., "Dividend Taxes, Corporate Investment and 'Q'," *Journal of Public Economics* (1983): 135–67.

Ramsey, F., "A Contribution of the Theory of Taxation," *Economic Journal* 37 (1927): 47–61.

Rizzuto, R., and Wachtel, P., "Further Evidence on the Returns to School Quality," *Journal of Human Resources* (spring 1980): 240–54.

Robins, P. K., "A Comparison of the Labor Supply Findings from the Four Negative Income Tax Experiments," *Journal of Human Resources* 20, no. 4 (fall 1985): 567–82.

Romer, T., "Individual Welfare, Majority Voting, and the Properties of a Linear Income Tax," *Journal of Public Economics* 4 (1975): 163–85.

Rothschild, M., and Stiglitz, J. E., "Equilibrium in Competitive Insurance Markets: An Essay on the Economics of Imperfect Information," *Quarterly Journal of Economics* 90 (1976): 629–50.

Salop, S., "Information and Monopolistic Competition," *American Economic Review* (May 1976): 240–45.

Sandmo, A., "The Effects of Taxation on Savings and Risk-Taking," in A. J. Auerbach and M. Feldstein (eds.), *Handbook of Public Economics*, vol. 1 (New York: Elsevier, 1987), pp. 293–309.

Schelling, T., "The Life You Save May Be Your Own," reprinted in T. Schelling, *Choices and Consequences* (Cambridge, Mass.: Harvard University Press, 1984).

Scholz, J., "Tax Policy and the Working Poor: The Earned Income Tax Credit," *Focus* (winter 1993–94): 1–12.

Shoepfle, G. K., Perez-Lopez, J. F., and Griego, E., "The Underground Economy in the United States," U.S. Department of Labor Occasional Paper on the Informal Sector, no. 2, September 1992.

Shoven, J., "New Developments in Corporate Finance and Tax Avoidance: Some Evidence," in L. Summers (ed.), *Tax Policy and the Economy*, National Bureau of Economic Research, 1987.

Showalter, M. H., and Thurston, N. K., "Taxes and Labor Supply of High-Income Physicians," *Journal of Public Economics* 66 (1997): 73–97.

Slavin, R., "School and Classroom Organization in Beginning Reading," in R. Slavin et al. (eds.), *Preventing Early School Failure: Research, Policy, and Practice* (Boston: Allyn and Bacon, 1994), pp. 122–30.

Slutsky, S., "A Voting Model for the Allocation of Public Goods: Existence of an Equilibrium," *Journal of Economic Theory* 11 (1975): 292–304.

Smith, A., *The Wealth of Nations* (New York: Modern Library, 1937).

Spence, A. M., "Job Market Signaling," *Quarterly Journal of Economics* 87 (1973): 355–74.

Spiegelman, R. G., and Yaeger, K. E., "The Seattle and Denver Income Maintenance Experiments: Overview," *Journal of Human Resources* 15, no. 4 (fall 1980): 463–79.

Starrett, D., "Principles of Optimal Location in a Large Homogeneous Area," *Journal of Economic Theory* 9 (1974): 418–48.

Stern, N. H., "On the Specification of Models of Optimum Income Taxation," *Journal of Public Economics* 6 (1976): 123–62.

Stern, N. H., "Optimum Taxation with Errors in Administration," *Journal of Public Economics* 17 (1982): 181–211.

Steuerle, E., "Is Income from Capital Subject to Individual Income Taxation?" *Public Finance Quarterly* (July 1982): 283–303.

Stigler, G. J., "The Theory of Economic Regulation," *Bell Journal Economics and Management Science* 2 (spring 1971): 3–21.

Stigler, G. J., "Free Riders and Collective Action: An Appendix to Theories of Economic Regulation," *Bell Journal Economics and Management Science* 5 (autumn 1974): 359–65.

Stiglitz, J. E., "The Effects of Income, Wealth and Capital Gains Taxation on Risk Taking," *Quarterly Journal of Economics* 83 (1969): 262–83.

Stiglitz, J. E., "Taxation, Corporate Financial Policy, and the Cost of Capital," *Journal of Public Economics* (February 1973): 1–34.

Stiglitz, J. E., "On the Irrelevance of Corporation Financial Policy," *American Economic Review* 64 (1974): 851–66.

Stiglitz, J. E., "The Theory of Screening Education and the Distribution of Income," *American Economic Review* 65 (1975): 283–300.

Stiglitz, J. E., "The Corporation Income Tax," *Journal of Public Economics* (April–May 1976): 303–11.

Stiglitz, J. E., "Theory of Local Public Goods," in M. Feldstein and R. Inman (eds.), *The Economics of Public Services* (New York: Macmillan, 1977), pp. 274–333.

Stiglitz, J. E., "Self-Selection and Pareto-Efficient Taxation," *Journal of Public Economics* 17 (1982): 213–40.

Stiglitz, J. E., "Utilitarianism and Horizontal Equity: The Case for Random Taxation," *Journal of Public Economics* 21 (1982): 257–94.

Stiglitz, J. E., "Public Goods in Open Economies with Heterogeneous Individuals," in J. F. Thisse and H. G. Zoller (eds.), *Locational Analysis of Public Facilities* (New York: Elsevier–North Holland, 1983).

Stiglitz, J. E., "Pareto Efficient and Optimal Taxation and the New Welfare Economics," in Alan J. Auerbach and Martin Feldstein (eds.), *Handbook of Public Economics* (New York: Elsevier, 1987), pp. 991–1042.

Stiglitz, J. E., "On the Relevance or Irrelevance of Public Financial Policy," in K. J. Arrow and M. J. Boskin (eds.), *The Economics of Public Debt* (New York: Macmillan Press, 1988), pp. 41–76.

Stiglitz, J. E., and Weiss, A., "Credit Rationing in Markets with Imperfect Information," *American Economic Review* 71, no. 3 (June 1981): 393–410.

Symposium on Contingent Valuation, *Journal of Economic Perspectives* 8, no. 4 (fall 1994).

Tiebout, C., "A Pure Theory of Local Expenditure," *Journal of Political Economy* 64 (1956): 416–24.

Tobin, J., "On Limiting the Domain of Inequality," *Journal of Law and Economics* 13 (1970): 263–77.

Triest, R. K., "The Effect of Income Taxation on Labor Supply in the United States," *Journal of Human Resources* (summer 1990): 491–516.

Viscusi, W. K., *Risk by Choice: Regulating Health and Safety in the Workplace* (Cambridge, Mass.: Harvard University Press, 1983).

Weiss, A., "Human Capital versus Signaling Explanations of Wages," *Journal of Economics Perspectives* 9, no. 4 (fall 1995): 133–54.

Wenglinsky, H., *When Money Matters: How Educational Expenditures Improve Student Performance and How they Don't* (Princeton, N.J.: Educational Testing Service, Policy Information Center, April 1997).

Wennberg, J., and Gittelsohn, A., "Small Are Variations in Health Care Delivery," *Science* 182 (1973): 1102–1108.

Willig, R., "Consumer's Surplus without Apology," *American Economic Review* 66 (1976): 589–97.

Windham, D., "Economic Analysis and the Public Support of Higher Education: The Divergence of Theory and Policy," in *Economic Dimensions of Education*, A Report of a Committee of the National Academy of Education, May 1979.

Zodrow, G. R., and Mieszkowski, P., "Pigou, Tiebout, Property Taxation, and the Underprovision of Local Public Goods," *Journal of Urban Economics* 19 (1986): 356–70.

INDEX